Postdigital Science and Education

This series is a new, international book series dedicated to postdigital science and education. It brings together a rapidly growing community of authors and the currently highly scattered body of research. The series complements the Postdigital Science and Education Journal and together they provide a complete, whole-rounded service to researchers working in the field. The book series covers a wide range of topics within postdigital science and education, including learning and data analytics, digital humanities, (digital) learning, teaching and assessment, educational technology and philosophy of education.

We no longer live in a world where digital technology and media are separate, virtual, 'other' to a 'natural' human and social life. Book series engaged with technology and education tend to view the research field as concerned with the 'effects' of digital media and other technologies on the existing activities of teaching and learning in education. This still assumes a clear division between an authentic educational practice and the imposition of an external, and novel, technology. The rapid growth of research and books and articles dealing with education and research in and for the postdigital age calls for a different approach that is no longer based on a division but rather on an integration of education and technology. This book series meets that need.

This book series

- Fills the gap in the scholarly community as the first academic book series in postdigital science and education
- Explicitly focuses on postdigital themes and research approaches
- Forms a hub for a growing body of scholarship in the field
- Enables communication, dissemination, and community building for researchers, authors, and students

Petar Jandrić • Alison MacKenzie • Jeremy Knox
Editors

Constructing Postdigital Research

Method and Emancipation

 Springer

Editors
Petar Jandrić (iD)
Department of Informatics and Computing
Zagreb University of Applied Sciences
Zagreb, Croatia

Alison MacKenzie (iD)
SSESW
Queen's University Belfast
Belfast, UK

Jeremy Knox (iD)
Moray House School of Education
and Sport
University of Edinburgh
Edinburgh, UK

ISSN 2662-5326 ISSN 2662-5334 (electronic)
Postdigital Science and Education
ISBN 978-3-031-35410-6 ISBN 978-3-031-35411-3 (eBook)
https://doi.org/10.1007/978-3-031-35411-3

This Springer imprint is published by the registered company Springer Nature Switzerland AG
The registered company address is: Gewerbestrasse 11, 6330 Cham, Switzerland

Paper in this product is recyclable.

Series Editor's Preface

At the age of 17, my scholarly interests revolved around physics, which I saw as the most fundamental of all natural sciences, and philosophy, which I saw as the most fundamental of all humanities. Physics prevailed, but not for long. After obtaining my BSc in physics, a master's degree in education, and a PhD in information science, I started my career as a researcher. Almost three decades later, I find myself asking the same questions about the nature of knowledge and human inquiry. I am still frustrated by the lack of dialogue between disciplines, and my interests still reach beyond entrenched knowledge infrastructures. *Postdigital Research: Genealogies, Challenges, and Future Perspectives* (Jandrić et al. 2023a) and *Constructing Postdigital Research: Method and Emancipation* (Jandrić et al. 2023b) are my latest attempts at making sense of these important questions.

My journey from physics to postdigital research, whatever that may be, was a bumpy one. Moving from natural sciences through social sciences to humanities, with an occasional detour into engineering, has required learning many new theories and approaches. However, the hardest part of that journey was not learning new things – it was *un*learning what everyone seems to know but no-one talks about: implicit assumptions, beliefs, and 'truisms' that appear in all disciplines. One such idea, that seems ubiquitous across the (natural and social) sciences and humanities, including education and EdTech research, is physics envy (Phillips 2014; Nelson 2015; Ackerman 2022).

Physics envy starts with the idea that physics is the most fundamental of all sciences and that physics research is methodologically superior to research in other disciplines. Consequently,

> [p]hysics has long been regarded as the model of what a science should be. It has been the hope, and the expectation, that if sufficient time, resources and talent were put into the sciences concerned with other phenomena—in particular the life sciences and the behavioral and social sciences—the kind of deep, broad and precise knowledge that had been attained in the physical sciences could be attained there too. … It is no wonder that scientists in other fields often suffer from physics envy, or that policymakers long for similar power in the sciences that bear on the problems they are trying to address. (Nelson 2015)

Physics envy dates at least from the nineteenth century. According to Philip Mirowski's classic, *More Heat than Light: Economics as Social Physics, Physics as Nature's Economics* (1989), 'neoclassical economic theory can be directly traced, through the mathematical formalism used, to the developments in nineteenth century physics. In this same thesis, the mathematical-physical link binds all past and present-day neoclassicals together' (Jolink 1993: 170). More recently, and closer to the theme of this volume, Eliezer Yudkowsky argues that

> [p]hysics envy in AI is the search for a *single, simple* underlying process, with the expectation that this one discovery will lay bare all the secrets of intelligence. The tendency to treat new approaches to AI as if they were new theories of physics may at least partially explain AI's past history of *overpromise* and *oversimplification*. (Yudkowsky 2007: 393) (emphases from the original)

Yudkowsky moves on to argue that '[t]he effects of physics envy can be more subtle; they also appear in the lack of interaction between AI projects' (393) and arrives to the definition of physics envy in AI as 'trying to replace the human cognitive supersystem with a single process or method' (394).

I could present many other examples, but that would expand this preface well beyond its scope. For my argument, it is enough to say that economics based on physical equations has epically failed (Mirowski 1989; Thomas and Wilson 2011), and that Yudkowsky's (2007) parallel does not hold water. Physics does not have its own unified theory (and there's no way to know whether it will ever get one); it is hard to envy thy neighbour on a car that she does not have.

Postdigital theory is transdisciplinary, yet this transdisciplinarity does not imply succumbing to the siren call of physics envy. Proverbial apples and oranges just do not mix; in the lingo of epistemology, some phenomena are incommensurable. According to Basarab Nicolescu (2008), transdisciplinarity is about trying to find a higher conceptual plane at which different theories may become at least partially commensurable – and that is a much more delicate matter than blending apples and oranges into a smoothie (see Jandrić 2016; MacKenzie 2022). However alluring, physics envy is just a popular epistemic fallacy, and the one in a need of demystification.

Postdigital Research: Genealogies, Challenges, and Future Perspectives (Jandrić et al. 2023a) and *Constructing Postdigital Research: Method and Emancipation* (Jandrić et al. 2023b) are explicitly positioned against and beyond physics envy, and, by extension, the pestiferous assumptions that a (post)digital science is somehow striving for a master algorithm, a fundamental axiom, or an underlying truth that will solve the mysterious universe of education. Their authors earnestly embrace postdigital messiness and uncertainty and develop theory and practice of postdigital research. While they actively learn and borrow from related theories and practices, in pursuit of higher transdisciplinary planes at which some theories might partially work together, they never attempt to keep up with the Joneses, and they humbly acknowledge that postdigitalism is not a theory of everything.

Constructing Postdigital Research: Method and Emancipation (Jandrić et al. 2023b) is focused on practical aspects of postdigital research, yet it looks and feels very differently from standard 'practical' research methods books. The book develops many great ideas and describes some important examples of postdigital research in diverse areas from cybernetics through design to feminism, yet its authors never prescribe how others should think about, or engage in, postdigital research. Messy and unpredictable by design, postdigital research proudly fails to create a level of coherence expected from a paradigm or school of thought (see Jandrić and Ford 2022). At its best, postdigital research could perhaps be understood as a collectively held attitude that accepts techno-social messiness and incoherence as fundamental characteristics of human existence.

Postdigital research may be hard to pin down, yet it still achieves some important results and deserves dedicated attention. I am thankful to all the authors who submitted their ideas under the big postdigital roof, and I feel compelled to stress that this roof is full of cracks and holes, and leaks numerous questions. While we cannot offer a physics-like theory of postdigital research, or even predict its advent in the most distant of futures, I do hope that these two volumes will lay out solid foundations for patching at least some of these cracks and holes in the times that come.

Zagreb University of Applied Sciences   Petar Jandrić
Zagreb, Croatia

References

Ackerman, G. (2022). Let's Loose the Physics Envy… We Might Be Better Users of Data if We Do. hackscience.education, 22 November. https://hackscience.education/2020/11/22/lets-loose-the-physics-envy-we-might-be-better-users-of-data-if-we-do/. Accessed 15 March 2023.

Jandrić, P. (2016). The methodological challenge of networked learning: (post)disciplinarity and critical emancipation. In T. Ryberg, C. Sinclair, S. Bayne, & M. de Laat (Eds.), *Research, Boundaries, and Policy in Networked Learning* (pp. 165–181). New York: Springer. https://doi.org/10.1007/978-3-319-31130-2_10.

Jandrić, P., & Ford, D. (2022). Postdigital Ecopedagogies: Genealogies, Contradictions, and Possible Futures. *Postdigital Science and Education, 4*(3), 672–710. https://doi.org/10.1007/s42438-020-00207-3.

Jandrić, P., MacKenzie, A., & Knox, J. (Eds.). (2023a). *Postdigital Research: Genealogies, Challenges, and Future Perspectives.* Cham: Springer. https://doi.org/10.1007/978-3-031-31299-1.

Jandrić, P., MacKenzie, A., & Knox, J. (Eds.). (2023b). *Constructing Postdigital Research: Method and Emancipation.* Cham: Springer. https://doi.org/10.1007/978-3-031-35411-3.

Jolink, A. (1993). "Procrustean Beds and All That": The Irrelevance of Walras for a Mirowski Thesis. *History of Political Economy, 25*(suppl_1), 157–174. https://doi.org/10.1215/00182702-1993-suppl_1017.

MacKenzie, A. (2022). Down to Earth transdisciplinarity. Response to the struggling towards a transdisciplinary metaphysics (Gibbs 2021). *Postdigital Science and Education, 4*(3), 676–682. https://doi.org/10.1007/s42438-022-00298-0.

Mirowski, P. (1989). *More Heat than Light: Economics as Social Physics, Physics as Nature's Economics.* Cambridge, UK and New York, NY: Cambridge University Press.

Nelson, R. R. (2015). Physics Envy: Get Over It. *Issues in Science and Technology, 31*(3). https://issues.org/physics-envy-get-over-it/. Accessed 15 March 2023.

Nicolescu, B. (2008). In vitro and in vivo knowledge – Methodology of transdisciplinarity. In B. Nicolescu (Ed.), *Transdisciplinarity – Theory and practice* (pp. 1–22). New York, NY: Hampton Press.

Phillips, D. C. (2014). Research in the Hard Sciences, and in Very Hard "Softer" Domains. *Educational Researcher, 43*(1), 9–11. https://doi.org/10.3102/0013189X13520293.

Thomas, H., & Wilson, A. D. (2011). 'Physics Envy', Cognitive Legitimacy or Practical Relevance: Dilemmas in the Evolution of Management Research in the UK. *British Journal of Management, 22*(3), 443–456. https://doi.org/10.1111/j.1467-8551.2011.00766.x.

Yudkowsky, E. (2007). Levels of Organization in General Intelligence. In B. Goertzel & C. Pennachin (Eds.), *Artificial General Intelligence* (pp. 389–501). Berlin and Heidelberg: Springer. https://doi.org/10.1007/978-3-540-68677-4_12.

Foreword

When reading *Constructing Postdigital Research: Method and Emancipation* (Jandrić et al. 2023a), the word 'emancipation' stood out for me. Emancipation is defined as being free from restraint, control, or the power of another (Merriam-Webster Dictionary n.d.). The five sections in this book – 'Postdigital Positionality', 'Constructing Postdigital Research', 'Postdigital Data and Algorithms', 'Exclusions and Inclusions', and 'Method and Emancipation' – are all advocates for research that is agentic, empowering, and democratic, alerting the reader to the fact that technologies are not neutral tools. Instead, technologies are foregrounded as a means for production and reproduction of existing (unequal) social structures, with effects that resonate throughout a wider socio-technical-environmental system.

Whilst technologies might have an enormous social impact, helping to overcome some of the complex challenges of our world, they might also have significant negative effects. With the digital so imbricated into the fabrics of society, those who are most disconnected are likely to encounter fewer opportunities for work, for learning, for socialising, for fully participating in society – and therefore be disadvantaged in some respects. Even those who are active members of a postdigital ecosystem, with full access and know-how to creatively and productively use technologies, are being exploited – given that they are also likely to have significant amounts of personal data collected on a daily basis, whether they are aware of it or not (Knox 2019; Hayes et al. 2023). This data can then be mined and aggregated, and might be sold or fed back to different institutions and organisations, raising questions about how data might be used, who owns it, how it might be shared and understood (Zuboff 2019).

Technologies can contribute to exclusion, enable digital surveillance, and provide the means for ongoing algorithmic control over people's lives (Sadowski 2019). Increasing proliferation of technological devices requires the creation and maintenance of a supporting infrastructure, with effects on natural resources, the environment, and the planet (Knox 2019). The ways the digital becomes tied up into socio-technical-environmental systems, influence and are shaped by broader social structures and cultural norms (Jandrić et al. 2018). And yet, there is insufficient critical understanding about the wider impact of technologies on society, on education, and on human rights, as well as how it raises ethical concerns, affects the environment, and contributes to inequality.

Constructing Postdigital Research: Method and Emancipation (Jandrić et al. 2023a) and its accompanying volume, *Postdigital Research: Genealogies, Challenges, and Future Perspectives* (Jandrić et al. 2023b), challenge readers to think differently. Numerous authors in this volume invite the reader to reflect on their own positionalities, to reflect on how traditional Western ways of knowing and being have influenced the ways we see relations between humans, technologies, and the environment. And so, in embracing the spirits of this book, particularly in the section 'Postdigital Positionality', I share a little bit of my own background to situate how I connect to the contributions in this volume, and to postdigital research more broadly.

I grew up in Brazil during the 1970s, a time when many spoke of this nation as being destined for prosperity. Life could be described through the colourful images of beautiful postcards depicting beach snaps in Copacabana, lush tropical greenery, the Amazon River, and exotic toucans. Brazil had recently relocated its capital to Brasilia, which was entirely architecturally designed and built from scratch. Brazilians were proud to be known as the best soccer players in the world and the creators of the beautiful sounds of Bossa Nova. They were easy going, creative, and innovative, living in a place where opportunities abounded. Against this very backdrop, however, the reality was that a military coup had recently taken over the government, marking the beginning of 21 long years of dictatorship. During this 'prosperous' period many were living in fear, constantly told to watch what they said in public. People could be persecuted and tortured, and indeed many disappeared or fled the country in a hurry, leaving family, friends, and their Brazilian lives behind.

I realised early on that things are not always what they seem. As a young person growing up during those years, it was hard to reconcile these contrasting elements: a perfect postcard depicting a prosperous nation against the lack of intellectual freedom, loss of democratic values, the fear, and the realisation that some individuals had so much more power and opportunity than others. I remember coming into adulthood towards the end of the dictatorship, with big questionings about freedom, social justice, and what was fair, trying to understand the functioning of structures in society and how multiple things connected and impacted not only a person's life, but also the ways the world goes round.

A key figure at this time was Paulo Freire, a Brazilian philosopher who influenced many in my generation all over the world, articulating an approach to education that went well beyond the notion of students waiting for the simple transfer of knowledge (Freire 1972, 1994). His work fiercely questioned the dominant structures of socio-economic and political relations, advocating ways to enable empowered people to discuss and find alternatives in order to create a better world. Education was foregrounded as a universal right, as a part of political processes, and therefore critical to the construction of just, democratic, and sustainable society for all (Roberts 2017). Emancipation in Freire's terms is about empowering people to be and to see themselves as active agents for social transformation.

Even though Freire's ideas emerged at a time that preceded the ubiquity of the digital as we know it today, some firm parallels can be traced with the notion of the postdigital and the ideas shared in this volume. The postdigital acknowledges that the digital has become an integral and inseparable part of people's lives (Jandrić et al. 2018). It also alerts us to notice how such constant presence is impacting people's identities and has effects that reverberate through inclusion and exclusion across social and political contexts (Hayes 2021).

In taking a postdigital stance, researchers are committing to the critical appraisal of the digital; they challenge simplistic assumptions and superficial understandings that do not probe into the complex relations between humans, technologies, and the environment (Jandrić and Hayes 2022). The postdigital encourages researchers to search for the role of technology and its effects on broader socio-technical structures. Postdigital lenses aim to reveal connections at multiple dimensions and scale levels – from how learning activities might unfold in classrooms to wider implications for curricula and education policy; from the need for a supporting infrastructure to the implications of such infrastructural support, and how it reverberates into the depletion of resources in the environment.

Constructing Postdigital Research: Method and Emancipation (Jandrić et al. 2023a) alerts readers to the need for critical awareness that does not shy away from understanding connections between the digital and social, political, and economic structures. The book raises questions about the postdigital condition, its relations to manifestations of power and control, and how these might create conditions and contradictions for actions and transformations. In so doing, it takes the reader through a reflective journey to consider ways of resisting, stretching boundaries, reflecting on ethical concerns, and interrogating existing assumptions about education and socio-political contexts.

Constructing Postdigital Research: Method and Emancipation (Jandrić et al. 2023a) is a much-needed addition to postdigital research, as it illuminates ways educators can change the social dynamics of the complex postdigital situations and circumstances that are part of our everyday experiences. The book offers useful analytical tools, methods, and insights to advance new frontiers of research that embrace knowledgeable action for social transformation. The chapters in this volume contribute to emancipating and empowering the education research community, as they foreground inquiry practices that go beyond discovery, towards embracing design, collaboration, co-creation, and action.

Massey University   Lucila Carvalho
Auckland, New Zealand

References

Merriam-Webster Dictionary (n.d.). Emancipation. https://www.merriam-webster.com/dictionary/emancipation. Accessed 26 April 2023.

Freire, P. (1972). *Pedagogy of the Oppressed*. Harmondsworth: Penguin.

Freire, P. (1994). *Pedagogy of Hope*. London: Bloomsbury.

Hayes, S. (2021). *Postdigital Positionality Developing Powerful Inclusive Narratives for Learning, Teaching, Research and Policy in Higher Education*. Leiden: Brill.

Hayes, S., Jopling, M., Connor, S., & Johnson, M. (Eds.). (2023). *Human Data Interaction, Disadvantage and Skills in the Community*. Cham: Springer. https://doi.org/10.1007/978-3-031-31875-7.

Jandrić, P., & Hayes, S. (2022). Postdigital Critical Pedagogy. In A. A. Abdi & G. W. Misiaszek (Eds.), *Palgrave Handbook on Critical Theories of Education* (pp. 321–336). Cham: Palgrave MacMillan. https://doi.org/10.1007/978-3-030-86343-2_18.

Jandrić, P., Knox, J., Besley, T., Ryberg, T., Suoranta, J., & Hayes, S. (2018). Postdigital Science and Education. *Educational Philosophy and Theory, 50*(10), 893–899. https://doi.org/10.1080/00131857.2018.1454000.

Jandrić, P., MacKenzie, A., & Knox, J. (Eds.) (2023b). *Postdigital Research: Genealogies, Challenges, and Future Perspectives*. Cham: Springer. https://doi.org/10.1007/978-3-031-31299-1.

Jandrić, P., MacKenzie, A., & Knox, J. (Eds.). (2023a). *Constructing Postdigital Research: Method and Emancipation*. Cham: Springer. https://doi.org/10.1007/978-3-031-35411-3.

Knox, J. (2019). What Does the 'Postdigital' Mean for Education? Three Critical Perspectives on the Digital, with Implications for Educational Research and Practice. *Postdigital Science and Education, 1*(2), 357–370. https://doi.org/10.1007/s42438-019-00045-y.

Roberts, P. (2017). Paulo Freire. In G. W. Noblit (Ed.), *Oxford Research Encyclopedia of Education*. Oxford: Oxford University Press. https://doi.org/10.1093/acrefore/9780190264093.013.10.

Sadowski, J. (2019). When data is capital: Datafication, accumulation, and extraction. *Big Data & Society, 6*(1), 205395171882054. https://doi.org/10.1177/2053951718820549.

Sinclair, C., & Hayes, S. (2019). Between the Post and the Com-Post: Examining the Postdigital 'Work' of a Prefix. *Postdigital Science and Education, 1*(1), 119–131. https://doi.org/10.1007/s42438-018-0017-4.

Zuboff, S. (2019). *The age of surveillance capitalism: The fight for a human future at the new frontier of power*. New York: PublicAffairs.

Introduction

Why This Book?

After a few years of publishing the *Postdigital Science and Education* journal, the book series, and the *Encyclopaedia*[1], it has become obvious that they consist in more than just another set of 'EdTech' publishing outlets. The rapidly growing body of research under a postdigital label, in the Postdigital Science and Education publishing ecosystem and elsewhere, has started to develop its own philosophy, theory, and a plethora of loosely connected research approaches, creating a network, and a community, of like-minded researchers (see Jandrić 2022; Jandrić et al. 2022, 2023c). Some aspects of this rapid development, such as the simple yet elusive question, 'What is the postdigital', have been addressed in considerable depth (see Jandrić et al. 2018; Knox 2019; Fawns 2019; Sinclair and Hayes 2019; and so on). Yet important questions, 'What is postdigital research?' and 'How should I do postdigital research?', have been addressed only sporadically (Jandrić 2020a, b, 2021; Jandrić and Knox 2022).

This lack of attention has not arrived by accident. Research is a thing of thinking while doing and cannot, of course, be addressed in a purely theoretical manner. However, the predominant assumption is that research *is* empirical. As primarily theoretical thinkers, we have often observed how the theoretical is added to (thrown at?) the findings to give some semblance of depth. The result is that the discussion can often be superficial, the theory misused, or the usual fare of a theoretical perspective trotted out. The best, or most compelling, research is a collective enterprise and requires collective appraisal and engagement. In 2023, coinciding with the fifth year of publication of the *Postdigital Science and Education* journal, the body of

---

[1] *Postdigital Science and Education* journal, https://www.springer.com/journal/42438, was incepted in 2018; Postdigital Science and Education book series, https://www.springer.com/series/16439, was incepted in 2021; and the *Encyclopedia of Postdigital Science and Education*, https://link.springer.com/referencework/10.1007/978-3-031-35469-4, was incepted in 2023. Accessed 16 July 2023.

postdigital research and the postdigital community have grown strong enough to allow for in-depth theoretical, practical, and collective engagement with fundamental questions pertaining to postdigital research.

As soon as Kairos appeared, we decided to collectively explore the many faces of postdigital research. Mindful of community needs, we spiced up this research-oriented collection with a slight pedagogical streak, offering readers an easy point of entry into postdigital theory and practice. Our practice-inspired approach also feels right theoretically, because we share an understanding of postdigital research and pedagogy as entangled and mutually interdependent (Jandrić et al. 2018). We wrote a short article explaining our main ideas for the project (Jandrić et al. 2022), launched the Call for Chapters, and hoped for the best.

The best was what we received – and in what numbers! – so much so that we needed to split the material between two volumes. *Postdigital Research: Genealogies, Challenges, and Future Perspectives* (Jandrić et al. 2023a) is slightly more oriented towards the theory of postdigital research, while *Constructing Postdigital Research: Method and Emancipation* (Jandrić et al. 2023b) tends more towards the practice of postdigital research. However, this common division does not imply that we believe in separations between theory and practice. On the contrary, we see postdigital research as critical praxis, where theory and practice are inseparable from each other (Jandrić et al. 2018), and is responsive to the world and its problems, old or new. Good theory is open to change and to new challenges, is flexible enough that it can be reformulated or restructured to absorb or reinterpret new problems – or, critically, recognise problems that have been wilfully or culpably ignored. Because of its general, abstract, and practical epistemological, ontological, and axiological nature, postdigital research is eminently responsive to a rapidly changing world. And, as these chapters reveal, produces research that is creative, imaginary, and boundary-pushing – perhaps even strange.

Consequently, we advise all readers to use these books in conjunction; or even better, to just understand them as one large book separated in two volumes for easier handling. The first volume, *Postdigital Research: Genealogies, Challenges, and Future Perspectives*, explores genealogies and challenges related to the concept of the postdigital, the ambiguous nature of postdigital knowledges, the many faces of postdigital sensibilities, and struggles related to postdigital agencies. The volume answers three key questions: What is postdigital knowledge? What does it mean to do postdigital research? What, if anything, is distinct from research conducted in other perspectives?

This volume, *Constructing Postdigital Research: Method and Emancipation*, explores postdigital positionality, the many ways of constructing postdigital research, questions pertaining to algorithms and analytics, the postdigital dynamic of inclusion and exclusion, and the relationships between method and emancipation. The volume answers three key questions: What is the relationship between postdigital theory and research practice? How can we construct emancipatory postdigital research? What is the relationship between method and emancipation?

What's in the Book?

Part I: Postdigital Positionality

The first chapter, Sarah Hayes' 'Positionality In Postdigital Research: The Power to Effect Change', explores the individual nature of postdigital research through positionality and considers the political economic structure that surrounds postdigital research alongside the potential role of postdigital decoloniality research. She presents a model of personal and community postdigital positionality, with attention in particular to where the language of postdigital positionality engages with the language of postdigital community. The second chapter, Nicola Pallitt and Neil Kramm's 'Beyond A 'Noticing Stance': Exploring Human and Nonhuman Positionalities in Postdigital Research', offers an overview of dominant educational technology research paradigms, how they conceptualise the relationship between humans and technology, and situate the researcher. Through reflective prompts, the authors engage readers in a journey to think about their own postdigital positionalities.

The third chapter, 'Mapping (Metaphorical) Journeys in And Against the Academy' by Mel M. Engman, Johanna Ennser-Kananen, and Jenna Cushing-Leubner, explores the use of hand-drawn 'maps' as a postdigital exercise in naming and spatialising researcher positionality, and academic career trajectories. The chapter highlights how the use of seemingly unchanged analog tools can allow for postdigital sense-making, acknowledging the ways in which our sense-making and subjectivities can be understood as postdigital assemblages in relation with the social and material world.

Part II: Constructing Postdigital Research

This section starts with 'Constructing Design Knowledge for Postdigital Science and Education' by Peter Goodyear, Lina Markauskaite, Cara Wrigley, Natalie Spence, Genevieve Mosely, and Teresa Swist. The authors draw upon their programme of research into interdisciplinary science and education to explore some relations between postdigital research and the construction of locally useful design knowledge. They introduce the Activity-Centred Analysis and Design framework (ACAD) and explain how design knowledge – knowledge that is useful for design work – can be constructed through alternating processes of collaborative analysis and design. The next chapter, 'Cyber-Social Research: Emerging Paradigms for Interventionist Education Research in the Postdigital Era' by Anastasia O. Tzirides, Akash K. Saini, Bill Cope, Mary Kalantzis, and Duane Searsmith, explores the processes of research-informed educational intervention and change at a time when much teaching and learning is pervasively mediated by digital tools and environments. Drawing on theories and practices of design research and agile research, they propose a model termed 'cyber-social research'.

James Lamb's 'Sociomateriality, Postdigital Thinking, and Learning Spaces Research' uses the example of emergent learning spaces research to argue that that while they work in complement, postdigital thinking goes beyond sociomateriality in pushing us to more resolutely examine the presence and influence of digital technologies more resolutely within our learning spaces. Lamb also suggests that the postdigital exists as a kind of research sensibility, which shapes how we understand our educational surroundings, and also our researcher selves. In 'Researching Interactional and Volumetric Scenographies – Immersive Qualitative Digital Research', Jacob Davidsen, Paul McIlvenny, and Thomas Ryberg introduce immersive qualitative digital research as an environment that facilitates a more qualitative, immersive, and emancipated way of working with audio-visual data. Using three examples of digital software, they present and discuss how researchers can come to a better and more nuanced understanding of the thickness of lived postdigital practice.

Part III: Postdigital Data and Algorithms

The first chapter for this section, 'Postdigital Student Bodies – Mapping the Flesh-Electric' by Paul Prinsloo, argues that while institutions have always, in one form or another, measured, collected, analysed, and used student data, the digitisation and datafication of higher education provide institutions access to greater volumes, varieties, velocity, and granularity of students' *digital* data resulting in learning analytics – a research focus and practice of measuring, collecting, analysing, and using students' digital data to, *inter alia*, (re)design pedagogy, student support strategies, and the allocation of resources.

The next chapter, Velislava Hillman's 'Algorithmic Systems Claim Education and The (Re)Production of Education', argues that algorithmic systems are increasingly used to infer, predict, and steer the education experience of children. Therefore, Hillman calls for more and systematic postdigital research to identify the needs of governance, scrutiny, and oversight of these advancing data-intensive systems and their owners to ensure that they are held accountable in their influence and impact on education.

In 'Negotiating Mnemotechnic Re-presentation', Greta Goetz extends the work of Bernard Stiegler on the capacity of the mnemotechnic tool to exteriorise, retain, and transmit re-presentations of knowledge – either automatically overtaking the human capacity for knowledge production or augmenting it. As mnemotechnics becomes increasingly abstracted from the social body and individual human subjects, potentially including researchers themselves, this raises the question of who or what the postdigital research observer is and what it means to re-present knowledge about the world in the ongoing pursuit of learning.

Part IV: Exclusions and Inclusions

The first chapter in this part, Felicitas Macgilchrist's 'Postdigital Validity: Peer Reviews on The Edges of Modernity', explores how to engage with today's muddy, lumpy, racist, scrappy, classist, glitchy, noisy sociotechnical practices to generate insights which are accepted as 'valid' by other scholars. The chapter suggests that a 'postdigital validity' draws on the rich tradition of rethinking validity, but also highlights the specific blurring of boundaries (e.g., digital/material binaries or epistemic demarcations) that is key to much postdigital research.

The next chapter, 'International Human Rights in The Posthuman Era' by Selman Özdan, answers two important questions: How should the basic elements that make people human be discussed in the posthuman and postdigital era? Will the discussion of the legal status of non-human entities (such as robots) within the framework of rights lead to a reshaping of the Universal Declaration of Human Rights?

The final chapter for this section, 'Understanding Children's Participation Rights Through a Postdigital Epistemology of Silence' by Amy Hanna, conceptualises the right to information in postdigital research through an epistemology of silence to better understand the misinformation, disinformation, and deceit that pervades our information sources. Hanna closes her chapter with a consideration of what this means for postdigital research methodology, arguing that children and young people should take a central role, given that they are growing up in the postdigital world.

Part V: Method and Emancipation

'A Feminist Postdigital Analysis of Misogyny, Patriarchy and Violence Against Women and Girls Online' by Alison MacKenzie offers a postdigital feminist analysis of misogyny and its harmful manifestations online. The chapter concludes with a tentative formulation of what feminist postdigital analysis could consist in and its relevance to the postdigital condition. Next, in 'Images of Incoming: A Critical Account of a (Mostly) Postdigital Photovoice Project with Rural Migrant Women in Northern Ireland and Canada', Tess Maginess, Amea Wilbur, and Elena Bergia offer a critical account of a postdigital, arts based, co- research project with rural migrant women in Canada and Northern Ireland. Their research positioning challenges neoliberal concepts of ownership and privatization of knowledge with a knowledge socialism ethos that research should not just be for the common good, but should be empowering, democratic, and agentic.

In 'Future Workshops as Postdigital Research Method', Juha Suoranta and Marko Teräs respond to the growing trend of future studies in educational research. They describe the future workshop as a viable postdigital research method that allows scholars methodological experimentation and switches from what is to what is not yet, but what could be. The final chapter of the book, Caroline Kuhn et al.'s 'Understanding Digital Inequality: A Theoretical Kaleidoscope', proposes a methodological toolkit: a theoretical kaleidoscope to examine and critique the constitutive elements and dimensions of digital inequalities. The authors argue that such a tool is helpful when a critical attitude to examine 'the ideology of digitalism', its concomitant inequalities, and the huge losses it entails for human flourishing seems urgent. The chapter describes different theoretical approaches that can be used for the kaleidoscope and gives relevant examples of each theory.

How to Use This Book?

No Gods, No Masters

As we have already written in the Introduction to *Postdigital Research: Genealogies, Challenges, and Future Perspectives* (Jandrić et al. 2023a), these books are not blueprints. They 'can indeed be used as points of entry into postdigital research, but they are not here to define what postdigital research is or how postdigital research should be done. They are here to challenge, inspire, and open new directions for inquiry.' Borrowing this section's title from anarchist philosophy and labour movements, we emphasise a crucial aspect of postdigital research: a strong focus on emancipation and social justice, with strong theoretical or philosophical underpinnings and analyses.

This focus does not imply that postdigital researchers should restrict their inquiry to political themes, that we should condemn religion, or that we should succumb to the terror of political correctness. Quite the contrary! Postdigital research should focus on any imaginable topic of human interest, regardless of its popularity and/or political economy (Jandrić and Knox 2022), if it responds to the kinds of problems, old or new, to the doxas, the excluded, overlooked, or marginalised, as we suggested above. To say that 'any imaginable topic' is relevant is not the same as saying postdigital research adopts an 'anything goes' approach. Rather, the point is that postdigital research challenges any ontological, epistemological, and methodological assumptions that would position other research enquiries as incongruent, and by extension, hopefully disincentivise any disciplinary gatekeeping about what is or isn't a 'postdigital concern'. For instance, postdigital theologies are an important area of inquiry into relationships between science, myth, and faith (Savin-Baden and Reader 2022). And political correctness is only as good inasmuch it does not restrict the freedom of thought and speech, or permits doxas – taken-for-granted assumptions and beliefs – to be challenged; else, when the weapons of cancel culture speak, the muses remain silent.

Here, we take an important lesson from Paulo Freire (1970), who insisted that the oppressors are also victims of (their own) oppression; and from bel hooks (2003), who ferociously argued, against mainstream feminist thinking of her time, that men are also victims of patriarchy. To live in the world is to live with the fact that it is fundamentally unjust and unequal, and that justice and equality are, contrary to classical theories of justice, the ideal. Our research should begin with that *fact*. So standing together with the oppressed should not imply oppressing someone else! While we deeply believe that postdigital research must always side with the weak and the oppressed, we also insist that it should not create new forms of oppression.

This can be applied at all levels. In everyday practice, postdigital research should be very mindful of ethics; epistemically, postdigital research should never attempt at dominating the research landscape. For better or worse, postdigital research needs to remain open to any and every theory and practice that may lead to a common good – including critique of postdigital research itself, and the inevitable replacement of postdigital research with the arrival of new *Zeitgeists*. It should be humble. In the words of Eric S. Raymond (2001), postdigital research is not the cathedral but a bazaar.

Towards a Critical Postdigital Research Praxis

These days, we can find the adjective 'critical' attached to almost anything, from all kids of pedagogies to advertisements for bank loans and swimwear. Similarly, the words 'postdigital' and 'praxis' mean different things to different people, even to the contributors in this volume. However, the intersection of three words in this section's title, 'critical', 'postdigital', and 'praxis', is nevertheless a productive starting point for describing what postdigital research should entail.

- The word 'critical' describes postdigital research's roots in (Freirean) critical pedagogies and a more general orientation to emancipation and social justice.
- The word, 'postdigital' describes the messy state of the human condition after the digital 'revolutions'.
- The word 'praxis' describes the (Aristotelian) inseparability between theory and practice, extending to the present through Freirean critical pedagogies.

Postdigital Research: Genealogies, Challenges, and Future Perspectives (Jandrić et al. 2023a) and *Constructing Postdigital Research: Method and Emancipation* (Jandrić et al. 2023b) present a remarkable diversity of the ways in which criticality, postdigitality, and praxis can be combined. For as long as these elements are present, in whatever shape or configuration, postdigital research will continue to productively contribute to understanding our world and changing it for the better.

Zagreb University of Applied Sciences   Petar Jandrić
Zagreb, Croatia

Queen's University Belfast   Alison MacKenzie
Belfast, UK

University of Edinburgh   Jeremy Knox
Edinburgh, UK

References

Fawns, T. (2019). Postdigital education in design and practice. *Postdigital Science and Education, 1*(1), 132–145. https://doi.org/10.1007/s42438-018-0021-8.

Freire, P. (1970). *Pedagogy of the oppressed.* New York: Continuum.

hooks, b. (2003). *Teaching Community: A Pedagogy of Hope.* New York: Routledge. https://doi.org/10.4324/9780203957769.

Jandrić, P. (2020a). Postdigital Research in the Time of Covid-19. *Postdigital Science and Education, 2*(2), 233–238. https://doi.org/10.1007/s42438-020-00113-8.

Jandrić, P. (2020b). Educational Research in The Postdigital Age. *Journal of South China Normal University (Social Science Edition), 6*, 1–14.

Jandrić, P. (2021). The postdigital challenge of critical educational research. In C. Mathias (Ed.), *The Handbook of Critical Theoretical Research Methods in Education* (pp. 31–48). Abingdon and New York: Routledge.

Jandrić, P. (2022). History of the Postdigital: Invitation for Feedback. *Postdigital Science and Education.* https://doi.org/10.1007/s42438-022-00345-w.

Jandrić, P., & Knox, J. (2022). The Postdigital Turn: Philosophy, Education, Research. *Policy Futures in Education, 20*(7), 780–795. https://doi.org/10.1177/2F14782103211062713.

Jandrić, P., Knox, J., Besley, T., Ryberg, T., Suoranta, J., & Hayes, S. (2018). Postdigital Science and Education. *Educational Philosophy and Theory, 50*(10), 893–899. https://doi.org/10.1080/00131857.2018.1454000.

Jandrić, P., MacKenzie, A., & Knox, J. (2022). Postdigital Research: Genealogies, Challenges, and Future Perspectives. *Postdigital Science and Education.* https://doi.org/10.1007/s42438-022-00306-3.

Jandrić, P., MacKenzie, A., & Knox, J. (Eds.). (2023a). *Postdigital Research: Genealogies, Challenges, and Future Perspectives.* Cham: Springer. https://doi.org/10.1007/978-3-031-31299-1.

Jandrić, P., MacKenzie, A., & Knox, J. (Eds.). (2023b). *Constructing Postdigital Research: Method and Emancipation.* Cham: Springer. https://doi.org/10.1007/978-3-031-35411-3.

Jandrić, P., MacKenzie, A., & Knox, J. (2023c). Introduction. In P. Jandrić, A. MacKenzie, & J. Knox (Eds.), *Postdigital Research: Genealogies, Challenges, and Future Perspectives.* Cham: Springer.

Knox, J. (2019). What does the postdigital mean for education? three critical perspectives on the digital, with implications for educational research and practice. *Postdigital Science and Education, 1*(2), 357–370. https://doi.org/10.1007/s42438-019-00045-y.

Raymond, E. S. (2001). *The Cathedral and the Bazaar: Musings on Linux and Open Source by an Accidental Revolutionary.* Sebastopol, CA: O'Reilly & Associates.

Savin-Baden, M., & Reader, J. (Eds.). (2022). *Postdigital Theologies: Technology, Belief, and Practice.* Cham: Springer. https://doi.org/10.1007/978-3-031-09405-7.

Sinclair, C., & Hayes, S. (2019). Between the post and the com-post: Examining the postdigital "work" of a prefix. *Postdigital Science and Education, 1*(1), 119–131. https://doi.org/10.1007/s42438-018-0017-4.

Acknowledgements

Republished Chapter

The last chapter in *Constructing Postdigital Research: Method and Emancipation* was originally published as: Kuhn, C., Khoo, S.-M., Czerniewicz, L., Lilley, W., Bute, S., Crean, A., Abegglen, S., Burns, T., Sinfield, S., Jandrić, P., Knox, J., & MacKenzie, A. (2023). Understanding Digital Inequality: A Theoretical Kaleidoscope. *Postdigital Science and Education.* https://doi.org/10.1007/s42438-023-00395-8. We are grateful to Springer publishers for the permission to republish.

The *CUC 2022 – Opening in a Closed World: Postdigital Science and Education* Conference

In 2022, Petar Jandrić was invited to chair the Programme Committee for the research section at the *CUC 2022 – Opening in A Closed World: Postdigital Science and Education* conference.[1] Jeremy Knox and Alison MacKenzie gave their keynotes at the conference, and most authors in *Postdigital Research: Genealogies, Challenges, and Future Perspectives* and *Constructing Postdigital Research: Method and Emancipation* presented working versions of their chapters only a month or so before submitting their manuscripts. This was a great opportunity for the authors and editors to meet, share ideas, and develop links between the chapters. We are grateful to the Croatian Academic and Research Network – CARNET – for the opportunity.

---

[1] See https://cuc.carnet.hr/2022/en/. Accessed 2 February 2023.

Contents

Part III   Postdigital Data and Algorithms

Part IV   Exclusions and Inclusions

Part V   Method and Emancipation

About the Editors

Petar Jandrić is Professor at the Zagreb University of Applied Sciences, Croatia. Petar's research interests are at the postdisciplinary intersections between technologies, pedagogies, and the society, and research methodologies of his choice are inter-, trans-, and antidisciplinarity. He is the Editor-in-Chief of *Postdigital Science and Education* journal, https://www.springer.com/journal/42438, Postdigital Science and Education book series, https://www.springer.com/series/16439, and *Encyclopedia of Postdigital Science and Education*, https://link.springer.com/referencework/10.1007/978-3-031-35469-4. His recent books include *The Methodology and Philosophy of Collective Writing* (2021), *Bioinformational Philosophy and Postdigital Knowledge Ecologies* (2022), *Postdigital Ecopedagogies: Genealogies, Contradictions, and Possible Futures* (2022), and *Postdigital Research: Genealogies, Challenges, and Future Perspectives* (2023). Personal website: http://petarjandric.com/.

Alison MacKenzie is a Reader at Queen's University, Belfast. Alison's research interests are in applied philosophy, particularly feminist and postdigital philosophy, epistemic injustice, and the related fields of epistemologies of ignorance and deceit. Alison has written on critical disability, the Capabilities Approach, and Bourdieusian analytical sociology. Alison is an Associate Editor of the *International Journal of Educational Research* and is on the editorial board of a number of journals, including *Postdigital Science and Education*. Her recent edited books are *Epistemology of Deceit in a Postdigital Era* (2021) and *Postdigital Research: Genealogies, Challenges, and Future Perspectives* (2023).

Jeremy Knox is Senior Lecturer and Co-director of the Centre for Research in Digital Education at the University of Edinburgh. His research interests include the relationships between education, data-driven technologies, and wider society, and he has led projects funded by the ESRC and the British Council in the UK. Jeremy's published work includes *Posthumanism and the MOOC* (2016), *Artificial Intelligence and Inclusive Education* (2019), *The Manifesto for Teaching Online* (2020), *Data Justice and the Right to the City* (2022), *AI and Education in China* (2023), and *Postdigital Research: Genealogies, Challenges, and Future Perspectives* (2023).

About the Authors

Sandra Abegglen is a Researcher in the School of Architecture, Planning and Landscape at the University of Calgary, Canada, where she explores online education and learning and teaching in the design studio. Sandra's interests are in collaboration, co-creation, and social justice. Her research focuses on digital education, hybrid pedagogy, academic literacies, creative learning and teaching methods, inclusion, and identity. She is the Principal Investigator for Playful Hybrid Higher Education and the Teaching and Learning Online Network (TALON), and she holds the project lead for several other education research projects. Sandra has been awarded for her inter-disciplinary, multi-stakeholder education work.

Elena Bergia is an independent researcher with a PhD in Anthropology\Irish Studies from Queen's University, Belfast. The primary focus of her research are the interconnections between gender and violence. Elena has authored peer-reviewed articles and op-ed pieces on gendered heroism and the unexpected rewards of political violence. Her publications also include studies on political bias in ethnographic research and on the ethical and political learning that our societies may extract from the Covid-19 pandemic. Her upcoming work includes 'Seductive Capital and Gendered Heroism' for the Encyclopedia of Heroism Studies, to be published by Springer in 2024.

Tom Burns is Senior Lecturer in the Centre for Professional and Educational Development at London Metropolitan University, UK, developing innovations with a special focus on praxes that ignite student curiosity and develop power and voice. Always interested in theatre and the arts, and their role in teaching and learning, Tom has set up adventure playgrounds, community events and festivals, and feeds arts-based practice into his learning, teaching, and assessment practices. He is co-author of *Essential Study Skills: The complete Guide to Success at University* (2022, 5th Edition), and other books and articles advocating for student success and creative practice.

Swati Jaywant Rao Bute is an Associate Professor at Jagran Lakecity University, India. Her research interests are in media and international relations, health communication, cross-cultural communication, print and electronic media. She is head of special interest group-health communication, Assistant Editor and Member of Southeast Asian Media Study Association (SEAMSA). Her recent edited books include *Media Diplomacy and its Evolving Role in the Current Geopolitical Climate* (2018) and *Intercultural Relations and Ethnic Conflict in Asia* (2016).

Bill Cope is a Professor in the Department of Education Policy, Organization & Leadership, University of Illinois, Urbana-Champaign, US, and an Adjunct Professor at Charles Darwin University, Australia. He is also a director of Common Ground Research Networks, a not-for-profit publisher and developer of 'social knowledge' technologies. His research interests include theories and practices of pedagogy, cultural and linguistic diversity, and new technologies of representation and communication. Among his publications are edited volumes on *The Future of the Academic Journal and e-Learning Ecologies*, and a book co-authored with Kalantzis and Magee, *Towards a Semantic Web: Connecting Knowledge in Academic Research.*

Dr. Aisling Crean is an award-winning Digital Education Developer at the University of St Andrews, UK, leading on the development of personalised learning and trustworthy learning analytics to support student learning and well-being. Recently, she has been developing an Open Educational Resource, Digital Educational Futures: Surveillance and Injustice, that aims to foster understanding of algorithmic injustice and its effects on marginalised groups in education. Her collaborative work on The Decolonial Classroom has won a number of awards. She holds a PhD in Philosophy from the Australian National University. Her co-authored work on trust and trustworthiness has been cited by the OECD.

Jenna Cushing-Leubner is an Associate Professor of Curriculum and Instruction at University of Wisconsin, Whitewater, United States. Jenna researches heritage language reclamation education, curriculum theory, and language teacher education. Her collaborative and community-driven approach to research as an act of participatory change-making includes work with language and knowledge keepers who are designing heritage language programs in both school-based and community settings. Her scholarship examines the relationship between settler colonialism, racial capitalism, and language justice, as well as how displaced communities live out theories of change, healing, and world-making in collective actions that are driven by desires for sustainable futures.

Laura Czerniewicz is Professor Emerita at the University of Cape Town in South Africa and the Founding Director of its Centre for Innovation in Learning and Teaching (CILT). She has a long-standing research and strategic focus on digital inequality and open education. Find Laura online at mastodon.social/@czernie. She blogs occasionally at https://czernie.weebly.com.

Jacob Davidsen is an Associate Professor in the Department of Communication and Psychology and Institute for Advanced Study in PBL at Aalborg University, Denmark. He is co-founder of the Video Research Lab (VILA), the Big Video Manifesto, the *QuiViRR* journal, and part of the BigSoftVideo team who develop software tools to enhance qualitative video research. He is currently working with collaborative immersive environments for learning, participation, and collaboration.

Mel M. Engman is a Senior Lecturer in Education and Applied Linguistics at Queen's University Belfast. She teaches on a wide range of topics related to language, education, and power, and she advocates for the maintenance and reclamation of Indigenous and minoritised languages in a variety of community-based contexts. Mel's research examines human-land relations, bilingual family learning, and anti-colonial approaches to language education. Her work can be found in the *Modern Language Journal, Linguistics and Education,* and *Language, Culture and Society.* She is on editorial boards for *Language and Education* and the *International Journal of Educational Research.*

Johanna Ennser-Kananen is an Associate Professor of English and Academy Research Fellow at the University of Jyväskylä's Department of Language and Communication Studies in Finland. Her work focuses on linguistically and culturally sustaining language and teacher education, particularly on epistemic justice in educational contexts. This entails the deconstructing of white, Eurocentric, and anthropocentric norms and the search for more sustainable and community-guided ways of being an academic.

Greta Goetz is Assistant Professor of Cultural Studies at the Faculty of Philology, Belgrade University. Her research is concerned with mnemotechnic hermeneutics, postdigital pedagogies, transnational and postdisciplinary dialogue, and networked learning. She has spoken and written about free software and Emacs as Design Pattern Learning and she iterates Stieglerian digital tools and approaches for her classes. A recent co-edited publication includes *Teaching and Learning to Co-Create,* and a recent chapter was published in *Bernard Stiegler and the Philosophy of Education II: Experiments in Negentropic Knowledge.* Her personal website is https://gretzuni.com.

Peter Goodyear is Emeritus Professor of Education at The University of Sydney in Australia. His research interests include professional education, networked learning, learning spaces, and educational design. Peter is a Senior Fellow of the Australian Learning and Teaching Council and an Australian Research Council Laureate Fellow. His most recent books are: *The education ecology of universities* (with Rob Ellis, 2019), *Spaces of teaching and learning* (with Rob Ellis, 2018), *Epistemic fluency and professional education* (with Lina Markauskaite, 2017), and *Place-based spaces for networked learning* (with Lucila Carvalho and Maarten de Laat, 2017).

Amy Hanna is a Lecturer at the University of Strathclyde, UK. Her research interests are in children's rights, children's rights theory, participation, and social epistemology. Amy is also interested in children's rights-based methodologies. She has published on the role of silence in both participation and 'voice' in education, what young people's silences can tell us about their (non) participation, and Epistemic Injustice in Childhood.

Sarah Hayes is Professor of Education and Research Lead in the School of Education at Bath Spa University, and a Principal Fellow of the HEA. She is an Honorary Professor at Aston University, Birmingham, UK, and an Associate Editor for *Postdigital Science and Education*. Sarah co-edited *Bioinformational Philosophy and Postdigital Knowledge Ecologies* (2022) with Michael Peters and Petar Jandrić. She also wrote *The Labour of Words in Higher Education* (2019) and *Postdigital Positionality* (2021), which opened debate on how disadvantage manifests in the disconnect between inclusivity policies and the widespread digitalisation and datafication of society.

Velislava Hillman (PhD) is a Visiting Fellow at the London School of Economics and Political Science and founder of Education Data Digital Sovereignty, an organisation that works at the intersection of research, education, and digital technologies. Velislava's research interests are in the integration of AI systems in schools, data-driven decision-making and children's rights and participation in increasingly digitalised classroom. Her recent work focuses on policy and governance of the EdTech sector with the aim to protect children's basic human rights and freedoms in the digitalised classroom.

Mary Kalantzis is a Professor in the Department of Education Policy, Organization and Leadership at the University of Illinois at Urbana-Champaign, US. From 2006 to 2016, she was Dean of the College of Education at the University of Illinois. Before then, she was Dean of the Faculty of Education, Language and Community Services at RMIT University, Melbourne, Australia, and President of the Australian Council of Deans of Education. With Bill Cope, she is co-author or editor of a number of books, including the two recent volumes on grammar of multimodal meaning: *Making Sense* and *Adding Sense* (2020).

Su-Ming Khoo is Associate Professor and Head of Sociology at the University of Galway, Ireland, and Visiting Professor in Critical Studies in Higher Education Transformation (CriSHET) at Nelson Mandela University, South Africa (2022–27). She researches, teaches, and writes about human development, human rights, public goods, development alternatives, decoloniality, global activism and learning, higher education and transdisciplinarity. She is co-editor with Helen Kara of *Researching in the Age of Covid-19, Volumes I Response and Reassessment, II Care and Resilience, III Creativity and Ethics* (2020), and *Qualitative and Digital Research in Times of Crisis* (2021). Personal website: https://www.nuigalway.ie/our-research/people/political-science-and-sociology/sumingkhoo/.

Neil Kramm is an Educational Technology Specialist and Lecturer in the Centre for Higher Education Research, Teaching and Learning (CHERTL) at Rhodes University in South Africa. He is currently reading for a PhD on the intersection of Generative Artificial Intelligence (GenAI) and assessment practices in higher education. Neil has co-published research with fellow researcher practitioners on various educational technology related topics ranging from online collaborative research to reimagining support for academics and how they can design more context appropriate learning experiences for students in resource constrained settings in higher education.

Caroline Kuhn holds a PhD in Education and works as a Senior Lecturer in Education at Bath Spa University, UK. She is particularly interested in open education and social justice framed under a critical pedagogy approach. She is a Fellow of the Higher Education Academy and an editor for the *Journal of Critical Realism*. Her research interest lies in the intersection of sociology, philosophy, technology, and social justice, with an interest in data justice. She is interested in how technology-driven solutions can be meaningfully integrated into resource constraint contexts so that different ways of knowing and beings are honoured and respected. She can be found online at @carolak, @Carolinekuhn@mastodon.social.

James Lamb is a Lecturer within the Centre for Research in Digital Education, and The Edinburgh Futures Institute, at the University of Edinburgh. His research and teaching particularly concerns the relationship between digital technologies and learning spaces. This includes research that has explored the postdigital learning spaces of higher education, the ways that online students conceptualise the campus, and mobile learning in urban settings. He is a co-author of the *Manifesto for Teaching Online* and has also published work advancing the case for multimodal assessment and feedback, and sonic methods within education research.

Warren Lilley is a Lecturer in the Psychology of Education at the School of Education, University of Cape Town, South Africa, where he focuses on developing meaningful educational praxis in the Global South. His continued research interests and publications, which draw on Cultural-Historical Activity Theory and participatory formative-intervention research, look towards how teaching and learning may be positively transformed through educational technologies. In addition, he continues to apply his expertise to educational technology integration efforts, including South African provincial teacher-training programmes, online courses, and research projects.

Felicitas Macgilchrist is Professor of Digital Education and Schooling at the University of Oldenburg, Germany. Her research explores the discourses and practices around educational technology, with a focus on critical, ethnographic, and speculative approaches. Felicitas is co-editor of *Learning, Media and Technology* and has recently published about automation/symmation in *Postdigital Science and Education*, rewilding EdTech in *on_education* and criticality in *Learning, Media* *and Technology.* Recent co-edited books include *Postdigital Participation in Education* (2023), *Schule und Unterricht im digitalen Wandel* (2023) and *Die datafizierte Schule* (2023).

Tess Maginess, Principal Fellow, Higher Education Academy, is Professor of Lifelong Learning at Queen's University, Belfast. A literature specialist, she has developed a range of innovative adult learning pedagogies over the course of 25 years, often using critical and creative digital approaches. Tess has gained many awards including a national Teaching Fellowship. She has gained funding to develop a wide spectrum of partnerships, local, national, and international. Her research spans World Literature, adult education, especially non-traditional learners, mental health and disability, and values and purposes of education. Otherwise, she gardens, cooks and sings. She lives on the family farm with her husband and dog.

Lina Markauskaite is a Professor of Learning Sciences at The University of Sydney, Australia. Her recent research projects have been mainly concerned with understanding the nature of complex professional knowledge work and learning in interdisciplinary and interprofessional spaces. Her recent books include *Epistemic Fluency and Professional Education: Innovation, Knowledgeable Action and Actionable Knowledge* (with Peter Goodyear, 2017), *Education for Practice in a Hybrid Space* (with Franziska Trede, Celina McEwen, and Susie Macfarlane, 2019), and *A Biophilic design guide to environmentally sustainable design studios* (with Niranjika Wijesooriya and Arianna Brambilla, 2022).

Paul McIlvenny is Professor in the Department of Culture and Learning at Aalborg University, Denmark, and research leader of the Centre for Discourses in Transition (C-DiT). He has published extensively on video-based analyses of talk and social interaction in a variety of settings. He is co-founder of the Video Research Lab (VILA), the Big Video Manifesto, the *QuiViRR* journal, and the BigSoftVideo team who develop software tools to enhance qualitative video research. He has crafted immersive visualisation technologies (XR) to investigate the relationship between mobilities, embodiments and mediated social interaction in complex environments.

Genevieve Mosely is a PhD Candidate in Architecture at The University of Queensland in Australia. Genevieve's research focuses on design education and the application of design thinking to help capture new value through better understanding users and their needs. Her PhD research utilises a qualitative approach to investigate current discourse on design practice, through specifically drawing attention to design facilitation. Genevieve's most recent book is *Design Thinking Pedagogy: Facilitating Innovation and Impact in Tertiary Education* (with Cara Wrigley, 2022).

Selman Özdan is an Associate Professor in the Department of Public International Law and Vice Dean of Law School at the Ondokuz Mayıs University, Turkey. Özdan's research interests are in international human rights law, diplomacy, jurisdictional immunities, fake news, and disinformation in the legal sense. Özdan is a member of the Society of Legal Scholars and Case Western Reserve University Law Alumni Association. He has previously published in *International Journal of Human Rights* and *Postdigital Science and Education*. His recent book is *The Human Rights Challenge to Immunity in International Law* (2022).

Nicola Pallitt is an Educational Technology Specialist and Senior Lecturer in the Centre for Higher Education Research, Teaching and Learning (CHERTL) at Rhodes University in South Africa. Nicola's recent research and collaborative projects include compassionate learning design, online professional development, online supervision, and digital pedagogies in resource constrained settings in higher education. Nicola is an Associate Editor for *Critical Studies in Teaching and Learning (CriSTaL)*. She is part of the e/merge Africa team, an educational technology network for educational technology researchers and practitioners in African higher education.

Paul Prinsloo is a Research Professor in the Department of Business Management at the University of South Africa. His research interests include the measurement, collection, analysis, and use of student data, student data privacy, student data sovereignty, data ethics, and student success. He has been Principal Investigator in grants funded by the Irish Research Council and the Volkswagenstiftung, Germany. Paul's published works includes *Open(ing) education: Theory and practice* (2020), *Learning analytics: a primer* (2021), and *Learning analytics in open, distance and distributed learning: Potential and challenges* (2022).

Thomas Ryberg is Professor of Problem Based Learning and Digital Learning and Director of Institute for Advanced Study in PBL (IAS PBL) at Aalborg University, Denmark. His primary research interests are within the fields of Networked Learning and Problem Based Learning. In particular, he is interested in Problem Based Learning, and how new media and technologies transform our ways of thinking about and designing for networked and hybrid learning. He is co-chair of the International Networked Learning Conference and co-editor of the Springer book series Research in Networked Learning.

Akash K. Saini is a Ph.D. student in the Learning Design and Leadership Program at the University of Illinois, Urbana-Champaign (UIUC), US. Prior to joining the Ph.D. program, he worked with multiple organizations (including UNESCO) and startups that concerns with harnessing new media and technology adapted for teaching-learning practices as well as policy advocacy for mainstream education. His research and practice focus on developing, designing, exploring, and testing digital tools (such as VR, AR, Games, etc.) to facilitate learning and assessment along with providing specialized instructions, training, and guidance for integrating such technologies into educational practices.

Duane Searsmith has developed writing analytics with the support of a series of IES and NSF grants in which Dr. Cope has been PI. As well as developing the CGMap software, he has worked with advanced natural language processing techniques and topic modelling. Searsmith has recently built prompt engineering software which recalibrates ChatGPT responses.

Christine Sinclair is an Honorary Fellow in the Centre for Research in Digital Education at the University of Edinburgh. Before retiring, she was Programme Director for the MSc in Digital Education. She graduated from this programme herself in 2010, when working as a Lecturer in Academic Practice at the University of Strathclyde. She enjoyed researching student experience through being a student and is the author of *Understanding University: A Guide to Another Planet* (2006) and *Grammar: A Friendly Approach* (2010).

Sandra Sinfield is Senior Lecturer in Education and Learning Development in the Centre for Professional and Educational Development at London Metropolitan University, UK, and a co-founder of the Association for Learning Development in Higher Education (ALDinHE). She has co-authored *Essential Study Skills: The complete Guide to Success at University* (2022, 5th Edition), *Teaching, Learning and Study Skills: A Guide for Tutors* (2004), and many other high-cited publications. Sandra is interested in creativity as liberatory and holistic practice in Higher Education; she has developed theatre and film in unusual places – and inhabited Second Life as a learning space.

Natalie Spence is a designer for learning at Macquarie University and postdoctoral research associate at The University of Sydney on the four-year Australian Research Council Discovery Project, Developing Interdisciplinary Expertise in Universities. In her research, she focuses on the sociomaterial aspects of knowledge creation. Natalie also has 13 years' experience supporting university academics in their use of technology and design of courses. Her current professional focus is on program-level design and associated workshops and practices.

Juha Suoranta is a Professor of Adult Education at Tampere University, Finland. He has studied and published critical pedagogy and public sociology. He has worked as a Visiting Scholar at the University of Illinois at Urbana-Champaign (1996–1997) and UCLA (2003–2004) and as Visiting Professor at the University of Minnesota (2005–2006). His books include *The Havoc of Capitalism* (2010), *Wikiworld* (2010), *Hidden in Plain Sight: How I Sheltered a Refugee* (2011), *Artistic Research Methodology* (2014), *Rebellious Research* (2014) (in Finnish language), *C. Wright Mills's Sociological Life* (2017) (in Finnish language), *Paulo Freire, A Pedagogue of the Oppressed* (2019) (in Finnish language), and *Militant Freire* (2021). Currently, he is working on the research project 'Speculative Social Science Fiction of Digitalization in Higher Education: Towards A Humanized Digital Future', funded by the Academy of Finland (2021–2025).

Teresa Swist is Research Associate at The University of Sydney in Australia and co-founder of the Education Futures Studio. Her inter/transdisciplinary research is focused upon participatory methodologies, knowledge and design practices, curriculum-making, and postdigital cultures. A particular interest is how people with diverse expertise can generate ideas, tools, and processes for collective learning and systemic change. Her work has been published in journals such as *Learning, Media and Technology, Higher Education Research & Development,* and *Computers & Education: Artificial Intelligence.*

Marko Teräs is a postdoctoral researcher in Social Sciences at Tampere University. He is the co-founder of Critical Applied Research of Digitalization in Education (CARDE) research group and CreditEd research network. His research interests include EdTech, HCI, digitalization, datafication, speculative methods, and utopian thinking. Marko has a broad professional history with research and development projects in online learning, HCI, digitalization, and datafication, in Tanzania, UAE, Southeast Asia, and Australia. His current research project is Speculative Social Science Fiction of Digitalization in Higher Education: Towards A Humanized Digital Future, funded by the Academy of Finland (2021–2025).

Anastasia O. Tzirides is a Visiting Lecturer at the University of Illinois Chicago, US, teaching online Modern Greek language and culture courses, and an academic researcher at the University of Illinois, Urbana-Champaign. She is also a User Experience Researcher at Google. Her research interests include advanced digital technologies, artificial intelligence, user experience research, learning design, online education, as well as language and culture learning. Her dissertation research project focused on exploring the potential of advanced digital technologies and artificial intelligence for collaborative language learning utilizing translanguaging and multimodal communication approaches.

Amea Wilbur (she, her, hers) is an Assistant Professor in Adult Education at the University of the Fraser Valley, Canada, and worked in the settlement sector for many years in Vancouver. She holds an EdD from the Department of Educational Studies at UBC. Her doctorate explored ways to make government-funded language training more inclusive for students who have experienced trauma. She has facilitated numerous workshops on trauma-informed practices for settlement and language providers both provincially and nationally. Her most recent writing collaboration, 'The Power of Narrative Storytelling: How Podcasts as An Arts-Based Practice Enhance Solidarity and Social Activism in Adult Education', was published in *Studies in the Education of Adults.*

Cara Wrigley is Professor of Design Innovation within the Faculty of Engineering, Architecture and Information Technology at The University of Queensland, Australia. She is Director of the Design Innovation Research Lab, leading a research team that focuses on design-led exploratory research, conducting applied and theoretical research into people, emotions, strategy, and business. Her most recent books include *Design Thinking Pedagogy: Facilitating Innovation and Impact in Tertiary Education* (with Genevieve Mosely, 2022).

Part I
Postdigital Positionality

Positionality in Postdigital Research: The Power to Effect Change

Sarah Hayes (iD)

1 Introduction

Postdigital research has a heritage (Jandrić et al. 2022) which includes its emergence from the arts, humanities, and creative subjects, which are currently under attack (Hall 2022). Through postdigital research there is an ongoing interchange between what is to come, as well as what has gone before. Postdigital researchers can reflect this ethos through honest, critically reflexive expressions of their positionality.

In discussing the topic of *Extinction Internet*, Geert Lovink (2022) argues that the Internet is accelerating the world's problems and that 'it is time to infuse the cold managerial approach of algorithmic governmentality with Mark Fisher's hauntology'. Adding that this calls for 'a new language to understand the present', I propose that the language and process of each individual's 'postdigital positionality' (Hayes 2021a, b) is one way to enact and express that hauntology. I like to think of postdigital positionality as a way to turn things 'inside out', surfacing what is often unseen and unheard throughout the joy and anguish of research. I perceive there to be a power to effect change in particular, where *the language of postdigital positionality* engages with *the language of postdigital community*.

In this chapter, the role of individual 'postdigital positionalities' in research will be examined, alongside the globally collaborative nature of the growing postdigital research community. Firstly, positionality as a statement or a process is considered. This is developed to suggest one form of language that could prompt reflection on a process for recognizing and expressing postdigital positionality. Then the idea of being postdigital is examined from a range of perspectives, recognizing the political economic structure that surrounds research.

S. Hayes (✉)
Bath Spa University, Bath, UK
e-mail: s.hayes@aston.ac.uk

© The Author(s), under exclusive license to Springer Nature
Switzerland AG 2023
P. Jandrić et al. (eds.), *Constructing Postdigital Research*, Postdigital Science
and Education, https://doi.org/10.1007/978-3-031-35411-3_1

The broader context of research and research methods arrive from a mainly Westernised approach, funding and publishing model in neoliberal society. Here 'the potential role of research methodology in decolonisation research' is acknowledged, along with related structural challenges and a need to 'synthesise existing work on decolonising methodologies' (Barnes 2018: 385). Challenges and assumptions will be discussed alongside *postdigital possibilities* to embrace what is often marginalised, in terms of research in global and local contexts of disadvantage. This includes, but is not limited to, recognising and addressing postdigital poverty as a barrier to participation. Here the idea of the postdigital is raised as a vehicle for change and a collaborative space where isolated researchers into decolonisation of different areas of postdigital life might gather in dialogue.

Finally, the more individual nature of postdigital research is examined once more through *positionality*. This includes exploring different stances that a human postdigital researcher might take and the critical reflexivity that is incumbent upon them to exercise. It also opens debate on how we might perceive the postdigital positionality of other 'entities' that are not (obviously) human, but that impact on humans and each other. This could include, but is not limited to, digital systems and data, algorithms, Artificial Intelligence (AI), Internet of Things (IoT), wearable technologies and all forms of tracking, surveillance, or interventions, digital or analog. It might refer to other species, biological or ecological forms of life, or geographical spaces.

Within our dominant Westernised approaches towards research, it is considered rigorous for researchers to resolve such issues with clarity from the outset, to explain their epistemological and ontological stances, and why they have chosen a certain related methodology. Yet researchers of postdigital society may also need to bring additional layers of reflexivity to this practice. They may need to provide somewhat uncertain and fluid accounts of the positionality of their minds and bodies in their research. I suggest that any *postdigital positionality statement* is an open, critical commentary that 'permits' researchers to honestly state their perceived relations to relevant factors, but as a fluid process rather than a static declaration. Researchers can disclose aspects of their identity, declare any potential bias but also point out where they may need to apply reflexivity and ongoing praxis, to later reposition some of their arguments.

As a community, it is necessary to appreciate both the *broader contexts* and *individual positions* involved in postdigital research as fluid. As such, we may open dialogue on what a *postdigital research manifesto* could look like. However, in a postdigital spirit (something we may each define differently too) such a manifesto may need to be dissolved as quickly as it is suggested, so that the power of the messy and open idea of 'the postdigital' is preserved. Therefore, the chapter concludes with this paradox in mind, outlining some possible features of a positional, postdigital research stance and approach. A suggested model of a process to engage with postdigital positionality in research is sketched out and presented for further postdigital dialogue (Jandrić et al. 2019). A cycle of questions or prompts are included, that might be adapted or applied in numerous ways, depending on the focus and context of the research/researcher(s').

The intention is not to assume anything about the research/researcher(s') postdigital positionality and environment, but instead to invite an emancipatory approach where such a model might be adapted or discarded. The example questions in the model might be asked of a human in a self-interrogatory way, or applied to non-humans or a hybrid assemblage, depending on the positioning of the research and researcher(s'). Such prompts may help to ensure (as part of any chosen methodology) that a continual interrogation of what is assumed about digital life, digital actors, positionality and the humanities takes place. As such, applying questions like these might help to capture what it means to 'think with postdigital noise' (Macgilchrist 2021: 663). Or they may further an understanding of the 'participation' of humans/non-humans or assemblages as they are positioned in a postdigital society.

2   Postdigital Positionality as Statement or a Process

Torres-Olave and Lee (2019) suggest that positionality is constructed around three main tenets: (1) identities are complex and fluid, (2) they are enmeshed in power relations, and (3) they are contextually bound. Yet often what is referred to as 'researcher positionality' is simply written into a brief statement early on in a thesis or a research article. Whilst it may refer to the personal role, values, context, position of power, or potential bias a researcher perceives they have brought to their study (Hayes 2021a, b: 211), it confines what is dynamic to something rather more static, failing to engage fully with the tenets Torres-Olave and Lee (2019) suggest. When positionality is considered as a process, then it enables researchers to consider ongoing and interesting tensions across these tenets and others they perceive to be relevant.

Developing and voicing our postdigital positionalities does not therefore set them in stone. I reserve the right to reflexively discuss my own positionality as interconnected with many entities, as I continue to relate to my identity, emotions, contexts, the positions of other people, objects, and theories. In contributing ideas that are not fully formed, researchers make themselves vulnerable, risking critique. Bringing the concept of vulnerability to bear on the postdigital is a topic that is explored by Michael Jopling (2023). He 'calls for us to access our postdigital vulnerability as researchers and educators in order to develop research that can help us better understand our entangled context and resist its more pernicious elements' (Jopling 2023: 168). This would seem to be valuable as part of any researcher's exploration of their postdigital positionality. It may even help to initiate resistance towards problematic rivalries amongst researchers in favour of community when vulnerabilities are openly voiced.

Furthermore, when postdigital positionalities are confronted to acknowledge who is disadvantaged, this helps to challenge exclusive funding or publishing models (Jandrić and Hayes 2019) or to ask 'whose or indeed what culture … we want to be funded?' (Hall 2022: 64) Furthermore, digitization, the humanities and social theory all have their place in popular culture. As Barron points out:

> The central issues that underpin classic social thought – class, conflict, sexual oppression, gender, power, consumerism, social relations and stability, ethnicity, the body, economic systems and social status – are all factors that can be readily discerned within the modern global world and everyday cultural life. (Barron 2013: 2)

Barron adds that these issues can be located in, and illuminated through, the 'stuff' of our culture, which includes 'popular music, cinema, celebrity, fashion, sport, television' (Barron 2013: 2). I would add that the many factors Barron lists above manifest too in our postdigital society via all manner of data-driven systems and media that now power and potentially control our lives (Hayes et al. 2023). From questions of design and programming, to access, operation, discrimination, and disadvantage, individuals are influenced and tracked, across these complex datafied contexts.

If positionality is perceived as an ongoing process, rather than a finite statement, then it offers a way for researchers to continually and reflexively discuss who, or what, intersects with their research, to potentially alter their positioning in postdigital society. Therefore, to apply this thinking, I will tentatively offer a *positionality process* and place myself in it.

3   My Own Postdigital Positionality

If I am to openly state what intimately connects me with this writing, I might disclose my circumstances to explain firstly any *position* that I am assuming. I could then discuss what *proposition* I am contributing and say if this sits in *opposition* to other theories. I may even anticipate what form of *composition* this writing will become, but also reflexively consider where I may need to *reposition* my arguments. Having stated these ideas let's give it a go.

3.1   *What* Position *Is Assumed?*

I am (I believe…) still a human, despite being immersed in postdigital-biodigital society, amid the 'many faces of postdigital' (Peters et al. 2023: 206). Yet I concur with the assertion made by Steve Matthewman that we have always been posthuman, that 'we are never prior to or independent of the very technologies, companion species and environments that help to constitute us' (Matthewman 2010: 176). As such, when I coined the phrase 'postdigital positionality' (Hayes 2021a, b), I imagined that *positionality* might easily have just as many 'faces' as *postdigital*; that it would constantly present in endless forms through the accounts of individual researchers, sharing their experiences of postdigital life, to develop our broader understanding as a diverse and inclusive global community.

However, sharing my own vulnerability as part of my postdigital position is far from easy at this time, raising questions for me of how much do I share? Personally,

I am experiencing the grief that accompanies the recent loss of a close family member, having been intimately involved in his palliative care. These emotions have become entangled too with the simultaneous loss of my institutional research role, as I and my colleagues have been faced with the recent closure of our successful research centre, the Education Observatory, at the University of Wolverhampton. Loss, though, invokes a powerful consideration of the past, as well as the future, prompting me to reflect on past writing that seems relevant to revisit here.

3.2 What Proposition *Is Contributed?*

In 2015, I wrote a chapter (Hayes 2015a, b) called: 'Encouraging the intellectual craft of *living* research' for a book called *Learning to Research – Researching to Learn* (Bartholomew et al. 2015). This drew on the approach suggested by C. Wright Mills (1959) 'that successful scholars do not split their work from the rest of their lives, but treat scholarship as a choice of how to *live*, as well as a choice of career' (Hayes 2015a, b: 126) (emphasis added). My chapter discussed how I designed the idea of *living* research into a final year Sociology undergraduate (UG) module I wrote and taught: 'Tattoos, TV and Trends: Understanding Popular Culture'.

My intention was to encourage UGs to see that they could connect all kinds of personal experiences and aspects of their identities with their chosen research projects. This was aimed too at students appreciating that they could resist the neoliberal structuring of their education, where each module of study becomes something chronological to simply tick off, disconnected from their lives, past and future experiences. My students chose topics in popular culture, such as modern genres of music, fashion, gender, interactions with smart phones, film, social media, sexting, affirmation, communicity (Cremin 2013), tattoos, and other areas of interest. They were asked to research their chosen subject through classical social theory first, before critiquing their findings via more contemporary theories.

Asking students to map their own life experiences on to what they research can liberate thought (Hayes 2015a, b: 148). I propose therefore that such a *process* that surfaces researcher connections with their object of study, aids a reflexive, ongoing appreciation of positionality. It is one way to 'anchor ourselves in ever changing postdigital situations, and to bring our individual experiences (past present and future) into both personal and collective dialogues' (Hayes 2021a, b: x). To what end though?

Taking the examples of research into disadvantage during the Covid-19 pandemic (see Jandrić et al. 2021a), or decolonisation research, there is a dilemma where findings are still surfaced via dominant westernized methods and funding models within neoliberal society. Surfacing the diverse positionalities of researchers and their contexts helps to draw attention to the decolonising of methodologies as ongoing. The job is never done. Yet a collaborative postdigital space can be cultivated where isolated researchers into decolonisation of different areas of postdigital life might gather in dialogue.

3.3 How Does This Sit in Opposition to Other Theories or Methods?

Adopting a *postdigital positionality process* that looks back as well as ahead reveals ways to resist any imposed chronological sequencing of life, education, and work in neoliberal society. A society indeed 'in which we are encouraged to become not just what Michel Foucault calls entrepreneurs of the self but micro-entrepreneurs of the self, acting as if we are our own, precarious, freelance microenterprises' (Hall 2016: 2). As universities are currently confronting apparent economic deficits in their income since the Covid-19 pandemic, there is much to notice, as 'uberfied' (Hall 2016) and datafied decisions are routinely taken to reduce costs, close courses and areas of research, as we in the Education Observatory experienced. With staff already employed on insecure contracts and subject to increased surveillance and measurement of their activities, Hall points out an increasing resemblance of university labour to that of the gig economy. Like mini cab drivers, academics are 'atomized, freelance microentrepreneurs in business for themselves' (Hall 2021: 15). Hall asks if this is really the academia that vice chancellors want?

In the absence of any immediate response to that question, and as newly redundant colleagues like myself routinely re-market themselves across LinkedIn as 'Open to Work', how such data-driven platforms also contribute to the construction of our postdigital positionalities is another key consideration in postdigital research. There is evidence, for example, that academics often differentiate their online identities, as they have become increasingly aware of the need to develop different strategies and user habits for every social networking site on which they have a presence (Segado-Boj et al. 2019). This fragmentation of online identities has implications for how each of us navigates and accounts for our positionalities in our research. Personally, I oppose this neoliberal division of different aspects of life in favour of *living* research that pulls the pieces back together. A good starting place can be to look back reflexively for potentiality and lost futures, when all else around us suggests forging ahead: 'When the present has given up on the future, we must listen for the relics of the future in the unactivated potentials of the past.' (Fisher 2013: 53)

3.4 What Form of Composition Will the Writing of This Chapter Become?

In anticipation now of the process of my writing to come, I return to the intellectual craft of 'living research' (Mills 1959; Hayes 2015a, b). I ponder ways of writing up more holistically, what is *live* or *lived* within postdigital research? When authors write collectively they may simply contribute isolated sections to a co-authored volume. Alternatively, they may each notice both their individual positionalities and also their collective postdigital cooperation and community.

Taking time to share these processes and tensions, to develop a dialogue about them and even to write into the composition some observations on these dynamics, holds a real power to effect change and develop positionality in writing. For me personally, this is a process of making connections and pointing to who/what I believe intersects with what. It is a gathering up of what seems fragmented, noticing and expressing ideas, undertaking analysis and also making unlikely analogies. This however requires each of us to be open to connections that may also unsettle our pre-existing beliefs in an uncomfortable manner. It can also take time. It is not easy though to resist the neoliberal structuring that leaves each of us living in the present and 'swiping the night away' (Lovink 2022), frequently disconnected from our past and future experiences.

3.5 Will There Be a Need to Reposition These Arguments?

I am reflecting here on how much failure, as well as fascinating findings might appear in the reporting of postdigital research. This feels to me to be an important and honest element of postdigital positionality when there are always alternative methodologies that might have been adopted, different topics studied, areas of bias that remain unexplored. Exposing such vulnerabilities takes courage when we are told that 'research excellence' and 'impact' are the dominant ingredients of a high-quality publication.

Having attempted to place my own postdigital positionality in this chapter I have dabbled with ideas that appeal to me and indulged my enjoyment of a play on words through the sections above on: *position, proposition, opposition, composition,* and *reposition* of arguments. Later in the chapter I will present this as a tentative model for critique from the postdigital community, but for now I am conscious that there may be readers who are unfamiliar with what is being discussed as 'postdigital' and why. Therefore, the next section explores some of the many faces of the postdigital (Peters et al. 2023: 206).

4 Being Postdigital

For quite some years now, the idea of the 'postdigital' has been explored and developed by a growing, global community of scholars (Pepperell and Punt 2000; Hall 2013, 2021; Cramer 2015; Jandrić et al. 2018). Some researchers have examined 'postdigital' as a concept to question, for example, how the term is differentiated from the 'digital', pointing to 'a contemporary disenchantment with digital information systems and media gadgets' (Cramer 2015: 12). Feenberg (2019: 8) suggests that '[t]he postdigital no longer opposes the virtual or cyber world to the world of face-to-face experience. The digital is integrated and imbricated with our everyday actions and interactions.' This would presumably then include our language, so there are questions of how various texts have changed in composition, as people have discussed their encounters with the digital. After all, to respond to Lovink's (2022) call for 'a new language to understand the present', an understanding of some of the issues of our current Internet-infused language is helpful. If digital discourse is giving us problems, what might a postdigital discourse offer?

4.1   Postdigital Discourse

In *The Labour of Words in Higher Education* I argued that the heavy emphasis on what the digital can be *used for* has distracted us from what digital inherently *is* (Hayes 2019: 89). In other words, expressions of economic value about what the digital apparently enhances is a 'limiting discourse'. It obscures the complexities of individual, positional encounters with technology as it intersects with policy and language (Hayes 2018: 110). The question is whether a postdigital discourse can disrupt decades of linguistic assumptions that marginalize human academic labour in educational technology policy (Hayes 2014, 2015a, b, 2019; Hayes and Bartholomew 2015; Jandrić et al. 2018). Tangentially, it has been asked what work the 'post' part of the concept of postdigital is doing anyway?

This is raised amid our 'postdigital reality' which is considered as 'a space of learning, struggle, and hope, where "old" and "new" media are now "cohabiting artefacts" that enmesh with the economy, politics and culture' (Sinclair and Hayes 2019: 119). If this is the case, then amongst concerns at the capabilities of new Artificial Intelligence (AI) tools, such as ChatGPT, that can now 'generate human-like text, making it capable of engaging in natural language conversations', we are presented too, with opportunities to creatively rethink what we do and how we do it (Illingworth 2023). Yet, when faced with a barely distinguishable replication of human creativity and language by an AI, there are challenging questions to face and debate, regarding any assumptions of 'equivalence'.

For example, can the proposition put forward by Pepperell and Punt (2000: 55) that 'language is a technology through which human desire is satisfied and generated' still be applied in cases of ChatGPT authorship, where any aspects of 'human desire' may be hard to determine? Concerns that our cohabiting AI tools like ChatGPT, Bard and Jukebox might replace or outwit us may be allayed by noticing where their digital discourse is only as good as the human programming that gives them a voice (Boulton 2023). Perhaps then a scrutiny of the values that underpin any alternative postdigital discourse is key. Rather than the linguistic separation of technology from people and their positionality that can be found in so many digital policies, postdigital dialogue brings value in disrupting forever, 'the myth that technology or indeed discourse, acts alone' (Hayes 2019: 147).

4.2 Postdigital Equivalence

Yet for some an equivalence between what is human and what is computational and more than just displacement, may be anticipated. This would bring implications for how we might understand and treat our own individual positionalities in postdigital research. Drawing on the work of Mark Poster, Gary Hall (2013: 2) has pointed out that computer science 'was the first case where "a scientific field was established that focuses on a machine" and not on an aspect of nature or culture, as is the case with the physical, life and social sciences'. Poster (1990: 147) argues that Computer Science found its first identity in its relation to the computer, but regardless of how that computer (and I would add too new data-driven online systems) have changed, what is digital remains misidentified as something 'inscribed with transcendent status'. Hall (2013: 2) points out that this has significant implications when discussing any so-called computational turn in the humanities (Berry 2012: 11) and that '[a]s a field computer science is not necessarily the best equipped to understand itself and its own founding object, let alone help those in the humanities with their relation to computing and the digital' (Hall 2013: 2).

This in itself is worth each postdigital researcher pausing for a moment to consider. Yes, as Feenberg (2019) argues, *the digital* is integrated and imbricated with our everyday actions and interactions, but what stance do each of us take on the extent to which *the human* is integrated and imbricated with the everyday actions and interactions of digital and data-driven systems? Indeed, if we take a theoretical 'position' on this notion, we may also (as humans) take a physical stance, such as refusing to engage with certain systems or data. Pallitt and Kramm, writing in this volume, suggest that taking a 'noticing stance' on the positionality of things as well as humans is 'an essential part of acknowledging what we bring to the assemblage of postdigital research we are involved in, and postdigital dialogue more broadly' (Pallitt and Kramm, this volume). I agree. However, what becomes challenging is the question of who decides what constitutes 'positionality' or 'stance' amongst technologies, objects, or non-humans, of any kind, as they gather and mutually constitute our areas of research?

If we can agree in this context that a human or a team of humans are conducting the research, can we also agree that the human researcher(s') are the ones who define their own positionalities, and perhaps suggest what positionalities or interconnected relationships any non-humans bring to bear on their positionalities? Alternatively, as a postdigital research community, should we agree to disagree on that point? Should we instead recognize that the existence of more automated, 'humanless research' raises questions of authorship, but also calls for fluid and open interpretations of postdigital positionality?

Related to such questions, Hall (2013: 3) proceeds to emphasize the importance of maintaining a distinction between what has come to be called the 'digital humanities' and any 'rigorous understanding of what the humanities can become in an era of networked digital information machines'. This seems to place reasoning concerning how we perceive research in the humanities and how this may need to adjust to digital changes, firmly with the humans, at least for now.

4.3 Postdigital-Biodigital

In the decade that has followed this debate around computing and the humanities, it has become necessary to also consider the place of 'biodigital' convergences in these arguments. A new paradigm, 'biodigitalism', refers to the mutual interaction and integration of digital information and biology, but this manipulation of biological systems in computational biology is now beginning to fundamentally reconfigure all levels of theory and practice (Peters et al. 2021a). Since the Covid-19 pandemic such biodigital reconfigurations have become even more apparent. If both old and new technologies remain with us, just as old and new philosophical theories reside together, then we have a lot of resources to draw on in seeking to understand through research what is integral to our postdigital lives and the lives of others. This enables us 'to question who and what humans and intelligences really are, in this shared context' (Jandrić and Hayes 2020: 297). Referring to such a context as 'the post-digital labyrinth', Blanco-Fernández (2022: 1421) concludes then that 'the worth of the post-digital resides in its heterogeneity. The lack of a narrow definition is precisely an opportunity for more diverse creation.'

I would suggest that in applying this fluid stance to the concept of the postdigital itself, it is worth maintaining a similar flow too when interpreting our own individual postdigital positionalities in research. This enables each researcher to take a critically reflexivity stance to approach their dynamic relationships and productive tensions with what is postdigital or biodigital from a position of openness to change.

5 Postdigital Political Economy

It is this diversity of position in the conducting of postdigital research that this chapter seeks to shed light on, given the apparently endless range of topics and possible methodological approaches that might be taken. Thus, where any postdigital researcher chooses to focus their postdigital arguments at the time is inextricably connected to the personal context that they themselves inhabit in our broader political economy. As such, a positional, postdigital research stance has both micro and macro elements to be considered.

At the macro level, scholars could be exploring the terminology and meaning of 'postdigital' as it plays out across society in different forms of research. Yet there will also be a personal stance or positionality that influences how their findings are interpreted at a micro level. Here the facets of a researcher's identity and context, their location, race, gender, values, political opinions, and many other factors all hold relevance. Equally, if a researcher takes time to explore deeply their own individual stance and values as they undertake research, there is also a political economic context surrounding us all, that frequently dictates the nature of the wider publication of any findings.

I perceive there to be a space of power and tension for researchers to explore between these *postdigital micro* and *postdigital macro* contexts. Though we cannot escape the postdigital political economy surrounding research, perhaps we can effect change where the language of postdigital positionality engages with the language of postdigital community.

5.1 Postdigital Publishing

In a paper called 'The Postdigital Challenge of Redefining Education from the Margins', Petar Jandrić and I (Jandrić and Hayes 2019) explored the question of *what makes a voice marginal in our postdigital reality?* We examined the process of publishing as a form of 'social production' that concerns everyone but that takes place across the economy, politics, and culture, all of which are in turn accommodating both old and new technology in our postdigital age. Looking backwards as well as ahead, we pointed to a 'need to understand relationships between yesterday's centres and margins, because they have set up the scene for our current situation, but we also need to understand that these relationships have significantly reconfigured' (Jandrić and Hayes 2019: 392).

We pointed to a powerful collaborative context that can help in developing a new language for what we mean by 'marginal voices' in the social relations between knowledge production and academic publication. Drawing on Fuchs (2016: 215), who argues that 'the logic of cooperation contradicts the logic of instrumental reason', the postdigital community, as a body of researchers, can counter neoliberal, instrumental models of publishing via collective writing that represents this cooperation.

5.2 Postdigital Collective Writing

Recent examples of postdigital collective writing have been led by Michael Peters and Petar Jandrić, and are discussed here as a revisiting of the concept of the 'edited collection' (Peters et al. 2021b). The notion of 'postdigital dialogue' (Jandrić et al. 2019) was fleshed out in a collective article, and in others that have followed, what it means to be 'public intellectuals in the age of viral modernity' (Peters et al. 2022) or to 'struggle for meaning-making' through collective writing (Jandrić et al. 2022a) have been expressed.

During the Covid-19 pandemic a longitudinal study of global teaching and learning experiences by a group of 84 authors from 20 countries was conducted through short testimonies and workspace photographs that were published into several collective articles (Jandrić et al. 2020, 2021b, 2022b). This material was then anal-ysed as both personal, positional narratives, but also for what these testimonies represent as data. As data, these mutually constitutive accounts offer a much larger, powerful commentary on the position of educators across the globe during the pan-demic (Jandrić et al. 2021a). Essentially, the Covid-19 testimonies project demon-strates where the postdigital community has the power to effect change through a new shared language that combines individual postdigital positionality with collec-tive postdigital cooperation and community.

5.3   Postdigital Poverty

The Covid-19 testimonies (Jandrić et al. 2020, 2021a, b, 2022) also revealed a clear disparity across authors in terms of their economic and cultural circumstances and postdigital spaces of work to be able to contribute to online teaching and research. The question of postdigital poverty, including differing levels of access to digital devices, skills, and spaces to be able to work is particularly relevant to understand-ing the positionality of marginalized researchers across the globe. There is a need to see beyond assumptions that everyone has a home office to use during a pandemic, that they can rely on stable Internet connections, or electricity, or access the latest articles and research databases via an institutional login.

The postdigital research community therefore can build on global and local find-ings concerning different forms of postdigital poverty as it arises in terms of infra-structure, bandwidth, connectivity, and unequal spaces in which to learn from, and contribute to, postdigital research (Traxler et al. 2020).

5.4   Postdigital Decoloniality

The strong emphasis on Westernized research environments, methods, and frame-works for esteem as well as commercial models of funding and publishing over-shadows research and researchers in the Global South and other parts of the world where contexts may vary considerably. For example, Onyango and Ndege (2021) point to the need to re-evaluate research funding flows, when Africa's research funding is dominated by foreign entities and skewed hugely in favour of agriculture and health sciences (Omungo 2018). They add that the grant application processes and the methodology used to assess these are considered flawed.

Picking up on such concerns in other continents such as Australia, Maclean et al. (2022: 333) argue that space is needed 'for Indigenous peoples to position them-selves as research leaders, driving agendas and co-designing research approaches, activities, and outputs'. They conceptualise researcher positionality as informing sustainability science, providing a 'way for scientists, practitioners, and research partners to consider the power that each project member brings to a project, and to make explicit the unique positioning of project members in how they influence project processes and the development of usable knowledge' (Maclean et al. 2022: 333)

Somerville and Turner (2020: 182) raise too the 'primacy of connections to place' that they say 'is vital to research conducted with Indigenous individuals and groups'. This means that all entities associated with these places are included in this understanding too: 'Researchers working in the Indigenous space identify the necessity of understanding the relationality between all entities in Indigenous ways of knowing, being and doing.' (Somerville and Turner 2020: 182)

Onyango and Ndege (2021) discuss decoloniality as multidimensional, requiring multiple layers of actions. The dialogical approach they suggest of exploring multiple world views, documenting concrete examples and challenging funding regimes and systems in which researchers operate seems to dovetail well with how postdigital research seems to be evolving. If the postdigital community seeks to effect change through a new language then it requires an ever-growing number of voices from diverse positionalities to shape this, via cooperation and community. There are questions to be raised concerning what the postdigital adds to decolonizing arguments, and indeed what such arguments bring to our developing understandings of what is postdigital? When culture wars can be observed unfolding across different forms of digital media and social networks, dialogue on how the postdigital intersects with both old and new cultural political theories and tensions is necessary.

Despite the complexities of decoloniality, these cannot sit apart from debates on postdigital positionality. Whilst much is currently written on equality, diversion, inclusion and different forms of decolonization, all too frequently there is a problematic disconnect between such policy agendas and the widespread (and also unequal) digitization of society (Hayes 2021a, b). Therefore, in considering the powerful political economic forces that shape research in its dominant form, it is necessary to look to the data-driven digital systems that support and reinforce these inequities.

We can though as a postdigital community raise attention towards alternative, indigenous methods and viewpoints. We can also, as Onyango and Ndege (2021) suggest, critique what is assumed as research methods and continually re-evaluate Eurocentric research funding flows, approaches, and grant application processes. As a community we can continually support alternative views, but as individuals we can also reflexively document our positionalities in postdigital research. It is only by surfacing and publishing real practical experiences and cases that we might better articulate *postdigital decoloniality* as integral to postdigital dialogue (Jandrić et al. 2019).

6 Enacting Postdigital Positionality

Returning to the question of a language and process for each individual's 'postdigital positionality' (Hayes 2021a, b), enacting and expressing a personal hauntology is one starting point. If we are to connect *the language of postdigital positionality* with *the language of postdigital community*, then each of us has individual responsibilities to draw connections with our positions as we write up research on others. Choosing one methodological approach always marginalizes others, but perhaps this needs explicitly stated, as each of us interrogate our current digital and postdigital assumptions.

As I have always enjoyed playing with language, I will be honest in adding that I have developed the question of 'position' in the model below in one way, at the expense of other possibilities. I have set up a series of questions in Fig. 1 that does not exclude others, but that I hope may be applied to people, objects, or assemblages as researchers see fit, depending on the positionalities of those involved in any research project.

When I mapped out my own responses to these questions in the first part of this chapter, I undertook this process as a way to make connections concerning who/what I believe intersects with who or what, as I construct this chapter. I found that I was noticing postdigital tensions at numerous intersections. In so doing, I was also seeking to recognize how my research is *lived* in order to resist a neoliberal structuring that leaves each of us focused mostly on the present, often disconnected from our contexts, past and future experiences.

Whilst this is a set of questions I applied to myself, these are questions that might be raised collectively by postdigital communities of scholars as they undertake collaborative research and writing. There is no intention though to distract from the messy complexities of postdigital research which attracts researchers to contribute

Fig. 1 A tentative model for developing a postdigital positionality process in research

to this open, edgeless community. The model is presented as incomplete and messy too. It is up for grabs, to be played with, discarded or developed, as individuals and groups may wish. It is though, I hope, thought provoking for the research that I have referred to as *postdigital decoloniality*. Given that the digital is integrated and imbricated with our everyday actions and interactions (Feenberg 2019: 8), even for those in digital or data poverty – via the agendas of others – no decoloniality research can sit apart from its encounters with digital bias in our economic and cultural political economy.

Postdigital dialogue (Jandrić et al. 2019) between decolonization researchers might be furthered and developed using the questions raised in Fig. 1. Indeed these are questions that might be examined further through decomposition to consider what others may be relevant. Concrete examples of these studies, that are in dialogue with the diverse, postdigital positionalities (Hayes 2021a, b) of each researcher will also strengthen our postdigital community. As mentioned earlier, Torres-Olave and Lee (2019) discussed positionality in terms of three main tenets: (1) identities are complex and fluid, (2) they are enmeshed in power relations and, (3) they are contextually bound. To their helpful framework I offer the questions above to reflect the intimate interactions that data-driven digital systems bring to each of these three categories.

7   Postdigital Esteem

In conclusion of a chapter that is anything but finished, I wanted to raise a question for further debate, given my assertion that there is power to effect change where *the language of postdigital positionality* engages with *the language of postdigital community*. What forms of *postdigital esteem*, if any, are we seeking as individual researchers and as an open inclusive community? For example, in the Western world, research is subject to measurement of 'excellence', impact and esteem. Are we, I wonder, prepared to adopt different routes to effect change, to even present postdigital research models and methods that we are also fully prepared to scrap, if necessary, explaining our reasons for any changed position? Then what do we do in the face of cancel culture by the very platforms we may be seeking to arrange a postdigital dialogue through? In one example, Sarah Phillimore claims that a clear breach of the Equality Act has taken place, as Eventbrite have removed her gender-critical book launch event from the platform because it was decided that it promoted 'violent' or 'hateful' content (Powell 2022). Whilst there may be challenges presented by Artificial Intelligence there are also challenges arising from the points where data-driven platforms meet with different forms of human intelligence and related political agendas.

My suggestion is for each of us to at least be bold in whatever individual stance we may take towards postdigital positionality, even if the structure in which we work confines to some extent how or where we publish our stance. A personal postdigital positionality may involve reference to beliefs, identity, values, or assumptions. It could be that positionality is written with flamboyance, creativity, humility, uncertainty, vulnerability, or involving painful and personal revelations. Hopefully though, as a research community, we might surface our postdigital positionalities authentically, and thus bring multiple diverse global perspectives into postdigital dialogue (Jandrić et al. 2019), for meaningful change.

On this basis, it is worth reflecting on whether postdigital research requires multiple theories of change as well as an interpretation of *postdigital impact and esteem*. At the very least it is worth considering where any tangible change from our activities might be noticed and considered, either in our individual postdigital positionalities or in our postdigital positionality as a community. Calling for a new language to understand the present is one thing, enacting and documenting it to critically and reflexively support postdigital change is another.

References

Barnes, B. R. (2018). Decolonising Research Methodologies: Opportunity and Caution. *South African Journal of Psychology*, *48*(3), 379–387. https://doi.org/10.1177/0081246318798294.

Barron, L. (2013). *Social Theory in Popular Culture*. Basingstoke: Palgrave.

Bartholomew, P., Guerin, C., & Nygaard, C. (Eds.). (2015). *Learning to Research – Researching to Learn*. London: Libri Publishing.

Berry, D. (2012). Introduction: Understanding the Digital Humanities. In David Berry (Ed.), *Understanding Digital Humanities* (pp. 1–20). London: Palgrave Macmillan. https://doi.org/10.1057/9780230371934_1.

Blanco-Fernández, V. (2022). The Post-digital Labyrinth. Understanding Post-digital Diversity through CGI Volumetric Aesthetics. *Convergence*, *28*(5), 1421–1437. https://doi.org/10.1177/13548565221077587.

Boulton, A. (2023). There's an explosion in AI interest but there's lots of life left in real human intelligence. SkyNews, 10 February. https://news.sky.com/story/theres-an-explosion-in-ai-interest-but-theres-lots-of-life-left-in-real-human-intelligence-adam-boulton-12807211. Accessed 8 March 2023.

Cramer, F. (2015). What is 'post-digital'? In D. M. Berry & M. Dieter (Eds.), *Postdigital aesthetics: Art, computation and design* (pp. 12–26). New York: Palgrave Macmillan. https://doi.org/10.1057/9781137437204_2.

Cremin, C. (2013). Communicity. *Ephemera*, *13*(3), 617–626.

Feenberg, A. (2019). Postdigital or Predigital? *Postdigital Science and Education, 1*(1), 8–9. https://doi.org/10.1007/s42438-018-0027-2.

Fisher, M. (2013). The Metaphysics of Crackle: Afrofuturism and Hauntology. *Dancecult: Journal of Electronic Dance Music Culture*, *5*(2), 42–55. https://doi.org/10.12801/1947-5403.2013.05.02.03.

Fuchs, C. (2016). *Critical Theory of Communication*. London: University of Westminster Press.

Hall, G. (2016). *The Uberfication of the University*. Minneapolis, MN: University of Minnesota Press.

Hall, G. (2021). Postdigital Politics. In S. Niederberger, C. Sollfrank, & F. Stalder (Eds.), *Aesthetics of the Commons* (pp. 153–177). Zurich and Berlin: Diaphenes. https://doi.org/10.4472/9783035803914.0008.

Hall, G. (2022). Defund Culture. *Radical Philosophy, 2*(12), 62–68.

Hall, G. (2013). Towards a post-digital humanities: Cultural analytics and the computational turn to data-driven scholarship. *American Literature, 85*(4), 781–809. https://doi.org/10.1215/00029831-2367337.

Hayes, S. (2014). The Political Discourse and Material Practice of Technology Enhanced Learning. PhD Thesis. Birmingham: Aston University. https://publications.aston.ac.uk/id/eprint/26694/1/Hayes_Sarah_L._2015.pdf. Accessed 14 January 2023.

Hayes, S. (2015a). Counting on the Use of Technology to Enhance Learning. In P. Jandrić & D. Boras (Eds.), *Critical Learning in Digital Networks* (pp. 15–36). Cham: Springer. https://doi.org/10.1007/978-3-319-13752-0_2.

Hayes, S. (2015b). Encouraging the Intellectual Craft of *Living* Research: Tattoos, Theory and Time. In P. Bartholomew, C. Guerin, & C. Nygaard (Eds.), *Learning to Research – Researching to Learn.* (pp. 125–150). London: Libri Publishing.

Hayes, S. (2018). Invisible labour: Do we need to reoccupy student engagement policy? *Learning and Teaching, 11*(1), 19–34. https://doi.org/10.3167/latiss.2018.110102.

Hayes, S. (2019). *The Labour of Words in Higher Education.* Leiden: Brill.

Hayes, S. (2021a). Postdigital perspectives on the McPolicy of Measuring Excellence. *Postdigital Science and Education, 3*(1), 1–6. https://doi.org/10.1007/s42438-020-00208-2.

Hayes, S. (2021b). *Postdigital Positionality: developing powerful inclusive narratives for learning, teaching, research and policy in Higher Education.* Leiden: Brill.

Hayes, S., & Bartholomew, P. (2015). Where's the Humanity? Challenging the Policy Discourse of Technology Enhanced Learning. In J. Branch, P. Bartholomew, & C. Nygaard (Eds.), *Technology Enhanced Learning in Higher Education* (pp. 113–133). London: Libri Publishing.

Hayes, S., Jopling, M., Connor, S., & Johnson, M. (2023). *Human Data Interaction, Disadvantage and Skills in the Community: Enabling Cross-Sector Environments for Postdigital Inclusion.* Cham: Springer. https://doi.org/10.1007/978-3-031-31875-7.

Illingworth, S. (2023). ChatGPT: students could use AI to cheat, but it's a chance to rethink assessment altogether. The Conversation. 19 January. https://theconversation.com/chatgpt-students-could-use-ai-to-cheat-but-its-a-chance-to-rethink-assessment-altogether-198019. Accessed 22 January 2023.

Jandrić, P, MacKenzie, A., & Knox, J. (2022). Postdigital Research: Genealogies, Challenges, and Future Perspectives. *Postdigital Science and Education.* https://doi.org/10.1007/s42438-022-00306-3.

Jandrić, P., & Hayes, S. (2019). The postdigital challenge of redefining education from the margins. *Learning, Media and Technology, 44*(3), 381–393. https://doi.org/10.1080/17439884.2019.1585874.

Jandrić, P., & Hayes, S. (2020). Postdigital We-Learn. *Studies in Philosophy of Education, 39*(3), 285–297. https://doi.org/10.1007/s11217-020-09711-2.

Jandrić, P., Bozkurt, A., McKee, M., Hayes, S. (2021a). Teaching in the Age of Covid-19 – A Longitudinal Study. *Postdigital Science and Education, 3*(3), 743–770. https://doi.org/10.1007/s42438-021-00252-6.

Jandrić, P., Fuentes Martinez, A., Reitz, C., Jackson, L., Grauslund, D., Hayes, D., Lukoko, H. O., Hogan, M., Mozelius, P., Arantes, J. A., Levinson, P., Ozoliņš, J., Kirylo, J. D., Carr, P. R., Hood, N., Tesar, M., Sturm, S., Abegglen, S., Burns, T., Sinfield, S., Stewart, G. T., Suoranta, J., Jaldemark, J., Gustafsson, U., Monzó, L. D., Batarelo Kokić, I., Kihwele, J. E., Wright, J., Kishore, P., Stewart, P. A., Bridges, S. M., Lodahl, M., Bryant, P., Kaur, K., Hollings, S., Brown, J. B., Steketee, A., Prinsloo, P., Hazzan, M. K., Jopling, M., Mañero, J., Gibbons, A., Pfohl, S., Humble, N., Davidsen, J., Ford, D. R., Sharma, N., Stockbridge, K., Pyyhtinen, O., Escaño, C., Achieng-Evensen, C., Rose, J., Irwin, J., Shukla, R., SooHoo, S., Truelove, I., Buchanan, R., Urvashi, S., White, E. J., Novak, R., Ryberg, T., Arndt, S., Redder, B., Mukherjee, M., Komolafe, B. F., Mallya, M., Devine, N., Sattarzadeh, S. D., & Hayes, S. (2022b). Teaching in the Age of Covid-19—The New Normal. *Postdigital Science and Education, 4*(3), 877–1015. https://doi.org/10.1007/s42438-022-00332-1.

Jandrić, P., Hayes, D., Levinson, P., Lisberg Christensen, L., Lukoko, H. O., Kihwele, J. E., Brown, J. B., Reitz, C., Mozelius, P., Nejad, H. G., Fuentes Martinez, A., Arantes, J. A., Jackson, L., Gustafsson, U., Abegglen, S., Burns, T., Sinfield, S., Hogan, M., Kishore, P., Carr, P. R., Batarelo Kokić, I., Prinsloo, P., Grauslund, D., Steketee, A., Achieng-Evensen, C., Komolafe, B. F., Suoranta, J., Hood, N., Tesar, M., Rose, J., Humble, N., Kirylo, J. D., Mañero, J., Monzó, L. D., Lodahl, M., Jaldemark, J., Bridges, S. M., Sharma, N., Davidsen, J., Ozoliņš, J., Bryant, P., Escaño, C., Irwin, J., Kaur, K., Pfohl, S., Stockbridge, K., Ryberg, T., Pyyhtinen, O., SooHoo, S., Hazzan, M. K., Wright, J., Hollings, S., Arndt, S., Gibbons, A., Urvashi, S., Forster, D. J., Truelove, I., Mayo, P., Rikowski, G., Stewart, P. A., Jopling, M., Stewart, G. T., Buchanan, R., Devine, N., Shukla, R., Novak, R., Mallya, M., Biličić, E., Sturm, S., Sattarzadeh, S. D., Philip, A. P., Redder, B., White, E. J., Ford, D. R., Allen, Q., Mukherjee, M., & Hayes, S. (2021b). Teaching in the Age of Covid-19—1 Year Later. *Postdigital Science and Education, 3*(3), 1073–1223. https://doi.org/10.1007/s42438-021-00243-7.

Jandrić, P., Hayes, D., Truelove, I., Levinson, P., Mayo, P., Ryberg, T., Monzó, L.D., Allen, Q., Stewart, P.A., Carr, P.R., Jackson, L., Bridges, S., Escaño, C., Grauslund, D., Mañero, J., Lukoko, H.O., Bryant, P., Fuentes Martinez, A., Gibbons, A., Sturm, S., Rose, J., Chuma, M.M., Biličić, E., Pfohl, S., Gustafsson, U., Arantes, J.A., Ford, D.R., Kihwele, J.E., Mozelius, P., Suoranta, J., Jurjević, L., Jurčević, M., Steketee, A., Irwin, J., White, E.J., Davidsen, J., Jaldemark, J., Abegglen, S., Burns, T., Sinfield, S., Kirylo, J.D., Batarelo Kokić, I., Stewart, G.T., Rikowski, G., Lisberg Christensen, L., Arndt, S., Pyyhtinen, O., Reitz, C., Lodahl, M., Humble, N., Buchanan, R., Forster, D.J., Kishore, P., Ozoliņš, J., Sharma, N., Urvashi, S., Nejad, H.G., Hood, N., Tesar, M., Wang, Y., Wright, J., Brown, J.B., Prinsloo, P., Kaur, K., Mukherjee, M., Novak, R., Shukla, R., Hollings, S., Konnerup, U., Mallya, M., Olorundare, A., Achieng-Evensen, C., Philip, A.P., Hazzan, M.K., Stockbridge, K., Komolafe, B.F., Bolanle, O.F., Hogan, M., Redder, B., Sattarzadeh, S.D., Jopling, M., SooHoo, S., Devine, N., & Hayes, S. (2020). Teaching in The Age of Covid-19. *Postdigital Science and Education, 2*(3), 1069–1230. https://doi.org/10.1007/s42438-020-00169-6.

Jandrić, P., Knox, J., Besley, T., Ryberg, T., Suoranta, J., & Hayes, S. (2018). Postdigital Science and Education. *Educational Philosophy and Theory, 50*(10), 893–899. https://doi.org/10.108 0/00131857.2018.1454000.

Jandrić, P., Luke, T. W., Sturm, S., McLaren, P., Jackson, L., MacKenzie, A., Tesar, M., Stewart, G. T., Roberts, P., Abegglen, S., Burns, T., Sinfield, S., Hayes, S., Jaldemark, J., Peters, M. A., Sinclair, C., & Gibbons, A. (2022a). Collective Writing: The Continuous Struggle for Meaning-Making. *Postdigital Science and Education.* https://doi.org/10.1007/s42438-022-00320-5.

Jandrić, P., Ryberg, T., Knox, J., Lacković, N., Hayes, S., Suoranta, J., Smith, M., Steketee, A., Peters, M. A., McLaren, P., Ford, D. R., Asher, G., McGregor, C., Stewart, G., Williamson, B., & Gibbons, A. (2019). Postdigital Dialogue. *Postdigital Science and Education, 1*(1), 163–189. https://doi.org/10.1007/s42438-018-0011-x.

Jopling, M. (2023). Postdigital Research in Education: Towards Vulnerable Method and Praxis. In P. Jandrić, A. MacKenzie, & J. Knox (Eds.), *Postdigital Research: Genealogies, Challenges, and Future Perspectives* (pp. 155–171). Cham: Springer. https://doi. org/10.1007/978-3-031-31299-1_9.

Lovink, G. (2022). Extinction Internet. https://networkcultures.org/wp-content/uploads/2022/11/ ExtinctionInternetINC2022Miscellanea.pdf. Accessed 28 January 2023.

Macgilchrist, F. (2021). Theories of Postdigital Heterogeneity: Implications for Research on Education and Datafication. *Postdigital Science Education, 3*(3), 660–667. https://doi. org/10.1007/s42438-021-00232-w.

Maclean, K., Woodward, E., Jarvis, D., Turpin, G., Rowland, D., & Rist, P. (2022). Decolonising Knowledge Co-production: Examining the Role of Positionality and Partnerships to Support Indigenous-led Bush Product Enterprises in Northern Australia. *Sustainability Science, 17*(2), 333–350. https://doi.org/10.1007/s11625-021-00973-4.

Matthewman, S. (2010). *Technology and Social Theory.* Basingstoke: Palgrave.

Mills, C. W. (1959). *The Sociological Imagination.* New York: Oxford University Press.

Omungo, R. (2018) Africa's science 'millionaires': survey spotlights top-funded researchers. Nature, 14 November. https://doi.org/10.1038/d41586-018-07418-6.

Onyango, J., & Ndege N. (2021). How do we 'Decolonise' Research Methodologies? Africa Research and Impact Network / African Centre for Technology Studies, STEPS Centre. https://steps-centre.org/blog/how-do-we-decolonise-research-methodologies/. Accessed 28 January 2023.

Pepperell, R., & Punt, M. (2000). *The postdigital membrane: Imagination, technology and desire.* Bristol: Intellect.

Peters, M. A., Jandrić, P., & Hayes, S. (2021a). Biodigital Philosophy, Technological Convergence, and New Knowledge Ecologies. *Postdigital Science and Education, 3*(2), 370–388. https://doi.org/10.1007/s42438-020-00211-7.

Peters, M. A., Jandrić, P., & Hayes, S. (2021b). Revisiting the Concept of the 'Edited Collection': Bioinformation Philosophy and Postdigital Knowledge Ecologies. *Postdigital Science and Education, 3*(1), 283–293. https://doi.org/10.1007/s42438-021-00216-w.

Peters, M. A., Jandrić, P., Fuller, S., Means, A. J., Rider, S., Lăzăroiu, G., Hayes, S., Misiaszek, G. W., Tesar, M., McLaren, P., & Barnett, R. (2022). Public intellectuals in the age of viral modernity: An EPAT collective writing project. *Educational Philosophy and Theory, 54*(6), 783–798. https://doi.org/10.1080/00131857.2021.2010543.

Peters, M. A., Jandrić, P. & Hayes, S. (2023). Postdigital-biodigital: An Emerging Configuration. *Educational Philosophy and Theory, 55*(1), 1–14. https://doi.org/10.1080/00131857.2020.1867108.

Poster, M. (1990). *The Mode of Information: Poststructuralism and Social Context.* Cambridge: Polity.

Powell, M. (2022). XCLUSIVE: British lawyer plans to sue US ticket-selling giant Eventbrite after it refused to sell tickets to her trans ideology debate with comedian Graham Linehan and branded it 'hateful' and 'dangerous'. DailyMail, 10 November. https://www.dailymail.co.uk/news/article-11412263/Lawyer-plans-sue-ticket-selling-giant-Eventbrite-pulling-tickets-trans-debate.html. Accessed 8 March 2023.

Segado-Boj, F., Díaz-Campo, J., Fernández-Gómez, E., & Chaparro-Domínguez, M. Á. (2019). Spanish Academics and Social Networking Sites: Use, Non-use, and the Perceived Advantages and Drawbacks of Facebook, Twitter, LinkedIn, ResearchGate, and Academia.edu. *First Monday, 24*(5–6). https://firstmonday.org/ojs/index.php/fm/article/view/7296/7806. Accessed 8 March 2023.

Sinclair, C., & Hayes, S. (2019). Between the post and the com-post: Examining the postdigital "work" of a prefix. *Postdigital Science and Education, 1*(1), 119–131. https://doi.org/10.1007/s42438-018-0017-4.

Somerville, W., & Turner, B. (2020). Engaging with Indigenous Research Methodologies: The Centrality of Country, Positionality and Community Need. *Journal of Australian Studies, 44*(2), 182–184. https://doi.org/10.1080/14443058.2020.1749869.

Torres-Olave, B., & Lee, J. J. (2019). Shifting Positionalities Across International Locations: Embodied Knowledge, Time-geography, and the Polyvalence of Privilege. *Higher Education Quarterly, 74*(2), 136–148. https://doi.org/10.1111/hequ.12216.

Traxler, J., Scott, H., Smith, M., & Hayes, S. (2020). Learning Through the Crisis: Helping decision-makers around the world use digital technology to combat the educational challenges produced by the current COVID-19 pandemic. DFID EdTech Hub. https://docs.edtech-hub.org/lib/CD9IAPFX/download/5N87EV2E/Traxler%20et%20al.%20-%202020%20-%20Learning%20through%20the%20crisis%20Helping%20decision-maker.pdf. Accessed 22 January 2023.

Beyond A 'Noticing Stance': Reflecting to Expand Postdigital Positionalities

Nicola Pallitt and Neil Kramm

1 Introduction

Postdigital researchers are being encouraged to engage with their own positionalities and that of others (Hayes 2021). However, this has been seen as a primarily human endeavour. Depending on our intellectual positionalities, we may view who or what as having various positionalities in different ways. Our social positionalities can also be entangled with our intellectual positionalities where some theories or concepts may be more accessible or attractive to us. Some of us may even be in the process of shifting our perspectives about our relationships with technology as we make sense of the disruptive impact of generative AI in our universities, for example.

In this chapter, we offer reflective prompts to enable practitioners and researchers to engage with their relationships with technology and positionalities. We adopt a posthumanist perspective and view postdigital research as part of a broader assemblage. We extend our discussion of intellectual positionalities to other perspectives in educational technology research and aim to contextualise postdigital research in a way that we hope will be useful to others joining the postdigital research community. In particular, we also hope that this chapter provides useful insights to postgraduate Educational Technology students who we encourage to reflect on and discuss their identities and sociomaterial encounters in relation to their empirical studies.

We believe that reflecting on our relationships with technology and positionalities can assist with further developing a 'noticing stance towards practice':

> A posthuman perspective potentially allows for a more focused, and accurate, account for what actually goes on, in the day-to-day of educational processes … it allows for the questioning of the fundamental assumptions underlying agency and the unfolding of epistemic

N. Pallitt (✉) · N. Kramm
Rhodes University, Makhanda, South Africa
e-mail: n.pallitt@ru.ac.za; n.kramm@ru.ac.za

P. Jandrić et al. (eds.), *Constructing Postdigital Research*, Postdigital Science
and Education, https://doi.org/10.1007/978-3-031-35411-3_2

practices in higher education, both digital and analog ... it allows for a move away from ideological assumptions and stereotypes, towards a profoundly ethnographic, observing, noticing stance towards practice. (Gourlay 2021: 8–9)

There are overlaps between postdigital and posthuman perspectives, with the main commonality being the inclusion of the non-human and a relational ontology that has implications for epistemology, as the researcher is not a separate self but part of the assemblage they are investigating (Gravett et al. 2021).

Coming from the global south, we see engaging with our positionalities as part of decolonising the Educational Technology field. We consider decolonial positionalities as part of such efforts and how it differs from a more general reflexive stance on positionality that involves recognising different aspects of our identities that intersect to make us who we are as practitioners and researchers.

2   What Is Positionality?

We encounter the term positionality across a range of university spaces worldwide, often with particular meanings depending on the country and situation. Postgraduate student researchers may engage with positionality to various degrees, particularly if it is required as part of a research proposal or dissertation in the form of a positionality statement or more detailed discussion. This practice varies across universities globally and between disciplines. Drawing on Savin-Baden and Major (2013), Holmes (2020) explains:

A good strong positionality statement will typically include a description of the researcher's lenses (such as their philosophical, personal, theoretical beliefs and perspective through which they view the research process), potential influences on the research (such as age, political beliefs, social class, race, ethnicity, gender, religious beliefs, previous career), the researcher's chosen or pre-determined position about the participants in the project (e.g., as an insider or an outsider), the research-project context and an explanation as to how, where, when and in what way these might, may, or have, influenced the research process. (Homes 2020: 4)

Articles and books are emerging that recognise that this is a complicated task for researchers who are doing this for the first time and provide useful guidance (such as Savin-Baden and Major 2013; Holmes 2020). Some universities (particularly in the US) request that their academic staff share positionality statements on their departmental websites. These can take various forms, from the superficial to the more authentic. US, Canadian, and Australian scholars sometimes include the land acknowledgement of their university as part of their positionality (Canadian Association of Education Teachers 2023). Land acknowledgments recognise that colonisation of land had taken place well as the indigenous people who originally inhabited the territory where the university is sited. It is commonplace for many researchers from Australian Universities to start any presentation and research with such acknowledgements.

Contrary to these very public opportunities, engaging in positionality involves reflexivity and even discomfort. Depending on the positionality of the researcher, there might be aspects that come up as part of the reflexive process that one might not want to share. It is important that we distinguish between these public forms and private reflexive processes that we might engage with alone or with fellow scholars.

Hayes (2021: 10) explains positionality as 'the intimate and ever-changing social, technological and political contexts that intermingle with, create and continue to influence a person's values, identity and opportunities'. She argues that this can include impacts on one's 'gender, race, sexuality, class, location, ability, prospects and many other factors, and so identity remains fluid within relations of power' (Hayes 2021: 10). According to Hayes (2021: 10), examining positionality through reflexivity makes a critical analysis of self-understandings possible and 'provides our individual route towards unpacking our postdigital positionality and considering the positionality of others'.

While Hayes' (2021) notion of postdigital positionality is useful, it centres the human. How might we broaden our understanding of positionality in postdigital research to the non-human, or even the more-than-human? As part of this process, we need to reflect on how the relationship between humans and technologies is conceptualised from different perspectives as a way to situate our own intellectual positionalities. In postdigital research, the terms non-human and more-than-human are used to discuss the complex relationships and interactions between humans, technology, and the environment. While they might seem similar at first glance, they are used to emphasise different aspects of these relationships.

The non-human pertains to aspects outside the human sphere, including animals, plants, objects, and technologies. In postdigital research, the focus on non-human elements helps to challenge anthropocentric perspectives, recognising that the world is not solely centred around human experiences and that non-human entities also have agency and significance. This perspective allows for the exploration of the diverse roles that non-human entities play in shaping the world, as well as their interactions and interdependencies with human actors.

The more-than-human goes beyond the simple distinction between human and non-human entities, emphasising the complex entanglements and hybridity that exist within the postdigital context. It acknowledges that our world is a network of interconnected human and non-human elements, all influencing and being influenced by each other. It highlights the ways in which technology, nature, and culture are interwoven, blurring the lines between what is considered human and non-human and encourages us to think about our relationships with technology and the environment in a more inclusive and holistic manner, understanding that these relationships are not just about human domination or control but also about collaboration, coevolution, and mutual shaping.

Overall, the distinction between non-human and more-than-human in postdigital research helps researchers investigate and understand the complex and intertwined relationships between humans, technologies, and the environment.

3 Intellectual Positionalities

Educational Technology is both a practice and an emerging field and there are professional and scholarly perspectives on what the field is where 'forms of knowledge can differ and overlap' (Czerniewicz 2008). While researchers are often more able to articulate their intellectual positionalities and the paradigms and theoretical perspectives that inform their work, practitioners and postgraduates also have tacit knowledge and beliefs about the role of technology in education based on their experiences. These may be influenced by solutionist perspectives popularised by mainstream media and the marketing of various educational technology related products and services and includes the unquestioned strategies by universities to adopt technology for the perceived benefits it provides to massify higher education and get more students into classes and the associated efficiencies of technologies.

We need to interrogate the metaphors and ideologies associated with different theoretical perspectives to better understand our intellectual positionalities in the field more broadly. This starts with reflecting on the different paradigms in educational technology research and their ontological and epistemological foundations regarding how the relationship between humans and technology is understood as well as the researcher's role when they are investigating this relationship.

Instrumentalism privileges the practical or functional use of technology, its utility, as a means to achieve educational goals. Technology is viewed as a neutral or value free tool, and the assumption is that teaching and learning will be enhanced and become more efficient. Researchers drawing on this perspective are interested in proving the effectiveness of various technologies by measuring its impact on student learning outcomes. Research tends to be uncritically positive, also known as techno-optimism. Educators are encouraged to adopt this perspective through formal study or professional development offerings, where they engage with how they may be using technologies in purposeful ways and evaluating the effectiveness of such use in helping them to achieve educational goals. Particular technology tools are found to be effective or not, often in decontextualised and deterministic ways (i.e., technology enhanced learning). The researcher is often positioned as an independent observer of their own practice or that of others.

Educational technology practitioners in various roles may find themselves thrust into this way of thinking when piloting a particular tool with educators or approaching new technologies in a pragmatic way initially. For example, at the time of writing many educators are being encouraged to think about how to leverage the affordances of generative AI for teaching, learning, assessment, and research. If you can't measure positive outcomes through student feedback or improved performance, then the tool is regarded as ineffective and unlikely to be institutionally supported or funded. While such processes may differ across universities, it is important to acknowledge that there are dominant practices underpinned by ways of thinking that might not align with the paradigms we are coming from. For example, a practitioner researcher holding a critical or postdigital perspective is likely to find such approaches uncomfortable and sometimes not have the understanding to articulate this discomfort.

By contrast, the interdisciplinary field of Science and Technology Studies (STS) explores the mutual shaping of science and technology and aspects of society such as modern culture, values, and institutions. The relationship between people and technologies are intertwined and socially constructed in ways that reflect the values, interests, and power dynamics of the societies in which it is created and used. Technologies are not neutral because they are imbued with meanings and shaped by social, economic, and political forces that inform their design and this in turn influences the ways people use these technologies and the impact thereof on society. Researchers in this field emphasise the social context in which technologies are used and the practices and relations that shape their use, thus being co-constructed through an interplay of the human and technological. STS seeks to understand the dynamic relationship between human and technologies in contextual ways, but these are seen as separate entities acting on each other.

There are overlaps between STS and critical perspectives of educational technologies that seek to explain the complex interplay between people and technologies in use in particular settings. Some of these theoretical orientations include critical, feminist, or postcolonial theories and perspectives from cultural studies. The research aims differ to STS as studies that adopt a critical perspective on educational technology not only use a critical lens to analyse social, political, and cultural implications of technology in education, but also seek to challenge and transform the underlying power dynamics and inequalities that shape its use and impacts. The relationship between humans and technology is studied in a particular setting and articulated in broader societal terms. Researchers may see themselves and their role in their studies as mutually shaping. Action research is an example of a research approach where researchers acknowledge how their social position may impact on the setting and their research more broadly.

Postdigital research paradigms draw on diverse theoretical lenses such as Actor Network Theory (ANT) or posthumanist perspectives. These involve different metaphors to explain the relationship between humans and technology, if we interrogate the concepts in use associated with different theoretical lenses within this paradigm. For example, ANT is interested in the ways that the human and nonhuman are interwoven through ties. By bringing the material to the fore, it decentres the human (Fenwick and Edwards 2010) and can be critiqued as not engaging with the complexity of entanglements in the way that posthumanist approaches might. While the notion of assemblages comes from ANT, posthumanists are more interested in the complexity of and interplay between different relationships. This involves recognising how 'technology is entangled with existing practices and economic and political systems' (Knox 2019).

Researchers who adopt a postdigital perspective are interested in better understanding the messy entanglements of technology, people, broader phenomena such as neoliberalism and its impact on universities, and so forth. They also see themselves as part of the assemblage they are investigating. In contrast to STS and perspectives in the critical paradigm, postdigital research involves a different understanding of context. Fawns (2022) cautions that context can be a 'dangerous shorthand'. Drawing on Nicolini (2013), he argues that context can obscure rather than illuminate important parts of the 'wider picture' that influences situated activity when context is used to include almost anything and potentially become a substitute for detailed analysis. The postdigital paradigm also encourages us to investigate the role of the non-human or more-than-human as part of entangled practices of which the digital, non-digital and the human are part of.

Rather than one paradigm being superior to the other by default, it is more about being able to recognise the differences between these and the implications for how we view the relationship between humans and technology and the studies that result from such conceptualisations. These positionalities are not fixed and may shift as we explore particular paradigms further.

3.1   Reflection

Think about your intellectual positionality in the educational technology field.

– Which of these paradigms resonate with you and why?
– Do you find yourself shifting between these paradigms or not?
– How do the paradigms you choose position you as a researcher?
– What might studies on AI for example look like, understood from these different paradigms?

4   Social Positionalities

Particular intellectual positionalities and their metaphors may be more or less attractive to us because of our social positionalities. Social, political, and material conditions affect how we view our world, which determines how we conceptualise our positionalities.

We work as Educational Technology Specialists in the Centre for Higher Education Research, Teaching and Learning (CHERTL) within the Faculty of Education at Rhodes University in Makhanda, located in the Eastern Cape of South Africa.[1] At our university, our roles are academic in addition to professional or support. We regard ourselves as practitioner-researchers, as we have both service and academic roles at our university. We do learning management system maintenance and support and design professional development opportunities and resources for lecturers. We also co-teach formal courses, short courses, and other structured opportunities.

Rhodes University is the only research-intensive university in South Africa not located in a major city and has experienced a change in its student profile over the past few years. The university now serves majority working-class students of whom

---

[1] See https://www.ru.ac.za/. Accessed 30 November 2022.

just over 50% are on financial aid. In terms of scale, it is one of the smallest South African universities with around 6600 undergraduate and 2000 postgraduate students.

Where we are situated shapes what we experience and perceive as worthy of research. Our previous jobs were at well-resourced but also research-intensive universities in the Western Cape. Coming to a university with less resources and to a town with many infrastructural challenges impacts on what we notice about our practice and those around us. We are both White[2] and middle class, working in an institution that is predominantly Black in terms of both its staff and student base. The city was founded by the 1820 settlers and has landmarks indicating 'frontier country' and a range of historical monuments and buildings that date back to colonial expansion.

Our whiteness is perceived as part of White settler colonialism even though neither of us have family ties to the settlers in this area. However, we were both born in South Africa and as White people growing up during apartheid, had privileges that others did not, such as access to quality government schooling and other socioeconomic advantages that shaped our future opportunities. Our identities are haunted by the histories of our country's colonial and Apartheid past and its racial and class relations; traces from the past that continue into the present. Because of this positionality, we cannot comprehend what it is like to be a first-year student who has grown up in a rural environment and never touched a computer. Some of our students' first contact with digital devices other than mobile phones is when they come to university.

Current quality of life for the broader Makhanda community depends on adaptations that require financial investments, such as installing water tanks and having these plumbed into one's home. The city is known for drought but also mismanagement of water resources and neglected infrastructure. We regularly experience scheduled water off days where municipal water is turned off. Nationally South Africa cannot produce enough electricity for the country's needs due to neglect and mismanagement of electrical production plants and the country has instituted rolling blackouts or what is known as loadshedding. As smaller cities and towns experience more extreme loadshedding schedules, some families invest in inverters, generators, LED light bulbs, solar panels, rechargeable lights, and so forth.

The university has equipped a number of buildings with generators and there are future plans for more sustainable energy sources. While campus Wi-Fi continues during power outages, network providers are sometimes affected if batteries do not have adequate time to charge or are stolen. The lack of basic services such as water and electricity impacts on how we can use technology. In an attempt to adapt to the protracted loadshedding duration, we have even purchased mobile projectors with rechargeable batteries to ensure teaching continuity in our department. Resilience

---

[2] We have capitalised racial groups in this chapter because in South African society, these terms are still used to categorise people for different purposes. We are conscious of this convention and past and present trauma of institutionalised/legalised segregation.

and adaptation have become part of our lives and extend to our teaching and learning practices.

The dominance of material challenges in our setting and how it intersects with our social positionalities led us to viewing the concept of sociomateriality as having descriptive and explanatory power. Many institutions and our government had an instrumentalist view of technology. They saw teaching continuity being enabled through simply 'pivoting' online which we wanted to problematise. In a recent paper, we examined Emergency Remote Teaching (ERT) during the Covid-19 lockdowns at our university which we describe as resource constrained that required lecturers to design for mobile by necessity (Pallitt and Kramm 2022). We reflected on the infrastructural challenges in the country, province, and town and the instrumental response from the government and the institution to provide basic connectivity and access as a primary response.

We argued that we need to understand the responses of teachers and ourselves as part of a sociomaterial assemblages. As people who supported lecturers during this time, we also acknowledge our roles as part of the approaches lecturers developed, and thus the broader assemblage we were investigating. Sociomateriality in particular was an attractive concept for us at the time and still is. We argue that it provides 'a lens for researchers and practitioners to better understand 1) ERT as shifting assemblages that involve complex negotiations and entanglements of the material, social and political, and 2) as mobile learning by necessity in resource constrained settings' (Pallitt and Kramm 2022).

We were aware that research on ERT was influenced by particular theorisations of the digital divide. As researchers in the global south, the use of this term by researchers in the global north in ways that overlook the complexities of digital exclusions often frustrates us. Just as postdigital scholars question the binary of digital and analog, online or offline, and so forth, we also need to recognise other framings that suggest binary thinking such as the digital divide. As a concept, the digital divide can be understood as a broader spectrum of digital inequalities where various inclusions and exclusions may be multidimensional (de Lanerollea et al. 2020). According to de Lanerollea et al. (2020), an information deficit is seen to underlie the 'less connected'. Rather than unequal access to information and how this creates conditions for inclusion or exclusion, they use the term network position and view it in social, economic, political and communication technology terms. We also need to question whose interests and agendas are served by the pervasiveness of particular framings of the digital divide and the assumption of 'deficit by default' that accompanies it.

Often taken for granted terms, such as data, may have different meanings depending on one's social positionality. Some researchers are interested in big data such as learning analytics in relation to data-driven practices and how these shape decision making, albeit with different perspectives of the ethics thereof (Thompson and Prinsloo 2023), how neoliberal agendas are served through particular practices, and so forth. However, recognising data as forms of connectivity and the role it plays in one's network position is also important. For example, lecturers at our university designed their low-tech response to emergency remote teaching during the pandemic around their awareness of their own network position and that of their students who relied on mobile data (Pallitt and Kramm 2022). It was only later that data analytics about 'engagement' became an interest. Rather than one being more important than the other, we see these as entangled. It was because of data in the form of learning management system usage statistics that we were able to identify the kinds of browsers and devices students were using and share this with lecturers to inform their approaches. Our network position and awareness thereof impacts what we bring to the assemblages we are involved in - it is part of our positionality.

4.1 Reflection

– How do you see your social positionality impacting on the research you do or are interested in?
– How does this influence the theories and concepts you find useful?
– Do you have a particular aspect of your social positionality that might enable you to notice something others might not?

5 More-Than-Human Positionalities

Our intellectual and social positionalities play a role in how we understand the non-human and more-than-human and whether these have positionalities independent of the human. These terms are defined in different ways by postdigital researchers. For example, some scholars may be drawn to Haraway's cyborg (1985) in thinking about the more-than-human, whereas others may prefer the ecological that includes our connection to the broader environment around us (Barad 2013). In Barad's terms, 'how matter matters' (2013) differs and it is important for postdigital researchers to become attuned to these subtle differences, including who decides.

The notion that the nonhuman has agency is not new and can be found across a range of fields, from philosophy (Heidegger 1977; Latour 2004) to science and technology studies (Haraway 1991) and ecocriticism (Dürbeck et al. 2015). Beinsteiner (2019) notes that 'transcending the human/nonhuman divide that shapes much of the western tradition of thought confronts these posthumanisms with the complex methodological problem of developing a unified vocabulary that is homogenously applicable to humans as well as to nonhumans' and that one way of approaching this is to conceptualise both the human and nonhuman as agents.

Forlano (2021) argues that engaging with 'critical gender, race, disability, and indigenous studies in what might be considered as radical humanism' may offer possibilities to expand our current notions of human experience and destabilise Western thought about the human. Western humanism has dehumanised women, Black, disabled, and indigenous people for centuries and enduring liberal Western

Eurocentric notions of individuality, rationality, and autonomy that are typically, White, male, and ableist continue to define 'the human' (Forlano 2021).

Forlano's (2021) interest is in alternative narratives around AI. Forlano notes that in the field of AI research, who is included and excluded as human matters; as well as the knowledges, practices, and modes of living that inform our analysis. There is power in deciding who is human or machine or nonhuman, who (or what) gets to decide where the boundaries lie, and whether these boundaries are firm or more fluid. Drawing on critical race theory one may argue that positionality alone is not enough and that we also need to engage with intersectionality and privilege. However, there may be a trace of the tension between posthumanism and radical humanist ideas, where applying positionality to the nonhuman means transplanting ideas from fields that have an existing complicated relationship.

A decolonial positionality involves reflecting 'on one's complicity, preconceived notions, and countering norms, behaviour, values, ideologies, language and policies that dehumanise marginalised populations' (Andreotti 2016). When applied to thinking about our relationships with technology, it involves recognising the ways that human and non-human positionalities can be complicit in valuing and legitimising certain practices and values that might not best serve students and educators.

Through engaging with our examples and questions, we hope this chapter takes you on a reflexive journey. As a reader, you may have different views about what it means to think of the nonhuman as having positionalities and how particular entanglements have implications for agency - of the non-human and more-than-human. This is okay. Can nonhuman actors have agency or enable or constrain the agency of humans in particular ways? While we present questions for reflection in the following sections, we encourage readers not to see these as exhaustive and to feel free to reframe or add questions as they wish to.

5.1 Reflection

- Thinking about our relationships with technology… How is something perceived as human, non-human or more-than-human?
- Under what circumstance does this become valued or legitimised?
- How do your intellectual and social positionalities impact on how you understand the non-human and more-than-human?

6 Non-Human Positionalities

In this chapter, we argue that since posthuman and postdigital perspectives view technologies as nonhuman actors with agency, they too have positionalities. If we extend our understanding of positionalities to the non-human, this has implications for the kinds of topics we consider to be worthy of study and how we conduct postdigital research. Rather than proposing a definitive approach, we see this chapter as a thought exercise to further develop a 'noticing stance' (Gourlay 2021) and part of an emerging conversation that has theoretical and methodological implications for postdigital research.

Sometimes the different positionalities of the human and non-human can be aligned and enable different activities while they may also clash with and constrain others. While some of these alignments and clashes may be more explicit, they can also be less visible and more difficult to notice. Blind spots are inevitable and we propose working from this assumption and that uncovering these are part of a broader reflexive journey.

In addition to positionality, we also need to consider the sociomaterialities of our worlds and rethink how we frame these. This is particularly important for scholars in the global south where notions of the 'digital divide' are accompanied by discourses that we internalise as part of our identities that can be disempowering. We argue that recognising decolonial positionality can open further opportunities for critical engagement with current understandings of positionalities in postdigital research. This chapter is also an attempt to decolonise academic writing in the field of postdigital research, as it straddles the theoretical, empirical, and reflective through questions that readers can engage with as part of a reflexive journey.

Many technologies in use in the global south come from elsewhere, of which many are imports from the global north. For example, Moodle's functionality to assign competencies to assignments and other activities is a digital trace of Australian Outcomes-based Education (OBE). It is hard coded into the fabric of the learning management system and cannot be removed. Users from other countries with different curricula can ignore this and use the rest of the functionality of the learning management system or invest in development capacity to customise the software. Moodle is one of the most widely used open source learning management systems worldwide. Commercial learning management systems have similar kinds of traces of where they come from. These traces might be thought of as echoes, shadows, ghosts embedded in the archive (Gallagher et al. 2022) or hauntology (Derrida 1994; Barad 2010; Bozalek et al. 2021).

Text-matching software, often erroneously understood as plagiarism detection tools, is also predicated on practices in the global north, more specifically English-speaking academia. McKenna (2022) argues that the ways plagiarism is discussed and addressed in the academy is shaped by the increased commodification of knowledge that is a by-product of neoliberal ideology and that it becomes a causal mechanism that enables plagiarism. Text-matching software is an example of 'Big EdTech' (Williamson 2022). In 2019 the global text-matching software market was $334 million and this is predicted to rise to $416 million per year by 2024 (Technavio 2021). McKenna (2022) mentions the 'catch and punish' approaches that many universities use rather than developmental approaches to academic writing and citation practices. While the values of a university might be about developing critically minded citizens, such 'catch and punish' punitive practices clash with the mission and aims of a university and purposes of higher education more broadly.

Selwyn et al. (2023) call on researchers to 'take an active stance by developing better understandings of how digital automations can be meaningfully integrated into education and adopting a sense of realism (rather than idealism) when reflecting on where we might like to be going next'. In addition to losses and gains, they also discuss digital automations of education in terms of power and acknowledging the futures and histories of such automations. With acknowledging power, we also need to consider local dynamics and practices. Being involved in choosing and purchasing various software at our university, we are privy to information that other researchers in the field are not. The cost of the text-matching software in use at our university is the single most expensive item on our budget; it costs more than the annual maintenance, upgrade and support of our learning management system and more than half of all the other supported teaching and research technologies at our university.

Many software taken for granted at universities in the global north are prohibitively expensive in the global south, especially for a university with a small student body, as the pricing is structured in such a way that the smaller the institution the larger the individual unit costs are for an individual user. Lecture recording and management platforms, analytics plugins, proctoring tools, text-matching software, and online conferencing tools are among the most expensive. These are globally recognised software that are near ubiquitous at many universities in the global north. South African universities make decisions about software informed by a range of local materialities rather than cost alone. The bandwidth intensive nature and differentiation of end user devices supported, means that proctoring tools are less viable at our institution due to the material arrangement of our students and their access off campus. Not all universities consider these constraints equally despite known inequalities among students. Local specialists prioritise mobile friendly alternatives when it comes to choosing contextually appropriate tools.

It's not just the cost of software, but the extension products and services they offer that shows up the market driven nature of various companies. One of these text-matching software companies provide a 'health check', initially as a free demo and afterwards as an additional paid for service, to interpret data from the software to make claims about the extent of an institution's academic integrity. This can be seen as part of a neoliberal logic where data is sold back to universities.

Analytics providers engage in similar activities. However, the practices that inform the design of reports and indicators often come from the global north. Working class South African students have different strategies when engaging in intentional academic dishonesty (i.e., cheating). These include using past student essays and notes bought from fellow students rather than essay mills. International essay mills are very expensive for South African students. Past essays or academic writing services are advertised in local groups from social networks to websites that allow for community sharing of advertisements and classifieds. These services present as legitimate and even include ratings by users and can range from consultants to corporate agencies. Some even advertise plagiarism removal, and say that potential student customers can free themselves from 'the unnecessary stress of writing up complex assignments'. Another common strategy that second and third language

English speaking students use that text-matching tools are unable to detect is translating text across languages or the use of AI writing assistant websites.

As part of our service role, we often engage with companies, attend demos, get quotes, etc. Whereas many researchers are writing about the consequences and practices of software in use, there are layers that come before this. If it's not part of your world, you don't notice it. We are part of the assemblages we study in a different way to others. This is why it is important for researchers in this field to hold and recognise various positionalities. It is not just what your position is in relation to educational technologies in the sense of a job, but also where you are located in the world that matters.

It is interesting to note that Selwyn et al. (2023) do not mention text-matching software by name, whereas McKenna (2022) does. This is likely because of the legal implications where countries have different positions on Strategic Lawsuit against Public Participation (SLAP) orders which are lawsuits aimed to intimidate individuals or groups from writing or speaking against powerful individuals, companies or governments (Pring and Canan 1996). How we talk about technologies, who can name these and what can be said about various platforms and companies differs geographically (Dawson 2021).

6.1 Reflection

- Are there technologies that you use that carry traces from elsewhere?
- How do these show up in broader university practices and policies?
- How do these align or clash with individual or collective values and beliefs i.e., positionalities?

7 Positionality as Part of a Global Postdigital Community

We, as the authors of this chapter, have joint positionalities that we share, as well as individual ones. In relation to a community of postdigital researchers globally, we were initially unsure about whether we 'fit in' with this collective. When we first heard the term 'postdigital' we understood it in terms of technological progress and well-resourced university infrastructures where data-driven practices had become the norm for fellow researchers in the global north. When we started to engage with some of the literature and debates and got a better sense of the postdigital through the Opening in A Closed World: Postdigital Science and Education conference,[3] we were better able to navigate our position as part of this collective and reflect on the value of our contribution to postdigital dialogue (Jandrić 2019).

---

[3] See https://cuc.carnet.hr/2022/en/. Accessed 30 November 2022.

We realised that we had internalised a digital deficit view that is associated with the global south through terms like the digital divide and journals that refer to resource constrained settings. Digital inequalities and the 'digital divide' are often used to brush over some of the things we encounter. Technicist levels of access (Deursen and van Dijk 2014) can also be read as not making enough of people and their agency or agency as being afforded by the absence or presence of particular materialities.

Material aspects often deemed insignificant in Higher Education research show up as powerful actors shaping our students' and educators' experiences and agency. Entangled materialities constitute relations and recast being, knowing and doing in Higher Education (Gravett et al. 2021). Rethinking human-technology relationships involves recognising how 'technology is entangled with existing practices and economic and political systems' (Knox 2019). This involves recognising assumptions (our own and that of others). Gourlay (2020) talks about sociomaterial activity as being 'messy, embodied, awkward, emotional, emergent, and difficult'. Perhaps it is this messiness that resonates with us because we find ourselves studying very messy human-technology relationships in our world that this appeals and a sociomaterial perspective offers explanatory power for us.

For fellow scholars from the global south, some of the postdigital literature may at first come across as indulgent navel-gazing by privileged others in the global north, but we later discovered sensibilities and concepts that are useful to better understand, frame, and analyse what we observe and experience. We also recognise that we share an anti-solutionist view of technology that has been part of critical educational technology research for a while. For fellow researchers from the global south: you are not alone and you can also be part of this dialogue. Don't let assumptions about fellow researchers in this community and their experiences discourage you from joining global postdigital dialogues.

7.1 Reflection

- How do you perceive your position as a member of a global postdigital community and beyond?
- What aspects make you feel more or less included in this field and its community?
- What are some of the assumptions you have that impact your participation in this field?

8 Conclusion

This chapter offers suggestions for how to expand understandings of positionality in postdigital research. We present concepts and questions for reflection to engage fellow researchers in this process which is an essential part of acknowledging what we bring to the assemblage of postdigital research we are involved in, and postdigital dialogue more broadly.

Theories and methods for a 'noticing stance' and the positionality of things has not been applied to the non-human and more-than-human and how it impacts the human experience. This changes the way a researcher identifies their own positionality and the positionality of things and practices as part of a socially situated assemblage they are investigating. We recognise various positionalities as part of such assemblages and the way these can be entangled and mutually shaping local settings. There will always be blind spots, as we as researchers have our own assemblages which consist of our intellectual and social positionalities, our role and our function in an institution. However, we need to think about how to mitigate these shortcomings in different ways by seeing assemblages not only of people but also beyond.

References

Andreotti V. (2016). The educational challenges of imagining the world differently. *Canadian Journal of Development Studies/Revue canadienne d'études du développement, 37*(1), 101–112. https://doi.org/10.1080/02255189.2016.1134456.

Barad, K. (2010). Quantum entanglements and hauntological relations of inheritance: Dis/continuities, spacetime enfoldings, and justice-to-come. *Derrida Today, 3*(2), 240–268. https://doi.org/10.3366/drt.2010.0206.

Barad, K. (2013). Ma(r)king time: Material entanglements and re-memberings: Cut-ting together-apart. In P. R. Carlile, D. Nicolini, A. Langley, & H. Tsoukas (Eds.), *How matter matters: Objects, artifacts, and materiality in organization studies* (pp. 16–31). Oxford, UK: Oxford University Press.

Beinsteiner, A. (2019). Cyborg agency: The technological self-production of the (post-) human and the antihermeneutic trajectory. *Thesis Eleven, 153*(1), 113–133. https://doi.org/10.1177/0725513619863855.

Bozalek, V., Zembylas, M., Motala, S., & Hölscher, D. (Eds.). (2021). *Higher Education Hauntologies: Living with Ghosts for a Justice-to-Come*. London: Routledge. https://doi.org/10.4324/9781003058366.

Canadian Assiociation of Education Teachers (2023). Guide to Acknowledging First Peoples & Traditional Territory. https://www.caut.ca/content/guide-acknowledging-first-peoples-traditional-territory. Accessed 30 November 2022.

Czerniewicz, L. (2008). Distinguishing the field of educational technology. *Electronic Journal of e-Learning, 6*(3), 171–178.

Dawson, P. (2021). *Defending assessment security in a digital world. Preventing e-cheating and supporting academic integrity in Higher Education*. London: Routledge

de Lanerolle, I., Schoon, A., & Walton, M. (2020). Researching Mobile Phones in the Everyday Life of the "Less Connected": The Development of a New Diary Method. *African Journalism Studies, 41*(4), 35–50. https://doi.org/10.1080/23743670.2020.1813785.

Derrida, J. (1994). *The Specters of Marx: The state of the debt, the work of mourning, and the new international*. Trans. P. Kamuf. London: Routledge.

Dürbeck, G., Schaumann, C., & Sullivan, H. (2015). Human and non-human agencies in the Anthropocene. *Ecozon@, 6*(1), 118–136. https://doi.org/10.37536/ECOZONA.2015.6.1.642.

Fawns, T. (2022). An Entangled Pedagogy: Looking Beyond the Pedagogy—Technology Dichotomy. *Postdigital Science and Education, 4*(3), 711–728. https://doi.org/10.1007/s42438-022-00302-7.

Fenwick, T., & Edwards, R. (2010). *Actor-network theory in education*. London: Routledge.

Forlano, L. (2021). Exploring the Boundaries of Humans and Machines. AI Now. https://ainowinstitute.org/publication/a-new-ai-lexicon-human. Accessed 2 June 2023.

Gallagher, M., Nicol, S., & Breines, M. (2022). Ghost Hunting in the Broken Archives: Re-Historicizing Digital Education in an Institutional Context. *Postdigital Science and Education.* https://doi.org/10.1007/s42438-022-00330-3.

Gourlay, L. (2020). Quarantined, Sequestered, Closed: Theorising Academic Bodies Under Covid-19 Lockdown. *Postdigital Science and Education, 2*(3), 791–811. https://doi.org/10.1007/s42438-020-00193-6.

Gourlay, L. (2021). *Posthumanism and the Digital University.* London: Bloomsbury.

Gravett, K., Taylor, C. A., & Fairchild, N. (2021). Pedagogies of mattering: re-conceptualising relational pedagogies in higher education. *Teaching in Higher Education.* https://doi.org/10.1080/13562517.2021.1989580.

Haraway, D. J. (1991). *Simians, Cyborgs, and Women. The Reinvention of Nature.* New York: Routledge.

Hayes, S. (2021). *Postdigital Positionality: Developing Powerful Inclusive Narratives for Learning, Teaching, Research and Policy in Higher Education.* Leiden: Brill.

Heidegger, M. (1977). *The Question concerning Technology and Other Essays.* New York: Harper and Row.

Holmes, A. (2020). Researcher Positionality – A Consideration of Its Influence and Place in Qualitative Research – A New Researcher Guide. *Shanlax International Journal of Education, 8*(4), 1–10. https://doi.org/10.34293/education.v8i4.3232.

Jandrić, P. (2019). We-Think, We-Learn, We-Act: the Trialectic of Postdigital Collective Intelligence. *Postdigital Science and Education, 1*(2), 257–279. https://doi.org/10.1007/s42438-019-00055-w.

Knox, J. (2019). What does the postdigital mean for education? Three critical perspectives on the digital, with implications for educational research and practice. *Postdigital Science and Education, 1*(2), 357–370. https://doi.org/10.1007/s42438-019-00045-y.

Latour, B. (2004). *Politics of Nature: How to Bring the Sciences into Democracy.* Trans. C. Porter. Cambridge, MA: Harvard University Press.

McKenna, S. (2022). Plagiarism and the commodification of knowledge. *Higher Education, 84,* 1283–1298. https://doi.org/10.1007/s10734-022-00926-5.

Nicolini, D. (2013). Bringing it all together: A toolkit to study and represent practice at work. In D. Nicolini (Ed.), *Practice Theory, Work, and Organization: An Introduction* (pp. 213–242). Oxford: Oxford University Press.

Pallitt, N., & Kramm, N. (2022). ERT as mobile learning by necessity: A sociomaterial perspective of lecturers' design journeys. *International Journal of Mobile and Blended Learning.* https://doi.org/10.4018/IJMBL.313975.

Pring, G. W., & Canan, P. (1996). *SLAPPs: Getting Sued for Speaking Out.* Philadelphia, PA: Temple University Press.

Thompson, T. L., & Prinsloo, P. (2023). Returning the data gaze in higher education. *Learning, Media and Technology, 48*(1), 153-165. https://doi.org/10.1080/17439884.2022.2092130.

Savin-Baden, M., & Major, C. H. (2013). *Qualitative Research: The Essential Guide to Theory and Practice.* London: Routledge.

Selwyn, N., Hillman, T., Bergviken-Rensfeldt, A., & Perrotta, C. (2023). Making Sense of the Digital Automation of Education. *Postdigital Science and Education, 5*(1), 1–14. https://doi.org/10.1007/s42438-022-00362-9.

Technavio. (2021). Anti-plagiarism Software Market for Education Sector by End-user and Geography – Forecast and Analysis 2021–2025. https://www.technavio.com/report/anti-plagiarism-software-market-for-education-sector-industry-analysis. Accessed 30 November 2022.

Van Deursen, A. J. A. M., & van Dijk, J. A. G. M. (2014). The digital divide shifts to differences in usage. *New Media & Society, 16*(3), 507–526. https://doi.org/10.1177/1461444813487959.

Williamson, B. (2022). Big EdTech. *Learning, Media and Technology, 47*(2), 157–162. https://doi.org/10.1080/17439884.2022.2063888.

Mapping (Metaphorical) Journeys in and Against the Academy

Mel M. Engman, Johanna Ennser-Kananen, and Jenna Cushing-Leubner

1 Introduction

This chapter considers postdigital possibilities toward an ongoing effort to understand our roles as academics producing 'critical research'. Embracing Knox's (2019: 358) characterisation of the postdigital 'not as a conclusive description of times to come, nor indeed a desired destination, but rather as a necessary junction for reflection', we reflect on how our relationships with one another and with knowledge creation are constructed with digital technology and in its absence. We build on previous work (Cushing-Leubner et al. 2021) that examined researcher choice in the academy by focusing on one particular aspect of our collective sense-making – the use of hand-drawn maps to name and spatialise experience.

Firstly, we briefly explore the nature of academic work and how our participation in it orients us to the technologies of empire (and possibilities for resistance to it). These technologies include material, discursive, ideological, and political processes. Examples of these include material and intellectual extraction, appropriation, and commodification; territorialization and privatization of land/air/waterways into property; conversion of land-knowledge relationship to debts and investments; and the use of academic archives as sites of defining and asserting power structures (see la paperson 2017: 4; Richards 1993). We then extend our attention to

M. M. Engman (✉)
Queen's University Belfast, Belfast, UK
e-mail: m.engman@qub.ac.uk

J. Ennser-Kananen
University of Jyväskylä, Jyväskylä, Finland
e-mail: johanna.f.ennser-kananen@jyu.fi

J. Cushing-Leubner
University of Wisconsin – Whitewater, Whitewater, WI, USA
e-mail: cushingj@uww.edu

P. Jandrić et al. (eds.), *Constructing Postdigital Research*, Postdigital Science
and Education, https://doi.org/10.1007/978-3-031-35411-3_3

'orientation' into a full embrace of the metaphors that we often use to describe our labour – metaphors such as navigating *academic terrain,* being on the *tenure track,* and progressing along *career paths.* We discuss the knowledge that emerged from the process of creating hand-drawn maps of our experiences in the academy (i.e., this metaphorical *terrain*), and the ways in which this exercise shifted our orientations to forms of inquiry, collaboration, and representation. Though hand-drawn maps are far from cutting-edge digital technology, our aim is to explore how their *use* served as a postdigital resource for sense-making.

As Peters et al. (2023) note, postdigital is an epistemological and ontological concept (rather than a chronological one). It refers to how we know what we know, and what we recognise as knowable. In the case of the informal, collective, imperfect mapping activities described in this chapter, postdigital refers to assemblages of phenomena in which digital technologies are entangled with technologies that existed long before digitisation. Humans have always related with technology in ways that are hybrid, partial, and entangled with the familiar; and these engagements with technology shape how we relate with the world. The emergence of new technologies need not displace/replace existing ways of knowing, but they may shape how we continue to use 'older' tools to make sense of 'new' ways of being/thinking/etc.

Our hand-drawn 'spatialised' texts represent an understanding of 'postdigital' as stepping *beyond* the digital and its binary code, its microprocessors, hyper-speed, synthetic neural networks, and invisibility (Negroponte 1998), for a critical embrace of the material, the inert, and the real (though with oft-invisibilised postdigital sensibilities). We examine the practices involved in experiential map-making and map-reading as a way of representing encounters in and with the academy as postdigital beings. It entails remembering and relating–humanising practices that invite ways of thinking which are slow, visible, fun, material (and imperfect), and it considers the ways in which the postdigital may be invisibilised and already deeply embedded in the social and material world.

2   Knowledge, Empire, and Terrain

Work in the academy tends to be portrayed as a labour of the mind whereby we inquire, analyse, and write to produce knowledge. Digital technologies are relatively recent additions to repertoires of scholarly practice in the academy. They may function as mediators of longstanding practices as well as disruptors of it (Hayes and Jandrić 2014; Jandrić and Kuzmanić 2015), or something else altogether (Kelly and Taffe 2022). Our 'outputs' are generated through engagement with humans and the digital, social, material world as well as through intellectual engagement with texts and their citational genealogies. In most cases, what we produce are 'thought knowledges' (de Sousa Santos 2018: 2), and this scholarly work is performed in the service of the imperial archive (Richards 1993) – a living record, a detailed handbook for maintaining the dominant configurations of power in the world.

Historically, as colonialism became an invaluable tool in the construction of empire (Heller and McElhinny 2017; Myers 2014), the accumulation of knowledge became important as both a product of biophysical expansion and a legitimisation of it (Lowe 2015; Richards 1993). Though some technologies of the empire have changed over time, the ongoing project of accumulation through the 'production' (Lowe 2015) of knowledge rolls on. Through the myth of epistemic neutrality (e.g., academia's 'zero-point'), empire itself is in part constructed by the imaginings and insistence that knowledge and relationality can be made 'empirical' through trials and tests (Cusicanqui 2012, 2019; Mignolo 2009). Through the conversion of living knowledge into discrete data items that can be organized and reorganized at will, archives of 'truth' can then be constructed to confirm the rationale and necessity of empire, as something capable of gathering, holding, and reconstructing knowledge in its most godly form: an all-seeing Truth of every thing and all complexities of relationships between every thing.

The research and teaching performed by employees (like us) of educational institutions in wealthy nations in Europe and North America aid in the collection and control of material and ideological phenomena that simultaneously construct an archive of the empire and legitimise it. For instance, research with speakers of minoritized languages may theorise creative languaging practices that reveal and resist power inequalities. Yet in so doing, this research likely also documents and collects knowledge about these languaging practices in the form of digital recordings and transcripts; keeping disembodied language (and knowledge about it) in the possession of the institutions that support and are supported by the imperial archive.

In a previous writing collaboration (Cushing-Leubner et al. 2021), we analysed key experiences in our development as academics alongside Ahmed's (2006) theorising of 'straightening devices' to better understand how we were/are apprenticed into doing this work. We showed how the colonial roots of the academy influence how we might (and might not) produce knowledge in and for the imperial archive. Various encounters in institutions and in disciplines expose us to everyday corrections and repetitions, assumptions about what is and is not legitimate. In both academic and everyday life, we are conditioned to have tendencies 'toward straight objects' (Ahmed 2006: 557), meaning we are socialised toward practices and ideas that are recognisable through specific 'straight' orientations.

Like many of our colleagues, we aim to see beyond the limited view afforded by disciplinary straightening devices, all while knowing that we are still very much 'produced colonialists' (la paperson 2017: xxiii), products of our environment. We are each teacher-researchers in critical language studies who were 'trained' academically through the same American public university at the same time. We emerged with PhDs and with shared social and professional networks, shared familiarity with specific theory and citational genealogies, as well as shared experiences in the neoliberal university, and shared 'impossible' (la paperson 2017: xxiii) desires for decolonisation. In spite of these shared experiences, our environments have not been and are not identical. Our positionalities are also differently constructed in relation to our communities and in our genealogies of migration and settlement.

Our experiences 'in' the academy (as if the academy is a *place*) orient us. They shape the angle of what is and is not visible, which in turn influences how we recognise the choices available to us at any given moment. We have written earlier of how these 'researcher choices exist within a terrain of options that persistently orient research in critical language studies towards empire entrenchments, white-Euro racial framing, and racial-linguistic capitalism' (Cushing-Leubner et al. 2021: 3). The word 'terrain' is significant here. It functions as a spatial metaphor that indexes varied ground to be traversed, with possible obstacles or areas of unevenness, and it is easily deployed to characterise professional, ideological, and discursive 'spaces'. Moreover, how a person is oriented surely influences how a person understands options available in a given terrain.

Terrain is useful for conceptualising the dynamic environment of academia because it calls to mind the forward motion academia requires of us (i.e., movement along our career *paths*) and the interrupted unevenness that we must often 'navigate'. Lakoff and Johnson (2008) note that this idea of movement along a path is a key entailment in the metaphor [noun] *is a journey*. In their analysis of the journey metaphor, they demonstrate how key entailments connecting the idea of a journey with motion along a material path lead to a shared sense that 'a journey defines a path / a path of a journey is a surface' (Lakoff and Johnson 2008: 80).

With these semantic linkages in mind, it is unsurprising that our group sought to represent key encounters and experiences in academia through a map – a surface view of the metaphorical journey in the academy along our career paths. A turn toward mapping in making sense of experience not only leans into the predominant *journey* metaphors, but also uses a familiar genre of text, or technology, to do so. A map – even a hand-drawn one – may be a viable means of representing what has come to be known of a given surface through observation. Importantly, maps have long been recognisable tools of the imperial archive, and continue to be used to note changing environmental geographies, to draw and maintain political boundaries, to visualise data, to aid in organising relationships between geographical, material, social, and/or theoretical phenomena.

Drawing a map not only collects named places into a single semiotic text, but it also relies on space to show relative distance and proximity between places; and it can illustrate pathways that connect or circumvent certain sites. These pathways are as important as the places they connect because of how they may reflect habitual use and, in so doing, instantiate further habitual use. As Ahmed (2019: 167) notes in her discussion of Lamarck's law of exercise: '(t)he more a path is used, the more a path is used'. If we may be more likely to walk a physical path through the woods that others have already created, would we not also be more likely to walk a metaphorical path through academic terrain? Or, at the very least, would certain well-worn paths not be more recognisable to us as individuals who have been oriented to the terrain in a specific way? In our ongoing attempt to understand how our orientations to researcher choice were shaped by straightening devices in the academy, we put pen to paper and drew some spatial representations of metaphorical terrain. We drew some maps.

3 Maps as Texts

In this brief overview of maps as texts, we consider what maps are and how they have been used and might be used in the future. Maps sit at the nexus of geography and art (Harmon 2004; Wood 2006). They are (usually) visual and (oftentimes, though not always) physical representations of real-world physical phenomena and the relations among them. Producing a map requires attending to 'data' as well as attending to aesthetic features and recognisability within shared semiotic systems. A single definition of maps is hard to come by, yet there tends to be a shared understanding of what a map is and is not.

As a starting point, Wood (2006) references Barthes in his description of five codes (iconic, linguistic, tectonic, temporal, presentation) that contribute to a map's map-ness, operating together within the map itself. Though he also notes five parallel codes that operate outside the map as part of human sense-making with the semiosis of the map. These codes control the ways in which certain features are drawn (or not drawn) on the map-s plane to aid in our understanding of the drawing as a representation of 'territory' first and foremost, rather than 'descriptions *of the behaviours linked through the territory*' (Wood 2006: 8) (emphasis from the original). This detachment of place from human action is part of what lends maps an air of objectivity. Objectivity invites a certain trustworthiness and invites us to (uncritically) accept their descriptions of terrain as static entities that can be known, traversed, and maybe even controlled – a problematic starting point.

Siegert (2011) writes about maps as 'cultural techniques' that function as representations as well as instruments. While Siegert is writing from the perspective of an art historian, the view of cartography as an epistemic and cultural product has been a part of discussions among geographers and mapmakers for quite some time. For instance, over 30 years ago Harley (1989) noted changes to British Cartographic Society's working definition for *cartographer* that emphasise the role of science and technology in interpreting geographic relationships. Specifically, Harley finds it 'surprising that the word "art"' (2) was removed from the revised definition. Harley points to this move toward technological precision in characterising cartography as an uncritical acceptance of an 'epistemological myth (created by cartographers) of the cumulative progress of an objective science always producing better delineations of reality' (15).

This distinction between the text and reality (and the blurriness that comes with assumptions of objectivity and neutrality) are incredibly important when thinking with maps. Maps can make a world. Fantasy author J. R. R. Tolkien says that he 'wisely started with a map, then made the story fit' with his *Lord of the Rings* trilogy (Fonstad 2006: 133), drawing villages and kingdoms alongside imagined geographical features with pen and paper before building the world of Middle Earth with prose. The ability of a map to *prescribe* how we perceive the world (as opposed to simply describing it) can help explain why cartographers, historians, and other researchers in the humanities and social sciences might be concerned about a cartography that uses discourses of objectivity and technology to think in terms of 'scientific integrity' as opposed to 'ideological distortion' (Harley 2009: 129).

Kitchin and Dodge (2007) go beyond Harley's (1989) desire for an exorcism of the human mapmaker's ideology and instead present maps as texts that possess no possibility of objectivity, neutrality, etc. They are semiotic texts that emerge through practice. From this point of view, 'the map reader becomes as important as the map maker' (Kitchin et al. 2011: 4), and the map can be seen as part of a dialogic meaning-making process rather than as a static cultural product.

This prescriptive possibility associated with map *use* is central to contemporary conversations in cartography and it is congruent with ongoing discussions we aim to participate in that pertain to postdigital scholarship and the imperial archive. Cartography has long played a dually prescriptive and descriptive role in the political world. Rose-Redwood et al. (2020) refer to this duality in their description of the roles that maps have played 'in the world-making practices of colonialism through the appropriation, demarcation, naming, and partitioning of territory as part of the process of colonisation and the assertion of imperial rule over peoples and places' (Rose-Redwood et al. 2020: 152). This history does not mean that all maps are only technologies of colonialism, however. Instead, Rose-Redwood et al. (2020) remind us that maps have also been important technologies of Indigenous peoples and call for a decolonising of the map.

This entails employing Indigenous methods of attending to obligations and relations with place such as with Enote's (2018) counter-mapping work that employs Zuni artists to reconnect Zuni people with ancestral knowledge of place. Indigenous ways of tracing connections with land may not always be legible to the colonial cartography audience, but a certain ambivalence about universal recognition can also be a decolonial practice. Similarly, la paperson (2017) writes about the world-making potential of the university as 'an amalgamation of first, second and third worlding formations' (xiv). His acknowledgement of the inequality and domination that comes from and with the university does not build a case for total rejection of engagement with scholarship, but it necessitates what la paperson calls 'theoriz(ing) in the break, that is, to refuse the master narrative that technology is loyal to the master' (5–6). We follow la paperson in seeking alternative practices that might subvert the use of a technology for anticolonial, if not decolonial purposes.

As a means for sense-making, or as postdigital technologies for learning, maps are not inherently innovative tools to radically alter how we represent knowledge. They are, however, a familiar genre of texts that we 'read' and 'write' on a regular basis. We wonder then, what is it about this way of representing that seemed to enable us to do something different than what we were already doing in academic writing and presentational speaking. What shifted when we oriented ourselves to the task of making a map rather than telling a story or writing an article?

4 Maps in *Use* (Maps as Method)

Our original aim was to find an alternative to the storytelling genre we had employed in our original efforts to examine our roles in the academy and perceived 'researcher choice'. We turned to maps as everyday, accessible texts (much like stories), and immediately saw the tone of our meetings and communications change. There was an enthusiastic, shared desire to continue messing about with hand-drawn maps so, in keeping with our academic training, we first looked to literature, starting with a search for existing 'maps of the academy'. Numerous empirical and conceptual works in the humanities and social sciences have titles that would indicate some map-making has been undertaken (e.g., 'mapping race and gender', 'mapping labour', 'mapping higher education') to conceptualise relationships across various features of a given metaphorical 'terrain'. Yet many publications claiming to 'map' things tend to be dominated by text (i.e., written accounts of relationships among specific phenomena) with few visual representations to make meaning with. It was rare to find image-based spatial representations of phenomena in research that aimed to be 'mapping' something.

Harmon's (2004) collection of 'maps of imagination' was one example of literature that de-centred text, relying more heavily on images to represent ideas, drawing on personal geography practices in hybrid texts exploring cartography and human experience. The maps we drew resembled these personal geographies in some respects, as they drew on memory and history. Though our maps were not drawn by professional artists and eventually our engagement with them had more to do with process than with the maps as products.

In our map-making processes, we crossed analog-digital boundaries so effortlessly that the only way for us to describe them is in retrospect. We remember, for example, drawing parts of our maps on paper with markers, sometimes using images on our phones for inspiration (Google search: 'drawing of volcano'). We took pictures of our first sketches, sent them to our chat group, from where Mel (first author) collected them and pasted them into a document that we all had access to. We resized, cut, and re/placed the pictures onto different backgrounds to build maps out of individual pictures. We presented our maps digitally, but also printed some as examples for an interactive conference session. In intra-action (Barad 2007) with our materials (paper, markers, phones, etc.) and with our memories, maps, and stories, both digital and analog, came into existence, and we emerged as mapmakers, pathbuilders, and storytellers. At no point in these processes of oscillating between digital and analog, or human and material, did we perceive our process as boundary crossing. Rather, we were naturally drawing on the available tools and practices to engage ourselves and our participants in meaning-making processes that were collaborative, personal, and critical. The construction of digital-analog and human-non-human boundaries only happened *a posteriori* in the reflective writing process for this paper.

Our ability to reconstruct and deconstruct these boundaries, and their *invisibility* in use is fed by a growing body of work in the area of postdigital (Jandrić and Knox

2022; Fawns et al. 2023), sociomaterial/new materialist (Fenwick 2015; Guerrettaz et al. 2021; Ennser-Kananen and Saarinen 2023), and posthumanist (Herbrechter 2013; Snaza and Weaver 2015) literature. In their collective reflection on conducting postdigital research, Fawns et al. (2023: 8) raise questions about the relationship between sociomaterial and digital approaches, admitting that 'we have not reached consensus on whether postdigital is necessarily sociomaterial or not'. Though we engage in this discussion without clear answers, we participate with an interest in inquiring about the possibilities for postdigital approaches to open spaces of resistance and change in the colonial project of epistemic control. In this sense, our maps are more than metaphorical representations of paths through the challenges of academia. They are instruments of sense-making and friends-making across cultural, intellectual, and vast physical distances, for which human-non-human and digital-analog boundaries had to be blurred.

Our maps first took the form of 2-dimensional representations of spatial relations among named 'geographies' of experience (see Fig. 1). The first attempt intentionally mimicked the style of Tolkien's map of Middle Earth,[1] drawn in pen with

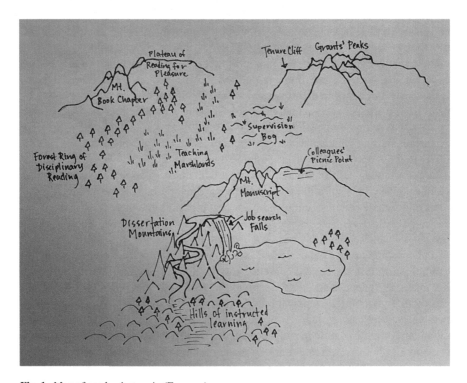

Fig. 1 Map of academic terrain (Engman)

---

[1] The idea for mapping initially came from an emailed conversation in which Jenna (third author) playfully suggested that we 'create a Tolkien-esqe map image' of our experiences in the academy as individual stories might take too long to share out in an academic presentation. Postdigital shenanigans ensued.

handwritten named 'places' (e.g., Job Search Falls) arranged and illustrated to indicate specific topographical and environmental features (e.g., mountain range, bog, marshland).

In terms of creating a recognisable product, the map in Fig. 1 is successful. It looks like a map and contains elements of most of Wood's (2006) five codes (i.e., iconic, linguistic, tectonic, temporal, presentational) of in-map properties (temporal code is unclear). Where its identity as a map starts to become questionable is in its utility for navigation. It is doubtful that this map of experiences through a journey metaphor could chart a clear course through 'academic terrain'. The named places on the map are not sites that one can travel to and between. They are metaphorical. Challenging academic labour (e.g., dissertation writing, job searching) is depicted through metaphors of perilous geography such as mountains, cliffs, waterfalls. Labour that is time-consuming or a grind that goes largely unlauded is depicted by indexing environmental features that are less perilous than a cliff but would be a slog to get through on foot (e.g., marshland, bog). There is one marked pathway on the map, but much of the metaphorical terrain is an open question as far as how to navigate it (emblematic of the mapmaker's early stage in her career).

This activity essentially reduced complex interconnected experiences and labours in the academy to discrete, named 'places' and hand-drawn doodles. Surprisingly this flattening appeared to be more generative than reductive in terms of promoting discussion and enquiry, so we tried it in other ways and in other settings (i.e., collaboratively and in our classrooms, respectively). While the map in Fig. 1 was created by one individual, collaborative mapping opened up communication channels, encouraging interpersonal negotiation and collective creativity as we dreamed up more 'places' and spatialised them strategically to allow for a more visible 'path' (see Fig. 2).

To create this collaborative map, discrete analog elements from the map in Fig. 1 were excised, uploaded, and incorporated in different spatial arrangements alongside other 'geographical features' that were dreamed up, named, and illustrated in isolation (see Figs. 3 and 4). We conspired with technology to digitise our drawings and clumsily drop them onto a digital image of a fantasy map pulled from the Internet.

The drawings of geographical features as representations of experiences, desires, and structures in higher education offered trade-offs with other ways of representing. Our maps conveyed both more and less about the experiences they represented in comparison with their academic text- and story-based versions. It was a surprise to find that the spatial relationships amongst the various features were not as useful for sense-making compared with the utility of the named locations. The matching of imagined place names to imagined geographies of key experiences and labour that dominated the mapping exercise in our first iterations were almost meme-like in their cohesion as culture-laden 'units that express specific contexts and meanings discernible to some and less discernable to others' (Iloh 2021: 3). When we shared our hybrid drawings with colleagues who also work in the academy, the named 'locations' such as The Mirage of Meritocracy were met with immediate recognition, emotion, and often suggestions for additional map features.

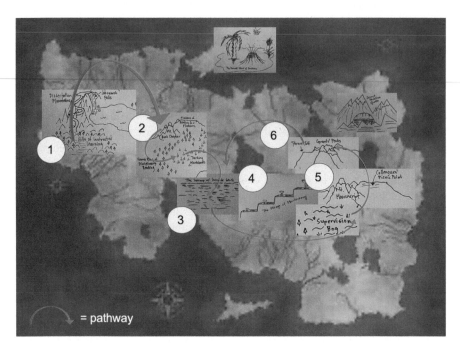

Fig. 2 Collective map with hand-drawn places superimposed on stock 'fantasy' map. Imagined pathways marked with red arrows. (Cushing-Leubner, Engman, Ennser-Kananen, Pettitt)

Fig. 3 The remote island of emotions (Ennser-Kananen)

Iloh (2021) writes about the use of memes in research as rapport-building and possibly an entry point for creativity and humour. In this respect, specific features of the metaphor maps were memetic in that they could be understood quickly given

Fig. 4 The mirage of meritocracy (Ennser-Kananen)

a shared frame for context, and they functioned sociably and encouraged participation (Marwick 2013). This reliance on assumptions and open participation runs counter to the features of sense-making practices that we have learned to associate with acceptable forms of knowledge dissemination as knowledge producers for the academy. Yet, as a means for communicating shared and shifting storylines it resonates with how we 'do culture' in the social world and indexes postdigital online interactions (Denisova 2019).

Subsequently, this metaphorical mapping was submitted as part of a colloquium addressing researcher choice and disciplinary straightening devices in critical language studies to our field's flagship conference [the American Association of Applied Linguistics (AAAL)] in spring 2022. Having learned that the maps seemed to generate more discussion and learning when created collectively, we brought art supplies to the colloquium and invited colleagues to map their experiences in the imperial archive. Session maps (see Figs. 5 and 6) took a wide variety of forms, with no adherence to shared semiotic conventions or scale, yet all depicted spatialised depictions of recognisable experiences and relations in the academy. Familiar paradigmatic and theoretical terms (from the academy) were overlaid atop hand-drawn renderings (and sometimes copious amounts of glitter).

Scholars well-known for their serious work on serious topics of race, Indigeneity, and social justice were on the floor with paints, passionately doodling maps of the metaphorical journeys they have taken as researchers and educators in service to the university. Many stayed well beyond the colloquium's allotted time, eager to wonder together about shared experiences with disciplinary tensions, states of precarity, and numerous other impossibilities. Discussions among conference goers involved a spontaneous hybrid grammar that integrated complex academic concepts with

Fig. 5 Glitter-bombing the academy at the American Association of Applied Linguistics annual conference 2022

everyday multilingual and multimodal repertoires, including Internet searches, digital file-sharing, and selfies with glitter-covered maps and mapmakers. This shared grammar necessitated a shared cultural frame which, in this case, came from within the postdigital academy – a site for sense-making that is not actually a place, but is also many places, not all of which take up space.

This activity was also brought into our teaching work. In Cushing-Leubner's class, comprised entirely of pre-service teachers, hand-drawn maps were used in an iterative way to help new teachers identify straightening devices in their professions. With an attention to the dynamism of educational environments, the students were invited to map their understandings of their work environment. Maps included material, social, and ideological phenomena, demonstrating the complexity of work in education. As with earlier attempts to make maps, the transformation of highly dynamic and complex systems to a 2-dimensional hand-drawn picture did not flatten discussion, inquiry, or understanding. Rather the maps seemed to provide generative starting points for allowing the pre-service teachers to decide the direction and extent of their sense-making. Cushing-Leubner also invited the students to add drawn revisions to one another's maps, adding a layer of dynamism (see Figs. 7 and 8).

The maps that were created and revised by pre-service teachers became heteroglossic texts as multiple voices contributed to capturing dynamic forces in educational 'terrain'. This heteroglossia, i.e., language that is internalised from others and

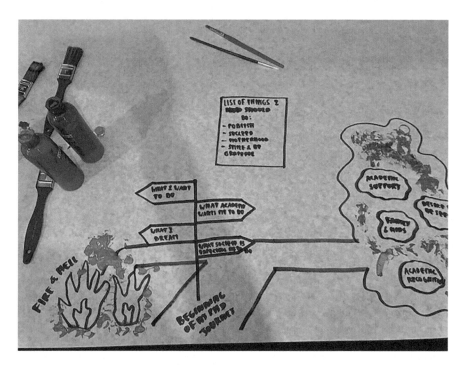

Fig. 6 Preparations for a journey metaphor at the American Association of Applied Linguistics annual conference 2022

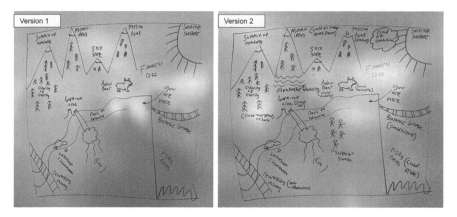

Fig. 7 Original student map and revised student map to include greater awareness of hazards

reused (Bakhtin 1934/1981) and its remembered and reused complexity is akin to the convergences and hybridity of Jandrić and Knox's (2022) characterisation of the postdigital. Further, the ludic nature of each of the mapping activities described here echoes the assertion made by Fawns et al. (2023) that 'postdigital inquiry is as much about creation as it is about discovery'. Importantly, while the maps provided

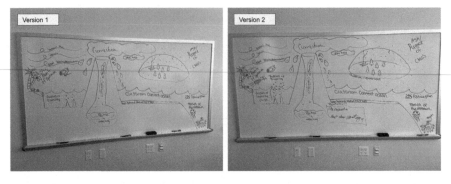

Fig. 8 Original student map and revised student 'water table map'

students with starting points for identifying straightening devices in their teaching environments, they ultimately functioned as multimodal creations for reckoning with postdigital subjectivities in a variety of educational contexts. Returning to Knox's (2019: 358) description of postdigital as 'a junction for reflection', we note that a significant portion of the value of the terrain maps resides not in their nature as descriptive or even prescriptive objects, but rather in their *use* as part of collective meaning-making.

Our experiences with different constellations of mapping activities with colleagues, strangers, and students, while initially focused on product, became more focused on process. They became a method of examination, reflection, and connection. Being *in process* with them (and with colleagues) felt good – these simultaneously analog and digital exercises cultivated postdigital practices that, in turn, cultivated human connection and enjoyment for the mapmakers. This shared experience of joy and lightness serving as possible companions for methods of critical inquiry is, for us, an unfamiliar surprise, in need of further examination. The creation and use of visual metaphors for the work we do (i.e., earnest, sardonic, glittery maps of the academy) facilitated 'un-straightened' views of experiences in the imperial archive. So we wonder how such postdigital products-as-processes can 'queer,' in Ahmed's sense (2006), our orientations against the colonising and straightening spirit of the academy?

5   Metaphorical Journeys Against the Spirit of the Academy

In examining the possibilities for postdigital mapping exercises that centre experiential knowledge, play, memory, and representation, we echo Knox's (2019: 357) suggestion that the 'post' in postdigital 'signal(s) a critical appraisal of the assumptions embedded in the general understanding of the digital'. Reflection on the use of our metaphorical maps of 'nowhere' highlights possibilities for postdigital multimodal methods to re-examine assumptions, or straightening devices, in the academy and to recognise possible countermoves.

First, our mapping opposed a spirit of constant, continuous movement. This felt counterintuitive after many years of socialisation on how and what to produce for the academy. More specifically, training in the schools of social constructionism/constructivism, has instilled an appreciation of hybridity, flexibility, and continuous motion in us. Language, most importantly (to us applied linguists), is always developing, never a fixed unity. In fact, we have learned to see fixity, stillness, and immobility as suspicious, likely fraught with normativity and violence. Understanding the world as fundamentally in-motion, as constantly being constructed and re/deconstructed, has been central to our scholarly identities in that it has offered us a starting point for undermining long-standing hierarchies of power. However, in its most radical forms, social constructivism, the lens we often used for this work of undermining, can also itself produce or reproduce normative spaces (e.g., Ennser-Kananen and Saarinen 2023), where fluidity and the speed of constant change make it difficult to engage with complex realities.

Metaphorical mapping taught us that the freezing or holding still of parts of our work can enable us to take a stance, to keep things safe, to orient ourselves, or to develop a sense of belonging. Adams et al. (2014) draw on the slow food movement to envision how 'slow research' may transform Global Health into a healthier field. As part of their suggestions to pause in the present, they describe anticipation as a force that impedes this:

> Anticipation eviscerates the impulse to remain local in time, or to remain attentive to immediacy and problem solving in the near tenses. Preparation and consumption carried out under the burden of anticipation become acts that are void of present meaning, abducted by a future that, even while structuring the present, often never comes to pass or is gone before it was comprehended. (Adams et al. 2014: 188)

When the speed of knowledge production renders our doings blurry and even invisible, a map disrupts the anticipation and the 'rhetoric of speed' (Adams et al. 2014: 188) by offering stable images which slow us down, invite us to become still, and linger with ourselves and the human and other-than-human beings around us. The hand-drawn maps of metaphor described here are postdigital objects insofar as (i) their creation and circulation required help from digital technologies and (ii) they are representations of experiences of postdigital subjectivities in the academy. At the very least, they embody the 'mixing up' of the analog and digital as discrete categories (Knox 2019: 359). These postdigital maps resist attempts to maintain a 'system in which the long-term temporal frames of basic sciences can be used to generate profits by configuring them into short-term transitional and temporary stopping points' (Adams et al. 2014: 188) and instead carve out space for patient engagements with our environment and encounters therein, for harking back to our values and orientations, and for 'the unexpected to reconfigure the research' (189). In this sense, mapping is a practice against the invisibility and blurriness that come with anticipation, a practice becomes particularly valuable as it anchors us in the present, when the institutional imperative is to speedily 'move along' on a 'track' to the goal of promotion or tenure.

Second, our mapping was fun. Ludic activities have been identified as a central and relevant part of learning and relating to the social world in a variety of contexts. For instance, within language education, Broner and Tarone (2001) have applied Cook's (2000) understanding of ludic language play (Cook 2000), i.e., play enjoyment and amusement as its sole purposes, and Lantolf's (1997) notion of language play as space for rehearsing target forms, to the immersion classroom context. They found that both can be observed in learner interactions and have a rightful place in language learning processes. Cook's (2000) drawing on Bakhtin's work to understand language play as carnivalesque resonated with us, as we observed ourselves and our colleagues, spreading pain and glitter on large pieces of paper at an academic conference (and partially the hotel room floor). Ennser-Kananen (2014) identified language play as a tool for claiming linguistic identity and legitimacy, and more generally, playful humour as a space where different and contradictory norms and expectations can be negotiated.

While the importance of play for identity construction and learning is widely accepted (e.g., Bowman 2010 on role-playing; Corbeil 1999 on simulation and games as learning; Stephen and Edwards 2017 on children playing in the digital age; Grindheim 2017 on playing as enacting citizenship, etc.), its subversive function is less recognised. Within education, Sutton-Smith's foundational work has documented the different ideologies and discourses around children's play, including play as self (identity), play as progress, play as imaginary, and play as power (Sutton-Smith 1997). Importantly, he noted that children's play is often nonhegemonic in the sense that it stretches, resists, and breaks the norms and rules of the adult world. Resistance to authority and gender stereotypes was also a major theme in Sanford and Madill's (2007) study on video gaming practices of male youth.

Prior research has also documented more explicitly nonhegemonic forms of play, including urban activism in the form of playfulness and creativity. For instance, Klepto (2004) describes initiatives that are driven by 'alternative urban visions' (403) such as the Clandestine Insurgent Rebel Clown Army (CIRCA) in Leeds, a group of political activists who foster and cherish the ability of clowning 'to disrupt, critique and heal society' (407). In a similar way, our mapping activities used humour to draw serious matters into the realm of ludicrousness, thus exposing their illegitimacy and debilitating their power over us. Relatedly, Flusty (2000) has documented play as resistance in the fringe spaces of Bunker Hill, LA. Their work includes portraits of skaters, musicians, and poetry performers who claim atypical or fringe spaces of the city (parking lots, trains, etc.) and resist being criminalised by the authorities. Also, Crossa (2013) has identified play and creativity as activism and protest in their work with street vendors and artisans in Mexico City, who claim the neighbourhood of Coyoacan as artistic space, engage their audience through personal and emotional connections, and resist the policy of gentrification.

In a similar vein, our mapping activities can be seen as a resistant form of space-making. Mapping creates spaces for the mappers, it carves out 'terrains of resistance' (Routledge 1997: Para 7 in Crossa 2013) and engages participants and bystanders emotionally. As Bosco (2007) in their work on emotional geographies of resistance state, 'emotions help create and sustain networks of collective action across time and space' (Bosco 2007 in Crossa 2013), and these emotions (e.g., belonging, anger, fear, identity, hope, connection) are activated and fostered through creativity and play. Our postdigital mapping as ludic activity was resistant in that it made space for humour within the seriousness of the academy. It made space for humour and play when we are otherwise expected to foreground our work, and it interrupted our daily doings with opportunities for remembering and longing for the places in the academy where we experience joy and safety. This critical playfulness resonates with postdigital turns toward storytelling and other artistic representations of the ambiguities and complexities of contemporary life (Jandrić and Knox 2022; Kitchin 2021).

Third, mapping of metaphor with pens, paint, Internet searches and memory seemed to engage the senses and inadvertently resist the physical intangibility demanded by 'cognitive empire' (de Sousa Santos 2018). In *The End of Cognitive Empire*, the sequel to *Epistemologies of the South*, de Sousa Santos explains:

> To take seriously the idea that knowledge is embodied implies recognizing that knowing is a corporeal activity potentially mobilizing the five senses. For the epistemologies of the North, valorizing the senses as sources of knowledge is out of the question. Only the mind knows; only reason is transparent regarding what is known; hence, only reason is trustworthy. The epistemologies of the South are at the antipodes of such a stance, which raises issues that have been barely charted. (de Sousa Santos 2018: 15)

To be clear, we don't claim for our mapping activities to have been intentional or even effective decolonising efforts, and we recognise our entanglement in the colonial work of our institutions. However, as our mapping evolved as sensually engaging collaboration, all the while occupying traditional academic spaces, our hope is that they helped embrittle what is a legitimate academic genre, behaviour, or tool, and crack open spaces for reimagining a different academy. During our mapping activities at the AAAL conference and in Jenna's classrooms with pre-service teachers, we exchanged our most common work tools of laptops and tablets, with pens, papers, brushes, scissors, glue, and glitter. This felt excitingly different from our work routine even though we were nevertheless gathered in spaces reserved by and for the postdigital academy, and it triggered a series of alternative engagements with materials. We worked on our maps in different places and postures (e.g., crouching on the floor of a hotel room), we contributed something concrete and visible to a collaborative activity (glitter and brush strokes vs text), and we repurposed academic spaces and postures.

For instance, the sterile presentation room at the conference was transformed into a chaotic, low-budget art space when we reconfigured furniture, using desks as places to paint and to dry our maps and chairs to hold paper, scissors, and brushes. Moving the furniture required a reconfiguration of how our bodies oriented to the space, lifting, sitting, kneeling, crouching on the floor, passing scissors to one another, acting as an easel for displaying large paper. Relating to materialities in this way engaged us as physical beings and in this way broke with the habit of the academy to reduce us to our cognitive or virtual/digital work.

As we are considering our mapping as embodied tangible-making of academic experience, we noticed that we are not alone in refocusing on embodied ways of being in the academy. For instance, the turning towards posthumanism, new materialism, and postdigital scholarship, has enabled a resurfacing of embodied approaches to research across many disciplines (e.g., Spatz 2017 on embodied research). Specifically, refocusing on bodily experiences and their entanglement or intra-action (Barad 2007) with the material world has facilitated scholarship through/with art (including dance, music, painting, and photography, e.g., Bolt and Barrett 2013; Hickey-Moody et al. 2016), fashion (Smelik 2018), media (Bruno 2014), sports (Markula 2019), and other ways of moving (e.g., walking: Springgay and Truman 2017), to name a few. These lines of work build on the recognition of human bodies being intrinsically intertwined with materialities and in fact coming into existence only through their intra-action (Barad 2007). Seen through this lens, in the entanglement of our own bodies with our materials (pens, brushes, paper, paint) we emerged as making and being made by our maps, and boundaries between 'object' and 'subject' became blurry.

Fourth, in all cases, though mobile phones, Internet searches, and editing software played important roles, our maps were hand-drawn. This unrefined, unpolished genre is a rare sighting in the academic contexts where we work. We have learned that research, in order to be legible, must be polished to the extreme through multiple processes of reviewing, revising, editing, and proofing, which supposedly ensure its compliance with linguistic, epistemological - for instance, reproducing genealogies of citations - and orthographic standards. Our hand-drawings interrupt this vetting process. Unlike hand-drawn fieldnotes or data, which sometimes hesitantly exist in academic contexts, they claim their space as centre of our work, that is not merely tolerated in its raw form and waiting to be lifted into more legitimate spheres of existence through analysis and theorisation. Instead, our imprecise and unscaled postdigital maps are presented here as *useful*, not awaiting any additional processing but saying what they say, unedited, unproofed. Their purpose is not to represent reality by approaching any norm of accuracy. Rather, they cross lines of time and space by combining and blurring reality with not-yet or not-anymore or maybe-never reality, so that aspirational, made-up, remembered, and empirically confirmed events and items can coexist and merge in our maps. As sense-making tools, hand-drawn postdigital maps of nowhere are the antithesis of the postdigital measurement technologies described by Williamson (2021: 361) as 'quantifiably objective, unambiguous, and precise'.

In all, mapping of metaphorical terrain in the postdigital academy has provided us with opportunities to resist the straightening towards our career goals by allowing for deviations from rhetorics of speed and production, encouraging enjoyment and humour, validating the embodied nature of our work, and centring things that are imperfect and raw. As we engaged in our collective mapping, we were thus reminded of Martin and Kamberelis' (2013) work on mapping as a research approach, and particularly their comment that '[e]ven the most intensely territorialised landscapes have some lines of flight' (671). Based on Deleuze and Guattari's (1987) rhizomatics and ontology of becoming, Martin and Kamberelis (2013: 671) understand such lines of flight as 'centrifugal, decentering, dispersing discourses and practices' and 'available means of escape from forces of repression and stratification'. Mapping, then, has the potential to repurpose the terrain of academic life by initiating processes of de- and reterritorialising. As the authors put it, '[m]apping … makes visible new possible organizations of reality; and it thus opens up new ways of organizing political resistance (praxis)' (Martin and Kamberelis 2013: 671).

6   Conclusion

We aimed to create visual representations that named and imagined navigation through the perils of participation in the academy (Cushing-Leubner et al. 2021). Analog (i.e., hand-drawn) mapping practices about and for the academy helped us bend back or 'queer' our straightened orientations (Ahmed 2006), 'seeing' the terrain from alternative (zoomed out/zoomed in) viewpoints and opening up alternative ways of relating to the work. The maps can be seen as postdigital assemblages (Macgilchrist 2021: 662) not because of the digital nature of their components but because of the ways in which the postdigital conditions of contemporary academic labour and subjectivities are 'drag(ged) inside them'. Though our maps were initially created to simply give a 'birds-eye view' of the critical academic events and encounters that we were analysing (i.e., a descriptive tool of representation), we found that our various engagements with creating and using maps led to shifts in how we oriented to text and to work. We can make specific and subversive meaning with texts that are 'open to interpretation', imprecise and subjective. The academic 'work' of knowledge production in the postdigital age can be playful, still, unfinished, and imperfect.

By examining map-making as a personal and collective process of creation, revision, and use, this project has implications for how we conceptualise the relationship between learning and institutions, and for postdigital constructions of language, sign, and space. Labelling the mapping activities here as 'postdigital' acknowledges the contemporary accumulations of power with colonial genealogies, and with more recent digital 'enhancements', that are still actively shaping our movement or lack thereof through physical and metaphorical space. It also invites curiosity about bringing these digital accumulations into contact with analog practices of text production.

How does our relationship with postdigital institutional labour and experience change when it is remembered and re-territorialised as still 'places' that are drawn, named, plotted as a visual artifact? How might the re-territorialising of postdigital memory shift orientations and, subsequently, perceptions of power and possibility?

The academy is a postdigital site of knowledge production that exists as both a physical and virtual reality, depending on the specifics of a given encounter. Experiences 'here' can be site-less yet also very much in a 'place' relative to other 'places'. We are optimistic about postdigital explorations of this 'terrain' because of the range of possibilities it presents us with to learn inductively about knowledge production and power using familiar tools that seem to move against the spirit of the academy while also reimagining it.

References

Adams, V., Burke, N. J., & Whitmarsh, I. (2014). Slow Research: Thoughts for a Movement in Global Health. *Medical Anthropology, 33*(3), 179–197. https://doi.org/10.1080/0145974 0.2013.858335.

Ahmed, S. (2006). Orientations: Toward a Queer Phenomenology. *GLQ: A journal of Lesbian and Gay Studies, 12*(4), 543–574. https://doi.org/10.1215/10642684-2006-002.

Ahmed, S. (2019). *What's the use?: On the uses of use*. Durham, NC: Duke University Press.

Bakhtin, M. (1934/1981). *The dialogic imagination: Four essays by M.M. Bakhtin*. Ed. M. Holquist. Trans. C. Emerson & M. Holquist. Austin, TX: University of Texas Press.

Barad, K. (2007). *Meeting the Universe Halfway: Quantum Physics and the Entanglement of Matter and Meaning*. Durham, NC: Duke University Press.

Barrett, E., & Bolt, B. (2013). *Carnal Knowledge: Towards a 'New Materialism' Through the Arts*. London: I. B. Tauris.

Bosco, F. (2007). Emotions that Build Networks: Geographies of Human Rights Movements in Argentina and Beyond. *Tijdschrift Voor Economische en Sociale Geografie, 98*(5), 545–563. https://doi.org/10.1111/j.1467-9663.2007.00425.x.

Bowman, S. L. (2010). *The Functions of Role-Playing Games: How Participants Create Community, Solve Problems and Explore Identity*. Jefferson, NC: McFarland.

Broner, M. A., & Tarone, E. E. (2001). Is it Fun? Language Play in a Fifth-grade Spanish Immersion Classroom. *The Modern Language Journal, 85*(3), 363–379. https://doi.org/10.1111/0026-7902.00114.

Bruno, G. (2014). *Surface: Matters of Aesthetics, Materiality, and Media*. Chicago, IL: University of Chicago Press.

Cook, G. (2000). *Language Play, Language Learning*. Oxford: Oxford University Press.

Corbeil, P. (1999). Learning from the Children: Practical and Theoretical Reflections on Playing and Learning. *Simulation & Gaming, 30*(2), 163–180. https://doi.org/10.1177/104687819903000206.

Crossa, V. (2013). Play for Protest, Protest for Play: Artisan and Vendors' Resistance to Displacement in Mexico City. *Antipode, 45*(4), 826–843. https://doi.org/10.1111/j.1467-833 0.2012.01043.x.

Cushing-Leubner, J., Engman, M. M., Ennser-Kananen, J., & Pettitt, N. (2021). Imperial straightening devices in disciplinary choices of academic knowledge production. *Language, Culture and Society, 3*(2), 201–230. https://doi.org/10.1075/lcs.21001.cus.

Cusicanqui, S. R. (2012). Ch'ixinakax utxiwa: A reflection on the practices and discourses of decolonization. *The South Atlantic Quarterly, 111*(1), 95–109. https://doi.org/10.12150/0382876-1472612.

Cusicanqui, S. R. (2019). Ch'ixinakax utxiwa: A reflection on the practices and discourses of decolonization. *Language, Culture and Society, 1*(1), 106–119. https://doi.org/10.1075/lcs.00006.riv.

de Sousa Santos, B. (2018). *The End of the Cognitive Empire: The Coming Age of Epistemologies of the South*. Durham, NC: Duke University Press.

Deleuze, G, & Guattari, F. (1987). *A Thousand Plateaus: Capitalism and Schizophrenia*. Trans. B. Massumi. Minneapolis, MN: University of Minnesota Press.

Denisova, A. (2019). *Internet memes and society: Social, cultural, and political contexts*. New York: Routledge. https://doi.org/10.4324/9780429469404.

Ennser-Kananen, J. (2014). The Right to be Multilingual: How Two Trilingual Students Construct their Linguistic Legitimacy in a German Classroom. https://conservancy.umn.edu/bitstream/handle/11299/164846/EnnserKananen_umn_0130E_14950.pdf?sequence=1&isAllowed=y. Accessed 7 March 2023.

Ennser-Kananen, J., & Saarinen, T. (2023). Towards Socio-material Research Approaches in Language Education. In J. Ennser-Kananen & T. Saarinen (Eds.). *New Materialist Explorations into Language Education* (pp. 3–17). Cham: Springer. https://doi.org/10.1007/978-3-031-13847-8.

Enote, J. (2018). Remapping a Place: How One Tribe's Art Reconnects Them to Their Land. Go Project Films, 9 December. https://emergencemagazine.org/story/counter-mapping. Accessed 7 March 2023.

Fawns, T., Ross, J., Carbonel, H., Noteboom, J., Finnegan-Dehn, S., & Raver, M. (2023). Mapping and Tracing the Postdigital: Approaches and Parameters of Postdigital Research. *Postdigital Science and Education*. https://doi.org/10.1007/s42438-023-00391-y.

Fenwick, T. (2015). Sociomateriality and learning: A critical approach. *The SAGE handbook of learning* (pp. 83–93). London: SAGE.

Flusty, S. (2000). Thrashing Downtown: Play as Resistance to the Spatial and Representational Regulation of Los Angeles. *Cities*, *17*(2), 149–158. https://doi.org/10.1016/S0264-2751(00)00009-3.

Fonstad, K. W. (2006). Writing "TO" the Map. *Tolkien Studies, 3*(1), 133–136.

Grindheim, L. T. (2017). Children as Playing Citizens. *European Early Childhood Education Research Journal*, *25*(4), 624–636. https://doi.org/10.1080/1350293X.2017.1331076.

Guerrettaz, A. M., Engman, M. M., & Matsumoto, Y. (2021). Empirically defining language learning and teaching materials in use through sociomaterial perspectives. *The Modern Language Journal, 105*(S1), 3–20.

Harley, J. B. (1989). Deconstructing the Map. *Cartographica: The International Journal for Geographic Information and Geovisualization, 26*(2), 1–20. https://doi.org/10.3138/E635-7827-1757-9T53.

Harley, J. B. (2009). Maps, Knowledge, and Power. In G. Henderson & M. Waterstone (Eds.), *Geographic Thought: A Praxis Perspective* (pp. 129–148). London: Routledge.

Harmon, K. (Ed.) (2004). *You are Here: Personal Geographies and Other Maps of the Imagination*. Princeton, NJ: Princeton Architectural Press.

Hayes, S., & Jandrić, P. (2014). Who is really in charge of contemporary education? People and technologies in, against and beyond the neoliberal university. *Open Review of Educational Research, 1*(1), 193–210. https://doi.org/10.1080/23265507.2014.989899.

Heller, M., & McElhinny, B. (2017). *Language, capitalism, colonialism: Toward a critical history*. Toronto: University of Toronto Press.

Herbrechter, S. (2013). *Posthumanism: A critical analysis*. A&C Black.

Hickey-Moody, A., Palmer, H., & Sayers, E. (2016). Diffractive Pedagogies: Dancing Across New Materialist Imaginaries. *Gender and Education*, *28*(2), 213–229. https://doi.org/10.1080/09540253.2016.1140723.

Iloh, C. (2021). Do it for the Culture: The Case for Memes in Qualitative Research. *International Journal of Qualitative Methods, 20*, 563–578. https://doi.org/10.1177/16094069211025896.

Jandrić, P., & Knox, J. (2022). The Postdigital Turn: Philosophy, Education, Research. *Policy Futures in Education, 20*(7), 780–795. 10.1177%2F14782103211062713.

Jandrić, P., & Kuzmanić, A. (2015). The wretched of the network society: Techno-education and colonisation of the digital. In R. Haworth & J. Elmore, (Eds.), *'Out of the ruins': The emergence of new radical informal learning spaces*. Oakland, CA: PM Press.

Kelly, M., & Taffe, S. (2022). When Digital Doesn't Work: Experiences of Co-Designing an Indigenous Community Museum. *Multimodal Technologies and Interaction, 6*(34), 1–11. https://doi.org/10.3390/mti6050034.

Kitchin, R. (2021). *Data Lives: How Data Are Made and Shape Our World*. Bristol, UK: Bristol University Press.

Kitchin, R., & Dodge, M. (2007). Rethinking Maps. *Progress in Human Geography, 31*(3), 331–344. https://doi.org/10.1177/0309132507077082.

Kitchin, R., Perkins, C., & Dodge, M. (2011). Thinking about Maps. In M. Dodge, R. Kitchin, & C. Perkins (Eds.), *Rethinking Maps: New Frontiers in Cartographic Theory* (pp. 19–43). London: Routledge.

Klepto, K. (2004). Making War with Love: The Clandestine Insurgent Rebel Clown Army. *City, 8*(3), 403–411. https://doi.org/10.1080/1360481042000313536.

Knox, J. (2019). What Does the 'Postdigital' Mean for Education? Three Critical Perspectives on the Digital, with Implications for Educational Research and Practice. *Postdigital Science and Education, 1*(2), 357–370. https://doi.org/10.1007/s42438-019-00045-y.

Lakoff, G., & Johnson, M. (2008). *Metaphors We Live By*. Chicago, IL: University of Chicago Press.

Lantolf, J. (1997). The Function of Language Play in the Acquisition of L2 Spanish. In W. R. Glass & A. T. Perez-Leroux (Eds.), *Contemporary perspectives on the acquisition of Spanish* (pp. 3–24). Somerville, MA: Cascadilla Press.

Lowe, L. (2015). *The Intimacies of Four Continents*. Durham, NC: Duke University Press.

Macgilchrist, F. (2021). Theories of postdigital heterogeneity: Implications for research on education and datafication. *Postdigital Science and Education, 3*(3), 660–667. https://doi.org/10.1007/s42438-021-00232-w.

Markula, P. (2019). What is New About New Materialism for Sport Sociology? Reflections on Body, Movement, and Culture. *Sociology of Sport Journal, 36*(1), 1–11. https://doi.org/10.1123/ssj.2018-0064.

Martin, A. D., & Kamberelis, G. (2013). Mapping Not Tracing: Qualitative Educational Research with Political Teeth. *International Journal of Qualitative Studies in Education, 26*(6), 668–679. https://doi.org/10.1080/09518398.2013.788756.

Marwick, A. (2013). Memes. *Contexts, 12*(4), 12–13. https://doi.org/10.1177/1536504213511210.

Mignolo, W. D. (2009). Epistemic disobedience, independent thought and decolonial freedom. *Theory, culture & society, 26*(7–8), 159–181. https://doi.org/10.1177/0263276409349275.

Myers, K. (2014). The intimacy of three settler nations: Colonialism, race, and child welfare. Gazillion Voices, November.

Negroponte, N. (1998). Beyond digital. Wired, 12. http://www.wired.com/wired/archive/6.12/negroponte.html. Accessed 10 February 2022.

la paperson. (2017). *A Third University is Possible*. Minneapolis, MN: University of Minnesota Press.

Peters, M. A., Jandrić, P., & Hayes, S. (2023). Postdigital-biodigital: An emerging configuration. *Educational Philosophy and Theory, 55*(1), 1–14. https://doi.org/10.1080/00131857.2020.1867108.

Richards, T. (1993). *The Imperial Archive: Knowledge and the Fantasy of Empire*. New York: Verso.

Rose-Redwood, R., Barnd, N. B., Hetoevėhotohke, A. Lucchesi, E., Dias, S., & Patrick, W. (2020). Decolonizing the Map: Recentering Indigenous Mappings. *Cartographica: The International Journal for Geographic Information and Geovisualization, 55*(3), 151–162. https://doi.org/10.3138/cart.53.3.intro.

Routledge, P. (1997). The Imagineering of Resistance. *Transactions of the Institute of British Geographers, 22,* 359–376. https://doi.org/10.1111/j.0020-2754.1997.00359.x.

Sanford, K., & Madill, L. (2007). Critical Literacy Learning Through Video Games: Adolescent Boys' Perspectives. *Elearning and Digital Media, 4*(3), 285–296. https://doi.org/10.2304/elea.2007.4.3.285.

Siegert, B. (2011). The Map is the Territory. *Radical Philosophy, 5,* 13–16. https://doi.org/10.25969/mediarep/13157.

Snaza, N., & Weaver, J. A. (Eds.) (2015). *Posthumanism and educational research*. New York: Routledge.

Smelik, A. M. (2018). New Materialism: A Theoretical Framework for Fashion in the Age of Technological Innovation. *International Journal of fashion studies, 5*(1), 22–54. https://doi.org/10.1386/infs.5.1.33_1.

Spatz, B. (2017). Embodied Research: A Methodology. *Liminalities, 13*(2).

Springgay, S., & Truman, S. E. (2017). *Walking Methodologies in a More-than-Human World: WalkingLab*. London: Routledge. https://doi.org/10.4324/9781315231914.

Stephen, C., & Edwards, S. (2017). *Young Children Playing and Learning in a Digital Age: A Cultural and Critical Perspective*. London: Routledge. https://doi.org/10.4324/9781315623092.

Sutton-Smith, B. (1997). *The Ambiguity of Play*. Cambridge, MA: Harvard University Press.

Williamson, B. (2021). Digital policy sociology: software and science in data-intensive precision education. *Critical Studies in Education, 62*(3), 354–370. https://doi.org/10.1080/1750848 7.2019.1691030.

Wood, D. (2006). Map Art. *Cartographic Perspectives, 53*(Winter), 5–14. https://doi.org/10.14714/CP53.358.

Part II
Constructing Postdigital Research

Constructing Design Knowledge for Postdigital Science and Education

Peter Goodyear, Lina Markauskaite, Cara Wrigley, Natalie Spence, Genevieve Mosely, and Teresa Swist

1 Introduction

This chapter is concerned with forms of knowledge that are useful to teams of people who are collaboratively learning how to improve ongoing scientific and/or educational activities in which they are directly involved. In other words, it has a primary pragmatic focus on situated actionable knowledge and secondarily on (research) methods used to construct such knowledge. In particular, we foreground *design knowledge*, understood broadly as knowledge tuned to the requirements of design work. Collaborative design activity, underpinned by design knowledge, is a way for a group of people to come to a shared understanding of complex issues arising in their collective work and to shape and agree on plans for better ways of working.

As with other chapters in the book, we aim to explore some of the ontological and epistemological issues that arise in conducting postdigital research.

Like many others contributing to this collection, we see rapidly diminishing returns from research that contrasts and compares digital and non-digital tools, artefacts or ways of working. In our experience, more productive questions emerge when one acknowledges that contemporary working practices, tools, infrastructures and so on involve complex mixtures or meshworks of digital, material and hybrid. Adding to this complexity, many of the scientific (and some of the educational) practices we observe in our studies have a strong flavouring of what can be called 'post-normal science' (see e.g., Funtowicz and Ravetz 1994; Farioli et al. 2022). They are practices in which epistemic uncertainty combined with a need for urgent

P. Goodyear (✉) · L. Markauskaite · N. Spence · T. Swist
The University of Sydney, Camperdown, Australia
e-mail: peter.goodyear@sydney.edu.au

C. Wrigley · G. Mosely
The University of Queensland, St Lucia, Australia

P. Jandrić et al. (eds.), *Constructing Postdigital Research*, Postdigital Science
and Education, https://doi.org/10.1007/978-3-031-35411-3_4

action make it imperative to bring together scientists, educators and other stakeholders in discussing and resolving ways to proceed. At the risk of overworking the 'post-' prefix, we should also add that we favour a post-critical stance, through which we (a) acknowledge that the scientific and educational practices we observe are the products of, and are enmeshed in, other practices that (also) reproduce inequality and injustice: physical, social and epistemic, while (b) locate possibilities for change firmly in the hands, hearts and minds of the real people who populate those practices (Goodyear 2021; Hodgson et al. 2020).

To illustrate the arguments, our account is grounded in two sites we have been researching through a large-scale, multi-year empirical study of interdisciplinary scientific and educational activity in a big, research-intensive university. One case is a Centre for Nanoscience; the other a Centre for Public Health.[1] In both settings, digital tools and technologies play widespread, substantial, diverse roles. They are woven into scientific and educational practices. Sometimes they are very much taken-for-granted, but occasionally they are the centre of collective attention. The practices we have been observing also draw on and hold together a variety of material technologies, social relations, divisions of labour, and epistemic challenges.

The fundamental questions in our research study are concerned with (a) the capabilities needed to participate successfully in interdisciplinary work and (b) methods for helping people strengthen such capabilities. We pursue these questions by linking three layers of observation and analysis: organisation, team and individual. How do research and innovation communities create interdisciplinary knowledge? How do interdisciplinary teams learn to function effectively? What constitutes the personal resourcefulness that enables individuals to participate in interdisciplinary work?

We use the Activity-Centred Analysis and Design framework (ACAD) to map out social, physical, and epistemic aspects of selected practices in the sites observed. We separate representations of emergent activities from representations of what might (next) be designed. We aim to show how a framework created for analysis and design in educational situations (ACAD) can also be used to construct design knowledge for improving scientific research settings – e.g., in supporting teams' conversations about the redesign of their lab spaces, tools, roles, goals and methods.

We advocate for forms of postdigital research that equip groups of people to understand, discuss and make decisions about the circumstances in which they work. Collectively designing for better ways of working can be complex and troubling. So, our chapter offers a reusable approach to constructing locally-useful design knowledge.

---

[1] Both centres are presented by pseudonyms.

2   Design Knowledge and Situated Action

We can start an explanation of our approach to research in this area by drawing on an observation from Raewyn Connell (2019). In describing how universities function, Connell insists that we must see them as real workplaces, within which real people do real work that has real effects. There is a strong tradition within the Anglophone literature on higher education of treating 'The University' as if it was human: capable of listening, reflecting, examining its conscience, mending its ways, and committing to making better decisions in the future. This is a dangerous fiction and Connell's careful decomposition of how universities actually do what they do is a useful corrective. Focussing on change in higher education, Goodyear develops the argument as follows:

> [C]hange occurs when people who work in universities change what they do, such that what they do has different effects. If we are interested in change now, or in the short to medium term, this means people in the current workforce have to change what they do. If course or curriculum designs, assessment or pedagogy are to change, real current members of the educational workforce have to think through the desired changes, discuss and agree what can be done, and change rules and documents to crystallise and communicate new expectations. Moreover, for a designed curriculum to become an experienced curriculum, students have to complete the work their teachers have begun. (Goodyear 2021: 38)

The same can be said of changes in the ways in which people engage in collectively-organised research. No critiques, proposals, or debates in journals on the philosophy of science (or of education) will have real effects on research or educational practice unless the real people who participate in science and education change what they do. This makes it important to understand both continuity and change in research and educational practices. How do we account for the ways in which practices are sustained and the ways in which they undergo significant transformation?

The research approach we describe in this chapter favours forms of explanation that acknowledge the roles played by social, physical, and epistemic relations in situating human activities (Dohn, Hansen, and Hansen 2020; Pink 2012; Suchman 1987, 2007). Changes in the ways activities unfold can often be attributed to situational changes: to the arrival of new team members, to the introduction of a new tool or instrument, or to a shift in the objects of an epistemic task, for example. If the changed activity persists, we can say there has been a shift in working practices. Such changes are sometimes accidental or unplanned or unremarked. Sometimes they are carefully rehearsed, deliberate choices, acknowledged by all and/or recorded in the biography of a teaching or research team. But such changes may also be complex and drawn out, involving mixtures of deliberation and serendipity, tacit acceptance and explicit recognition, differentially distributed across the people involved.

We are especially interested in ways of strengthening the capacities of such people, whether they be involved in educational or research work or both, to engage with each other in analysing and improving upon their working practices. In this we include their workplaces, the tools they use, the infrastructures they rely on, the ways they divide up tasks and distribute responsibilities and the ways they determine what is worth working on. This adds a recursive quality to our approach – not least because we aim to pass on some of the tools and ideas we use for our analyses to the participants in our research, for them to use in their own analysis and improvement work.

Going one step further, we aim to make it easier for the participants in our research to pass on similar tools and ideas to the people whose lives they are committed to enhancing: whether they be students, or the end-users and intended beneficiaries of research. This recursive ambition makes most sense in the context of strongly 'participatory' forms of research and education, such as when research aims and outcomes are co-designed or when students 'as partners' co-design courses, curricula and assessments (Cook-Sather et al. 2018; Cottam 2019). Discontinuities in conceptions of knowledge construction (e.g. ontological framings and epistemological commitments) make the passage of tools and ideas much more uncertain.

In the next section, we sketch a framework for thinking about analysis and design – the ACAD (Activity-Centred Analysis and Design) framework. After that, we illustrate aspects of the use of this framework in researching our two case study sites, making some observations about theoretical and methodological concerns as we do so.

An important characteristic of our approach is to insist on the use of two related but distinguishable ontologies: ways of conceptualising what exists. In our approach, *analysis* aims at explaining real mechanisms, relations, and causal paths while *design* eventually has to limit itself to what is amenable to deliberate change. (One can hope that good results will flow, but valued outcomes are rarely directly designable.) Design discussions enable a team of people with a stake in the situated practice(s) at hand to make decisions about how to improve their ways of working, including through changes they can make to the situation(s) in which their activities will unfold.

Such design discussions and decisions can be *informed* by analyses and representations of existing ways of working, but the things that can be represented and transformed into objects in and of design must not be mistaken for what actually exists or will exist. Design discussions necessarily disentangle designable from undesignable things, even though those things only exist as entanglements in reality. Subscription to this dual ontology is part of what constitutes the design knowledge we aim to pass on to others: it is a way of thinking about analysis and design that we find productive and which we hope others will find useful. For one thing, it gives permission to think and talk about 'the digital' at design time, while not forgetting the entanglement of digital and material in the everyday experiences of scientists, students and others.

3   Activity-Centred Analysis and Design (ACAD)

What has become known as the Activity-Centred Analysis and Design framework, or ACAD, has its deepest theoretical roots in Lucy Suchman's account of plans and situated action – derived from anthropologically-inspired field research undertaken in technology-rich workplaces (see e.g., Suchman 1987, 2007) – and in a related corpus of ethnographic studies in the emerging area of Computer-Supported Co-operative Work (CSCW) (see e.g., Beaudouin-Lafon 1998). An important conceptual bridge between ethnographically-informed studies of work and ACAD can be found in French-language ergonomics, especially in the writing of the late Alain Wisner (see especially Wisner 1995a, b).

ACAD can be described as 'a meta-theoretical framework for understanding and improving local, complex, learning situations' (Goodyear, Carvalho, and Yeoman 2021: 446). In this chapter, we set out to expand the scope of the framework to cover a much broader range of instances of academic work, including collective *research* work – while not implying that such work takes place without the occurrence of incidental (and often intentional) workplace learning. In other words, we propose that ACAD can be applied to a wide range of situations in which peoples' activity involves learning and work. We aim to show how it can be useful for researching such situations, especially where some or all of the people involved in the learning-working have a strong interest in the research being done: as when they help shape research questions, data-gathering strategies, interpretation and/or use of the research findings. Figure 1 can be used to explain how ACAD may help in researching such situations from a perspective sensitised by ideas about the postdigital, post-disciplinary, and postcritical.

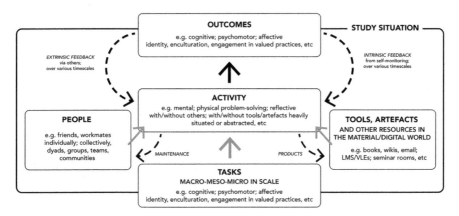

Fig. 1 ACAD framework applied to researching working-learning situations. (Adapted from Goodyear and Ellis 2008: 147.)

Firstly, Fig. 1 shows how we focus on a temporally bounded, naturally occurring, collaborative *activity* that is of significance to those participating in it – and which is of an extent that is manageable within the practical constraints applying to the (research) team who are seeking to understand it.[2] Typically, these qualities of significance and observational stamina mean that activities will unfold over hours rather minutes or days. It will never be possible to observe all that happens as an activity unfolds. For example, there will typically be very little observer access to what participants are thinking or feeling, though there may be occasional opportunities to prompt concurrent or retrospective 'thinking aloud'.

Secondly, as Fig. 1 suggests, activities can have multiple outcomes and these outcomes can be of different kinds. Some outcomes may be of the kind that we conventionally associate with learning: the creation of new insights, fine-tuning a skill, a sharpening of perceptions, etc. Some outcomes may be examples of personal and/or collective knowledge creation. Some outcomes may provide data for feedback to current or future activities, intrinsically (e.g., through participants' evaluative judgements – their thoughts about the quality of what they are producing) or extrinsically (e.g., through comments from more experienced others, such as teachers or managers).

Thirdly, activity is always situated. There are numerous ways one could classify the phenomena that comprise the situation. ACAD typically divides them into three kinds, saying that activity is situated by (i) structures of place, (ii) social structures, and (iii) epistemic/task structures. Putting it crudely but concisely, activity is shaped by where it unfolds, who is involved, and what (epistemic and other) tasks are being tackled. Mapping it to more familiar language, we might also say that activity is physically, socially, and epistemically situated. [For an alternative decomposition of situated laboratory work, see Wershler, Emerson, and Parikka (2021), who propose a six-part model embracing: space, technique, imaginaries, people, policy and infrastructure, and apparatus.]

In Fig. 1, the visual separation of activity from structures of place, social structures, and task/epistemic structures allows us to point out that some side-effects of an activity may create new tools and artefacts, or reconfigure a (work/learning) place and some side-effects may modify social relations, including through processes of group strengthening and maintenance. Also, distinguishing activity and the three kinds of phenomena that situate it makes particular sense when thinking about and discussing arrangements *at design time* (see below). But the visual separation does not capture the fact that *when the activity is unfolding* it is deeply entangled with the physical, social and epistemic, which are themselves tangled together.

Those things which might be said to *physically* situate work-learning activities include tools and artefacts that may be material or digital or hybrid. Tracing the entanglement of networks of tools and artefacts (etc.) in an activity necessitates a postdigital sensibility. The digital is virtually ubiquitous – especially in the kinds of

---

[2] Unlike Activity Theory (Engeström and Sannino 2021), ACAD does not insist on defining an activity by its intended goals.

research and educational situations and activities that we have been studying – but that does not mean that digital capabilities become uninteresting; not worthy of note (Sinclair and Hayes 2019). Moreover, digital devices normally have material qualities whose affordances can be consequential. Tracing these entanglements also requires us to have a spatial sensibility. (It would be helpful to have 'platial' as a term-of-art.) The complex, nested configurations, structures, boundaries, and access points that afford privacy, visibility, community, and exclusion can be hard to detect and depict, but it is necessary to try – while also being alert to the fact that activities and divisions of labour readily spill out to other places, near and remote.

Such nesting is also characteristic of the social and epistemic. Teams sit within organisations and tasks sit within larger programs of work, for example. One can be tempted to apply a structuralist's magical thinking when contemplating nested relations, but ACAD often leans towards networked forms of explanation – patiently piecing together the webs or meshworks in which socially, physically, and epistemically situated activity unfolds.

Figure 2 helps shift the perspective to 'design time', e.g., when the participants in a research team or centre are working together to improve some aspects of how, where and/or on what they work in the future.

Three key points can be added to the argument, using Fig. 2. First, at 'design time', a team of people – such as one of the research or teaching teams we are studying – can make shareable representations of a situation in which activities they see as problematic unfold, and can use these representations to reason about and discuss the logical connections between things they can (re)design, outcomes they value, and intervening processes.

Secondly, Fig. 2 acts as a reminder that valued outcomes emerge from activity and have no direct causal connection to things that are themselves directly amenable

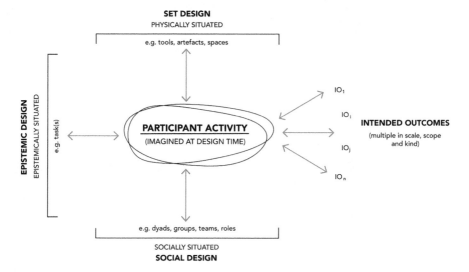

Fig. 2 ACAD framework applied 'at design time'. (Adapted from Goodyear et al. 2021.)

to (re)design – such as the physical arrangement of a shared laboratory, the software tools used for data analysis, or the sequencing of a set of related experiments.

Thirdly, Fig. 2 suggests that while (re)designable arrangements that have an influence on activity can be grouped into different kinds (e.g., set, social, epistemic), their real effects come about through entanglements in activity. At design time, it can be helpful to separate digital tools from divisions of labour, for example, because implementing design decisions is qualitatively different for these two kinds of design component. Reasoning about the affordances of two candidate digital tools is different from reasoning about what people may do, when asked to work in different configurations. Therefore, it can make sense to spend some time and effort considering the inherent attributes of tools, or places, or people, or tasks – but eventually decisions about what to do in the future will depend upon reasoning about relations *between* tools, tasks and people, meshed together in situated activity.

We see ACAD, and frameworks like it, functioning as epistemic tools in at least two senses. First, ACAD encapsulates some reusable design knowledge in the way it helps people find an initial, perhaps provisional, shared structure for representing analysis and design issues of interest to them. Then, people start constructing local design knowledge, based on their joint inquiries into how and why their working-learning activities unfold as they do, what it is they really value (and why), and what might need to be changed (redesigned) in order to make improvements.

In the next section, we describe our current program of research into interdisciplinary expertise, with special attention to how ACAD helps represent some important relationships.

4   Illustrations from Our Field Studies

Understanding what constitutes interdisciplinary expertise and even how to theorise and describe such expertise, so that successful interdisciplinary learning and work practices become more scalable, is not easy. None of the disciplinary, theoretical, or methodological perspectives can handle this level of heterogeneity. Our analytical approaches, at best, can be described as belonging to a general move to build on and integrate cultural, social, material, cognitive, and embodied accounts of knowledge work and learning (Clark 2011; Hutchins 2010; Malafouris 2012; Markauskaite and Goodyear 2017; Nersessian 2005, 2022). (Such accounts have made some inroads in, and across, philosophy, anthropology, organisational and workplace studies, science and technology studies, learning sciences, and some other domains.) This, then, is supplemented by design. At the core of this approach are two theoretical and methodological principles.

4.1 Theoretical Framing

We approach innovative knowledge work and learning *as a practice* by specifically drawing on Knorr Cetina's (1999, 2007) notion of 'epistemic practice'. As Knorr Cetina (2007: 361) notes, those who construct new knowledge often face the need to construct 'machineries of knowledge construction'. These machineries are amalgams of tools, technologies, people, objects, social agreements, and other arrangements and mechanisms that enable one to do knowledge work. The notion of epistemic practice emphasises the non-routine, creative, and relational character of complex knowledge-producing practices (Knorr Cetina 2001). Such practices cannot be understood by looking at rule-governed routines or habits commonly implied in the notions of established practices. Indeed, those who engage in interdisciplinary work often face the need to create the practice itself.

To understand how interdisciplinary practices are created and function in large interdisciplinary research centres and what enables people to participate in them skilfully, we study these practices at and across three intertwined levels:

- At a macro (organisational) level, we want to understand how institutional research cultures look, emerge and function in large interdisciplinary research centres. Here we aim to depict characteristic features, infrastructures, and ways of organising interdisciplinary work.
- At a meso (team) level, we want to understand what different interdisciplinary groupings within these labs actually do—particularly how they learn—when they engage in complex interdisciplinary activities. Here we are primarily interested in depicting what provides a tangible foundation for boundary-crossing activities focusing on the nature of objects, tools, and environments that interdisciplinary teams use and co-create as well as epistemic strategies that they enact.
- At a micro (individual) level, we want to understand what kinds of personal resourcefulness enable people to contribute to shared interdisciplinary knowledge work. Here, we are interested in depicting diverse personal resources (formal knowledge, skills, concrete experiences, emotions, dispositions, etc.), including disciplinary knowledge, on which people draw in critical interdisciplinary teamwork moments.

This kind of conceptual and analytical framing broadly mirrors the main strands of human cognitive–cultural development: community-wide (macro), activity-wide (meso), and individual (micro) (Markauskaite and Nerland 2019; Saxe 2018). To keep the account concise, the illustrations we give in this chapter are primarily from the analysis of practices taking the macro level perspective. However, it is important not to forget that these levels are neither ontologically nor analytically independent. It is the *conjunction* of insights across these levels that allows us to get a rounded understanding of the interdisciplinary practices and learning in natural, technology-rich settings.

4.2 Methodological Framing

Our overarching approach is informed by Nicolini's (2009, 2012) strategy of 'zooming in' to certain aspects of practice by choosing particular theoretical lenses, and 'zooming out' from practices by examining interconnections and looking at larger emerging phenomena.

To capture arrangements and mechanisms that underpin interdisciplinary practices, we must move inside the settings within which people engage in these kinds of work. The key challenge is to capture arrangements and mechanisms in ways that acknowledge the contingency of situated knowledge work and multiplicity of practices – vital characteristics of interdisciplinarity (Barry and Born 2013; Frickel, Albert, and Prainsack 2017) – while simultaneously revealing how they combine to form a coherent whole and how we (and others) can design for supporting productive practices. To make this transition possible, much of our empirical work focuses on depicting the kinds of social and physical arrangements and activities which facilitate joint working, learning and inquiry, as such arrangements and activities provide the tangible basis for design work.

In our earlier studies, we have been capturing key features of epistemic practices by identifying characteristic strategies used by professional communities to conduct inquiries and construct actionable knowledge – their main 'epistemic games' (Markauskaite and Goodyear 2017; Collins and Ferguson 1993). We also have been developing ways of capturing sociomaterial arrangements for professional knowledge practices and learning by identifying infrastructures and tools that professionals use and construct for complex knowledge work. Epistemic infrastructures are basic, shared conceptual, physical, and organisational arrangements that underpin and provide the backbone for the broadly distributed and diverse knowledge practices within a given area or field. Epistemic tools are specific conceptual, symbolic, and material devices that professionals use to conduct inquiries and solve particular problems. Organisational structures, committee meetings, organisational bulletins, shared research facilities, online sites and databases are very familiar examples of infrastructures found in many large research organisations, including those that do interdisciplinary work. Specific tools – templates, software, physical instruments – often complement this.

Studying interdisciplinary practices at each level, and in the relationships between levels, involves a set of approaches, but all of them require looking deeply into the workings of mundane interdisciplinary work. We attend management meetings and public events, analyse documents, interview leaders, managers and members, attend research team meetings, visit labs, and record and collect other data that give insights into everyday working activities that shape shared intellectual labour in interdisciplinary labs. Such research work is neither theoretically clean nor methodologically easy. Still, it gives glimpses of how and why things are done in particular ways, and what kinds of consequences they have. It helps see how tasks, tools and people come together into distinct configurations that make sense and how joint reflections on (re)design could help improve activities, practices and outcomes.

4.3 About the Centres

Our research has been situated in two large multidisciplinary research centres: Health and Nano, for short. One centre focuses on 'combatting' global health challenges – 'diabetes, obesity, cardiovascular disease and their related conditions'; the other concentrates on 'transforming' everyday human lives and society through 'nanoscale science and technology'. In terms of their general characteristics, both centres have significant similarities. Both multidisciplinary centres emerged together with purpose-built modern buildings – called 'hubs' – hosting state-of-the-art research facilities for doing research that underpins their missions. The Health hub is a 50,000 m^2 facility with wet and dry labs, shared core research facilities, a clinic and teaching spaces. (The Centre also has three small regional hubs created later in local hospitals.) The Nano hub is designed as a facility for research in the fields of nanophotonics and quantum science. In 900m^2 it contains 'some of the best cleanroom and nanofabrication facilities in the world' – tightly controlled labs enabling precise measurement for studying phenomena at the nanoscale; 32 laboratories plus 10,000m^2 of teaching spaces.

The centres have extensive memberships: between 1000 and 1100 people from across the university are engaged in each of the centres. In both centres, most people come from science and engineering, health and medicine; other disciplines account for less than 20% of the membership.

Both centres describe the scope of their research activity as a matrix of *domains*, representing broad disciplinary areas (e.g., biology, quantum science) and *themes* that cut across the domains and give strategic focus (e.g., physical activity, exercise and energy expenditure; communication, computing, and security).

Below the surface level, when we look at epistemic practices, the two centres have more differences than similarities. The ACAD framework helps depict some. To illustrate, we use ACAD to unpack the strategic practices of the centres (looking at the macro level).

4.4 Analysis

The Health Centre articulates a core part of its mission as 'to ease the burden of obesity, diabetes, cardiovascular disease and related conditions *by collaborative research and education that translates into real-world solutions*' (emphasis added). This joint task comes together with evident attention to the need to construct a new epistemic practice. Their core tool is the modern physical building—the hub— described by its director as 'the most complex integrated facility' within the university. It hosts around 900 occupants and is designed to foster collaborative research. The main ways for organising research activities and people are informed by the view of the Centre as 'a complex adaptive system'. The Centre tries to function as a 'niche' within the disciplinary, often over-managed, university structures – to help

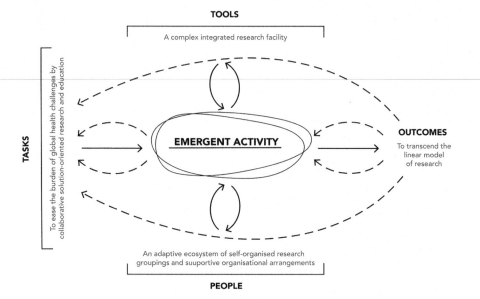

Fig. 3 ACAD framework – Health Centre

people from different disciplines come together and self-organise by creating so-called 'nodes' for joint interdisciplinary projects (see Fig. 3). The Centre's leadership put significant thought and effort into creating conditions that would inspire, motivate, and enable diverse autonomous groupings to function successfully and collaborate (e.g., sharing 'good practices' in node leaders' meetings).

However, there is no anticipation that one size may fit all; thus, beyond some basic expectations about how the nodes should be constituted and operate, day-to-day functioning is left to emerge. There is no fear of supporting 'slow boiling' or more risky ideas, as there is no illusion that all nodes will produce immediate, measurable outcomes. One of the Health Centre's key aspirations is: 'to *transcend the linear model* that conceives research as travelling from discovery research to applied to real-world implementation of research outcomes' (emphasis added). Truly transformative things take effort and time to emerge. Over 10 years, the Centre has been successful in demonstrating the productivity of this design in terms of traditional outcomes (publications, external income, awards, etc.) and has continued to reinvent itself as a very distinctive epistemic space. One clear outcome has been a shift in strategic focus from disease-centred research, focused on treatments, to prevention-centred research, focused on discovering and preventing causes of chronic conditions. This has been accompanied by a repositioning of 'multidisciplinarity', from being the *purpose* of the Centre to being a *tool* to achieve its mission, as well as a rhetorical shift from 'multidisciplinary research' to 'mission-driven research'.

In the Nano Centre, the joint task is different: 'to enable, facilitate and promote *transformational activities and translational outcomes* in nanoscience and technology that would otherwise not be possible through existing faculty and university structures'(emphasis added). One of the key issues for Nano is that the actual challenge it is tackling is not well defined or widely understood (in the general public or the university). Beyond the fact that its solution should be related to nanoscience and nanotechnologies, finding important interdisciplinary challenges that can be solved using nano is an integral part of the solution. In terms of tools, the language of 'nano' serves as the major 'attractor' for organising joint work, but the Nano Centre is primarily a symbolic rather than a physical space.

The Nano hub is a highly specialised and controlled research space, used only by those who do core nanoscience (just over 150 people). So, it is deliberately separated from the interdisciplinary activities sponsored by the Nano Centre. (The Nano hub is a highly specialised facility and is not a physical space suitable for researchers to 'hang out' together to let new collaborations serendipitously emerge. Nor is it suitable for translational and transformational research.) The fine-tuned academic program and arrangements for organising people and activities, therefore, form the core of the Nano Centre's practice. Different types of nodes and other groupings – Grand Challenges, Kickstarters, Frontiers, Catalysts, Networks – different types of leadership positions and events (e.g., design thinking workshops, townhall meetings, partnership events, Early Career Research ambassadors) each designed with a particular purpose – have their own particular roles in the Nano Centre's arrangements.

In contrast to the Health Centre, whose main aspiration is to transcend and find new ways of framing and solving the challenge, the Nano Centre's outcomes are primarily designed to make the linear science model work well and to align their activities and projects with national and global priorities and challenges (e.g. the United Nations Sustainable Development Goals) (see Fig. 4). While the Nano

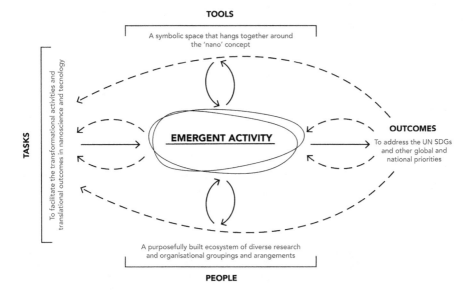

Fig. 4 ACAD framework – Nano Centre

Centre was created a few years later than the Health Centre, there is no lack of evidence to show that this design – while being finetuned and refined regularly – generates promised outputs and outcomes.

Each of the two centres offers a different balance between what is already designed (and why) and what is left for others to complete and emerge. Four main points are worth noting.

First, much of this designerly work that is done in the centres is deeply epistemic – it is firmly focussed on creating 'machinery' for creating interdisciplinary knowledge. This work is an essential part of knowledge work, without which interdisciplinarity cannot function. It is not deeply scientific, but neither is it a-scientific. It cannot really be done by someone who has no 'skin in the game' or who does not understand how science functions, and how things could work at the intersections of science and society.

Second, the buildings, with their state-of-the-art facilities, play essential roles in the identities of the two centres, yet there are deep ambiguities in each case. The Nano Centre uses the prestige of the associated Nano (hub) building as a springboard to create an exciting and vibrant *symbolic space* around the 'nano' concept. In practice, there is a significant gap between what's happening in the labs of the Nano building and what the Nano Centre does. As some participants noted, this organisational fiction is not such a big problem for those who work in the building or the Centre: the existence of the interdisciplinary centre was an essential condition for building the hub, which was needed for frontier research in physics, and the hub makes the Centre visible. Each symbiotically helps the other and each does what it does very well. Of course, the lack of shared physical space that would enable the serendipity of interdisciplinary collaboration has to be compensated by a much stronger focus on social and epistemic design.

In contrast, the core Health hub is *the* key part of the Health Centre's activities and identity and the benefits of physical proximity in enabling collaborations are noticeable. However, this creates a further challenge. Physical walls, between those who are housed in the core Health Hub and those who are not, unintentionally create a barrier. For example, the leaders of the smaller regional hospital-based hubs regularly remind people that there is more to the Health Centre than the central hub; and some members of the Centre who do not have space in any hub say they do not *really* feel a part of the Centre. Others see the core facilities as the only valuable thing, dismissing the added value of other multidisciplinary activities. Those who are inside face the challenges of having to share labs, office spaces, and other facilities. These tensions constantly need to be corrected by tweaking social arrangements and designs at various levels of the Centre's ecosystem (e.g. at the macro level, the Centre has created a Diversity and Inclusion Committee to drive its inclusion agenda). In comparison, the issue of belonging has not been such a noticeable matter in the Nano Centre, where most members have offices (and labs) outside the hub and the questions related to the occupancy and management of the hub are solved separately from the questions about the Centre.

Third, neither of the two centres is markedly 'digital'. Both have virtual spaces for their members, but these are not busy spaces, or where the 'real' action takes place. At the same time, digital technologies are deeply embedded in their interdisciplinary practices. This includes the use of Zoom and Miro for collaboration and regular newsletters and emails to keep engaged with the members: strengthening identity around the Centres in the absence of all-inclusive shared material spaces. Also, complex scientific visualisations generated by machines are a common feature of research presentations in both centres. They are routinely used when people are explaining their research to others who may have no clue how things actually work. But some of the interdisciplinary research is digital through and through.

For example, one of the Health Centre's themes is dedicated to integrative systems modelling, featuring research using large data sets to investigate a range of phenomena, from biological systems to social networks. Such research is full of technical complexities and not free from serious epistemic frictions. What is a ground-breaking research question for a biologist may not be the most interesting research question for a modeller. The entanglement between digital and physical becomes even more acute when we look more closely at research in quantum computing or computational materials discovery, where researchers describe their research in one of the annual reports as follows: 'Simulating new materials from a single atom to fully functioning devices using quantum computers, multiscale simulation, artificial intelligence and machine learning'.

Fourth, the leaders of these centres are often deeply aware that their macro visions and designs do not translate neatly into practices. 'Yes, being in the same space does not always result in collaboration'; 'Yes, this building was not suitable for collaboration right from the start'; 'Yes, the solution to this particular problem is deeply disciplinary'; 'Yes, some nodes do not produce the expected outcome: So what?' Making such interdisciplinary centres function productively is a hard task. It is not just, or mainly, a matter of design at the macro level. It is not just a matter of imagining what would be better or even ideal. Such centres and their sub-units are co-configured from many distributed activities, each with its own design. For example, what does it take to create a successful node that brings different people together? How can one help this happen organically yet reliably? How can productive collaborations be sustained over time?

The many people working (and learning) in our two research sites are well aware that they have to find short and long-term resolutions in order to periodically and provisionally reconcile competing forces or demands. They know, for example, that there are disputes about the respective merits of disciplinary and interdisciplinary research, about publishing in disciplinary or interdisciplinary journals, about the merits of basic (curiosity-driven) and applied (use-inspired) research. They know that there is not a simple alignment between working on projects aimed at social benefit and advancing one's career as an academic scientist or between individual and collective success. Such tensions are endemic in their worlds. Researchers studying laboratory life, or analysing the workings of science more generally, are free (of course) to point out these contradictions and diagnose their origins.

But, from our point of view – and from the point of view of many of the participants in our research – this should be the start and not the end of a line of inquiry. (It is no longer interesting to conclude that 'X is contested' or 'Y is an inevitable consequence of managerialism' or 'Z is performative'.) Rather, we want to know how people develop the personal resourcefulness needed to work with others in such complex circumstances. What does it take to strengthen the capacities of people, teams, labs, universities, and other organisations to thrive in complicated worlds? How can design and designerly ways of thinking help with this?

We think about the answers to such questions in at least two complementary and intertwined ways: (a) interdisciplinary research as design, and (b) design for interdisciplinary research. Design is not an uncommon activity in interdisciplinary research settings (White and Deevy 2020), including in our research sites, and senior leaders in such interdisciplinary research centres are often skilful, usually self-taught, intuitive designers. But it takes years for them to learn. A different way is to use design to co-create tools for interdisciplinary teams – tools that help teams engage in the co-design of situated actionable knowledge for their interdisciplinary work (see, e.g., Hubbs, O'Rourke, and Orzack 2021 and also Wrigley 2017 for methods). It is this intertwinement – between interdisciplinarity *as* design and design *for* interdisciplinarity – where postdigital ways of thinking have a significant potential to make a practical difference.

5   Concluding Comments

In this chapter, we have tried to use some of our experiences of researching complex sites of intellectual inquiry – notably some multidisciplinary university centres – to illustrate an argument about doing postdigital research through constructing design knowledge. Our stance is shared with some others who carry out research with and for participants, to enable them to deal with problematic situations and/or collectively design improvements to aspects of their work. Readers may see some similarities with (participatory) action research, soft systems methodology, Change Laboratory methods, design-based implementation research, formative evaluation, and other kinds of formative intervention, for instance (Checkland and Poulter 2006; Engeström et al. 2014; Penuel et al. 2011; Gutierez et al. 2016; Penuel 2014; Virkkunen and Newnham 2013; Whyte 1991; Wrigley 2017).

Finding, naming, and analysing structural barriers to better ways of working can be an absorbing complement to such engagement, but it does not always help find opportunities for movement or delineate spaces within which valued changes can be pursued. Moreover, planning, discussing, critiquing, improving, and agreeing on desirable courses of action are themselves inherently complex and can benefit from supportive tools and ideas. Among these, methods and constructs associated with collective design have a role to play. In all this, technologically-mediated epistemic practices turn out to be pervasive, important, complicated and intriguing: fit subjects for postdigital research.

Acknowledgement This work was funded by the Australian Research Council through Discovery Project grant DP200100376 (Developing interdisciplinary expertise in universities).

References

Barry, A., & Born, G. (2013). *Interdisciplinarity: Reconfigurations of the social and natural sciences*. London: Routledge.

Beaudouin-Lafon, M. (Ed.). (1998). *Computer Supported Co-operative Work (CSCW)*. London: John Wiley & Sons.

Checkland, P., & Poulter, J. (2006). *Learning for action. A short definitive account of soft systems methodology and its use for practitioners, teachers and students*. Chichester: Wiley.

Clark, A. (2011). *Supersizing the mind: Embodiment, action and cognitive extension*. Oxford: Oxford University Press.

Collins, A., & Ferguson, W. (1993). Epistemic forms and epistemic games: structures and strategies to guide inquiry. *Educational Psychologist, 28*(1), 25–42. https://doi.org/10.1207/s15326985ep2801_3.

Connell, R. (2019). *The good university: what universities actually do and why it's time for radical change*. Clayton, VI: Monash University Publishing.

Cook-Sather, A., Matthews, K. E., Ntem, A., & Leathwick, S. (2018). What we talk about when we talk about students as partners. *International Journal for Students as Partners, 2*(2), 1–9. https://doi.org/10.15173/ijsap.v2i2.3790.

Cottam, H. (2019). *Radical Help: How we can remake the relationships between us and revolutionise the welfare state*. London: Little Brown.

Dohn, N. B., Hansen, S. B., & Hansen, J. J. (Eds.). (2020). *Designing for situated knowledge transformation*. Abingdon: Routledge.

Engeström, Y., & Sannino, A. (2021). From mediated actions to heterogenous coalitions: four generations of activity-theoretical studies of work and learning. *Mind, Culture, and Activity, 28*(1), 4–23. https://doi.org/10.1080/10749039.2020.1806328.

Engeström, Y., Sannino, A., & Virkkunen, J. (2014). On the methodological demands of formative interventions. *Mind, Culture, and Activity, 21*(2), 118–128. https://doi.org/10.1080/10749039.2014.891868.

Farioli, F., Funtowicz, S., & Mayer, M. (2022). Post-Normal Science, transdisciplinarity, and uncertainty in relation to educators' competences: a conversation with Silvio Funtowicz. In P. Vare, N. Lauselet, & M. Reickmann (Eds.), *Competences in education for sustainable development: critical perspectives* (pp. 61–67). Cham: Springer. https://doi.org/10.1007/978-3-030-91055-6_8.

Frickel, S., Albert, M., & Prainsack, B. (Eds.). (2017). *Investigating interdisciplinary collaboration: Theory and practice across disciplines*. New Brunswick: Rutgers University Press.

Funtowicz, S. O., & Ravetz, J. R. (1994). Uncertainty, complexity and post-normal science. *Environmental Toxicology and Chemistry, 13*(12), 1881–1885. https://doi.org/10.1002/etc.5620131203.

Goodyear, P. (2021). Realising the good university: social innovation, care, design justice and educational infrastructure. *Postdigital Science and Education, 4*(1), 33–56. https://doi.org/10.1007/s42438-021-00253-5.

Goodyear, P., & Ellis, R. (2008). University students' approaches to learning: rethinking the place of technology. *Distance Education, 29*(2), 141–152. https://doi.org/10.1080/01587910802154947.

Goodyear, P., Carvalho, L., & Yeoman, P. (2021). Activity-Centred Analysis and Design (ACAD): core purposes, distinctive qualities and current developments. *Educational Technology Research and Development, 69*(2), 445–464. https://doi.org/10.1007/s11423-020-09926-7.

Gutiérrez, K. D., Engeström, Y., & Sannino, A. (2016). Expanding educational research and interventionist methodologies. *Cognition and Instruction, 34*(3), 275–284. https://doi.org/10.1080/07370008.2016.1183347.

Hodgson, N., Vlieghe, J., & Zamojski, P. (Eds.). (2020). *Post-critical perspectives on higher education: reclaiming the educational in the university*. Cham: Springer. https://doi.org/10.1007/978-3-030-45019-9.

Hubbs, G., O'Rourke, M., & Orzack, S. H. (2021). *The toolbox dialogue initiative: the power of cross-disciplinary practice*. Boca Raton, FL: CRC Press. https://doi.org/10.1201/9780429440014.

Hutchins, E. (2010). Cognitive ecology. *Topics in Cognitive Science, 2*(4), 705–715. https://doi.org/10.1111/j.1756-8765.2010.01089.x.

Knorr Cetina, K. (1999). *Epistemic cultures: how the sciences make knowledge*. Cambridge, MA: Harvard University Press.

Knorr Cetina, K. (2007). Culture in global knowledge societies: knowledge cultures and epistemic cultures. *Interdisciplinary Science Reviews, 32*(4), 361–375. https://doi.org/10.1179/030801807X163571.

Knorr-Cetina, K. (2001). Objectual practice. In T. R. Schatzki, K. Knorr Cetina, & E. von Savigny (Eds.), *The practice turn in contemporary theory* (pp. 175–188). London: Routledge.

Malafouris, L. (2012). *How things shape the mind: A theory of material engagement*. Cambridge, MA: The MIT Press.

Markauskaite, L., & Goodyear, P. (2017). *Epistemic fluency and professional education: innovation, knowledgeable action and actionable knowledge*. Dordrecht: Springer. https://doi.org/10.1007/978-94-007-4369-4.

Markauskaite, L., & Nerland, M. (2019). An ecological framework for studying interdisciplinary learning: Linking culture, activity and mind. Paper presented at The 18th biennial EARLI conference for research on learning and instruction, Aachen, Germany.

Nersessian, N. J. (2005). Interpreting scientific and engineering practices: Integrating the cognitive, social, and cultural dimensions. In M. E. Gorman, R. D. Tweney, D. C. Gooding, & A. P. Kincannon (Eds.), *Scientific and technological thinking* (pp. 17–56). Mahwah, NJ: LEA.

Nersessian, N. J. (2022). *Interdisciplinarity in the making: Models and methods in frontier science*. Cambridge, MA: The MIT Press.

Nicolini, D. (2009). Zooming in and out: Studying practices by switching theoretical lenses and trailing connections. *Organization Studies, 30*(12), 1391–1418. https://doi.org/10.1177/0170840609349875.

Nicolini, D. (2012). *Practice theory, work and organization*. Oxford: Oxford University Press.

Penuel, W. (2014). Emerging forms of formative intervention research in education. *Mind, Culture, and Activity, 21*(2), 97–117. https://doi.org/10.1080/10749039.2014.884137.

Penuel, W., Fishman, B., Cheng, B. H., & Sabelli, N. (2011). Organizing research and development at the intersection of learning, implementation, and design. *Educational Researcher, 40*(7), 331–337. https://doi.org/10.3102/0013189X11421826.

Pink, S. (2012). *Situating everyday life: practices and places*. London: Sage.

Saxe, G. B. (2018). Conceptual change: A cultural-historical and cognitive-developmental framework. In T. G. Amin & O. Levrini (Eds.), *Converging Perspectives on Conceptual Change* (pp. 51–60). Oxon: Routledge.

Sinclair, C., & Hayes, S. (2019). Between the post and the com-post: examining the postdigital 'work' of a prefix. *Postdigital Science and Education, 1*(1), 119–131. https://doi.org/10.1007/s42438-018-0017-4.

Suchman, L. (1987). *Plans and situated actions: the problem of human-machine communication*. Cambridge: Cambridge University Press.

Suchman, L. (2007). *Human-machine reconfigurations: plans and situated actions*. 2nd Ed. Cambridge: Cambridge University Press.

Virkkunen, J., & Newnham, D. (2013). *The Change Laboratory: a tool for collaborative development of work and education*. Rotterdam: Sense Publishers.

Wershler, D., Emerson, L., & Parikka, J. (2021). *The lab book: situated practices in media studies*. Minneapolis, MN: University of Minnesota Press.

White, P. J., & Deevy, C. (2020). Designing an interdisciplinary research culture in higher education: A case study. *Interchange, 51*, 499–515. https://doi.org/10.1007/s10780-020-09406-0.

Whyte, W. F. E. (1991). *Participatory action research*. Thousand Oaks, CA: Sage Publications, Inc.

Wisner, A. (1995a). Understanding problem building: ergonomic work analysis. *Ergonomics, 38*(3), 595–605. https://doi.org/10.1080/00140139508925133.

Wisner, A. (1995b). Situated cognition and action: implications for ergonomic work analysis and anthropotechnology. *Ergonomics, 38*(8), 1542–1557. https://doi.org/10.1080/00140139508925209.

Wrigley, C. (2017). Principles and practices of a design-led approach to innovation. *International Journal of Design Creativity and Innovation, 5*(3–4), 235–255. https://doi.org/10.108 0/21650349.2017.1292152.

Cyber-Social Research: Emerging Paradigms for Interventionist Education Research in the Postdigital Era

Anastasia O. Tzirides, Akash K. Saini, Bill Cope, Mary Kalantzis, and Duane Searsmith

1 Introduction

First, a note about the 'postdigital' in the title of our chapter and this book. As Jandrić and colleagues explain,

> the contemporary use of the term 'postdigital' ... describe[s] human relationships to technologies that we experience, individually and collectively, in the moment here and now. It shows our raising awareness of blurred and messy relationships between physics and biology, old and new media, humanism and posthumanism, knowledge capitalism and bio-informational capitalism. (Jandrić et al. 2018: 896)

Clearly, we are not postdigital in the sense that digital is in the past; we're postdigital in the paradoxical sense that the digital has become so pervasively embedded in our biomaterial and social lives to have become ubiquitous and as such nearly invisible. The digital is now part of the infrastructure of our lives across many domains, from personal to professional. In its nature, say Geoffrey Bowker and colleagues, infrastructure 'typically exists in the background'. It is 'frequently taken for granted' (Bowker et al. 2010: 98). Infrastructure, says Leigh Starr, is 'a system of substrates' that often slips into invisibility, like plumbing or railroad lines. Because infrastructure is 'boring', we willingly leave 'the nerds' to take an interest in it and to attend to it (Star 1999: 379–80).

Precisely the problem of much educational technology is that we have left it to the engineers to create the infrastructure of our lives as learners and teachers. All-too-frequently, the result has been to replicate existing pedagogical relations rather than to reform them, or worse still, to give unwarranted new life to the learning experiences of the engineers' past experience (Cope and Kalantzis 2023).

A. O. Tzirides (✉) · A. K. Saini · B. Cope · M. Kalantzis · D. Searsmith
College of Education, University of Illinois, Champaign, IL, USA
e-mail: aot2@illinois.edu; aksaini2@illinois.edu; billcope@illinois.edu;
marykalantzis@illinois.edu; dsearsmi@illinois.edu

P. Jandrić et al. (eds.), *Constructing Postdigital Research*, Postdigital Science
and Education, https://doi.org/10.1007/978-3-031-35411-3_5

Cyber-social research as we theorize and exemplify it in this chapter is about integrating the projects of education research with the design—not just the implementation—of digital learning environments.

A note too about 'cyber-social': against techno-determinism where the implementation of technology fashions social change, we propose a dialectical model more appropriate to the contemporary conditions of digital technology (Cope and Kalantzis 2022). The cyber-social concept points to a techno-social relationship where the shape of human action is within the scope of technological 'affordances' (Gibson 1977; Kalantzis and Cope 2020: 90–94) including possibilities that may or may not be fully exploited. The education research we describe in this chapter is about pushing these affordances—pushing the technical into new frontiers of the social/educational, and pushing the social/educational based on emerging possibilities in the technical.

2 Changing Paradigms for Software Development: Lessons for Education Research

Ironically perhaps, in a cyber-social frame of reference, software development processes have in recent decades become more socially responsive than education research in the traditional experimental model. The term most frequently used to describe today's leading edge software development methodologies is 'agile'. This contrasts with earlier paradigms for software development that have been characterized retrospectively by the metaphor 'waterfall'.

Waterfall software development is a methodical, linear, and necessarily slow process of: customer and stakeholder consultation > requirements specification > technical specification > alpha development software > developer testing > beta testing with a small group of users > version release (Royce 1970). New versions might subsequently be built by repeating this cycle. The way in which the general population of users experienced these processes was the box of CDs and instructions that came out every few years, version 1.0 to version n. If you wanted to stay up-to-date, you bought the new box and reinstalled the software on your computer. In the industrial era, washing machines, cars, and buildings were designed, developed, and delivered to consumers in much the same way.

As a technical development and social design process, these processes were slow, typically requiring years in a full design cycle. They involved minimal engagement with a small sample of users (if at all), and only at the beginning of the process. Engineers ruled! Innovation was expensive, requiring considerable capital input and so restricting the design of innovation to the capital-rich. And the measures of success were determined by the logic of mass production, market demand for a uniform, mass produced product with little scope for varied use and no scope beyond the crudest overall demand metric for a generic product. This is how the logic of Fordism was ported into software development. The waterfall was a precipitously one-way drop: the water of a product poured over the edge to take its place in the river of life, but there is no way that the ripples in the post-waterfall river can ever forewarn the waters before their fall.

With the rise of cloud-based software and online code repositories, a new paradigm for software development emerged in the early 2000s: 'agile software development' (Martin 2009; Stober and Hansmann 2009). It is hard to overestimate the depth and scale of this paradigm change. New software projects could begin with only the most general of expectation of software function. The unit of design is small—the 'user story'. These are short narratives which describe fragments of human interest and desire, typically of the form, 'As a user, I want to...' (Cohn 2004). A software project may have quite a few stories. These can be combined into 'epics', and a software application may be constituted by a number of such epics.

As early as possible in the design/development process, fragments of code representing separate stories or epics are released to users. Design-release cycles are frequently reduced to one or two weeks—or even less. Instead of big-number versioning in slow waterfall cycles, agile programming is characterized by rapid, small, incremental story > coding > release cycles. These can be continuous, and from a user point of view, seamless. So, from 1 day to the next, when you return to a cloud application or social media platform, you may find small and subtle changes. A user suggestion has become a user story, translated into code, released ... and later reversed if it does not work or if enough users complain. If there is some doubt about the value of a change, an A/B study will leave code unchanged for the 'A' sample while changing it for a 'B' sample in order to ask the 'B's what they think of the new code. The range and diversity of user engagement can be addressed, because the needs of edge-cases and outliers are captured and become worthy of attention. The result is what we would call cyber-social learning, integrating users into an integrated process of research-design.

Compare this now to traditional experimental designs for education research, such as those employed in randomized, controlled trials. Frequently canonized as the 'gold standard' for establishing the efficacy of educational interventions, these are more like the metaphorical waterfall than the agile methodologies prevailing today in software development. Research is expensive, so educational researchers look for grants, preferably big ones, to support sufficiently large sample sizes and for a time-period long enough to implement an innovation with effect. The process is linear: design the intervention > implement the intervention > evaluate the results. At best it is long cycle, in the unusual case where the results of one intervention can be constructively used for a revised implementation. It is disengaged: the researcher must set in place protocols such that their otherwise obvious interests do not influence the outcomes.

Fidelity of implementation is demanded. To prove an intervention works and that its effects are replicable, every teacher in the experiment should apply the intervention in the same way and for every student—an entirely unrealistic expectation, not to mention inappropriate one that over-writes the professionalism of teachers and the diversity of learners. Results are processed for overall populations as if they were more-or-less homogenous. (Does this intervention work for a significant portion of the students in a sample?) If there is to be demographic breakup, that needs a bigger sample size and more expense, and even then, the sample can only realistically be broken up according to the grossest of demographics, such as gender or race/ethnicity, so homogenizing in another way. The insights of outliers and edge cases are lost; diversity is erased in the interest of generalization (Cope and Kalantzis 2020; Erikson and Gutierrez 2002). Of course, there are other methodologies in education, but it is these kinds of experimental or quasi-experimental methods that get the lion's share of federal education research funding in the US, where we work. We use them here as a methodological counterpoint.

For these reasons, we propose a model of cyber-social research that applies to education research insights parallel to the agile critique of waterfall software development. Here, we build upon and extend two research methods literatures: design research and agile research. Both these underpin the principles of what we term cyber-social research.

3   Agile and Design-Based Research

Agile and design-based research methods allow for a more flexible, adaptive, and collaborative approach to research. By using these approaches, we can continually evaluate and improve educational practices to ensure that they are relevant, effective, and well-suited to the needs of students and educators in a rapidly changing postdigital world.

Design-based research is intended to support the development of tools, curriculum, and theories in order to understand how learning takes place and by aiming to support it (Barab and Squire 2004). As a research approach, it aims to develop and refine educational interventions through an iterative cycle of design, implementation, and evaluation. Design-based research is well-suited for the field of educational technology in the postdigital era because it allows researchers and educators to adapt to the rapidly changing landscape of digital technologies and explore the effectiveness of these technologies in real-world educational contexts. It focuses on practical, real-world problems and seeks to create innovative solutions that are grounded in theory and evidence. By combining elements of design, evaluation, and theory-building, design-based research offers a flexible and adaptive framework for researchers and educators to explore the complex relationships between technology, learning, and teaching.

The origins of design-based research can be traced back to the work of Ann Brown and Allan Collins who argued that laboratory educational research, detached from the real educational practice in classrooms by its artificially constructed laboratory conditions, could rarely resemble real classroom conditions (Brown 1992; Collins 1992). More recently, Gutierrez and colleagues have conceptualized 'social design research' that is sensitive to learner diversity and is focused on equity objectives (Gutiérrez and Jurow 2016).

A design-based research approach, according to Barab and Squire (2004), aims to create new theories, artifacts, and practices to influence learning and teaching in natural contexts. Context, they argue, is critically important for design-based research, as the setting for all learning and cognition. Similarly, McKenney and Reeves contend that educational design researchers aim to solve problems of the real world, in real settings, by using the already-known theory of the field, and simultaneously by trying to create new knowledge to be used by others that experience similar issues (McKenney and Reeves 2014).

According to the Design-Based Research Collective (2003), design-based research should not be considered just as the design and testing of specific interventions. They articulate that design-based research presents the following five characteristics: (1) combining the goals of designing learning environments and creating theories to promote and support the wider scientific understanding; (2) iterative cycles of design, implementation, analysis, and refinement; (3) taking a pragmatically flexible approach, justifiable through the outcomes of sharable theoretical knowledge and solutions that can be used by practitioners and educational designers; (4) accounting for and record all salient issues (positive and negative) involved in learning in authentic contexts even when some at first seem tangential to the focus of the research; (5) using appropriate methods to record the implementation process and communicate it to those interested. In addition to these characteristics, McKenney and Reeves (2014) claim that design-based research is: (1) grounded, since it uses theory and empirical findings to drive the task; (2) interventionist, because it aims to change an educational setting; (3) collaborative, as it requires the joint involvement and work of researchers, teachers, and other professionals; (4) adaptive, since the research and intervention design are subject to alterations based on emerging insights from the process and the scientific knowledge. It is the hope and aspiration of design-based research to broaden the range of participation in the design process and deepen its sensitivity to diversity.

Agile research, as proposed by Twidale and Hansen (2019), is a flexible and adaptive approach to research designed to keep up with the fast-paced changes in technology and digital advancement. It involves an iterative and collaborative approach to research that is based on the principles of agile software development. Agile research is ideal for the field of educational technology because it allows for ongoing improvement and refinement of educational practices and digital tools based on the changing needs of learners and educators.

Twidale and Hansen (2019) argue that agile principles can be applied to research studies since software development and research projects present various similarities (e.g., uncertain requirements beforehand, unexpected delays, cost, and complexities). Agile research can be particularly useful for projects that are mostly exploratory, where it is unclear from the beginning what needs to be done to make progress at any specific point, as well as the fact that it is almost completely unknown what the final research outcomes will be. Agile research can well serve this research type since it does not require heavy planning in advance, and in this respect is unlike conventional research processes.

For Twidale and Hansen (2019), the main characteristics of agile research are: (1) research in tight iterative cycles with focus on individuals and interactions; (2) incremental delivery of operational outcomes; (3) collaboration of all the stakeholders involved; and (4) embracing and implementation of changes during the process. In these respects, it is similar to design-based research, in the general sense that it is a flexible and adaptive approach, based on the current context of the research implementation, and one that acknowledges and embraces the errors, unexpected circumstances, and diversity of responses that occur in real-life. To address this issue, agile research focuses on constructing and testing an intervention iteratively—designing implementing and evaluating small subcomponents of that intervention quickly in order to catch any problems, designing and gradually adding supplementary features as required. The combination of agile and design-based research approaches allows for a continuous evaluation of the impact of technology in education.

Both agile and design-based research emphasize collaboration and teamwork, by involving stakeholders, including students, educators, and researchers, in the research process. The diversity of participants is designed-in, and principles of parity of participation are included in the design process. For example, an agile research study could be conducted to evaluate the effectiveness of a new educational technology tool that involves the students in the research process and incorporates their feedback to improve the tool. Such a collaborative approach allows for a continuous evaluation of the tool's effectiveness, ensuring that the research is relevant and meaningful to all stakeholders and leading to better outcomes. It is assumed that responses will cross a wide range of perspectives, and the methods are looking for the range of responses rather than averaged or normed responses.

Such approaches are essential nowadays in the development of new tools for computer-mediated learning. In part, this is simply a pragmatic matter of aligning educational research with contemporary software development processes, or the application of existing tools and platforms when they offer multiple pathways for implementation. In the most general of terms, we would argue that this is a valuable approach for all educational interventions in contexts of deep social diversity and rapid social change. In this sense, such approaches stand as a critique of traditional experimental education research with its long-cycles and population-based analyses.

McKenney and Reeves (2014) state that design-based research is more than a methodology. Rather it is a framework that uses other methods and methodologies to address research questions. Similarly, agile research is considered by Twidale and Hansen (2019) to be a metamethod, meaning that is a different way of utilizing already established methods. For that reason, when conducting research studies, a method or methods should be selected based on the research study objectives, such as qualitative methods for collecting in-depth and detailed insights, quantitative methods for gathering data to uncover trends, and mixed-methods combining the benefits of both qualitative and quantitative methods.

However, design-based and agile research frameworks do not come without their limitations or challenges. One of the main criticisms is their close connections to context, which can be assumed to make it difficult to generalize the outcomes to other settings (Design-Based Research Collective 2003). Design-based research aims to realize Stake's 'petite generalization' objective, demonstrating with evidence-based claims that make explicit relevance of the specific context with other contexts (Stake 2005). According to Barab and Squire (2004), design-based researchers need to generate flexible theories and design principles that have been created in a naturalistic context and can be easily adapted to other contexts while keeping their robustness and rigor. Adaptability is the key to address the close relation of the outcomes to one specific type of context in design-based research.

Similarly, McKenney and Reeves (2014) argue that design-based research outcomes provide insights and guidelines that can be considered and inform the work of others, following Yin's notion of 'analytic generalization' in which 'the investigator is striving to generalize a particular set of results to a broader theory' (Yin 1994: 36). To achieve this, Barab and Squire (2004) suggest that researchers take into account the general constraints and characteristics of the broad type of setting in which the specific research context belongs in order to increase generalizability and add validity to the study.

Meanwhile the agile research framework that Twidale and Hansen (2019) articulate, as they themselves argue is still being defined. A risk with agile research is that it can be perceived as too easy to implement. Its aim is to make less complicated and intimidating the protocols of a monolithic research project by separating an immense workload into smaller pieces and removing the necessity to plan everything in advance. Implementing multiple iterations, structure, and guidance is still needed, and reflection on what has been learned and how to proceed is key to achieving effectiveness. However, reflection and subsequent decisions are always demanding and never simple. The benefit, though, derives from dealing with problems on a smaller scale that can be addressed in a more manageable way, instead of having to deal with the same problem for the full research project. Therefore, research projects following the agile research framework in combination with the design-based research framework can have the necessary structure and plan for the multiple iterations and refinements that occur in practice. This combination provides the necessary flexibility that the complexity of the postdigital research designs requires.

Addressing the question of the validity of the research study's findings, the Design-Based Research Collective (2003) suggests that this can be strengthened through the collaboration of various researchers, practitioners, and professionals, and through the iterative character of the study which leads to better calibration of theory, design, practice, and measurement. Concerning the reliability of the data and the outcomes, the Design-Based Research Collective argues that this measure can be addressed through the triangulation of multiple data sources, the use of standardized instruments, and the repetitive cycles of design, implementation, analysis, and refinement.

At the end of this chapter, we will propose a synthesis and extension of these approaches that we call 'cyber-social learning research'.

4   A Cyber-Social Research Study

In this section we describe the application of agile and design-based research in the field of higher education, bringing these together into an approach we term 'cyber-social research'. Our aim is to demonstrate the importance of these research approaches in assessing the impact of digital technology on educational practices.

To do this, we present a case study that uses these approaches to evaluate the effectiveness of an innovative, browser-based peer review and concept mapping tool in two online higher education courses at the University of Illinois. Online learning requires particular ways and means to enhance engagement, foster community and sustain presence. The pedagogy of these courses have at their core peer to peer feedback and formative assessment. The experimental nature of the courses and the platform in which they are delivered is made explicit. Learners opt into this collaborative orientation to research and development. By involving students and researchers in the design, implementation, and incremental development processes, the goal is for the tool to progressively evolve, meeting course goals and addressing students' needs.

To set this tool in a larger context, peer review is an essential element in the validation of knowledge claims, used extensively in a number of high-stakes epistemic contexts, including scholarly journals and competitive research application review. In teaching and learning, peer review has the advantage of training learners to participate in these canonical knowledge processes. In conventional educational terms, peer review provides a channel for formative assessment. It also contributes to the formation of epistemic community, where students learn to give and take on board constructive feedback (Montebello et al. 2018; Pinheiro 2018).

Peer review has been extensively studied and researched, with many reports highlighting the benefits it brings to academic achievements and behavioral change (e.g., increased confidence, engagement, etc.) (Double et al. 2020; Gamage et al. 2021). Moreover, peer review has been shown to enhance student learning through the diffusion and exchange of knowledge and ideas (Kalantzis and Cope 2016).

The increasing use of peer review in education is part a larger trend, moving away from assessment methods that are unidirectional (solely from teachers to students) to multidirectional, encompassing peer-to-peer and self-assessment approaches. If the traditional summative assessment discourse was summative, retrospective, and judgmental, the new assessment discourse as exemplified in peer- and self-review is formative, prospective, and constructive. Meanwhile, new technologies of assessment and learning analytics empower students to assume responsibility for their self-evaluation and learning.

In response to these opportunities and challenges, we developed a new visual review tool as a medium for peer feedback and learning, CGMap. This web application is connected with CGScholar (Common Ground Scholar), a digital social learning platform developed by our research laboratory.[1] The CGMap tool allows users to create concept maps or visual representations of ideas and concepts linked together through a network of linked nodes (Cope et al. 2022; Novak 2010). This visual approach enables reviewers to provide feedback that goes beyond the surface level of the text, identifying connections and relationships among thoughts and ideas as well as suggesting ways to strengthen the overall argument and its structure. By using such a visual review tool, peer review can become a more dynamic, interactive, and collaborative process.

The CGMap tool enables users to create graphical representations of interconnected concepts or ideas. Unlike other concept mapping software, it allows the user to map something in particular—in this case a multimodal scholarly work. To achieve this, it has a split screen architecture (Fig. 1). On the left side is an extended multimodal work. On the right is a concept mapping palette. CGMap allows students to review their peers' works with maps that use a predefined rubric, add coded annotations to specific parts of the text, and provide general comments for feedback. Reviewers highlight text on the left side of the screen, which generates a color-matched node on the right that corresponds to the rubric criterion. In this node, they can also comment on the work based on the rubric criteria. In this case study, the review rubric included specific categories drawn from the Learning by Design Framework including Experience, Conceptualization, Analysis, and Application (Cope and Kalantzis 2015). In each review node, reviewers can add a rating and provide an explanation and suggestions for improvement for their peers to consider.

The CGMap tool also allows the creation of coded annotations that correspond to predefined categories aligned with the review rubric or general annotations for text formatting, grammatical errors, and so forth. To create the coded annotations, students highlight the text they want to reference and tap the corresponding 'Select'

[1] US Department of Education, Institute of Education Sciences: 'The Assess-as-You-Go Writing Assistant' (R305A090394); 'Assessing Complex Performance' (R305B110008); 'u-Learn.net: An Anywhere/Anytime Formative Assessment and Learning Feedback Environment' (ED-IES-10-C-0018); 'The Learning Element' (ED-IES-10-C-0021); and 'InfoWriter: A Student Feedback and Formative Assessment Environment' (ED-IES-13-C-0039). Bill and Melinda Gates Foundation: 'Scholar Literacy Courseware.' National Science Foundation: 'Assessing 'Complex Epistemic Performance' in Online Learning Environments' (Award 1,629,161); Utilizing an Academic Hub and Spoke Model to Create a National Network of Cybersecurity Institutes, Department of Homeland Security, contract 70RCSA20FR0000103; Infrastructure for Modern Educational Delivery Technologies: A Study for a Nationwide Law Enforcement Training Infrastructure, Department of Homeland Security, contract 15STCIR00001–05-03; Development of a Robust, Nationally Accessible Cybersecurity Risk Management Curriculum for Technical and Managerial Cybersecurity Professionals, Department of Homeland Security, contract 70SAT21G 00000012/70RCSA21FR0000115; MedLang: A Semantic Awareness Tool in Support of Medical Case Documentation, Jump ARCHES program, Health Care Engineering Systems Center, College of Engineering, contracts P179, P279, P288.

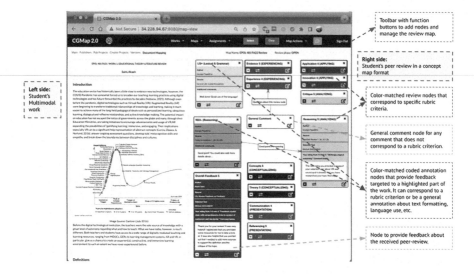

Fig. 1 Example of a CGMap peer review with additional explanations from authors about the different elements

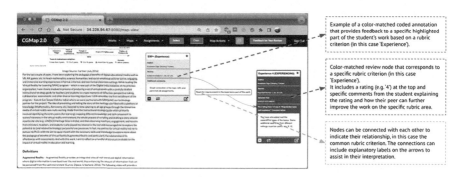

Fig. 2 Examples of CGMap coded annotations with additional explanations from authors about them

button of the toolbar at the top to add the annotation node, which corresponds to a highlighted part of the text.

The nodes in CGMap can be connected to indicate the conceptual links between review comments and annotations. Labels can be added to the connected arrows to help students understand the connections, as shown in Fig. 2. Additionally, the tool allows for the creation of general comments that are not part of any rubric or predefined annotation category. These comments can be added at any time during the course and can also be connected with arrows with any of the other review nodes to indicate any conceptual connection required.

The overall peer review functionality that the CGMap tool supports, enables reviewers to provide feedback that goes beyond the surface level of the text, by identifying connections and relationships among thoughts and ideas as well as suggesting ways to strengthen the overall argument.

As a cyber-social research and development activity, this project aimed to explore the benefits and difficulties of using CGMap to organize and reimagine peer feedback in higher education courses and by extension in the academic peer review process. The objective of the study was to develop and evaluate the innovative CGMap as a digital peer review tool that leverages concept mapping and collaborative features to enhance the effectiveness and efficiency of the peer review process as compared to the conventional peer review.

Iterative design and development processes were deployed across two cohorts of four graduate-level courses offered in the Learning Design and Leadership program at the University of Illinois. With the methodologies used in this project, the distinction between researcher/developer and subject/user became blurred. The best characterization of the relationship is co-design and co-research—appropriate also, because the project participants were graduate students in education. In each course, students were asked to use separate peer-review feedback systems for each two of their projects, one using a conventional form-based design, and the other the innovative visualization tool. Students were then asked to submit their feedback on the two peer review tools by completing a survey questionnaire about their experience.

The participants of this study consisted of 30 students from two different cohorts: the first cohort included 13 Masters and 7 Doctoral students, while the second cohort consisted of 9 Masters students and 1 non-degree student. Supplementing the incremental design process, a survey instrument collected students' feedback. Additionally, during the study, a group of four educational technology researchers at the University of Illinois Urbana-Champaign were engaged to provide additional feedback on the design-development process and to triangulate their perspectives with those of learners. The data from the student survey and the feedback of the research group were utilized to assess the effectiveness of the tool and to identify areas for improvement. The student participants were adults representing a range of ages, levels of digital savvy, academic backgrounds, as well as power and authority in their working or community lives. It is also noteworthy to mention that all stakeholders, students and researchers, participated in the study voluntarily. Participation occurred without any compulsion or influence on their course scores or grade.

5   Research Insights

This section summarizes the results of the iterative research-design process used in the development of the CGMap tool. The section also sheds light on the areas for improvement identified during the two implementations.

In the course of this research-design process, CGMap underwent multiple iterations based on feedback obtained from both students and the research group. User feedback was framed in terms of user stories, recorded in the agile project development software, JIRA. Revised iterations of the software were frequently released, as often as daily in the first weeks of deployment (at midnight, to minimize disruptions to student work!). Feedback was also collected through surveys and feedback forms, helping to identify areas of improvement that could enhance the overall user experience and effectiveness of the tool. User stories were prioritized according to a set of criteria that included urgency, difficulty of implementation, and significance in terms of overall functionality. Following are some examples of changes related specifically to these criteria that were made as a consequence of findings.

5.1 First Cohort

5.1.1 User Interface Changes

A significant issue pointed out by student feedback related to the aesthetic of the tool's interface that was said could hinder the review process'efficiency. Another issue was associated with the tool's navigational system which allowed access to the map and getting started with the peer review. These observations/suggestions lead to a number of user interface revisions, providing more detailed documentation, and improving the validation message generated for missing rubric items in order to be more explicit about which ones were still required before submission of the map.

5.1.2 Functionality Changes

Other important suggestions from feedback sources related to the technical issues that were deemed to result in reduced efficiency for students, instructors, and reviewers—for example, the load function and 'error' messages while refreshing the page, challenges whilst dragging and connecting nodes, and collapsing or stacking of nodes. The primary response in the functional area were stories addressing glitches and errors, improving the load function, fixing page refresh errors, and resolving other issues that were impeding the tool's usability.

5.1.3 Customization Options

Options for customization were also raised, that is, the ability to customize the tool to fit specific user needs. This included options to change the layout, color scheme, and font size, among other system changes. These changes included commenting, options for turning off the overall feedback function, and specificity of what remains missing or incomplete, among others. These requests were logged, prioritized and progressively addressed during the research-design process.

5.1.4   Feature Requests

The issue of additional features that would further improve user learning experience also arose. Recommended features included the ability to attach files, more advanced commenting options, linkage with the CGScholar's analytics system of formative assessment, zoom in and out functionality in the concept mapping area, counting the number of nodes, notification when the feedback is available on CGMap, and more. Again, these were logged, prioritized and addressed as time for coding became available.

5.2   Tackling the Key Challenges

Most of the navigation issues raised by the first cohort related to the criteria of urgency, difficulty of implementation and overall functionality. Some of these requests were addressed immediately; glitches and errors (including the load function), others such as dragging and connecting nodes, and issues with collapsing or stacking nodes were moved to the backlog of stories as a consequence of time constraints. The second cohort worked in the recalibrated tool.

5.3   Second Cohort

5.3.1   User Interface Changes

New issues emerged, related to the limited space for organizing the nodes, and the similar colors of elements of different categories.

5.3.2   Functionality Changes

Challenges persisted with dragging and connecting nodes, and issues with collapsing or stacking nodes.

5.3.3   Customization Options

Feedback related to customization suggestions from the first cohort were expanded with additional feedback received during the implementation with the second cohort. Suggestions included the options to change the layout (inclusive of one-sided or two-sided work options if available), color scheme, and font size, among other system changes, such as commenting all the way through, word limit requirement, etc.

5.3.4 Feature Requests

Features requested from the first cohort included advanced commenting options, functionality of zoom in and out, counting of node, and notifications when feedback is available on CGMap. The second cohort added in-text suggestions, submitted works/review column, capacity to edit the work while reading the reviews and annotations, instead of going back and forth between the pages.

5.4 Future Action

Based on this feedback and following the agile and design-based research approaches, the tool is constantly being redesigned to address the best, more pressing, and most achievable user suggestions. Moving forward, the plan is to further refine the user interface of CGMap in order to make it more intuitive and accessible. Second, there is an intention to incorporate additional features that enable reviewers to provide more detailed and specific feedback to their peers including explicit notes on what items are missing and/or need more text to meet the requirements. Third, the goal is to enhance the tool's ability to track scores and reviews, including linkage with the CGScholar formative assessment analytics and with notifications to reviewers. Fourth, more importantly, the aim to develop robust AI review capabilities, allowing students to receive consistent and personalized feedback that is influenced by minimal bias.

This case study demonstrates by way of example, design-research and agile approaches—in this case, evaluating the processes employed for the development of the CGMap tool in higher education. The development of this tool was motivated by the growing significance of technology in shaping modern assessment practices and the need to develop more dynamic and inclusive learning and assessment processes. The study was conducted in a collaborative and iterative manner, involving stakeholders from different backgrounds, age, levels of expertise and authority, such as students and educational technology researchers. Through the iterative process of gathering data from both student feedback and expert research group evaluations, the tool was refined and improved to better meet the needs of its users.

The research approaches we deployed gave us the ability to adapt to changing circumstances (as highlighted in the areas of improvement subsection), and the flexibility to incorporate feedback and suggestions from diverse stakeholders. The overall emphasis was on collaboration and iterative development. In the case study, the involvement of students and the members of the research group was key in the process of evaluating and improving CGMap, as it provided a more holistic view from multiple perspectives, of the tool's design, functionalities, and essential instructional support materials. Through the flexibility and adaptiveness of the research framework, we achieved a more comprehensive and nuanced understanding of the research problem, enabling us to develop solutions that can better address the needs of learners and educators, while utilizing state-of-the-art digital artifacts.

However, it is important to note that there are also some drawbacks to the approach that should be considered in future studies. The iterative nature of the research process can be time-consuming and may require significant resources. In our case study, we had only one software developer working on the CGMap tool. The implementation of some of the requests proved significantly time-consuming due to their complexity. Therefore, we had to prioritize the issues that need to be addressed based on the resources that were available to our research group. Nevertheless, through each iteration, we made progress that demonstrably helped users and their learning.

Another challenge to be considered is the involvement of multiple stakeholders with differing experiences, opinions, and perspectives, which may need to be reconciled. Addressing this challenge, we carefully planned and communicated the research process to all stakeholders from the beginning; we clearly defined their roles and responsibilities; and we were transparent in the data collection and analysis procedures.

6   Towards Cyber-Social Research for Learning

Extending theorizations of research methods under the rubrics of design-based research and agile research and drawing upon our experience in the case study just described, we want to outline by way of conclusion four principles for cyber-social research. This is our reframing and modest extension of the design-based research and agile research paradigms in the context of 'postdigital times'. Incidentally, by 'cyber', we don't (just) mean technology. To return to the creator of the 'cyber' metaphor, Norbert Weiner, cyber is not about technology *per se*—as illustrated by the *kubernētēs* or steersman on the ancient Greek ship (Wiener 1948/1961). It is about feedback relationships that may be between humans and machine as much as relationships within more or less intelligent machines. Beyond computer-mediation and machines, 'cyber' turns on the iterative, recursive relationships that can motivate social action and drive forward designs for social change (Cope and Kalantzis 2022).

Cyber-social learning research, to conclude, is grounded in the following four propositions:

1. **Research for Postdigital Media.** When so much of today's educational change is supported by digital media and digital media are so profoundly imbricated in the embodied experience of our material lives, the knowledge-design processes for innovation in education would benefit from alignment with those used in the development of now-ubiquitous media.
2. **Participatory Design Processes.** Design-development of educational innovations in general and educational technology developments in particular are not well supported by long-cycle, linear, experimental methodologies. Cyber-social research consists of short design-implementation cycles, supporting incremental,

iterative development. The key is flexible, user-driven development, where the end points of the process are interim at best and may be turn out to be quite different from those originally anticipated.

3. **An Epistemology of Inclusion.** Not only do cyber-social research processes put users at the center of the design process. That process is itself to be conceived as collaborative and participatory research and design. Some people may assume the role of 'admins' (if we are to import that role definition from social media groups). Their role is just to keep things moving. But from the point of view of knowledge generation and innovation, everyone is a participant and everyone is a researcher. Call this co-research for co-design.

4. **Agency to Leverage Diversity.** Cyber-social learning research validates diversity. Instead of averaging or norming results across statistical populations, it positions edge cases and outliers as contributors to design. At times these are even more valuable than normed or averaged perspectives. The methods of cyber-social learning research should consciously call out and validate edge and outlier views. If the injunction 'everyone should be involved' is not to be mere rhetoric, cyber-social research demands that diversity is built into the participatory design process and that all designed outcomes are genuinely inclusive of the full range of current and potential users.

References

Barab, S., & Kurt Squire, K. (2004). Design-Based Research: Putting a Stake in the Ground. *Journal of the Learning Sciences, 13*(1), 1–14. https://doi.org/10.1207/s15327809jls1301_1.

Bowker, G. C., Baker, K., Millerand, F., & Ribes, D. (2010). Toward Information Infrastructure Studies: Ways of Knowing in a Networked Environment. In J. Hunsinger, L. Klastrup, & M. Allen (Eds.), *International Handbook of Internet Research* (pp. 97–117). Cham: Springer. https://doi.org/10.1007/978-1-4020-9789-8_5.

Brown, A. L. (1992). Design Experiments: Theoretical and Methodological Challenges in Creating Complex Interventions in Classroom Settings. *Journal of the Learning Sciences, 2*(2), 141–78. https://doi.org/10.1207/s15327809jls0202_2.

Cohn, M. (2004). *User Stories Applied.* Boston, MA: Addison-Wesley.

Collins, A. (1992). Toward a Design Science of Education. In E. Scanlon & T. O'Shea (Eds.), *New Directions in Educational Technology* (pp. 15–22). Berlin: Springer. https://doi.org/10.1007/978-3-642-77750-9_2.

Cope, B., & Kalantzis, M. (2015). The Things You Do to Know: An Introduction to the Pedagogy of Multiliteracies. In B. Cope & M. Kalantzis (Eds.), *A Pedagogy of Multiliteracies: Learning by Design* (pp. 1–36). London: Palgrave. https://doi.org/10.1057/9781137539724_1.

Cope, B., & Kalantzis, M. (2020). Editorial: Futures for Research in Education. *Educational Philosophy and Theory, 53*(11), 1732–1739. https://doi.org/10.1080/00131857.2020.1824781.

Cope, B., & Kalantzis, M. (2022). The Cybernetics of Learning. *Educational Philosophy and Theory, 54*(14), 2352–2388. https://doi.org/10.1080/00131857.2022.2033213.

Cope, B., & Kalantzis, M. (2023). Platformed Learning: Reshaping Education in the Era of Learning Management Systems. In D. A. Thomas & V. Laterza (Eds.), *Varieties of Platformisation: Critical Perspectives on EdTech in Higher Education.* London: Palgrave Macmillan.

Cope, B., Kalantzis, M., Zhai, C-X., Krussel, A., Searsmith, D., Ferguson, D., Tapping, R., & Berrocal, Y. (2022). Maps of Medical Reason: Applying Knowledge Graphs and Artificial Intelligence in Medical Education and Practice. In M. A. Peters, P. Jandrić, & S. Hayes (Eds.), *Bioinformational Philosophy and Postdigital Knowledge Ecologies* (pp. 133–159). Cham: Springer. https://doi.org/10.1007/978-3-030-95006-4_8.

Design-Based Research Collective. (2003). Design-Based Research: An Emerging Paradigm for Educational Inquiry. *Educational Researcher, 32*(1), 5–8. https://doi.org/10.3102/0013189X032001005.

Double, K. S., McGrane, J. A., & Hopfenbeck, T. N. (2020). The Impact of Peer Assessment on Academic Performance: A Meta-analysis of Control Group Studies. *Educational Psychology Review, 32,* 481–509. https://doi.org/10.1007/s10648-019-09510-3.

Erikson, F., & Gutierrez, K. (2002). Culture, Rigor and Science in Educational Research. *Educational Researcher, 31*(8), 21–24. https://doi.org/10.3102/0013189X031008021.

Gamage, D., Staubitz, T., & Whiting, M. (2021). Peer Assessment in MOOCs: Systematic Literature Review. *Distance Education, 42*(2), 268–289. https://doi.org/10.1080/01587919.2021.1911626.

Gibson, J. J. (1977). The Theory of Affordances. In R. Shaw & J. Bransford (Eds.), *Perceiving, Acting, and Knowing: Toward an Ecological Psychology* (pp. 67–82). Hillsdale, NJ: Lawrence Erlbaum Associates.

Gutiérrez, K. D., & Jurow, S. (2016). Social Design Experiments: Toward Equity by Design. *Journal of the Learning Sciences, 25*(4), 565–598. https://doi.org/10.1080/10508406.2016.1204548.

Jandrić, P., Knox, J., Besley, T., Ryberg, T., Suoranta, J., & Hayes, S. (2018). Postdigital Science and Education. *Educational Philosophy and Theory, 50*(10), 893–899. https://doi.org/10.1080/00131857.2018.1454000.

Kalantzis, M., & Cope, B. (2016). New Media and Productive Diversity in Learning. In S. Barsch & N. Glutsch (Eds.), *Diversity in der LehrerInnenbildung* (pp. 310–325). Münster: Waxmann.

Kalantzis, M., & Cope, B. (2020). *Adding Sense: Context and Interest in a Grammar of Multimodal Meaning.* Cambridge, UK: Cambridge University Press. https://doi.org/10.1017/9781108862059.

Martin, R. C. (2009). *Agile Software Development, Principles, Patterns, and Practices.* Upper Saddle River, NJ: Prentice Hall.

McKenney, S., & Reeves, T. C. (2014). Educational Design Research. In J. M. Spector, M. D. Merrill, J. Elen, & M. J. Bishop (Eds.), *Handbook of Research on Educational Communications and Technology* (pp. 131–140). New York: Springer. https://doi.org/10.1007/978-1-4614-3185-5_11.

Montebello, M., Pinheiro, P., Cope, B., Kalantzis, M., Amina, T., Searsmith, D., & Cao, D. (2018). The Impact of the Peer Review Process Evolution on Learner Performance in e-Learning Environments. In S. Klemmer & K. Koedinger (Eds.), *Proceedings of the Fifth Annual ACM Conference on Learning at Scale (L@S 2018).* New York: Association for Computing Machinery. https://doi.org/10.1145/3231644.3231693.

Novak, J. D. (2010). *Learning, Creating and Using Knowledge: Concept Maps as Facilitative Tools in Schools and Corporations.* New York: Routledge. https://doi.org/10.4324/9780203862001.

Pinheiro, P. (2018). Text Revision Practices in an e-Learning Environment: Fostering the Learning by Design Perspective. *Innovation in Language Learning and Teaching, 14*(1), 37–50. https://doi.org/10.1080/17501229.2018.1482902.

Royce, W. W. (1970). Managing the Development of Large Systems: Concepts and Techniques. In *9th International Conference on Software Engineering: Proceedings of IEEE WESCON* (pp. 328–338). http://www-scf.usc.edu/~csci201/lectures/Lecture11/royce1970.pdf. Accessed 3 March 2023.

Stake, R. E. (2005). *The Art of Case Study Research.* Thousand Oaks, CA: Sage.

Star, S. L. (1999). The Ethnography of Infrastructure. *American Behavioral Scientist, 43*(3), 377–391. https://doi.org/10.1177/00027649921955326.

Stober, T., & Hansmann, U. (2009). *Agile Software Development: Best Practices for Large Software Development Projects.* Berlin and Heidelberg: Springer. https://doi.org/10.1007/978-3-540-70832-2.

Twidale, M., & Hansen, P. (2019). Agile Research. *First Monday, 24*(1), 1–18.

Wiener, N. (1948/1961). *Cybernetics, or the Control and Communication in the Animal and the Machine.* Cambridge MA: MIT Press,

Yin, R. K. (1994). *Case Study Research: Design and Methods.* Thousand Oaks, CA: Sage Publications.

Sociomateriality, Postdigital Thinking, and Learning Spaces Research

James Lamb

1 Introduction

A central assumption of postdigital thinking is that digital technologies, and the practices they engender or support, are embedded within the fabric of everyday society. This naturally includes those settings where teaching and learning take place. My interest within this chapter concerns the relationship between sociomateriality and postdigital thinking, explored through the growing body of research around the learning spaces of higher education. I am going make three points that, I hope, can help us to better understand what 'postdigital research' might be.

First, I will propose that there is a considerable amount of conceptual compatibility between some of the key ideas that have emerged within postdigital thinking, and the more consolidated principles of sociomateriality. Second, I will argue that postdigital thinking goes beyond sociomaterial approaches to education research by more forcefully pushing us to recognise the presence and influence of digital resources and practices, for instance in those settings where teaching and learning happen. Where a considerable strength of sociomateriality is its flexibility in enabling us to recognise the full range of human and non-human actors that shape our educational spaces and activities, postdigital research can be more resolute in examining the significance of digital resources within our everyday lives and surroundings. Third, I will propose that postdigital thinking can work as a kind of research sensibility, as it shapes the questions we ask, and more fundamentally, how we see our educational world.

The Call for Chapters that originally announced this edited collection challenged authors to examine the scope and significance of postdigital thinking within research. In writing the chapter presented here, I have been attentive to the editors'

J. Lamb (✉)
Moray House School of Education and Sport, University of Edinburgh, Edinburgh, UK
e-mail: James.Lamb@ed.ac.uk

P. Jandrić et al. (eds.), *Constructing Postdigital Research*, Postdigital Science and Education, https://doi.org/10.1007/978-3-031-35411-3_6

wish for this to be a research-oriented volume with a pedagogical flavour, rather than a manual or textbook. To this end, in the pages that follow I will regularly discuss or point towards published studies and critical commentary, but always with the purpose of exploring the relationship between sociomateriality and postdigital thinking, and to more broadly help us consider what postdigital research might be.

This is a relationship that can be productively explored through the growing body of critical work that is seeking to understand the complex and changing nature of those spaces where teaching and learning are performed. A feature of the growing body of learning spaces research is a clear focus on the future, typically pursued by exploring how and where digital technologies might contribute towards the creation of accessible, equitable and positive learning environments. As I will come on to show, postdigital thinking and sociomateriality can be usefully combined to support this work.

2   Taking a Position on 'The Postdigital'

When I began to draft the structure for this chapter, I debated whether a discussion of the postdigital would end up retreading ground covered elsewhere in this volume. After some reflection, I decided that this would assume postdigital thinking to have consolidated into a universally agreed collection of assumptions. In fact, as an idea (or collection of ideas), the postdigital is understood and deployed in different ways. The postdigital refers to 'a state of becoming where the human and the digital are interacting, co-creating, and merging in ways that are beyond imagining' (Ball and Savin-Baden 2022: 754), but also describes 'a state in which the disruption brought upon by digital information technology has already occurred' (Cramer 2015: 20). Even within the context of higher education research, and as I will come on to discuss, the postdigital can be a subject of study, an outlook, and also a way of being.

That the postdigital is differently understood and used within education research is perhaps to be expected when it existed as a way of informing thinking around art and aesthetics prior to providing a way of supporting the study of learning practices, spaces and organisations. It is also a concept that continues to evolve, something that is captured particularly well by Cormier et al. (2019) as they map their own shifting stances over the period of a decade. This includes noting a move away from evangelising the possibilities of digital technologies, to unquestioningly accepting their presence, with both positions being problematic in their own ways. The meaning attached to the postdigital has evolved to reflect changes happening within the wider social and natural world that it serves to critique.

In the absence of a single, fixed understanding of the postdigital, it falls on individual researchers to take a position on what it means within the context of their own work. In my case, this concerns the relationship between higher education learning spaces and digital technologies. Before sharing my own stance, I am conscious that 'the digital' is also a term that benefits from some explanation. In seeking to make sense of what he regards as the complex and problematic concept of the postdigital, Cramer (2015) points towards an unquestioning acceptance of the term 'digital' to describe any kind of electronic computation device. This is a definition, in Cramer's view, that is convenient for the marketing and advertising of products, but does little to encourage a critical take on the relationship between traditional and emergent technologies, and their associated practices. A lack of nuance and sophistication is also to be found in the fairly commonplace reference to digital technologies as 'tools' that exist to fulfil pre-determined pedagogical outcomes. As I will come on to discuss, this framing denies the ways that digital resources influence learning spaces and practices, while at the same time disregarding the often untidy and unpredictable reality of higher education.

At some point, however, there is a need to commit to a working definition, and in my research around learning spaces, I have taken 'digital technologies' to refer to all the devices, platforms, data flows and infrastructures that enable the storage, processing and presentation of data. The term 'learning space' also accommodates a range of interpretations, however for the purpose of this chapter, it refers to any setting where teaching or learning happens. This includes those parts of the campus with an advertised educational function (laboratories, libraries, and lecture theatres, for example) but also any other setting across or beyond the campus where writing, reading, reflection, teaching or other educational activity is performed. For a more comprehensive discussion of learning space from a postdigital perspective, see Lamb et al. (2022).

2.1 The Digital Within Our Everyday Surroundings and Practices

A central proposition of postdigital thinking is that the proliferation of digital technologies over the last two decades has at some point reached the point where these resources have become an accepted part of the fabric of our everyday surroundings and practices. This cannot be pinpointed to a single moment in time, simply because the spread of digital technologies has been experienced differently across social and global contexts. What we *can* say, is that the emergence of the Internet as a public resource in the 1990s, the mass ownership of mobile devices that followed in the 2000s, and then the rapid expansion of social media in the 2010s, have contributed to a situation where digital technologies in their different forms are commonplace. Where these and other digital technologies, and the practices they enabled, once seemed remarkable, they are now accepted as a regular part of our surroundings and of our being.

The postdigital provides a useful way of reflecting how our attitudes towards technologies have changed over time, for instance as we have gone from enthusiastically proclaiming their possibilities, to more moderately accepting their presence alongside pre-existing objects and practices (Cormier et al. 2019). In this way, the postdigital refers to a state of being less in thrall to digital technology than was once the case. We can still become excited at the development of a new device or platform, but we do so with the awareness that it will merge together with, rather than transform, our educational and everyday activities and existence. The digital, as Jandrić et al. (2018) explain, is bound together with the biological, informational, and technological. Therefore, rather than somehow standing apart from other resources, we might describe digital technologies as being subsumed into our wider surroundings and practices.

Being subsumed into something greater does not remove the significance of those pieces of software and hardware that we readily draw on in the performance of our day-to-day lives: rather, it is a recognition of their existing together with other objects and practices. Within the postdigital discourse, digital technologies are variously described as 'entangled', 'integrated', or having 'coalesced' together with other human and non-human bodies and practices. Feenberg (2019) meanwhile refers to the digital as being 'imbricated' with everyday activities and actions, thereby pointing towards an overlapping of newer technological resources with pre-existing objects and practices. The terminology varies but the overall meaning is the same: the postdigital recognises digital technologies as existing together with other technological, informational, biological, and material bodies.

Recognising that digital technologies are integrated within our everyday surroundings and actions should not, however, be mistaken for assuming their even distribution. Access to digital resources can vary within a single classroom of students, let alone between socio economic groups, between urban and rural contexts, and across different global contexts. We may be experiencing a 'postdigital era' (Örtegren 2022), inhabiting a 'postdigital world' (Gravett et al. 2022) and participating in 'postdigital society' (Thorén et al. 2019), but access to devices, the availability of data, and the digital practices they help to engender, are by no means uniform. As researchers working with the postdigital, perhaps we have a duty to more stridently make the point that the ubiquity of digital technologies should not be conflated with there being even opportunity to take advantage of these resources.

2.2   The Digital Reconfiguration of University Space

A trope that punctuates conversation around education and technology is that advances in digital resources have revolutionized our learning spaces and practices. This suits the interests of companies hoping to encourage us to purchase their devices and download their software apps. However, perpetuating the idea of a tech-enabled revolution of education does little to help us understand the complex reality of what happens across and beyond the classroom. A revolution, after all, implies a displacement of old with new. It points towards a moment where there occurred some kind of radical transformation of our practices. It suggests that digital products have swept away pre-existing educational technologies and resources. A cornerstone of postdigital thinking, and something that has tremendous value in supporting meaningful critiques of contemporary learning spaces, is Pepperell and

Punt's (2000) proposition that the postdigital enables us to reflect upon the presence and influence of technology, but in a way that rejects the abruptness implied by a digital revolution.

Two decades on, the proof of Pepperell and Punt's (2000) argument can be found in our lecture theatres, libraries, laboratories, and almost every other corner of the campus. Let us imagine you are reading this chapter in a seminar room. If it is a reasonably modern space, there will be a data projector attached to the ceiling above you, which is controlled by a desktop computer situated on a presentation console at the front of the room. The console will almost certainly have a built-in dashboard that allows the presenter to switch between projecting from the desktop PC, their laptop, or a document camera. There might also be a wall-mounted smart board. What you cannot see but know to be present are the Wi-Fi, cabling and other resources that support an instant connection to the Internet.

This quick survey might immediately seem to lend some credibility to the idea of a digital revolution, as we imagine members of the university's estates team dispensing with the overhead projector, chalkboard, television and video trolley, and other educational resources that were previously here. Further scrutiny of the seminar room, though, shows this not to be case. Look behind the presentation console, and within its storage cavity you will find a partially used roll of flip chart paper. It will be resting beneath a collection of marker pens, sticky notes, and other kinds of analog paraphernalia. On the adjacent wall there will be a whiteboard that, judging by a spider diagram left over from a previous class, is perhaps used as frequently as the smartboard equivalent at the front of the class. In the postdigital setting of the seminar room, digital technologies sit alongside, and together with, more traditional teaching resources.

If this exercise were to be interrupted by the arrival of students, you would observe them working across these and other analog and digital resources, discussing and developing ideas as they perform a kind of postdigital knowledge production. From a postdigital research perspective, you would conclude that as the seminar room has gradually been equipped with digital technologies, there has been a steady *reconfiguration* of the space and the activities it engenders, but that no revolution has taken place here.

2.3   Exploring the Postdigital Learning Spaces of Higher Education

It is important at this point to make clear that understanding digital technologies to be part of the fabric of our everyday educational surroundings does not mean they can be disregarded as a subject of critical interest. On the contrary, their being commonplace gives us even more cause to consider their presence and influence. Solely from a learning spaces perspective, it is important that research questions investigate the intrusiveness of proctoring technologies when students sit exams from home. We should consider whether the growing ease of attending class online potentially decentres the physical university campus. There is a need to explore whether digitally-enabled hybrid spaces and pedagogies widen access to programmes of study, or simply extend existing inequalities. It is vital that we better understand the experience of connecting with the university via the smartphone, as is the case for many thousands of learners in the Global South.

These kinds of questions were the motivation behind a special issue of *Postdigital Science and Education* where Lucila Carvalho, Michael Gallagher, Jeremy Knox and I invited contributions that explored the relationship between digital technologies and higher education learning spaces (Lamb et al. 2022). The papers collected within the special issue provide evidence of the value that postdigital thinking, and more generally the concepts of postdigital space and the postdigital university, offer in helping us to interrogate the complexity of those settings where teaching and learning take place. The postdigital provides a critical route into pursuing questions around accessibility, engagement, presence, pedagogical innovation, soundscapes and other themes that in some way help us to make sense of those settings where we teach and learn.

The significance of postdigital thinking to the study of learning spaces has been further shown by recent work that argues for the continued importance of the physical campus in spite of the growing emphasis on digital platforms and pedagogies (Allen and McLaren 2022; Spire 2022), and as a way of theorising outdoor education (van Kraalingen 2022; Reed 2022). While the relationship between digital technologies and learning spaces has often been considered from the student perspective, Gravett et al. (2022) have instead looked towards the teacher, as they explore spaces of connection in the post-Covid landscape. With an interest in methodology meanwhile, I suggest that by revealing how students use streaming services to negotiate personalized learning spaces, the music playlist exists as an ethnographic artefact and a postdigital object (Lamb 2022). I have already noted that postdigital thinking has evolved alongside the social world that it serves to critique: there is a clear sense within emergent learning spaces scholarship that it is also productive in providing different ways of making sense of our educational surroundings.

3   Sociomateriality and Education Research

Although sociomateriality is firmly established within education research, particularly among those with an interest in understanding the presence and influence of digital technologies, I am conscious that it may not be familiar to the growing body of researchers turning towards the postdigital to support their work. Partly for the benefit of those coming new to sociomateriality here, but also in order to help explain the conceptual ground it shares with the postdigital, I am going to spend a bit of time setting out some of its key assumptions.

To begin, sociomateriality is not a discrete theory in itself, something that I would suggest it shares with the postdigital. Rather, as Fenwick et al. (2011)

discuss, it is a term which captures the common interest of a range of social science theories including, but not limited to, Complexity Theory, Cultural Historical Activity Theory, Spatial Theory and New Materialist theory. With a guiding principle that actions and entities cannot be solely attributed to human interest or agency, it also informs critical posthumanism and post-anthropocentric thought. Where social inquiry has traditionally approached meaning-making as depending on human interests and actions, sociomateriality is interested in the network of human and non-human discourses and phenomena that are implicated in these processes. Rather than seeing objects as dormant traces of culture, sociomateriality instead looks to the ways that they are entangled within the performance of action.

Casting an eye across the wider body of higher education research, it is often the case that attention falls upon the attitudes, experiences and interests of the teacher and student. Sociomateriality instead broadens our critical attention to a wider range of visible and invisible resources, constraints and opportunities that shape our educational practices and surroundings. Or as Fenwick et al. put it:

> Sociomaterial studies try to reveal the minute dynamics and connections that are continuously enacting the taken-for-granted in educational events: the clothing, timetables, passwords, pencils, windows, stories, plans, buzzers, bubble gum, desks, electricity and lights – not as separate objects, but as continually changing patterns of materiality. These patterns comprise human and non-human energies, each with historical trajectories, continually combining with (and dissolving away from) other assemblages. (Fenwick et al. 2011: xii)

In short summary, explored through the context of education, the key assumptions of sociomateriality are as follows: in common with work around critical posthumanism, sociomateriality recognizes educational spaces and practices to be more-than-human. From a sociomaterial perspective, education is performed through a 'constellation' or 'entanglement' of 'actors'. These human and non-human actors form 'assemblages', which Müller (2015) suggests in his discussion of sociomaterial power and space, to be relational, productive, heterogenous, desired and bound to ongoing deterritorialisation and reterritorialization. Müller's description usefully captures the fluid and co-constituting interweaving of different social and material actors, as human and non-human bodies come together in continually shifting patterns. The assemblage, and sociomateriality more broadly, provides a way of acknowledging the dynamics and linkages between objects and processes that create educational activities and artefacts (Fenwick et al. 2011).

Brought together, these sociomaterial assumptions provide a conceptual framework that has supported a varied body of educational research. This includes work around teacher professional learning (see for example Mulcahy 2012), policy (Landri 2015), digital literacies (Bhatt and de Roock 2014) and learner identity (Aberton 2012). This is far from being an exhaustive account of sociomateriality within the study of higher education, but it points towards its value across a varied body of inquiry. Through the way that it 'carefully illuminates the junctures, tensions and lived practice of spatial-social relationships' (Acton 2017: 1442), sociomateriality is also particularly suited to the study of those settings where teaching and learning happen. The proof can be found for instance in Gourlay and Oliver's

(2016) use of sociomateriality to examine the learning spaces and literacy practices of postgraduate students at a UK university, Mulcahy et al.'s (2015) exploration of the relationship between policy, pedagogy and physical learning spaces, and Robinson's use of assemblage to explore rural learning environments (2018).

4   Conceptual Common Ground

Having taken a position on the postdigital, and then summarized the central ideas of sociomateriality, I want now to discuss the conceptual ground they share, and how they can work in concert. Their complementarity can be found in a number of recent studies concerned with higher education learning spaces. Carvalho and Freeman (2022) bring together sociomateriality and the postdigital as a way of exploring how the learning spaces of Doctoral students in a New Zealand university were bound together with issues of professional identity. The experiences and practices of students are also a part of Wardak et al.'s research (2022) as they draw on Actor Network theory to explore the postdigital learning spaces of undergraduates at an Australian university during Covid-times. Elsewhere, Gravett et al. (2022) make use of sociomaterial assemblage and entanglement as a way of exploring questions of connection amid the spaces and places where teachers learn within the postdigital university. Meanwhile Goodyear (2022) discusses sociomaterial practices alongside postdigital infrastructure in asking how we might nurture learning spaces in ways that realise a more just and caring university. The combining of sociomateriality and the postdigital within these and other recent examples of learning spaces research is dependent on their conceptual compatibility.

4.1   The More-Than-Human Learning Spaces of Higher Education

Perhaps the clearest similarity between sociomateriality and postdigital thinking is in the shared assumption that educational spaces and practices cannot be adequately conceptualised or investigated by focusing solely on human bodies, interests, and actions. In order to recognize that a learning space is more complex than layout, dimensions and furniture, researchers have sometimes proposed that educational settings instead need be understood through the activities they support. This is helpful up to a point in recognizing that the function of a single physical setting varies depending upon the activity happening at a particular moment in time.

The emphasis on human activity also leaves the door open for the non-institutional spaces of the student flat and café to be recognised as an extension of the campus, for instance when the learner logs into an online class or platform. However, sociomateriality and postdigital thinking go beyond this human-centric focus to also question the presence and influence of a wider body of actors. A classroom (whether on or beyond the campus) does indeed depend on physical location, objects, and pedagogy, but from a sociomaterial and postdigital perspective might also simultaneously be digital, political, commercial and contingent on more influences, pressures, constraints, and resources besides.

This shared interest in the more-than-human make-up of educational spaces and events means that the concept of assemblage is to be found both in sociomaterial and postdigital education research. The assemblage, as I explained earlier, is an important part of sociomaterial research, through the way that it recognizes the co-presence and relationality of different actors in shaping objects, activities and our wider surroundings. Building on this work, there has recently emerged the possibility of a 'postdigital assemblage'. Writing on the subject of postdigital research around education and datafication, Macgilchrist (2021) advances the idea of postdigital assemblage through the example of an interview conversation with a teacher around the ways that her students use software in the completion of learning tasks. Reflecting on this research process, Macgilchrist concludes that the postdigital assemblage acts as a kind of guide against systematically listing the different actors or elements that were reported, and instead to consider them as 'a complex, heterogeneous and historicised story anchored in that teacher's account' (2021: 662).

Using Macgilchrist's proposition, Reed (2022) deploys the postdigital assemblage as a way of reckoning with the countless disparate yet connected elements that comprise the performance of outdoor environmental education. Elsewhere, Matthews (2022) uses the idea of postdigital assemblage to counter the narrative that digital technologies will inevitably conclude with the demise of the (human) lecturer and lecture that for centuries have been central to the working and understanding of the university. These examples demonstrate how postdigital thinking can productively draw on a key assumption of sociomateriality in order to specifically critique the presence and influences of digital technologies.

4.2 Working with Mess in Our Educational World

The assemblage usefully allows us to recognize and examine the unpredictability – the messiness – of educational activity. Thinking in particular about how we perform social science inquiry, Law (2004) argues for approaches that embrace the messy reality of our social world, over research that strives for 'definiteness' (25), attempts to reduce the complexity of our world into 'a set of fairly specific, determinate and more or less identifiable processes' (5), and thus becomes a 'methodological version of auditing' (6). Turning attention to postdigital research around education, the relevance of mess can be found in, among other places, Jandrić et al.'s (2018) recognition of the disparate and unpredictable coming together of digital, analog, biological, and other elements that are central to our human condition.

Meanwhile, reflecting on the importance of retaining the human touch within the postdigital university, Cureton et al. (2021: 238) recognise student lives as a 'messy fusion of both digital and non-digital elements'. Elsewhere, Allen and McLaren (2022) argue that we should value and seek to preserve the productive moments of mess that happen on the physical campus, compared with the sterile online environments they see as being given strategic importance in our postdigital age.

Mess refers to more than the haphazard scattering of paraphernalia that can characterize some classrooms and personal learning spaces beyond the campus: instead, it talks in a fundamental way about the unpredictability of educational contexts. As I noted earlier, research with a human-centric emphasis can sometimes present education as something of a closed communion between teacher and learner, with the effect of excluding other objects or resources that might be significant to our knowledge and understanding. In contrast, through an interest in the more-than-human, research informed by sociomateriality or postdigital thinking recognises the multitude of resources and interests that variously enable, constrain and otherwise shape the university.

At the time of writing, the teaching and learning taking place across UK universities (and the universities themselves) are being shaped by pedagogy and technology, but also by the varying influence and disruption of commercialisation, politics, industrial action, climate crisis, and a host of other influences beyond the immediate concerns of the academic project. Furthermore, the presence and prominence of these biological, informational, technological, and other actors is continually shifting, meaning they are beyond the educator's or the university's anticipation, much less their control (and the profound impact of the Covid-19 pandemic upon the higher education sector is the obvious recent example of this being the case).

4.3   Reckoning with the Complex Relations Between Education, Space and the Digital

By acknowledging that learning spaces, activities and organisations are contingent on an assemblage of human and non-human actors, which in turn allows us to recognize their fluidity and unpredictability, sociomaterial and postdigital thinking encourages the kind of meaningful critique that is required to make sense of our complex educational surroundings. This includes bringing critical depth and nuance to the discourse around education and digital technologies, which often defers to a simplistic instrumentalism where digital resources are presented as tools for realizing pre-determined educational objectives.

Taking as an example the design of physical university learning spaces, this kind of instrumentalism is evident when the installation of technology is presented as a positive outcome in itself, with the assumption that equipping the classroom with intelligent microphones or motion-sensitive cameras will necessarily lead to an enhanced learner experience. From a sociomaterial or postdigital stance, we understand things to be considerably less clear-cut than the marketing claims of ed. tech companies, or of the university itself when investment in facilities is conflated with high quality education. If the introduction of these resources coincides with a reported rise in student satisfaction, or an assumed improvement in academic performance or acquisition of knowledge, we will know the success to have been contingent also on a wider body of human and non-human influences, and how they were entangled with the newly introduced classroom technologies.

5 Beyond Sociomateriality

In light of this conceptual common ground, the obvious question we need to ask is what, if anything, can postdigital thinking do that is not already performed by the key assumptions of sociomateriality? Are we attempting to carve out a discreet postdigital research space without really venturing beyond the conceptual ground covered by sociomateriality? I am reminded here of a criticism that has been levelled at autoethnographers, which posits that they have attached to themselves a new label when their focus on personal experience and being situated in a field of individual significance is perhaps already accommodated within the established practices of ethnography more broadly. Exactly what original work is the postdigital doing in the study of learning spaces, and can there truly be a postdigital research in its own right? I am going to suggest that we can answer these questions by considering the limitations of sociomateriality in the study of educational spaces and practices.

In their discussion of learning entanglement in innovative learning spaces, Carvalho and Yeoman (2018) recognise the value of sociomateriality within education research, for instance in challenging the often-assumed neutrality of interactions between humans and technologies. At the same time however, they argue that a sociomaterial focus on tracing the relations between different actors falls short of explaining how they more holistically contribute towards learning activity. Knox and Bayne (2014) likewise draw on sociomateriality while also noting its methodological limitations, discussed within their work around the digital and multimodal literacy practices associated with a Massive Open Online Course. Citing a wider critique of sociomateriality by Mutch where he points towards an inadequate attention to the specifics of technological resources, combined with an underconsideration of broader social structures (2013), Knox and Bayne warn against viewing sociomateriality as an 'all seeing eye' (4) for research.

The critiques described here suggest that sociomateriality provides a kind of conceptual starting point for critical inquiry, but that it stops methodologically short on the specifics needed to really advance our research questions. The lack of specificity would seem to make sense in light of Fenwick et al.'s (2011) position that sociomateriality refers to the common interests of a range of social science theories, rather than being a single theory in itself. We might see sociomateriality as the wide-angle lens that needs to be augmented by something more pointed. Taking Mutch's critique surrounding the lack of focused attention on the specifics of technologies within sociomateriality, the postdigital propositions I set out above would seem well equipped to drive this kind of critical work. Once again, I think it will be helpful to explore the meaning and value of postdigital thinking through the example of a fairly typical educational setting.

Let us imagine that we have moved from the seminar room we visited earlier in this chapter, and are now seated somewhere towards the back of a lecture theatre like that in Fig. 1, which is drawn from my own research. From a sociomaterial perspective, we can see the presence of a varied constellation of actors: the artificial lighting, hierarchical layout, fixed seating and desks, students, laptop computers, lecturer, projection screen, and a host of other human and non-human objects. A postdigital position, though, more forcefully pushes us to consider how digital technologies are entangled with these and other actors.

If the lecture we are sitting in now resembles that in Fig. 1, the presence of digital technologies will be obvious. The banks of laptop screens might be reminiscent of NASA's Mission Control Room or the Operation Centre for Rio de Janeiro's smart city, as much as they resemble a traditional teaching auditorium. On closer inspection of the desks either side of us, we see laptops, smartphones and tablets, but also ring binders, A4 refill notepads, pencil cases, and highlighter pens. With our postdigital stance, we immediately question what the co-existence of these traditional and more modern technologies has to say about the learning practices of these students, and the lecture environment itself. Turning our attention again towards the front of the auditorium, we notice occasional splashes of on-screen colour amid the glowing grey-white hue of the Office interface. We assume these to be a digitally

Fig. 1 The postdigital setting of the modern lecture theatre

mediated deviation away from the lecture topic. A student is following the fortunes of the England cricket team via a livestream: physically present in the lecture theatre, but mentally occupied with action unfolding on the far side of the world. Where we notice a student browsing lines of vintage clothing on eBay, we see an entanglement between commerce and technology that repositions the lecture theatre from learning space into marketplace, if only until a bid is placed and attention switches back to the academic subject matter in hand.

In these moments, we recognise digital technologies as being enmeshed within everyday educational surroundings, existing alongside and relational to pre-existing technologies. From there we begin to see how their existence contributes towards different learning practices as the digital combines with analog. We are pushed also to consider what it means to be 'present' on the postdigital campus. We consider how the ability to seamlessly connect to networked materials, locations and activities beyond the classroom reveals the complexity and fluidity of the lecture theatre as a postdigital learning space.

Therefore, where a strength of sociomateriality is its recognition that learning spaces and practices are performed through shifting patterns of human and material interests and objects, postdigital thinking would seem to be more resolute in providing a set of assumptions to drive our research into making sense of the presence and influence of digital technologies.

6 Conclusion: A Postdigital Research Sensibility

In concluding this chapter, I want to consider whether the ideas advanced across the preceding pages have taken us any closer to establishing the existence of something that we might call 'postdigital research'. Taking higher education learning spaces research as my example, I have shown that postdigital thinking has recently started to become popular as a way of reckoning with the complex and changing nature of our educational surroundings, often with a view to understanding the presence and influence of digital technologies. Surveying the output of this work, the postdigital has clear conceptual value, while the existence of the postdigital university and postdigital learning spaces are themselves subjects of interest. The postdigital, though, is not presented as a method in itself. This does not deny the possibility of there being postdigital methods, however at least in the context of learning spaces research, postdigital thinking works as an outlook or lens, rather than a defined, practical way of generating and analysing research material.

Looking back to the postdigital propositions that inform my own research, I see them as combining to form a kind of sensibility: that is, they influence how I see and seek to interrogate my surroundings and the subjects of my research. Where an 'ethnographic sensibility' refers to a way of studying peoples and cultures, can there not also a be a postdigital sensibility which starts from the position that human actors are bound to the digital, biological, informational and technological? In the context of learning spaces research, a postdigital sensibility starts from the position that digital technologies are established within our everyday surroundings and practices, before then pushing us to consider how these resources coalesce with other human and non-human bodies. In raising the possibility of there being a distinct postdigital sensibility, I take encouragement from Thompson's (2012) discussion of 'sociomaterial sensibilities', which itself looks towards Law's suggestion that we might understand Actor Network Theory as a kind of diverse union of 'material-semiotic tools and sensibilities' (2009: 141).

I would suggest that the notion of a postdigital sensibility is also supported through it having an ontological dimension which moves it beyond being a methodological apparatus. At the point that we accept the postdigital as a way of questioning our reality, it becomes more than an academic exercise (Cormier et al. 2019). This being the case, if as researchers we truly commit to the postdigital, we accept our human researcher bodies as being entangled, imbricating or coalescing with technological, political, strategic and other interests. From there we need to reflexively reconsider some of the assumptions we may previously have held about ourselves and our scholarship. The postdigital recognises that 'the ways we live, think, and interact are shaped by digital configurations' (Ackerman et al. 2020: 417), which cuts much deeper than questions of research design, to instead demand some kind of reflection upon the researcher-self.

This provides a further opportunity to look towards sociomateriality as we seek to understand what postdigital research might be. Of the different theories that fall within Fenwick et al.'s (2011) explanation of sociomateriality, Actor Network Theory has particularly found a place within education research, and especially as a way of interrogating how digital technologies affect learning practices, spaces and organisations. Thompson and Adams (2013) also use Actor Network Theory as lens to critique research practice itself, and in so doing raise intriguing questions around whether the recording devices and coding software that feature in the generation and analysis of data need to be recognised as co-researchers. In light of the postdigital assumption of an entanglement between the biological and digital, there would seem to be a case for postdigital researchers to similarly consider the implications of their being enmeshed with the wider human and non-human objects of their work.

This leads us towards a more holistic appreciation of postdigital research, whether it is concerned with learning spaces or another part of the higher educational ecosystem. The postdigital provides a way of recognizing that digital technologies exist within the fabric of our educational surroundings, it resolutely pushes us as researchers to critically interrogate how these resources shape our learning spaces and practices, but it also operates as a sensibility and more fundamentally prompts us to reflect on our researcher-selves.

References

Aberton, H. (2012). Material enactments of identities and learning in everyday community practices: implications for pedagogy. *Pedagogy, Culture & Society, 20*(1), 113–136. https://doi.org/10.1080/14681366.2012.649418.

Ackermann, J., Egger, B., & Scharlach, R. (2020). Programming the Postdigital: Curation of Appropriation Processes in (Collaborative) Creative Coding Spaces. *Postdigital Science and Education, 2*(2), 416–441. https://doi.org/10.1007/s42438-019-00088-1.

Acton, R. (2017). Place-people-practice-process: Using sociomateriality in university physical spaces research. *Educational Philosophy and Theory, 49*(14), 1441–1451. https://doi.org/10.1080/00131857.2017.1309637.

Allen, R. M., & McLaren, P. (2022). Protecting the University as a Physical Place in the Age of Postdigitization. *Postdigital Science and Education, 4*(2), 373–393. https://doi.org/10.1007/s42438-021-00276-y.

Ball, J., & Savin-Baden, M. (2022). Postdigital Learning for a Changing Higher Education. *Postdigital Science and Education, 4*(3), 753–771. https://doi.org/10.1007/s42438-022-00307-2.

Bhatt, I., & De Roock, R. (2014). Capturing the sociomateriality of digital literacy events. *Research in Learning Technology, 21*. https://doi.org/10.3402/rlt.v21.21281.

Carvalho, L., & Freeman, C. G. (2022). Materials and Places for Learning: Experiences of Doctoral Students in and around University Spaces. *Postdigital Science and Education*. https://doi.org/10.1007/s42438-022-00328-x.

Carvalho, L., & Yeoman, P. (2018). Framing learning entanglement in innovative learning spaces: connecting theory, design and practice. *British Educational Research Journal, 44*(6), 1120–1137. https://doi.org/10.1002/berj.3483.

Cormier, D., Jandrić, P., Childs, M., Hall, R., White, D., Phipps, L., Truelove, I., Hayes, S., & Fawns, T. (2019). Ten Years of the Postdigital in the 52group: Reflections and Developments 2009–2019. *Postdigital Science and Education, 1*(2), 475–506. https://doi.org/10.1007/s42438-019-00049-8.

Cramer, F. (2015). What is 'post-digital'? In D. M. Berry & M. Dieter (Eds.), *Postdigital aesthetics: Art, computation and design* (pp. 12–26). New York: Palgrave Macmillan. https://doi.org/10.1057/9781137437204_2.

Cureton, D., Jones, J., & Hughes, J. (2021). The Postdigital University: Do We Still Need Just a Little of That Human Touch? *Postdigital Science and Education, 3*(1), 223–241. https://doi.org/10.1007/s42438-020-00204-6.

Feenberg, A. (2019). Postdigital or predigital? *Postdigital Science and Education, 1*(1), 8–9. https://doi.org/10.1007/s42438-018-0027-2.

Fenwick, T., Edwards, R., & Sawchuk, P. (2011). *Emerging approaches to educational research: Tracing the sociomaterial.* Abingdon: Routledge.

Goodyear, P. (2022). Realising the good university: Social innovation, care, design justice and educational infrastructure. *Postdigital Science and Education, 4*(1), 33–46. https://doi.org/10.1007/s42438-021-00253-5.

Gourlay, L., & Oliver, M. (2016). Students' Physical and Digital Sites of Study: Making, Marking and Breaking Boundaries. In L. Carvalho, P. Goodyear, & M. de Laat (Eds.), *Place- based spaces for networked learning* (pp. 73–86). New York: Routledge.

Gravett, K., Baughan, P., Rao, N., & Kinchin, I., (2022). Spaces and Places for Connection in the Postdigital University. *Postdigital Science and Education*. https://doi.org/10.1007/s42438-022-00317-0.

Jandrić, P., Knox, J., Besley, T., Ryberg, T., Suoranta, J., & Hayes, S. (2018). Postdigital Science and Education. *Educational Philosophy and Theory, 50*(10), 893–899. https://doi.org/10.1080/00131857.2018.1454000.

Knox, J., & Bayne, S. (2014). Multimodal profusion in the literacies of the Massive Open Online Course. *Research in Learning Technology, 21,* 21422. https://doi.org/10.3402/rlt.v21.21422.

Lamb, J. (2022). The Music Playlist as a Method of Education Research. *Postdigital Science and Education, 5*(5), 1–12. https://doi.org/10.1007/s42438-022-00319-y.

Lamb, J., Carvalho, L., Gallagher, M., & Knox, J. (2022). The postdigital learning spaces of higher education. *Postdigital Science and Education, 4*(1), 1–12. https://doi.org/10.1007/s42438-021-00279-9.

Landri, P. (2015). The sociomateriality of education policy. *Discourse: Studies in the Cultural Politics of Education, 36*(4), 596–609. https://doi.org/10.1080/01596306.2014.977019.

Law, J. (2004). *After Method: Mess in Social Science Research.* Oxford: Routledge.

Law, J. (2009). Actor network theory and material semiotics. In B. S. Turner (Ed.), *The new Blackwell companion to social theory* (pp. 141–158). Chichester: Wiley-Blackwell.

Macgilchrist, F. (2021). Theories of postdigital heterogeneity: implications for research on education and datafication. *Postdigital Science and Education, 3*(3), 660–667. https://doi.org/10.1007/s42438-021-00232-w.

Matthews, A. (2022). Death of the Lecture(r)? *Postdigital Science and Education, 4*(2), 253–258. https://doi.org/10.1007/s42438-021-00239-3.

Mulcahy, D. (2012). Thinking teacher professional learning performatively: a socio-material account. *Journal of Education and Work, 25*(1), 121–139. https://doi.org/10.1080/1363908 0.2012.644910.

Mulcahy, D., Cleveland, B., & Aberton, H. (2015). Learning spaces and pedagogic change: envisioned, enacted and experienced. *Pedagogy, Culture & Society, 23*(4), 575–595. https://doi.org/10.1080/14681366.2015.1055128.

Müller, M. (2015). Assemblages and Actor-networks: Rethinking Socio-material Power, Politics and Space: Assemblages and Actor-networks. *Geography Compass, 9*(1), 27–41. https://doi.org/10.1111/gec3.12192.

Mutch, A. (2013). Sociomateriality — Taking the wrong turning? *Information and Organization, 23*(1), 28–40. https://doi.org/10.1016/j.infoandorg.2013.02.001.

Örtegren, A. (2022). Digital Citizenship and Professional Digital Competence — Swedish Subject Teacher Education in a Postdigital Era. *Postdigital Science and Education, 4*(2), 467–493. https://doi.org/10.1007/s42438-022-00291-7.

Pepperell, R., & Punt, M. (2000). *The postdigital membrane: Imagination, technology and desire.* Bristol: Intellect Books.

Reed, J. (2022). Postdigital Outdoor and Environmental Education. *Postdigital Science and Education.* https://doi.org/10.1007/s42438-022-00323-2.

Robinson, P.A. (2018). Learning spaces in the countryside: university students and the Harper assemblage. *Area, 50*(2), 274–282. https://doi.org/10.1111/area.12379.

Spire, Z. (2022). University estates and postdigital higher education: Space, place, and being a university. *Postdigital Science and Education.* https://doi.org/10.1007/s42438-022-00314-3.

Thompson, T. L. (2012). I'm deleting as fast as I can: negotiating learning practices in cyberspace. *Pedagogy, Culture & Society, 20*(1), 93–112. https://doi.org/10.1080/14681366.2012.649417.

Thompson, T. L., & Adams, C. (2013). Speaking with things: encoded researchers, social data, and other posthuman concoctions. *Distinktion: Journal of Social Theory, 14*(3), 342–361. https://doi.org/10.1080/1600910X.2013.838182/.

Thorén, C., Edenius, M., Lundström, J. E., & Kitzmann, A. (2019). The hipster's dilemma: What is analogue or digital in the post-digital society? *Convergence, 25*(2), 324–339. https://doi.org/10.1177/1354856517713139.

van Kraalingen, I. (2022). Theorizing Technological Mediation in the Outdoor Classroom. *Postdigital Science and Education.* https://doi.org/10.1007/s42438-022-00315-2.

Wardak, D., Vallis, C., & Bryant, P. (2022). #OurPlace2020: Blurring boundaries of learning spaces. *Postdigital Science and Education, 4*(1), 116–137. https://doi.org/10.1007/s42438-021-00264-2.

Researching Interactional and Volumetric Scenographies – Immersive Qualitative Digital Research

Jacob Davidsen, Paul McIlvenny, and Thomas Ryberg

In a university building, a group of students work on their project. They have found a room with a table and chair for each of the group members physically present today. They live a nomadic life as they must find a new place to work every day. There are not enough power outlets in this room, so they need to take turns charging their laptops and tablets. Two of the group members write in a shared Google document about the theoretical perspective of their project, while two other members work on the digital data visualization from their scraping of Twitter posts. The sixth member puts different tangible materials together to prepare their analog visualization of the Twitter posts for an upcoming design review session. They are excited about their presentation and hope that the different visualisations will work out well. While the five of them sit together, the final group member is travelling from the university city to visit his parents at the other end of the country. He is constantly online – sometimes through a video service, but all the time available on chat and present in their shared documents. He makes comments on the theory section, and the students working on the digital data visualization are often asking him about technical issues as he is the expert on the software the group is using. After lunch, the supervisor joins the group for a scheduled meeting. She provides feedback to the group on their method section which they sent to her a week ago. There are many things to discuss. The supervisor uses the room's blackboards to facilitate a discussion on the chosen methodological perspective. She writes questions and makes drawings about their chosen method. She also points to specific sentences in their written text to underline some of her critical remarks. At some point, she asks the students to join her for a walk around the university building to spark some energy into their conversation.

1 Introduction

Researching learning in the age of postdigital circumstances is a complex task as social interaction is mediated through various media and takes place across many different physical and virtual locations. The concept of mediation (Vygotsky 1978) is not new, but in the postdigital age, conditions seem to be accelerated and are even

J. Davidsen (✉) · P. McIlvenny · T. Ryberg
Aalborg University, Aalborg, Denmark
e-mail: jdavidsen@ikp.aau.dk; paul@ikl.aau.dk; ryberg@ikp.aau.dk

P. Jandrić et al. (eds.), *Constructing Postdigital Research*, Postdigital Science
and Education, https://doi.org/10.1007/978-3-031-35411-3_7

more complex than a few years ago (Rosa 2013). Therefore, we need to find and develop ways of capturing, archiving, and analysing 'the messy, entangled and unpredictable nature of the socio-technical relationships that constitute education' (Jandrić and Knox 2022: 784).

The most straightforward approach for researching learning in the postdigital age would be to ask people what they do. We could ask the students what it is like to work in a group or send out a questionnaire to the entire student cohort at the university to get some indications of what it is like to be a student in a postdigital learning environment. Most likely we would learn something very general about what students do when they are working together, but their situated 'interactional work' (Davidsen et al. 2020a, b) will remain in the dark. Ethnographers of work refer to this as the 'say/do problem' (Blomberg et al. 1993), which contends that people will only tell more general details and anecdotes about what they do and not the specific details that constitute their everyday activities. Ethnographers are also being immersed in the site of study in the moment, but they will have to rely on their written notes and their experience of being there in their research dissemination. The 'interactional work' we are referring to includes all the situated, embodied, and multimodal work that students perform to navigate in the complex, entangled and unpredictable postdigital practices.

Another methodological approach could be to use algorithms and artificial intelligence to track and trace the students' behaviour on the online platforms they use, but what about all the interactional work they do next to or outside the purview of the platforms being tracked, and what about the connections between their mixed use of analog and digital resources? In this chapter, we suggest that postdigital research could focus on students' work through interactional and volumetric scenographies using complex video recording setups and software for working with the data qualitatively and immersively. The main plot is that postdigital research should emancipate the researcher from being a spectator of abstract data to a participant that can inhabit and reactivate the data immersively. To do that, we need to return to principles and ideas located in ethnography, ethnomethodology and interaction analysis.

2   From Algorithms and Data Visualization to Interactional and Volumetric Scenographies

In the current methodological landscape of educational research, there is a profound interest in algorithmic, automated, and computational approaches to studies of educational practice (Cerratto Pargman et al. 2022; Jandrić and Ford 2022). The volumes of data have increased dramatically in the last decade, but in some cases, the data is used for control and economic goals, and not for supporting better and more sound pedagogies. The tracking of digital activities is feeding the algorithms, but it is not clear how this data will support students' learning activities or support the teachers in developing new pedagogical activities. The current landscape of research methodology with digital tools is not entangled, but very polarised. Computational methods and techniques in educational research have gained momentum as big data sets can be systematised, archived, and analysed. In contrast, qualitative and immersive research methodologies have yet to be empowered and revitalised with digital tools. Before we introduce our perspective on immersive qualitative digital research environments that focus on systematising, archiving, and analysing interactional and volumetric scenographies, we will focus on the computational perspective in educational research.

Computational methods and techniques such as Learning Analytics (LA), Multimodal Learning Analytics (MMLA), and Data Visualization seemingly provide 'visualized facts' of human actions (Kitchin et al. 2015; Williamson 2017). According to Blikstein and Worsley (2016: 233), MMLA is 'a set of techniques employing multiple sources of data (video, logs, text, artifacts, audio, gestures, biosensors) to examine learning in realistic, ecologically valid, social, mixed-media learning environments'. However, human actions are not bound to a specific platform or interface and can be tricky to decipher through and with a piece of code. While the visualized facts hold tremendous persuasive power, it is also clear that interactional practice is reduced, recoded or abstracted into proxies of the event (Crescenzi-Lanna 2020).

Following the clicks and strokes of people in a system is, of course, telling us something about the digital traces people produce (Wise et al. 2021), but the context-sensitivity is poorly understood and the sequential order of the students' interactional work is transformed into visualizations that leave few traces of the interactional production of meaning and learning. Additionally, the data collected and analysed is logo-centric and click-centric, which means that multimodal and embodied (Davidsen and Ryberg 2017; Goodwin 2017) aspects of interaction and learning are often subtracted from the situated practice. These multimodal and embodied actions with and through mediational resources are fundamental elements of learning processes (Vygotsky 1978). Neglecting or abstracting these actions is problematic for research on postdigital science and education, which is grounded in the overlapping and entangled ecotones of analog and digital practices (Fawns 2022; Ryberg et al. 2021). Worryingly, the abstracted digital traces cover up the situated and fluid interactional work that students do that are constitutive of postdigital practices.

To grasp the situated, multimodal, and embodied interactional work in postdigital scenographies, we strategically return to an ethnomethodological understanding of practice (Garfinkel 2002). Eisemann and Lynch (2021) outline an ethnomethodological understanding of practice as 'a field of embodied actions, in the thickness of lived space and time, populated by things, irreducibly intersubjective, infused with language, inhabited by the presence and absence of other beings' (2021: 14). As discussed by McIlvenny and Davidsen,

> [s]tudying members' ethno-methods using audio-visual documents should *not only* be restricted to the careful analysis of talk-centred transcripts; we also need to develop practices and tools that allow us to study this 'field' that get at other dimensions of the *thickness* of lived space and time, such as volumetricity. (McIlvenny and Davidsen 2023) (emphasis in the original)

With a profound interest in understanding the thickness of lived space and time, we move beyond the thin, logo-centric, and click-centric measures of postdigital practice. To capture and understand aspects of the thickness of lived practice, we focus on the interactional and volumetric scenographies that people inhabit using different mediational resources. Further, if we consider postdigital practices as interactional and volumetric scenographies, we need to move beyond questionnaires and pre/post-test, and instead return to ethnographic and interactional positions. Furthermore, we need to critically examine and develop immersive qualitative research environments that will allow us to study the situated, multimodal, and embodied interactional work that students do.

Recent theories on theatrical scenography are precisely trying to capture and analyse the complex, entangled, and unpredictable relationship between the actors, the audiences and the specific staging of a theatrical production or live performance. The director, actors, scenographers, and everyone/everything else involved in the re-documentation of the manuscript are all doing analysis and interpretation of the manuscript[1] Howard notes that '[s]cenography is the seamless synthesis of space, text, research, art, actors, directors and spectators that contributes to an original creation' (2002: 160). That conceptualisation of scenography has a bearing on the postdigital practices researchers are trying to capture, analyse, and theorize. The postdigital scenographies researchers are studying are, of course, not staged in the same way as a screenplay, but they are based on the 'natural' activities, for example, that students are doing in the setting they are inhabiting. Another important remark on the qualities of scenography is made by Lotker and Gough:

> We engage with scenography, with the performative environments, not only by observing and mentally engaging with them, but by 'observing' with our whole bodies; these environments, these scenographies move us. They disturb us, challenge us and affect us. Depending on how scenographies are built – whether 'human'-made (cat-walk, public square or theatre) or 'god'-made (Everest) – they can make us do things; they make us perform. Scenography is not as benign as has been previously perceived. Whether we enter them consciously knowing that they are scenographies or whether we enter them without that knowledge, scenographies have power over us they, command our attention and affect our emotion. (Lotker and Gough 2013: 4)

We turn to research on scenography and theatre (Burian 1974; Howard 2002; Lotker and Gough 2013) to highlight that a postdigital research environment should be about actualizing, inhabiting, and sensing the educational practice more than a matter of producing visualized and cartographic facts. Of course, the analysis of the interactional and volumetric scenographies is still aided by the production of detailed transcripts of the interaction between the participants and their use of mediational resources, but it is also a matter of developing immersive qualitative digital research environments that will allow researchers to re-enter the situated, multimodal, and embodied practice for 'another next first time' (Garfinkel 2002).

---

[1] As researchers, we are not necessarily acting out the data [see Sormani's (2016) work on practice-based video analysis for an interesting counterexample], but we are analysing and interpreting the data based on methodological and theoretical stances.

McIlvenny (2020a) points towards the need for technologies that allow this type of re-documentation of the interactional and volumetric scenographies through a critical discussion of how new recording and analytical technologies are built on different assumptions about human social interaction. Algorithms, AI, and data visualisations are positioning the researchers as spectators of a re-coded practice, and often the original practices are not recoverable. In contrast, immersive qualitative digital research environments are built to position the researchers as emancipated spectators (Rancière 2011). Rancière engaged in a critique of theatrical staging and proposed that theatre should emancipate the audience and make them 'active participants as opposed to passive voyeurs' (2011: 4). Rancière continues his critique of the passivity of the spectator:

> Being a spectator is a bad thing for two reasons. First, viewing is the opposite of knowing: the spectator is held before an appearance in a state of ignorance about the process of production of this appearance and about the reality it conceals. Second, it is the opposite of acting: the spectator remains immobile in her seat, passive. To be a spectator is to be separated from both the capacity to know and the power to act. (Rancière 2011: 2)

With this chapter, we develop and outline a postdigital research perspective on interactional and volumetric scenography. The idea of moving 'beyond video' (McIlvenny and Davidsen 2023) is allowing us to introduce a new methodological orientation to postdigital research. This is a methodological perspective in which researchers are not just consuming at a distance the interactional work of the participants, but a perspective in which researchers are actively engaged in inhabiting and reliving the situated, multimodal, and embodied practice.

3   A Brief History of Video-Based Research

Since the invention of the camera, and later the digital video camera, researchers have developed ways of using this sophisticated technology for capturing, documenting, and analysing human social practices in very diverse settings (Broth et al. 2014; DeLiema et al. 2021; Derry et al. 2010). The story has often been told of Leland Stanford hiring Edward Muybridge to develop a photographic technology that could document if a horse is ever not touching the ground with all four legs (Broth et al. 2014). In the 1880s, Étienne-Jules Marey developed a 'chronotropic gun' used for capturing everyday life in France. Many years later in the 1960s, Sacks (1995) started to use the tape machine to document and analyse human social interaction. These three examples illustrate the close link between the development of technology and the development of new research practices (Hirschauer 2007). Presently, new technologies are also pushing the boundaries of research practice. In this chapter, we are particularly concerned with how immersive technologies such as Virtual Reality and 360° video can shape future postdigital research practices.

The use of audio-visual records in science and education has a long history, with examples from Bateson et al.'s (1971) work on the natural history of an interview,

Mehan's (1979) identification of the Input-Response-Evaluation structure in class-rooms, Goodwin's (1981) work on conversational structures, and more recent work on embodied instructions (Lindwall and Ekström 2012) and meta-imaging (Steier and Kersting 2019). Video has also been used in detailed analysis of students learning processes with digital and analog materials (Davidsen et al. 2020a, b), to give voices to marginalized people in society (Harris 2016) and as a means for engaging vulnerable people in design processes (Karadechev et al. 2021). In other words, video has played a prominent role in the last four decades as researchers have obtained new ways to access to learning in situ (Hall and Stevens 2015; Jordan and Henderson 1995).

In her work on sensory ethnography, Pink (2015, 2017) also explores how video can be used to document and research the everyday practices of people. Pink brings a camera into people's homes and uses it to document how people live in their homes, e.g., the practical use of electrical appliances. Pink notes that sensory ethnography should 'bring researchers and their audiences close to other people's multisensory experiences, knowing, practice, memories and imaginations' (2015: 132). In some of her later work, Pink (2017) points towards the potential of video for giving researchers access to the immersive experiences of being and participating in situated, multimodal, and embodied interaction.

In all the above mentioned examples, the researcher is using one (or more) cameras that have been positioned on a tripod or are mobile. This type of individual or collaborative videoing is still the standard in much interactional research (Mondada et al. 2022). However, these traditional video cameras are still producing flat 2D video representations of the interactional and volumetric scenographies (McIlvenny 2020a). With the introduction of new recording technologies and software for capturing and replaying the data in Virtual Reality, it is now possible to conduct a different type of postdigital research focusing on how the interactional and volumetric scenographies can be inhabited and re-documented.

4 Immersive Everyday Realities: 360° Video, Volume, and Scene

Virtual Reality is mostly associated with computer-generated worlds in which the user through a laptop, head-mounted display, or a cave system, gets access to an alternate version of reality (Pirker and Dengel 2021; Radianti et al. 2020). The computer-generated worlds can give access to exotic or dangerous places – and the participant is allowed to practice their skills in a risk-free environment (Abich et al. 2021). Currently, there is much interest in creating photo-realistic avatars and space in virtual reality learning environments (Alldieck et al. 2022; Kasapakis and Dzardanova 2022), which should support a more immersive experience in Virtual Reality. Compared to situated, multimodal, and embodied practice, the computer-generated worlds are more like a basic-level map, not a detailed and complex representation of the entangled and unpredictable nature of postdigital practices. The scenographies that the computer-generated worlds are trying to imitate are still not giving us access to the mundane everyday practice and the 'thickness of lived practice' (Eisenmann and Lynch 2021).

With 360° video and head mounted displays for Virtual Reality a new type of immersive reality is made possible. Gómez Cruz (2017) argues that this can lead to a higher degree of immersive reflexivity for researchers studying a practice. While the classical video format gives audio-visual access to the event as it plays out on a moment-to-moment basis, it is also clear that a traditional 2D video consists of 'dumb' flat pixels (McIlvenny 2020a) that do not contain volumetric information about the recorded scene. 2D videos reduce the complexity of the lived postdigital practice; thus, it is important to explore other ways of engaging with collecting, archiving, and analysing audio-visual data. This is possible through developing immersive qualitative digital research environments that will allow researchers (and their collaborators) to investigate the thickness, entangled and unpredictable nature of the lived practice. While we cannot capture everyday postdigital practices volumetrically yet, 360° video Virtual Reality allows us to inhabit the interactional and volumetric scenography in ways that allow us to move beyond text-based transcripts and click-centric statistics. In the future, we will be able to capture practices volumetrically in real settings using Lidar scanners and other spatial capture technologies, which will create a different texture of the scenography and new ways of re-activating the lived practice (see Possible Bodies et al. 2022 for a critical perspective).

With the advent of head mounted displays for Virtual Reality and the introduction of 360° video cameras, we are on the threshold of a new way of staging interactional events (McIlvenny and Davidsen 2017) – a scenographic turn aided by the affordances of networked 360° Virtual Reality (McIlvenny and Davidsen 2023). The possibility to record practice with one or more 360° cameras is fascinating, but the qualitative difference of using 360° video is not just the spatial recording of the situated, multimodal, and embodied human social actions, but the possibility to work with the data in new unexplored ways. Watching a 360° video using a traditional media player, however, is like driving an electric bike without using the battery – the full potential is not unleashed. Therefore, it is important that researchers develop new immersive qualitative digital research environments for researching postdigital practices as we get a substantially different kind of access to the situated, multimodal, and embodied practice when compared to the use of traditional video methods and big data approaches. Tabački (2021) is directing us to what he terms 'virtual scenography':

> Using virtual scenography as a tool to provoke changes in the viewer's perception may challenge them to reconsider the concept of space and how it comes into being, providing preconditions for widening the scope of spatial sensory experience. Understanding an HMD [head-mounted display] as an extension of the body, instead of as a passive instrument for achieving quick thrills, and actively engaging the user in the production of space, opens perspectives for scenographic agency to unfold its potential for merging physical and digital realities in a new way and to expand possibilities for spatial experimentation. (Tabački 2021: 14)

The Virtual Reality industry has steered us towards a limited understanding of immersive experiences as a way to achieve 'quick thrills'. In contrast, immersive qualitative digital research environments engage the researcher in understanding the interactional and volumetric scenography through a variety of different tools. The degree of agency for the researcher in these environments is substantially different to the classic viewing and analysis of the video on a flat screen or text-based transcripts on paper. To consider the head-mounted display 'as an extension of the body' in immersive qualitative research is important, but it is also clear that new tools and ways of engaging with an analysis of postdigital practice are required.

5 Immersive Qualitative Digital Research Environments

Performing immersive qualitative digital research is closely coupled with recent technological developments that allow a different type of engagement and involvement with postdigital practices. With head mounted displays, 360° video data, and virtual environments, we move towards an interactional and volumetric scenographic perspective in postdigital research. In this section, we present three different software packages we have developed that together delineate the contours of an immersive qualitative digital research environment.

The BigSoftVideo group at Aalborg University, Denmark, have pioneered immersive qualitative digital research environments with software packages like DOTE (McIlvenny et al. 2022), AVA360VR (McIlvenny et al. 2021), SQUIVE (McIlvenny 2020a), and CAVA360VR (Davidsen and McIlvenny 2022). In AVA360VR, individual researchers can work with complex audio-visual data sets in Virtual Reality. With CAVA360VR researchers are offered a networked Virtual Reality environment for postdigital research – originally used for live distance video data sessions (McIlvenny 2020b; Vatanen et al. 2022). In CAVA360VR researchers can watch and annotate a 360° video recording with peers who are not physically present in the same space but are virtually present in a shared scenography. SQUIVE (McIlvenny 2020a) is the first attempt to develop a spatial re-documentation of the staging of a lived practice using both computer-generated techniques and audio-visual data collected from a live art event.

5.1 AVA360VR

The free software package AVA360VR (Annotate Visualise Analysis 360° video in Virtual Reality) attempts to build an immersive qualitative digital research environment (McIlvenny 2018; McIlvenny et al. 2021) using 360° video and Virtual Reality. AVA360VR allows a single-user to analyse their audio-visual data in Virtual Reality. Inside AVA360VR (see Fig. 1) the researcher is presented with a range of different tools supporting an immersive analysis of postdigital practice. Among other things, the researchers can play/pause 360° video, jump between different 360° cameras, draw on the 360° video, capture and export frame-grabs, create comic strips, view a synced transcript, etc. In AVA360VR, the researcher is not only analysing a single 360° video but can import other synced/unsynced 360° videos, 2D videos, images, sound, and 3D models. The participants in Fig. 1 and Fig. 2 all gave consent to publish the data, and the data is accessible in an open archive (Davidsen et al. 2020a, b).

Instead of being a passive spectator of the video, the researcher is presented with tools that shape the design of a personalised immersive qualitative digital research environment. AVA360VR is thereby supporting the creation of a research environment in which the researcher is given the freedom to use different audio-visual resources and different tools for analysing postdigital practices. There is no study that directly compares the difference between analysing audio-visual data inside AVA360VR and using more conventional tools (e.g. a media player on a standard laptop), but research indicates that there is a qualitative difference between learning new skills with 2D video and immersive 360° Virtual Reality tools (Kosko et al. 2021).

While the experience of being inside AVA360VR is immersive for the individual researcher, it is also clear that researchers will face troubles when trying to communicate analytical points to an audience not in VR (Paulsen et al. 2022) or with traditional screen recordings. What is transmitted or recorded on the screen is not exactly the same experience as being inside Virtual Reality – the interactional and volumetric scenography is usually recoded into a flat 2D image (as seen in Fig. 2). However, with AVA360VR, the researcher is offered an alternative way of documenting and presenting analytical work through Volumetric Capture (VolCap) and RePlay (Davidsen et al. 2022; McIlvenny 2020a).

Fig. 1 View from inside AVA360VR

Fig. 2 VolCap RePlay output

In Fig. 2, a composite image from a reactivated VolCap is visible in the quad image. A new researcher examines an analysis made by another researcher of a cooperative learning exercise recorded with several 360° cameras and microphones. The green avatar head is the RePlayer and the blue is the VolCapper. When the VolCap is re-activated, the RePlayer will see a blue avatar head in the scene (and his/her controllers), which represents the user who performed the original VolCap. Hence, the RePlayer will be able to follow every action of the original VolCapper – and can even teleport around the VolCapper to obtain the best possible position for following the analysis by the VolCapper in 3D. In addition, several of the same 3D tools and views available to the VolCapper are also available to the RePlayer.

In Fig. 2, the top left image is the viewport from the original VolCapper and at the top right is the 2D viewport of the RePlayer. The two images in the lower part of the quad image show outputs from two different virtual cameras that can be positioned where the RePlayer wants to. In a VolCap, every action of the researcher doing the analysis in VR is captured volumetrically in Virtual Reality, and the voice of the researcher is also recorded. This capture of the analysis allows a future RePlayer to reactivate the analysis again, yet immersively.

Through the reactivation of the VolCap, a RePlayer is not only gaining a new perspective on the original audio-visual record of the event, but also the embodied analysis of the original VolCapper. Thus, VolCaps preserve the interactional and volumetric analytical work a researcher is doing in a postdigital practice. VolCaps are only RePlayable in AVA360VR, which of course makes them less accessible as one needs a Head Mounted Display and Virtual Reality ready computer to engage with the VolCap.

5.2   CAVA360VR

The software prototype CAVA360VR (Collaborate Annotate Visualise and Analyse 360° video in Virtual Reality) (Davidsen and McIlvenny 2022; McIlvenny 2020b) is a collaborative, immersive and networked research environment for studies of post-digital educational practice. In CAVA360VR, researchers in distant locations can actualise the interactional and volumetric scenography of an educational setting recorded with a 360° camera (see Vatanen et al. 2022 for examples). Compared to AVA360VR fewer tools are available to aid the analysis of the audio-visual data of the event, but in CAVA360 the co-present researchers in the shared virtual space can play/pause the video, draw on the 360° video, look at an additional image or an additional 2D video and use the 'mirror-cam' to view in two directions at the same time (see Fig. 3).

In Fig. 3, there are two images – the top image is showing what R1 is seeing and the image at the bottom shows what R2 is seeing in the virtual scene. R1 and R2 are seeing the same slices of time of the video, but they are also seeing and using

Fig. 3 Two researchers (R1 and R2) using CAVA360VR

different additional resources. R2 looks at a transcript and the timeline, whereas R1 only looks at the video.

CAVA360VR offers both an individual and shared research environment – each person is represented as an avatar with hands (linked to the controller) and the voice of each person is transmitted to the other participants. When one researcher is playing the 360° video it is also playing at the other locations and when someone is drawing it is also visible to the rest of the participants. CAVA360VR offers a way of inhabiting the educational practice repeatedly and together with fellow peers in Virtual Reality.

5.3   SQUIVE

In AVA360VR and CAVA360VR the researcher is working directly with the audio-visual data collected in a practice, but in SQUIVE (Staging Qualitative Immersive Virtualisation Engine) the researcher is accessing the audio-visual data through a digital twin (Jones et al. 2020) with animated avatars and virtual spaces that represent the physical setting. SQUIVE is a virtual volumetric simulation of the scenography of the physical space and the recording technologies, in which you can play with both the simulation and the original audio-visual data recorded in the setting. To explain the affordances of SQUIVE, an example from McIlvenny (2020a) is introduced.

After the collection of a massive and complex audio-visual data set from the esteemed interactive exoskeleton theatre performance called Inferno,[2] McIlvenny (2020a) developed the software prototype called SQUIVE. Based on a close inspection of the 360° video recordings and ethnographic experiences, McIlvenny recreated the interactional and volumetric scenography using a Virtual Reality software engine (Unity) (see Fig. 4) with 'avatars, lighting, furniture and props were styled to reflect the ambience and actants in the relevant spaces in which the performances took place' (McIlvenny 2020a: 806).

The re-documentation of the space and the insertion of the 360° video data created a new version of the event that allows researchers to sense and navigate the spatial organisation of the event in a Virtual Reality version as well as the interactional details in the collected audio-visual data. As shown in (McIlvenny 2020),

> a user can walk around the simulated theatre and encounter the different rooms and connecting spaces that the participants interacted in and moved through. A user can interact with the cameras that were used to record scenes and they can hear spatial sound in the space as it was recorded. Footage from the physical cameras can be selected, played, cloned and clipped. (McIlvenny 2020a: 806)

---

[2] Inferno is designed, choreographed, composed, and realized by Louis-Philippe Demers and Bill Vorn (see http://prix2016.aec.at/prixwinner/19611/, accessed 30 November 2022). The data shown here were collected by the research group EXACT (Exoskeletons, Art, Choreography and Training) (Jochum et al. 2018). Consent was granted by all participants for the full recordings to be used for research purposes.

Fig. 4 View from inside SQUIVE of one of the performance spaces

Another interesting perspective when using SQUIVE is that the data is an ano-nymised version of the event, which means 'the user can alternate between navigat-ing the staged virtual volumetric reconstruction and re-viewing the physical camera footage from actual locations in the space of the event' (McIlvenny 2020a: 806). Producing a digital twin of a postdigital practice is, of course, not the same as see-ing/hearing the original audio-visual recordings or the experience of being physi-cally present, but it offers an alternative volumetric archival entry point for researchers.

As stated by McIlvenny (2020a: 806), '[t]he virtual models are a tool to organise qualitative enquiry; they are not a substitute for ethnography, skilled camerawork and originary sources'. SQUIVE gives researchers a new perspective on the spatial organisation of the event and the relation between the space and the recorded audio-visual data, which works more like a spatial memory device for the researcher. Instead of looking for the audio-visual data in a folder structure on a computer, the researcher can now use SQUIVE as the primary entrance to the spatialised data archive.

6 Researching Postdigital Science and Education

With the increasing interest in computational methods in educational research, there is a need to envision an alternative stance grounded in qualitative methodological perspectives. Theoretically, postdigital research has strived to blur the lines between analog and digital technologies (Ryberg et al. 2021) and technology and pedagogy (Fawns 2022), but how should we study the complex, entangled and unpredictable nature of postdigital activities? The story in the prologue of the chapter shows that students constantly and iteratively reorganise their ways of working – there is not just one digital platform for their work – they are patchworking a mesh of different resources that support their specific way of working.

In this chapter, we argue that postdigital practices could be studied through the perspective of interactional and volumetric scenography using immersive qualitative digital research environments. To do that we need to develop and sustain immersive qualitative digital research environments for experimenting with postdigital research methodologies. We have presented three different software packages (AVA360VR, CAVA360VR and SQUIVE) that show how researchers can use immersive technologies for researching the situated, multimodal, and embodied interactional work students do. Moreover, we stress that postdigital research must find solutions to represent learning spaces that move beyond 'dumb' flat pixels and offer ways of inhabiting the interactional and volumetric scenographies.

We are aware of the hype towards the artificial intelligence and automated research futures (Pink 2022; Pink et al. 2022), but we strongly advocate for another emerging postdigital future for qualitative research. For us, immersive qualitative digital research is primarily human labour supported by smart and immersive software. With the three different software packages, the general motivation is to activate the researcher in the analysis of postdigital practices, not to rely on automated outcomes based on pre-established categories or what the machine has 'learned' about the postdigital practice.

To get a deeper understanding of the entangled and unpredictable interaction in postdigital practices researchers to need to explore and develop other research approaches and environments. Deeply rooted in qualitative research, we offer a different 'future-focused practice in the qualitative social sciences and humanities' (Pink 2022: 752), which is immersive, spatial and volumetric. In the future, it may be possible to couple automated analytics with the immersive qualitative digital research we are proposing, which could lead to another understanding of the complex and unpredictable nature of postdigital science and education.

Returning to Rancière (2011), the goal of establishing an immersive qualitative digital research environment is to emancipate and empower researchers with tools that transgress the limitations of passive spectatorship. The different software presented in this chapter all promote active participation by the researcher in re-activating the postdigital practice – the complexity of the recorded events requires that the researchers make decisions about 'where-to-watch' and 'how-to-hear' the audio-visual recordings of the event. For example, the ability to compose a scenography using different audio-visual data or to have discussions about which video or audio track will give the best possible access to the practice will be essential in the future.

Of course, while engaged in the immersive qualitative digital environment, the researcher does not participate in the 'original event' and cannot interfere with the participants' historical actions. Nevertheless, the researcher gets a much better sense of the thickness of the situated, multimodal, and embodied interactional work that students do in their local setting in unpredictable ways. We are not claiming that researchers can obtain full sensorial, embodied and volumetric access to the recorded event through immersive digital research environments, but we see emerging trajectories towards a more emancipated position that allows researchers to inhabit the complex, mediated, and unpredictable postdigital practices.

Like any other methodological position, immersive qualitative digital research will also have limitations, but it will provide a new way of researching the interactional and volumetric scenographies. Currently, there is an important issue of uneven accessibility to immersive technologies, but as these technologies become better integrated in education and research in the near future there is an opportune moment for developing and maintaining immersive qualitative postdigital research environments.

References

Abich, J., Parker, J., Murphy, J. S., & Eudy, M. (2021). A Review of The Evidence for Training Effectiveness With Virtual Reality Technology. *Virtual Reality*. https://doi.org/10.1007/s10055-020-00498-8.

Alldieck, T., Zanfir, M., & Sminchisescu, C. (2022). Photorealistic Monocular 3D Reconstruction of Humans Wearing Clothing. In *Proceedings of the IEEE/CVF Conference on Computer Vision and Pattern Recognition* (pp. 1506–1515). https://openaccess.thecvf.com/content/CVPR2022/html/Alldieck_Photorealistic_Monocular_3D_Reconstruction_of_Humans_Wearing_Clothing_CVPR_2022_paper.html. Accessed 28 November 2022.

Bateson, G., Birdwhistell, R., Brosin, H. W., Hockett, C. F., McQuown, N. A., Smith, H. L., & Trager, G. L. (1971). *The Natural History of an Interview*. Chicago, IL: University of Chicago Library.

Blikstein, P., & Worsley, M. (2016). Multimodal Learning Analytics and Education Data Mining: Using Computational Technologies to Measure Complex Learning Tasks. *Journal of Learning Analytics*, *3*(2), 220–238. https://doi.org/10.18608/jla.2016.32.11.

Blomberg, J., Giacomi, J., Mosher, A., & Swenton-Wall, P. (1993). Ethnographic Field Methods and Their Relation to Design. In D. Schuler & A. Namioka (Eds.), *Participatory Design: Principles and Practices* (pp. 123–155). Hillsdale, NJ: Lawrence Erlbaum Associates.

Broth, M., Laurier, E., & Mondada, L. (Eds.). (2014). *Studies of Video Practices: Video at Work*. New York and London: Routledge.

Burian, J. (1974). *The Scenography of Josef Svoboda*. Middletown, CN: Wesleyan University Press.

Cerratto Pargman, T., Lindberg, Y., & Buch, A. (2022). Automation Is Coming! Exploring Future(s)-Oriented Methods in Education. *Postdigital Science and Education*. https://doi.org/10.1007/s42438-022-00349-6.

Crescenzi-Lanna, L. (2020). Multimodal Learning Analytics Research with Young Children: A Systematic Review. *British Journal of Educational Technology*, *51*(5), 1485–1504. https://doi.org/10.1111/bjet.12959.

Davidsen, J., & McIlvenny, P. (2022). Towards Collaborative Immersive Qualitative Analysis. In A. Weinberger, W. Chen, D. Hernández-Leo, & B. Chen (Eds.), *CSCL2022 Conference Proceedings*. Hiroshima: International Society of the Learning Sciences.

Davidsen, J., & Ryberg, T. (2017). "This is the Size of One Meter": Children's Bodily-Material Collaboration. *International Journal of Computer-Supported Collaborative Learning*, *12*(1), 65–90. https://doi.org/10.1007/s11412-017-9248-8.

Davidsen, J., Ryberg, T., & Bernhard, J. (2020a). "Everything comes together": Students' Collaborative Development of a Professional Dialogic Practice in Architecture and Design Education. *Thinking Skills and Creativity*, *37*, 100678. https://doi.org/10.1016/j.tsc.2020.100678.

Davidsen, J., Thomsen, M., & McIlvenny, P. B. (2020b). Lego Project Data: An Open Data Archive for Qualitative Video Research. *QuiViRR: Qualitative Video Research Reports, 1.* https://doi.org/10.5278/OJS.QUIVIRR.V1.2020.A0003.

Davidsen, J., McIlvenny, P., & Kovács, A. B. (2022). Volumetric Capture and Replay in Virtual Reality – Entering the age of immersive and volumetric analysis in CSCL. In A. Weinberger, W. Chen, D. Hernández-Leo, & B. Chen (Eds.), *CSCL2022 Conference Proceedings.* Hiroshima: International Society of the Learning Sciences.

DeLiema, D., Hufnagle, A., Rao, V. N. V., Baker, J., Valerie, J., & Kim, J. (2021). Methodological Innovations at the Intersection of Video-Based Educational Research Traditions: Reflections on Relevance, Data Selection, and Phenomena of Interest. *International Journal of Research & Method in Education.* https://doi.org/10.1080/1743727X.2021.2011196.

Derry, S., Pea, R., Barron, B., Engle, R., Erickson, F., Goldman, R., et al. (2010). Conducting Video Research in the Learning Sciences: Guidance on Selection, Analysis, Technology, and Ethics. *Journal of the Learning Sciences, 19*(1), 3–53. https://doi.org/10.1080/10508400903452884.

Eisenmann, C., & Lynch, M. (2021). Introduction to Harold Garfinkel's Ethnomethodological "misreading" of Aron Gurwitsch on the Phenomenal Field. *Human Studies, 44*(1), 1–17. https://doi.org/10.1007/s10746-020-09564-1.

Fawns, T. (2022). An Entangled Pedagogy: Looking Beyond the Pedagogy—Technology Dichotomy. *Postdigital Science and Education.* https://doi.org/10.1007/s42438-022-00302-7.

Garfinkel, H. (2002). *Ethnomethodology's Program: Working out Durkheim's Aphorism.* Lanham, MD: Rowman & Littlefield.

Gómez Cruz, E. (2017). Immersive Reflexivity: Using 360° Cameras in Ethnographic Fieldwork. In E. Gómez Cruz, S. Sumartojo, & S. Pink (Eds.), *Refiguring Techniques in Digital Visual Research* (pp. 25–38). Springer International Publishing. https://doi.org/10.1007/978-3-319-61222-5_3.

Goodwin, C. (1981). *Conversational Organization: Interaction Between Speakers and Hearers.* New York: Academic.

Goodwin, C. (2017). *Co-operative action.* Cambridge: Cambridge University Press.

Hall, R., & Stevens, R. (2015). Interaction Analysis Approaches to Knowledge in Use. In A. A. diSessa, M. Levin, & N. J. S. Brown (Eds.), *Knowledge and Interaction a Synthetic Agenda for the Learning Sciences* (pp. 72–108). Abingdon: Routledge.

Harris, A. M. (2016). *Video as Method.* Oxford and New York: Oxford University Press.

Hirschauer, S. (2007). Puttings Things into Words. Ethnographic Description and the Silence of the Social. *Human Studies, 29*(4), 413–441. https://doi.org/10.1007/s10746-007-9041-1.

Howard, P. (2002). *What is Scenography?* London and New York: Routledge.

Jandrić, P., & Ford, D. R. (2022). Postdigital Ecopedagogies: Genealogies, Contradictions, and Possible Futures. *Postdigital Science and Education, 4*(3), 692–710. https://doi.org/10.1007/s42438-020-00207-3.

Jandrić, P., & Knox, J. (2022). The Postdigital Turn: Philosophy, Education, Research. *Policy Futures in Education, 20*(7), 780–795. 10.1177%2F14782103211062713.

Jochum, E. A., Demers, L-P., Vorn, B., Vlachos, E., Mcilvenny, P. B., & Raudaskoski, P. L. (2018). Becoming Cyborg: Interdisciplinary approaches for exoskeleton research. In *EVA Copenhagen 2018 – Politics of the Machines – Art and After* (pp. 1–9). [40] British Computer Society. Electronic Workshops in Computing Vol. EVA Copenhagen No. 2018. https://doi.org/10.14236/ewic/EVAC18.40.

Jones, D., Snider, C., Nassehi, A., Yon, J., & Hicks, B. (2020). Characterising the Digital Twin: A Systematic Literature Review. *CIRP Journal of Manufacturing Science and Technology, 29,* 36–52. https://doi.org/10.1016/j.cirpj.2020.02.002.

Jordan, B., & Henderson, A. (1995). Interaction Analysis: Foundations and Practice. *The Journal of the Learning Sciences, 4*(1), 39–103. https://doi.org/10.1207/s15327809jls0401_2.

Karadechev, P., Kanstrup, A. M., & Davidsen, J. (2021). Digital Producers with Cognitive Disabilities: Participatory Video Tutorials as a Strategy for Supporting Digital Abilities and Aspirations. In C. Ardito, R. Lanzilotti, A. Malizia, H. Petrie, A. Piccinno, G. Desolda, &

K. Inkpen (Eds.), *Human-Computer Interaction - INTERACT 2021* (pp. 170–191). Cham: Springer. https://doi.org/10.1007/978-3-030-85623-6_12.

Kasapakis, V., & Dzardanova, E. (2022). Virtual Reality Learning Environments: Using High-Fidelity Avatars to Enhance Distance Learning Experience. *Interactive Learning Environments*. https://doi.org/10.1080/10494820.2022.2146140.

Kitchin, R., Lauriault, T. P., & McArdle, G. (2015). Knowing and Governing Cities through Urban Indicators, City Benchmarking and Real-Time Dashboards. *Regional Studies, Regional Science, 2*(1), 6–28. https://doi.org/10.1080/21681376.2014.983149.

Kosko, K. W., Ferdig, R. E., & Zolfaghari, M. (2021). Preservice Teachers' Professional Noticing when Viewing Standard and 360 Video. *Journal of Teacher Education, 72*(3), 284–297. https://doi.org/10.1177/0022487120939544.

Lindwall, O., & Ekström, A. (2012). Instruction-in-Interaction: The Teaching and Learning of a Manual Skill. *Human Studies, 35*(1), 27–49. https://doi.org/10.1007/s10746-012-9213-5.

Lotker, S., & Gough, R. (2013). On Scenography: Editorial. *Performance Research, 18*(3), 3–6. https://doi.org/10.1080/13528165.2013.818306.

McIlvenny, P. (2018). Inhabiting Spatial Video And Audio Data: Towards A Scenographic Turn In The Analysis Of Social Interaction. *Social Interaction. Video-Based Studies of Human Sociality, 2*(1). https://doi.org/10.7146/si.v2i1.110409.

McIlvenny, P. (2020). Virtual Cameras, Avatars and Real Footage of a Focus Group Staged in SQUIVE. https://doi.org/10.5281/ZENODO.3954026.

McIlvenny, P. (2020a). The Future Of 'Video' In Video-Based Qualitative Research Is Not 'Dumb' Flat Pixels! Exploring Volumetric Performance Capture And Immersive Performative Replay. *Qualitative Research*, 146879412090546. https://doi.org/10.1177/1468794120905460.

McIlvenny, P. (2020b). New Technology And Tools To Enhance Collaborative Video Analysis *QuiViRR: Qualitative Video Research Reports, 1*, a0001–a0001. https://doi.org/10.5278/ojs.quivirr.v1.2020.a0001.

McIlvenny, P., & Davidsen, J. (2017). A Big Video Manifesto: Re-sensing Video and Audio. *Nordicom Information, 39*(2), 15–21.

McIlvenny, P., & Davidsen, J. (2023). Beyond Video: Using Practice-based VolCap Analysis to Understand Analytical Practices Volumetrically. In P. Haddington (Ed.), *Methodological explorations in and for EMCA: Emerging directions for the study of social order*. London: Routledge.

McIlvenny, P., Davidsen, J., Christensen, N. H., Tanderup, S. H., & Kovács, A. B. (2021). AVA360VR: Annotate, Visualise, Analysis 360 Video in Virtual Reality. https://vbn.aau.dk/da/publications/ava360vr-annotate-visualise-analysis-360-video-in-virtual-reality. Accessed 20 January 2020.

McIlvenny, P., Davidsen, J. G., Kovács, A. B., & Stein, A. (2022). DOTE: Distributed Open Transcription Environment. Aalborg: Github. www.dote.aau.dk. Accessed 30 November 2022.

Mehan, H. (1979). *Learning Lessons: Social Organization in the Classroom*. Cambridge, MA: Harvard University Press.

Mondada, L., Monteiro, D. T., & Tekin, B. S. (2022). Collaboratively Videoing Mobile Activities. *Visual Studies*. https://doi.org/10.1080/1472586X.2022.2086614.

Paulsen, L., Davidsen, J., & Steier, R. (2022). "Do you see what we see?" – Perspective-taking Across Realities. In A. Weinberger, W. Chen, D. Hernández-Leo, & B. Chen (Eds.), *CSCL2022 conference proceedings*. Hiroshima: International Society of the Learning Sciences.

Pink, S. (2015). *Doing Sensory Ethnography*. London: Sage.

Pink, S. (2022). Methods for Researching Automated Futures. *Qualitative Inquiry, 28*(7), 747–753. https://doi.org/10.1177/10778004221096845.

Pink, S., Sumartojo, S., Lupton, D., & Heyes LaBond, C. (2017). Empathetic Technologies: Digital Materiality and Video Ethnography. *Visual Studies, 32*(4), 371–381. https://doi.org/10.1080/1472586X.2017.1396192.

Pink, S., Berg, M., Lupton, D., & Ruckenstein, M. (Eds.). (2022). *Everyday Automation: Experiencing and Anticipating Emerging Technologies*. London: Routledge. https://doi.org/10.4324/9781003170884.

Pirker, J., & Dengel, A. (2021). The Potential of 360° Virtual Reality Videos and Real VR for Education—A Literature Review. *IEEE Computer Graphics and Applications*, *41*(4), 76–89. https://doi.org/10.1109/MCG.2021.3067999.

Possible Bodies, Pujals, B., Rocha, J., Snelting, F., Seifee, S., Malevé, N., Niquille, S. C, Dada, M., Langley, P., Pritchard, H. V., Ward, K., Spec Boiron, S., Huyghebaert, P., Morrison, R. R., The Underground Division, & Berends, M. (Eds.) (2022). *Volumetric Regimes: Material Cultures of Quantified Presence*. London: Open Humanities Press.

Radianti, J., Majchrzak, T. A., Fromm, J., & Wohlgenannt, I. (2020). A Systematic Review of Immersive Virtual Reality Applications for Higher Education: Design Elements, Lessons Learned, and Research Agenda. *Computers & Education*, *147*, 103778. https://doi.org/10.1016/j.compedu.2019.103778.

Rancière, J. (2011). *The Emancipated Spectator*. London: Verso.

Rosa, H. (2013). *Social Acceleration: A New Theory of Modernity*. Trans. J. Trejo-Mathys. New York: Columbia University Press.

Ryberg, T., Davidsen, J., Bernhard, J., & Larsen, M. C. (2021). Ecotones: a Conceptual Contribution to Postdigital Thinking. *Postdigital Science and Education*, *3*(2), 407–424. https://doi.org/10.1007/s42438-020-00213-5.

Sacks, H. (1995). *Lectures on Conversation: Volumes I & II*. Oxford: Blackwell.

Sormani, P. (2016). Practice-based Video Analysis: A position Statement. *SocietàMutamentoPolitica*, *7*(14), 103–120. https://doi.org/10.13128/SMP-19698.

Steier, R., & Kersting, M. (2019). Metaimagining and Embodied Conceptions of Spacetime. *Cognition and Instruction*, *37*(2), 145–168. https://doi.org/10.1080/07370008.2019.1580711.

Tabački, N. (2021). Into the Nebula: Embodied Perception of Scenography in Virtual Environments. *Performance Research*, *26*(3), 9–16. https://doi.org/10.1080/13528165.2021.1977491.

Vatanen, A., Spets, H., Siromaa, M., Rauniomaa, M., & Keisanen, T. (2022). Experiences in Collecting 360° Video Data and Collaborating Remotely in Virtual Reality. *QuiViRR: Qualitative Video Research Reports*, *3*, a0005. https://doi.org/10.54337/ojs.quivirr.v3.2022.a0005.

Vygotsky, L. (1978). *Mind in Society: The Development of Higher Psychological Processes*. Cambridge, MA: Harvard University Press.

Williamson, B. (2017). *Big Data in Education: The Digital Future of Learning, Policy and Practice*. Thousand Oaks, CA: SAGE.

Wise, A. F., Knight, S., & Shum, S. B. (2021). Collaborative Learning Analytics. In U. Cress, C. Rosé, A. F. Wise, & J. Oshima (Eds.), *International Handbook of Computer-Supported Collaborative Learning* (pp. 425–443). Cham: Springer. https://doi.org/10.1007/978-3-030-65291-3_23.

Part III
Postdigital Data and Algorithms

Postdigital Student Bodies – Mapping the Flesh-Electric

Paul Prinsloo ⓘ

1 Prologue

Understanding student learning, and particularly student success or attrition, has been part and parcel of twenty-first century educational research since the early models of Spady (1970) and Tinto (1975) that emerged from discourses about student 'mortality' referring to the failure of students to stay in college (McNeely 1938). The use of the notion of 'mortality' to describe students' failure to remain in college or university, however peculiar, was an established diagnostic term in, among others, the work of Bourdieu and Passeron (1990), referring to 'the differential educational mortality rate of the different social classes' (154). The notion of describing (and counting) students' *bodies* (alive or dead) to explain student success became infused with research into student learning. Spady (1970), for example, relied on Durkheim's Theory of Suicide to explain students' decision to drop out of college. According to this theory, suicide rates emerge from individual's relations within a particular group structure, and the levels of integration into groups (e.g., number and density of ties) and the 'controls and coordinates' of the collective's moral order over the individual (Mueller et al. 2021). The model developed by Tinto (1975) used Van Gennep's ethnographic research into rites of passage to propose a model for understanding student decisions to leave college.

One of the earliest reports on student mortality in the context of the United States is the report by McNeely (1938) on the characteristics of those 'bodies' that drop out of education in terms of gender (as binary), age, the home location of the body, the place of lodging, participation in extracurricular activities, and engagement in part-time work. McNeely (1938) does not refer to any rationale for specifically

P. Prinsloo (✉)
University of South Africa, Pretoria, South Africa
e-mail: prinsp@unisa.ac.za

© The Author(s), under exclusive license to Springer Nature   139
Switzerland AG 2023
P. Jandrić et al. (eds.), *Constructing Postdigital Research*, Postdigital Science
and Education, https://doi.org/10.1007/978-3-031-35411-3_8

selecting these characteristics but mentions that the Office of Education 'furnished the specific items for which information was to be collected by the institutions' (2).

The centrality of student *bodies* in thinking about student success and attrition took an uncomfortable turn from the 1940s to the 1960s if one attended Yale, Mount Holyyoke, Vassar, Smith, or Princeton (Rosenbaum 1995). Nude 'posture photos' were taken of all freshmen as part of their orientation. Students' future achievement was linked to the shape and dimensions of their bodies. Even more disturbing, is that this 'research' was envisaged to eventually 'control and limit the production of inferior and useless organisms' or worse, 'enforce better breeding – getting those in Exeter and Harvard men together with their corresponding Wellesley, Vassar and Radcliffe girls' (Prof Hersey in Rosenbaum 1995) (see also Belden-Adams 2022; Vertinsky 2007).

Documenting the preferred somatotype also meant defining the 'other'; the 'crooked backs of working (lower class) immigrants' (Vertinsky 2007: 300). As such, physique became destiny (Vertinsky 2002, 2007). Though there is no evidence that somatotyping has been used to determine admission into higher education or to determine risk of failure or educational mortality, there is ample evidence of how other bodily characteristics such as race, age and gender have been used and continue to be used to classify students' potential and risk (e.g., Clancy and Goastellec 2007).

2   Introduction

Lawn (2013: 11) points out that nation states started to produce education data 'from the mid 1850s or thereabouts' and the 'measurement of education became a defining element of the governing of education'. According to Lawn (2013: 11), the need for educational data expanded exponentially since the 1950s 'with the use of testing and selecting, comparisons and productivity audits, and the rise of powerful digital technologies'. Since then, and especially after Covid-19, the digitization and datafication of higher education expanded and offer, *inter alia,* potential increased understanding of students' learning processes, their progress as well as opportunities to offer personalized and just-in-time support (Selwyn and Gašević 2020). The increased digitization of higher education however also results in concerns about the ever-increasing digital surveillance of students and the seemingly insatiable data hunger by data brokers, Silicon Valley, and learning platform providers (Fawns et al. 2021; Gourlay 2022; Williamson et al. 2020).

While concerns about the datafication of learning should not be taken lightly, it is easy to forget that the collection of student data has always been part of education (see Lawn 2013). Monitoring students' learning through class attendance, as well as formative and summative assessment, were some of the ways educators and institutions used to ensure, *inter alia*, students' engagement and achievement of the learning outcomes. Dan Knox (2010) distinguishes between monitoring and surveillance by claiming that while both actions rely on data, not all monitoring counts as surveillance, but all surveillance entails monitoring.

Prior to the digitization of education, data were collected at various parts of students' journey and the type and range of data included, but were not limited to, demographic and prior learning data at registration, students' class attendance, formative and summative assessment, as well as other data such as library use, disciplinary records, extracurricular activities, etc. Depending on the administrative efficiencies of the educational context, the data were collected and stored in centrally administered files, teachers' lockers, filing systems, and were also found in manually filled in registers, attendance sheets, access records kept in a variety of formats and locations. While it is obvious that many of current concerns about student data e.g., privacy, bias in the interpretation and use of data, and data leaks and sharing of data with unauthorized individuals and organizations have become germane to *digital* education, these issues have also been part of predigital education.

Fast forward to the first Learning Analytics and Knowledge (LAK) conference in Banff, Canada, when learning analytics was defined as 'the measurement, collection, analysis and reporting of data about learners and their contexts, for purposes of understanding and optimising learning and the environments in which it occurs' (Long et al. 2011). It is interesting to note that the context and rationale for learning analytics are stated as follows:

> Learning institutions and corporations make little use of the data learners 'throw off' in the process of accessing learning materials, interacting with educators and peers, and creating new content. In an age where educational institutions are under growing pressure to reduce costs and increase efficiency, analytics promises to be an important lens through which to view and plan for change at course and institutions levels. (Long et al. 2011) (emphasis added)

3 Postdigital Learning Analytics

Since 2011, the field of learning analytics has grown (if not matured) and with the naturalisation of digital teaching and learning due to Covid-19 (Williamson 2021), the 'digital' (in education) has become like the air we breathe, and the water in which fishes swim. Our offline and online educational lives, as well as our teaching and learning became inseparable resulting in a realization that the 'the digital is noticed only by its absence, not its presence' (Jandrić et al. 2018). The continued use of notions of 'offline' and 'online' is becoming untenable and it seems more appropriate to speak of 'onlife' (Floridi 2015). As such 'the postdigital no longer opposes the virtual or cyber world to the world of face-to-face experience. The digital is integrated and imbricated with our everyday actions and interactions.' (Feenberg 2019: 8).

This corresponds with Hayes (2021: 6) who states: 'The overlap and parallels across physical and virtual environments, as well as across space and time, are more aptly observable now in the notion of a postdigital society that all of us inhabit.' Lewis (2020: 265) therefore suggests that '[i]nstead of assuming as a starting point a dichotomy between analog and digital educational forms of life, it assumes that they are always already plugged into one another: *a flesh electric*' (emphasis added). While Lewis (2020) does not expand on the notion of the 'flesh electric', he uses it in his argument to describe how the analog ('flesh') and the digital ('electric') are inseparable. The notion of postdigital learning analytics may therefore help us 'to complicate the terms "digital" and "analog", particularly in the humanities and social sciences' (Cramer and Jandrić 2021: 985).

Proceeding from the entanglement of the physical and the digital, we must consider not only the entanglements of inequalities found in the physical realm with the digital, but also digital inequalities' entanglement within the physical. As such, '[d]igital inequality is a pluralistic construct, multidimensional, and contextual' (Kuhn et al. 2023). How do we make sense of this 'flesh electric' in the context where 'abysmal inequality in broadband access and educational gaps in the ability to operate a digital culture tend to reproduce and amplify class, ethnic, race, age, and gender structures of social domination between countries and within countries' (Castells 2009: 57)? And, if technology 'has built the house in which we all live' and where '[m]ore and more of human life takes place within its walls, so that today there is hardly any human activity that does not occur within this house' (Frankli 2004: 10), how do we account for those who enter this house through the backdoor, whether as slaves or hackers? How do we make sense of students' digital lives when their digital lives are irreversibly entangled in intergenerational material legacies of inequality? (See the work on data poverty by Hayes et al. 2022.)

The focus of this chapter is to reconsider learning analytics' focus on and beliefs surrounding students' digital data as proxies for their learning without considering, for example, the unevenness in digital access and the entanglement of students' digital and physical lives or their 'flesh electric' the implications for our understanding, explanation, prediction, and prescription of student learning. The chapter unfolds as follows: I will firstly share a personal sensemaking of the changing datascape in higher education before looking at evidence regarding nondigital data – the oral, analog, and non-digitized student data in learning analytics. From this basis I proceed to map notion of postdigital data and the tentative contours of postdigital learning analytics.

4 Making Sense of the Changing Datascape in Higher Education

If student data has always been part and parcel of teaching and learning (see Lawn 2013), how do we understand the evolution of the use of student data in higher education specifically and what are the implications for understand the 'flesh electric' in education?

There are several differences pertaining to the collection, analysis and use of student data resulting from the digitization and subsequent intensification of the datafication of higher education (see Table 1). The differences refer to (1) data sources; (2) data formats; (3) who/what did/does the collection and analysis of the data; (4) who/what used/uses the data; (5) the purpose of the collection of data; (6) the temporal aim; (7) scope of data collection; and (8) oversight and governance.

Table 1 The evolution of student data collection and analysis in higher education

	Aspect of student data collection	Predigital education	Digital education
1	**Data sources**	Specific 'points' of collection such as student enquiries, registration, formative and summative assessment.	Continuous, directed, gifted, and automated collection of data from a range of data sources/systems – student administration, learning management system (LMS), sources outside of the LMS (e.g., multimodal data (Garaizar and Guenaga 2014).
2	**Data format**	Oral and analog data.	A combination of oral, analog, and digital data noting that only digital data and digitized data are used (e.g., Rodriguez-Triana et al. 2016).
3	**Who/what did/does the collection, analysis?**	Humans – Researchers, educators, administrators.	Plus … supervised and unsupervised algorithmic decision-making systems (Prinsloo et al. 2023a, b).
4	**Who/what uses the data?**	Humans – Researchers, educators, administrators. Institutions. Departments. National bodies.	Plus… Data brokers/cartels. Platform providers. Venture capital (e.g., Komljenovic 2021; Lamdan 2023; Prinsloo et al. 2023a; Thompson and Prinsloo 2023).
5	**Purpose of collection of data**	Reporting purposes, operational planning on cohort, group level by management and institutional researchers. Descriptive, diagnostic, predictive, and prescriptive on group/cohort level.	Plus… individualized, often real-time use of data to inform pedagogy, curriculum, assessment, student support by faculty, students and support staff. Data-as-service, commercialization of data (e.g., Prinsloo 2017a, b, 2020; Prinsloo et al. 2022).
6	**Temporal aim**	Retrospective/historical data to make predictions regarding operations, future enrollments, and resource allocation on institutional level.	Plus … real-time data for real-time interventions. Real-time collection and use with analyses shaping what is remembered, as well as immediate and long-term futures (e.g., Thompson and Prinsloo 2023).
7	**Scope of data collection**	Data needed to determine admission, student advising, course selection, monitoring course progress and achievement of course outcomes.	Plus… geolocation and a range of multimodal data – emotions, eye tracking, brain activity, etc. (e.g., Garaizar and Guenaga 2014).

(continued)

Table 1 (continued)

	Aspect of student data collection	Predigital education	Digital education
8	**Oversight and governance**	*Administrative* use of data was informed by keeping files and data in secure cabinets. Access control to data was most probably governed on a need-to-know-basis. Data collection, analysis, and use for *research purposes* governed by ethics review boards (ERBs) and policies.	*All* collection, analysis and use of personal data protected and governed by (national and/or regional legislation (e.g., GDPR). Data collection, analysis and use for *research purposes* governed by Ethics Review Boards (ERBs), and policies. All digital platforms have Privacy and Fair Use policies (often obscured in legalese, long, etc.). The exchange with data brokers, and combination of personal data from a variety of sources by commercial platform providers makes the definition of 'personal data' and 'identity' as related to a specific physical person difficult if not untenable (e.g., Prinsloo et al. 2023a; Willis et al. 2016).

Underpinning Table 1 is Kitchin's (2014a) distinction between three sources of data namely directed, automated, and volunteered data. Directed data 'are generated by traditional forms of surveillance, wherein the gaze of the technology is focused on a person or place by a *human* operator' (Kitchin 2014a: 5) (emphasis added) such as, in the case of predigital education, points of registration, formative and summative assessment, or surveys and traditional research. The second source of data is automated data is where 'data are generated as an inherent, automatic function of the device or system' (Kitchin 2014a: 5). In predigital times it is hard to imagine automated data sources, while in digital education the automatic collection and analysis of data is integral from pre-enrolment to post-enrolment. Interestingly, the automated gathering and collection of data can also be *directed* – harvesting specific data points, or specific behavioral data. The last source of data, according to Kitchin (2014a: 5), is 'volunteered data' referring to data 'gifted by users' such as, in the case of higher education, sharing of information on discussion forums, comments on social media, and/or email communication to the university (also see Thompson and Prinsloo 2023).

Despite the possible value added by looking at the evolution of student data collection and analysis as presented in Table 1, there is a danger that it perpetuates thinking in terms of binaries – predigital and digital. As indicated in the preceding section, looking at Table 1 through the lens of the *postdigital* petitions us to appreciate the intersections of oral, analog, digital, and digitized data at various points in students' learning journeys.

While the definition of learning analytics explicitly makes mention of students' *digital* data, this chapter is an invitation to think of what we miss when we only consider the digital and even more, when we think that students' digital lives are separate and separable from their bodily entanglements in the nexus of human and non-human actors, as well as political, economic, social, environmental, legal, and technological relations and forces.

5 The Oral, Analog, and Non-Digitized Student Data in Learning Analytics

While it falls outside the scope of this chapter to provide the findings of a scoping review, adhering to PRISMA guidelines (e.g., Cooper et al. 2021), a tentative, exploratory search on the collection, analysis, and use of student data *prior* to the official advent of learning analytics with the first Learning Analytics and Knowledge Conference in 2011 using the following search string – ['student data' AND 'higher education' NOT 'learning analytics'] [no limitation on dates or source type] did not yield any appropriate results. The search string – ['student' AND 'analog* data' AND 'higher education'] yielded relatively disappointing results with only Marcum-Dietrich and Ford (2002) reporting on the role of computers to collect student analog data and converting the data into digital input, resulting in a graphical model that can be used to improve teaching.

So, are there any traces in the early history of learning analytics of any consideration of oral, the analog, and/or non-digitized teaching and learning data or of the entanglement of students' digital data with their being-bodies-in-contexts?

5.1 Learning Analytics: A Short Early History

While the emergence of learning analytics as a distinct research focus and practice is officially marked as having taken place at the first Learning Analytics and Knowledge Conference in 2011 in Banff, Canada, the term 'learning analytics' had been used *prior* to 2011. Three of the earliest references to 'learning analytics' are found in articles by Boggon (2004), Retalis et al. (2006), and a presentation by Siemens and Graf (2010) on 'Learning analytics: Personalizing and adapting the learning process' at Athabasca University.

Interestingly, Boggon (2004: 12) does not refer to learning analytics from the context of education, but rather from business/industry and states: 'Just as companies have learned to measure the effectiveness of their sales and marketing programs it is also possible to measure the effectiveness of learning and human capital.' In the context of networked learning environments, Retalis et al. (2006: 2) refer to Learning Management Systems (LMSs) as allowing access to learning data and with the use of 'specialised analysis tools that collect actions of the users' and 'provide efficiently feedback to their users (either learners, lecturers, or evaluators)'. While the use of basic access logs may provide lecturers insights into which course materials are accessed and by whom, it is only when combined with 'data from a detailed and reasonably accurate interpretation of a learners' interaction with the peers, the use of the provided resources/objects as well as with data from content analysis' (Retalis et al. 2006: 2) that insights would emerge.

Bach (2010: 1) also refers to the fact that the use of advanced analytics by major industries to support their decision-making and goals served as stimulus for higher education institutions to adapt these methods 'to target fund raising, inform enrolment decisions, target marketing efforts, improve student support processes, and to better understand retention/persistence patterns'. Combined with efforts by regional and national bodies to focus on measurable outcomes, learning analytics emerged (Bach 2010).

Interestingly, neither Boggon (2004) nor Bach (2010) refer to the fact that collecting and using student data have always been part of education (e.g., Lawn 2013), but they emphasize the need to transfer data practices from industry and the world of business, to education. While Bach (2010) mentions different kinds of student data (e.g., test scores, class grades, demographic and psychographic data, learning styles, characteristics or preferences, data LMS/CMS activity data, as well as survey data), he does not refer to any nondigital or analog data.

In another two articles pre-dating the formal launch of learning analytics in 2011, Worsley and Blikstein (2010) and Knox (2010) link learning analytics to forms of assessment. Worsley and Blikstein (2010: 1) refer to learning analytics as 'a set of multi-modal sensory inputs, that can be used to predict, understand and quantify student learning' serving the purpose to assist educators to 'adhere to learning recommendations when they are given the proper tools'. It is noteworthy that in this early article, the authors refer to one of the modalities of learning analytics namely, speech – 'leveraging the tools of text and speech analysis, we are able to identify domain independent markers of expertise' (Worsley and Blikstein 2010: 1).

In a nod to the predigital era, these authors state that advanced tools have become available 'to truly measure the nature of student progress that takes place' in order 'to study learning processes in large scales, *instead of simply looking at learning products'* (Worsley and Blikstein 2010: 2) (italics added). Reporting on the use of these different types of data in this research is one of the first instances of 'multimodal' data in the context of learning analytics – a year before the official launch of learning analytics in 2011.

Interestingly, Lodge (2011) refers to a 'learning health framework' in his use of an epidemiological approach to understanding student success. Such as approach, according to Lodge (2011: 2), 'does not take a deficit approach to understanding outcomes. Good health is not just about increasing life expectancy, it is also about enhancing day-to-day living.' The framework refers to a number of indicators of 'learning health' as well as data sources – and it is important to note that none of the data sources are nondigital. Lodge and Lewis (2012) also refer to early reports of the collection of digital student data from learning management systems, and the use of data from the National Survey of Student Engagement, a student, self-assessment survey (Kuh 2001). Despite a brief mention of the research by

B. F. Skinner, there is no recognition of the use of data before the digital era or early educational research.

In the early learning analytics literature, it is rather surprising not to have found any consideration of the long history of the use of analog data prior to the emergence of learning analytics, such as, but not limited to, educational data and statistics (e.g., Lawn 2013) and research in behavioural psychology such as the work by B. F. Skinner (Lindsley 1990). Early literature in learning analytics (as discussed above) do, however, refer to evidence-based management practices in industry (Boggon 2004), and the corporate sector (Bach 2010) prompted a consideration of the looking for and use of evidence to improve learning.

Evidence-based education (EBE) links to the development of evidence-based management (EBM) which emerged in the medical establishment. Pfeffer and Sutton (2006: 1) report on EBM as 'a bold new way of thinking [that] has taken the medical establishment by storm in the past decade'. These authors therefore proposed that '[i]t's time to start an evidence-based movement in the ranks of managers'. Pfeffer and Sutton conclude that in order to become evidence-based, managers need to 'demand evidence' (2006: 7), 'examine logic' and 'treat the organization as an unfinished prototype' (9), and embrace 'the attitude of wisdom' (10). They warn that '[e]vidence-based practice changes power dynamics, replacing formal authority, reputation, and intuition *with data*' (1) (emphasis added).

Very interesting is the finding by Reay et al. (2009: 10) that the earliest publication regarding EBM was in 1948 and focused on 'technology decision making in industries reliant on primary research in the basic sciences'. According to Reay et al. (2009), Drucker's (1955) paper was the first to map the central characteristics and aims of 'management science'. The growth in EBM is traced to have started in 1998, spiking in between 2005 and 2008 (Reay et al. 2009). Despite the increased academic interest in EBM, the majority of evidence (53%) provided in these publications were 'based on the author's opinion, sometimes backed up by anecdotes' (11). None of the articles in this study produced evidence based on 'large-scale studies adhering to principles of random assignment or meta-analysis of previously published research' (Reay et al. 2009; see also Briner et al. 2009).

To what extent EBM informed the growth in institution research (IR) is open for interpretation (Taylor et al. 2013). These authors acknowledge the 'clamour for evidence-based decision making … among politicians and university leaders' they warn that data should 'not [be] used as excuses to avoid individual or institutional responsibilities' (71). Elliot (2001) reflects on evidence-based practice and its claims to improve educational outcomes and the 'obsession' with finding out 'what works' through experimental research.

While it falls outside the scope of this chapter to consider Elliot's criticism against evidence-based practice and his proposal for research-based teaching, it does have implications for our thinking about *data* – whether analog and/or digital. According to Elliot (2001), the question is 'what counts as evidence' and he proposes that evidence is not the 'instrumental effectiveness of the strategies employed to secure certain learning outcomes, but evidence about the extent to which teaching strategies are ethically consistent with *educational* ends' (570) (emphasis from the original) (see also Biesta 2007, 2010; Beer 2016; Fawns et al. 2021). So, what (data) counts as evidence?

6 Postdigital Data

As data is central to evidence, as well as all the discourses surrounding evidence, we move now to consider what postdigital data looks like. As far as I could ascertain, there is no 'definition' of postdigital data which should not come as a surprise considering the lack of definition of postdigital as phenomenon (Feenberg 2019). If the notion of the postdigital is not defined or definable, why would we expect the proposition of postdigital data to be defined?

The first attempt, as far as I could establish to map the notion of postdigital data, is by Hayes et al. (2022) who propose that 'data takes many different forms in postdigital society, and all of these are relevant, in matters of digital inequality and disadvantage' (237). Many policies and strategies do not consider 'the complex forms that data now takes. Nor do they address the diverse and unequal ways in which people have capacity to interact with, or understand their relations with, data.' (238) These authors refer to the new field of Human-Data Interaction (HDI) and its three key tenets: agency, legibility, and negotiability focusing not only on 'how humans recognise and interact with the data they are creating in physical and virtual spaces, [but also] their rights in relation to data created about them' (329).

If data 'takes many different forms', as proposed by Hayes et al. (2022: 237), what are the implications of only valuing digital data? How much agency do humans have to negotiate meaning over their data? How it is used to create data-doubles or digital twins (Haggerty and Ericson 2000; Ruckenstein 2014), that take on lives of their own creating fluid, intersectional digital layers with/in physical bodies/lives? And more importantly, what is considered to be 'real', in a context where '[k]nowledge is not produced about the world anymore, but from the digital world' (Rouvroy 2013: 4)?

Postdigital data also highlights 'more hidden forms of data about individual citizens' are now collected 'in digital systems, whether they themselves interact online, or not' (Hayes et al. 2022: 240). The notion of digital exclusion links to 'data poverty' highlighting 'matter of affordability, infrastructure, choices, privacy and security, quantity, skills, and usability' (241). Even when people are provided with access to hardware and software, as well as skills training to increase employability, these individuals do not develop '*agency* in relation to their data, or how *legibility* or *negotiability* will be improved' (242) (emphases from the original). There is also no evidence of forms of resistance in relation to personal data and human rights.

In addition to the work by Hayes et al. (2022), there are also other glimpses towards what postdigital data might resemble, even for a fleeting moment in postdigital time. As early as 2010, Lewis and Kahn (2010), proposed the notion of *exopedagogy* that is founded on the belief that the gap between human and non-human animals is 'an artifact of the anthropological machine underwriting the educational project writ large … reminding us that the cut separating hand from hoof is never so clear, precise, or stable as one might want it to be?' (Lewis 2020: 265). The porousness of the boundaries between human and non-human animals is also found between the analog and the digital which are, as referred to in the Introduction, '*always already* plugged into one another' resulting in a 'flesh electric' (Lewis 2020: 265) (emphasis in the original). To speak of analog data in opposition, or as supplement to digital data (or vice versa), ignores the implications of Lewis' (2020) understanding of the postdigital. What is the digital other than the analog, however momentarily?

Massumi (2002) argues that the digital is 'actually a hybrid' (Griffin 2022: 52) and proposes that the digital is 'sandwiched between the analog functions [e.g., perceptions] allowing it to appear' (Massumi 2002: 135). As such, 'the digital must always be actualised in the analog and has not superseded it' (Griffin 2022: 52). The analog/digital distinction is an 'after-the-fact-illusion' (Geoghegan and Galloway 2021 in Griffin 2022: 52).

> In electronic terms, analog is infinite and continuous (a waveform) whereas digital is finite and discrete (a point) but digital circuits will have analog elements to allow them to interface and translate, and digital signals must be interpreted by our analog perception; so, it is necessarily interconnected, not oppositional. (Griffin 2022: 52)

As such, the digital and the analog are 'archipelagos that blur into one another' (Griffin 2022: 53 referring to the work of Eduard Glissant) (see also Geoghegan and Galloway 2021). *All is flesh and all is electric* – the postdigital 'evinces this entanglement and undermining of binaries' (Griffin 2022: 58). Destabilising Cartesian binaries is furthermore in line with the work of Karen Barad's theory of 'diffraction' – meaning 'cutting together apart' as an alternative and 'generative way to make distinctions' (Griffin 2022: 59).

While the above is anything but a comprehensive exposition of what can be thought of as the nature and scope of postdigital data, it is also important to consider postdigital data as *performative* in the context of higher education.

7   On the Contours of Postdigital Learning Analytics

Student learning, and students' learning journeys, are complex entanglements between physical, non-physical, and increasingly non-human actors and ecologies, intersectional inclusions, exclusions, and discriminations – which makes it hard, if not impossible to render a combination of data points in a students' learning journey as representing *the* student experience. Hayes (2021: 162) suggests that 'data can be rich and qualitative, as well as descriptive and summative, or it can be both, depending on how it is collected and with what purposes, in a cultural political economy'. In the context of higher education and specifically learning analytics, this data is limited to the digital or digitized, and the analysis of this data increasingly assumed to be authoritative, objective, revealing, panoramic, prophetic, and smart providing speedy and accessible information at the push of a button (Beer 2018; Williamson et al. 2021).

Learning analytics, as such, is 'a structuring device, not neutral, informed by current beliefs about what counts as knowledge and learning, coloured by assumptions about gender/race/ sexual orientation/ class/capital/literacy and in service of or perpetuating existing or new power relations' (Prinsloo and Slade 2017). The datafication of the students' learning experience often precludes and/or excludes alternative ways of description, of understanding, and intervention, and 'new identities [are] 'being ascribed to students where they routinely require therapeutic interventions to counter the emotionally difficult aspects of learning' (Hayes 2021: 162). Using (only) digital and digitized data to explain, and predict student experiences, does not only result in and depend on classifications of vulnerability and risks but also in skewed and incomplete accounts of students' learning.

Learning analytics currently allows institutions to narrate a particular understanding of students' learning based on what was digital or digitized, measurable, accessible and/or visible (on the LMS). As such this narration is a voice-over of students' experiences (Broughan and Prinsloo 2020; Prinsloo 2017a, b). The institutional narration of the student learning journey performs an act of ventriloquism where the learning journey is presented as a 'student voice', and as representing their journey, but actually, the voice is coming from somewhere else, from an increasingly black box at the intersections of human and non-human actors. Hayes (2021) warns that when students are understood and classified only in terms of their data, data become facts and 'facts (along with their associated metrics) can form a basis for all kinds of calculations and reasoning that can easily bypass the complications of human positionality' (163), resulting in an 'iron cage' (169) of the student journey. Institutions and regulatory bodies 'can no longer treat "data" as isolated from the interconnected cultural and technological spheres of civic life' (Hayes 2021: 65).

Hayes (2021) poignantly states that 'any generalised description of the 'shared trauma' of being a student along with a set of prescribed antidotes is not the same thing as an individual narrative from a person who has overcome challenges to learning' (163). Much of the current narratives in higher education emerging from the collection, analysis, and use of their data, focuses on what students did not do, lack, or don't have, or don't have enough of, or don't do enough of. Archer and Prinsloo (2020) refer to the early conceptual and empirical models (e.g., Spady 1970; Tinto 1975) on student success and state 'they made specific reference to what students lack, what they don't have resulting in them not fitting in' (Archer and Prinsloo 2020: 891). In their analysis of Spady's (1970) understanding of student drop-out, they identified several 'lacks' such as 'lack of exposure and mastery of the fundamental skills'; a lack of adaptability; lack of 'deep emotional commitments', 'self-esteem and self-confidence'; 'lack [of] insight and capacities for self-analytic, critical thinking'; 'a lack at least some of the attributes commonly associated with psychological maturity'; a lack of social support, a lack of integration, and 'a lack of consistent, intimate interaction with others'; and a lack of 'a sense of compatibility with the immediate social system' (Spady 1970 in Archer and Prinsloo 2020: 891). 'Belonging' or 'fitting in' focuses on only 'a single aspect of a person's identity, such as their gender or their race' without any consideration (or understanding) of students' identities and experiences being *intersectional* (Hayes 2021: 172) (emphasis added) (see Hayes 2021 for an analysis and critique of 'the student experience').

'Deficit models of understanding student ability in higher education often underpin institutional responses to students who do not correspond to the norm of often white, first-language English-speaking students.' (Broughan and Prinsloo 2020: 618) The way data are defined and selected, as well as the categories and the way the analyses are used, flow from an *ontological* stance of deficiency and of not *being* enough, resulting in 'hyphenated' identities (Broughan and Prinsloo 2020: 618) such as 'at-risk'. When deficit understandings of student identity and learning are combined with, and/or informs the design of learning analytics, it not only provides legitimacy of such deficit understandings, but potentially becomes self-fulfilling prophecies (Archer and Prinsloo 2020).

8   What Are the Contours of Postdigital Learning Analytics?

Understanding learning analytics as data ecology (Prinsloo et al. 2023a) points to the flows and different data interests as students' learning spills over outside the increasingly porous boundaries of institutional learning management systems (LMSs). While such an understanding does provide sobering views on students' data privacy and agency, as well as institutional data governance, the proposal by Prinsloo et al. (2023a, b) only refers to the digital, without regard for student data as 'flesh electric'.

Contrary to the approach by Prinsloo et al. (2023a, b), Fawns et al. (2021) propose 'an ecological view, in which evaluation must take account of those aspects of teaching, learning, and educational context, missing from digital data' (65). They propose 'the cross-fertilization of diverse kinds of data and non-datafied understandings, along with greater involvement of teachers and students in ways that enhance their agency and develop their evaluative judgement of the quality of educational practices' (65). Should an understanding of learning analytics not only consider the porous boundaries and digital layers and interests as proposed by Prinsloo et al. (2023a, b), but also consider the 'flesh electric' as suggested by Fawns et al. (2021), it will provide more holistic views of the complexity of students' learning, and help to destabilise deficit understandings of student agency and learning.

For example, when we use the 'flesh electric' as heuristic or point of departure, students' engagement data, assessment submissions, download histories, etc., cannot be understood as neither adequate proxy of their learning, potential and/or risk, nor representing the 'reality' of their learning worlds. *Their* data and *our* analysis and categorisation of their data is rather an invitation for a discussion with students, not as an act of benevolence, or nosiness, but as recognition of students' data sovereignty (Prinsloo and Slade 2018). Recognising the impossibility to separate their digital data from physical lives, our collection and analysis of their digital data must take cognisance of us 'cutting together apart' (Griffin 2022: 59).

Postdigital learning analytics furthermore acknowledges and embraces education as an open recursive system and not a closed, laboratory setting where causal relations can be mapped and predicted without external inferences (Biesta 2007, 2010). The success of teaching and learning depends on much more than teachers' efforts (Fawns et al. 2021), or students' grit and effort (Credé et al. 2016; Fosnacht et al. 2019; Muenks et al. 2017), and emerge from a range of often mutually constitutive factors, human and non-human actors in the nexus between students' habitus, dispositions and prior learning experiences, the institutional and disciplinary contexts, cultures and efficiencies and broader current and inter-generational societal structures and relations (e.g., Subotzky and Prinsloo 2011). Postdigital learning analytics do not only consider the framing of student learning data as technological, economical, ethical, spatial, and philosophical, but also understand that student learning data do not exist 'independently of the ideas, instruments, practices, contexts and knowledges used to generate, process and analyse them' (Kitchin 2014b: 2). As such, Fawns et al. (2021: 70) call for 'analytics that are part of a wider, ecological view of education, where relationships and holistic conceptions of practice are valued above individual variables'.

Where learning analytics inherently focuses on the measurement, collection, analysis, and use of *student* data, postdigital learning analytics student outcomes are not 'reduced to the merits of individual elements' but necessitates 'a holistic analysis of the wider system' (Fawns et al. 2021: 72). 'In a postdigital ecology, data is only one element, and is entangled in nondigital (physical, social, economic, political) activity.' (Fawns et al. 2021: 72; see also Subotzky and Prinsloo 2011). We must consider datafied as well as non-datafied understandings of student learning as part of a broader educational deeply material ecology consisting of human and increasing, autonomous nonhuman actors.

Taylor (2019) proposes that feminist new materialism allows us to recognize 'human and nonhuman bodies are entangled and co-constitutive equal partners' (39) and where 'agency is not an attribute of a person, is not possessed by individuals as free will but is, rather, an ongoing becoming and reconfiguring of practices of mattering, in both senses of the word' (42) (referring to the work of Karen Barad). Analysing students' engagement data in combination with their demographic and previous learning data necessitate that we accept students' intensity and quality of interaction not as the result of their individual agency and effort, but rather as emerging from 'intra-action' (Barad 2014) between human, non-human, institutional, disciplinary, environmental, political, social, economic, legal and technological factors and forces (Subotzky and Prinsloo 2011).

In essence, following Taylor's (2019) and Barad's (2014) proposal of 'intra-action' instead of interaction, the 'flesh electric' in postdigital learning analytics does not refer to the interaction between, on the one hand, what students do (or don't do) and what institutions do or don't do, and on the other hand, digital and nondigital and non-digitized data. Students' learning is a material-discursive phenomenon – *the flesh electric* – that does not consist of 'separate and separable entities prior to their coming together' (Taylor 2019: 42).

9   (In)Conclusions

There is a rich and long history of research into understanding student success and attrition. For very long researchers were looking for (collections of) variables, mostly focused on student demographics, dispositions, orientation (e.g., grit), and time as predictors for 'fit' or as basis for identifying students who become hyphened identities such as 'at-risk' (Broughan and Prinsloo 2020).

As higher education has become increasingly digitized and datafied, institutions have access to increased volumes, velocity of the flow and processing of data, and varieties and nuances of student digital data resulting in ever-more detailed data profiles used to understand, explain, predict, and prescribe student learning. These data profiles are based on the measurement, collection, analysis, and use of students' *digital* data and assumed authoritative and declarative power shaping student choices and futures. Learning analytics focuses on digital traces of students' actions or inactions, in combination with students' demographic, prior learning and other data (directed, automated, and/or gifted). Analog, oral, and other data are considered when digitized, often in experimental multimodal learning analytics research settings (Garaizar and Guenaga 2014). Even though one could celebrate the inclusion of other forms of data in multimodal learning analytics, the core attention of multimodal learning analytics is still one what *students* do or don't do in combination with, *inter alia*, their demographic, prior learning, and circumstantial data (e.g., peer group discussions).

In somewhat stark contrast, this chapter's proposal for considering the potential of *postdigital* learning analytics offers a different understanding of students' learning journeys (and education), the relation between the digital and the analog, and finally the notion of the 'flesh electric' to make sense of students' learning journeys as material-discursive phenomena. Postdigital learning analytics emerge from an understanding of education and students' learning journeys as relational, emerging in the nexus, or intra-action of broader societal (current and intergenerational) human and (automated) non-human relations and actors.

10   Epilogue

Bodies. Student bodies. Bodies producing data. Data becoming different bodies. Bodies that graduate. Bodies that don't.

Those bodies that, somehow, did not and still don't make it 'through' the system as expected in the expected minimum time, fascinated, and continue to fascinate educational researchers, policymakers, funders, data analysts, and increasingly data brokers, and sellers of analytic software providing one-stop solutions to occupied educational bureaucrats looking for interventions that work and provide a return-on-investment.

Bodies were/are seen as entering higher education, staying separate through their journeys but interacting with the institution, lecturers, support, admin, and other staff who also remained/remain separate. Throughout this journey, we collect(ed) interaction (digital and digitized) data through our directed and automated gaze, also not allowing the data students 'throw off' (Long et al. 2011) or gift to us, to go to waste. We use(d) the data to understand how bodies fit(ted) in, explain why some bodies didn't/don't, predict which bodies will (not) fit in, and prescribe steps to help bodies fit in. We measure(d) their postures, archive(d) and categorise(d) their documented vulnerabilities, before recording student mortality to whoever wanted/wants to know and then turn our gaze to new intakes using insights from performed autopsies of dead data bodies which we assumed were the same bodies we no longer see on campus.

Postdigital learning analytics, in following Hayes (2021), Lewis (2020), and Torres-Olave and Lee (2020), proposes a re-imagining of student positionality in the intersections of human and non-human actors where student identities are assumed to be 'complex and fluid', entangled in power relations and 'contextually bound' (Hayes 2021).

Acknowledgement I would like to acknowledge and thank the editorial team and reviewers for their critical engagement and support.

References

Archer, E., & Prinsloo, P. (2020). Speaking the unspoken in learning analytics: troubling the defaults. *Assessment & Evaluation in Higher Education*, *45*(6), 888–900. https://doi.org/1 0.1080/02602938.2019.1694863.

Bach, C. (2010). Learning analytics: Targeting instruction, curricula and student support. In *Proceedings of the 8th International Conference on Education and Information Systems, Technologies and Applications: EISTA 2010.* https://www.iiis.org/CDs2010/CD2010SCI/ EISTA_2010/PapersPdf/EA655ES.pdf. Accessed 13 March 2023.

Barad, K. (2014). Diffracting diffraction: Cutting together-apart. *parallax*, *20*(3), 168–187. https:// doi.org/10.1080/13534645.2014.927623.

Beer, D. (2016). *Metric power.* London: Palgrave Macmillan. https://doi. org/10.1057/978-1-137-55649-3.

Beer, D. (2018). *The data gaze: Capitalism, power and perception.* London, UK: Sage.

Belden-Adams, K. (2022). 'We did what we were told': The 'compulsory visibility' and de-empowerment of US College women in nude 'posture pictures', 1880–1940. *Miranda, 25.* https://doi.org/10.4000/miranda.44430.

Biesta, G. J. (2007). Why "what works" won't work: Evidence-based practice and the democratic deficit in educational research. *Educational theory*, *57*(1), 1–22. https://doi.org/10.1111/j.1741-54 46.2006.00241.x.

Biesta, G. J. (2010). Why 'what works' still won't work: From evidence-based education to value-based education. *Studies in philosophy and education*, *29*(5), 491–503. https://doi.org/10.1007/ s11217-010-9191-x.

Boggon, R. (2004). Analytics: understanding the economics of learning. *Training and Development in Australia*, *31*(4), 12–15.

Bourdieu, P., & Passeron, J-C. (1990). *Reproduction in education, society and culture.* Trans. R. Nice. London, UK: Sage.

Briner, R. B., Denyer, D., & Rousseau, D. M. (2009). Evidence-based management: concept clean-up time?. *Academy of management perspectives, 23*(4), 19–32. https://doi.org/10.5465/amp.23.4.19.

Broughan, C., & Prinsloo, P. (2020). (Re) centring students in learning analytics: in conversation with Paulo Freire. *Assessment & Evaluation in Higher Education, 45*(4), 617–628. https://doi.org/10.1080/02602938.2019.1679716.

Castells, M. (2009). *Communication power.* Oxford: Oxford University Press.

Clancy, P., & Goastellec, G. (2007). Exploring access and equity in higher education: Policy and performance in a comparative perspective. *Higher Education Quarterly, 61*(2), 136–154. https://doi.org/10.1111/j.1468-2273.2007.00343.x.

Cooper, S., Cant, R., Kelly, M., Levett-Jones, T., McKenna, L., Seaton, P., & Bogossian, F. (2021). An evidence- based checklist for improving scoping review quality. *Clinical Nursing Research, 30*(3), 230– 240. https://doi.org/10.1177/1054773819846024.

Cramer, F., & Jandrić, P. (2021). Postdigital: A term that sucks but is useful. *Postdigital Science and Education, 3*(3), 966–989. https://doi.org/10.1007/s42438-021-00225-9.

Credé, M., Tynan, M. C., & Harms, P. D. (2016). Much ado about grit: A meta-analytic synthesis of the grit literature. *Journal of Personality and Social Psychology, 111,* 492–511. https://doi.org/10.1037/pspp0000102.

Drucker, P. F. (1955). "Management Science" and the Manager. *Management Science, 1*(2), 115–126. https://doi.org/10.1287/mnsc.1.2.115.

Elliott, J. (2001). Making evidence-based practice educational. *British educational research journal, 27*(5), 555–574. https://doi.org/10.1080/01411920120095735.

Fawns, T., Aitken, G., & Jones, D. (2021). Ecological teaching evaluation vs the datafication of quality: Understanding education with, and around, data. *Postdigital Science and Education, 3*(1), 65–82. https://doi.org/10.1007/s42438-020-00109-4.

Feenberg, A. (2019). Postdigital or predigital?. *Postdigital Science and Education, 1*(1), 8–9. https://doi.org/10.1007/s42438-018-0027-2.

Floridi, L. (2015). *The onlife manifesto: Being human in a hyperconnected era.* Cham: Springer. https://doi.org/10.1007/978-3-319-04093-6.

Fosnacht, K., Copridge, K., & Sarraf, S. A. (2019). How valid is grit in the postsecondary context? A construct and concurrent validity analysis. *Research in Higher Education, 60,* 803–822. https://doi.org/10.1007/s11162-018-9524-0.

Franklin, U. M. (2004). *The real world of technology.* Toronto, ON: House of Anansi Press Inc.

Garaizar, P., & Guenaga, M. (2014). A multimodal learning analytics view of HTML5 APIs: technical benefits and privacy risks. In F. J. Garcia-Peñalvo (Ed.), *Proceedings of the Second International Conference on Technological Ecosystems for Enhancing Multiculturality* (pp. 275–281). New York, NY: Association for Computing Machinery. https://doi.org/10.1145/2669711.2669911.

Geoghegan, B. D., & Galloway, A. (2021). Shaky distinctions: A dialogue on the analog and the digital. *e-flux, 121.* https://www.e-flux.com/journal/121/423015/shaky-distinctions-a-dialogue-on-the-digital-and-the-analog/. Accessed 13 March 2023.

Gourlay, L. (2022). Surveillance and datafication in higher education: Documentation of the human. *Postdigital Science and Education.* https://doi.org/10.1007/s42438-022-00352-x.

Griffin, J. (2022). Aura in the post-digital: a diffraction of the curatorial archive. Doctoral dissertation. Sheffield: Sheffield Hallam University. https://doi.org/10.7190/shu-thesis-00481.

Haggerty, K. D., & Ericson, R. V. (2000). The surveillant assemblage. *The British Journal of Sociology, 51*(4), 605–622. https://doi.org/10.1080/00071310020015280.

Hayes, S. (2021). *Postdigital positionality. Developing powerful inclusive narratives for learning, teaching, research and policy in higher education.* Leiden: Brill.

Hayes, S., Connor, S., Johnson, M., & Jopling, M. (2022). Connecting cross-sector community voices: Data, disadvantage, and postdigital inclusion. *Postdigital Science and Education, 4*(2), 237–246. https://doi.org/10.1007/s42438-021-00251-7.

Jandrić, P., Knox, J., Besley, T., Ryberg, T., Suoranta, J., & Hayes, S. (2018). Postdigital science and education. *Educational Philosophy and Theory, 50*(10), 893–899. https://doi.org/10.108 0/00131857.2018.1454000.

Kitchin, R. (2014a). The real-time city? Big data and smart urbanism. *GeoJournal, 79,* 1–14. https://doi.org/10.1007/s10708-013-9516-8.

Kitchin, R. (2014b). *The data revolution.* London, UK: Sage.

Knox, D. (2010). Spies in the house of learning. Paper presented at Edge 2010: e-Learning: The horizon and beyond, 12–15 October. Newfoundland, CA: University of Newfoundland.

Komljenovic, J. (2021). The rise of education rentiers: Digital platforms, digital data and rents. *Learning, Media and Technology, 46*(3), 320–332. https://doi.org/10.1080/17439884.202 1.1891422.

Kuh, G. D. (2001). Assessing what really matters to student learning inside the national survey of student engagement. *Change: The Magazine of Higher Learning, 33*(3), 10–17. https://doi. org/10.1080/00091380109601795.

Kuhn, C., Khoo, S.-M., Czerniewicz, L., Lilley, W., Bute, S., Crean, A., Abegglen, S., Burns, T., Sinfield, S., Jandrić, P., Knox, J., & MacKenzie, A. (2023). Understanding Digital Inequality: A Theoretical Kaleidoscope. *Postdigital Science and Education.* https://doi.org/10.1007/ s42438-023-00395-8.

Lamdan, S. (2023). *Data cartels. The companies that control and monopolize our information.* Stanford, CA: Stanford University Press.

Lawn, M. (Ed.). (2013). *The rise of data in education systems: Collection, visualization and uses.* Symposium Books Limited.

Lewis, T. E. (2020). Everything you always wanted to know about being postdigital but were afraid to ask a vampire squid. *Postdigital Science and Education, 2*(2), 265–266. https://doi. org/10.1007/s42438-019-00082-7.

Lewis, T., & Kahn, R. (2010). *Education out of bounds: Reimagining cultural studies for a posthuman age.* Cham: Palgrave Macmillan. https://doi.org/10.1057/9780230117358.

Lindsley, O. R. (1990). Precision teaching: By teachers for children. *Teaching Exceptional Children, 22*(3), 10–15. https://doi.org/10.1177/004005999002200302.

Lodge, J. (2011). What if student attrition was treated like an illness? An epidemiological model for learning analytics. In *Proceedings of ASCILITE-Australian Society for Computers in Learning in Tertiary Education Annual Conference* (pp. 822–825). Tugun: Australasian Society for Computers in Learning in Tertiary Education. https://research-repository.griffith.edu.au/bit-stream/handle/10072/61188/95812_1.pdf?sequence=1. Accessed 27 March 2023.

Lodge, J., & Lewis, M. (2012). Pigeon pecks and mouse clicks: Putting the learning back into learning analytics. In M. Brown, M. Hartnett, & T. Stewart (Eds.), *Future challenges, sustainable futures. Proceedings Ascilite Wellington* (pp. 560–564).Tugun: Australasian Society for Computers in Learning in Tertiary Education. https://www.ascilite.org/confer-ences/Wellington12/2012/images/custom/lodge,_jason_-_pigeon_pecks.pdf. Accessed 27 March 2023.

Long, P. D., Siemens, G., Conole, G., & Gašević, D. (Eds.). (2011). *Proceedings of the 1st International Conference on Learning Analytics and Knowledge (LAK'11).* New York: Association for Computing Machinery.

Marcum-Dietrich, N. I., & Ford, D. J. (2002). The place for the computer is in the laboratory: An investigation of the effect of computer probeware on student learning. *Journal of Computers in Mathematics and Science Teaching, 21*(4), 361–379. https://www.learntechlib. org/primary/p/9527/. Accessed 13 March 2023.

Massumi, B. (2002). *Parables of the Virtual: Movement, Affect, Sensation.* Durham, NC & London, UK: Duke University Press.

McNeely, J. H. (1938). College student mortality (No. 11). Washington, DC: US Government Printing Office.

Mueller, A. S., Abrutyn, S., Pescosolido, B., & Diefendorf, S. (2021). The social roots of suicide: Theorizing how the external social world matters to suicide and suicide prevention. *Frontiers in psychology, 12.* https://doi.org/10.3389/fpsyg.2021.621569.

Muenks, K., Wigfield, A., Yang, J. S., & O'Neal, C. R. (2017). How true is grit? Assessing its relations to high school and college students' personality characteristics, self-regulations, engagement, and achievement. *Journal of Educational Psychology, 109*(5), 599–620. https://doi.org/10.1037/edu0000153.

Pfeffer, J., & Sutton, R. I. (2006). Evidence-based management. *Harvard Business Review, 84*(1), 1–12. https://hbr.org/2006/01/evidence-based-management. Accessed 13 March 2023.

Prinsloo, P. (2017a). Fleeing from Frankenstein's monster and meeting Kafka on the way: Algorithmic decision-making in higher education. *E-Learning and Digital Media, 14*(3), 138–163. https://doi.org/10.1177/2042753017731355.

Prinsloo, P. (2017b). Guidelines on the ethical use of student data: a draft narrative framework. Johannesburg: Siyaphumelela. https://www.siyaphumelela.org.za/documents/5a61c7b737ff5.pdf. Accessed 13 March 2023.

Prinsloo, P. (2020). Of 'black boxes' and algorithmic decision-making in (higher) education–A commentary. *Big Data & Society, 7*(1), 1–6. https://doi.org/10.1177/2053951720933994.

Prinsloo, P., & Slade, S. (2017). Building the learning analytics curriculum: Should we teach (a code of) ethics? Learning Analytics and Knowledge Conference LAK'17 Workshop. https://www.slideshare.net/prinsp/building-the-learning-analytics-curriculum-should-we-teach-a-code-of-ethics. Accessed 13 March 2023.

Prinsloo, P., & Slade, S. (2018). Student consent in learning analytics: The Devil in the Details? In J. Lester, C. Klein, A. Johri, & H. Rangwala (Eds.), *Learning Analytics in Higher Education: Current Innovations, Future Potential, and Practical Applications* (pp. 118–139). New York and Abingdon: Routledge. https://doi.org/10.4324/9780203731864-6.

Prinsloo, P., Slade, S., & Khalil, M. (2022). The answer is (not only) technological: Considering student data privacy in learning analytics. *British Journal of Educational Technology, 53*(4), 876–893. https://doi.org/10.1111/bjet.13216.

Prinsloo, P., Khalil, M., & Slade, S. (2023a). Learning analytics as data ecology: a tentative proposal. *Journal of Computing in Higher Education*. https://doi.org/10.1007/s12528-023-09355-4.

Prinsloo, P., Slade, S., & Khalil, M. (2023b). At the intersection of human and algorithmic decision-making in distributed learning. *Journal of Research on Technology in Education, 55*(1), 34–47. https://doi.org/10.1080/15391523.2022.2121343.

Reay, T., Berta, W., & Kohn, M. K. (2009). What's the evidence on evidence-based management?. *Academy of Management Perspectives, 23*(4), 5–18. https://doi.org/10.5465/amp.23.4.5.

Retalis, S., Papasalouros, A., Psaromiligkos, Y., Siscos, S., & Kargidis, T. (2006). Towards networked learning analytics–A concept and a tool. In S. Banks, V. Hodgson, C. Jones, B. Kemp, D. McConnell, & C. Smith (Eds.), *Proceedings of the fifth international conference on networked learning* (pp. 1–8). https://www.lancaster.ac.uk/fss/organisations/netlc/past/nlc2006/abstracts/pdfs/P41%20Retalis.pdf. Accessed 13 March 2023.

Rodriguez-Triana, M. J., Matinez-Moés, A., & Villagrá-Sobrino, S. (2016). Learning analytics in small-scale teacher-led innovations: Ethical and data privacy issues. *Journal of Learning Analytics, 3*(1), 43–65. https://doi.org/10.18608/jla.2016.31.4.

Rosenbaum, R. (1995). The great Ivy league nude posture photo scandal. The New York Times Magazine, 15 January. https://www.nytimes.com/1995/01/15/magazine/the-great-ivy-league-nude-posture-photo-scandal.html. Accessed 13 March 2023.

Rouvroy, A. (2013). The end (s) of critique: Data behaviourism versus due process. In M. Hildebrandt & K. de Vries (Eds.), *Privacy, due process and the computational turn* (pp. 143–165). London, UK: Routledge.

Ruckenstein, M. (2014). Visualized and interacted life: Personal analytics and engagements with data doubles. *Societies, 4*(1), 68–84. https://doi.org/10.3390/soc4010068.

Selwyn, N., & Gašević, D. (2020). The datafication of higher education: Discussing the promises and problems. *Teaching in Higher Education, 25*(4), 527–540. https://doi.org/10.1080/13562517.2019.1689388.

Siemens, G., & Graf, S. (2010). Learning analytics: Personalizing and adapting the learning process. Athabasca, AB: Athabasca University. http://sgraf.athabascau.ca/slides/ABCTech10_graf.pdf. Accessed 13 March 2023.

Spady, W. G. (1970). Dropouts from higher education: An interdisciplinary review and synthesis. *Interchange, 1*(1), 64–85. https://doi.org/10.1007/BF02214313.

Subotzky, G., & Prinsloo, P. (2011). Turning the tide: A socio-critical model and framework for improving student success in open distance learning at the University of South Africa. *Distance Education, 32*(2), 177–193. https://doi.org/10.1080/01587919.2011.584846.

Taylor, C. A. (2019). Diffracting the curriculum: Putting "new" material feminism to work to reconfigure knowledge-making practices in undergraduate higher education. In M. Tight & J. Huisman (Eds.), *Theory and Method in Higher Education Research* (pp. 37–52). London, UK: Emerald Group Publishing. https://doi.org/10.1108/S2056-375220190000005004.

Taylor, J., Hanlon, M., & Yorke, M. (2013). The evolution and practice of institutional research. *New Directions for institutional research, 157,* 59–75. https://doi.org/10.1002/ir.20039.

Thompson, T. L., & Prinsloo, P. (2023). Returning the data gaze in higher education. *Learning, Media and Technology, 48*(1), 153–165. https://doi.org/10.1080/17439884.2022.2092130.

Tinto, V. (1975). Dropout from higher education: A theoretical synthesis of recent research. *Review of Educational Research, 45,* 89–125. https://doi.org/10.2307/1170024.

Torres-Olave, B., & Lee, J. J. (2020). Shifting positionalities across international locations: Embodied knowledge, time-geography, and the polyvalence of privilege. *Higher Education Quarterly, 74*(2), 136–148. https://doi.org/10.1111/hequ.12216.

Vertinsky, P. (2002). Embodying normalcy: Anthropometry and the long arm of William H. Sheldon's somatotyping project. *Journal of Sport History, 29*(1), 95–133.

Vertinsky, P. (2007). Physique as destiny: William H. Sheldon, Barbara Honeyman Heath and the struggle for hegemony in the science of somatotyping. *Canadian bulletin of medical history, 24*(2), 291–316. https://doi.org/10.3138/cbmh.24.2.291.

Williamson, B. (2021). Education technology seizes a pandemic opening. *Current History, 120*(822), 15–20. https://doi.org/10.1525/curh.2021.120.822.15.

Williamson, B., Bayne, S., & Shay, S. (2020). The datafication of teaching in Higher Education: critical issues and perspectives. *Teaching in Higher Education, 25*(4), 351–365. https://doi.org/10.1080/13562517.2020.1748811.

Williamson, B., Macgilchrist, F., & Potter, J. (2021). Covid-19 controversies and critical research in digital education. *Learning, Media and Technology, 46*(2), 117–127. https://doi.org/10.1080/13562517.2020.1748811.

Willis, J. E., Slade, S., & Prinsloo, P. (2016). Ethical oversight of student data in learning analytics: A typology derived from a cross-continental, cross-institutional perspective. *Educational Technology Research and Development, 64,* 881–901. https://doi.org/10.1007/s11423-016-9463-4.

Worsley, M., & Blikstein, P. (2010). Towards the development of learning analytics: Student speech as an automatic and natural form of assessment. Paper Presented at the Annual Meeting of the American Education Research Association (AERA). http://marceloworsley.com/papers/aera_2011.pdf. Accessed 13 March 2023.

Algorithmic Systems Claim Education and The (Re)Production of Education

Velislava Hillman ⓘ

1 Introduction

Access to education has remained the focus in debates surrounding the digital divide and sustainability development goals. However, issues in education have never been merely about connectivity but are in fact the root cause of political forces affecting the distribution of knowledge (in its full truth). Yet, a new force arises as a dominant contender: one that is likely to surpass and diminish the expertise of policymakers. Or at least that is a possible risk.

As education becomes increasingly dependent on EdTech and digital connectivity, their owners have the capacity to claim control over not only the distribution of knowledge but also over societies and individuals with regards to who will occupy what professional role in society. In this chapter, I wish to draw attention to the postdigital education ecosystem emerging in Western societies as a result of EdTech's prevalence, and a new pedagogic authority – that of data-driven algorithmic systems – emerging with its promise to innovate, and even re-define learning and pedagogy. Specifically, I wish to highlight the necessity for further research and systematic investigation of these systems' impact on the educational processes, individuals, and the kind of 'postdigital' learning environment they establish.

As a prerequisite for a postdigital research, systematic investigation is needed to make clear whether data-intensive advancing algorithmic systems in education are held to account (Jandrić et al. 2018; Jandrić 2022) for their impact in education or whether a postdigital education is simply experimental products of neoliberal markets. This chapter, therefore, concretises the agenda for postdigital research that focuses on governance, benchmarking, and scrutiny of the digital technology sector

V. Hillman (✉)
London School of Economics and Political Science, Media and Communications Department, London, UK
e-mail: v.hillman@lse.ac.uk

© The Author(s), under exclusive license to Springer Nature Switzerland AG 2023
P. Jandrić et al. (eds.), *Constructing Postdigital Research*, Postdigital Science and Education, https://doi.org/10.1007/978-3-031-35411-3_9

with particular focus on advancing data-intensive algorithmic systems whose role in education continues to grow.

To demarcate this new authority, I adopt one concrete line of analysis. Drawing from Bourdieu's *Reproduction in Education, Society and Culture* (Bourdieu and Passeron 2000), I argue that EdTech, with focus on data-intensive algorithmic systems, are beginning to occupy a certain *pedagogic power* as they increasingly mediate educational processes. This pedagogic power is accrued through the means of *pedagogic action* and *pedagogic work,* both of which are articulated by the ability of EdTech to extract student data for algorithmic pedagogising. The pedagogic action and pedagogic work legitimise the datafication processes and raise EdTech to the level of *pedagogic authority.* As an authority, the businesses of EdTech products and services have the capacity to legitimate their own pedagogic dominance and therefore influence the (re)production of education.

This new pedagogic authority arises on the grounds of educational institutions with little resistance, critique, and governmental oversight. Moreover, this new pedagogic authority positions educational institutions in the postdigital environment as ones that have slowly ceded to a sense of inevitabilism. Data-driven algorithmic systems are seen as the way to progress and innovation. While nuances of resistance and critique exist, educational institutions, are often positioned to cede to this inevitabilism either because they fail to recognize the new power gripping their infrastructures, or because they do not present an honest account of why it happens without resistance and what alternative postdigital – and even non-digital – learning milieu can be imagined and realised.

Using the concept of symbolic violence (Bourdieu and Passeron 2000), I view data-driven algorithmic systems in education as becoming

> the delegation which establish[es] the pedagogic action, in addition to a delimitation of the content inculcated, a definition of the mode of inculcation (the legitimate mode of inculcation) and of the length of inculcation (the legitimate training period), which define the degree of completion of pedagogic work considered necessary and sufficient to produce the accomplished form of the habitus, i.e., the degree of cultural attainment (the degree of legitimate competence) by which a group or class recognizes the accomplished man. (Bourdieu and Passeron 2000: 34)

In other words, driven by data and hosted by educational institutions, EdTech products (and their business owners) become the legitimate pedagogic power but also one that can 'secure a monopoly of legitimate symbolic violence' (Bourdieu and Passeron 2000: 6). Furthermore, with their advancement into education, EdTech has begun to emerge as the pedagogic power with techno-monopolistic tendencies (Srnicek 2017). Put otherwise, EdTech can grow from a mediator of education to an influencer in the (re)production of education, to a monopolist through the 'expansion of [data] extraction, positioning as a gatekeeper, convergence of markets, and enclosure of ecosystems' (Srnicek 2017: 98).

This chapter's first objective is to describe the present digitalised education, which becomes subjugated not only by the owners of the digital systems but also to their inanimate and decontextualised data-driven algorithmic decision-making. While the concept 'postdigital education' is hard to pin down to a concrete definition, even 'messy' (Jandrić et al. 2018: 895), this chapter draws attention to the need to move away from seeing education as merely digitalised (i.e., EdTech are integrated into teaching and learning processes) to a postdigital which has advancing algorithmic systems held accountable and undergo systematic scrutiny, assessments, and appropriate external validation that govern them and minimise any of the risks that come with digitalising education (unjust algorithmic inferencing, data surveillance and so on). In other words, postdigital education is one in which integrated technologies and their developers and owners are held to account about the impact these products have on the learning and teaching processes. A postdigital learning environment should have a regulatory system in place that mandates minimum standards and prerequisites for these products and their businesses.

The growing dependence of educational processes on data-intensive algorithmic systems challenges the idea of seeing technologies as merely an independent supplement. To this end, it becomes imperative to call for further investigation into and even systematic assessment of how algorithmic systems mediating educational processes legitimate their position and what impact they have on education. Seen as 'beyond the digital', a postdigital education assumes that as technologies becomes ingrained deeply into the fabric of societies, including education, technologies begin to be 'taken for granted, and [their] connotation will become tomorrow's commercial and cultural compost for new ideas' (Negroponte 1998). It is these 'new ideas' that lack solid evidence of their impact that demand further research and understanding of to what ends they are transforming education and to whose benefit. Crucially, however, they also require regulatory oversight to ensure that as their legitimate power in education grows, this power comes with responsibility.

The digital systems with their data pipelines are serving policy machinations of plotting industry labour demands with education's output. Thus, the systems grip the educational infrastructure and establish a postdigital form of control. However, their algorithmic decision-making capabilities conceal the responsibility and identity of these new non-human decision-makers and empowers them to act not only as pedagogic powers, but also as regulatory and normative authorities. For example, they have the capacity to assess a student, however, they are not held responsible if the student fails an exam. Algorithmic systems' regulatory and normative power is also expressed through their design interfaces, algorithms adapting the learning content, and through their inferencing, assumption or prediction values given about students – imposing new identities for and on behalf of students (e. g., when EdTech applications such as Thrively label students as 'depressed', 'likely to cheat' etc.).

This rather oppressive postdigital educational ecosystem is depicted for two reasons. First, the chapter draws attention to a possible postdigital design that EdTech have envisioned for education, here described in its worst manifestation. And second, a gloomy picture of worst outcomes for a postdigital education aims to call for a collective conscience and resistance through critical action against systems whose outcomes can indeed manifest the worst for children and the future of democratic societies. Unconsciousness about EdTech's growing legitimate power in education, while there is a lack of scrutiny and governance of the EdTech market, allows for their naturalization, and challenges efforts to understand and mitigate the subsequent risks to children's education and futures.

This chapter continues with the theoretical framework I have chosen to define the role of EdTech in education. Next, it lays out the claim EdTech businesses make for education, which is deconstructed to reveal its techno-deterministic foundations. This section is then followed by a proposal for the governance of EdTech and, therefore, the defence of a postdigital education that does not merely relinquish pedagogic power to businesses selling algorithms in exchange for data collection but maintains an honest and independent capacity to steer its own course of development through co-partnership with teachers and learners.

2   Theoretical Background

In their *Reproduction in Education, Society and Culture,* the French cultural sociologists Pierre Bourdieu and Jean-Claude Passeron (2000) explore, among other aspects of public education, scientific and technical education to examine the foundations of Bourdieu's theory of symbolic violence. When a dominant power is able to impose its own meanings through pedagogy and impose them as *legitimate* by veiling the power relations which have established it as a dominant power in the first place, it contributes even more to the maintenance of those power relations (Bourdieu and Passeron 2000). Once a dominant power is secured in the education system, it can also secure its monopoly, which adds to the symbolic and structural violence imposed in that system.

As a monopoly, this dominant power then has the ability to design, impose, and reproduce only the sort of pedagogy and curriculum that serve, reinforce, and secure its dominant position, but also to design, impose, and reproduce the sort of legitimising language, discourse, and symbolism that add to the imposition and reproduction efforts. The dominant power in the education system then becomes the *pedagogic authority* (Bourdieu and Passeron 2000), which then has the power to control – i.e., never produce the full truth of its means, objectives, and content – of its own being.

This authority will make use of powerful communication strategies to conceal the 'power relations which make it possible and thereby adding the specific force of its legitimate authority to the force it derives from those relations' (Bourdieu and Passeron 2000: 12). As a legitimate power, it then has the ability to (re)establish the laws that it may be breaking, never admitting its errors or flawed work, adding to the structural and symbolic violence that is now encapsulated in a powerful system of legitimation and monopoly.

The envoy that establishes this new legitimate pedagogy is expressed through digital platforms and data systems that have now become a legitimate *mode of inculcation.* This same envoy also has the legitimate and dominant power to decide upon the length of inculcation, area of specialisation, and ultimately the individual student who will be inculcated. The envoy therefore represents two powerful systems.

On the one hand, the data systems can specify *what* and *who* will be inculcated. On the other hand, a curriculum of hyper-specialization system can be designed that can decide *where* and *how* inculcation will happen.

These two systems define the pedagogic authority's *pedagogic work* (Bourdieu and Passeron 2000). In the hands of the dominant power, the two systems become the mode of cultural, educational, and class reproduction – an educational system that can perpetuate inequalities and diminish human agency, voice, and rights. Put otherwise, this system represents a symbolic and structural violence that occurs in education through the power of data-driven algorithmic systems.

The argument of symbolic and structural violence is not new (Freire 1970). The legitimisation of such violent structures, however, is expressed through the legitimation of capable and advancing digital data systems of precision and their predictive analytics for human control. If oppressive pedagogies were imposed by dominant forces of ideologies before (Freire 1970), today such structures are backed by computer systems that are not only hard to understand by the many in an educational system; but are also inaccessible due to their proprietary nature.

With this theoretical backdrop, this chapter sheds light on the power data-intensive algorithmic systems accumulate and the authoritative role they begin to occupy in educational institutions as they increasingly work to maintain monopoly over rulemaking in the absence of governance and policy scrutiny, and to deliver not only postdigital education but also their vision for postdigital futures. Next, the chapter delves into what kind of postdigital pedagogy and future that might be.

3   Postdigital Education – Algorithmic Systems' Promise for Pedagogy and Futures

EdTech businesses promise successful futures including that of their users in the hope of investment and minimal political barriers to market entry – and educational institutions. These same businesses promise to 'personalise' the educational experience through the means of datafication – by converting student activities into granular data for profiling and prediction. For example, Panorama Education,[1] a platform, collects granular and sensitive information about students through surveys on anything from personal feelings to how much potential they think they have. The harvested data is then integrated with a school district's data systems to bring together a 'panorama' of information about children to enable personalisation of students' learning pathways (Azavedo 2021). Naviance, another platform used in schools, 'track[s] students as they move through elementary school, college and beyond' to provide college and career planning (Straumsheim 2015). Profiling and prediction, the promise goes, will support accurate decision-making and steering of individuals

---

[1] See https://www.panoramaed.com/. Accessed 25 January 2023.

to the right learning and skills acquisition and from there – to the right professional paths.

Recent research (Hillman and Bryant 2022) has shown how vocational education is a particularly appealing part of education where data pipelines development has been proposed through policies and the promises of EdTech with the aim to align educational 'output' with industry's labour demands. While these initiatives target a more technical strand of education, vocational education still affects substantial proportion of society and more concretely its less privileged members. For instance, in Europe, close to half (48.4%) of upper secondary school students follow vocational programs (Eurostat 2020). In the United States, 98% of public-school districts offer vocational education programs (Haviland and Robbins 2021).

Vocational education is an opportunity for many underserved and underemployed individuals – students and adult workers – who rely on and seek postsecondary training (Bragg et al. 2006). In the United States, such programs target the most disadvantaged individuals who fall within the federally funded, Title I program (US Department of Education 2020a), non-English-speaking immigrants and their children. To this end, vocational education is an important subject within the wider debates and research on education, digital technologies and young people's future job security and wellbeing.

Job security is a particularly powerful factor that EdTech and big technology corporations (Big Tech) use to articulate their importance and promises, and the capacities of their products in and for education. For instance, Amazon through its Amazon Future Engineer (Niehoff 2021), Ford the motor company through its Ford Academies (Ford NGL n.d.) and Meta (Asiedu 2022) offer students courses and subsequently – job opportunities at their corporations. The perceived need for innovation in education has led policymakers across the UK and the US to welcome EdTech's propositions with little substantial oversight and scrutiny (Fouad 2022), which can have wider implications for the Global South communities where similar proposals with Silicon Valley-made products have been influencing the digital transformation of education (Kwet 2018).

Such policies in the United States, for instance, envision data pipelines and digital infrastructures that will capture data from the 'cradle' to work and streamline the supply and demand of workers. The California's Cradle-to-Career Data System Act (California Cradle-to-Career Data System Act 2019: 4) envisages 'state-wide data infrastructure that integrates data from various partner entities' from K-12 data to college, student financial aid agencies, state labour agencies and so on. The Act proposes identifying and tracking predictive indicators for the provision of appropriate interventions, identifying the impact of early education on student success, college access and completion, and so on.

Individual States are also developing 'datamarts' – dashboards – for access to 'targeted sets of data related to specific topics or questions' (National Centre for Education Statistics 2019b: 1). Kentucky, Minnesota, and North Dakota, for example, have datamarts connecting secondary, postsecondary and workforce data (National Centre for Education Statistics 2019a). Others are introducing data 'lakes', an euphemism for a warehouse or a repository, 'capable of ingesting, storing, and providing data from a large number of sources and for a wide range of users and uses' (National Centre for Education Statistics 2019b: 1). Yet others are promoting data 'backpacks' or electronic student records that contain all sorts of academic and personal student data – test scores, behavioural patterns, 'non-cognitive variables that impact achievements, as well as an 'early warning system', self-management skills, behaviour/character education, and a record of community service' (Bailey et al. 2012: 2).

In the United Kingdom, too, data pipelines and interoperability, learner, and workforce data alignment are envisioned (United Kingdom, Department for Education 2021). The European Union has similarly set up strategies for harvesting skills intelligence through the development of a 'permanent online tool for real-time information' for 'all interested stakeholders' to tailor careers and inform education policy based on industry demands (European Commission 2020: 8). The goal is, as these policies envision and EdTech systems propose, to track children, and steer them into a career path. EdTech systems already not only track but also predict and suggest what students could become in the future. Naviance, PowerSchool, Panorama Education,[2] and similar other 'big tech' platforms enable student profiling and career pathway suggestions (Hillman and Bryant 2022).

Perhaps some education and career guidance would not necessarily hurt anyone. However, the risks emanating from the capabilities of such systems are present before they even make their judgment call about individuals, their education, and or their futures. First, the granular data collection, inferencing, and prediction not only perpetuates an already dehumanised process. The dehumanisation of education did not suddenly come along with data-driven platforms; it existed with standardised paper-based surveys and assessment tests before these processes were digitalised. However, digital products have enabled an automation and digitalisation of learning and teaching processes at scale) that spews some kind of verdict about the student. For instance, Naviance (2019) provides career cluster such as 'games dealer', following substantial personality surveys and other data gathered from academic records, personal student journaling and so on, creating a quasi-legitimate data output that may have permanence and weight on the student's education and future.

For example, the platform Naviance designs career journeys without the student knowing or understanding how the algorithm generates the pathway and based on what data. In fact, the data the platform collects can be highly sensitive and granular such as information about students' parental income and educational background, their present interests and thoughts about college or career choice, and so on. Similarly, Thrively,[3] a platform used in compulsory education in the US measures 'how hopeful' a student is. The algorithm first determines students' level of 'hopeful' by combining two components: students' 'agency' – their determination to reach a goal and 'pathways' – students' routes to the goal (Team Thrively 2022). In

---

[2] See https://www.naviance.com/, https://www.powerschool.com/, and https://www.panoramaed.com/. Accessed 25 January 2023.

[3] See https://www.thrively.com/. Accessed 25 January 2023.

addition, neither the students nor their teachers know how the system has arrived at the said components and there is no way to know how the system determines a student's level of hopefulness.

Second, the spewed verdict may be generated from bias that is already baked into the code of the system, which no one can tell and know for certain. We have already seen algorithmic bias discriminating against individuals (according to gender or ethnicity) in employment advertising (Ali et al. 2019) and in selecting job applicants (Chen et al. 2018). How can we know that algorithmic systems are not discriminating against individual students when they measure their levels of hopefulness and abilities, or when they carve career pathways for them? Third, any inferencing and prediction is an arbitrary algorithmic output. For the growing child or the young individual, even if algorithms are made transparent, they can still be hard to understand. Moreover, even if the algorithmic output suggests a career or college pathway that seems like a good fit according to a child's present interests and preferences, it does not mean that these will carry on into the future.

With platforms like Naviance and Panorama Education, we see algorithmic systems' pedagogic work in action. The data systems deployed in education can now define *what* and *who* will be inculcated; it can drive a hyper-specialization with precision, which is designed to seek ways to maximise efficacy.

Hyper-specialisation that aims to maximise efficacy only presents structural violence which diminishes individuals to the dictates of the industry (and the data systems). The structural violence bears on workers' 'unremitting commitment [which] is obtained by sweeping away all temporal guarantees' (Bourdieu 1998: 98). The rise of the gig (task-oriented) and casual (on-demand) worker (Moore 2019; Stuart 2020) are examples of how the micro-economic model and policy of flexibility first and foremost benefit industries' interests and help them address their vulnerabilities. Algorithmic management has enabled flexible hours for workers but also have empowered employers to decide at what moment they may need a worker which leads them to hire part-timers and avoid all the complexities and social responsibility that comes with full-time employees (O'Conner 2016).

For instance, with Amazon Future Engineer[4] offered aggressively across the United States, India and UK, students are offered training and future jobs at Amazon. Yet, Amazon's recent sacking of thousands of employees and change of business tactics may leave all these trainees with no job guarantee by the time they come out of the training courses. The casual workers might be earning something but might equally need retraining at any moment, if, say, Amazon changes its mind about opening new headquarters in Virginia in the US. They are left to 'hang on an arbitrary decision of a power responsible for the 'continued creation' of their existence – as is shown and confirmed by the threat of plant closure, disinvestment, and relocation' (Bourdieu 1998: 99); and, indeed, the dictates of data systems.

We witness this hyper-specialisation through the casualisation of work. When individuals become hyper-specialised in one area, they become highly vulnerable to

---

[4] See https://www.amazonfutureengineer.com/. Accessed 25 January 2023.

the changes of the market. Accelerating technological development leaves them with no rest and no sense of security. They become highly competitive not with others but with themselves – self-exploitation, self-regulation and self-control are the only forms of striving to maintain job security. This is not subjugation from the top, but self-subjugation where the individual workers, insecure about their jobs, become self-focused and apolitical, demotivated, and de-opinionated. They think of food for the next day but not beyond. Hyper-narrow specialisation offered by the infernal machine and its algorithm-powered products invisibly shackle individuals to a unique structure that they cannot escape (Bourdieu 1998).

Fourth, as a legitimate pedagogic power, data-driven algorithmic systems (and their business owners) have little governmental scrutiny (Fouad 2022) to be held accountable for any risks their products may incur. EdTech businesses have the opportunity to never admit to their own flaws or when they transgress, even if they can realise it. For they become the agents and the domain experts and so they themselves can steer not only societies and education at large but also the laws that are supposed to govern and control them. In the face of laissez-faire authorities [see for instance the repealing of the UK GDPR (Hern 2021)], such scenarios are realistic. We see examples of algorithmic transgression, e.g., algorithms giving unfair A-level results (Coughlan 2020) and biases in hiring workers (Ajunwa 2020) with little consequences for the owners of the algorithms, or the sector that runs on similar business models.

Fifth, the intention of aligning industry demands with educational output may mean that these systems are already biased to make inferences that steer students towards some professions rather than others. In Bordieuan terms, the alignment is created through the data-driven algorithmic systems, which select who will be 'the holder of the principles (e.g., the engineer) and the mere practitioner (e.g., the technician)' (Bourdieu and Passeron 2000: 50). Thus, for instance, we witness policy and industry's call for (more) STEM specialists, assuming a specific 'skills gap' persists in the market and impacts the competitiveness and economic growth of neoliberal countries.

The narrative of STEM-specialized workforce has been consistent since at least the 1950s in the United States when its public education was cast as a national security 'crisis' (Klein et al. 2012). While the STEM program imperative has been created largely on the myth that the American labour market is plagued by a 'skills gap' that employers in STEM fields cannot find skilled employees (Weaver 2022), there is the conflicting rhetoric that 'jobs of the future' are yet to be created (DeVos 2017). Others have looked at the perceived 'skills gap' in STEM arguing that it is rather inflated (Zaloom 2019).

Therefore, one can argue that it is not necessarily the gap of specific kind of labour that industry demands, but the gap for *cheap* labour of a specific kind. The highest paid jobs, some argue, come from the STEM sector (Choksi 2021), suggesting that industry demands are not merely for skilled workers but for cheap ones. The logic goes that if educational output is more STEM-oriented, a growing supply of such labour will drive their value (i.e., their salary) down.

And sixth, if data systems' work is the product of policy and industry demand for specific type of labour, they risk generating a highly insecure postdigital future for individuals. As research has shown (Hillman and Bryant 2022), when Amazon decided to set up new headquarters in Virginia, in the United States, it was policy leadership that promised educational institutions for Amazon to use to train their future workforce (Moret 2019). Within this arrangement, data systems capture educational infrastructures and convert education into mere factories of labour. However, this leads to a structural violence which reduces individuals to the dictates of the industry (and the data systems, instated by policy). The structural violence bears on workers' 'unremitting commitment [which] is obtained by sweeping away all temporal guarantees' (Bourdieu 1998: 98). This structural violence is compounded by the lack of rigorous evidence that the data systems aligning industry with education works (Mulder 2017). In a word, the promise of EdTech systems for postdigital education and futures can be bleak and uncertain.

To this end, there is a dangerous flaw in EdTech's promise in and for education. First, there is no governmental scrutiny and oversight of the EdTech (and Big Tech) industry and their work in education. It is difficult to tell exactly what happens as their infrastructures are imposed onto educational systems. Big Tech's say has entered both governments in the UK and the US through lobbying and through direct contractual influence. See for example the leading EdTech working group in the UK (Snowdon 2019), with Microsoft, Apple, Google, and Amazon Web Services as members among others, which grants them the privilege to exercise their pedagogic, authoritative, and even quasi-regulatory powers.

Similarly, DXTera Institute (2022) in the US have grown their lobbying efforts in the European Union through their EdTech Alliances. EdTech companies paying membership to belong to this exclusive club have managed to obtain a contract from the European Commission to establish a Community of Practice for the support of a new digital hub for education. This industry-led effort positions EdTech businesses from the position of power before any government scrutiny or licensing regimes are established to govern and regulate what they do and how they influence education. The needs therefore for governance and scrutiny of the EdTech and Big Tech's workings in education are highly needed. The next section focuses on how such governance can be achieved.

4   Necessary Governmental Scrutiny of the New Pedagogic Powers in a Postdigital Education

There is no doubt that the recent health pandemic accelerated the digitalisation of education. The common need and understanding according to governments (U.S. Department of Education 2017) and powerful supranational organisations (Fullan et al. 2020; United Nations Educational, Scientific and Cultural Organisation 2020), continues to be that EdTech will help deliver quality education for all. The harder argument has been to clearly understand who is doing what and what 'quality' education entails. To this end, little oversight has been offered to ensure that EdTech companies deliver their promises. How EdTech products are chosen also remains debatable. Moreover, digital technologies are not neutral tools but private offerings of business organisations who seek financial profit and market growth.

This begs the question, what are the primary motivations of such business organisations in offering their digital innovations in education? Little is known about it other than the propositions and prospects debated publicly (Peters et al. 2019). For instance, the scenarios Peters, Jandrić, and Means offer are those in which (1) AI can lead everyone to permanent economic insecurity and joblessness; (2) a scenario in which individuals remain in firm control over their future course regardless of the advancement of intelligent systems; and (3) a scenario of business-as-usual where AI does not impose any significant predetermined futures for individuals, rather a tech-hype project with meagre impact on the future of education or work.

However, what is known is how businesses operate and the conditions under which they survive. In the case with EdTech, even if companies are motivated by improving educational processes, any such goal must also make business sense. If Google give free Chromebooks to children (Elias 2020), what business model sustains this generosity? There can be at least three speculative answers based on what has been witnessed in the wider technology sector. The first two concern the motivation to attract investment and the motivation to sell a product, whatever that may be. These are short-term motivations. The third, long term motivation is that industry will capture markets as early as the 'cradle', from where a future labour force can be moulded to fulfil specific needs, as predicted by algorithmic systems, which are now settling in the arteries of educational systems.

If this is nothing more than a speculative argument, first, research in this area is necessary. And second, what governmental scrutiny exists to prevent these business motivations from happening in education? Therefore, it is relevant and necessary to identify the conditions and regulations that the EdTech sector, like any other business, should be subject to. If, say, advertising agencies are subject to specific regulation and licensing (i.e., Advertising Standards Authority 2018), so should the businesses of EdTech. Within this context, the EdTech sector may not only target underage individuals but also claim the privilege to provide a service for something considered a human right. Businesses must earn the privilege to sell products in education, be licensed to operate and undergo scrutiny to ensure that they do not infringe on children's basic human rights [United Nations (1989) Convention on the Rights of the Child]. Yet, the EdTech sector continues to grow with little meaningful oversight, code of practice, and clear evidence of their value to education.

4.1   The Present State of Governing EdTech

Current legal frameworks only partially achieve scrutiny and governance as EdTech companies continue to exploit existing loopholes (Palfrey et al. 2020). Education data collection and use practices undergo no prior ethical reviews. And at a personal level, students have no agency over the practices of data extraction and use. In other words, there is no coherent and meaningful oversight, control, and data governance mechanism that ensures accountable, transparent, and ethical collection and processing of education data (Jim and Chang 2019). While general data protection laws provide a baseline for making data privacy impact assessments, these are seen as insufficient (Mantelero 2022) and within the education context – chaotic and limited (Hillman 2022b). First, compliance does not provide external validation of what data privacy mechanisms and security controls are implemented by technology companies to guarantee the minimisation or repurposing of data use. Even when companies are more transparent about the data they collect, this still leaves a grey area about their ability to repurpose the collected data. And second, data privacy assessments do not address the societal consequences of the technologies (Mantelero 2022).

EdTech products generate large quantities of data that are siloed across disparate digital systems beyond the reach of educational institutions or students (Hillman 2022a). Much of the data collected can remain with EdTech providers leaving the door open for further concerns and even speculation as to what happens to the data now and in the future (Barassi 2020). Advancing EdTech applications already have the capacity to produce continuous algorithmic profiling, prediction, and modification of user behaviour without their knowledge and awareness (Breiter and Hepp 2018). Additionally, a student has limited or no choice but to sign into the classroom technologies and acquiesce to behavioural tracking by third parties.

Added to that, students are a particularly vulnerable group. The vulnerability can be based on age, language, cultural differences, although some researchers consider research on the basis of responsive, reflexive, and relational ethics whereby all students should always be considered vulnerable whether they are competent and knowledgeable on the research question or not (Lahman et al. 2011). Many algorithmic systems used in schools do not go through any prior ethical review. Algorithmic systems adapt content by 'learning' from their users. They conduct continuous research about their user at a speed that does not 'await' ethical approval. We have seen past examples where companies, in educational settings (Hillman 2022a) repurpose the use of collected data, conduct experiments without the awareness and consent of their products' users and the ethical pitfalls of adaptive learning where data can be mishandled (Kramer et al. 2014).

Additionally, as companies change terms and conditions frequently, they may begin to collect data that students remain unaware of, such as keystroke cadence (which could be exploited further outside of the learning context), thus breaching ethical and legal obligations (Johanes and Lagerstrom 2017). This demonstrates the gap in ethical regulation and robust scrutiny of the private sector selling these algorithmic systems. As the private sector of EdTech become increasingly present, such gaps must be addressed with urgency.

4.2   Framework for Governing EdTech: Ethical Benchmarking

There are no clear ethical review procedures that EdTech companies undergo for their product deployment or data processing and use as shown in research (Hillman 2022a). The conditions in which ethical go-ahead is given are often based on the imposition of legal frameworks such as those of Children's Online Privacy Protection Act (COPPA) and Family Educational Rights and Privacy Act (FERPA) in the United States, and the General Data Protection Regulation (GDPR) (through data privacy impact assessments) in the UK and Europe. However, while FERPA provisions control for what data can be used, once collected, repurposing its use still remains a grey area (Zeide 2017). It is also hard to find data misuse. In one case (Hillman 2022a), the vendor of a popular math product used the collected data to carry out research on student learning and publishing papers while the students were unaware of the repurposing of the collected data. Even if there was no harm done, repurposing data remains unethical.

Ethical complexities are also economically sensitive. Conducting research with economically deprived communities without any prior due ethics review process can cross ethical lines. Paying homeless black people to test a facial recognition technology (Fussell 2019) for example, has demonstrated not only how a giant technology company like Google successfully skips ethical scrutiny but also preys on human vulnerabilities. Google Opinion Rewards, an app that runs surveys, offers payment in exchange for completed surveys (Google Play 2021). Yet, no ethical consideration supplements the application to clarify the objectives behind the surveys; what data may be collected and how that data may be used. A research project necessitates not only external ethical review but also special care.

It remains unclear if and what kind of ethical clearance edtech companies using student data for research, product quality and development, student profiling, and predictive analytics undergo. With the acceleration of artificial intelligence (AI), research and development, many larger technology companies have their own ethics committees (Vincent 2019), yet it remains relatively unknown who or what their processes and structures are – and how, therefore, objectively and ethically they scrutinise their companies' research projects. Ethical reviews and conditions can form part of a coherent EdTech governance framework not only for the purpose of transparency but also to provide a more meaningful data education for stakeholders (students and teachers).

4.3   Governing EdTech for Their Pedagogical and Socio-Structural Value

Governing EdTech should be conceptualised with data education and literacy in mind, not only as to what data EdTech products collect and why, but also for the implications of data processing and long-term impact on the structure and even purpose of education. What is the value proposition of EdTech for pedagogy and learning? The claims EdTech products make for enhancing learning remain speculative with little evidence for consistent improvement across educational institutions, individuals, and the learning process.

Education as a social structure determines the process of what is taught, how it is taught, and what is learned (Dornbusch et al. 1996). Re-thinking governance of EdTech through a social-structural lens demands a critical view of how education data may impact what is conceptualised as learning and the social structure of the learning processes. It follows to ask: what data can learning processes go without? For example, what is the purpose of collecting ethnicity data in order to generate score reports as in the case with Pearson's Q-global platform (Hillman 2022a)? Within the social structure of the learning processes whose interests does such data serve?

Not only lax governmental scrutiny (Fouad 2022), but governments also support the initiative of infrastructure development for data interoperability, open data markets, and further data economy imperatives that data will drive innovation everywhere (European Commission 2018; US Department of Education 2020b). However, this architectural drive for data interoperability in education demands further critical analysis and governance. Data interoperability enables granular data assembly from various systems which further advance the development of predictive analytics. In education, this can be translated as student profiling and behavioural modification.

In the US, the Common Education Data Standard (Common Education Data Standards n.d.) (CEDS) is a data interoperability template available for districts and states to adopt and implement (NCES n.d.). CEDS is a state-wide 'initiative … to streamline the understanding between and across P-20W' (National Centre for Education Statistics 2019a, b) – data across the early years, kindergarten, primary, postsecondary and workforce institutions and sectors. CEDS's proposed 'common language' (National Centre for Education Statistics 2019a, b: 2) contains hundreds of data elements. However, this common language of data raises a number of concerns.

First, this common language of data not only streamlines what information to collect and how to organise it; it also determines what counts in education and how to count it. However, if education is seen as a social structure of what is taught, how it is taught, and what is learned with the primary goal of serving the interests of the child, then does this data language serve these same interests? Therefore, a meaningful governing framework also requires pedagogical and curriculum expertise to critically evaluate how the data-driven language and its capacity to enable predictive analytics, student profiling, and behavioural modification may be impacting or even transforming education. The data-driven language imposes its own 'grammars of action' (Agre 1994: 747) on the structural and social arrangement of education to the extent that data can 'oversimplify the activities they are intended to represent'.

Second, the language of data interlocks an expanding network of third parties that adopt it. The CEDS Data Warehouse (Common Education Data Standards 2021) 'has the capacity to support the full P-20W data pipeline'. It partners with learning agencies, public and private higher education institutions, the US Department of Education, the US Health and Human Services and the US Department of Labour; education data standards organisations, as well as powerful members of the private sector (Common Education Data Standards 2021: 3). Some are directly related to education; others are not (InnovateEDU 2021). For example, the Gates Foundation of the Microsoft founder has long been a proponent of common data standards in education, and funds various projects dedicated to this goal. Project InBloom for collecting student data failed following parental outcry (Bulger et al. 2017). However, two others that are striving for 'pathways data' (Data Quality Campaign 2021) – the Data Quality Campaign (2012, 2014, 2021) and Chiefs for Change (CFC), a bipartisan lobby group (The Gates Foundation 2019) – carry on. DQC and CFC push aggressively for data alignment and student tracking (Chiefs for Change 2021) while they also partner with CEDS.

Third, the language of data enabling data interoperability has led to data pipeline development across districts and states and a new way of thinking about education. As pointed out earlier, data pipelines have become the conduit between labour market demand and education supply. In other words, the language of data and the capacities stemming from data interoperability have enabled a direct link to be made between education and industry (the labour market). For example, aligning education with industry through the common language of data has led to clustering Washington (Workforce Training and Education Coordinating Board 2019, 2021) and Virginia (GO Virginia Foundation 2020) into industrial zones. From there, education policies propose hyper-specialised education and training depending on which zone a student comes from (Virginia Business Higher Education Council 2021). In the UK, learning-to-earning models that align education with industry demands with the help of data are also on the way (Department for Education 2021). In short, a common data-driven language allows policy and industry to 'speak' about what needs training depending on what labour is presently in demand.

This model, however, suggests that education data, enabled through EdTech, serve first and foremost industry and its labour demands, which may not necessarily align with the interests and demands of a young learner. This model therefore begs to question whether data pipelines reduce public education to the sole means for labour production – and therefore even class (re)production (Hillman and Bryant 2022).

Lastly, the language of data has the capacity to modify the conditions that shape a learner's behaviour. Education data present learning as the function by which what is taught, how it is taught and what is learned is quantified through numbers. The learning process becomes an If–Then uniform pattern that is formulaically predetermined since everything, no matter what, has to amount to a quantifiable number – data. This assumes that education data, generated through the means of EdTech, will benefit the system – be that of education or industry – on which the student is a reactive, modifiable participant (a node). If data become the central voice of expression and force that drives one's learning trajectory it can limit the agency of a developing individual whose interests can change at any time.

The promise of algorithmic systems with data interoperability is for a greater visibility of the teaching and learning processes – an opportunity to adapt the learning process, deliver timely intervention, improve efficacy, and improve the overall learning experience, than as a concern that students will be pushed aside as reactive participants in their education. However, there is not enough evidence that the former is happening and not the latter.

5 Conclusion

EdTech are not merely neutral tools for connection and access to education; they have also been transformed to become a means for production in education and a powerful actor whose role and influence continues to grow precisely because of the lack of government scrutiny and oversight.

Through policy support and often dominant discourses about innovation and progressiveness, schools have become ever more dependent on devices, applications, data collection, algorithmic analysis, data, and information visualisation on digital dashboards, and generally EdTech products' capabilities for nudging, managing, storing, and mediating communication. With that, concerns grow regarding their unregulated impact on education (Decuypere et al. 2021). The digitalisation of educational processes has infused the education landscape with products that blur the lines between school and the marketplace (Williamson and Hogan 2020; Williamson 2021).

However, the data-extracting systems are changing and disrupting society and economies unpredictably. By its very nature, the new pedagogic authority (industry through the reins of data-driven systems) seeks to sustain itself and continue to grow. Their political promise for prediction with precision enables their legitimation in schools; in return, their algorithmic capacities are beginning to offer an unprecedented and untested alignment of industry demands with educational goals, with a promised employability as the promised output (and therefore political stability).

This formula's sustainability depends on and leads to an 'absolute reign of flexibility' (Bourdieu 1998: 97) and the need for constant upskilling and reskilling of employees – the lifeline of industry. Businesses adjust 'ever more rapidly to the demands of the markets' which leads to a 'recruitment on short-term contracts or on a temporary basis and repeated "downsizing", and the creation, within the company itself, of competition … between teams … between individuals' (Bourdieu 1998: 97). The permanent threat further triggers competition with oneself through 'responsibilisation' (Bourdieu 1998: 97), self-exploitation, and constant stress. The employee, even at the highest echelons, has a sense of insecurity. In this 'Darwinian world' (Bourdieu 1998: 98), with the state and its market-driven policies in its base, individuals are constantly threatened with extinction if their skills and knowledge do not guarantee them employment.

The scenarios proposed elsewhere (Peters et al. 2019), including the absolute reign of flexibility scenario that this chapter depicts, ultimately demand further research: in which fields or sectors and how likely is it that any of these scenarios will become the postdigital reality? Furthermore, is there room for fourth and fifth scenarios whereby, in one foreseeable instance, as described in this chapter, the owners of intelligent systems can entirely take control over everyone else's conditions, and in another scenario where intelligent systems entirely outpace everyone else to unknown unknowns that cannot even be anticipated?

As Brunton and Nissenbaum argue (2016), the risks of data collection and misuse can be known knowns (e.g., the student may be aware that the EdTech collects sensitive data about him), unknown knowns (the student may not know how that data may be used later in his life), and a category of unknown unknowns (any other impossible to anticipate unknowns as a result of this data collected about a student when he was in school). These questions demand not only further investigation but also creative and critical thinking about the direction, speed, and magnitude with which data-intensive algorithmic systems are integrated into all aspects of life, and specifically in education.

However, encouraged by actionable rationale, this chapter describes the need to develop meaningful and coherent governance of digital technologies and their business owners. Such meaningful and systematic governance should depart from robust evidence about who benefits from these new dominant works and action.

This chapter describes a rather pessimistic picture of a postdigital education where EdTech continue to assert their visions for a labour supply and demand equilibrium, while it also called for a coherent and concerted effort to monitor and scrutinise the EdTech sector's ambitions in education by looking through ethical and social-structural lenses. However, more research is needed to drive away from the pessimistic view of a postdigital educational ecosystem, towards a positive one where EdTech companies are held accountable, use data responsibly, and are dedicated to ethical practices, clear standards, and benchmarks.

First, more empirical research is necessary to understand teachers' and students' knowledge, attitudes, and perceptions towards EdTech and a digitalised education. What sort of learning environment do students wish to be a part of and what learning environments do teachers, education policymakers, school leaders and parents wish to promote? Answers to these questions will help navigate the kind of governance and policies for EdTech these same stakeholders can design.

Second, well-thought out governing and oversight of EdTech should account for further substantial evidence of EdTech products' effectiveness and for whom (Boninger et al. 2020).

Third, at a conceptual and social-structural level, data interoperability for predictive analytics, profiling, and behavioural modification can lead to further consequences for the social order and sociality of a postdigital educational ecosystem. Data-driven adaptive EdTech products can challenge older forms of knowledge, expertise, and judgement and risk side-lining educators and learners by reducing their autonomies. It follows that data interoperability has the potential to re-structure not only how learning happens, for whom, and why in whichever way it does, but also the social organisation and governance under which it happens (opening doors to commercial entities to build their own worker pipelines through the means of public educational institutions). Addressing what forms of EdTech governance are needed in a postdigital educational ecosystem therefore demands deliberation on many fronts simultaneously. It is an ambitious project that requires stakeholder, expert, and policy participation regardless of what the technologies of the day may be.

Collective effort must underpin an innovative governance architecture including education scholars, EdTech critics, and experts who have long worked in the space and continue to provide evidence about the influence and impact of EdTech specifically and in the educational processes more broadly. For that, this chapter has called for further postdigital research and effort in the area of what governance mechanisms are necessary to put in place and ensure that EdTech, specifically data-intensive algorithmic systems, are held to account for how they influence and impact educational processes.

Education partially is meant to provide and generate more knowledge; motivate and lead individuals to find their sense of purpose. The focus of learning therefore should remain the departure point on which governing and appropriate scrutiny of EdTech and Big Tech businesses should be re-thought. Moreover, governance and scrutiny should include ethical, technological, and social-structural considerations to prevent and protect education from any structural and symbolic violence from occurring as advancing data-intensive algorithmic systems continue to encroach on education. A postdigital research should look into what frameworks, benchmarks, standards, and governing mechanism exist or can be developed and implemented to provide the necessary oversight and scrutiny of EdTech and ensure a postdigital education where these products and their owners demonstrate accountability and ethical practices.

References

Advertising Standards Authority. (2018). More impact online: Advertising Standards Authority Committees of Advertising Practice Annual Report 2018. https://www.asa.org.uk/static/upload ed/563b3e3c-1013-4bc7-9c325d95c05eeeb7.pdf. Accessed 7 September 2022.

Agre, P. E. (1994). Surveillance and Capture: Two Models of Privacy. *The Information Society, 10*(2), 101–127. https://doi.org/10.1080/01972243.1994.9960162.

Ajunwa, I. (2020). The "black box" at work. *Big Data & Society, 7*(2). https://doi.org/10.1177/2053951720938093.

Ali, M., Sapiezynski, P., Bogen, M., Korolova, A., Mislove, A., & Rieke, A. (2019). Discrimination through Optimization. *Proceedings of the ACM on Human-computer Interaction, 3*(CSCW), 1–30. https://doi.org/10.1145/3359301.

Asiedu, K. G. (2022). Meta's next big bet: the 'metaversity'. Protocol, 20 July. https://www.protocol.com/enterprise/metaverse-in-education-morehouse-meta. Accessed 15 January 2023.

Azevedo, A. M. (2021). Panorama raises $60 million in General Atlantic-led Series C to help schools better understand students. TechCrunch, 2 September. https://techcrunch.com/2021/09/02/panorama-raises-60m-in-general_atlantic-led-series-c/. Accessed 15 January 2023.

Bailey, J. C, Carter, S., Schneider, C., & Ark, V. T. (2012). Data Backpacks: Portable Records and Learner Profiles. *Digital Learning Now: Smart Series*. http://digitallearningnow.com/site/uploads/2012/10/Data-Backpacks-FINAL. Accessed 10 October 2022.

Barassi, V. (2020). *Child, citizen, data: how tech companies are profiling us from before birth.* Cambridge, MA: The MIT Press.

Boninger, F., Molnar, A., & Saldaña, C. (2020). Big Claims, Little Evidence, Lots of Money: The Reality Behind the Summit Learning Program and the Push to Adopt Digital Personalized Learning Platforms. Boulder, CO: National Education Policy Centre. https://nepc.colorado.edu/publication/summit-2020. Accessed 5 October 2022.

Bourdieu, P. (1998). *Acts of resistance: against the myths of our time.* Cambridge, UK: Polity Press.

Bourdieu, P., & Passeron, J. C. (2000). *Reproduction in education, society and culture.* 2nd Ed. London, UK: SAGE Publications.

Bragg, D. D., Kim, E., & Barnett, E. A. (2006). Creating Access and Success: Academic Pathways Reaching Underserved Students. *New Directions for Community Colleges, 135,* 5–19. https://doi.org/10.1002/cc.243.

Breiter, A., & Hepp, A. (2018). The complexity of datafication: putting digital traces in context. In A. Hepp, A. Breiter, & U. Hasebrink (Eds.), *Communicative figurations. Transforming communications – studies in cross-media research* (pp. 387–405). Cham: Palgrave Macmillan. https://doi.org/10.1007/978-3-319-65584-0_16.

Brunton, F., & Nissenbaum, H. (2016). *Obfuscation: a user's guide for privacy and protest.* Cambridge, MA: The MIT Press.

Bulger, M., McCormick, P., & Pitcan, M. (2017). The legacy of InBloom (Working Paper 02.02.2017). New York: Data & Society Research Institute. https://datasociety.net/pubs/ecl/InBloom_feb_2017.pdf. Accessed 12 October 2022.

California Cradle-to-Career Data System Act. (2019). Cradle-to-Career Data System Act [1-850-10874], Ch.51, Sec.14.

Chen, L., Ma, R., Hannak, A., & Wilson, C. (2018). Investigating the impact of gender on rank in resume search engines. In M. Perry & A. Cox (Eds.), *CHI '18: CHI conference on human factors in computing systems* (pp. 1–14). New York: Association for Computing Machinery. https://doi.org/10.1145/3173574.3174225.

Chiefs for Change. (2021). The Role of Governance in Supporting Learner Pathways. Chiefs for Change. https://chiefsforchange.org/resources/?r-category=61. Accessed 26 January 2023.

Children's Online Privacy Protection Act (COPPA). (2016). *15 U.S.C. §§ 6501–6506.*

Choksi, H. (2021). Top 10 Highest Paying Jobs in 2022 brings to you the top-paying jobs that you could upskill for. And with 2022 rolling in, If you are giving your care. LinkedIn, 29 November. https://www.linkedin.com/pulse/top-10-highest-paying-jobs-2022-brings-you-top-paying-haren-choksi?trk=organization-update-content_share-article. Accessed 20 October 2022.

Common Education Data Standards. (2021). CEDS Data Warehouse: Expansion Project. https://ceds.ed.gov/. Accessed 10 October 2022.

Common Education Data Standards. (n.d.). Related Efforts. https://ceds.ed.gov/relatedInitiatives.aspx. Accessed 9 October 2022.

Coughlan, S. (2020). Why did the A-level algorithm say no? BBC News, 14 August. https://www.bbc.co.uk/news/education-53787203. Accessed 10 October 2022.

Data Quality Campaign. (2012). Pivotal Role of Policymakers as Leaders of P-20/Workforce Data Governance. https://dataqualitycampaign.org/wp-content/uploads/2016/03/DQC_Governance-June27.pdf. Accessed 3 October 2022.

Data Quality Campaign. (2014). Who Uses Student Data? https://dataqualitycampaign.org/resource/infographic-uses-student-data/. Accessed 3 October 2022.

Data Quality Campaign. (2021). It's Time to Make Linked Data Work for K-12 Leaders. https://chiefsforchange.org/wp-content/uploads/2021/11/It's-Time-to-Make-Linked-Data-Work-for-K-12-Leaders.pdf. Accessed 2 October 2022.

Decuypere, M., Grimaldi, E., & Landri, P. (2021). Introduction: Critical studies of digital education platforms. *Critical Studies in Education, 62*(1), 1–16. https://doi.org/10.1080/1750848 7.2020.1866050.

Department for Education. (2021). DfE outcome delivery plan: 2021 to 2022. Corporate Report. Department for Education. https://www.gov.uk/government/publications/department-for-education-outcome-delivery-plan/dfe-outcome-delivery-plan-2021-to-2022. Accessed 26 January 2023.

DeVos, B. (2017). Betsy DeVos on preparing youth for future jobs. The Wall Street Journal, 19 November. https://www.wsj.com/articles/betsy-devos-on-preparing-youth-for-future-jobs-1510782958. Accessed 10 October 2022.

Dornbusch, M. S., Glasgow, L. K., & Lin, I-C. (1996). The Social Structure of Schooling. *Annual Review of Psychology, 47*(1), 401–429. https://doi.org/10.1146/annurev.psych.47.1.401.

DXTera Institute. (2022). DXTera team awarded Digital Education Hub community of practice. https://dxtera.org/news/news-dxtera-joins-digital-education-hub-community-of-practice/. Accessed 26 January 2023.

Elias, J. (2020). California governor says, 'We need more Googles' as company offers free Wi-Fi and Chromebooks to students. CNBC, 1 April. https://www.cnbc.com/2020/04/01/coronavirus-google-offers-wi-fi-chromebooks-to-california-students.html. Accessed 10 October 2022.

European Commission. (2018). Elements of the European data economy strategy 2018. Brussels: European Commission. https://digital-strategy.ec.europa.eu/en/library/elements-european-data-economy-strategy-2018. Accessed 10 October 2022.

European Commission. (2020). Communication – European Skills Agenda for Sustainable Competitiveness, Social Fairness and Resilience. Brussels: European Commission. https://ec.europa.eu/migrant-integration/library-document/european-skills-agenda-sustainable-competitiveness-social-fairness-and-resilience_en. Accessed 10 October 2022.

EUROSTAT. (2020). Vocational Education and Training Statistics. https://ec.europa.eu/eurostat/statistics-explained/index.php?title=Vocational_education_and_training_statistics. Accessed 10 October 2022.

Family Educational Rights and Privacy Act (FERPA) (2016). 20 U.S.C. § 1232g; 34 CFR Part 99.

Ford Next Generation Learning. (n.d.) https://www.fordngl.com/data. Accessed 10 October 2022.

Fouad, N. S. (2022). The security economics of EdTech: vendors' responsibility and the cyber-security challenge in the education sector. *Digital policy, Regulation and Governance, 24*(3), 259–273. https://doi.org/10.1108/DPRG-07-2021-0090.

Freire, P. (1970). *Pedagogy of the oppressed.* London: Penguin.

Fullan, M., Quinn, J., Drummy, M., & Gardner, M. (2020). Education reimagined: The future of learning. A collaborative position paper between new pedagogies for deep learning and Microsoft education. http://aka.ms/HybridLearningPaper. Accessed 15 January 2023.

Fussell, S. (2019). How an attempt at correcting bias in tech goes wrong. The Atlantic, 9 October. https://www.theatlantic.com/technology/archive/2019/10/google-allegedly-used-homeless-train-pixel-phone/599668/. Accessed 10 October 2022.

Gates Foundation. (2019). Committed Grants: Chiefs for Change. https://www.gatesfoundation.org/about/committed-grants/2019/10/inv004270. Accessed 10 October 2022.

General Data Protection Regulation (GDPR). (2016). Regulation (EU) 2016/679 of the European Parliament and the Council of 27 April 2016 on the protection of natural persons with regard to the processing of personal data and on the free movement of such data, and repealing Directive 95/46/EC. *Official Journal of the European Union, 119,* 1–88. http://data.europa.eu/eli/reg/2016/679/oj.

GO Virginia Foundation. (2020). Virginia Growth and Opportunity Foundation. https://govirginia.org/about/go-virginia-foundation/. Accessed 10 October 2022.

Google Play. (2021). Google opinion rewards. Google LLC. https://play.google.com/store/apps/details?id=com.google.android.apps.paidtasks&hl=en_GB&gl=US&pli=1. Accessed 10 October 2022.

Haviland, S., & S. Robbins. (2021). Career and Technical Education as a Conduit for Skilled Technical Careers: A Targeted Research Review and Framework for Future Research. *ETS Research Report Series, 21*(1), 1–42. https://doi.org/10.1002/ets2.12318.

Hern, A. (2021). UK to overhaul privacy rules in post-Brexit departure from GDPR. The Guardian, 26 August. https://www.theguardian.com/technology/2021/aug/26/uk-to-overhaul-privacy-rules-in-post-brexit-departure-from-gdpr. Accessed 10 October 2022.

Hillman, V. (2022a). Bringing in the technological, ethical, educational and social-structural for a new education data governance. *Learning, Media and Technology*. https://doi.org/10.1080/17439884.2022.2052313.

Hillman, V. (2022b). Edtech procurement matters: it needs a coherent solution, clear governance and market standards. Social Policy Working Paper 02-22, London: LSE Department of Social Policy. https://www.lse.ac.uk/social-policy/Assets/Documents/PDF/working-paper-series/02-22-Hillman.pdf. Accessed 10 October 2022.

Hillman, V., & Bryant, J. (2022). Families' perceptions of corporate influence in career and technical education through data extraction. *Learning, Media and Technology*. https://doi.org/10.1080/17439884.2022.2059765.

InnovateEDU. (2021). InnovateEDU's Project Unicorn Releases Inaugural School Data Interoperability Update. InnovateEDU. https://www.innovateedunyc.org/internal-news. Accessed 10 October 2022.

Jandrić, P. (2022). History of the postdigital: invitation for feedback. *Postdigital Science and Education*. https://doi.org/10.1007/s42438-022-00345-w.

Jandrić, P., Knox, J., Besley, T., Ryberg, T., Suoranta, J., & Hayes, S. (2018). Postdigital Science and Education. *Educational Philosophy and Theory, 50*(10), 893–899. https://doi.org/10.1080/00131857.2018.1454000.

Jim, K. C., & Chang, H. (2019). The Current State of Data Governance in Higher Education. *Computer Science, 55*(1), 190–206. https://doi.org/10.1002/pra2.2018.14505501022.

Johanes, P., & Lagerstrom, L. (2017). Adaptive learning: the premise, promise, and pitfalls. Paper presented at 2017 ASEE Annual Conference & Exposition, Columbus, Ohio. https://doi.org/10.18260/1-2-27538.

Klein, J. I., Rice, C., & Levy, J. (2012). U.S. Education Reform and National Security. Council on Foreign Relations. http://www.jstor.org/stable/resrep05781. Accessed 10 October 2022.

Kramer, D. I. A., Guillory, E. J., & Hancock, T. J. (2014). Experimental evidence of massive-scale emotional contagion through social networks. *Proceedings of the National Academy of Sciences of the United States of America (PNAS), 111*(24), 8788–8790. https://doi.org/10.1073/pnas.1320040111.

Kwet, M. (2018). Digital colonialism: South Africa's education transformation in the shadow of Silicon Valley. PhD dissertation. Grahamstown: Rhodes University. https://doi.org/10.2139/ssrn.3496049.

Lahman, M., Geist, M., Rodriquez, K. L., & Graglia, P. (2011). Culturally responsive relational reflexive ethics in research: the three Rs. *Quality & Quantity, 45*(6), 1397–1414. https://doi.org/10.1007/s11135-010-9347-3.

Mantelero, A. (2022). *Beyond data: human rights, ethical and social impact assessment in AI*. Berlin: Springer. https://doi.org/10.1007/978-94-6265-531-7.

Moore, M. T. (2019). The Gig Economy: A Hypothetical Contract Analysis. *Legal Studies, 39*(4), 579–597. https://doi.org/10.1017/lst.2019.4.

Moret, S. (2019). How did Virginia win Amazon HQ2? Other States Pitched Incentives; We Pitched Our Educated Workforce. https://twitter.com/chamberrva/status/1151859322483335168. Accessed 10 October 2022.

Mulder, M. (Ed.). (2017). *Competence-Based Vocational and Professional Education: Bridging the Worlds of Work and Education*. Cham: Springer. https://doi.org/10.1007/978-3-319-41713-4.

National Centre for Education Statistics. (2019a). Statewide Longitudinal Data System (SLDS) topical webinar summary: infrastructure series 3: data lakes, data science, and preparing an

SLDS to meet emerging data needs. National Centre for Education Statistics. https://slds.ed.gov/services/PDCService.svc/GetPDCDocumentFile?fileId=34963. Accessed 10 October 2022.

National Centre for Education Statistics. (2019b). SLDS Topical Webinar Summary: Benefits and Use Cases for Employment Outcome Datamart. https://slds.ed.gov/services/PDCService.svc/GetPDCDocumentFile?fileId=34211. Accessed 10 October 2022.

National Centre for Education Statistics. (n.d.). Common Education Data Standards: CEDS 101. https://ceds.ed.gov/pdf/ceds-101-presentation.pdf. Accessed 10 October 2022.

Naviance. (2019). Naviance student Part 1: overview, about me, careers [YouTube Video]. https://youtu.be/UwEo89AGGf8. Accessed 10 October 2022.

Negroponte, N. (1998). Beyond digital. Wired, 12. http://www.wired.com/wired/archive/6.12/negroponte.html. Accessed 10 October 2022.

Niehoff, M. (2021). With an eye toward the future, this program connects students to tech careers. EdSurge, 13 September. https://www.edsurge.com/news/2021-09-13-with-an-eye-toward-the-future-this-program-connects-students-to-tech-careers. Accessed 15 January 2023.

O'Connor, S. (2016). When your boss is an algorithm. Financial Times, 8 September. https://www.ft.com/content/88fdc58e-754f-11e6-b60a-de4532d5ea35. Accessed 10 October 2022.

Palfrey, Q., Good, N., Ghamrawi, L., Monge, W., & Boag, W. (2020). Privacy Considerations as Schools and Parents Expand Utilization of EdTech Apps during the Covid-19 Pandemic. International Digital Accountability Council. https://digitalwatchdog.org/wp-content/uploads/2020/09/IDAC-Ed-Tech-Report-912020.pdf. Accessed 5 October 2022.

Peters, M. A., Jandrić, P., & Means, A. J. (Eds.). (2019). *Education and Technological Unemployment*. Singapore: Springer. https://doi.org/10.1007/978-981-13-6225-5.

Srnicek, N. (2017). *Platform capitalism*. Cambridge: Polity.

Snowdon, K. (2019). Paralympic swimmer to chair new edtech expert group. Schools Week, 3 June. https://schoolsweek.co.uk/paralympic-swimmer-to-chair-new-edtech-expert-group/. Accessed 10 October 2022.

Straumsheim, C. (2015). Completing the 'student life cycle'. Inside Higher Ed, 23 January. https://www.insidehighered.com/news/2015/02/23/student-success-company-hobsons-acquires-starfish-retention-solutions. Accessed 15 January 2023.

Stuart, D. (2020). The Rise of Casual Worker Puts Us All At Risk. The Jacobin, 23 August. https://jacobinmag.com/2020/08/casual-work-australia-part-time-jobs. Accessed 5 October 2022.

Team Thrively. (2022). Well-being index. [YouTube video]. https://www.youtube.com/watch?v=Q79nM8SD9k0. Accessed 25 January 2023.

U.S. Department of Education. (2017). Reimagining the role of technology in education: 2017 national education technology plan update (Report). https://tech.ed.gov/files/2017/01/NETP17.pdf. Accessed 15 January 2023.

United Nations Educational, Scientific and Cultural Organization. (2020). Global education coalition: Members. Paris: UNESCO. https://globaleducationcoalition.unesco.org/members. Accessed 15 January 2023.

United Nations. (1989). United Nations Convention on the Rights of the Child. Geneva: United Nations. http://www.ohchr.org/EN/ProfessionalInterest/Pages/CRC.aspx. Accessed 5 October 2022.

US Department of Education. (2020a). Education for the Disadvantaged – Grants to Local Educational Agencies. https://www2.ed.gov/programs/titleiparta/index.html. Accessed 10 October 2022.

US Department of Education. (2020b). US Department of Education data strategy. US Department of Education. https://www.ed.gov/sites/default/files/cdo/ed-data-strategy.pdf. Accessed 10 October 2022.

Vincent, J. (2019). The problem with AI ethics. The Verge, 3 April. https://www.theverge.com/2019/4/3/18293410/ai-artificial-intelligence-ethics-boards-charters-problem-big-tech. Accessed 5 October 2022.

Virginia Business Higher Education Council. (2021). Growth 4 VA: A Campaign of the Virginia Business Higher Education Council. https://growth4va.com/wp-content/uploads/2021/09/2021Policy.pdf. Accessed 5 October 2022.

Weaver, A. (2022). Who has trouble hiring? Evidence from a national IT survey. *ILR Review, 75*(3), 608–637. https://doi.org/10.1177/0019793920985261.

Williamson, B. (2021). Making markets through digital platforms: Pearson, edu-business, and the (e)valuation of higher education. *Critical Studies in Education, 62*(1), 50–66. https://doi.org/10.1080/17508487.2020.1737556.

Williamson, B., & Hogan. A. (2020). Commercialisation and Privatisation in/of Education in the Context of Covid-19. Brussels: Education International Research. https://go.ei-ie.org/GRCovid-19. Accessed 10 October 2022.

Workforce Training and Education Coordinating Board. (2019). Future of Work Task Force 2019 Policy Report. https://www.wtb.wa.gov/wp-content/uploads/2019/12/Future-of-Work-2019-Final-Report.pdf. Accessed 10 October 2022.

Workforce Training and Education Coordinating Board. (2021). House College and Workforce Development Committee: Overview. Workforce Training and Education Coordinating Board. https://app.leg.wa.gov/committeeschedules/Home/Document/226010#toolbar=0&navpanes=0. Accessed 10 October 2022.

Zaloom, C. (2019). STEM is overrated. The Atlantic, 10 September. https://www.theatlantic.com/ideas/archive/2019/09/college-not-job-prep/597487/. Accessed 10 October 2022.

Zeide, E. (2017). The structural consequences of big data-driven education. *Big Data, 5*(2), 164–172.

Negotiating Mnemotechnic Re-presentation

Greta Goetz

1 Introduction

In the postdigital age of Artificial Intelligence (AI), questions being explored include how it is possible for a brain, 'whether biological or electronic, to perceive, understand, predict, and manipulate a world far larger and more complicated than itself' as well as how to build intelligent entities with those properties (Russell and Norvig 1995: 3). This can be described as the possibility to program machines to think—whether this implies imitating humans (Boesch 2022), or not imitating humans (Christiano 2015), or (non-) agentic simulation (janus 2022).[1] It is related to ancient concerns with 'how seeing, learning, remembering and reasoning could, or should, be done' (Russell and Norvig 1995: 3), which are of 'infinite importance' (Whitehead 1948: 89). This chapter is concerned with how computational 'intelligence' should be negotiated within the evolving network of learning and research.

The field of AI is very broad, with many sub-fields 'focusing on *measurable* performance in specific *applications*' (Russell and Norvig 2022: 50) (emphases added) and 'components of agents' (Russell and Norvig 2022: 79) that have largely been developed less theoretically than with a view to economic utility (game theory

---

[1] Authoratative texts on AI like Russell and Norvig (1995, 2022) cited in this paper refer to AI agents, as AI can act such as through decision-making. However, janus (2022) argues—within the context of self-supervised learning—that the word agent can be misleading. As this conversation is beyond the scope of this chapter, an attempt has been made to use the word agent in contexts where decision-making outputs are significant.

G. Goetz (✉)
English Department, Faculty of Philology, University of Belgrade, Belgrade, Serbia
e-mail: greta.goetz@fil.bg.ac.rs

P. Jandrić et al. (eds.), *Constructing Postdigital Research*, Postdigital Science and Education, https://doi.org/10.1007/978-3-031-35411-3_10

is important here)[2] and practical applications,[3] distinguishing it from philosophy (Sowa 2000). It is defined as 'the science of designing computer systems to perform tasks that would normally require human intelligence'. These tasks today include 'information retrieval, stock-market trading, resource allocation, circuit design, virtual reality, speech recognition, and machine translation' (Sowa 2000). As it has been suggested that '[a]ll the researcher has to do is look in the mirror to see an example of an intelligent system' (Russell and Norvig 1995: 3), this endeavour can be considered a problem of re-presentation, inclusive of tensions related to mimesis.

Briefly, AI is defined as 'machines thinking and/or acting humanly and/or rationally' (Russell and Norvig in Malone et al. 2019: 4). The features of AI that enable it to act or *seem* human (cf. janus 2022), if not think humanly or necessarily rationally, through the laws of thought of logic, include natural language processing (NLP) 'to communicate successfully in a human language', knowledge representation 'to store what it knows or hears', automated reasoning to 'answer questions and to draw new conclusions', and machine learning 'to adapt to new circumstances and to detect and extrapolate patterns' (Russell and Norvig 2022: 20)—though pattern learning is an overlapping but 'closely-allied' field (Russell and Norvig 2022: 738).

In the specific class of algorithms modelled after the neural networks of the human brain, processing nodes are interconnected in 'deep' layers, with each cell processing inputs and producing an output that is sent to other neurons. A deep learning model that has led to great advances in generative AI and NLP is the transformer, which can figure out the rules in one language and map them[4] to another.

---

[2] The approach to much decision-making in AI is taken from John von Neumann and Oskar Morgenstern's game theory, outlined in *The Theory of Games and Economic Behavior* (1944) (in Russell and Norvig 2022: 28). Game theory was critiqued (but not necessarily invalidated) by thinkers like Gregory Bateson (in Halpern 2017) and Norbert Wiener for being harmful to learning and broader outcomes (Wiener 1950/1989: 185; Wiener 1960: 1356; Heims 1991: 109–110).

[3] 'The discipline imposed in AI by the need for one's theories to "work" has led to more rapid and deeper progress than when these problems were the exclusive domain of philosophy (although it has at times also led to the repeated reinvention of the wheel).' (Russell and Norvig 2022: 356) This can be compared with the classical philosophical view of *theoria*, which was valued more highly than progress. A human's ultimate goal was to be able to articulate their place in the universe by recreating the heavens as best they could, through the proper use of *tékhnē* (e.g., Randall 1967/1970: 150).

[4] Mapping is an important technique in AI. It is the symbolic re-presentation of knowledge or data. Put informally, because there are different ways of naming things in the real world with symbols because the real world is 'just so *huge* (especially if you include symbols describing mathematics)' and because certain symbols can refer to 'parts of other symbols' objects, or overlap with them somehow, scientists avoid this through a type of interpretation called mapping. Using interpretation in this way 'we basically say to ourselves: "The real world is too messy for us to name things directly. Instead, we'll just create an imaginary structure that *maps* things in the real world to symbols- But we just won't worry too much about what objects in the real world map to our symbols, because doing so is impossible to do perfectly anyway"' (Barski 2007) (emphasis in first quote in original).

Transformer models can be trained on large quantities of textual training sets called large language models, which include data collected from the web. They can learn new behaviours by being shown new training data[5] and are used not just in translation but in artificial neural networks like generative pre-trained transformers (GPT), which can output new words in response to inputs of words (Huang 2023). More generally, transformer models can learn the pattern represented in a 'language' (Chowdhery et al. 2022 in janus 2022), *harnessing pre-existing abstractions* (janus 2022). This can include the possibility to learn a 'language' to represent images through latent representation which uses *compressed* 'latent space' representations of extracted aspects of images or 'languages' (Huang 2023).

The word 'pattern' is highly suggestive and points to the essence of a functioning structure (Cunningham and Mehaffy 2013: 7) or the essence of regularities (Bishop 2006: 1). It is central to understanding both machine and human learning, including learning how to program machines and the continued generation and re-presentation of knowledge. A distinction will be made in this chapter between those patterns and pattern languages ('language-like networking') (Cunningham and Mehaffy 2013: 7)[6] that are *used to solve problems* (Russell and Norvig 2022: 332) and those whose essence is ultimately extra-linguistic (Gabriel 1996), although both definitions can be found in the work of architect and designer Christopher Alexander and can be related to programming (e.g., Gabriel 1996). While Alexander (1977) did seek the core of a solution to a problem that can be used in many ways within a field of expertise, this was decidedly *human-centered* and sought 'the quality without a name', which is to say, sought that which is beautiful, comfortable, free, and eternal (in Gabriel 1996: 36–39).[7] This raises the question of whether learning, made possible through the exteriorization of memory (cf. Ross in Stiegler 2018: 17), seeks to model openness towards a collective working out of the learning process and reach knowledge that is imbued with this human-centered quality.

The problem of mediating retentions through mnemotechnology is addressed in ubiquitous computing (ubicomp) design principles that seek computing design that is convenient, calm, and informed:

---

[5] However, a lot of data is required for patterns to be recognized and this in turn requires great amounts of computational power (Thompson et al. 2022).

[6] 'Much of the early work in knowledge representation (the study of how to put knowledge into a form that a computer can reason with) was tied to language and informed by research in linguistics, which was connected in turn to decades of work on the philosophical analysis of language.' (Russell and Norvig 2022: 35)

[7] The laws of human logic extend to *extra-linguistic* objects of human apprehension as Aristotle (2008) showed in his 'Categories' (Studtmann 2007/2021), a work in the *Organon* which explains the tools of logic that are used to understand the branches of human knowledge. Certain extra-linguistic objects can also be extracted and classified through pattern recognition: for example, one industry overview suggests it capable of emotion recognition (Boesch 2022)—but this raises questions of how 'comfortable' this is (cf. Alexander in Gabriel 1996: 36–39).

> Besides the daunting computational and infrastructural problems, we must also find the
> balance between control and simplicity, between unlimited power and understandable
> straightforwardness, between the seduction of smooth digital mediation and the immediacy
> of those complex fellow workers called humans. But in the end, it is hard to imagine a more
> important task for twenty-first century technologists. (Weiser et al. 1999: 693)

Suffice to say in this introduction, there is tension between computing as an amplifier for individual human reach and programming system design (Kay 1993).[8] At present, it is recognised that the large language models that made generative pre-trained transformers possible can lead to societal harms, such as 'stereotyping, denigration, increases in extremist ideology, and wrongful arrest' (Bender et al. 2021). Significantly, 'AI models are fundamentally stochastic', trained with an algorithm that compares the training data input to the model's output and calculates how to move closer to the right answer (Huang 2023).[9] This means that it cannot distinguish between right and wrong but only proximity to preferred output.

The ancient practice of using artificial memory and techniques to re-present reality through mnemotechnics (Yates 1966/1999) today involves mnemotechnologies that not only re-member and classify but are transformative on a massive, global scale (Stiegler 2018: 51). They have clear social implications and require negotiation to mitigate their applications. For example, an as-yet unanswered question asks: 'Even with fair, socially justifiable data, what kinds of algorithms would best support human flourishing and, in Dignum's terms, uphold accountability, transparency, and our own responsibility?' (Dignum 2017 in Kasenberg et al. 2018: 189). Other papers already describe applying computational simulacra to social contexts (e.g., Park et al. 2022).

It is thus proposed that a mission statement for postdigital research seek 'e-quality of opportunity' that promotes co-participatory relational dialogue through the experience of assembling people, tools, activities, and outcomes in mnemotechnic networked learning (Beaty et al. 2002; also see Markauskaite and Goodyear 2017: 610). A co-participatory approach could be designed such that participants learn 'to use symbols and knowledge in new ways, across groups, across cultures' by opening our minds 'to full, complete use of computers to augment our most human of capabilities' (Engelbart 2002). In this context, networked learning, a field that has worked in the space for decades, can be called on to 'problematize' (cf. Gourlay in

---

[8] Thanks to my informal mentor Fernando Boretti for directing my attention to this text in summer 2022 (personal correspondence).

[9] The director of the Tufte University's Human-Robot Interaction Laboratory explains: 'Moral competence can be roughly thought about as the ability to learn, reason with, act upon, and talk about the laws and societal conventions on which humans tend to agree … The question is whether machines—or any other artificial system, for that matter—can emulate and exercise these abilities.' (Scheutz in Collins 2014). For example, 'agents would have to infer an observed person's goals, assess costs and benefits for the person and for other individuals, and compare actual to counterfactual actions (e.g., the agent's foregone benefits as an indicator of prescription norms). Thus, artificial agents would need to have social-cognitive capacities to ground their norm competence.' (Malle et al. 2019: 26).

Networked Learning Editorial Collective 2021: 328) questions of classification and control in network patterns.

To work through this, socio-humanist-materialist paradigms (e.g., Latour 1987; Barnett 2017) could be used to place technology within 'a broader understanding of the socio-technical systems within which the project of education is constituted', entangled in capitalism and the emerging data economy, metrification, algorithmic ranking, and material labour practices and natural resources (Knox 2019). Such an approach could uphold postdisciplinarity (Peters et al. 2021). This chapter expands that aim. Drawing on the work of Bernard Stiegler on mnemotechnics (and extending currents of Whiteheadian process philosophy that figure in his work), this chapter questions claims of the augmentation or conservation of the retentional process through the use of the mnemotechnic tool within in the larger historical context of what it means to know.

The legitimacy of departing from conventional research approaches and paradigms is today supported in more conservative environments such as at the World Economic Forum which in its 2020 initiative invalidates 'silo thinking' (Schwab and Malleret 2020: 22). The authors describe 'highly interconnected and uncertain, incredibly complex' interrelated components that are further complicated by the 'position of the observer' (Schwab and Malleret 2020: 29). In the context of postdigital research, it may be asked who or what the position of the 'research observer' is and what this means to the continued circulation and production of knowledge. This is critical in the age of ubiquitous computing, as the distribution of knowledge among its networks involves 'dumb' terminals[10] as computing architecture is removed from individual humans' hardware to the cloud in feedback loops designed for containment and control (e.g., Nielson and Rossiter 2014; Nowotny 2021).

2   Re-presenting Knowledge

Knowledge representation moves through the social and symbolic relationship which 'speaks for'—'as in political representation' where a delegate takes the place of a larger collective, and as a process of 'returning to presence', despite the threat of the difference between what is re-presented and its re-presentation disappearing (van Loon 2007: 279). This problem can be seen in the difficulty of 'returning to

---

[10] A 'dumb terminal' is a simple output device that is basically a monitor that accepts data from a central processing unit and has limited processing power and features. As much processing happens in the cloud today, the client-server model can be used to overlay many centralized assets and services onto the distributed Internet, effectively making these assets available only as a 'time-limited loan' (Stokel-Walker 2022). As such, dumb terminals are a metaphor for the state of computing for individuals. 'As more and more of the connected world comes to depend on Whatever as a Service, "the cloud" and other remote and centralized services, the very idea of distributed capacities on standalone open-source (or open-source-based) hardware and software that individuals or organizations fully control as independent and sovereign entities in the world, seems terribly retro, utopian, or both.' (Searls 2016)

presence' exteriorized memory and knowledge ex-pressed in ideas, words, audio files, and images but also symbols, including code. Mnemotechnologies have the power to re-member, classify, and transform knowledge re-presentations.

The attempt to 'frame a coherent, logical, necessary system of general ideas in terms of which every element of our experience can be interpreted' (Whitehead 1978: 3) has historically been the work of philosophy and philology (Gadamer 1975/2006: 470). As it is possible that AI can or will at some point attempt to perform the task of interpreting experience (janus 2022; Malle et al. 2019), it is therefore possible to speak of competing knowledge representations. This is especially true given the particular context of knowledge representation in AI which is often designed with utilitarian goals, through utility-maximization and game theory. Ongoing learning can iteratively modify an AI technology's output action goals. The re-presentation of the technology's background knowledge can be generative: producing something not there before (whether simulation, re-presentation, text, image, etc.). This raises questions about 'reality' and imitation.[11]

There is a *difference* in exteriorized memory where it is not classified according to the performance measure of the attempted automatization or predictability of utility (Gadamer 1975/2006: 318). The latter can be achieved through the certainty effect which reduces computational burden by choosing 'certain' outcomes, for example (Russell and Norvig 2022: 528), or by using game theory. Bateson, while not categorically against game theory, understood such games as 'producing conditions for action—but not for different possible actions, only repetitive cycles culminating in potentially genocidal violence' (Bateson in Halpern 2017). In the long run, 'the application of the theory of games can only … [force] people to regard themselves and each other as Von Neumannian robots' (Bateson in Halpern 2017).

> The horror of such computational approaches, therefore, is not at the locus of representation, but rather in their automation of the process of relationality—their standardization of communication, and technologization of change itself as a process to be modelled, replicated, repeated. Such systems take the collapse between materiality and representation—the vitality of their process—literally, making the world and the game the same, always reacting, but never changing. This is the destruction of temporality in its own name. … Bateson's analysis implies that proximity physically may be desirable, but distance temporally is necessary for emergence. (Halpern 2017)

---

[11]The question of what is real is only touched on in this chapter. Suffice to say, Plato warns of opinion-imitation, as opposed to scientific imitation (based on the experience of doing the methodical work of discovering knowledge imaginatively-as opposed to doing so for utilitarian ends-as ex-pressed in words such as ποιητικός [creative]; φαντάζω [imagined in the mind], μουσική [muse-inspired art] used throughout). Plato divides imitation into uncertainty as to the truth vs. dissemblance, with sophistry belonging to the latter (1921: 267d-8b). A more contemporary example of such discussion is Jean Baudrillard's suggestion in *Simulacra and Simulation* (1983) that reality can be replaced by symbols and signs to become a simulation. Reality, where it is revealed through a faithful image or copy (first stage) can be masked by images that do not reveal reality faithfully (stage two) or replaced by copies that are arbitrary images with no relation to what they claim to represent, masking the absence of a profound reality (stage three). Ultimately, the simulacrum has no relationship to reality but becomes a regime where any claims are expected to be artificial.

Through automated processes of relationality, the programmable tool can shape 'the one who trains himself in its usage, just as the words we use shape our thoughts and the instrument forms the violinist' (Dijkstra 1982; also see McLuhan in Kay 1993).

There is a difference where exteriorized memory is negotiated before becoming re-presentations of knowledge. Traces of networked knowledge representations can be further collectively 're-presenced' by individuals that interiorize and exteriorize them (Goetz 2023; van Loon in Johnson 2020).

2.1 Re-presencing the Knowledge Trace

The trace, through its exteriorization, can threaten to liquidate knowledge as a price can be put on it and an attempt can be made to capture it and re-produce it automatically. However, it can also promote new knowledge production through an admittedly risky continuing process of discovery (e.g., Hesiod 1914: 1.25; Plato 1925b: 47d). Utilitarian, liquidating designs on knowledge inform 'today's globalized industry of reticulated [networked] traces'. The organ of these traces 'is the *reticulated computer*, operating on the basis of the network effect, the self- and autogeneration of traces' (Stiegler 2018: 46), i.e. operating on and through data traces that are 'modeled, replicated, repeated' (cf. Bateson in Halpern 2017) according to 'real time calculation applied to these traces on a planetary scale' (Stiegler 2018: 46). This can forget the importance of temporal distance to perspective and subjectivity (Bateson in Halpern 2017), cited in long-form above, and effectively re-present rather than '[return] to presence' (van Loon 2007 : 279) or re-presence.

To take a view of knowledge as a series of traces that are both near and far is one way to arrive at 'patterns which connect' (Bateson 1979: 8). In human-centered design, participants in the learning process can learn to look for patterns of networks that connect and negotiate the relation between people, things, and ideas across disciplines, culture, and individual barriers as they re-presence them:

> Revealing such patterns requires empathy and openness. What common sense of humanity do we share? What things do we care about and share in common? These and many more questions are a start to the development of patterns that connect people to people. In a way that is similar to patterns that connect us to our world, we can begin to explore our similarities across expressions of difference. (Bloom 2004: 17)

A focus on traces allows for consideration of ways of re-presencing understandings (written and spoken languages, mathematics, etc.) across disciplines and relating them to the individual through a process of *personal* transformation (Gadamer 1975/2006: 153–154).

Where *education* is taking place, not *training,* 'traces' of the learning process are not always visible until they are evoked.

> Training is for the purpose of passing on specific information necessary to perform a specialized activity. Education is the building of the person. To *educe* means to draw out or evoke that which is latent; education then means drawing out the person's latent capacities for understanding and living, not stuffing a (passive) person full of preconceived knowledge. (Nachmanovitch 1990: 118)

Only the 'hack' views everything through the script of the textbook case. To not be a hack means seeing beyond the textbook to the subject before one: using training but not allowing it to blind one to the person or the subject 'sitting in front of you. In this way, you pass beyond competence to *presence'* and 'create *through* your technique and not *with* it' (Nachmanovitch 1990: 21). To re-presence is to educe and experience the process of 'forming concepts through working out' a common meaning (Gadamer 1975/2006: 361).

Such enlargement of thought transforms contradictions and agreements into 'partial aspects of wider points of view' (Whitehead in Borden 2017: 89). The re-presencing of traces is also a search for causality and thus also explainability, providing a view to multiple avenues for meeting and dealing with other things or people (Bateson in Halpern 2017).[12]

To re-presence is to reclaim knowledge capital by retracing, as a human individual, ex-pressions of knowledge. This could, for example, involve reverse engineering or seek to recover moral values (cf. Gadamer 1975/2006: 318) in programming even where programs that emerge through the product of human intelligence are not designed to return any of this knowledge back to humans, though this is not to undermine the immense work that goes into the creation of programs, which should be rewarded.[13]

To re-presence is to move from the external mark (like the code in a program) to the thing that made it (like conceptual frameworks behind the code, or an individual context in a dialogue) to isolate the significance of the possible or probable causal relation of vestige to passage. It is a process. Following a trace means being as self-effasive as receptive and open, tracing anew in the ongoing work of forming new connections, readings, interpretations (Ricoeur 1991: 130–131), moving forwards and backwards (cf. Whitehead 1929: 4). In other words, as a trace is generative of an expression issued from the presence in a new present (cf. Whitehead 1978: 68–9), following it is a form of productive knowledge (cf. Plato 1921: 265b). Ideally, there is receptive, open space for new knowledge to emerge (cf. Plato 1925b: 47d; Beaty et al. 2002; Markauskaite and Goodyear 2017: 610). New knowledge can include making sense of new information in terms of the old (Beghetto and Schuh in Beghetto 2021a: 476).

The possibility to bring things to presentation is an opportunity to bring expression to multiple comparable perspectives (e.g. Gadamer 1975/2006: 361–362). It allows for consideration of what it means to re-present one expression through

---

[12] This attempt can involve the production of 'novel togetherness' through the importance of memory and causality (cf. Whitehead 1948: 89, 1978: 21) or finding traces and then re-presencing them to arrive at 'the mass of thoughts that are generated by interaction' (Bateson 1954/2017: 119).

[13] 'Reverse engineering is a big job; will we have programmers with sufficient determination to undertake it? Yes—if we have built up a strong feeling that free software is a matter of principle, and non-free drivers are intolerable.' (Stallman 2002: 29) The moral principles of free software seek the freedom to run, modify, redistribute copies of, and distribute modified versions of a program (Stallman 2002: 20). Notably, '"Free software" is a matter of liberty, not price. To understand the concept, you should think of "free" as in "free speech," not as in "free beer".' (Stallman 2002: 43) This could be linked to the relevance of the 'anticipated future' (Whitehead 1978: 21).

another like in structural linguistics, algebra, philosophy (e.g., Plato 1921: 236), programming, and machine learning.

That is not to imply that comparable re-presentations are 'equal'. This tension is revealed by post-structuralist philosophy (Derrida 1972/1982) as well as by programming challenges in compiling, writing test suites, and cryptography—which can also be related to philosophical concerns (Krishnamurthi 2019). This point is relevant to the possible displacement of human activity through AI task performance—without minimizing the paradigm-shifting accomplishments of transformer-based learning models that can extrapolate the semantics of arbitrary natural language structures. The purpose of this chapter is to point to the negotiation for 'the production of novel togetherness' (Whitehead 1978: 21).

2.2   Exteriorizing the Memory of Knowledge

It has been posited that even cave walls and papyrus, in addition to pixels, have all functioned as types of mnemotechnic 'writing screens', used to present ex-pression (Stiegler 2018: 175) so that it can be shared, even transgenerationally as memory, and become knowledge that can be conserved or augmented through original thought.

Historically, the conditions for exteriorizing thought have been made possible by the technical tool and the desire for learning (Plato 1967: 81a-e). This is what is known as mnemotechnic—or 'hypomnesic'—tertiary-retention (Stiegler 2018: 154). Tertiary retention, or remembering, is exteriorized and exosomaticized (occurring outside the human body). It is 'tertiary' as it conditions the relationship between the memory of (secondary) seized (primary) apprehensions (Stiegler 2018: 93).

'Exosomatic ages' (Stiegler 2018: 146) emerge through the history of the *different* 'science[s] of intellectual facts, or the facts of the intellect (Fleming 1860: 347), i.e., noologies, reflected in the multiplication of all manner of expressions and exteriorizations. Exosomatic ages emerge because they are increasingly unified by a shared understanding of mnemotechnic retentions, or the 'logical ideal of the ordered arrangement of concepts' (Gadamer 1975/2006: 431), which allow powers to form that are trans-individual and 'that cultivate forms of knowledge, which, over millennia, eventually become what we still today call the sciences' (Stiegler 2018: 246–247).

The exteriorization of knowledge through the mnemotechnic tool enables but does not guarantee trans-individual, trans-generational knowledge transmission and production. Where knowledge is transformed to become a set of closed, entropic systems and is liquidated into a computational system of speculative capital (Stiegler 2018: 146), structural insolvency can ensue (Stiegler 2018: 51–52). But knowledge is not only that which is liquidated and automated: knowledge is an open system (Stiegler 2018: 51).

The problem of seizing re-presentations (of simulations, shadow images) projected onto a hypomnesic screen (whether that of a cave wall or digital screen) is of political significance where it fails to raise questions of the authenticity of (re-) presented knowledge (Plato 1969: 514a). It is only the wise ruler who, through education, comes to understand a code of interpretation that is beyond not only shadows but also things. The mnemotechnic screen, while appearing to hold knowledge, is not necessarily the ultimate tool for learning. Learning involves something more and is not automatic. Given the immensity of the transformation underway on a global scale during the Anthropocene, a postdigital research mission could seek 'e-quality of opportunity' (Beaty et al. 2002) involving the dialogic exploration of the quality of retentions. This could further, and more constructively, involve co-participation among all actors 'to use symbols and knowledge in new ways, across groups, across cultures' by opening our minds 'to full, complete use of computers to augment our most human of capabilities' (Engelbart 2002). This is to re-presence traces of the shared ongoing process of learning made possible by exteriorized memory and its tools in the open system of knowledge (cf. Stiegler 2018: 51) and not just re-present them.

The repetition or 'reduplication' of knowledge re-presented on the mnemotechnic screen could be understood in the vocabulary of thermodynamics to express either 'the entropic tendency towards equalization and effacement of energetic differences in the world' or the bright light of iconic augmentation (Ricoeur 1991: 131). If reduplication expresses 'the entropic tendency towards the equalization and effacement of energetic differences in the world, iconic activity merits the name negentropic' in so far as it stems the inclination to entropy and 'fights against the tendency to annul contrasts and differences in the universe' (Ricoeur 1991: 131). Exteriorized knowledge that is negentropic serves to 'condense, spell out, and develop reality', augmenting it (Ricoeur 1991: 130).

Problematic exteriorized knowledge can be augmented through negotiation: 'People … might have different understandings of what has been brought and taken', additionally, they may 'bring different things to the table and may take different things away.' (Irani et al. 2010: 1318)

That which is of infinite importance (Whitehead 1929: 86), or the 'heart of reality' (Ricoeur 1991: 133) of extra-linguistic types (Aristotle 2008), can comprise new, shared ex-pressions of the 'quality without a name' (Alexander in Gabriel 1996: 36–39). If it may be agreed that reality is also supra- or extra-, it extends the *true value* of purported complete knowledge capture to the possibility of knowledge production not informed by preceding knowledge. Significantly, preceding knowledge, or its containment and control, can inform the choice of mnemotechnological media available for ex-pression. This can be augmented by re-presencing lost traces, such as by returning to the 1987 Hypertext Proceedings (Smith and Halasz 1987) to revisit different ways of thinking about bi-directional links (employed on MediaWiki) or hypertext on creative writing or non-lineal thinking, etc. (Boretti 2023).

While the mnemotechnic tool can aid re-membering previously exteriorized knowledge, it can also lead to forgetting (Stiegler 1998: 183–184; Plato 1967: 320–322), productive of 'forgetfulness in the minds of those who learn to use it'. This is because '[t]heir trust in writing, produced by external characters which are no part of themselves, will discourage the use of their own memory within them'

(Plato 1925a: 275). The mnemotechnic invention is not deemed one 'of memory, but of reminding', 'the appearance of wisdom, not true wisdom'. A lesson of situated learning (e.g., Vygotsky in Lave 1991) is that knowledge must be actively and reflexively internalized, not automatically repeated.

This can be explained in terms of individuation according to which individuals have access to interpreting retentional systems to be able to continue to be productive. In Stiegler's words, 'code must *become knowledge* in order to be a law or right, which must in turn be that of a social body' (2018: 251) (emphasis in the original). The difficulties of social encodification of the effects of ever-larger learning models and automation systems can be seen not just in the problems of fair AI (Barocas et al. 2022) but also in the problems with legacy software, where tacit knowledge embodied in previous generations of programmers can be lost (Naur 1985; Cockburn 2002: 239–240). It can further be seen in how the architecture of the cloud is displacing individual knowledge and becoming incomprehensible to individual human beings (e.g., Crawford and Joler 2018) or by how knowledge is becoming a set of closed, entropic systems (Stiegler 2018: 51). Such fragmentation is in need of negotiating and re-presencing 'patterns that connect' (cf. Bateson 1979: 8).

2.3   (Automatic) Knowledge That (Dis)sociates

For mnemotechnics to be fully effected, 'continual arbitration' is needed among psychosomatic organisms (psychic individuals), artificial organs (technical individuals), and social organizations (collective individuations) (Stiegler 2018: 55). This is to say that within the process of human understanding where it is assisted by prosthesis (an artificial device augmenting the human body), three organs are involved: the biological/psychic, the social, and the technical (through tools). Understanding mnemotechnics requires stepping back to ask questions not just about the media but the individual and social.

Collective individuation involves the psychic individuation of individuals as well as a technical and artificial dimension (Stiegler 2018: 55). Stiegler notes that mnemotechnics is being 'profoundly transformed' as devices attempt to 'short-circuit' both the mnemotechnic individuation of 'psychic individuals that are psychosomatic organisms' and the 'collective individuation of social organizations' together with 'the social systems of which they are composed' (2018: 247). Mnemotechnological devices attempt to seize hold of digital tertiary retention in order to re-member and reconfigure social units.

Milieus that do not allow for co-participation are dissociated milieus as they are no longer the medium or vector of a biological person's individuation. In such contexts, individuals consume and do not produce symbols (Stiegler in Petit 2013) and automatized mnemotechnics become a form of entropy. The irreversible dissipation of energy is hastened where the hyper-standardization of automatization submits individual and collective intelligence to the law of averages (Stiegler 2018: 40). Even where this is 'more than the parametrized distribution of agents' (janus 2022), regression ensues where it is not co-individuating. This compression of the universe into a generative rule (janus 2022), as a form of reductionsim, is a 'study of which we may estimate the character and propensities of an imaginary being called the Mean Man' (Maxwell in Campbell 1882: 213) no matter how granular or deep[14] the learning model is. It is always a re-presentation while education is a co-ex-pressive process.

This can be compared to the pursuit of 'originary' knowledge (Stiegler 1998: 99; Plato 1925a: 248c-e, 1967: 80e) with all of its associated problems of truth-seeking, morality, and ethics. The rescue of this knowledge is not received by the individual human thinking soul from outside but is found within itself (Stiegler 1998: 99), relating from within. True knowledge is the recollection of this *a priori* originary knowledge.

This is a critical point about learning versus understanding, wherein the anamnesic recollection of knowledge can be threatened by the 'writing screen', which can disable the active learning of the thinking soul (Stiegler 2018; cf. Plato 1925a: 275a). To paraphrase an illustrative joke, knowledge cannot be taught but must be learned. From this 'opening to the world' (cf. Bateson in Halpern 2017), thoughts are originary in the productive sense (cf. Plato 1921: 265b), so dis-automatized (Stiegler 2016: 72; also see Aristotle in Matuschak and Nielsen 2019).

What is meant by automatization here is encapsulated by 'the Google way of science' which is the stipulation that through the sheer volume of (programmed) data collected, patterns can be recognized without the need for a theoretical model which was previously a human-proposed explanation or (narrative) process of thought. 'It may turn out that tremendously large volumes of data are sufficient to skip the theory part in order to make a predicted observation. Google was one of the first to notice this.' (Kelly 2008; cf. Stiegler 2016: 51–55).

Individuals can be denied the possibility to interpret (explain or describe) their psychic collective retentions (Stiegler 2018: 44–52). An illustration of this are the search systems that provide answers instead of supporting a user's ability to find and make sense of information, explore, stumble, and learn through the process of querying and discovery (Shah and Bender 2021). Another is how Bateson (in Halpern 2017) anticipated the weakening of the human 'too closely married to one perceptual condition', which could be compared to what, from a pedagogical standpoint, is the 'persona' used in user design (Gray 2017) which prioritizes definition even of desires and fears over the latent potential of pedagogical change (Nachmanovitch 1990: 118). To understand patterns only as solutions to problems can be a narrow view of patterns (Gabriel 2022).

While knowledge gained through the automatization of thought through data collection can be seen as the solution to disagreement and conflict (Stiegler 2018: 17), such as by ostensibly (O'Neil 2016; Noble 2018; Nowotny 2021) being unbiased through the 'performativity of fact', it replaces semantic and causal analysis,

---

[14] This is a ML model that contains 'deep' layers of nodes that process input data-of exteriorized knowledge-and transmit outputs to the next layer, learning by cumulative pattern recognition.

as well as hypotheses, models, and experiments (Stiegler 2018: 49) and other processes of learning in the pursuit of knowledge.

2.4   Mnemotechnics as Anthropological Device

It was suggested above that human understanding has historically been assisted by mnemotechnic prosthesis, an artificial device augmenting (or threatening) the human physical being, or organism. The evolution of the human species (its ethnicity) differs from the natural selection relevant to animals (their specificity). It is 'humankind', not the animal species, that continually trans-forms itself. 'Specific' memory is internal to the (animal) organism and thus endosomatic. The human capacity for technical memory is epiphylogenetic: external to the organism, exosomatic. As it is externalized, it is tertiary.

Technicity can succeed social organizations. In such cases, those in the 'technical group' exceed those in the 'ethnic group' by holding (having 'seized') the technicity that constitutes the ethnic milieu while also exceeding it (Stiegler 2018: 216–217), trans-forming it. This can be illustrated by the difference in use-cases between those who know how to use the technology and those who do not (janus 2022).

The technological and mechanical, as a 'sustained focus' and product of science, alters material life, industry, systems, and society (cf. Whitehead 1948: 130–131), changing the ethnic milieu. Stiegler developed a 'grammatology' in order to analyse the process of successive technical development, such as by perceiving a 'writing *screen*' (emphasis added) in the cave wall (e.g. Stiegler 2018: 146).

'Exosomatic incursions' of recent digital technicity all over the globe has meant that there are almost no remaining 'ethnic communities in the strict sense' that remain unexposed. This in turn leads to the eradication of diversity of thought through the subduing of psychic singularities (Stiegler 2018: 222) as individuals 'throughout the entire world grammatize their own behaviour by interacting with computer systems operating in real time' (Stiegler 2018: 46). That is to say, 'once we've shaped tools', in McLuhan's words, 'they turn around and "reshape us"' (Kay 1993; cf. Dijkstra 1982). Re-presentation is bi-directional (Nelson in Smith and Halasz 1987). Individuals inscribe themselves into the technological constitutive forces that condition the possibilities of human becoming as they use technology, being trans-formed by it. At the same time, technical tendencies become emancipated from ethnic milieus and become concretized as technical facts (Stiegler 2018: 192). Technicity as an emergent universifying power privileges technical fact over the human species with all of its inherent differences.

If all of the world's humans, or ἄνθρωπος (*anthropos*), are subsumed to the same technological development, this raises questions of noodiversity. Noodiversity pertains to νοῦς (*nous*, related to *noein, noetics, noology*), intellectual *perception* (Gadamer 2001: 105); the intellect or faculty of the human mind to understand what is true or real and think rationally, where human understanding can at once intuit or apprehend divine order and create it (e.g., Aristotle 1934: 1142a; Whitehead 1978: 21). Noetic heritage[15] comprises 'its languages, archives, works, knowledge and noetic exteriorities in general' (Stiegler 2018: 79). Difference of *local* ex-pression is related to productive difference in human thought (Stiegler 2018: 222). As stated earlier, the exteriorization of memory through the mnemotechnic tool enables but does not guarantee trans-individual, trans-generational memory transmission and knowledge production. However, the very concept of information (data that is *retained*), which is 'concretized and put in play as fixed capital … tends to eliminate noetic *différance* itself … as well as vital *différance*, and does so through the generalized proletarianization [liquidation of knowledge] not just of production and consumption but of conceptualization' (Stiegler 2018: 201). The generalized automation of fixed capital is constituted by the algorithm that replaces human workers who had previously reduced their knowledge of how to work to merely adapt to tasks and the system that realizes them (cf. Taylor 1919).

One point here is to perceive whether the knowledge re-presented by the technical organs that are capacitated by the *anthropos* produce entropic possibilities, or the opposite, negentropic possibilities (Stiegler 2018: 142). A question for postdigital research is how receptive it is to different ways of knowing. This has implications for epistemological pluralism, such as how different learners learn in different ways (Turkle and Papert 1991).

The entropic tendencies of the Anthropocene—of the tension between mnemotechnologies and knowledge re-presentation, the place of human activity like work, and the calculated monetization of exteriorized knowledge—call for the bifurcation of negentropic *différance* (cf. Stiegler 2018: 92), exceeding every expectation and understanding through the play of imagination (Stiegler 2018: 98). Such bifurcation could prioritize more care-ful relations between mnemotechnics and humans and negotiate the place of the former such that it supports the authentic learning process.

3 Narrative-Code Shift

In the context of the organological relations outlined above, according to which it is necessary to negotiate between mnemotechnologies, psychic/biological individuals, and social organizations, such that they are able to co-individuate, it is significant that digitalized knowledge representation provides machines with traces of memory that humans possess, as a form of mnemotechnics, so that *AI systems* can become better. Yet the ultimate goal of *learning agency* is to enable *humans* to attain practical knowledge that is in line with the goals (*telos*) that serve the common good (Aristotle 1944: 1337a-b).

---

[15] The term was used by Ampère (1838) to designate the diversity of the sciences of the human mind.

Can aggregated standardizing or statistical approaches 'drill down into each sub-population' (Hu 2023), especially where emergent categories are not anticipated?[16] And can AI systems produce dissociated milieus—*particularly if we are talking about individual human understanding of the more complex generative transformer and pattern recognition technologies?* Long before such developments in AI, algorithmic approaches to understanding human culture were critiqued (Geertz 1973: 11). A danger to the *ethnicity* of the human being in the present context can be seen by considering the mnemotechnic achievements in AI that are bred to maximize certain variables to suit a complex purpose. In exchange for reaching these variables, diversity and flexibility are bred out. 'But if conditions change, the species is locked into a narrow range of variety. Monoculture leads invariably to a loss of options, which leads to instability.' (Nachmanovitch 1990: 118)

There has been an expansion of both the feedback loops developed through work in cybernetics (e.g., in the Macy Conferences 1946–1953) and the network of connections (Bateson 1979: 8). These are manifested in the supervised and unsupervised learning of AI—but also through networks of infrastructure, labour, zones, optimization, and contingency. This 'produces circulatory regimes of containment' as global infrastructural and software standards stitch spaces, labour, and operational procedures together across diverse geographical scales and modalities of time (Nielson and Rossiter 2014). Calculation can be performed through the repetition of certain symbols and performed without fully understanding the displacement of what is represented by the symbol (Stiegler 2018: 52), like the quality of or 'sensibility' (Ito 2018) for life.

This needs to be considered in the contexts of how even though code is privileged above narrative *tékhnē*, narrative technique (cf. Aristotle 1926: 1357a) is critical to learning and how humans learn how to learn. This (so-called 'deutero learning') requires more than just responding to changes in an environment, and, perhaps most significantly, is worked out through trial and *error* (Bateson 1972/1987). The attempt to formally overcome error has the potential to remove a view of the importance of error in learning—which, acknowledged in digital learning, has led to innovations in the field (Beghetto 2021b). There is a *difference* in human knowledge where it involves the process of self-deliberation (Gadamer 1975/2006: 318) and is not classified according to pre-determined performance measures. This has been recognised by teachers and researchers who note a lack of original thought and motivation in connection with the metrics of grading (Tommel 2020) and assessment (Sanford 2018) and who make use of AI in teaching to promote creative thinking (e.g. Schiappa and Montfort 2023; Mollick and Mollick 2022).

---

[16] 'One thing I learned about modern medicine is that it mostly looks at groups and treatment in aggregate. Due to funding, most studies lack statistical power to drill down into each subpopulation and causal factors. Doctors use these studies as the source of truth, but these studies are incomplete. Specialists augment this with experience, and the consequence is that not all specialists are created equal and can properly diagnose and treat a patient. I have to root cause complex issues frequently in my work in tech. But root causing self issues requires a high level of disciplined self-analysis.' (Hu 2023)

Disequilibrium, the state of imbalance that occurs in the face of new information that requires us to develop a new conceptual re-presentation ('schema') or modify an existing one and that can be a sign of incorrect thinking, is what sparks new learning (Piaget 1952). Along these lines, mistakes can be catalysts for collaborative discussion where errors are viewed as part of 'works in progress' (Staples and Colonis 2007: 259), re-presencing better ways forward. By contrast, expectations of 'smooth digital mediation' (Weiser et al. 1999: 693) can give rise to new (possibly false) expectations of the environmental elimination of error (O'Neil 2016; Noble 2018; Nowotny 2021).

Judgment or deliberation were once resolved through philosophical or rhetorical reflection (e.g., Aristotle 1926: 1357a, 1934). Dissatisfaction with error in human thought led to the formalization of a codified *mathêsis universalis* in an attempt to reduce error (e.g., Descartes 1641/1901: 22; Descartes 1637/1927: 19–20). But there are ways in which the displacement of ideas, or schemas by mathematics or engineering can be problematic. On the level of 'equivalences'—mentioned as being problematic in the section on re-presentation—it is noted that in practice assumptions can be made that are more for 'mathematical convenience than faithfulness to actual human data' (Russell and Norvig 2022: 865). Similarly, the purpose of technical expansion, which all forms of knowledge were mobilized by and brought closer to, approaches the field of instrumentality, to which science, 'with its ends determined by the imperatives of economic struggle or war, and with its epistemic status shifting accordingly, became more and more subject' (Stiegler 1998: 2).

The technicization of science can constitute 'its eidetic *blinding*. While in the Leibnizian (1672/1951) project of a *mathêsis universalis*, the ensuing displacement of meaning leads to an elaboration of method that is metaphysical', algebraic arithmetic subsumes nature to 'systematic "instruction" and instrumentalization' (Stiegler 1998: 3) (emphasis in the original).

The question is whether the automation of the reduced process of relationality (Bateson in Halpern 2017) will lead to new horrors.

Automatization in this chapter has largely been considered in relation to 'individuation', according to which individuals have access to interpreting retentional (re-membering) systems to be able to continue to be productive as members of society. 'Code must *become knowledge* in order to be a law or right, which must in turn be that of a social body.' (Stiegler 2018: 251) (emphasis in the original).

By contrast, the belief in Singularity is 'that AI will supersede humans with its exponential growth, and that everything we have done until now and are currently doing is insignificant' (Ito 2018; also see Nowotny 2021). The Dalai Lama once suggested that human consciousness could be transferred to machines as part of the continuum of consciousness (1992: 152–153). This aligns with the goal to create learning patterns that mimic consciousness. But conscious appearance could also just be an impression or falsely generated recognition (γένηται ἀναγνώρισις) (cf. Plato 1921: 193b).

It is the human job to practice their own skills of perception, including the process of re-cognizing themselves with respect to the context of their technical tools and their environment through the care-ful work of re-presencing the digital trace.

While this takes place naturally where extracurricular knowledge is circulated among individuals in a social body, the skill of re-cognition can be dulled. 'Poor, reduced contextualization produces levelled language, deprived of significance for both interlocutor and speaker alike. Learning how to contextualize is the first step in learning how to learn.' (Trocmé-Fabre 1999: 206) Cognitive levelling is already a problem in the application of words such as 'believes' and 'thinks' to large language models (Shanahan 2022).

4   Mnemotechnic Entropy

Entropy can also be found in the architectures of digital code. Today 'everything is libraries developing on top of libraries, all of which, in the cloud, need network configuration as big cloud vendor network topologies determine the shape of our applications' (Boykis 2022). Modern programming is 'becoming complex, uninteresting, full of layers that just need to be glued' (Sanfilippo n.d.) and a lot of it is 'just plugging in magic incantations—combine somebody else's software and start it up' (Siebel 2009; see also Dullien 2019; Branwen 2010/2021). Much of the knowledge of this stack is hidden in proprietary code that is illegal to read or hardwired into parts that are illegal to fix. This mnemotechnic stack, from the hardware up, in addition to being harmful to the environment and certain workers (cf. Knox 2019), does not foster the movement for code to become knowledge. However, today as a researcher re-presences the digital trace through digital research, they are *equally* being traced by EdTech spyware, and thus every move can arguably already digitally anticipated through (frequently game-playing) generative technologies.

Computers are not easier to use or less isolating or require less attention than they did before the advent of so-called 'calm computing' and ubicomp that tried to address ways to push the technical body of mnemotechnics into the background to foreground the ongoing process of knowledge work (Weiser et al. 1999). The attempt to balance control and simplicity or smooth digital mediation and the immediacy of other humans, or unlimited power and understandable straightforwardness (Weiser et al. 1999) was also part of the promise of general-purpose computing. This gist was encapsulated by Michael Crichton (1983: Introduction) who wrote that 'it's easy to use computers, which is fortunate because everyone's going to have to learn. It's not easy to use computers wisely, which is unfortunate because everyone's going to have to learn.' Instead of everyone having a personal computer with smart processing power giving them full control over knowledge work, ever more people use 'dumb' terminals as computing is done 'in the cloud' when there is greater processing power but a lack of privacy, autonomy, and the pedagogical value of minimal implementations (e.g. Suckless software n.d.). What has become of the goal for digital tools to 'have great thinking patterns' and beauty 'built-in' (Kay 1993)?

Even in the field of postdigital learning, mnemotechnic interfaces are often oversimplified or do not give options for customization and personal control. Learning software is often not created by actual teachers even though good tools for representing thought 'arise mostly as a byproduct of doing original work on serious problems' who are motivated less by money than a genuine interest in the problem (Matuschak and Nielsen 2019; also see Groom et al. 2019). Mnemotechnic 'iconic augmentation' could consider how to re-present 'symbols and knowledge in new ways, across groups, across cultures' by opening our minds 'to full, complete use of computers to augment our most human of capabilities' (Engelbart 2002; e.g., Strasser 2021). In practice, however, the mnemotechnological design seems to solidify systems in place.

The 'normativity' of code (Stiegler 2016: 209) or the 'repetition without difference' (Bateson in Halpern 2017) such as the internalization of instrumentalist patterns (cf. Dijkstra 1982; McLuhan in Kay 1993), has impacted social relations, such as where humans 'bin' other humans into categories without a second thought—even though the code of the digital mnemotechnic tool is itself a narrow representation of greater knowledge. 'The analogies between automata and servomechanisms and human thought and actions sanctioned the adoption of mechanical metaphors, which in turn fostered thinking of oneself and one's community as mechanical systems.' (Heims 1991: 41) Pathologies emerge 'when the subject has no other, different communicative situations to compare, contrast, or use, outside of the immediate message'; the cure is diachronicity (Bateson in Halpern 2017). Where knowledge turns into non-knowledge it becomes toxic (Stiegler 2018: 194).

5   Anthropological Difference

Many thinkers (e.g., Plato, Whitehead, Ricoeur) suggest that there is knowledge that exists beyond the physical world of 'manipulable objects' that must be sought through learning. This could be 'uncognitive apprehension' (Whitehead 1929: 86) comprising uncognitive essential relational connections that are grasped if not knowledge-based, not unlike the secondary retention or originary knowledge mentioned earlier. Such apprehensions can be 'felt' relationships to the rest of the world (Whitehead 1978: 219–282; also see Bateson 2015). This is related to the intuition of *noeîn* (Gadamer 2001: 36), a relational component that can make a difference (the human receptor being one of the organs in organology, capable of noetic *différance*: difference in human thought).

It is humans who can feel; computers can simulate. There is a human a code of interrelation and interpretation beyond the shadows and things; this is the 'novel togetherness' that can be experienced (cf. Whitehead 1978). Humans make the computer programs even when they do not understand them; humans are also capable of the bifurcation of negentropic *différance* (cf. Stiegler 2018: 92), 'exceeding every expectation' (Stiegler 2018: 98). If predicted, it would not be a bifurcation. However, without bifurcation, knowledge becomes a closed and entropic system; mnemotechnics does not support that which is '*beyond any possible analysis*'

(Stiegler 2018: 98) (emphasis in the original). The language used here is deliberate, as poetry also points to such a 'beyond' (cf. Whitehead 1929: 108). Even if readers disagree with this line of thought, it introduces a different schematic possibility for the re-presentation of knowledge. An example of something 'beyond' can be as rudimentary, in the digital realm, as the creative iteration of a domain of one's own (Groom et al. 2019; Goetz 2022). It does not preclude digital technology but is an extra- aspect to it, enriching it.

Just as computation supports *applications* of knowledge (Sowa 2000), the philosophical method can also involve 'the *utilization* of specific notions, applying to a restricted group of facts, for the divination of the generic notions which apply to all facts' and the search for patterns (Whitehead 1978: 5) (emphasis added). Both aim to introduce and rationally coordinate 'direct insight into depths as yet *unspoken*' (Whitehead 1968: 174) (emphasis added). But human-generated philosophical, philological reason has its place even as we do not necessarily mirror or live up to its principles. Philosophical linguistically ex-pressed systems explain our place in the world and how each actual entity and member of society are involved in the process of novel togetherness that may be inexplicable but can be intuited (cf. the νοῦς in noology) (Gadamer 2001; Whitehead 1978). It brings the idea of a co-creative holistic system with which we can co-create and re-presence (as mortals cf. Whitehead 1978), if we are willing to interpret the code by understanding philological meaning from given contexts (Gadamer 1975/2006: 470).

Where the source code is opaque, it can conceal contexts and functions despite claiming openness (e.g., Deceptive Design n.d.). Yet applications of this type of knowing about the world are used to make deeply troubling social and personal decisions such as loan approval or racial profiling (e.g., O'Neil 2016; Noble 2018; Nowotny 2021). It is argued that this does not mean that machines should be responsible for people as 'transferring ever more control over complex processes to intelligent machines—outsourcing our thinking and decision making' may 'work against the empowerment of individual human beings' and 'even prevent them from taking the responsibilities we would expect to go together with having human rights' (Birhane and van Dijk 2020: 212).

If postdigital research is truly motivated towards shared good, it can be suggested, for example, that 'bioethicists could benefit from more abstract, theoretical reflection about meaning in general. However, on the other hand, there is probably another essay to write, on how philosophers of life's meaning would benefit from considering the concrete implications of their views for bioethical matters.' (Metz 2021: 451)

In the narrative-code shift, where the knowledge re-presentation used for an increasing amount of decision-making impacts human, organological lives, a problem for postdigital research will be how to keep spaces open for negotiation, discourse, and exploration especially that which is respective of *local* difference through an attention to mutual engagement, recognising the presence of the digital 'encounter as an intentional, motivated, and power-laden act (rather than as an inherent consequence of an impersonal process)' (Irani et al. 2010: 1318). This gives a different perspective to how data 'capture' might view 'users as active participants and partners rather than as passive repositories of 'lore' to be mined' (Irani et al. 2010: 1318). Digital technology could, after Kay's early vision, mirror users' intelligence and experiences—not weaknesses! (also see Gadamer 1975/2006: 361)—being 'co-extensive' (Simon in Kay 1993) to the range of human thought.

It would hardly be a technological advance if what is captured is at the expense of any human place. It would be less of an epistemological advance if it were claimed that all knowledge *could* be captured, like birds in a room (Plato 1921: 197c-d), or if any language could 'pin down' all experience—including 'slavery, genocide, war'. All users and makers are responsible for the demise of human memory and the tools we have to keep it alive (cf. Morrison 1993), to say nothing of augmenting it.

6 Conclusion

The context of ever more ubiquitous computational knowledge representation in AI brings challenges in how to think through the seduction of digital mediation smoothing over the immediacy of complex fellow workers and humans in general. But in order to continue to learn how to learn, individuals need access to the interpretation and interrelation with retentional systems and others. Mnemotechnics, which can be used to re-member and trans-form, can threaten local, human *différance* through the capacity of the technical tool to exceed the human being through its universifying powers (Stiegler 2018). This can lead to entropic equalization and effacement (Ricoeur 1991).

The mnemotechnic tool most capable of the greatest combinatorial proliferation of meanings (cf. janus 2022) today constitutes transformer-based deep learning models in AI. AI is the science of designing computer systems to overtake human tasks (Sowa 2000). In the context of postdigital research, it may be asked who or what the task of the 'research observer' is and what this means to the continued circulation of memory and knowledge.

The chapter calls learning professionals to think of ways to use the digital tool to re-presence (Goetz 2023) 'symbols and knowledge in new ways, across groups, across cultures' by opening our minds 'to full, complete use of computers to augment our most human of capabilities' (Engelbart 2002). This is critical in the age of ubiquitous computing, or ubiquitous programmable network terminals, as the distribution of knowledge among its networks increasingly involves 'dumb' terminals in feedback loops that can be designed for containment and control. Without practice in the contextualization that occurs through interrelational communication, humans might imitate and repeat such narrowed applications of knowledge (Bateson in Halpern 2017; McLuhan in Kay 1993) and become closed to the pursuit of learning that exists beyond the world of manipulable objects (Whitehead 1929), trading different tongues to mine what has been captured until structural insolvency is reached (cf. Plato 1925b; Stiegler 2018).

Code is a mirror, for better or worse. In the narrative-code shift, knowledge representation is increasingly used to make automated decisions that impact human, organological lives despite categorical differences. Consequently, a problem for postdigital research is how to keep spaces open for negotiation, discourse, and exploration especially that which is respective of difference through an attention to mutual engagement, recognising users of technology 'as active participants and partners rather than as passive repositories of 'lore' to be mined' (Irani et al. 2010: 1318). This would evoke users' own contexts and intelligence (Coleridge in Kay 1993) and challenge mnemotechnic ex-pression to re-presence the 'quality without a name' (Alexander in Gabriel 1996) on individual, social, and technical terms, beyond the closed system of the mnemotechnic tool's pre-programmed image (Dijkstra 1982; McLuhan in Kay 1993).

References

Alexander, C. (1977). *A Pattern Language*. New York: Oxford University Press.

Ampère, A. (1838). *Essai sur la philosophie des sciences*. Paris: Bachelier.

Aristotle. (1934). Nicomachean Ethics. In H. Rackham (Ed. and Trans.), *Aristotle in 23 Volumes, Vol. 19*. Cambridge, MA: Harvard University Press.

Aristotle. (1944). Politics. In H. Rackham (Ed. and Trans.), *Aristotle in 23 Volumes, Vol. 21*. Cambridge, MA: Harvard University Press.

Aristotle. (1926). Rhetoric. In J. Freese (Ed. and Trans.), *Aristotle in 23 Volumes, Vol. 22*. Cambridge, MA: Harvard University Press.

Aristotle. (2008). *The Categories*. https://www.gutenberg.org/files/2412/2412-h/2412-h.htm. Accessed 30 January 2023.

Barnett, S. (2017). *Rhetorical Realism: Rhetoric, ethics and the ontology of things*. New York: Routledge.

Barocas, S., Hardt, M., & Narayanan, A. (2022). Fairness and Machine Learning. https://fairmlbook.org/. Accessed 30 January 2023.

Barski, C. (2007). How To Tell Stuff To A Computer. https://www.lisperati.com/tellstuff/index.html and https://www.lisperati.com/tellstuff/scientist.html. Accessed 30 January 2023.

Bateson, G. (1979). *Mind and Nature*. New York: E. P. Dutton.

Bateson, G. (1954/2017). "Minimum Constellation Necessary For Type Confusion": Letters to Norbert Wiener. *Grey Room 66*, 115–11. https://doi.org/10.1162/GREY_a_00214.

Bateson, G. (1972/1987). *Steps to an Ecology of Mind*. New Jersey: Jason Aronson Inc.

Bateson, N. (2015). Symmathesy: a word in progress. https://norabateson.wordpress.com/2015/11/03/symmathesy-a-word-in-progres. Accessed 20 August 2022.

Baudrillard, J. (1983). Simulacra and Simulation. Trans. P. Foss, P. Patton, & P. Beitchman. New York: Semiotext(e).

Beaty, L., Hodgson, V., Mann, S., & McConnell, D. (2002). Towards E-quality in Networked E-learning in Higher Education. http://www.networkedlearningconference.org.uk/past/nlc2002/manifesto.htm. Accessed 1 July 2020.

Beghetto, R. A. (2021a). Creative learning in education. In M. L. Kern & M. L. Wehmeyer (Eds.), *The Palgrave Handbook of Positive Education* (pp. 473–491). Cham: Palgrave Macmillan. https://doi.org/10.1007/978-3-030-64537-3_19.

Beghetto, R. A. (2021b). My favorite failure: Using digital technology to facilitate creative learning and reconceptualize failure. *Tech Trends, 65*, 606–614. https://doi.org/10.1007/s11528-021-00607-7.

Bender, E., Gebru, T., McMillan-Major, A., & Mitchell, M. (2021). On the Dangers of Stochastic Parrots: Can Language Models Be Too Big? In L. Irani, S. Kannan, M. Mitchell, & D. Robinson (Eds.), *FAccT '21: Proceedings of the 2021 ACM Conference on Fairness, Accountability, and Transparency* (pp. 610–623). New York: Association for Computing Machinery. https://doi.org/10.1145/3442188.3445922.

Birhane, A., & van Dijk, J. (2020). Robot Rights? Let's Talk about Human Welfare Instead. In Markham, J. Powles, T. Walsh, & A. L. Washington (Eds.), *2020 AAAI/ACM Conference on AI, Ethics, and Society (AIES'20)* (pp. 207–213). New York: Association for Computing Machinery. https://doi.org/10.1145/3375627.3375855.

Boretti, F. (2023). Roam, Twenty Years Before Roam. https://borretti.me/article/roam-twenty-years-before-roam. Accessed 1 February 2023.

Bishop, C. (2006). *Pattern Recognition and Machine Learning*. New York: Springer.

Bloom, J. (2004). Patterns That Connect: Rethinking Our Approach to Learning and Thinking. *Curriculum and Teaching, 19*(1), 5–26.

Boesch, G. (2022). What is Pattern Recognition? A Gentle Introduction. https://viso.ai/deep-learning/pattern-recognition/. Accessed 30 January 2023.

Borden, R. (2017). Gregory Bateson's Search for "Patterns Which Connect" Ecology and Mind. *Human Ecology Review, 23*(2), 87–96. https://doi.org/10.22459/HER.23.02.2017.09.

Boykis, V. (2022). The cloudy layers of modern-day programming. https://vickiboykis.com/2022/12/05/the-cloudy-layers-of-modern-day-programming/. Accessed 1 January 2023.

Branwen, G. (2010/2021). How many computers are in your computer? https://gwern.net/Computers. Accessed 20 November 2022.

Campbell, L. (1882). *The Life of James Clerk Maxwell*. London: Macmillan and Co.

Christiano, P. (2015). Against Mimicry. https://ai-alignment.com/against-mimicry-6002a472fc42. Accessed 30 December 2022.

Cockburn, A. (2002). *Agile Software Development*. Boston, MA and San Francisco, CA: Addison-Wesley.

Collins, P. (2014). Teaching Robots Right from Wrong. Tufts Now. https://web.archive.org/web/20220617150137/https://now.tufts.edu/2014/05/09/teaching-robots-right-wrong. Accessed 30 January 2023.

Crichton, M. (1983). *Electronic Life*. New York: Knopf.

Crawford, K., & Joler, V. (2018). Anatomy of an AI System. https://anatomyof.ai/. Accessed 30 January 2023.

Cunningham, W., & Mehaffy, M. W. (2013). Wiki as Pattern Language. In C. Köppe (Ed.), *Proceedings of the 20th Conference on Pattern Languages of Programs (PLoP'13)* (pp. 1–14). The Hillside Group.

Dalai Lama. (1992). Buddhist reincarnation and AI. In J. Hayward & F. Varela (Eds.), *Gentle Bridges: Conversations with the Dalai Lama on the Sciences of Mind* (pp. 152–153). Boston, MA: Shambala.

Deceptive Design. (n.d.). Deceptive Design. https://www.deceptive.design/. Accessed 20 November 2022.

Derrida, J. (1972/1982). *Margins of Philosophy*. Chicago, IL: University of Chicago Press.

Descartes, R. (1637/1927). *A Discourse on Method*. New York: Everyman's Library.

Descartes, R. (1641/1901). *Meditations on First Philosophy*. Lancaster: Lancaster University.

Dignum, V. (2017). Responsible autonomy. *arXiv:1706.02513*. https://doi.org/10.48550/arXiv.1706.02513.

Dijkstra, E. (1982). A Letter from Dijkstra on APL. https://www.jsoftware.com/papers/Dijkstra_Letter.htm. Accessed 1 January 2023.

Dullien, T. (2019). Security, Moore's law, and the anomaly of cheap complexity. CyCon Keynote. https://thomasdullien.github.io/about/#talks. Accessed 20 November 2021.

Engelbart, D. (2002). Improving our ability to improve: a call for investment in a new future. Keynote address, World Library Summit, April 23–26, 2002, Singapore. https://www.dougengelbart.org/content/view/348/000/. Accessed 1 November 2022.

Fleming, W. (1860). *The Vocabulary of Philosophy: The mental, moral, and metaphysical.* Philadelphia, PA: Smith, English & Co.

Gabriel, R. (1996). *Patterns of Software*. New York and Oxford: Oxford University Press.

Gabriel, R. (2022). Personal correspondence.

Gadamer, H. (1975/2006). *Truth and Method*. London and New York: Continuum.

Gadamer, H. (2001). *The Beginning of Philosophy*. New York: Continuum Press.

Geertz, C. (1973). *The Interpretation of Cultures*. New York: Basic Books.

Gray, D. (2017). Updated Empathy Map Canvas. https://medium.com/the-xplane-collection/updated-empathy-map-canvas-46df22df3c8a. Accessed 30 December 2022.

Goetz, G. (2022). A song of Teaching with Free Software in the Anthropocene. *Educational Philosophy and Theory, 54*(5), 545-556. https://doi.org/10.1080/00131857.2021.1962706.

Goetz, G. (2023). Re-presencing the network in networked learning. In M. Johnson, F. Healey-Benson, N. Bonderup Dohn, & C. Adams, C. (Eds.), *Phenomenological Perspectives on Networked Learning*. Singapore: Springer.

Groom, J., Taub-Pervizpour, L., Richard, S., Long-Wheeler, K., & Burtis, M. (2019). Seven things you should know about a domain of one's own. Educause, 18 October. https://library.educause.edu/resources/2019/10/7-things-you-should-know-about-a-domain-of-ones-own. Accessed 18 July 2020.

Halpern, O. (2017). Schizophrenic Techniques: Cybernetics, the Human Sciences, and the Double Bind. *S & F Online, 10*(3). https://web.archive.org/web/20160715055240/http://sfonline.barnard.edu/feminist-media-theory/schizophrenic-techniques-cybernetics-the-human-sciences-and-the-double-bind/0/#footnote_39_603. Accessed 1 January 2023.

Heims, S. (1991). *The Cybernetics Group 1946-1953: Constructing a Social Science for Postwar America*. Cambridge, MA: MIT Press.

Hesiod. (1914). Theogony. In H. Evelyn-White (Ed. and Trans.), *The Homeric Hymns and Homerica with an English Translation*. Cambridge, MA: Harvard University Press.

Hu, S. (2023). How Poor Sleep Drove Me Insane, and My Long Path to Recovery. https://writing.samsonhu.com/how-poor-sleep-drove-me-insane-and-my-long-path-to-recovery/. Accessed 27 February 2023.

Huang, H. (2023). The Generative AI Revolution Has Begun – How did we get here? Ars Technica, 30 January. https://arstechnica.com/gadgets/2023/01/the-generative-ai-revolution-has-begun-how-did-we-get-here/. Accessed 30 January 2023.

Ito, J. (2018). Resisting Reduction: A Manifesto. *Journal of Design and Science*. https://doi.org/10.21428/8f7503e4.

Irani, L., Vertesi, J., Dourish, P., Philip, K., & Grinter, R. (2010). Postcolonial Computing: A Lens on Design and Development. In G. Fitzpatrick, S. Hudson, K. Edwards, & T. Rodden (Eds.), *CHI 2010: Proceedings of the SIGCHI Conference* (pp. 1311–1320). New York: Association for Computing Machinery. https://doi.org/10.1145/1753326.1753522.

janus. (2022). Simulators. https://www.lesswrong.com/posts/vJFdjigzmcXMhNTsx/simulators#fnrefbjl6s2y0l5a. Accessed 30 January 2023.

Johnson, M. (2020). Phenomenology and networked learning: mobilage glimpsed from the inside through an online focus group. In M. De Laat, T. Ryberg, N. Bonderup Dohn, S. Børsen Hansen, & J. Jørgen Hansen (Eds.), *Proceedings of the 12th International Conference on Networked Learning*. Aalborg: Aalborg University. https://orca.cardiff.ac.uk/id/eprint/132075/1/826410_25.-johnson-phenomenology-and-networked-learning-mobilage-glimpsed-from-the-inside-through-an-online-focus-group.pdf. Accessed 25 October 2021.

Kasenberg, D., Arnold, T., & Scheutz, M. (2018). Norms, Rewards, and the Intentional Stance: Comparing Machine Learning Approaches to Ethical Training. In J. Furman, G. Marchant, H. Price, & F. Rossi (Eds.), *AIES '18: Proceedings of the 2018 AAAI/ACM Conference on AI, Ethics, and Society* (pp. 184–190). New York: Association for Computing Machinery. https://doi.org/10.1145/3278721.3278774.

Kay, A. (1993). The Early History of Smalltalk. *SIGPLAN Notices 28*(3), 69–95. https://doi.org/10.1145/155360.155364.

Kelly, K. (2008). The Technium: The Google way of science. https://kk.org/thetechnium/the-google-way/. Accessed 20 November 2022.

Knox, J. (2019). What Does the 'Postdigital' Mean for Education? Three Critical Perspectives on the Digital, with Implications for Educational Research and Practice. *Postdigital Science and Education, 1*(2), 357–370. https://doi.org/10.1007/s42438-019-00045-y.

Krishnamurthi, S. (2019). On the Expressive Power of Programming Languages. Papers We Love Conference, 12 September, St. Louis, Missouri. https://github.com/papers-we-love/pwlconf-info/blob/master/2019/shriram-krishnamurthi/Shriram%20Krishnamurthi%20PWL2019.txt. Accessed 20 November 2022.

Lave, J. (1991). *Situated Learning.* Cambridge, UK: Cambridge University Press.

Latour, B. (1987). *Science In Action.* Cambridge, MA: Harvard University Press.

Leibnitz, G. (1672/1951). *Leibnitz: Selections.* New York: Charles Scribner's Sons.

Malle, B., Bello, P., & Scheutz, M. (2019). Requirements for an Artificial Agent with Norm Competence. In V. Conitzer, G. Hadfield, & S. Vallor (Eds.), *AIES '19: Proceedings of the 2019 AAAI/ACM Conference on AI, Ethics, and Society* (pp. 21–27). New York: Association for Computing Machinery. https://doi.org/10.1145/3306618.3314252.

Malone, T., Rus, D., & Laubacher, R. (2019). Artificial Intelligence and the Future of Work. https://workofthefuture.mit.edu/wp-content/uploads/2020/12/2020-Research-Brief-Malone-Rus-Laubacher2.pdf. Accessed 30 January 2023.

Markauskaite, L., & Goodyear, P. (2017). *Epistemic Fluency and Professional Education: Innovation, knowledgeable action and actionable knowledge.* Dordrecht: Springer. https://doi.org/10.1007/978-94-007-4369-4.

Matuschak, A., & Nielsen, M. (2019). How can we develop transformative tools for thought? https://numinous.productions/ttft/. Accessed 20 November 2022.

Metz, T. (2021). Meaning and Medicine: An underexplored bioethical value. *Ethik in der Medizin, 33,* 439–453. https://doi.org/10.1007/s00481-021-00662-x.

Mollick, E., & Mollick, L. (2022). New Modes of Learning Enabled by AI Chatbots: Three Methods and Assignments. https://papers.ssrn.com/sol3/papers.cfm?abstract_id=4300783. Accessed 30 January 2022.

Morrison, T. (1993). Nobel Lecture. https://www.nobelprize.org/prizes/literature/1993/morrison/lecture/. Accessed 1 January 2023.

Nachmanovitch, S. (1990). *Free Play: Improvisation in life and art.* New York: Jeremy P. Tarcher/Putnam.

Naur, P. (1985). Programming As Theory Building. *Microprocessing and Microprogramming, 15*(5), 253–261.

Nielson, B., & Rossiter, N. (2014). Logistical Worlds 1. https://logisticalworlds.org/publications. Accessed 20 November 2022.

Networked Learning Editorial Collective. (2021). Networked Learning: Inviting Redefinition. *Postdigital Science and Education, 3*(2), 312–325. https://doi.org/10.1007/s42438-020-00167-8.

Noble, S. (2018). *Algorithms of Oppression.* New York: NYU Press.

Nowotny, H. (2021). *In AI We Trust.* Cambridge: Polity.

O'Neil, J. (2016). *Weapons of Math Destruction.* New York: Crown.

Park, J. S., Popowski, L., Cai, C. J., Morris, M. R., Liang, P., & Bernstein, M. S. (2022). Social Simulacra: Creating Populated Prototypes for Social Computing Systems. https://arxiv.org/pdf/2208.04024.pdf. Accessed 1 January 2023.

Peters, M. A., Jandrić, P., & Hayes, S. (2021). Postdigital-Biodigital: An Emerging Configuration. *Educational Philosophy and Theory.* https://doi.org/10.1080/00131857.2020.1867108.

Petit, V. (2013). Vocabulaire d'Ars Industrialis. In B. Stiegler, *Pharmacologie du Front National* (pp. 369–411.) Paris: Flammarion.

Piaget, J. (1952). *The Origins of Intelligence in Children.* New York: International Universities Press.

Plato. (1921). Sophist. In H. N. Fowler (Ed. and Trans.), *Plato In Twelve Volumes: Vol. 12.* London: William Heinemann Ltd.

Plato. (1925a). Phaedrus. In H. N Fowler (Ed. and Trans.), *Plato in Twelve Volumes: Vol. 9*. London: William Heinemann Ltd.

Plato. (1925b). Timaeus. In H. N Fowler (Ed. and Trans.), *Plato In Twelve Volumes: Vol. 9*. London: William Heinemann Ltd.

Plato. (1967). Meno. In W. R. M. Lamb (Ed. and Trans.), *Plato in Twelve Volumes, Vol. 3*. Cambridge, MA: Harvard University Press and London: William Heinemann Ltd.

Plato. (1969). The Republic. In P. Shorey (Ed. and Trans.), *Plato in Twelve Volumes, Vols. 5 & 6*. Cambridge, MA: Harvard University Press.

Randall, J. (1967/1970). *Plato: Dramatist of the Life of Reason*. New York: Columbia University Press.

Ricoeur, P. (1991). *A Ricoeur Reader: Reflection and Imagination*. Toronto: University of Toronto Press.

Russell, T., & Norvig, P. (1995). *Artificial Intelligence: A Modern Approach*. New Jersey: Prentice Hall.

Russell, T., & Norvig, P. (2022). *Artificial Intelligence: A Modern Approach*. 4th Ed. London: Pearson.

Sanfilippo, S. (n.d.). Aka antirez. https://web.archive.org/web/20230102123630/http://invece.org/. Accessed 1 December 2023.

Sanford, C. (2018). *No More Feedback*. Edmonds: InterOctave.

Schiappa, E., & Montfort, N. (2023). Advice Concerning the Increase in AI-Assisted Writing. https://nickm.com/schiappa_montfort/ai_advice_2023-01-10.pdf. Accessed 30 January 2023.

Schwab, K., & Malleret, T. (2020). *COVID-19: The Great Reset*. Geneva: Forum Publishing.

Searls, D. (2016). Giving Silos Their Due. Linux Journal, 2 February. https://www.linuxjournal.com/content/giving-silos-their-due. Accessed 30 January 2023.

Shanahan, M. (2022). Talking about large language models. *arXiv:2212.03551*. https://doi.org/10.48550/arXiv.2212.03551.

Siebel, P. (2009). *Coders At Work*. New York: Apress.

Smith, J., & Halasz, J. (1987). Hypertext '87: Proceedings of the ACM Conference on Hypertext. New York: Association for Computing Machinery. https://dl.acm.org/doi/proceedings/10.1145/317426.

Sowa, J. (2000). *Knowledge Representation: Logical, Philosophical, and Computational Foundations*. Pacific Grove: Brooks Cole Publishing.

Stallman, R. (2002). *Free Software, Free Society*. Boston, MA: GNU Press.

Staples, M., & Colonis, M. (2007). Making the Most of Mathematical Discussions. *Mathematics Teacher, 101*(4), 257–261. https://doi.org/10.5951/MT.101.4.0257.

Stiegler, B. (1998). *Technics and Time 1: The Fault of Epimetheus*. Stanford, CA: Stanford University Press.

Stiegler, B. (2016). *Automatic Society: The Future of Work*. Cambridge: Polity Press.

Stiegler, B. (2018). *The Neganthropocene*. London: Open Humanities Press.

Stokel-Walker, C. (2022). Adobe Just Held a Bunch of Pantone Colors Hostage. Wired, 2 November. https://www.wired.com/story/adobe-pantone-color-subscription-fee/. Accessed 30 January 2023.

Strasser, M. (2021). The business of extracting knowledge from academic publications. https://markusstrasser.org/extracting-knowledge-from-literature/. Accessed 20 November 2022.

Studtmann, P. (2007/2021). Aristotle's Categories. In E. N. Zalta (Ed.), *Stanford Encyclopaedia of Philosophy*. https://plato.stanford.edu/entries/aristotle-categories/. Accessed 30 January 2023.

Suckless software (n.d.). https://suckless.org/. Accessed 30 January 2023.

Taylor, F. (1919). *The Principles of Scientific Management*. New York: Harper & Brothers Publishers.

Thompson, N., Greenwald, K., Lee, K., & Manso, G. (2022). The Computational Limits of Deep Learning. *arXiv:2007.05558*. https://doi.org/10.48550/arXiv.2007.05558.

Tommel, J. (2020). Ungrading: A Bibliography. https://www.jessestommel.com/ungrading-a-bibliography/. Accessed 30 January 2022.

Trocmé-Fabre, H. (1999). *Réinventer le métier d'apprendre*. Paris: Éditions d'organisation.

Turkle, S., & Papert, S. (1991). Epistemological Pluralism and the Revaluation of the Concrete. In I. Harel & S. Papert (Eds.), *Constructionism* (pp. 161–192). New York: Ablex Publishing.

Van Loon, J. (2007). Ethnography: A critical turn in cultural studies. In P. Atkinson, A. Coffey, S. Delamont, J. Lofland, & L. Lofland (Eds.), *Handbook of Ethnography* (pp. 273–284). Los Angeles, CA and London, UK: Sage Publications.

Weiser, M., Gold, R., & Brown, J. (1999). The Origins of Ubiquitous Computing Research at PARC in the Late 1980s. *IBM Systems Journal, 38*(4), 693. https://doi.org/10.1147/sj.384.0693.

Whitehead, A. (1948). *Essays in Science and Philosophy*. New York: Rider and Company.

Whitehead, A. (1968). *Modes of Thought*. New York: Free Press.

Whitehead, A. (1978). *Process and Reality*. New York: Free Press.

Whitehead, A. (1929). *Science and the Modern World*. Cambridge: Cambridge University Press.

Wiener, N. (1950/1989). *The Human Use of Human Beings*. London: Free Association Books.

Wiener, N. (1960). Some Moral and Technical Consequences of Automation. *Science, New Series, 131*(3410), 1355–1358. https://doi.org/10.1126/science.131.3410.1355.

Yates, F. (1966/1999). *The Art of Memory*. London and New York: Routledge.

Part IV
Exclusions and Inclusions

Postdigital Validity: Peer Reviews on the Edges of Modernity

Felicitas Macgilchrist

1 Introduction

How to assess the validity of the claims made by research publication? Are classic modes of validity still helpful? Which new proposals have been suggested? Or is validation itself a remnant of modernist times and no longer necessary? This chapter explores the intelligibility of validity under the conditions of postdigitality (see Lather 1995). It suggests that adding the adjective 'postdigital' to 'validity' reminds scholars of key issues which have been long discussed, and may also open up new ways of discussing the matter. The key could lie in the blurring of traditional boundaries among forms of making knowledge.

'Postdigital' is thus used in this chapter, firstly, as a diagnosis of our contemporary world, i.e., the muddy, lumpy, racist, scrappy, classist, glitchy, noisy everyday practices of lives in which digital technologies thread through much of what we do, whether it is online, networked, or as ostensibly physical and offline as sitting in a park and listening to birds (where the walk in the park is surveilled by networked CCTV cameras and the birdsong has been captured in a citizen science app for identifying birds).

'Postdigital' is also used in this article, secondly, as a critical perspective on this world. In this latter sense, using the term 'postdigital' flags a turn away from seeing digital technology as a solution or a technical fix for social, economic, political, educational, or other problems. Instead, the term flags a turn towards critical approaches which engage with 'the mud' (Jandrić et al. 2018), 'glitches' (Russell 2020), 'failure' (Cascone 2000), 'noise' (Macgilchrist 2021a), 'broken data' (Pink et al. 2018), and 'scrappy realities' (Selwyn and Jandrić 2020) of contemporary life. Postdigital is one of the perspectives interested in blurring traditional (modernist)

F. Macgilchrist (✉)
University of Oldenburg, Oldenburg, Germany
e-mail: felicitas.macgilchrist@uni-oldenburg.de

P. Jandrić et al. (eds.), *Constructing Postdigital Research*, Postdigital Science and Education, https://doi.org/10.1007/978-3-031-35411-3_11

epistemic demarcations, hierarchies, and boundaries [see Striano (2019) for several uses of 'postdigital' and Jandrić et al. (2022) for a genealogy of the research field].

This chapter first reflects on how 'validity' is entangled with 'modernity' and hegemonic modernist notions of progress, development, and knowledge. As modernity is dying (Machado de Oliveira 2021), some scholars cling more strongly to these notions, while others seek alternatives. Discussions around the postdigital condition are part of these alternatives. Second, the chapter sketches recent methodological approaches for engaging with these realities, from baroque, inventive and speculative methods to classic ethnographies (Lather 1993; Law 2016; Lury and Wakeford 2014; Ross 2023; Small 2009). These methods do not, however, always sit comfortably with the blind peer review process in social science journals.

Third, and in the tradition of sharing steps in research processes that are often less visible (Walford 1991; Addey and Piattoeva 2022), the chapter provides three snapshots of peer reviews, and reflects on how the authors engaged with the reviewers' queries about validity: (i) a piece on the narrativity of academic publications (Macgilchrist 2021b); (ii) an article on the perplexity and complicity of postdigital participation (Poltze et al. 2022); and (iii) a speculative account of future histories based loosely on discourse analysis of contemporary debates (Macgilchrist et al. 2020). In this way, the chapter reflects on ways of negotiating and demonstrating the 'validity' of postdigital research, which can include realigning predominant understandings of validity in the social sciences.

2   Validity and Modernity/Coloniality

From the Latin *validus* (strong, effective, powerful) and *valere* (strong), the meaning of 'validity' as 'sufficiently supported by facts or authority' was first recorded in the seventeenth century. Contemporary questions in the social sciences revolving around these notions of facts and authority include: Do these methods *accurately* test what they are supposed to test? Do the methods measure what they *intend* to measure? Have they been applied *correctly*? Are the cases *representative* of the whole? Can the findings be *generalised*? However, the understanding of validity has changed over time, with the concept critiqued most intensely in the wake of debates about postmodern, posthuman, postpositivist, postcolonial, poststructural, postfoundational and post-qualitative approaches in the 1980s and 1990s (see St. Pierre 2013, 2019 for an overview of the key issues and references in these debates).

'Accuracy', 'intentions' 'correctness', 'representativity', and 'generalisability' have been shown to be deeply political concepts, rooted in histories of oppression, exclusion and hierarchisation. I thus borrow from decolonial thought to describe this universalising, rationalist mode of knowing not only as entangled with 'modernity' but with modernity/coloniality, since modernity is not thinkable without coloniality (Machado de Oliveira 2021; Maldonado-Torres 2007). And now, with the planet 'on the verge of destruction' (Law 2016: 18), and social science seeking creative means to engage with life in these 'capitalist ruins' (Tsing 2015), seems another good time to revisit the critique of this mode of knowledge production and current alternatives.

As modernity/coloniality dies, and its common-sense and hegemonic ways of knowing change, Vanessa Machado de Oliveira (2021) writes of 'hospicing modernity' to remind us not to discard everything, but to learn as much as we can as we help it to die gracefully. As Patti Lather (1993, 1995) has argued, this means not relinquishing the concept of validity, no matter how problematic it is, but revisioning it after the collapse of the traditional conditions of the legitimation of knowledge. We can ask with Jean-Francois Lyotard (1984: xxv): 'Where, after the metanarratives, can legitimacy reside?'

Critical engagement with validity has proposed a host of alternative concepts, too broad to be comprehensively mapped here. Some suggest replacing validity with alternatives such as verisimilitude, persuasiveness, trustworthiness, authenticity, credibility, or transferability (e.g., Lincoln and Guba 1985). Others add adjectives to revision the classic notion, including pragmatic validity, catalytic validity, process validity, democratic validity, or dialogic validity (e.g., Anderson and Herr 1999). These proposals draw to differing extents on the argument that 'in the social sciences and the humanities there is only interpretation' (Denzin 2003: 258). Rather than trying to be as statistical as possible with qualitative materials, which is invariably never statistical 'enough', the goal is to embrace the interpretive, diagnostic mode of drawing inferences known from e.g., doctors (Macgilchrist 2016). Inferences and interpretation are situated (Haraway 1988), conducted by scholars differently marked within the matrix of oppression (Collins 1990) in social, political, cultural, and economic contexts. Some publications reflect more on [or play more excessively or 'outrageously' (Greco 2017) with] the interpretive aspects of their research, others less so.

In reflections of validity after post-structuralism, Lather (1993) posits 'validity' as an incitement to discourse 'to help chart the journey from the present to the future' (Lather 1993: 673). She seeks a generative methodology, and proposes transgressive 'open-ended and context sensitive validity criteria' (Lather 1993: 674): (i) simulacra/ironic validity, (ii) paralogical/neo-pragmatic validity, (iii) rhizomatic validity, and (iv) situated/voluptuous validity.

> In creating a nomadic and dispersed validity, I employ a strategy of excess and categorical scandal in the hope of both imploding ideas of policing social science and working against the inscription of another 'regime of truth.' (Lather 1993: 677)

The critique is self-critical, observing its own process of inscription as it deconstructs other inscription practices, and working with, not against, the *aporia*, dead-ends, and constitutive contradictions that emerge with any form of validation, including scandalous, excessive and/or contrapuntal validity practice (see Boger and Castro Varela 2021: 11). If theory in what has been called the 'land of the posts' invites us to explain and deconstruct apparently self-evident global, capitalist relations of exploitation and extraction, for Leila Haghighat, postcolonial education aims to create new images, new self-evidencies, and new systems of meaning (Haghighat 2021). Thus, the land of the posts, including postdigital research, deconstructs and generates new systems of validity.

Rather than remaining with traditional distinctions between, for instance, explanatory, interpretive, and critical modes of research, in which technical action requires deductive reasoning, practical action requires interpretive approaches, and emancipatory action requires critical knowledge-making, each with its own forms of validity (see, e.g., Habermas 1973), the blurring of distinctions at the heart of postdigital research reminds scholars to also blur these boundaries. Traditional forms of policing social science and truth claims are, as Lather (1993) might say, 'imploded', when the technical becomes social and the sociotechnical becomes critical.

While I am using the concept of 'validity' to frame this chapter, the implications are broader. As Karin Priem and Lynn Fendler (2019) have argued, further terms, such as 'rigour', 'discipline', and even 'systematic', are inventions of a rational, modernist Enlightenment spirit. In the face of critique from philosophy and the arts, as well as from within the (hard and social) sciences, these terms have shifted their meanings. For Priem and Fendler, digital humanities provides a particular provocation for rethinking the epistemologies brought into research with these terms: it deals with large data-sets, yet, unlike classic quantitative research, focuses on uncertainties, ambiguities, and the materiality of data accumulation. This connection of digital technologies and the messy contingent underworld of thinking, reflecting, and making decisions reiterates, in my reading, one of the core impulses from research on the postdigital.

3   Inventive Methodologies

In response to the critique of modernity/coloniality (albeit often discussed in terms of modernity alone), a host of inventive methodologies have been proposed over the past decades of social science research. Performative social science, for instance, foregrounds the performative aspects of 'doing' social science, drawing on practices, techniques, and technologies from drama, filmmaking, poetry, photography, dance, music, and fiction (Gergen and Jones 2008; Jones 2022). This arts-led research is not only used to disseminate findings but throughout the research process, often in collaborations across science and arts.

Scholars from Science and Technology Studies (STS) have explored nonstandard modes of knowing outwith the settled, institutional, standardised Enlightenment modes of knowing by thinking through, for instance, the baroque. John Law introduces the baroque as a mode of knowing that was materially heterogeneous, that recognised different kinds of realities, and that acknowledged otherness; the baroque sat on the split between rationalist and non-rationalist, emotional, affective, spiritual, embodied modes of knowing (Law 2016: 23). The baroque folds the inside and outside together, displacing within and outwith, rendering the outside continuous with the inside (Law 2016: 36). Techniques of baroque knowing are 'explicit about their own performativity': as they describe or represent the world, they also intervene, seeking to create change (Law 2016: 42). In this way, whether drawing on Leibniz, Deleuze, Benjamin, or Foucault, the baroque can be a resource for (academic) modes of knowing today beyond traditional, rationalist, modernist validity claims.

Others have proposed the word 'device' to reflect critically on ways of making knowledge (Lury and Wakeford 2014). Devices include the list, the event, the pattern, the phrase, the screen, and the anecdote (see also Law et al. 2013 on the unfinished list). In this view, devices operate as 'hinges' between epistemology and ontology, between theory and practice, and between phenomena and invention. Mapping to the concerns of postdigital research, this approach invokes sociotechnical assemblages in which agency is no longer only assigned to human actors, but also to the things, relations, connections, nodes, non-human, and more-that-human actors (see also Hofhues and Schütze 2023). Remnants of theory in the earlier days of digital culture remain in these reflections on inventive methods, however, when a distinction is made been 'the actual and the virtual' (Lury and Wakeford 2014: 9). If devices both make and unmake the social, then the difference held to pertain between an 'actual' and a 'virtual' can be unmade as recent research has shown how the production of the virtual is tethered to very material actual practices of, e.g., ecological and labour exploitation (Bender et al. 2021).

At the same time, speculative methods invite researchers to attend to the 'not-yetness' of the complex issues analysed in social and cultural research, including the 'unintended consequences and emergent properties of technologies in use' (Ross 2023: 169). Speculation can be understood as 'a struggle against probabilities' (Stengers 2010: 17). Not the statistically probable, nor the logically plausible, stands at the forefront of this mode of knowing. Instead, in 'reclaiming' speculation, these methods aim to step out of 'the problem-space of the normal, the probable and the plausible', and to step into the 'speculative possibilities' that 'emerge out of the eruption of what, from the standpoint of the impasse of the present seems, in all likelihood, to be *impossible*' (Savransky et al. 2017: 7) (emphasis from the original). If postdigital research understands this 'impasse of the present' as combining not only onto-epistemological fragilities but also the ethico-political dimensions of research involving digitality at the verge of planetary destruction, and the demise of modernity/coloniality, then the 'speculative sensibility' that researchers can cultivate 'in our engagements with the empirical' (Greco 2017: 218) will also be enacted as deeply political (Suoranta et al. 2021).

This writing on inventive methods, baroque modes of knowing, speculative research, performative social science, and similar concepts often describes itself as outrageous, excessive, risky. These adjectives may also sit well with research describing itself as post- (whether postfoundational, posthumanist, postpunk, post-digital, or other posts). In conversation with a social scientist recently, the deconstruction of validity that is familiar to me was indeed (still) made to feel outrageous, excessive, and risky.

Nevertheless, I would prefer to return to what I see as a central concern across postdigital research: the muddy, lumpy, racist, scrappy, classist, noisy, glitchy everyday practices of postdigital lives. Engaging with these practices is not outrageous, excessive, or risky. The issues are banal, but by no means benign. As cultural or social anthropologists have said, anthropology, rooted in close observations of situated, contextualised practices, is a form of applied philosophy: looking closely at everyday practices to address broad philosophical issues (Schiffauer 2008). However, precisely because there is no claim to risk, we need these inventive, speculative methodologies, alongside thick ethnographic research, to gain insights into the postdigital heterogeneities of everyday practices.

4 Peer Reviews

These methodologies do not, however, always sit comfortably with the blind peer review process in social science journals. Double-blind peer reviews, in which reviewers do not know the name of the authors' they are reviewing and are not named in the process of publication, remaining invisible to all but the editors, are a core feature of contemporary academic service. While commercial services such as Publons[1] and non-profits such as ORCID[2] aim to accord recognition for the number of reviews, this only counts some reviews (primarily English-language publications), and the person behind a specific review remains anonymous.

Scholarly writing on the review process has pointed to its function as a mode of policing the boundaries of knowledge-making and circulation (Lather 1999). Media historians trace a trajectory from the burning of books to a Foucaldian 'disciplining of a text and its author' (Biagioli 2002: 11). Sociolinguists consider the role of face, gender, language, and values in the genre of peer reviews (Paltridge 2017). Reviews are both repressive and productive. By foregrounding specific work to be cited, and rendering other positions invisible, reviewers shape what counts as a field of scholarship. Reviewers operate as gatekeepers, which can lead to a conservative bias in reviewing if, for instance, reviewers do not attend to citational bias (Dion et al. 2018): 'It is this fragile, double-blinded choreography of methodology that produces science.' (Gorur 2022: 67).

Open or networked peer review processes in online spaces have aimed to open up this choreography to scrutiny and have been found to slightly improve the quality of reviews (Kowalczuk et al. 2015). The journal of *Discourse Analysis Online* launched in 2002 with named reviewers posting their reviews as threaded comments to the article on a private site.[3] Authors were encouraged to respond, and reviewers to respond to the responses. After these discussions, articles that were deemed suitable for the journal were published as preprints for public open review among interested research communities. Debate, participation and visibility were key to this phase of the reviewing process.

---

[1] See https://publons.com/wos-op/. Accessed 16 March 2023.

[2] See https://orcid.org/. Accessed 16 March 2023.

[3] The legacy website for the DAOL journal is here: https://extra.shu.ac.uk/daol/about. Accessed 16 March 2023.

Further online open review processes have been utilized for books/collections (e.g., Malone and Bernstein 2022; Davies et al. 2020), journals such as *Public History Weekly*[4] or for collectively authored articles in, for instance, *Postdigital Science and Education*,[5] in which reviews are included in the article, and reviewers are listed as co-authors. Projects such as CommentPress, Digress.it, Hypothes.is, Commons in a Box, and Peer Review Personas have sought to turn reviewing/commenting from an individual action into networked conversations (see Belojevic et al. 2014). Collective projects, open reviewing, and other 'knowledge socialism' initiatives (Peters et al. 2020) do not remove power hierarchies or gate-keeping from academia. The issues of patriarchy, diversity, prejudice, capital, and power associated with peer reviewing as a central practice in academic publishing are relevant for all forms of review (Jackson et al. 2018). Open reviews do, however, change the way these power relations are performed.

Overall, double-blind reviews continue to dominate the field of social science. Bearing in mind all that has been said about 'vituperative feedback' from peer reviewers, in particular in the double-blind review (Comer and Schwartz 2014: 141),[6] the warmth and support offered by some reviewers to fellow academics, without reputational gain or visibility, has often reassured me of scholars' interest in 'simply' creating better scholarship and a more expansive critical understanding of the world. Done like this, peer review is not an academic play between rivals or a mode of picking holes in another's argument; instead, peer review is understood as a conversation, a way of 'thinking with' others (PoLAR 2022).

With this background, and with thanks to the reviewers who took time to read our articles and formulate critique, this section reflects on three sets of comments from peer reviews. These comments point to challenges of inventive methodologies, when they are written for, or read by, scholars adhering to more classic forms of validity.

4.1   Essaying

In an article for a special issue on narrative and critical discourse analysis in *Critical Discourse Studies*,[7] I drew on social and cultural theory to unfold the assumption that critical discourse analyses are always already narrative (Macgilchrist 2021b). The article suggests that narrative permeates the humanities and social sciences. Social and cultural researchers could thus embrace the storytelling qualities of our

---

[4] See https://public-history-weekly.degruyter.com/. Accessed 16 March 2023.

[5] See https://www.springer.com/journal/42438. Accessed 16 March 2023.

[6] See, for instance, the Facebook page dedicated to sharing the pain inflicted by destructive reviewers, 'Reviewer 2 must be stopped', https://de-de.facebook.com/groups/reviewer2/. Accessed 16 March 2023.

[7] See https://www.tandfonline.com/journals/rcds20. Accessed 16 March 2023.

research, rather than excusing it. The point of departure was that contemporary scholarship is being pulled in two directions.

> On one side, in the age of validity, inter-rater reliability and evidence-based research, it can seem subversive when researchers 'tell stories' (rather than 'write reports', 'produce findings' or 'demonstrate effectiveness'). On the other side, public relations departments encourage researchers to use 'storytelling' techniques to engage public audiences. (Macgilchrist 2021b)

By foregrounding the storytelling dimensions of scholarship, critical analysis would, suggests the paper, perform its own critical approach by undermining the traditional power hierarchy between 'research' and 'the public'. It is important, however, while reflecting on telling stories, to avoid producing hero-centred or monovocal stories.

When the manuscript was reviewed, both reviewers provided very helpful feedback, most of which I integrated in revisions. One issue is particularly relevant to this chapter and visible in an early sentence in one of the reviews. This reviewer, who had reviewed several of the manuscripts in the special issue, responded:

> This piece has much more of an essayistic style, but is essentially sound in its core message (that narration should be admitted as a core dimension of how we do 'worlding' in the humanities and social sciences).

Interesting for this chapter is the 'but' in this extract. The article was submitted to a journal which usually publishes empirically-rich analyses. This article does not analyse original empirical materials, instead drawing on previous research and YouTube critics to critically reflect on the politics and positionality of knowledge-making. Nevertheless, the presupposition in the extract is that an essayistic style will not be as 'sound in its core message' as other styles.

In my response to this review, I allowed myself to focus on the second part of the sentence ('essentially sound') and ignored the 'essayistic … but'. Can 'essayistic', however, perhaps be grasped as a key aspect of postdigital validity? Etymologically, the verb essay has been traced to the late fifteenth century, from the French *essaier*, from *essai,* 'trial, attempt'. Is scholarship, across all hard and soft sciences, not indeed always an attempt: an attempt to see, to conceptualise, to examine, to observe, to ascertain, to conclude? Yet since postmodern theory, we have learnt that these attempts are invariably limited, positioned, situated. If we agree that the 'god trick' of seeing everything from nowhere is problematic (Haraway 1988), then research *essays.* Research flagged as 'post-' would then wear the adjective essayistic to create a sound argument without a 'but'. We essay (i.e., try, attempt), albeit in the limited sphere of academic texts, to provoke thought, stimulate debate and/or move to action.

The fast-moving world of technology addressed by postdigital research is, one could suggest, constitutively engaged in essaying; for instance, the attempt to blur a clear boundary between what is digital and what is not digital. Scholars try to shape arguments about novel technologies and media. We attempt to examine the digital-material-bio-socio-physical-cultural-political-economic-affective-spiritual   practices that constitute these media. We *essai* to decelerate, to draw on historical research, cultural theory, philosophy, etc., to generate knowledge about digital culture, digital education, digital democracy, which simultaneously uses and complicates the notion of the 'digital'.

4.2   Creating Pointillist and Pixel Art

How to draw on observations of one's own empirical research to generate conceptual contributions to the field? Without taking recourse to auto-ethnography, our aim in a reflective paper that we submitted to peer review was to generate concepts to think about the practices of conducting participatory postdigital research (Poltze et al. 2022). We wanted these concepts to be rooted in our lived experience of collaboration in a design research project on FabLabs and schools. We thus recorded a set of conversations in which two social scientists in the project and the team running the project's FabLab reflected together on how the project was unfolding. The goal was to recall particularly memorable, challenging, enjoyable, frustrating, successful, and confusing moments in the project (which at the time of the conversations was still ongoing). Listening to the audio recordings, we identified four aspects and concluded that participation unfolds as a messy, unsystematisable experience that enables both a formatting of participation as tamed and limited consensus-building and its reformatting as situated, conspiratorial perplexity.

Again, much of the feedback helped us to clarify our argument. One comment, however, drew on a binary rooted in modern understandings of scholarship:

> The empirical basis seems to be too thin for the statements made. Only the observations of the authors are referred to. However, the statements made suggest that a validation or external validation is necessary, at least by referring to comparable findings, better still by a broader basis or the analysis of collected data by other researchers. This may not be possible immediately, but it is to be expected that further analyses will be presented anyway within the framework of the project in which the study was conducted, so that it may be better to concentrate on purely conceptual presentations of the work at this stage.

A distinction is drawn here between an empirical basis, which needs to be thicker and requires validation, and purely conceptual presentations, which would not require any empirical basis. Our goal, shared by much work in postdigital research, was to draw on experience (which is a form of empiricism broadly understood) to present conceptual insights. The notion of external validation by, for instance, having multiple scholars analyse the data, is deeply rooted in classic qualitative methods, and flagged by terms such as inter-rater reliability. As noted above, post-qualitative research has questioned whether this kind of validity is at all relevant for qualitative inquiry, since external validation reproduces a quantitative, experimental and/or decontextualised stance in which interpretation should be reduced rather than enhanced.

Postdigital validity, when taken as a critical perspective (see above), dissolves binaries. Elements thought to be separate – biology and technology, digitality and materiality, empirical and conceptual – are seen to be parts of a whole. This guided our response to the review. First, we made our goal in the article more explicit, and second, we increased the use of non-standard vocabulary. Inspired by the work on inventive and baroque methods noted above, but aiming for a metaphor which captured our approach of zooming in on spots of a larger picture, we describe our method in the article as pointillism. Pixel art is similar. If a viewer looks from a distance, they see a figure. If they zoom in, the whole disappears and individual points/pixels become visible. Each individual dot is important for the whole picture, whether it is in the centre or at the edge. However, a single point alone would mean nothing. It is only in combination that the picture comes into being. In this sense, the article discusses only four individual points. Together, we suggested, these form part of the overall pointillist figure of participatory research. Other points have been discussed in previous research, and further points will be added in future research and practice.

This approach resonates with and encourages research on the postdigital condition and/or research adopting a postdigital perspective to zoom in on specific aspects, to generate complex accounts that make space to observe and reflect on the ambivalence and tensions. But to also consider these aspects explicitly as dots making up a larger picture. The dots are unbounded. This interweaving of individual practices, locations, or technologies beyond the site of research, beyond the specific concept under consideration or beyond the politics being discussed, is a second key to postdigital validity.

4.3   Drawing Inferences

Social science fiction is the most speculative of methods in the three articles on which this chapter reflects. In an article speculating about education and technology in the 2020s, we positioned ourselves in 2040 and wrote the 'history' of the 2020s (Macgilchrist et al. 2020). Since history is not linear, the article offered three alternative histories. Each arose from a different set of political, legal, structural, infrastructural, economic, cultural, personal, and institutional decisions that 'were made' about education and technology in the early 2020s (and none of the histories included a global pandemic). The first scenario shaped 'smooth and competent users'. Students were encouraged by policymakers and educational institutions to use new technologies as tools to become more efficient, effective, productive; to continually optimise themselves. The second scenario created 'digital nomads' in which freedom and individualism frame solopreneurs' sense of self. They use their understanding of algorithmic data-aggregating commercial processes to withdraw from social systems of solidarity. The third prioritised 'collective agency', and active participation in designing a future that the planet can sustain. Community, solidarity, conflict, and collective organising were core, as was a recognition of our entanglement with our human and more-than-human kin across the planet.

The article was fairly detailed, as historical accounts are, with the role of institutions, politics, commercial entities described and relations explored. Both reviewers suggested the discussion following the three scenarios be deepened and extended.

> If the purpose of speculative fiction in the social sciences is to excite or otherwise stimulate the 'sociological imagination', then I would expect this exercise to outline a few openings for further theorising or empirical work (or both). (R1)
>
> I thought the discussion could make a lot more of what was covered in the main sections of the article (i.e., the three types of student). For example, what can we learn about the future of education and technology from these three scenarios? Who are the winners and losers? Are there opportunities to resist these? (R2)

Complicit with the authors, these two reviewer comments already 'implod[e] ideas of policing social science', they work against 'the inscription of another "regime of truth"' (Lather 1993: 677). Instead, they expect openings, recommend making more of the main sections, suggest making the learnings clearer. They ask for a more explicit politics of resistance.

This indicates a third key to a postdigital validity in the ruins of modernity: drawing inferences that blur lines of demarcation between technical, social, and critical action or between explanatory, interpretive, and emancipatory research approaches; just as postdigital thinking has blurred lines between on- and offline, virtual and real, digital and material. More specifically, Mario Small's (2009) reflection on the role of inference in ethnographic or qualitative work is helpful here. To decide if an analysis is valid or not, Small suggests qualitative social scientists operate with 'logical' rather than 'statistical' inference, where the former draws on deep insights into stories, relations, and contexts generated through case research. Validity lies in providing convincing (logical, narrative) inferences. Inference is not understood here as reason and deduction, which are too reminiscent of modern, rationalist, Enlightenment thought. Instead, Small's approach can remind us that the etymology of *infer* also refers to 'carrying in', 'carrying forwards'. It carries across sociotechnical criticality. Publications arising from postdigital research carry descriptions forward. But the direction of 'forward' is not given. These publications would bring in the politics, the infrastructures, the systems, the sociomaterialities and heterogeneous assemblages and carry them somewhere. To carry the muddy, lumpy, racist, scrappy, classist, noisy, glitchy everyday practices of today's world forward.

5 Concluding Thoughts

Can it be that, in the mid-2020s, the social sciences are still struggling over what counts as valid research? Lyotard's (1984) *Postmodern Condition* was first published in the late 1970s. Lather (1993) considered 'validity after poststructuralism' in the early 1990s. Scholars across the social sciences have worried this problem for decades. Speculative methods are the most recent incarnation, opening new perspectives for social science at the nexus of the arts and humanities. And yet peer reviewers continue to distinguish between scholarship and essaying; they continue to press for external validity. The (double-blind) peer review process sketched in this chapter also, however, illustrates changes in the way validity is being done in social science.

In each case described here, we made a more or less inventive or 'forward-carrying' revision to the manuscript, which was then accepted for publication. Two of the three journals welcome research from the post-traditions (postfoundational, postdigital, etc.). There is space for negotiation, for conversation, in the response to reviewers. We took on board many but not all recommendations. This – negotiation, conversation, emergent spaces – is perhaps precisely what enacts postdigital research today. Reviewers may desire, hope for, and suggest different onto-epistemological commitments. Boundaries around methodological communities are built and guarded. Reviewers will reject the invitation to review. Other journals would have rejected these articles outright as unsuitable or unsound. But in many journals, reviewers are not always (or, are no longer) able to *police* those onto-epistemological commitments. This goes not only for newer formats that seek to de-police these scholarly practices, such as open reviews or networked comments, but also for the mainstay of contemporary academic publishing, the double-blind peer review.

To respond to the questions raised in the introduction: How can we engage with the muddy, lumpy, racist, scrappy, classist, glitchy, noisy everyday practices of postdigital lives to generate new insights which are accepted as 'valid' by other scholars? Or is this validation itself a remnant of modernist times, and no longer necessary? This chapter – partial, positioned, and debatable as academic chapters are – has suggested that classic modernist validity continues to hold relevance across the social sciences, but the spaces for scholarly exchange have broadened. Some spaces enable far more unconventional scholarship than the papers described here. There is a danger of creating ever more research silos across which communication does not flow. Validity claims remain crucial throughout as a situated community-based practice that, however, also reaches across silos. Scholarship, including poststructuralist, inventive and speculative approaches, has pushed the boundaries of what is considered legitimate.

Postdigital validity can be flagged by an essayistic style when examining emergent technologies, practices, and politics; by gathering specific points into a larger picture; by drawing inferences which carry findings across technosocial criticality towards indeterminate locations. In each case, postdigital validity is enacted as a blurring of clear boundaries, binaries, and demarcations. Postdigital research is one mode of reworking validity as an attempt (an *essai*) at research, as voluptuous, inventive, or excessive, and as the need to carry analysis forwards – perhaps in playful, artistic or speculative ways; often in political ways – towards further theory and practice.

Acknowledgements Part of the research reported here was funded by the German Ministry for Education and Research, grant number 01JD1902C (*FaBuLoUS*). Many of the thoughts have been inspired by colleagues at the *Leibniz ScienceCampus – Postdigital Participation – Braunschweig*. The author remains responsible for the content.

References

Addey, C., & Piattoeva, N. (Eds.). (2022). *Intimate Accounts of Education Policy Research: The Practice of Methods*. London: Routledge. https://doi.org/10.4324/9781003123613.

Anderson, G. L., & Herr, K. (1999). The New Paradigm Wars: Is There Room for Rigorous Practitioner Knowledge in Schools and Universities? *Educational Researcher, 28*(5), 12–21. https://doi.org/10.3102/0013189X028005012.

Belojevic, N., Sayers, J., & the INKE and MVP Research Teams. (2014). Peer Review Personas. *The Journal of Electronic Publishing, 17*(3). https://doi.org/10.3998/3336451.0017.304.

Bender, E. M., Gebru, T., McMillan-Major, A., & Shmitchell, S. (2021). On the Dangers of Stochastic Parrots. In *Proceedings of the 2021 ACM Conference on Fairness, Accountability, and Transparency (FAccT '21)* (pp. 610–623). New York: Association for Computing Machinery. https://doi.org/10.1145/3442188.3445922.

Biagioli, M. (2002). From Book Censorship to Academic Peer Review. *Emergences: Journal for the Study of Media & Composite Cultures, 12*(1), 11–45. https://doi.org/10.1080/1045722022000003435.

Boger, M.-A., & Castro Varela, M. d. M. (2021). Was ist postkoloniale Bildung (überhaupt)? In bildungsLab* (Ed.), *Bildung, Ein postkoloniales Manifest* (pp. 11–16). Unrast.

Cascone, K. (2000). The Aesthetics of Failure: "Post-Digital" Tendencies in Contemporary Computer Music. *Computer Music Journal, 24*(4), 12–18. https://doi.org/10.1162/014892600559489.

Collins, P. H. (1990). *Black Feminist Thought: Knowledge, Consciousness, and the Politics of Empowerment*. London: Unwin Hyman.

Comer, D. R., & Schwartz, M. (2014). The Problem of Humiliation in Peer Review. *Ethics and Education, 9*(2), 141–156. https://doi.org/10.1080/17449642.2014.913341.

Davis, R. F., Gold, M. K., Harris, K. D., & Sayers, J. (2020). *Digital Pedagogy in the Humanities: Concepts, Models, and Experiments*. Modern Language Association. https://digitalpedagogy.hcommons.org/. Accessed 16 March 2023.

Denzin, N. K. (2003). Reading and Writing Performance. *Qualitative Research, 3*(2), 243–268. https://doi.org/10.1177/14687941030032006.

Dion, M. L., Sumner, J. L., & Mitchell, S. M. (2018). Gendered Citation Patterns across Political Science and Social Science Methodology Fields. *Political Analysis, 26*(3), 312–327. https://doi.org/10.1017/pan.2018.12.

Gergen, M., & Jones, K. (2008). Editorial: A Conversation about Performative Social Science. *Forum Qualitative Sozialforschung / Forum: Qualitative Social Research, 9*(2), 43.

Gorur, R. (2022). Opening the Black Box of Peer Review. In C. Addey & N. Piattoeva (Eds.), *Intimate Accounts of Education Policy Research: The Practice of Methods* (pp. 62–76). London: Routledge.

Greco, M. (2017). Afterword: Thinking with Outrageous Propositions. In A. Wilkie, M. Savransky, & M. Rosengarten (Eds.), *Speculative Research: The Lure of Possible Futures*. London: Routledge. https://doi.org/10.4324/9781315541860.

Habermas, J. (1973). *Erkenntnis und Interesse*. 2nd Ed. Berlin: Suhrkamp.

Haghighat, L. (2021). Kompliziertes Lernen. In bildungsLab* (Ed.), *Bildung, Ein postkoloniales Manifest* (pp. 59–61). Unrast.

Haraway, D. (1988). Situated Knowledges: The Science Question in Feminism and the Privilege of Partial Perspective. *Feminist Studies, 14*(3), 575–599. https://doi.org/10.2307/3178066.

Hofhues, S., & Schütze, K. (Eds.). (2023). *Doing Research – Wissenschaftspraktiken zwischen Positionierung und Suchanfrage*. Berlin: transcript.

Jackson, L., Peters, M. A., Benade, L., Devine, N., Arndt, S., Forster, D., Gibbons, A., Grierson, E., Jandrić, P., Lazaroiu, G., Locke, K., Mihaila, R., Stewart, G., Tesar, M., Roberts, P., Ozoliņš, J., & Ozoliņš, J. (2018). Is Peer Review in Academic Publishing Still Working? *Open Review of Educational Research, 5*(1), 95–112. https://doi.org/10.1080/23265507.2018.1479139.

Jandrić, P., Ryberg, T., Knox, J., Lacković, N., Hayes, S., Suoranta, J., Smith, M., Steketee, A., Peters, M., McLaren, P., Ford, D. R., Asher, G., McGregor, C., Stewart, G., Williamson, B., & Gibbons, A. (2018). Postdigital Dialogue. *Postdigital Science and Education, 1*(1), 163–189. https://doi.org/10.1007/s42438-018-0011-x.

Jandrić, P., MacKenzie, A., & Knox, J. (2022). Postdigital Research: Genealogies, Challenges, and Future Perspectives. *Postdigital Science and Education.* https://doi.org/10.1007/s42438-022-00306-3.

Jones, K. (Ed.) (2022). *Doing Performative Social Science. Creativity in Doing Research and Reaching Communities.* London: Routledge. https://doi.org/10.4324/9781003187745.

Kowalczuk, M. K., Dudbridge, F., Nanda, S., Harriman, S. L., Patel, J., & Moylan, E. C. (2015). Retrospective Analysis of the Quality of Reports by Author-suggested and Non-author-suggested Reviewers in Journals Operating on Open or Single-blind Peer Review Models. *BMJ Open, 5*(9), e008707. https://doi.org/10.1136/bmjopen-2015-008707.

Lather, P. (1993). Fertile Obsession: Validity after Poststructuralism. *Sociological Quarterly, 34*(4), 673–693. https://doi.org/10.1111/j.1533-8525.1993.tb00112.x.

Lather, P. (1995). The Validity of Angels: Interpretive and Textual Strategies in Researching the Lives of Women With HIV/AIDS. *Qualitative Inquiry, 1*(1), 41–68. https://doi.org/10.1177/107780049500100104.

Lather, P. (1999). To Be of Use: The Work of Reviewing. *Review of Educational Research, 69*(1), 2–7. https://doi.org/10.3102/00346543069001002.

Law, J. (Ed.) (2016). *Modes of Knowing: Resources from the Baroque.* Manchester: Mattering Press.

Law, J., Afdal, G., Asdal, K., Lin, W.-y., Moser, I., & Singleton, V. (2013). Modes of Syncretism: Notes on non-coherence. CRESC Working Paper 119. Manchester: Centre for Research on Socio-Cultural Change. http://www.cresc.ac.uk/publications/modes-of-syncretism-notes-on-non-coherence. Accessed 16 March 2023.

Lincoln, Y., & Guba, E. G. (1985). *Naturalistic Inquiry.* Sage.

Lury, C., & Wakeford, N. (Eds.). (2014). *Inventive Methods: The Happening of the Social.* London: Routledge. https://doi.org/10.4324/9780203854921.

Lyotard, J.-F. (1984). *The Postmodern Condition: A Report on Knowledge.* Manchester: Manchester University Press.

Macgilchrist, F. (2016). Fissures in the Discourse-scape: Critique, Rationality and Validity in Postfoundational Approaches to CDS. *Discourse & Society, 27*(3), 262–277. https://doi.org/10.1177/0957926516630902.

Macgilchrist, F. (2021a). Theories of Postdigital Heterogeneity: Implications for Research on Education and Datafication. *Postdigital Science and Education, 3*(3), 660–667. https://doi.org/10.1007/s42438-021-00232-w.

Macgilchrist, F. (2021b). When Discourse Analysts Tell Atories: What Do We 'Do' When We Use Narrative as a Resource to Critically Analyse Discourse? *Critical Discourse Studies, 18*(3), 387–403. https://doi.org/10.1080/17405904.2020.1802767.

Macgilchrist, F., Allert, H., & Bruch, A. (2020). Students and Society in the 2020s: Three Future 'Histories' of Education and Technology. *Learning, Media and Technology, 45*(1), 76–89. https://doi.org/10.1080/17439884.2019.1656235.

Machado de Oliveira, V. (2021). *Hospicing Modernity: Facing Humanity's Wrongs and Implications for Social Activism.* Berkeley, CA: North Atlantic Books.

Maldonado-Torres, N. (2007). On the Coloniality of Being. *Cultural Studies, 21*(2–3), 240–270. https://doi.org/10.1080/09502380601162548.

Malone, T. W., & Bernstein, M. S. (Eds.). (2022). *Handbook of Collective Intelligence.* Cambridge, MA: MIT Press. https://cci.mit.edu/cichapterlinks/. Accessed 16 March 2023.

Paltridge, B. (2017). *The Discourse of Peer Review. Reviewing Submissions to Academic Journals.* London: Palgrave Macmillan. https://doi.org/10.1057/978-1-137-48736-0.

Peters, A. M., Besley, T., Jandrić, P., & Zhu, X. (Eds.). (2020). *Knowledge Socialism. The Rise of Peer Production: Collegiality, Collaboration, and Collective Intelligence*. Singapore: Springer. https://doi.org/10.1007/978-981-13-8126-3.

Pink, S., Ruckenstein, M., Willim, R., & Duque, M. (2018). Broken Data: Conceptualising Data in an Emerging World. *Big Data & Society*. https://doi.org/10.1177/2053951717753228.

PoLAR. (2022). PoLAR Directions Digital Roundtable Discussion on Peer Review: "Thinking With" When Peer Reviewing. PoLAR: Political and Legal Anthropology Review. https://polarjournal.org/2022/06/13/polar-directions-digital-roundtable-discussion-on-peer-review-thinking-with-when-peer-reviewing/. Accessed 16 March 2023.

Poltze, K., Demuth, K., Eke, S., Moebus, A., & Macgilchrist, F. (2022). Erfahrungen des Partizipierens. Reflexionen zu partizipativen Forschungs- und Gestaltungsprozessen. *bildungsforschung, 2022*(2), 1–14. https://doi.org/10.25539/bildungsforschung.v0i2.900.

Priem, K., & Fendler, L. (2019). Shifting Epistemologies for Discipline and Rigor in Educational Research: Challenges and Opportunities from Digital Humanities. *European Educational Research Journal, 18*(5), 610–621. https://doi.org/10.1177/1474904118820433.

Ross, J. (2023). *Digital Futures for Learning: Speculative Methods and Pedagogies*. Abingdon and New York: Routledge.

Russell, L. (2020). *Glitch Feminism: A Manifesto*. London and New York: Verso.

Savransky, M., Wilkie, A., & Rosengarten, M. (2017). The Lure of Possible Futures. On Speculative Research. In A. Wilkie, M. Savransky, & M. Rosengarten (Eds.), *Speculative Research: The Lure of Possible Futures* (pp. 1–17). London: Routledge.

Schiffauer, W. (2008). *Parallelgesellschaften*. Berlin: transcript.

Selwyn, N., & Jandrić, P. (2020). Postdigital Living in the Age of Covid-19: Unsettling What We See as Possible. *Postdigital Science and Education, 2*(3), 989–1005. https://doi.org/10.1007/s42438-020-00166-9.

Small, M. L. (2009). How Many Cases Do I Need?: On Science and the Logic of Case Selection in Field Based Research. *Ethnography, 10*(1), 5–38. https://doi.org/10.1177/1466138108099.

St. Pierre, E. A. (2013). The Posts Continue: Becoming. *International Journal of Qualitative Studies in Education, 26*(6), 646–657. https://doi.org/10.1080/09518398.2013.788754.

St. Pierre, E. A. (2019). Post Qualitative Inquiry, the Refusal of Method, and the Risk of the New. *Qualitative Inquiry, 27*(1), 3–9. https://doi.org/10.1177/1077800419863005.

Stengers, I. (2010). *Cosmopolitics I*. Minneapolis, MN: University of Minnesota Press.

Striano, F. (2019). Towards "Post-Digital". A Media Theory to Re-Think the Digital Revolution. *Ethics in Progress, 10*(1), 83–93. https://doi.org/10.14746/eip.2019.1.7.

Suoranta, J., Teräs, M., Teräs, H., Jandrić, P., Ledger, S., Macgilchrist, F., & Prinsloo, P. (2021). Speculative Social Science Fiction of Digitalization in Higher Education: From What Is to What Could Be. *Postdigital Science and Education*. https://doi.org/10.1007/s42438-021-00260-6.

Tsing, A. L. (2015). *The Mushroom at the End of the World. On the Possibility of Life in Capitalist Ruins*. Princeton, NJ: Princeton University Press.

Walford, G. (Ed.). (1991). *Doing Educational Research*. London: Routledge. https://doi.org/10.4324/9780203409480.

Don't Leave Artificial Intelligence Alone: It Could Hurt Human Rights

Selman Özdan

1 Introduction

When a person starts to lose their sense of reality and naturality, they may also be losing genuineness, experience, the opportunity to make mistakes and, probably, a degree of consciousness. Perhaps humanity is experiencing its last moments now that seemingly organic ideas can be written by a non-human. Perhaps someone, by using the ChatGPT application[1] right now, may be overestimating her/his own intelligence – or feel compelled to cheat because an exam is looming.

These opening sentences could be considered quite dystopian, even overstated. They nevertheless reflect a concern not to criticise Artificial Intelligence (AI), but to set the person firmly in the posthuman and postdigital age and within the realities of AI.

Supporting and promoting democratic values and human rights in the posthuman and postdigital world is as difficult as it is important. The posthuman world is based on the self-directed principle and the concept of conscious evolution. The self-directed principle 'asserts the conviction that it is not only possible, but desirable, to decide our evolutionary destiny both as a species and as individuals through the use of technology, which means enhancing the human biological make-up' (Silva 2011: 1). It is at this point that AI tools come to the fore. While not denying the contribution of AI tools to humanity, it should be taken into account that these tools can lead to human rights violations.

---

[1] See https://openai.com/blog/chatgpt. Accessed 1 March 2023.

S. Özdan (✉)
Ondokuz Mayıs University School of Law, Samsun, Turkey
e-mail: selman.ozdan@omu.edu.tr

© The Author(s), under exclusive license to Springer Nature   227
Switzerland AG 2023
P. Jandrić et al. (eds.), *Constructing Postdigital Research*, Postdigital Science
and Education, https://doi.org/10.1007/978-3-031-35411-3_12

The posthuman and postdigital age, which was once the focus of science fiction movies, is now subject to an interdisciplinary examination and the future of human existence is discussed in many fields from medicine to law. This chapter discusses how AI tools challenge the protection of fundamental human rights and what steps and measures should be taken in a legal sense. Malcolm Murdock, in his novel of *The Quantum Price*, underlines that 'AI doesn't have to be sentient to kill us all. There are plenty of other scenarios that will wipe us out before sentient AI becomes a problem' (Murdock in Bajema 2022). While worse scenarios are more likely to impact us than AI, it is nevertheless of primary importance to identify the challenges of the posthuman and postdigital world to human rights. AI is the result of blending human characteristics with the benefits of technology. Therefore, we can neither explain AI by ignoring human beings, nor can we explain it based only on the blessings of leading-edge technology. Accordingly, the postdigital and posthuman period can be explained through the interaction of humans and technology. In this sense, Petar Jandrić et al. (2018: 896) underline that the 'contemporary use of the term "postdigital" does describe human relationships to technologies that we experience, individually and collectively, in the moment here and now'. Indeed, the human brain plays a guiding role in the development of AI systems and these systems are also extensively applied in genetic research (Peters and Jandrić 2019: 197).

This chapter will first draw attention to the leading definitions of AI. Then, the challenge to international human rights as a result of AI applications will be analysed. In order to properly address this issue, human rights such as the right to freedom of expression, the right to privacy, and the principle of non-discrimination which are threatened by the AI tools and applications, will be examined. After defining the problem in question, the steps to be taken in the legal sense will be emphasised. First, the international legal personality of AI will be discussed in order to discuss whether it is possible to attribute responsibility to AI tools. Then, the importance of creating and codifying legal regulations regarding AI will be underlined. In line with this objective, soft law and hard law instruments on AI will be discussed. When these instruments are examined, it will be observed that states play a primary role in preparing and creating international regulations on AI. In international law, the consent factor of the states is deemed to be essential element for the formation of these regulations. The consent factor arises from the sovereign power of states. So, examining the compatibility of the internal and external sovereignty of the state in the age of AI is the missing piece of the human rights struggle.

2   Artificial Intelligence

There is no universally accepted common definition of AI. However, it is clear that definitions of AI generally refer to the posthuman age. High-Level Expert Group on Artificial Intelligence defines AI as follows:

(AI) refers to systems that display intelligent behaviour by analysing their environment and taking actions – with some degree of autonomy – to achieve specific goals. AI-based systems can be purely software-based, acting in the virtual world (e.g. voice assistants, image analysis software, search engines, speech and face recognition systems) or AI can be embedded in hardware devices (e.g. advanced robots, autonomous cars, drones or Internet of Things applications). (AI HLEG 2019: 1)

AI can be considered a technological development that points to the posthuman age. When describing the societies of the future, we may think that AI is an indispensable product that could even replace (perhaps already has replaced) the human being. According to Ryan Calo (2017: 404), AI is 'a set of techniques aimed at approximating some aspect of human or animal cognition using machines'. Considering this definition, we can posit that the posthuman world has created a new type of person, one that is distinct from the real and legal person of international law. AI is a technology that offers features very close to human beings. In 1987, Robert Schank claimed that for an entity to be attributed as AI, it is expected to have the following five characteristics:

Communication – An intelligent entity can be communicated with … Internal Knowledge – We expect intelligent entities to have some knowledge about themselves They should know when they need something, they should know what they think about something, and they should know that they know it … World Knowledge – Intelligence also involves being aware of the outside world and being able to find and utilize the information that one has about the outside world … Intentionality – Goal-driven behavior means knowing when one wants something and knowing a plan to get what one wants ... Creativity – [E]very intelligent entity is assumed to have some degree of creativity. (Schank 1987: 60–61)

The abovementioned five features are roughly equivalent to the definition of AI system in a 2021 report by the European Parliament's Committee on Legal Affairs. According to the report's Rapporteur, Gilles Lebreton, AI means 'a system that is either software-based or embedded in hardware devices, and that displays behaviour simulating intelligence by, inter alia, collecting and processing data, analysing and interpreting its environment, and by taking action, with some degree of autonomy, to achieve specific goals' (European Parliament 2021: 6). While both a modern and more inclusive definition of AI was eventually proposed in the Report, I would like to include a final definition that does not contradict these definitions but which expresses AI in a very comprehensive and concise way: Jacob Turner (2019: 16) describes AI as 'the ability of a non-natural entity to make choices by an evaluative process'.

The potential impact of world-changing AI technology on societies is unpredictable. AI is a double-edged sword. AI may ethically turn into a harmful product but may also be revolutionary in a positive way. Paul Timmers (2022: 45) sums it up as follows: 'AI is wonderful. AI is scary. AI is the path to paradise. AI, it is the path to hell.' AI offers convenience in many fields such as medicine, education and investment. But it is no longer a secret that AI is used to spy on people, that it erodes and infringes on their privacy, is used to monitor their movements and behaviours and determine their preferences. Oren Etzioni (2017), the chief executive of the Allen Institute for AI, lists three rules for regulating AI systems to avoid the harms of

AI. First, an AI system must be subject to all laws that apply to human behaviour. In particular, AI should not be engaged in cyberbullying, stock manipulations, or terrorist threats. AI systems that drive people to commit crimes should not be allowed to circulate freely in either the hard or soft ecosystem.

Second, AI systems should unambivalently declare that they are not human to ensure that people know when a bot impersonates someone, and that by doing so, the content produced by bot accounts that impersonate public figures in social media can be consciously eliminated. Finally, Etzioni's (2017) third rule is that AI systems 'cannot retain or disclose confidential information without explicit approval from the source of that information. Because of their exceptional ability to automatically elicit, record and analy[s]e information, [AI] systems are in a prime position to acquire confidential information'.

AI poses some challenges to the fundamental principles of international human rights law. In the posthuman age, which develops under the influence of AI, the need for new mechanisms, new policies, and new regulations is obvious in order to protect human rights and overcome the challenges faced by international human rights law. In the following section, how certain principles of international human rights law are being violated by means of AI tools will be discussed.

3 Protection of International Human Rights in the Age of Artificial Intelligence

Following the atrocities unleashed by the Second World War, the United Nations (UN) member states in 1948 decisively signed the Universal Declaration of Human Rights (UDHR). The UDHR promised a set of rights, such as the right not to be tortured, the right to seek asylum, and the right to life. Further the UDHR, 'has been supplemented by a raft of treaties and conventions guaranteeing civil and political rights, social and economic rights, and the rights of refugees, women, and children' (Strangio 2017). A year after this document, the Geneva Convention was adopted, taking into account the principles of international humanitarian law, to protect the lives of civilians in situations of war and to guarantee the right of medics to work freely on battlefields. With the 1951 Refugee Convention and the absolute prohibition of torture, a number of principles of human rights were incorporated into international law. While thousands of immigrants and asylum seekers waiting at the borders are waiting for asylum offers from European countries to be accepted, we can state that these countries are reluctant and unwilling to meet this basic human right need. However, considering the present, we can argue that the human rights ideals proposed by the UDHR are now outdated or antiquated.

In the 2016 Presidential Campaign, Donald Trump openly supported torture at an event in South Carolina. During the question and answer session of the event, Trump was asked if he approved of the waterboarding technique. As Trump has repeatedly stated, he answered this question 'absolutely'. He said:

I said I'll approve it immediately, but I'll make it also much worse ... I said they're chopping off our heads in the Middle East. They want to kill us. They want to kill us. They want to kill our country. They want to knock out our cities. And don't tell me it doesn't work. Torture works, okay folks? ... Believe me, it works. (Deb 2016)

Article 3 Common to the four Geneva Conventions explicitly prohibits torture. Unfortunately, there are some who claim that the waterboarding technique is not a form of torture. Trump (in Deb 2016) said: 'Waterboarding is your minor form ... Some people say it's not actually torture. Let's assume it is. But they asked me the question. What do you think of waterboarding? Absolutely fine. But we should go much stronger than waterboarding. That's the way I feel.'

With official tolerance for the admissibility of torture, the targeting and bombing of civilians and medics on battlefields around the world prompts us to question where human rights are going. With the reservation that existing documents need to be updated, there are some concrete human rights regulations that we can at least consider to be violations in these discourses and practices. However, existing human rights documents do not have any regulation or detailed provision regarding the new threats that humanity has faced and/or may encounter.

The issues that international human rights law struggles with are transboundary problems, such as poverty, oppressive state regimes, and terrorism, which are directly caused by the negligence of states. However, in the posthuman age, besides these conventional threats, new threats have emerged beyond states. Threats such as AI, climate change, nuclear wars and cyber-attacks pose a great risk to all humanity. These posthuman threats require international consensus since they are threats that transcend national borders.

Since I do not have the space to address each of these threats separately, I will focus on AI, one of the most radical effects of the posthuman world. For this reason, I will talk about the protection of human rights in the age of AI. Indeed, and as I underlined before, AI is double-edged sword for human rights. In this sense, Bachelet, in the report to the UN High Commissioner for Human Rights, rightly states that:

No other technological development of recent years has captured the public imagination more than ... AI. ... Indeed, these technologies can be a tremendous force for good, helping societies overcome some of the great challenges of the current time. However, these technologies can also have negative, even catastrophic, effects if deployed without sufficient regard to their impact on human rights. (UN High Commissioner for Human Rights 2021: 2)

Dunja Mijatović (2019) states that 'ensuring that human rights are strengthened and not undermined by ... AI is one of the key factors that will define the world we live in'. AI may negatively affect a number of international human rights. This problem, further, can be 'compounded by the fact that decisions are taken on the basis of these systems, while there is no transparency, accountability and safeguards on how they are designed, how they work and how they may change over time' (Mijatović 2018).

The question of whether the use of AI can interfere with freedom of expression, information, and thought is a fundamental human rights concern. There are various types of interferences with freedom of expression and opinion using AI tools. Some of them are listed below based on Brkan's (2019) analysis regarding the impact of AI on the freedom of expression and information.

The first one is about personalisation of online users. Internet search engines create a profile based on their users' past searches and other data collected about the user. Hence, as the information and news reaching the users pass through filters, users will be exposed to a less diverse information ecosystem. Similarly, in profiles created based on users' social media usage, information close to the users' interest can be detected and this information can be displayed more frequently in the social media stream (Brkan 2019: 2). Undoubtedly, users can benefit from certain aspects of content personalisation. For example, users can quickly access pre-prepared information that suits their needs. The user who wants to buy a new coffee maker would most likely encounter coffee maker campaigns as a result of her/his searches on the Internet. Content personalisation may also create echo chambers. Therefore, the right to freedom of expression and receiving information would indirectly be restricted.

The automatic blocking and removal of online content can be referred to as the second AI intervention to freedom of expression and information (Brkan 2019: 4). Digital platforms can interfere with online content using AI tools to block or remove content that provokes violence, contains hate speech, or incites xenophobia. According to Article 19(3)[2] of the International Covenant on Civil and Political Rights (United Nations General Assembly 1966), the right to freedom of expression and information may be subject to certain restrictions under limited circumstances. However, due to algorithms that fail to properly analyse the expression context, specified limitations may go beyond their intended purpose. When AI cannot fully define the context of the conversation taking place on the online platform, it cannot distinguish between a genuinely violent discourse and an ironic one (Kaye 2018: Para. 29). As a result, it may happen that the AI tool unnecessarily blocks content that is neither socially nor legally problematic.

The third type of intervention is the detection of content such as fake news or disinformation through AI tools and removing them from the online ecosystem, even if it does not consist of illegal content (Brkan 2019: 5). In the democratic state system, there should be no interference that hinders the circulation of such content in the Internet ecosystem. Fake news or disinformation content undoubtedly has its drawbacks. However, these drawbacks cannot be repelled by removing or banning such content from the Internet. There are alternative democratic methods for this struggle. We have also seen that such methods are used in extraordinary times. One of the closest examples is the measures taken to prevent the sharing of fake cures and fake news in the digital ecosystem during the Covid-19 epidemic. Indeed, using

---

[2] Article 19(3) reads: 'The exercise of the rights provided for in paragraph 2 of this article carries with it special duties and responsibilities. It may therefore be subject to certain restrictions, but these shall only be such as are provided by law and are necessary: (a) For respect of the rights or reputations of others; (b) For the protection of national security or of public order (*ordre public*), or of public health or morals.'

AI tools, disinformation and fake news content can be separated from the information ecosystem. However, when using these tools, correct information content may also be mistakenly labelled as disinformation, which may inadvertently lead to the restriction of the freedom to receive information. Further, AI tools 'could be deliberately misused to downplay allegedly undesirable content such as condemnatory, challenging, surprising or distressing opinions. This could lead to a potentially unjustified impairment of freedom of expression and could hence affect democratic political structures.' (Brkan 2019: 6)

The right to privacy, one of the fundamental human rights, is particularly affected by AI technologies. The right to privacy is protected by article 17[3] of the International Covenant on Civil and Political Rights (United Nations General Assembly 1966) and article 8[4] of the European Convention on Human Rights (Council of Europe 1950). The right to privacy is essential for an individual to lead a safe and dignified life. Further, the right to privacy is a 'gateway to the enjoyment of other rights, particularly the freedom of opinion and expression' (Kaye 2015: Para. 16). However, while people are in the digital ecosystem, a significant amount of personal data is collected whether they know it or not. This collected data can be used to profile individuals and to make predictions about their behaviour, choices or preferences. Elements such as the right not to disclose personal information, the right to make personal decisions on their own, the right not to reveal their personal tendencies, and the right to individual life without interference are components of the fundamental right to privacy (Manheim and Kaplan 2019: 116). However, AI methods, particularly on social media platforms, 'are used to infer and generate sensitive information about people that they have not provided or confirmed, such as sexual orientation, family relationships, religious views, health conditions or political affiliation' (Kaye 2018: Para. 34).

In a report prepared by the UN High Commissioner for Human Rights on 13 September 2021, the right to privacy in the digital age was analysed and the threats and risks posed by AI to the right to privacy are discussed. These risks include:

(a) AI, which has a great impact on the collection of personal data, facilitates interference with the right to privacy and paves the way for the violation of other rights.
(b) The collection and long-term storage of personal data may reveal other violations of rights in a chain. The report sums it up as follows:

> Long-term storage of personal data also carries particular risks, as data are open to future forms of exploitation not envisaged at the time of data collection. Over time, the data can become inaccurate, irrelevant or carry over historic misidentification, thereby causing biased or erroneous outcomes of future data processing. (UN High Commissioner for Human Rights 2021: 5)

---

[3] 'No one shall be subjected to arbitrary or unlawful interference with his privacy, family, home or correspondence, nor to unlawful attacks on his honour and reputation.'
[4] 'Everyone has the right to respect for his private and family life, his home and his correspondence.'

(c) AI tools can be used to gain insights by observing people's behaviour patterns. By accessing accurate data sets, 'it is possible to draw conclusions about how many people in a particular neighbourhood are likely to attend a certain place of worship, what television shows they may prefer and even roughly what time they tend to wake up and go to sleep' (UN High Commissioner for Human Rights 2021: 5).

(d) By analysing people's preferences and ideas with AI tools, people's political, social or other tendencies can be disclosed. This situation violates not only their right to privacy, but also their right to freedom of expression and thought.

Another issue to be considered in the use of AI tools is the principle of non-discrimination. Even if there was no intention to discriminate when an AI tool was designed, it could have discriminatory effects. The Finnish Non-Discrimination Ombudsman (Non-Discrimination Ombudsman n.d.) provides some of the reasons why AI is potentially discriminatory: 'errors and inadequacies in algorithmic teaching data; poorly selected algorithmic forecast variables and sorting criteria; [and] the algorithm is designed to give meaning to a ground for discrimination, such as age, language or gender'. The so-called unintentional effect of AI tools is called 'AI bias' in the literature, whereby the output of a machine learning model can provoke the discrimination against certain individuals or groups (Belenguer 2022: 773). These individuals or groups are often historically discriminated against and marginalised on the basis of social class, gender, sexual orientation, or race.

The reason for the AI bias is not always intentional.[5] AI bias can manifest in many different ways that can lead to discrimination. For example, Joy Buolamwini and Timnit Gebru (2018), working on leading facial recognition[6] software packages, found an AI bias based on gender and racial discrimination. They tested on four subgroups: darker females, darker males, lighter females, and lighter males. They found that these facial-recognition software packages 'performed best for lighter individuals and males overall'. The packages 'performed worst for darker females' (88). Following similar studies, the Association for Computing Machinery US Technology Policy Committee (ACM USTPC) published a statement in 2020 on face recognition technologies that lead to discrimination. It 'urges an immediate suspension of the current and future private and governmental use of [facial-recognition] technologies in all circumstances known or reasonably foreseeable to be prejudicial to established human and legal rights' (USTPC 2020: 1).

Another example is the recruitment algorithm developed by Amazon. In 2015, Amazon realised that the algorithm they used to recruit was biased against women. After this incident came to light, Amazon decided to shut down the tool. Amazon created an AI tool to identify potential candidates on the web, rating them from 1 to 5 stars. However, the company realised that this hiring algorithm was not ranking

---

[5] 'It is important to highlight that bias means a deviation from the standard and does not necessarily lead to discrimination.' (Belenguer 2022: 773) For a detailed reading on this subject, see Ferrer et al. (2021).

[6] To figure out how Facial Recognition Technologies work, see Davide (2020).

candidates for software developer and other technical positions because it had learned to systematically downgrade women's résumés for those jobs. So, what was the reason that this algorithm discriminated against women? The reason lay in the algorithm's reliance on the number of résumés submitted to the company over the past 10 years to identify the best candidates which came predominantly from men; the algorithm was trained to prefer men over women. In other words, this algorithm detected male dominance and accepted this ratio as a factor in success (Lavanchy 2018). As Jandrić (2019a: 27) underlined, 'Amazon AI's bias against women is not a technical glitch, or even an error in design – AI's "independent mind" is a feature built in the very essence of its workings'. Therefore, it is important to protect human rights against biases independently generated by AI. The following section will accordingly examine what actions should be taken in order to eliminate the conflict between AI tools and international human rights law.

4 A Step Forward

The application of AI tools certainly supports social development and contributes to the continuation of a prosperous society. However, AI may also cause serious security problems and human rights violations as observed in the previous discussion. It should not be overlooked that AI can also be used for illegal purposes. Therefore, both national and international regulation for AI tools and applications is urgently needed. It is of great importance to analyse the development of AI and its impact on society, the individual, and the state, through the principles of international law.

The international community should work for the safe use of AI. While providing the necessary conditions for the development of AI, states should keep this process under surveillance so that it does not harm the state, society, and individuals. In this sense, Elon Musk has called for the regulation of AI as soon as possible. Musk has said before that AI is 'the most serious threat to the survival of the human race ... I'm increasingly inclined to think that there should be some regulatory oversight, maybe at the national and international level, just to make sure that we don't do something very foolish.' (Musk in Gibbs 2014).

Existing legal regulations are not prepared for the needs or problems of the virtual world or posthuman world. Therefore, the principles and documents of international law in the posthuman age should be re-evaluated. Existing national and international legal regulations are not sufficient to cope with the negative effects of AI tools. Particularly, international society should discuss what actions should be taken in this regard. In line with this objective, first, the international legal personality of AI should be examined. In a system where AI can be accepted as an actor, it is important to determine its legal personality. Subsequently, the necessity of both soft and hard law instruments should be examined in order to ensure that AI tools are subject to legitimate control and do not cause gross human rights violations. It will be observed that the sovereign existence of the state plays a fundamental role in such a legal regulation (soft or hard law). While the state is the main actor of international law, it is also an indispensable element in concluding international agreements. The consent, granted by states to become a party to multilateral agreements with their sovereign powers, is the sole reason for the formulation of multilateral agreements. Hence, before concluding this chapter, the necessary arrangements for AI tools in the field of internal and external sovereignty of states should be discussed.

4.1   Legal Personality of Artificial Intelligence in International Law

In a society where activities with legitimate impact are overwhelmingly performed by AI systems, do AI entities need to be granted a kind of legal personality? This question is important in terms of defining the new actors of the posthuman world and legitimising their place in the society.

In the language of law, the concept of person should not be understood only as a natural person, namely a human being. A person is legally divided into two groups: natural persons and legal entities/juridical persons. The former group refers to a human being as an individual who can assume obligations and hold rights. The latter group refers to such entities endowed with legal personality, generally known as collective persons or social persons (Adriano 2015: 366).

It is controversial whether AI has a personality in the legal sense. Since AI is a relatively new concept, it would not be realistic to expect an international consensus on its legal status. AI cannot be considered a human being in the biological sense. AI does not have the rational thinking and morality with which humans are endowed. Therefore, the transformation of an AI entity into a natural human may be nothing more than a utopian proposition.

Some scholars believe that AI could become a legal entity under the jurisdiction of national law when it met the standards set by legal entities. For example, Thomas Burri (2017: 95) claims that 'an artificially intelligent entity is a legal person governed by national law that "houses" an [AI]'. Some scholars state that the recognition of AI as a legal entity is very real and promising, stating that this will provide AI with a legal electronic identity/entity status (Eduardovich 2017: 137–139). For some scholars, granting a legal personality to AI would create legal problems and serve no purpose. Bringing a critical perspective to this issue, Kasap (2022: 542) notes that one of the most prominent obstacles in granting personality to the AI tools is the concept of consciousness. He underlines that an AI tool which is unaware of its existence can neither be entitled nor be liable; hence, granting legal personality to AI would likely cause ambiguities in a legal manner.

Based on the fact that AI can compete with real human intelligence, we cannot deny that it has the potential to surpass human intelligence. Since AI might have the ability to make decisions like humans, we should open up discussions about treating AI as a legal subject and assigning rights and obligations to it in certain situations.

The standards and principles on acquiring citizenship for an AI entity cannot be the same as natural and legal persons.

The AI entity that acquires legal personality will be able to benefit from the rights granted to it by the relevant national law and will be able to assume some legal responsibilities to the extent of its ability and capacity. After acquiring this legal entity, how is the status of AI considered within the framework of international law?

In public international law, there are certain conditions to be accepted as an international legal person. However, 'there are no international rules prohibiting legal personality for AI' (Turner 2019: 180). Conventionally, the primary subject of international law is the state. State practices play a primary role in the formation of sources of international law, such as customary rules and international treaties. In addition, states have a leading role in the formation, amendment or abandonment of fundamental norms in international law. However, we cannot regard states as the only actors in the modern international legal order. Alongside states, international organisations and individuals also have an international legal personality. However, it should be noted that the protection of something by international law with certain regulations does not necessarily make it a subject of international law. For example, even if there are many international agreements to protect wildlife and cultural heritage, they are considered protected and regulated structures, not subjects of international law (Hárs 2021: 331). As Hárs (2021: 332) states, '[l]acking a supranational entity, or proper branches of power, subjects of international law and the characteristics of the legal personality they possess 'organically evolve' as stated by the – usually numerous – documents that support their legal personality'.

According to Talimonchik (2021: 89), '[s]olving the problem of the international legal personality of [AI] using established approaches to the international legal personality of legal entities is more optimal than the development of completely new approaches'. International legal personality can be granted by states to another entity as long as the relevant provisions are included in an international treaty or an international customary rule is established. In this sense, for the sake of figuring out the expectations and trends regarding the international legal personality recognition of AI, we need to draw a parallel between AI and non-state actors. As a matter of fact, the 'closest analogy to [AI] in international law is a legal entity' (Talimonchik 2021: 86). By analysing the international legal entities of non-state actors, we could make a proper determination about the said legal entity of AI. In this respect, Talimonchik (2021: 93) reminds us that the 'international legal personality of non-state actors can be recognised only in public international law and only by states through an international treaty or an international custom'.

In this case, there are some ways to follow. First, '[s]tates that grant the rights of legal entities to certain objects of civil rights in their civil law may grant the rights of a legal entity to [AI] ... second ... states may conclude that [AI] will be granted the rights of a legal entity or rights sui generis, a new legal fiction, by participating in discussions organised by various international organizations' (Talimonchik 2021: 93). In this context, it is an important development that international organisations have practices in regulating AI with its legal dimensions.

The irrefutable role of AI in commerce was highlighted in a 2017 report by the European Parliament's Committee on Legal Affairs. The Committee considered that 'the civil liability for damage caused by robots is a crucial issue which also needs to be analysed and addressed at Union level' (European Parliament 2017: 16). Further, regarding the legal status of AI, the European Parliament has called on the Commission to discover and analyse all possible legal solutions such as 'creating a specific legal status for robots in the long run, so that at least the most sophisticated autonomous robots could be established as having the status of electronic persons responsible for making good any damage they may cause, and possibly applying electronic personality to cases where robots make autonomous decisions or otherwise interact with third parties independently' (European Parliament 2017: 18).

If we define objects as tools that serve a purpose, it is highly likely that AI will be considered an object (Hárs 2021: 333). Basically, given the unreal or inanimate person characteristics of AI, the practice of giving a special kind of legal personality to inanimate objects such as ships, planes or rivers in international law can also be applied to the inanimate object AI. Therefore, we can make an inference about the international legal personality of AI by referring to the criteria in international law for determining the nationality of such inanimate objects.

A few prominent examples from international conventions may serve as an example on this issue. Article 91 of the UN Convention on the Law of the Sea deals with the nationality of ships. It reads as follows:

> (1) Every State shall fix the conditions for the grant of its nationality to ships, for the registration of ships in its territory, and for the right to fly its flag. Ships have the nationality of the State whose flag they are entitled to fly. There must exist a genuine link between the State and the ship. (2) Every State shall issue to ships to which it has granted the right to fly its flag documents to that effect. (United Nations General Assembly 1982: Art. 91)

Regarding the nationality of aircraft, the Chicago Convention includes the following provisions in its relevant articles (articles 17–20):

> Aircraft have the nationality of the State in which they are registered.
> An aircraft cannot be validly registered in more than one State, but its registration may be changed from one State to another.
> The registration or transfer of registration of aircraft in any contracting State shall be made in accordance with its laws and regulations.
> Every aircraft engaged in international air navigation shall bear its appropriate nationality and registration marks. (International Civil Aviation Organization 1944: Arts. 17–20)

Considering the above articles, a recommendation or a determination could be made for the legal status of AI. AI is 'looked upon as either a tool or a threat that is not to be protected, but either used, or its growth potential limited so as not to cause a threat to humanity' (Hárs 2021: 334). Therefore, since it will be important to determine who/what will be responsible under international law, the method followed for aircraft and ships, which are inanimate entities, can also be followed (although not exactly) for AI entities. In order to properly exercise jurisdiction, it is necessary to determine the legal status of the AI, and for this, the place where the AI entity is registered can be designated as its nationality.

Each country should have the right to independently determine the conditions for registration of an AI entity. In addition, each country should have the right to authorise the AI entity to be registered in its own territory. Considering the relevant articles of international agreements above, each country should have the right to fly the flag of the country showing its nationality to the AI entity and issue the necessary certificates. In short, treating an entity as a special subject of international law is not a new case.

An international regulation regarding the international legal personality of AI has become essential. For example, the legal status of the Moon was determined by an international agreement and a *sui generis* status was attributed to the Moon. According to Article 11 of the 1979 Moon Treaty,

> The moon and its natural resources are the common heritage of mankind ... The moon is not subject to national appropriation by any claim of sovereignty, by means of use or occupation, or by any other means. ... Neither the surface nor the subsurface of the moon, nor any part thereof or natural resources in place, shall become property of any State, international intergovernmental or non-governmental organization, national organization or non-governmental entity or of any natural person. (United Nations 1979: Art. 11)

For the international legal personality of AI, it will eventually be necessary to provide the consensus of the international community on either the establishment of an international treaty or the development of international customary rule. The International Law Commission may launch its first attempts for the sake of creating a draft multilateral treaty, although the formation of international customary rule on AI's legal personality seems unlikely in the near future.

4.2   Soft Law Instruments on Artificial Intelligence

The first step to be taken regarding the regulation of AI tools should be the determination and codification of certain principles on the international plane. Further, it is essential to adopt relevant legislation at the national level. It is also essential, furthermore, to avoid conflicts between national and international regulations. The most practical and fastest step to be taken at the international level is to create soft law instruments regarding AI tools. Anna Jobin (in Clarke 2021) is surely correct when she says that 'for new technologies, soft law precedes hard law because it can be accomplished much faster ... because it can be created ad hoc, by different stakeholders, initiatives can reach across sectors or even national borders, and their implementation can be very flexible'.

The formation and adaptation of new rules in the field of law is an intricate and difficult task. For this reason, the rules are first approved in the form of soft law, then in hard law which provides strict, binding and clear provisions. The concept of soft law is used to indicate statements that are not legally binding. Soft law documents and other instruments are predominantly found on the international plane, such as UN General Assembly resolutions. Hard law instruments, on the other hand, refer to legal provisions that bind the parties and are legally enforceable before a judicial body (ECCHR n.d.). Soft law instruments have some advantages over hard law instruments, especially for states. Soft law instruments do not impose binding responsibilities on states. Thus, these instruments are easier to negotiate. States may assume that the privacy of their absolute sovereignty will not be compromised under any circumstances, while being party to soft law instruments. Further, soft law instruments are directly available to non-state actors such as NGOs and international or regional organisations. Thus, the variety in the soft law instruments is relatively large (Shaffer and Pollack 2010: 719). Furthermore, soft law 'constitutes international norms, principals, and procedures that lack the requisite degree of normative content to create enforceable rights and obligations but are still able to produce certain legal effects. Soft law functions as a gap-filler, giving guidance to states and other stakeholders in the absence of binding legal norms.' (ECNL 2019: 1).

AI is still an emerging field – a fact of the postdigital world which asserts that there is no 'rupture' between the digital and the *post*digital (Jandrić et al. 2018: 895). As a matter of fact, AI technology has not fully fledged and is still at embryonic stage for many countries. Even if states enact national guidelines or rules on AI, such as a code of ethics, it is a very difficult task to establish internationally binding norms for states. Soft law instruments are available to non-state actors and therefore many actors other than the state can be effective in the formation of soft law rules. Non-governmental organisations, multinational or regional companies, research and development centres, governmental organisations, and all other stakeholders, can take the lead or have an active role in some way in formulating rules and standards regarding the safety, ethics, and application of AI. Although soft legal instruments are not binding, they can be useful in solving some technical and ethical problems.

It should be emphasised that one of the most important stages of the formation of hard law texts is to reach a consensus on soft law rules. Therefore, the soft law text in question may lead to a multilateral and binding agreement or convention to be formed in the future. For example, the Institute of Electrical and Electronics Engineers (IEEE) is working to standardise ethical principles internationally. In particular, IEEE works on AI bias, transparency, privacy, and inequality created by algorithms (Burri 2017: 105–106). The Public Voice coalition, established by the Electronic Privacy Information Center (EPIC) in 1996, is another entity that offers universal guidelines for AI. The Public Voice coalition was formed to encourage public participation in decisions about the future of the Internet. Main purpose of the proposed universal guidelines is 'to maximize the benefits of AI, to minimise the risk, and to ensure the protection of human rights' (The Public Voice 2018). To name a few of the Universal Guidelines issues: Right to transparency, right to human determination, identification obligation, public safety obligation, cybersecurity obligation, prohibition on secret profiling (The Public Voice 2018).

4.3 The Need for Hard Legal Instruments on Artificial Intelligence

The ideal way to resolve disputes, potential problems and conflicts between states on the subject of AI is to conclude multilateral agreements. In this way, some, if not all, of the soft law rules mentioned above may become binding rules for states. Thus, AI could be regulated effectively, and legal loopholes could be avoided. Ultimately, an international risk prevention and control mechanism can be established by making a multilateral agreement. However, today neither states nor human rights organisations are concerned about the evolution of autonomous AI into advanced and super-intelligence (Castel and Castel 2016: 10–11). This is an issue that may have major and perhaps unpredictable consequences for the present and future of humanity. For this reason, it was an issue that needed to be considered long before we succeeded in creating super-intelligent or autonomous AI tools (Castel and Castel 2016: 11). But it is not too late. We still have the opportunity to create regulations by which we can reach international consensus. Castel and Castel emphasise that international cooperation on AI can prevent potential conflicts as follows:

> International collaboration at all stages of development of autonomous artificial super-intelligence would also reduce the possibility of an international conflict in a post-transition multipolar world, especially if several states were trying to develop competing autonomous artificial super-intelligent machines at the same time. (Castel and Castel 2016: 12)

With the growth of AI technology, the potential dangers and harms of AI applications, which contain high risk factors, have begun to be noticed. For this reason, awareness of policy makers on creating new laws regarding AI has increased. However, due to the lack of international consensus on AI tools, binding multilateral regulations face some challenges. There are currently no international legal binding documents which specifically focus on AI. However, a number of existing international legal frameworks are closely related to AI. For example, European Convention on Human Rights and International Bill of Human Rights can be considered as prominent frameworks (Leslie et al. 2021: 25). These legal frameworks have provisions on a number of fundamental human rights, such as the right not to be discriminated against or the right to privacy, which clearly concern AI applications. As AI is also closely related to issues that the state has to deal with individually or by international consensus, such as cybercrime and the dissemination of fake news or disinformation, a binding legal framework governing AI is required.

Although the approach to the regulation of AI is generally taken by following the soft law method, the international community should make an effort to establish hard law on AI. There are two main methods to create and adopt a hard law instrument on AI. For the sake of explaining these methods, I cite the work of Leslie and others (2021) that was prepared to support the Feasibility Study published by the Council of Europe's Ad Hoc Committee on AI. The first option is modernising relevant existing legal documents; the second option is creating and adopting a binding new legal instrument.

What can be done about the first option? For example, a protocol or a set of rights can be added to the European Convention on Human Rights regarding AI. This method is, of course, open to criticism since additional protocols 'are only binding on States that ratify them, which may make oversight more fragmented' (Leslie et al. 2021: 29). As an alternative to this option, existing legal instruments can be modified to cover concerns and other issues raised by AI.

The second option is to create and adopt an entirely new set of binding rules, obligations and rights for AI. Two methods can be followed in this regard: a framework convention and a regular convention. A framework convention could broadly provide a code of ethics and key principles about AI tools, applications, and effects. However, states would exercise considerable discretion in the implementation of the rules and principles in question. Thus, a practical solution could be produced for ethical problems and other concerns raised by AI. In fact, such framework conventions could be regarded as a directive or guidelines for states. States can determine or amend their national policies according to these guidelines for the sake of ensuring international cooperation and consensus on AI.

Regular conventions, on the other hand, contain more comprehensive and detailed regulations. Regarding AI, 'a convention could identify the rights and obligations that would safeguard human rights, democracy, and the rule of law, and give greater legal protection to people as a result' (Leslie et al. 2021: 29). Adopting binding multilateral conventions on AI would encourage states to enact relevant national laws and regulations. Thus, common policies in the international plane would be adopted and followed by states. However, such a multilateral agreement should not be limited to European countries. If so, other countries would make their own regulations on AI. Thus, patchwork agreements could emerge, and an atmosphere would be created that is far from international consensus (Leslie et al. 2021: 29–30).

Although binding international rules have not been concluded in the field of AI yet, some national policies and rules have emerged on this issue. So how can these national arrangements help to make a multilateral agreement? For the sake of formulating and concluding a multilateral agreement on AI covering international obligations and rights, states should attempt to reach an international consensus by concluding bilateral or regional agreements on ethical codes and technical standards. One of the best methods, which plays an important role in reaching international consensus, is for states to establish high-level institutions on AI. For example, a ministry dedicated to AI could be established within the government (Turner 2019: 282). In October 2017, the United Arab Emirates (UAE) established the world's first Ministry of AI: Minister of State for Artificial Intelligence. In July 2020, the position was renamed to Minister of State for Artificial Intelligence, Digital Economy and Remote Work Applications (The UAE Government n.d.). In an interview, the first minister his Excellency Omar bin Sultan Al Olama, emphasised that AI is in a grey area and invited everyone to talk about it. Al Olama continued:

> People need to be part of the discussion. It's not one of those things that just a select group of people need to discuss and focus on. ... At this point, it's really about starting conversations — beginning conversations about regulations and figuring out what needs to be implemented in order to get to where we want to be. I hope that we can work with other

governments and the private sector to help in our discussions and to really increase global participation in this debate. With regards to AI, one country can't do everything. It's a global effort. (Galeon 2017)

With these sentences, Al Olama emphasises that a regulation on AI should be provided by international consensus, and also underlines that other states, organisations and individuals interested in this issue should play an active role in this process.

4.4 State Sovereignty and Artificial Intelligence

Among actors with international legal personality, the position of states differs from other actors since sovereignty is a notion attributed to the state. Non-state actors may have rights and obligations under public international law. For instance, individuals have rights under international human rights conventions. In addition, individuals may potentially be subject to criminal jurisdiction under a number of specific international crimes. International governmental organisations can 'act on the international plane vis-à-vis states, making treaties, bringing claims, litigating, even governing territory under specific mandates' (Crawford 2013: 118). These entities have international legal personality to the extent of their powers. However, apart from the state, none of these personalities can be considered as sovereign (Crawford 2013: 119).

Sovereignty is a notion bestowed only on the state. The principles of sovereignty and sovereign equality apply to all states, regardless of their power (economic, military, political, intelligence, social, etc.). According to UN Charter articles 2(1) and 78, all States are sovereign, and the sovereign equality principle is applied to all States. These articles respectively read as follows:

> The Organization is based on the principle of the sovereign equality of all its Members. ... The trusteeship system shall not apply to territories which have become Members of the United Nations, relationship among which shall be based on respect for the principle of sovereign equality. (United Nations 1945)

The sovereignty and sovereign equality of states have some corollaries: a) Exclusive jurisdiction over a territory and the permanent population living in that area; b) A duty of the non-interference within the exclusive jurisdiction area of other States; and c) Obligations arising from customary law or international agreements ultimately depend on the consent of states (Crawford 2019: 431). Specifically, the first two of these corollaries are issues that need to be re-examined in the posthuman and postdigital age, where AI permeates everything and is everywhere. In other words, states need to make some regulations on internal sovereignty and external sovereignty in order to both fight AI and operate AI under its own control.

The concept of internal sovereignty reflects the relationship between the state, which legitimately has authority and power, and its citizens. Internal sovereignty refers to the monopoly of the governing authority. Crawford clearly summarises what is meant by internal sovereignty. The state's.

governmental authority extends to determining who may enter the territory, who belongs to the state as its nationals, what the law of the state shall be on any matter and how (or when) it is to be enforced, what taxes shall be paid and on what the proceeds shall be spent, what armaments the state shall have and how they will be deployed, and so on across the spectrum of possible matters for government. (Crawford 2013: 121)

This is the exclusive authority of the state. Any governmental activity carried out in the territory of another state is considered lawful and legitimate only if that state consents to the activity in question (Crawford 2013: 121).

There is more than one exclusive authority in the international relations. The existence of more than one state with exclusive authority naturally gives rise to the principle of non-intervention in domestic affairs. This principle is the basis of external sovereignty. The primary justification for external sovereignty is the idea of recognising the right of states not to be invaded (Prokhovnik 1996: 9). Therefore, sovereign equality of states and independence of states are prominent features of the concept of external sovereignty.

As can be seen, internal and external sovereignty are concepts that occur with the existence of the basic tenets of states. Thus, in the posthuman age, states should make the necessary arrangements and amendments for the sake of preserving and maintaining their internal and external sovereignty. The existing limited structure of AI technologies can shape and change the balance of power among states in international law (Hárs 2021: 327). Power differences would arise among states, which are the main actors of international law, in direct proportion to their capacity to own and use AI technologies in matters they dominate, such as military, intelligence, strategy, and economy. States should adopt specific regulations on the AI in terms of both internal and external sovereignty in order to close this power gap or to maintain their power.

States should have legislative, judicial and administrative jurisdiction over AI technology. Specific legal frameworks and technical systems must be developed to regulate AI. In the context of external sovereignty, states have the right to develop and protect the AI industry. In order to enjoy this right properly, states should be able to create independent plans and policies without interference from foreign states. Therefore, other states cannot interfere, hinder, and control the development of AI in a country. Otherwise, this intervention would be considered to be disrespectful of the external sovereignty of that state and the principle of non-intervention in domestic affairs, which is the basic principle of international law, will be directly infringed.[7]

States must ensure national information security as a result of their internal sovereignty. In other words, states should also have sovereign power over the data and information ecosystem. AI 'works best when large amounts of rich, big data are available' (Ismail 2018); building and deploying effective AI systems requires large datasets (McKendrick 2021). The broader in scope the data is drawn from, 'the faster the algorithms can learn and fine-tune their predictive analysis' (Ismail 2018). According to Philip Russom,

[t]he development of a machine learning algorithm depends on large volumes of data, from which the learning process draws many entities, relationships, and clusters. To broaden and

---

[7] It must be noted that if international law does not contain provisions on these issues, states must respect the fundamental principles of international law, such as the principle of sovereign equality.

enrich the correlations made by the algorithm, machine learning needs data from diverse sources, in diverse formats, about diverse business processes. (Russom 2018)

Issues such as ensuring the flow of information/data and whether it is served outside the national borders of the state should fall within the domain of the sovereignty of the state, and particularly internal sovereignty. Ultimately, adopting regulations on AI and protecting the AI industry from intervention of foreign states are important for states to ensure national information security. After all, AI is such a technology that creates a number of challenges to the concept of sovereignty. The necessity of making and regulating the policies regarding AI and the necessity of protecting the national AI industry are issues related to the sovereign power of the state. Darrell West and John Allen (2018) offer some recommendations regarding the regulations that the State should make on the AI industry. Before listing them, I would like to point out that we can claim that these recommendations should also be compatible with the national interests of the states and that when these recommendations are implemented, states can maintain their sovereign power in the posthuman age. West and Allen's (2018) recommendations can be summarised as follows:

- Promoting greater data access for researchers without violating users' right to privacy: states should develop strategies that support AI innovation and protect consumers. Certain standards should be adopted in terms of data access, data sharing, and data protection.
- Allocating government funding for AI research: Emphasising that the investment to be made in AI would be long-term, West and Allen (2018) claim that the investment will pay for itself many times over thanks to the social and economic benefits it will bring.
- Creating an AI advisory commission to make policy recommendations and recommendations.
- Establishing guiding principles on AI.
- Establishing and maintaining mechanisms for surveillance and control by real human beings.
- Promoting cybersecurity to prevent malicious AI behaviour: In the posthuman period, the software of the developing technology should be prevented by some deterrent measures if the software is contrary to humanitarian purposes or is programmed in a way that violates fundamental human rights (Brundage et al. 2018). Governments should be careful to protect their own cyber security and not to harm the cyber security of other countries. In fact, the issue of cyber security breach is a problem that transcends national borders. Therefore, countries should act together to ensure cyber security.

In the posthuman and postdigital age, it would be outdated and useless to confine the concept of sovereignty to a territorial understanding the concept of sovereignty, so responsibilities of states should be updated. I would like to draw particular attention to the fact that state sovereignty can also extend to the digital ecosystem (for example AI). In addition, within the framework of the updated understanding of sovereignty, states should resort to innovative and modern methods rather than classical methods to protect fundamental human rights (for example, protecting the right to privacy in the digital ecosystem).

5   Conclusion

In the postdigital age, a natural human and social life cannot be separated from digital technologies and cannot marginalise each other (Jandrić et al. 2018: 893). Accordingly, as Jandrić (2019b: 276) rightly observed, 'we have no other choice but develop new postdigital forms of collective intelligence'. Thus, it is clear that we need a new human rights approach in the posthuman and postdigital age. As Albert Einstein (BrainyQuote.Com n.d.) once reminded us, we cannot tackle today's human rights problems by applying the same thinking method we used to create them. We can overcome the challenges we experience regarding human rights, by going beyond outdated and conventional methods, with modern and contemporary practices and codified texts.

The world's need for a global leadership on human rights is exponentially growing. There are various multilateral conventions that directly concern humanity, such as the rights of refugees, the right not to be tortured or the rights of the children. Although human rights are still violated, many countries have reached a consensus on these issues. However, there has not yet been a consensus on the impact of AI on human rights in the sense of hard law.

The doctrine of human rights has been shaped according to the human species and has been developed based on the human species. AI will never be a truly natural human being. So, even if existing human rights documents still appeal to the human species, how to protect against new threats should also be considered. However, it should not only be resolutions if the provisions regarding the regulation or legal status of AI were codified in the human rights document; a multilateral convention on AI and human rights should also be considered.

Ultimately, this chapter aimed to reveal the tension between human rights and AI. I explained this tension with some specific case studies that basic human rights can be violated by AI tools. For the sake of preventing or mitigating this tension, I offered a number of steps should be taken in this regard, reminding the need for an international consensus on AI.

References

Adriano, E. A. Q. (2015). The Natural Person, Legal Entity or Juridical Person and Juridical Personality. *Penn State Journal of Law & International Affairs*, 4(1), 363–391.

AI HLEG. (2019). A definition of AI: Main capabilities and scientific disciplines. Brussels: European Commission.

Bajema, N. (2022). AI's 6 Worst-Case Scenarios. IEEE Spectrum, 3 January. https://spectrum.ieee.org/ai-worst-case-scenarios. Accessed 30 November 2022.

Belenguer, L. (2022). AI bias: Exploring discriminatory algorithmic decision-making models and the application of possible machine-centric solutions adapted from the pharmaceutical industry. *AI and Ethics*, 2(4), 771–787. https://doi.org/10.1007/s43681-022-00138-8.

BrainyQuote.Com. (n.d.). Albert Einstein Quotes. https://www.brainyquote.com/quotes/albert_einstein_385842. Accessed 30 November 2022.

Brkan, M. (2019). Freedom of expression and Artificial Intelligence: On personalisation, disinformation and (lack of) horizontal effect of the Charter. *Maastricht Faculty of Law Working Papers*. https://doi.org/10.2139/ssrn.3354180.

Brundage, M., Avin, S., Clark, J., Toner, H., Eckersley, P., Garfinkel, B., Dafoe, A., Scharre, P., Zeitzoff, T., Filar, B., Anderson, H., Roff, H., Allen, G. C., Steinhardt, J., Flynn, C., Ó hÉigeartaigh, S., Beard, S., Belfield, H., Farquhar, S., Lyle, C., Crootof, R., Evans, O., Page, M., Bryson, J., Yampolskiy, R., & Amode, D. (2018). The Malicious Use of Artificial Intelligence: Forecasting, Prevention, and Mitigation. https://www.repository.cam.ac.uk/bitstream/handle/1810/275332/1802.07228.pdf?sequence=1&isAllowed=y. Accessed 30 November 2022.

Buolamwini, J., & Gebru, T. (2018). Gender Shades: Intersectional Accuracy Disparities in Commercial Gender Classification. *Proceedings of Machine Learning Research*, *81*, 77–91.

Burri, T. (2017). International Law and Artificial Intelligence. *German Yearbook of International Law*, *60*, 91–108. https://doi.org/10.2139/ssrn.3060191.

Calo, R. (2017). Artificial Intelligence Policy: A Primer and Roadmap. *UC Davis Law Review*, *51*(2), 399–435. https://doi.org/10.2139/ssrn.3015350.

Castel, J. G., & Castel, M. E. (2016). The Road to Artificial Super-Intelligence: Has International Law a Role to Play? *Canadian Journal of Law and Technology*, *14*(1), 1–15.

Clarke, L. (2021). AI is mostly governed by 'soft law'. But that is set to change. TechMonitor, 21 September. https://techmonitor.ai/policy/ai-mostly-governed-by-soft-law-but-set-to-change. Accessed 30 November 2022.

Council of Europe. (1950). Convention for the Protection of Human Rights and Fundamental Freedoms. In Council of Europe Treaty Series 005. Council of Europe.

Crawford, J. (2013). Sovereignty as a Legal Value. In J. Crawford & M. Koskenniemi (Eds.), *The Cambridge Companion to International Law*. 3rd Ed. (pp. 117–133). Cambridge: Cambridge University Press.

Crawford, J. (2019). *Brownlie's Principles of Public International Law*. 9th Ed. Oxford: Oxford University Press.

Davide, C. (2020). Is facial recognition too biased to be let loose? *Nature*, *587*, 347–349. https://doi.org/10.1038/d41586-020-03186-4.

Deb, S. (2016). Donald Trump: 'Torture works'. CBS News, 17 February. https://www.cbsnews.com/news/donald-trump-torture-works/. Accessed 30 November 2022.

ECCHR. (n.d.). Hard law/soft law. https://www.ecchr.eu/en/glossary/hard-law-soft-law/. Accessed 30 November 2022.

ECNL. (2019). Counter-Terrorism & Human Rights: Soft Law, Hard Consequences. https://www.ohchr.org/sites/default/files/Documents/Issues/Terrorism/SR/UNSRCTbrieferSoftLaw.pdf. Accessed 30 November 2022.

Eduardovich, R. O. (2017). Criminal Liability of the Artificial Intelligence. *Problems of Legality*, *138*, 132–141.

Etzioni, O. (2017). How to Regulate Artificial Intelligence. The New York Times, 1 September. https://www.nytimes.com/2017/09/01/opinion/artificial-intelligence-regulations-rules.html. Accessed 30 November 2022.

European Parliament. (2017). Report with recommendations to the Commission on Civil Law Rules on Robotics (2015/2103(INL)). https://www.europarl.europa.eu/doceo/document/A-8-2017-0005_EN.html. Accessed 30 November 2022.

European Parliament. (2021). Report on artificial intelligence: Questions of interpretation and application of international law in so far as the EU is affected in the areas of civil and military uses and of state authority outside the scope of criminal justice (2020/2013(INI)). https://www.europarl.europa.eu/doceo/document/A-9-2021-0001_EN.pdf. Accessed 30 November 2022.

Ferrer, X., Nuenen, T. van, Such, J. M., Coté, M., & Criado, N. (2021). Bias and Discrimination in AI: A Cross-Disciplinary Perspective. *IEEE Technology and Society Magazine*, *40*(2), 72–80. https://doi.org/10.1109/MTS.2021.3056293.

Galeon, D. (2017). An Inside Look at the First Nation With a State Minister for Artificial Intelligence. Futurism, 12 November. https://futurism.com/uae-minister-artificial-intelligence. Accessed 30 November 2022.

Gibbs, S. (2014). Elon Musk: Artificial intelligence is our biggest existential threat. The Guardian, 27 October. https://www.theguardian.com/technology/2014/oct/27/elon-musk-artificial-intelligence-ai-biggest-existential-threat. Accessed 30 November 2022.

Hárs, A. (2021). AI and International Law – Legal Personality and Avenues for Regulation. Hungarian Journal of Legal Studies, 62(4), 320–344. https://doi.org/10.1556/2052.2022.00352.

International Civil Aviation Organization. (1944). Convention on Civil Aviation—Chicago Convention, 7 December 1944, 15 UNTS 295. https://www.icao.int/publications/documents/7300_orig.pdf. Accessed 8 March 2023.

Ismail, N. (2018). The Success of Artificial Intelligence Depends on Data. Information Age, 23 April. https://www.information-age.com/success-artificial-intelligence-data-10142/. Accessed 30 November 2022.

Jandrić, P. (2019a). The Postdigital Challenge of Critical Media Literacy. The International Journal of Critical Media Literacy, 1(1), 26–37. https://doi.org/10.1163/25900110-00101002.

Jandrić, P. (2019b). We-Think, We-Learn, We-Act: the Trialectic of Postdigital Collective Intelligence. Postdigital Science and Education, 1(2), 257–279. https://doi.org/10.1007/s42438-019-00055-w.

Jandrić, P., Knox, J., Besley, T., Ryberg, T., Suoranta, J., & Hayes, S. (2018). Postdigital Science and Education. Educational Philosophy and Theory, 50(10), 893–899. https://doi.org/10.1080/00131857.2018.1454000.

Kasap, A. (2022). Güncel Gelişmeler Işığında Türk Hukukunda Yapay Zekâ Varlıkları ve Hukuki Kişilik. Türk-Alman Üniversitesi Hukuk Fakültesi Dergisi, 4(2), 485–556.

Kaye, D. (2015). Report of the Special Rapporteur on the Promotion and Protection of the Right to Freedom of Opinion and Expression (A/HRC/29/32). https://digitallibrary.un.org/record/798709. Accessed 30 November 2022.

Kaye, D. (2018). Promotion and protection of the right to freedom of opinion and expression (A/73/348). https://digitallibrary.un.org/record/1643488. Accessed 30 November 2022.

Lavanchy, M. (2018). Amazon's sexist hiring algorithm could still be better than a human. The Conversation, 1 November. https://theconversation.com/amazons-sexist-hiring-algorithm-could-still-be-better-than-a-human-105270. Accessed 30 November 2022.

Leslie, D., Burr, C., Aitken, M., Cowls, J., Katell, M., & Briggs, M. (2021). Artificial intelligence, human rights, democracy, and the rule of law: A primer. Brussels: The Council of Europe.

Manheim, K., & Kaplan, L. (2019). Artificial Intelligence: Risks to Privacy and Democracy. Yale Journal of Law & Technology, 21, 106–188.

McKendrick, J. (2021). The Data Paradox: Artificial Intelligence Needs Data; Data Needs AI. Forbes, 27 June. https://www.forbes.com/sites/joemckendrick/2021/06/27/the-data-paradox-artificial-intelligence-needs-data-data-needs-ai/?sh=1d0d7ff571a5. Accessed 30 November 2022.

Mijatović, D. (2018). In the era of artificial intelligence: Safeguarding human rights. Open Democracy Blog, 3 July. https://www.coe.int/en/web/commissioner/view/-/asset_publisher/ugj3i6qSEkhZ/content/in-the-era-of-artificial-intelligence-safeguarding-human-rights/pop_up?inheritRedirect=true. Accessed 30 November 2022.

Mijatović, D. (2019). Unboxing artificial intelligence: 10 steps to protect human rights. Open Democracy Blog, 14 May. https://www.coe.int/en/web/commissioner/-/unboxing-artificial-intelligence-10-steps-to-protect-human-rights. Accessed 30 November 2022.

Non-Discrimination Ombudsman. (n.d.). Artificial intelligence and equality. https://syrjinta.fi/en/artificial-intelligence-and-equality. Accessed 30 November 2022.

Peters, M. A., & Jandrić, P. (2019). AI, Human Evolution, and the Speed of Learning. In J. Knox; Y. Wang; & M. Gallagher (Eds.), Artificial Intelligence and Inclusive Education: speculative futures and emerging practices (pp. 195–206). Singapore: Springer Nature. https://doi.org/10.1007/978-981-13-8161-4_12.

Prokhovnik, R. (1996). Internal/external: The state of sovereignty. Contemporary Politics, 2(3), 7–20. https://doi.org/10.1080/13569779608454736.

Russom, P. (2018). Data Requirements for Machine Learning. TDWI, 14 September. https://tdwi. org/articles/2018/09/14/adv-all-data-requirements-for-machine-learning.aspx. Accessed 30 November 2022.

Schank, R. C. (1987). What Is AI, Anyway? *AI Magazine, 8*(4), 59–65. https://doi.org/10.1609/ aimag.v8i4.623.

Shaffer, G. C., & Pollack, M. A. (2010). Hard Vs. Soft Law: Alternatives, Complements, and Antagonists in International Governance. *Minnesota Law Review, 94*(3), 706–799.

Silva, D. F. (2011). From Human Rights to Person Rights: Legal Reflection on Posthumanism and Human Enhancement. In Goethe University Frankfurt am Main Department of Law (Ed.), *25th IVR World Congress: Law Science and Technology*. Frankfurt am Main: Goethe University.

Strangio, S. (2017). Welcome to the Posthuman Rights World. Foreign Policy, 7 March. https:// foreignpolicy.com/2017/03/07/welcome-to-the-posthuman-rights-world/. Accessed 30 November 2022.

Talimonchik, V. P. (2021). The Prospects for the Recognition of the International Legal Personality of Artificial Intelligence. *Laws, 10*(4), 85.

The Public Voice. (2018). Universal Guidelines for Artificial Intelligence. 23 October. Brussels: The Public Voice. https://thepublicvoice.org/ai-universal-guidelines/. Accessed 30 November 2022.

The UAE Government. (n.d.). Artificial Intelligence Office. https://ai.gov.ae/about_us/. Accessed 30 November 2022.

Timmers, P. (2022). AI Challenging Sovereignty and Democracy. *Transatlantic Policy Quarterly, 20*(4), 45–55.

Turner, J. (2019). *Robot Rules: Regulating Artificial Intelligence*. Cham: Palgrave Macmillan. https://doi.org/10.1007/978-3-319-96235-1.

UN High Commissioner for Human Rights. (2021). The right to privacy in the digital age (A/ HRC/48/31). Paris: United Nations. https://www.ohchr.org/en/documents/thematic-reports/ ahrc4831-right-privacy-digital-age-report-united-nations-high. Accessed 30 November 2022.

United Nations. (1945). Charter of the United Nations, 24 October 1945, 1 UNTS XVI, https:// www.un.org/en/about-us/un-charter/full-text. Accessed 8 March 2023.

United Nations. (1979). The Moon Treaty. Paris: United Nations. https://www.unoosa.org/oosa/en/ ourwork/spacelaw/treaties/intromoon-agreement.html. Accessed 30 November 2022.

United Nations General Assembly. (1966). International Covenant on Civil and Political Rights. Treaty Series, 999, 171. https://www.ohchr.org/sites/default/files/ccpr.pdf. Accessed 8 March 2023.

United Nations General Assembly. (1982). Convention on the Law of the Sea, 10 December 1982, 1833 UNTS 397. https://www.un.org/depts/los/convention_agreements/texts/unclos/unclos_e. pdf. Accessed 8 March 2023.

USTPC. (2020). Statement on Principles and Prerequisites for the Development, Evaluation and Use of Unbiased Facial Recognition Technologies. Washington, DC: ACM U.S. Technology Policy Committee. https://www.acm.org/binaries/content/assets/public-policy/ustpc-facial-recognition-tech-statement.pdf. Accessed 30 November 2022.

West, D. M., & Allen, J. R. (2018). How Artificial Intelligence is Transforming the World. Brookings, 24 April. https://www.brookings.edu/research/how-artificial-intelligence-is-transforming-the-world/. Accessed 30 November 2022.

Understanding Children's Participation Rights Through a Postdigital Epistemology of Silence

Amy Hanna

1 Introduction

The Covid-19 pandemic has underlined the role of technology in adapting to emergency events, but technology is not merely a tool for enhancing our experiences or solving our problems (Jandrić and Knox 2022). Recognition that technology is part and parcel of human and non-human interactions that range from education to the intricacies of our social lives demands a theory that moves beyond understanding technology as merely a solution or enhancement: the postdigital (see Feenberg 2019). The postdigital evades disciplinary silos and troubles distinctions between disciplines; and perhaps owing to this disciplinary refusal (Jandrić and Ford 2022; MacKenzie 2022), is 'messy; unpredictable; digital and analog; technological and non-technological; biological and informational' (Jandrić et al. 2018: 895) – very much like the messy and complex lives of children (Spyrou 2011) who live in the postdigital world.

Children have a right to 'seek, receive and impart information and ideas of all kinds' under Article 13 of the UN Convention on the Rights of the Child (CRC), and the right to access information under article 17 CRC. Inhabiting a postdigital space that comprises both online and offline environments, information and communication technology is a central aspect of children's daily lives (U.N. Committee on the Rights of the Child 2013: Para. 45). The digital environment is children's most common source of vast swathes of information and therefore affords opportunities for the realisation of children's rights and in particular their 'civil, political, cultural, economic and social rights' (U.N. Committee on the Rights of the Child 2021: Para. 3–4), which are exercised online as well as offline. The distinction between the digital and analog space in which children live and grow up is increasingly blurred.

A. Hanna (✉)
University of Strathclyde, Glasgow, UK
e-mail: amy.hanna@strath.ac.uk

P. Jandrić et al. (eds.), *Constructing Postdigital Research*, Postdigital Science
and Education, https://doi.org/10.1007/978-3-031-35411-3_13

Children's access to information under Article 17 CRC, and their right to adult direction and guidance in accordance with the evolving capacities of the child under Article 5 CRC, are crucial cornerstones for the information children require to be able to participate in research processes – and to reach informed views in order to do so (Lundy and McEvoy 2011). While the postdigital situates itself in the idea of knowledge as a common construct (Peters et al. 2020), postdigital research methodology – how this knowledge is created and examined – is the 'elephant in the room' and questions remain about postdigital research methods (Jandrić 2018).

The postdigital, therefore, is about 'dragging digitalisation and the digital … down from its discursive celestial, ethereal home and into the mud. It is about rubbing its nose in the complexities of everyday practice' (Ryberg in Jandrić et al. 2018: 166); in this case, research. In this chapter, the postdigital will be used as a lens for troubling the dichotomy of 'digital' and 'analog' (Cramer in Cramer and Jandrić 2021: 985) alongside the 'voiced' and the 'silent' in the lives of children, and in particular with regard to their access to, and sharing of, information. Further, this conceptualisation of the postdigital will be employed as a guiding principle for examining postdigital research (Jandrić et al. 2022).

This chapter will examine Article 13 freedom of expression and its inclusion of the right to seek, receive, and impart information because this Article centres the right to be *informed*. I will consider two silences central to an epistemology of silence – omission and concealment; and bullshit – before examining the revelatory features of some silences. The chapter will close with an exploration of what this means for children's rights in postdigital research. First, it is necessary to present Goldberg's (2010) epistemology of silence, which this chapter seeks to build upon.

2 Social Epistemology and an Epistemology of Silence

Traditional epistemology focuses on the individual: it assumes that normative standards of rationality and justification possess some level of objective validity (Goldman 2010). Inherent in this focus upon the individual are assumptions about homogeneity and universal replicability of individual knowers, and the 'known' (Code 2010). Yet, curiously, a very small proportion of what people come to 'know', both as individuals or as a collective, is verifiable by first-hand experience (Code 2010); we rely on others conveying what they know to us. Indeed, our education systems rely on such impartation of knowledge from teachers to students; what Freire (1974) called the 'banking model' of education where knowledge is transmitted from teacher to student.

Social epistemology is a branch of traditional epistemology that studies the epistemic features of individuals that arise from their relations to others, including groups and social systems (Goldman 2010). Social epistemology focuses on our communal knowledge practices that are engaged in particular social, political, geographical, and ethical contexts; it recognises that it is our 'situatedness' that makes knowledge possible, and grants a central place to testimony where these factors are particularly relevant (Code 2010). Indeed, Fricker (2006: 225) observes that 'it is not clear that we do or could possess any knowledge at all which is not in some way, perhaps obliquely, dependent upon testimony'.

Social epistemologists have also become increasingly interested in systemic preservation of ignorance about inconvenient truths (Tanesini 2018; Mills 2007; Tuana 2004, 2006; Alcoff 2007), and therefore with implications for power in epistemic interactions. Commonly understood to be a state of not knowing (see MacKenzie 2023), ignorance is not a failure of knowledge, but modes of not knowing, and knowing inadequately, that are oftentimes cultivated and reinforced (Code 2010; MacKenzie 2023) for the purposes of exclusion and inequality. Ignorance is therefore a powerful force of resistance to testimonial knowledge and a sociopolitical phenomenon produced or sustained in ways that parallel knowledge and the inherent power relations of such production.

There can be a vested interest in maintaining conditions of not knowing or uncertainty about a particular subject, or paternalistic protectiveness against certain truths entering public knowledge. These conditions emerge in the withholding, suppression, or distortion of knowledge to cultivate distrust or confusion about the veracity of knowledge claims (MacKenzie 2023). With respect to this ignorance, social epistemologists have also become intrigued by the role of silence in knowledge and ignorance.

In Goldberg's *Epistemology of Silence* (2010), he explores and characterises the epistemic significance of two kinds of belief based on the 'silence' of a *trusted source*. The first is belief based on memory, and the second belief based on testimony (what Goldberg calls the interpersonal case). Goldberg argues that the presence of 'silence' in the sources relied upon by a hearer should be understood as influencing their belief, in conjunction with other indirect evidence. For example, if a hearer already doubts the existence of weapons of mass destruction in Iraq and is suspicious of George W. Bush's motivations in going to war in Iraq, the fact that the hearer has not come across any reports of any weapons of mass destruction will necessarily be interpreted through this other indirect evidence (Goldberg 2010).

To appreciate the epistemic significance of silence, Goldberg begins with the idea of epistemic reliance on an information source that offers a 'report' or testimony (i.e., is not silent). In this case of testimony there are two forms of reliance: on the source; and on the process of content transmission. In testimony, the source of information is another person; that person may or may not choose to provide the audience with information, and may or may not be reliable in doing so. Reliance therefore refers to both the source of information, and the process by which information is conveyed to the subject.

Goldberg goes on to explore epistemic reliance in cases where a subject relies upon a source that remains silent, asking how having *not* received a report might ground a justification for acquiring a specific belief. He does this by examining two conditionals. The first conditional is as follows:

(i) If a source were to present something as true, then it would be the case that something is true. (Goldberg 2010)

This is what Burge (1993) (cited in Goldberg 2010) calls 'presentation-as-true', and so this conditional is the 'presentational-as-truth' conditional. Goldberg (2010) clarifies the conditional to: a source would present something as true only if it were that case that something is true. The presentation of something as true is what we understand as testimony.

In contrast, in the case of silence, the conditional is not presentation-as-true, but the 'truth-to-presentational' conditional:

(ii) If something is true, then a source would present it as true. (Goldberg 2010)

This captures the idea that if something is true, then there will be relevant coverage of that idea. Goldberg probes this conditional, however, pointing out that it is the *implication* of this conditional, the underside of this claim, more than the conditional itself, that is used in our reasoning:

(iii) If no source has presented that one thing is true, then the alternative must be true. (Goldberg 2010)

Goldberg's (2010) epistemology of silence is explored by examining this statement and reducing this to the question: what does it take to be justified in believing the relevant instance of *iii.*? Where a subject cannot acquire silence-supported knowledge unless *iii.* is true, justification does not require *iii.* to be true as much as it requires that a subject *believes* it to be true. The epistemology of silence, Goldberg argues, involves reliance on other sources and so there are occasions on which the epistemic assessment of an individual will be incomplete without accounting for the members of a community and how they play a role in acquiring, storing and transmitting information. This applies to information in both analog and digital environments whilst acknowledging that remaining silent online does not have the same significance or consequences as it has in face-to-face communications (Brown 2019).

Accounting for collective roles in information spanning the digital and analog spaces is central to postdigital research in order to combat the pitfalls of relying on silence for our beliefs. Goldberg (2010) locates his epistemology of silence in social epistemology because where a subject is assuming coverage of an idea by others, reliable silence-supported belief is not warranted by one individual alone. Instead, the social conditions that endorse such a silence-supported belief are crucial background conditions for the formation of such a belief.

Goldberg (2020) has gone on to argue that there is a default entitlement to take silence as acceptance (see also Pettit 2002), and that most people will worry about what silences will be interpreted to mean if they don't speak up. Some suggest there is an epistemic obligation to voice disagreement (Johnson 2018; Langton 2018). Langton (2018: 161) suggests that 'back door speech acts' usher in assumptions which must be criticised with counter speech. However, these assertions are built on a model of speech acts that are face to face, and in which speakers are positioned as equals (Saul 2021; Lackey 2018). We know from Fricker's (2007) work, for example, that this is not the case and testimony is permeated with discrimination and power disparities.

Taking silence to indicate acceptance also overlooks how frequently silence is used to make known an interlocutor's dissent (Tanesini 2018). These assumptions are also built on a model of speech acts that disregard silence as a speech act of itself. Communication is frequently understood as a matter of information exchange where a speaker encodes thoughts into language and transmits them through speech, received and decoded by a listener (Wakeham 2017). This code model ignores how little is often 'said' in conversations, however (Sperber and Wilson 1995; Goffman 1959). For example, silence can be a speech act through protest (Goldberg 2020): it can be used to *reveal* as well as conceal.

In advancing the epistemic significance of silence, Goldberg (2010) emphasises innovative thinking about testimony itself: it is not only what others tell us, but what they do *not* tell us (see also Fricker 2007). The silence of others can back our claims to knowledge and therefore silence should be located alongside testimony as a manifestation of our epistemic reliance on social peers. Despite there being several types of silence, however, no definition of silence is presented in Goldberg's account, and his epistemology only deals with the silence of a trusted source – one acting in good faith.

The remainder of this chapter therefore seeks to build upon Goldberg's (2010) proposal to expound children's right to information through a postdigital lens. This lens incorporates the multivariate silences that exist in the postdigital environment, including those that incorporate acting in bad faith – what MacKenzie et al. (2021) suggest is an epistemology of deceit – as well as those that reveal. This consideration will therefore understand silence as both a literal absence of dissenting speech, and an expression of dissent in different circumstances. In doing so, I will add troubling knowledge and information as 'voiced' and 'unvoiced' to Jandrić et al.'s (2018) definition of the postdigital. Before applying this to a discussion of a postdigital epistemology of silence, it is necessary to consider children's participation rights in more depth.

3 Children's Participation Rights

McGregor (2015) emphasises that to confront the complexity of the world's wicked problems, many perspectives are needed, and that by employing methodologies that work beyond traditional boundaries, with multiple perspectives, new knowledge is created. I suggest that integrating children's perspectives is a vital component in a postdigital methodology, and requires one that is rights-respecting.

The term 'participation' does not appear in the United Nations Convention on the Rights of the Child (CRC), but children's rights to participation have evolved to include processes of information sharing and dialogue between children and adults (United Nations Committee on the Rights of the Child 2009: Para. 3). Information is a central component of children's participation rights in the CRC, and is enshrined as part of the right to freedom of expression under Article 13, in tandem with Article 17 'access to information and material'. It is access to *accurate* information that underpins this right, and the obligations upon States parties to regulate misinformation and disinformation available to children has not been well explored to date. Effective implementation of administrative participation rights under Article 12 CRC (State obligations to hear children's views on matters that affect them to inform decision making) relies on the state obligation under Article 13 (Lundy et al. 2019; United Nations Committee on the Rights of the Child 2009: Para. 80–81) not to interfere in the expression of those views or access to information, subject to necessary restrictions provided for in law.

In contrast to the administrative obligations under Article 12, which impose an active obligation to facilitate the expression of views and to give them due weight, Article 13 places an obligation on the state and state actors to refrain from *interfering* in the expression of a child's views:

1. The child shall have the right to freedom of expression; this right shall include freedom to seek, receive and impart information and ideas of all kinds, regardless of frontiers, either orally, in writing or in print, in the form of art, or through any media of the child's choice.
2. The exercise of this right may be subject to certain restrictions, but these shall only be such as are provided by law and are necessary:

    (a) For respect of the rights or reputations of others; or
    (b) For the protection of national security or of public order (order public), or of public health or morals. (UN 1989)

The right to freedom of expression is central to autonomy, but social expectations about children's capacity have marginalised the structures and mechanisms with which to enjoy it (Tobin and Parkes 2019); a social context that directly engages social epistemology. Without these social structures and mechanisms, of course, children's expressions remain silent. The 'information of all kinds' under Article 13 is not limited to statements of fact, but includes opinions, criticisms, and speculation (Tobin and Parkes 2019) – what amounts to 'testimony' under social epistemology. The Committee on the Rights of the Child (the Committee) is clear that both Article 13 on the right to freedom of expression and Article 17 on access to information 'assert that the child is entitled to exercise those rights on his or her behalf, in accordance with her or his evolving capacities' (United Nations Committee on the Rights of the Child 2009: Para. 80). Article 17 provides that:

> States Parties recognize the important function performed by the mass media and shall ensure that the child has access to information and material from a diversity of national and international sources, especially those aimed at the promotion of his or her social, spiritual and moral well-being and physical and mental health.

To this end, States Parties shall:

> (a) Encourage the mass media to disseminate information and material of social and cultural benefit to the child and in accordance with the spirit of article 29 […] (UN 1989)

Generally, the right to seek and receive information has been understood as a right to access information held by public authorities, but Tobin and Parkes (2019) argue that it goes beyond accessing personal information to denote 'active inquiry' on the part of the child. Conceptualising the right to information in this way highlights its instrumental role in equipping children to be 'informed' in order to understand and articulate their experiences. This is bolstered by the Article 17 right to access information 'aimed at the promotion of his or her social, spiritual and moral well-being': an essential prerequisite for not only understanding social and political experiences, but expressing them (Hanna 2022).

Shaub (2012: 209) observes that 'children use media and other expressive outlets to listen to, and participate in, expression that entertains and satisfies them … [and] to experience the autonomous pleasure and emotional fulfilment of catharsis' which, Tobin and Parkes (2019) suggest, offers expression uninhibited by the expectation of dialogue with adults. It is also a crucial means of young people 'coming to know' (Hanna 2022) – coming to informed positions on topics under debate, including the wicked problems of the twenty-first century (McGregor 2015). Consequently, Articles 13 and 17 provide for young people to access social and cultural information with which to understand their experiences, and to inform their exercise of human rights.

The Committee is explicit in stating that children are under no obligation to exercise their participation rights, and expressing their views is a choice; States parties must ensure that children have the necessary information to form a view, and make a decision whether or not to participate in their own best interests (United Nations Committee on the Rights of the Child 2009: Para. 16, 25). Using this information, they can express themselves through a medium of their choice, about a subject of their choice, allowing for the possibility that this expression need not be 'encumbered by the need for a conversation' (Tobin and Parkes 2019: 473) – silence.

It is here that children's right to information intersects with social epistemology. Children's positioning as knowers (or 'non-knowers') takes place in a specific social-epistemic environment in which social norms and practices mediate what adults know, or *think* they know (Buchanan 2020). The information that children can attain is contingent on their social experience and identities which are interpreted through the medium of shared epistemic norms and cultural values – the essence of Article 17 access to information. Buchanan (2020) examines the social epistemology of human rights, using gender discrimination as a worked example, by asking why in some societies, many hold false beliefs about the epistemic 'capacity' of women. He argues that changing these false beliefs is unlikely to be achieved by presenting information to the contrary, but by shifting social practices and experiences in order for the epistemic collective to be one in which they are viewed as 'knowers'. Buchanan's (2020) arguments also apply to children's right to information. Social understandings of children as lacking in capacity for knowledge, and pervasive perceptions of children as being the objects of 'information' remain widespread in society (see Hanna 2022) and it is here that postdigital research can be instrumental in shifting social norms that position children as non-knowers.

Buchanan (2020) argues that reliable judgements about individual capacities include realisation of human rights to non-discrimination, freedom of association, expression, and participation. Social conditions in which there is discrimination on the basis of age limits children's exercise and development of 'capacity', and therefore creates a social milieu that produces and reinforces ignorance about children's capacity. In this discriminatory social milieu, therefore, social experiences are not reliable indicators of children's capacity. Buchanan (2020) argues that such societies are poor epistemic environments in which to ascertain children's capacity because discrimination creates social experiences that appear to confirm lack of capacity, the effects of which are mistaken (or distorted in the production of ignorance) as valid grounds for discrimination. In postdigital research, children can be engaged as co-researchers with their own research questions, in spaces that transcend the traditional dichotomy of digital and analog, and positioned as having capacity to engage with the wicked problems of the twenty-first century (McGregor 2015).

Perceptions of children's 'capacity' are frequently bonded with forms of silence. In many cases, children's silences are interpreted as lack of capacity or ignorance. Fricker (2007) identifies two forms of silence regarding participation in knowledge practices: epistemic 'objectification' and 'pre-emptive silence'. Epistemic objectification occurs where the subject is 'ousted' from participation in the capacity for knowledge, and relegated to 'passive bystander' (Fricker 2007: 132). This serves to wrong someone in their capacity as an inquirer by confining them to a 'passive capacity as a source of information' (Fricker 2007: 132). In young people's experience, such silences may emerge in the education system where their silence is required for knowledge transmission from teachers, but young people themselves are not viewed or treated as subjects of knowledge or epistemic agents – only as sources from whom information is to be gleaned. Such information is not authentic young person testimony, but the repeated testimony of teacher speakers: it is regurgitated or rehearsed testimony, and is not, therefore, authentic exchange of knowledge.

Pre-emptive silence occurs, according to Fricker (2007: 130), when 'markers of trustworthiness' lead to a 'tendency for some groups simply not to be asked for information in the first place'; this information includes 'their thoughts, their judgements, their opinions' whereby these individuals' word is not taken seriously and is, therefore, not asked for. This 'advance' silencing confirms pre-conceived notions of children lacking capacity in advance of their expression of any views or opinions, meaning they are not free to impart ideas and express themselves. Moreover, their silences are interpreted in deficit, instead of considered as a form of expression (see Tanesini 2018).

The operation of both objectification and pre-emptive silences can, therefore, control whose contributions are expressed, whose are not, whose are expressed in and through silence, and how these multivarious silences are interpreted. Fricker (2007: 171–172) urges that such silences require a more socially aware, and remedial, kind of listening: 'listening as much to what is *not* said as to what is said' which resonates with young people's broad participation rights, and the postdigital world in which they are exercised. This demands a methodology that attends to silence as both concealment and revelation, conformity and dissent; one which the postdigital, in its problematisation of boundaries and dichotomies is ideally placed to do.

4 A Rights-Based Postdigital Epistemology of Silence

Rights based approaches to children's engagement in the digital environment have grown steadily, offering a lens for research and policy that balances children's need for protection in the online world with the benefits of day to day lives that span the online and offline worlds (Livingstone and Third 2017). In a study by Third et al. (2014), children suggested that the binary between the online and offline worlds had already been transcended by the diversity of communicative modes and settings that make up children's lives. This forms the basis for the means through which young people exercise their right to information and participation (Livingstone 2016). What is essential, is a digital literacy that builds children's capacity to access and participate online, and to exercise their rights in the digital environment (Livingstone 2016). I go further to argue that what is essential, is a methodology that builds children's capacity to access and impart information and knowledge in both digital and analog spaces, which takes account of their capacity to participate in these spaces.

Two tensions that quickly become apparent, however, are those between children's protection and participation rights, and between rights asserted in the online and offline worlds (Livingstone and Third 2017). The UN Committee on the Rights of the Child (the Committee) is clear that meaningful access to digital technology can support children in the realisation of their 'civil, political, cultural, economic and social rights' (U.N. Committee on the Rights of the Child 2021: Para. 4). As drawing the distinction between the online and offline in children's lives is increasingly impossible (Stoilova et al. 2016), this demands new theory (Livingstone and Third 2017): the postdigital.

A postdigital lens is apt because it conceptualises the digital sphere as a communal space that provides access to knowledge through collective knowledge sharing, but also because it encompasses the digital and analog (Jandrić et al. 2018). It is also fitting because, as McGregor (2015) and MacKenzie (2022) point out, the problems we face in society in the twenty-first century cannot be tackled through single disciplines, stakeholders, or sectors. A postdigital research methodology requires working in connection with others, including children.

A further contemporary challenge is the common adoption of a technologically determinist view of digital technology and the digital environment which focus reductively on the causal impacts of technology on particular aspects of children's lives (Stoilova et al. 2016). This overlooks the social structures and contexts that also shape children's lives, such as the meaning children associate with not only digital technology, but social contexts (Mansell 2012; Manyozo 2011); a space emerges here for a postdigital social epistemology. With the postdigital's notorious resistance to definition and disciplinary refusal (Jandrić and Ford 2022; MacKenzie 2022), it is an apt lens through which to consider children's rights spanning the digital and analog environments, and the tensions which arise between protecting children from harm and their right to participate in civic society – both online and offline. These harms include the epistemic vice of deceit.

Where humans engage in communication, some form of deceit commonly occurs (MacKenzie and Bhatt 2021). Social media, and the digital environment generally, is the source of several epistemic vices such as lies, wilful ignorance, and vast swathes of misinformation, disinformation, and discrimination (U.N. Committee on the Rights of the Child 2021: Para. 54; MacKenzie and Bhatt 2021; Deibert 2019); what has been conceptualised elsewhere as the *epistemology* of deceit (see MacKenzie et al. 2021). Technology is a broker of information from sources in the digital and analog spaces and children have themselves stated that they want help in managing untrustworthy information presented online (U.N. Committee on the Rights of the Child 2021: Para. 3). Information that is untrustworthy, however, is rarely accompanied by an indication that it is deceptive, and the modes employed in disseminating such untrustworthy information frequently deploy forms of silence in doing so. MacKenzie et al. (2021) raise epistemological questions about how we respond to the silence of, for example, omission in its myriad forms.

I have asserted that silence illuminates an epistemology of children's participation rights because it is often taken to occlude children's right to freedom of expression (Hanna 2022). That is, it frustrates the act of imparting knowledge, but also the seeking and receiving of information; information that enables young people to make sense of their own experiences. Deserving of further attention is how silence can be used to highlight deception and misinformation, and what this might mean for postdigital research in the children's rights field.

4.1 Testimony in Bad Faith

Deception is directly related to our ideals of truth, and is woven throughout our epistemological, technological, and social worlds, according to Rose (2021). Testimony depends on relationships in which we trust others to tell the truth and there is therefore an assumption that our interlocutors act in good faith (Rose 2021). What we know of the world comes from social sources, which means we are vulnerable to others' deception and incompetence, and indeed we all participate in others' white lies, embellishments, and ambiguities (Wakeham 2017). Of course, as Rose (2021) asserts, it is not possible to verify the truth or epistemic validity of all the information we consume, and learning from others is how we acquire such information: knowledge is socially constructed and disseminated. It is perhaps for this reason, that silences can tell us something about testimony and the transmission of 'information'. What is necessary to advance Goldberg's (2010) epistemology of silence based on silences from trusted sources, is a contemplation of types of information that may not be in 'good faith': misinformation and disinformation.

According to Wardle and Derakhshan (2017), misinformation is false information shared without the intention of harm; what the World Health Organisation termed an 'infodemic' during Covid-19 due to the volume of misinformation about coronavirus. Disinformation is false information shared with the intention of harm. Jiang and Vetter (2021) also propose categories of false information: misinformation being that whose accuracy is unintentional, and disinformation that whose accuracy is deliberately false or misleading. I suggest that disinformation also includes sharing of false information with disregard as to whether it harms others or not, and foreground Jiang and Vetter's (2021) conceptualisation of these terms because they couch information in terms of accuracy, which neatly parallels children's right to *accurate* information.

Silences form a crucial part of the various transmissions of information in bad faith. Most accounts of lying for example, argues Rose (2021), feature a speaker who makes a statement that is false (and therefore silence on the truth), and which intends to deceive, resulting in the listener acquiring a false belief. As such, the flow of knowledge or information is frustrated. However, as Rose (2021) suggests, the reasons why people lie are just as numerous as the methods they choose to do so, which makes this most prominent account of lying only one type of deception. Partial silences can also be deceptive, and half-truths are difficult to categorise because they are not entirely believed to be false, but not entirely believed to be true either (Marsili 2019). Indeed, humans can be skilled at exploiting the difference between saying explicitly that a statement is not believed, and conveying information we do not believe in other ways (Rose 2021): uses of silence in the form of 'doublespeak' (Sinclair 2021).

4.2   Omission and Concealment

Omissions can be misleading, and have far reaching implications, even if not premeditated and I therefore argue that they confound the dichotomy of 'misinformation' and 'disinformation'. O'Sullivan (2021) argues that epistemic practices that produce omissions can also constitute untruthfulness, particularly where there are patterns of omission akin to what Mark Twain calls the 'silent lie' (Twain 1992): misleading by not mentioning something. Omissions differ from lies because a lie requires a statement, but withholding information that the hearer might need to know can be similarly deceptive (Rose 2021), and more difficult to identify. These withheld pieces of information are packaged in euphemistic silences including 'alternative facts' and discreetly withheld truths (Maginess 2021). Such examples of silence can be deceptive when a person knows their silence will be interpreted as agreement (cf. Goldberg 2020), intends their silence to be understood as such, and remains silent intentionally for the purpose of deception (Fallis 2019).

O'Sullivan (2021) suggests that concerning ourselves with the absence of information might prompt us to think more carefully about information that *is* available. Perhaps, then, part of the cure for misinformation and disinformation when it comes to children is to teach them to look for what is absent: no small task, and one which might benefit from an epistemic consideration of questioning. Knowledge may not be so much about speech acts of 'information', but about omissions as constitutive of untruthfulness, because conceptualisations of 'information' are based on a model of truthfulness through speech acts that fail to consider 'truth' as incomplete or inchoate. Deception can occur by concealment easily perpetrated in analog, and perhaps even more easily in the digital environment, by withholding information that the hearer might need to know in order to reach an informed position. Postdigital methods can foreground analysis of such silences to elicit the nuances of the role of silence in testimony, building upon work already begun in this area (Presser 2022).

These silences have long been exploited in politics by opportunistic politicians who claim to represent the unspoken views of the majority. In a speech delivered on 3 November, 1969, Richard Nixon popularised the notion of the 'silent majority' when garnering support for war in Vietnam.[1] Yet, if enough people are silent in a democracy, this can deprive others of crucial information about where majority opinion actually lies (Kuran 1995) with a consequent 'spiral of silence' that gives the false impression of popular support for a government's decisions and politics, precisely because nobody is willing to say otherwise (Noelle-Neumann 1993); a danger inadequately examined by social epistemology to date.

4.3   Bullshitting and Gaslighting

Wakeham (2017) argues that bullshit is a problem of social epistemology distinctive from lying and is a problematic form of deception in itself. The problem of bullshit emerges from, he argues, the tension between our individual need to have true beliefs, and our simultaneous need for cooperation with others. Bullshitting differs from lying or overt concealment because where the liar does not consider his statements to be true, the bullshitter is not on the side of the true or the false – he seeks to convince the audience that questions of truth or falsity are immaterial or irrelevant (Frankfurt 2005; Wakeham 2017). In some cases, interlocutors themselves do not take a position on truth or falsehood, and this uncertainty is exploited by trolls – extremely common in digital spaces.

Wright (2021) argues that the success of trolling depends on the target individual's uncertainty of what to believe and the lack of clarity about what the troll believes. Trolls' claims are made to elicit reaction, and often involve ambiguities that allow an ironic distance. Any claims that their speech acts (or silent exceptions) are inappropriate can therefore be met with a suggestion that the interlocutor misinterpreted the troll's statement: what we might understand as gaslighting. Such gaslighting distracts (and therefore deceives) others from the fact that claims are

---

[1] See https://www.americanrhetoric.com/speeches/richardnixongreatsilentmajority.html. Accessed 23 January 2023.

harmful because of their deception. This gaslighting is a form of avoidance and therefore of silence: manipulation by withholding information or distracting attention, intending to make a person doubt their beliefs, knowledge, and experience.

Fake news works in a similar way: false information is intentionally produced and disseminated with the aim of deceiving the public to believe in false statements and doubt verifiable truths (Özdan 2021). In the postdigital era, communication technologies may cause distortions in freedom of expression and opinions and other democratic rights such as protest, to the extent that they reduce people's belief in democracy and eventually obscure the difference between information and dis/misinformation. Of course, such an effect creates a society where when people don't know what to believe, they don't believe anything, or perhaps more dangerously, they believe everything. Green (2021) suggests that gaslighting the public creates epistemic destruction because they doubt their judgement and are consequently afraid to speak up and express themselves. This is a direct consequence of what Green calls a 'propaganda feedback loop': a self-reinforcing media ecosystem that delivers partisan narratives, while labelling dissenting accounts as biased and untrustworthy. Indeed, Noelle-Neumann (1993) conceptualised such echo-chambers as a 'spiral of silence'.

Ultimately, forms and modes of silence are instrumental in the value of truth: implicit and tacit uses of silence deliberately mislead and deceive interlocutors. This deception uses ambiguity to weaponize speech by abusing the listeners' assumptions that interlocutors are acting in good faith; omission and bullshitting weaponize silence to mask acting in bad faith. The postdigital has a crucial role to play here because its disciplinary abstinence allows it to draw together these seemingly ironic and paradoxical uses of silence to mislead with the silences employed as a medium of revelation and clarification through social epistemology.

4.4   Revelatory Silence

Silence is not always expressive of acceptance (Tanesini 2018; cf. Goldberg 2020). Moreover, conceptions of silence as omission only are reductive; silence can be deployed as a means of *voicing* protest, refusal, and dissent (Tanesini 2018; Jungkutz 2012). Whilst there are cooperative silences, other forms of silence are an effective means through which to convey a lack of cooperation (Tanesini 2018). For example, our society frequently obliges citizens to produce speech about themselves; speech that discloses personal information to authorities. In such a society, silence becomes a medium, in certain circumstances, for dissent, expressions of boredom, and disagreement (Tanesini 2018).

One of the most notable applications of silence is its role in exposing truths as well as concealing or omitting them; not all silences are conducive to malice in the postdigital era. For example, Sinclair (2021) discusses uses of humour such as satire in calling out hierarchies of power, without naming such hierarchies, and in pointing out unflattering truths about society without directly confronting them. Tanesini (2018) highlights the use of silence for disapproval and censure. Humour might thus be considered a further use of silence in highlighting how deception is central to many of our social foibles and holding them up to ridicule.

Sinclair (2021) further exemplifies the use of doublespeak: deliberately obscure and ambiguous language, and the use of deliberate silences and omissions to direct or distract attention to and from certain aspects of stories – often a feature of the stage. Sinclair adeptly highlights the irony of such doublespeak and satire in exposing what might have been muffled or implicit and in doing so, reveals how we might be deceived by the silences which have distracted our attention elsewhere.

Such nuanced conceptualisation of silence is directly congruent with the postdigital's troubling of dichotomies and its refusal to be siloed in its approach to the wicked problems of the twenty-first century (McGregor 2015). Using this refusal as a starting point for research with children is a sound starting point for building children's capacity, including children's testimony, and respecting their rights, in postdigital research methods.

5   Children's Rights and Postdigital Research

The postdigital is concerned with how knowledge practices take shape in the digital environment, given the rapidity and magnitude at which information, misinformation, and disinformation flow in the online environment (MacKenzie 2023). This has prompted vital debate on the relationship between education and digital technology, particularly given the postdigital position that digital technologies are not neutral instruments (see Mörtsell and Gunnarsson 2023; Jandrić and Knox 2022). Buchanan (2020) further suggests that the postdigital is a useful lens for considering teaching and learning, and the messiness of teaching and learning processes and relationships (see Jopling 2023; Jandrić 2023). The remaining elephant in the room, however, is how the postdigital approaches research methodologies (Jandrić 2018).

The development of communication technologies has provided wider access to information than ever before, and in doing so has introduced some distortions to freedom of expression, the right to information and to privacy (Özdan 2021) – rights which apply to the ethics of research. For example, in research that transcends the dichotomy of the analog and digital spaces, researchers must recognise that participant testimony in the digital sphere does not have the same meaning as testimony in person; remaining silent on social media does not have the same significance or consequences as it has in face-to-face communications (Brown 2019). Postdigital research acknowledges these nuances of testimony through its refusal to be categorised.

When it comes to rights-respecting research with children, the digital environment provides an opportunity for children to exercise their right to access to information, and so digital media and online content performs a crucial function

(U.N. Committee on the Rights of the Child 2021: Para. 50). Notwithstanding this vital epistemic function, however, the digital environment also includes misinformation and disinformation which may come from multiple sources. The Committee emphasises that States Parties should protect children from harmful and untrustworthy content, and enable children to safely access diverse content, recognizing children's rights to information and freedom of expression (U.N. Committee on the Rights of the Child 2021: Para. 54), which captures a key tension in realising children's rights in the postdigital milieu.

Opportunities offered by the digital environment play a vital role in children's development, but the digital environment also poses risks and potential harm to children. Postdigital research much therefore 'ensure that children have access to a wide diversity of information, including information held by public bodies, about culture, sports, the arts, health, civil and political affairs and children's rights' (U.N. Committee on the Rights of the Child 2021: Para. 51). In balancing the opportunities and the risks to children, the Committee is explicit in stating that:

> States parties should protect children from harmful and untrustworthy content and ensure that relevant businesses and other providers of digital content develop and implement guidelines to enable children to safely access diverse content, recognising children's rights to information and freedom of information, while protecting them from such harmful material in accordance with their rights and evolving capacities. (U.N. Committee on the Rights of the Child 2021: Para. 54)

States parties should also encourage digital providers to label online content, for example, on its trustworthiness, and encourage provision of guidance, training, and education for children. When considering the postdigital research through the lens of human rights as this chapter has sought to do, therefore, questions regarding state obligations around information and dis/misinformation must be raised. Given the tension between protecting children from information that is inaccurate and injurious, and children's right to information under Articles 13 and 17, a fruitful balance might be reached by considering children's best interests under Article 3 CRC. The best interests principle stipulates that in all actions that affect children, the best interests of the child shall be a primary consideration (United Nations 1989). It is here that there are direct implications for research.

For postdigital research, rights-based research with children is that in which children's experiences in the postdigital era are foregrounded – they are the 'multiple' in McGregor's (2015) call for multiple perspectives. To carry out research in this manner, the postdigital must view children as having rights entitlements, as well as being creators and consumers of meaning (Lundy and McEvoy 2011; Beazley et al. 2009). This requires a methodology that develops deliberate strategies for building children's capacity to form their views (Lundy and McEvoy 2011), which requires a critical approach to the swathes of information they have at their fingertips. Postdigital research must put an onus on building children's capacity to engage with substantive issues that underpin research using a constructivist position (Lundy and McEvoy 2011) – not merely use them as conduits of information. This demands interpreting children's testimony in line with their right to be guided and supported by adults under article 5 CRC, their information rights under article 13 and 17 CRC, and creating a space in which children can grapple and interact with information, adults and their peers (Lundy and McEvoy 2011; Lundy et al. 2011).

Lundy and McEvoy (2011) clearly argue for accurate information, and in the postdigital era there are vast swathes of disinformation and misinformation that children must learn to identify and analyse. The Committee states that the media are obliged to take all appropriate steps to encourage the dissemination of information that will have social and cultural benefit to children, as stated under Article 17(a). Yet, this obligation will not always be realised by the media who operate in partisan and political spaces (see MacKenzie et al. 2021 for multiple examples). What is needed – and what postdigital research can deliver – is guidance for children to respond to epistemic uncertainty. For this to be effective, they need exposed to falsehoods in a safe environment so they can learn the hallmarks of epistemologies of deceit and in so doing, benefit from the inoculation effect of learning epistemic virtues.

These virtues may include: epistemic humility – not falling into the trap of assuming or thinking they 'know' something definitively; and reflexivity – seeing things from others' perspectives, questioning information sources, and questioning and reflecting on themselves. From a rights-based perspective, this also demands education about human rights, and some myth-busting about freedom of expression. The right to freedom of expression does *not* include an obligation upon anyone else to listen or amplify certain messages, and children's right to information must include the right to education on mis/disinformation, as well as skills that build their capacity to critically analyse such information.

One way of meeting this obligation, I suggest, is teaching skills pursuant to social epistemology as a collective endeavour, such as questioning and probing knowledge practices and exchanges. Jandrić et al. (2018) highlight postdigital critical pedagogy in a reclamation of the digital sphere as a commons that brings people tougher and provides them with access to human knowledge through horizontal communication. Critically, this horizontal communication enriches knowledge through testimony: receiving and imparting information, sharing ideas and debating (Jandrić et al. 2018).

Essential for such a pedagogy is questioning because it is quintessentially collaborative skill for gathering knowledge and information (Watson 2020) and informs collective debate, without stipulating the need for consensus (Jandrić et al. 2018). Such collective debate engages not only social epistemology, but also goes to the centre of research methodology. Postdigital research – given its proclivity for confronting dissent, and the use of silence in doing so – has a unique opportunity to foreground methods that emphasise the skill of disagreement, and acceptance that there does not always need to be a correct answer, or consensus, to such questions. Ultimately, postdigital methods must model critical skills for seeking and receiving information, and build capacity for young people to impart that information and their ideas in research encounters that may be met with dissent or censure.

6   Conclusion

Falling back on our education system for teaching young people critically aware digital practices in an overwhelming digital landscape might be futile (MacKenzie and Bhatt 2021), partly because the skills children need to navigate this postdigital world are lacking in curriculums, and partly because the digital environment advances at a pace that is difficult to keep up with. We must teach our children critical thinking: a willingness to interrogate what they hear through others' testimony, both online and offline, and to challenge their own prejudices with a range of perspectives (Maginess 2021; McGregor 2015). This chapter has built upon postdigital pedagogy posited elsewhere (Jandrić et al. 2018) to suggest a postdigital children's rights-based methodology which centres capacity building (see Lundy and McEvoy 2011), through which tensions between the rights to protection and to participation, and the pivotal role of accurate information, may be navigated productively in research encounters.

As highlighted by the Committee, the digital environment includes discrimination and exploitation, as well as 'false narratives, misinformation and disinformation' (U.N. Committee on the Rights of the Child 2021: Para. 54). Yet these epistemic vices also occur in analog. This chapter employed a theoretical lens of social epistemology to engage in a 'postdigital dialogue' (McLaren and Jandrić 2021) about how the silences, omissions, and partialities of information in the postdigital incorporate both the online and offline to form a postdigital epistemology of silence. Developing a postdigital social epistemology with a focus on the increasing indistinction between the online and offline worlds in children's lives illuminates how silence can both reveal deception and ignorance, and frustrate it.

Such a lens allows an examination of issues such as what is voiced, what remains unvoiced, and what is voiced through silence to enter the discourse to better understand and messy and unpredictable postdigital milieu (see Jandrić et al. 2018). Ignorance, for example, can be sustained and exploited through silence. Alternatively, silence can be employed as an expression of dissent and censure – a resistance to ignorance. As children grow up in the postdigital world, postdigital research must employ a rights-respecting methodology that builds children's capacity to scrutinise uses of testimony and information, including silence, as voiced and unvoiced, truth and deceit, in order to share their perspectives on the postdigital challenges we all face.

References

Alcoff, L. M. (2007). Epistemologies of Ignorance: Three Types. In S. Sullivan & N. Tuana (Eds.), *Race and Epistemologies of Ignorance* (pp. 39–57). Albany, NY: State University of New York Press.

Beazley, H., Bessell, S., Ennew, J. and Waterson, R., 2009. The right to be properly researched: Research with children in a messy, real world. *Children's Geographies, 7*(4), pp. 365–378.

Brown, A. (2019). The meaning of Silence in Cyberspace. In S. Brison & K. Gelber (Eds.), *Free Speech in the Digital Age* (pp. 207-223). New York: Oxford University Press. https://doi.org/10.1093/oso/9780190883591.003.0013.

Buchanan, A. (2020). The Reflexive Social Epistemology of Human Rights. In M. Fricker, P. J. Graham, D. Henderson, & N. J. L. L. Pedersen (Eds.), *The Routledge Handbook of Social Epistemology* (pp. 284–292). Abingdon: Routledge.

Burge, T. (1993). Content Preservation. *The Philosophical Review, 102*(4), 457–488. https://doi.org/10.2307/2185680.

Code, L. (2010). Testimony, Advocacy, Ignorance: Thinking Ecologically about Social Knowledge. In A. Haddock, A. Millar, & D. Pritchard (Eds.), *Social Epistemology* (pp. 29–50). New York: Oxford University Press. https://doi.org/10.1093/acprof:oso/9780199577477.003.0002.

Cramer, F., & Jandrić, P. (2021). Postdigital: A Term That Sucks but Is Useful. *Postdigital Science and Education, 3*(3), 966–989. https://doi.org/10.1007/s42438-021-00225-9.

Deibert, R. J. (2019). The Road to Digital Unfreedom: Three painful truths about social media. *Journal of Democracy, 30*(1), 25–39.

Fallis, D. (2019). Lying and omissions. In J. Meibauer (Ed.), *The Oxford Handbook of Lying* (pp. 183–192). New York: Oxford University Press. https://doi.org/10.1093/oxfordhb/9780198736578.013.13.

Feenberg, A. (2019). Postdigital or Predigital? *Postdigital Science and Education, 1*(1), 8–9. https://doi.org/10.1007/s42438-018-0027-2.

Frankfurt, H. (2005). *On Bullshit*, Princeton, NJ: Princeton University Press

Freire, P. (1974). *Pedagogy of the oppressed*. Trans. M. B. Ramos. New York: Seabury Press.

Fricker, E. (2006). Testimony and Epistemic Autonomy. In J. Lackey & E. Sosa (Eds.), *The Epistemology of Testimony* (pp. 225–250). https://doi.org/10.1093/acprof:oso/9780199276011.003.0011.

Fricker, M. (2007). *Epistemic Injustice. The Power and Ethics of Knowing*. Oxford: Oxford University Press. https://doi.org/10.1093/acprof:oso/9780198237907.001.0001.

Goffman, E. (1959). *The Presentation of Self in Everyday Life*. New York: Anchor Books.

Goldberg, S. C. (2010). The Epistemology of Silence. In A. Haddock, A. Millar, & D. Pritchard (Eds.), *Social Epistemology* (pp. 243–261). New York: Oxford University Press. https://doi.org/10.1093/acprof:oso/9780199577477.003.0012.

Goldberg, S. C. (2020). *Conversational Pressure: Normativity in Speech Exchanges*. New York: Oxford University Press. https://doi.org/10.1093/oso/9780198856436.001.0001.

Goldman, A. I. (2010). Why Social Epistemology Is *Real* Epistemology. In A. Haddock, A. Millar, & D. Pritchard (Eds.), *Social Epistemology* (pp. 1–28). New York: Oxford University Press. https://doi.org/10.1093/acprof:oso/9780199577477.003.0001.

Green, B. (2021). US Digital Nationalism: A Habermasian critical discourse analysis of Trump's 'Fake News' approach to the First Amendment. In A. MacKenzie, J. Rose, & I. Bhatt (Eds.), *The Epistemology of Deceit in a Postdigital Era: Dupery by Design* (pp. 95–117). Cham: Springer. https://doi.org/10.1007/978-3-030-72154-1_6.

Hanna, A. (2022). Silent Epistemologies. *The International Journal of Children's Rights*. https://doi.org/10.1163/15718182-30040003.

Jandrić, P., Knox, J., Besley, T., Ryberg, T., Suoranta, J., & Hayes, S. (2018). Postdigital Science and Education. *Educational Philosophy and Theory, 50*(10), 893–899. https://doi.org/10.1080/00131857.2018.1454000.

Jandrić, P. (2018). Post-truth and critical pedagogy of trust. In M. A. Peters, S. Rider, M. Hyvönen & Tina Besley (Eds.), *Post-Truth, Fake News: Viral Modernity & Higher Education* (pp. 101–111). Singapore: Springer. https://doi.org/10.1007/978-981-10-8013-5_8.

Jandrić, P. (2023). Histories of the Postdigital. In P. Jandrić, A. MacKenzie, & J. Knox (Eds.), *Postdigital Research: Genealogies, Challenges, and Future Perspectives*. Cham: Springer. https://doi.org/10.1007/978-3-031-31299-1_2.

Jandrić, P., & Ford, D. (2022). Postdigital Ecopedagogies: Genealogies, Contradictions, and Possible Futures. *Postdigital Science and Education, 4*(3), 672–710. https://doi.org/10.1007/s42438-020-00207-3.

Jandrić, P., & Knox, J. (2022). The Postdigital Turn: Philosophy, Education, Research. *Policy Futures in Education, 20*(7), 780-795. https://doi.org/10.1177%2F14782103211062713.

Jandrić, P., MacKenzie, A., & Knox, J. (2022). Postdigital Research: Genealogies, Challenges, and Future Perspectives. *Postdigital Science and Education*. https://doi.org/10.1007/s42438-022-00306-3.

Jiang, J., & Vetter, M. (2021). Writing Against the 'Epistemology of Deceit' on Wikipedia: A feminist new materialist perspective towards critical media literacy and Wikipedia-based education. In A. MacKenzie, J. Rose, & I. Bhatt (Eds.), *The Epistemology of Deceit in a Postdigital Era: Dupery by Design* (pp. 159–176). Cham: Springer. https://doi.org/10.1007/978-3-030-72154-1_9.

Johnson, C. R. (2018). Just Say 'No': Obligations to Voice Disagreement. *Royal Institute of Philosophy Supplement, 84*, 117–138. https://doi.org/10.1017/S1358246118000577.

Jopling, M. (2023). Postdigital Research in Education: Towards Vulnerable Method and Praxis. In P. Jandrić, A. MacKenzie, & J. Knox (Eds.), *Postdigital Research: Genealogies, Challenges, and Future Perspectives* (pp. 155-171). Cham: Springer. https://doi.org/10.1007/978-3-031-31299-1_9.

Jungkutz, V. (2012). The Promise of Democratic Silences. *New Political Science, 34*, 127–150. https://doi.org/10.1080/07393148.2012.676393.

Kuran, T. (1995). *Private truths, public lies: The social consequences of preference falsification.* Cambridge, MA: Harvard University Press.

Lackey, J. (2018). Silence and Objecting. In C. R. Johnson (Ed.), *Voicing Dissen t: The Ethics and Epistemology of Marking Disagreement Public* (pp. 82–96). New York: Routledge.

Langton, R. (2018). Blocking as Counterspeech. In D. Harris, D. Fogal, & M. Moss (Eds.), *New Work on Speech Acts* (pp. 144–164). New York: Oxford University Press. https://doi.org/10.1093/oso/9780198738831.003.0006.

Livingstone, S. (2016). Reframing media effects in terms of children's rights in the digital age. *Journal of Children and Media, 10*(1), 4–12. https://doi.org/10.1080/17482798.2015.1123164.

Livingstone, S., & Third, A. (2017). Children and young people's rights in the digital age: An emerging agenda. *New Media and Society, 19*(5), 657–670. https://doi.org/10.1177/1461444816686318.

Lundy, L., & McEvoy, L. (2011). Children's rights and research processes: Assisting children to (in)formed views. *Childhood, 19*(1), 129–144. https://doi.org/10.1177/0907568211409078.

Lundy, L., McEvoy, L., & Byrne, B. (2011). Working with young children as co-researchers: An approach informed by the United Nations Convention on the Rights of the Child. *Early education & development, 22*(5), 714–736. https://doi.org/10.1080/10409289.2011.596463.

Lundy, L., Tobin, J., & Parkes, A. (2019). Article 12. The Right to Respect for the Views of the Child. In J. Tobin (Ed.), *The UN Convention on the Rights of the Child: A Commentary* (pp. 397–434). New York: Oxford University Press.

MacKenzie, A. (2022). Down to Earth Transdisciplinarity. *Postdigital Science and Education, 4*(3), 676–682. https://doi.org/10.1007/s42438-022-00298-0.

MacKenzie, A. (2023). Postdigital Epistemology of Ignorance. In P. Jandrić (Ed.), *Encyclopaedia of Postdigital Science and Education*. Cham: Springer.

MacKenzie, A., & Bhatt, I. (2021). Bad Faith, Bad Politics, Bad Consequences: The Epistemic Harms of Online Deceit. In A. MacKenzie, J. Rose, & I. Bhatt (Eds.), *The Epistemology of Deceit in a Postdigital Era: Dupery by Design* (pp. 3–20). Cham: Springer. https://doi.org/10.1007/978-3-030-72154-1_1.

MacKenzie, A., Rose, J., & Bhatt, I. (Eds.). (2021). *The Epistemology of Deceit in a Postdigital Era: Dupery by Design.* Cham: Springer. https://doi.org/10.1007/978-3-030-72154-1.

Maginess, T. (2021). Duperation: Deliberate lying in postdigital, postmodern political rhetoric. In A. MacKenzie, J. Rose, & I. Bhatt (Eds.), *The Epistemology of Deceit in a Postdigital Era: Dupery by Design* (pp. 63–75). Cham: Springer. https://doi.org/10.1007/978-3-030-72154-1_4.

Mansell, R. (2012). *Imagining the Internet: Communication, Innovation and Governance.* New York: Oxford University Press.

Manyozo, L. (2011). Rethinking communication for development policy: Some considerations. In R. Mansell & M. Raboy (Eds.), *The Handbook of Global Media and Communication Policy*. Chichester: Wiley-Blackwell. https://doi.org/10.1002/9781444395433.ch20.

Marsili, N. (2019). Lying and certainty. In J. Meibauer (Ed.), *The Oxford Handbook of Lying* (pp. 170–182). New York: Oxford University Press. https://doi.org/10.1093/oxfor dhb/9780198736578.013.12.

McGregor, S. L. T. (2015). Integral Dispositions and Transdisciplinary Knowledge Creation. *Integral Leadership Review, 15*(1). http://integralleadershipreview.com/12548-115-integral-dispositions-transdisciplinary-knowledge-creation/. Accessed 25 January 2023.

McLaren, P., & Jandrić, P. (2021). Scallywag Pedagogy. In A. MacKenzie, I. Bhatt, & J. Rose (Eds.), *The Epistemology of Deceit in a Postdigital Era: Dupery by Design* (pp. 215–232). Cham: Springer. https://doi.org/10.1007/978-3-030-72154-1_12.

Mills. C. (2007). White Ignorance. In S. Sullivan & N. Tuana (Eds.), *Race and Epistemologies of Ignorance* (pp. 39–55). Albany, NY: State University of New York Press.

Mörtsell, S., & Gunnarsson, K. (2023). Caring Cuts: Unfolding Methodological Sensibilities in Researching Postdigital Worlds. In P. Jandrić, A. MacKenzie, & J. Knox, (Eds.), *Postdigital Research:Genealogies, Challenges, and Future Perspectives*. Cham: Springer. https://doi.org/10.1007/978-3-031-31299-1_10.

Noelle-Neumann, E. (1993). *The spiral of silence: Public opinion: Our social skin*. Chicago, IL: University of Chicago Press.

O'Sullivan, V. (2021). A Project of Mourning: Attuning to the impact of 'anthropocentric-noise disorder' on non-human kin. In A. MacKenzie, J. Rose, & I. Bhatt (Eds.), *The Epistemology of Deceit in a Postdigital Era: Dupery by Design* (pp. 119–136). Cham: Springer. https://doi.org/10.1007/978-3-030-72154-1_7.

Özdan, S. (2021). The Right to Freedom of Expression Versus Legal Actions Against Fake News: A case study of Singapore. In A. MacKenzie, J. Rose, & I. Bhatt (Eds.), *The Epistemology of Deceit in a Postdigital Era: Dupery by Design* (pp. 77–94). Cham: Springer. https://doi.org/10.1007/978-3-030-72154-1_5.

Peters, M. A., Besley, T., Jandrić, P., & Zhu, X. (Eds.). (2020). *Knowledge Socialism. The Rise of Peer Production: Collegiality, Collaboration, and Collective Intelligence*. Singapore: Springer. https://doi.org/10.1007/978-981-13-8126-3.

Pettit, P. (2002). *Rules, Reasons, Norms*. Oxford: Clarendon Press. https://doi.org/10.1093/0199251878.001.0001.

Presser, L. (2022). *Unsaid: Analyzing Harmful Silences*. Oakland, CA: University of California Press.

Rose, J. (2021). An Epistemology of False Beliefs: The role of truth, trust and technology in Postdigital deception. In A. MacKenzie, J. Rose, & I. Bhatt (Eds.), *The Epistemology of Deceit in a Postdigital Era: Dupery by Design* (pp. 21–37). Cham: Springer. https://doi.org/10.1007/978-3-030-72154-1_2.

Saul, J. (2021). Someone is Wrong on the Internet: Is there an obligation to correct false and oppressive speech on social media? In A. MacKenzie, J. Rose, & I. Bhatt (Eds.), *The Epistemology of Deceit in a Postdigital Era: Dupery by Design* (pp. 139–157). Cham: Springer. https://doi.org/10.1007/978-3-030-72154-1_8.

Shaub, J. (2012). Children's Freedom of Speech and Expressive Maturity. *Law and Psychology Review, 36,* 198–210.

Sinclair, C. (2021). Learning from the Dupers: Showing the Workings. In A. MacKenzie, J. Rose, & I. Bhatt (Eds.), *The Epistemology of Deceit in a Postdigital Era: Dupery by Design* (pp. 233–249). Cham: Springer. https://doi.org/10.1007/978-3-030-72154-1_13.

Sperber, D., & Wilson D. (1995). *Relevance: Communication and Cognition.* 2nd Ed. Malden, MA: Blackwell Publishing.

Spyrou, S. (2011). The Limits of Children's Voices: From authenticity to critical, reflexive representation. *Childhood, 18*(2), 151–165. https://doi.org/10.1177/0907568210387834.

Stoilova, M., Livingstone, S., & Kardefelt-Winther, D. (2016). Global Kids Online: Researching children's rights globally in the digital age. *Global Studies of Childhood, 6*(4), 455–466. https://doi.org/10.1177/2043610616676035.

Tanesini, A. (2018). Eloquent silences: silence and dissent. In C. R. Johnson (Ed.), *Voicing Dissent: The Ethics and Epistemology of Making Disagreement Public* (pp. 109–128). New York: Routledge.

Third, A., Bellarose, D., Dawkins, U., Keltie, E., & Pihl, K. (2014). *Children's Rights in the Digital Age: A Download from Children Around the World.* Melbourne: Young and Well Cooperative Research Centre.

Tobin, J., & Parkes, A. (2019). Article 13. The Right to Freedom of Expression. In J. Tobin (Ed.), *The UN Convention on the Rights of the Child: A Commentary* (pp. 435–474). New York: Oxford University Press.

Tuana, N. (2004). Coming to Understand: Orgasm and the Epistemology of Ignorance. *Hypatia: A Journal of Feminist Philosophy, 19*(1), 194–232. https://doi.org/10.1111/j.1527-2001.2004. tb01275.x.

Tuana, N. (2006). The Speculum of Ignorance: Women's Health Movement and Epistemologies of Ignorance. *Hypatia: A Journal of Feminist Philosophy, 21*(3), 1–19. https://doi. org/10.1111/j.1527-2001.2006.tb01110.x.

Twain, M. (1992). On the decay of the art of lying. In L. J. Budd (Ed.), *Mark Twain: Collected tales, sketches, speeches, and essays, 1852–1890* (pp. 824–829). New York: Library of America.

United Nations. (1989). United Nations Convention on the Rights of the Child. Geneva: United Nations. https://www.ohchr.org/en/instruments-mechanisms/instruments/convention-rights-child. Accessed 20 January 2023.

United Nations Committee on the Rights of the Child. (2009). General Comment No. 12, The Right of the Child to be Heard (CRC/C/GC/12). Geneva: United Nations. https://www2.ohchr. org/english/bodies/crc/docs/advanceversions/crc-c-gc-12.pdf. Accessed 20 January 2023.

U.N. Committee on the Rights of the Child. (2013). General Comment No. 13 on the right of the child to rest, leisure, play, recreational activities, cultural life and the arts (art. 31). CRC/C/ GC/17. Geneva: United Nations. https://digitallibrary.un.org/record/778539?ln=en. Accessed 20 January 2023.

U.N. Committee on the Rights of the Child. (2021). General Comment No. 25 on children's rights in relation to the digital environment. CRC/C/GC/25. Geneva: United Nations. https:// www.ohchr.org/en/documents/general-comments-and-recommendations/general-comment-no-25-2021-childrens-rights-relation. Accessed 20 January 2023.

Wakeham, J. (2017). Bullshit as a problem of social epistemology. *Sociological Theory, 35*(1), 15–38. https://doi.org/10.1177/0735275117692835.

Wardle, C., & Derakhshan, H. (2017). Information Disorder: Toward an Interdisciplinary Framework for Research and Policy Making. Strasbourg: Council of Europe. https://edoc.coe. int/en/media/7495-information-disorder-toward-an-interdisciplinary-framework-for-research-and-policy-making.html. Accessed 20 January 2023.

Watson, L. (2020). Educating for Good Questioning as a Democratic Skill. In M. Fricker, P. J. Graham, D. Henderson, & N. J. L. L. Pedersen (Eds.), *The Routledge Handbook of Social Epistemology* (pp. 437–446). Abingdon: Routledge.

Wright, J. (2021). Towards a Response to Epistemic Nihilism. In A. MacKenzie, J. Rose, & I. Bhatt (Eds.), *The Epistemology of Deceit in a Postdigital Era: Dupery by Design* (pp. 39–59). Cham: Springer. https://doi.org/10.1007/978-3-030-72154-1_3.

Part V
Method and Emancipation

A Feminist Postdigital Analysis of Misogyny, Patriarchy and Violence Against Women and Girls Online

Alison MacKenzie 🅭

1 Introduction

The abuse of women and girls online is extensive and persistent. Women and girls across the world are expressing concerns at the 'harmful, sexist, misogynistic and violent content and behaviour online', according to the UN Rapporteur on Violence Against Women and Girls (VAWG) (UN General Assembly 2018: 5). In the UK, for example, one in five women have experienced online abuse or harassment on social media or another online platform, 62% of which is experienced by young women (Amnesty International 2017). 85% of women who experience online abuse from a partner or ex-partner also experience abuse offline (Women's Aid 2021). Young women and girls are not safe from online abuse either. The Girls' Attitude Survey (Girlguiding 2021) of over 2000 women and young girls aged 7–21, found that 82% of 11–21-year-olds experienced online harm (any kind) and 50% were subject to sexist comments. And the abuse is intersectional. Black women are 84% more likely to experience this abuse than white women (Amnesty International 2018), a form of racist misogynistic abuse targeted specifically against black women, which the African American feminist scholar and activist Moya Bailey (2010) termed 'misogynoir'.

The Internet is a potent tool in the systemic and structural discrimination and gender-based violence against women and girls, the most common target for online hate. It offers a highly fertile, contagious, and disinhibited environment for the easy, swift, and wide-spread amplification of Internet violence and abuse. In its digital dimension, violence against women and girls includes technology-facilitated harmful behaviour, along with technological tools to stalk, bully, harass, surveil, and control the perpetrators' victims. These tools include smartphones, cameras,

A. MacKenzie (✉)
SSESW, Queen's University Belfast, Belfast, UK
e-mail: a.mackenzie@qub.ac.uk

© The Author(s), under exclusive license to Springer Nature Switzerland AG 2023
P. Jandrić et al. (eds.), *Constructing Postdigital Research*, Postdigital Science and Education, https://doi.org/10.1007/978-3-031-35411-3_14

global positioning systems (GPS); Internet-connected devices such as smart watches, fitness trackers and smart home devices; and software such as spyware that may facilitate violence (Grevio 2021: 13).

Despite the colossal scale and prevalence of digital gender-based violence, misogyny and sexism, social media platforms are currently under little to no legal obligation to address the abuse, though they are coming under increasing legal and moral pressure to do so. As a matter of justice and equality, it is imperative that legal pressure is brought to bear on Big Tech because of the unambiguous, long-lasting, and profound harms that online abuse can cause. These harms violate women and girls' human rights, undermine any progress on gender equality, and erode their offline quality of life.

I will offer a postdigital critique of these harms in this chapter. Postdigital analysis, I will argue, offers perspicuous insight, a 'critical attitude (or philosophy) that inquires into the digital world, examining and critiquing its constitution, its theoretical orientation and its consequences' (Peters and Besley 2019: 30). The digital, Feenberg (2019: 8) explains, 'is integrated and imbricated with our everyday actions and interactions.' For the vast majority of us, there is virtually no separation between the online and offline worlds: they intermesh, are coterminous, conjoined, and porous; and we are totally dependent on the online world and the devices by which we access it. We carry our mobile phones in our pockets and are rarely away from the computer, which means that vulnerability and exposure to abuse can be mere inches away and needs only our digital or password sign-in. It is, therefore, often difficult to distinguish the consequences of actions that begin in online environments from their effects offline, and vice versa.

As many of the authors in the edited collection of Jandrić et al. (2023a, b) attest, 'postdigital' evades distillation to a single definition, even to a concept, a dissatisfying state for those who like to work with settled definitions or conceptions. While I am clearly referring to violence and abuse online, on social media platforms and ICT-facilitated devices, some explanation needs to be offered as to why the postdigital is hard to define. Simply, it is a very messy, complex thing. The clearest explanation for this state of affairs is expressed by some of the seminal thinkers in the field – Jandrić et al. (2018: 895): 'The postdigital is hard to define; messy; unpredictable; digital and analog; technological and non-technological; biological and informational. The postdigital is both a rupture in our existing theories and their continuation.' This is actually helpful. We have freedom to conceptualise as the occasion demands. Gender based violence always finds new ways to express itself and the infinity of the online environment is perfectly suited to its prodigiously malign intent (it also has the power to contest and call out abuse, but hatred is more arresting).

The particular perspective I will take here is that of feminist postdigital analysis, wherein I argue that women and girls' freedom should be supported by coercive anti-discrimination laws, by measures that foster greater parity in participation in the online sphere, and which criminalise some forms of online harms. Big Tech should take action to change how their algorithms work; that they have been so reluctant to control or reconfigure how algorithms work testifies to the dopamine seduction of money. (As Jandrić wryly comments in the Preface to this edited collection, money is like the ring in the Lord of the Rings. People die and must die in order for the ring to be possessed. Those who possess it cannot resist its powers, no matter its evil intent.) Abuse is profitable. Social media platforms promote algorithms that encourage trolling because they swiftly gain traction and generate advertising revenue. As a result, the platforms prioritise profit over safety (McKay 2021; The Centre for Humane Technology 2022).

Online gender-based violence is part of the 'postdigital condition'; a condition which presents, as Jandrić et al. (2019: 1) have observed, 'one of today's grand challenges'. The great and enduring challenge for women and girls in this condition is how we retain autonomy and agency, our human rights, states of freedom-being that women and girls have fought so hard to obtain, when misogyny proliferates with baneful fecundity in the online environment. This problem is one of the foci of this chapter. The incontrovertibility and inventiveness of the postdigital is such that life online can persist even beyond the death of offline individuals, living on as 'virtual' humans existing permanently in the 'digital afterlife' – an achievement of 'digital immortality' (Savin-Baden and Burden 2019). The online is practically inescapable and its life forms (can be) inerasable. These facts of the postdigital condition explain why deep fakes and mal/dis/misinformation are so threatening and so unjust, and why far more concerted international efforts are required to safeguard human rights and entitlements on- and off-line (see MacKenzie et al. 2021). We need measures that challenge gendered prejudicial stereotypes about who women supposedly *are*, and what women can supposedly *do*. In this feminist postdigital analysis, I also critically engage with the narrow conception of misogyny as hatred of all women. This, as I will explain, is naïve, indiscriminate, and exculpatory.

The structure of the chapter is as follows: I begin with a discussion of the scale of gender-based violence that women in the online sphere must confront. Next, I provide a conceptual, descriptive, and analytical account of the term misogyny,[1] followed by an epistemic account of the same, drawing on Fricker's (2007) seminal construction of epistemic injustice. Simply explained, epistemic injustice is the harm caused to a speaker when her telling of her experiences is deflated on account of her status (as a woman, in this case), and who lacks the interpretive resources to name or convey a significant experience owning to structural prejudice and inequality (Fricker 2007; MacKenzie 2022). This is the feminist analysis that underpins the postdigital description of the harms that are facilitated, disseminated, or aggravated by ICT, the Internet, and Big Tech. I then switch to the offline world to discuss first the Online Harms Bill making its way through the parliament of the UK, and second, the necessity of a Code of Practice to specifically protect women and girls online from misogyny and sexism. This combined approach is the feminist postdigital analysis I present in this chapter, and which I commend in the conclusion.

Before I begin my analysis, the 'post' in 'postdigital' should not be taken to mean 'after' or to mark a break from 'digital', as the 'post' in, for example,

---

[1] My account of misogyny is heavily indebted to Kate Manne's (2017) account.

postmodernism does. It signals, on the contrary, even ironically, continuity (see, for example, Jopling 2023; Sinclair 2019). The prefix, for me, indicates that the postdigital is incontrovertible, durable, constantly evolving and intelligent, and as necessary as the essential goods of life (Jandrić 2022) – this is the postdigital condition. The technology, devices, cyber environment and infrastructure that I discuss in this chapter, along with all the social and commercial activities that take place online, are all encompassed by the capacious idea we term the 'postdigital'.

2   The Scale of Gender-Based Violence Online

The Human Rights Council of the UN General Assembly defines violence against women as

> a form of discrimination against women and a human rights violation falling under the Convention on the Elimination of All Forms of Discrimination and other international and regional instruments, according to which violence against women includes gender-based violence against women, that is, violence directed against a woman because she is a woman and/or that affects women disproportionately. Article 1 of the Declaration on the Elimination of Violence against Women further specifies that violence against women is any act of gender-based violence that results in, or is likely to result in, physical, sexual or psychological harm or suffering to women, including threats of such acts, coercion or arbitrary deprivation of liberty, whether occurring in public or in private life. (UN General Assembly 2018: 6)

This definition extends to any kind of harm that is facilitated, assisted, or aggravated by digital technology, the Internet, social medial platforms, email, artificial intelligence (AI) or any other form of ICT that is directed at women simply because they are women. These gendered acts of violence occur in contexts of persistent structural inequality, discrimination, and patriarchy, in which misogyny and sexism are invariably manifest.

As in the offline environment, the online environment offers diverse forms of gender-based violence that can result in physical, sexual, psychological, and economic harms. These harms are especially pernicious because of the exponential speed at which information passes – the virality of the environment – the global reach of Internet transmissions and search engines, the replicability and scalability of information, and the ease with which behaviours are amplified. This situation is unique in the inordinately long history of gender-based violence and discrimination. Women can be targeted not just by one person (as might happen in their offline worlds), by but hundreds or thousands, or millions, particularly if well-known, across the world. Redacting, taking down content or eliminating false information, is near impossible given these features of the Internet and the digital appliances on which are so reliant. The consequences to their health and wellbeing, to their status as persons is that women and girls can suffer fear, depression, anxiety, suicidal thoughts, humiliation, or loss of jobs (UN General Assembly 2018).

The sheer variety of violence and abuse is staggering and inventive. The Special Rapporteur (UN General Council 2018) on violence against women has reported on the kinds of digital threats and gender-based violence that women and girls disproportionately experience online. For example, threats of or incitements to rape or kill; unwanted and harassing online communications; dissemination of reputation damaging lies; impersonations of the victims; abusive emails, blogs, posts, or tweets. ICT is used for trafficking women and girls, and to coerce them into trafficking through threats of violence to their families or disclosure of personal information. New forms of harassment have emerged specifically as a result of Internet ICT – 'doxing' (the publication of private information with malicious intent), 'trolling' (the posting of messages or the creation of hashtags, for example, to harass or incite violence), and 'sextortion' (blackmail by threatening to release intimate pictures or videos unless the victim complies by sending more explicit images or videos). Familiar forms of offline abuse have the prefix 'online' to denote new versions of the harm: 'online mobbing', 'online stalking' and 'online sexual harassment'. Non-consensual pornography which involves the distribution of sexually explicit images, and revenge porn which is the dissemination of images for the purpose of humiliating or harming the victim (see also Ruvalcaba and Eaton 2020; Eaton et al. 2022), also proliferate.

Every form of violence perpetrated online creates a permanent digital record that cannot be easily deleted, resulting ongoing, repeated harm to the victims. With respect to non-consensual pornography, research by Ruvalcaba and Eaton (2020) of 3044 US adults, 54% of whom were women, showed that women victims had lower psychological well-being and higher somatic symptoms than women nonvictims. The female participants also had higher somatic symptoms than the male victims, findings support research that nonconsensual pornography is a gendered form of sexual abuse (Ruvalcaba and Eaton 2020).

Amnesty International's findings from the Troll Patrol Project on online Twitter abuse against 778 female politicians and journalists in the US and UK is also alarming (if, sadly, not surprising). Between January and December 2017, Amnesty International (2018) found that 7.1%, or 1.1 million tweets were problematic or abusive, regardless of where the women were located on the political spectrum, and that black women in particular were disproportionately affected – misogynoir (Bailey 2010). The role of female journalists as public watchdogs in democratic societies in Europe is being seriously undermined because they are 'inundated with threats of murder, rape, physical violence and with graphic imagery via digital means' (Mijatović 2022). 'Free speech' is silencing many women (and, of course, minority voices) because they fear violence and abuse, degrading, infantilising and humiliating attacks, online mobbing by real people, bots, and trolls, while amplifying the voice of others – the powerful and aggressive abusers and misogynists.

The violence often results in self-censorship or withdrawal from social media. As Mijatović (2022) has found and directly experienced as Commissioner for Human Rights and as a former Organisation for Security and Co-operation Representative on Freedom of the Media, public figures, politicians, journalists, video game players and creators, environmental and other activists, and women's rights defenders who speak out and engage in the digital sphere to 'document and expose human rights violations, access and share information, gain visibility and mobilise people for action' (Mijatović 2022), are at risk of being attacked, harassed, and exposed to smear campaigns. Public women also risk having their work discredited or delegitimised, in addition to many other types of gender-based violence – simply because they are women.

The violence against women and girls online is a manifestation and continuum of offline gender-based violence that tracks them in all spheres of life. Violence and the threat of violence, silencing and self-censorship represent a threat to democracy, to epistemic diversity, and to the visibility of women and minorities online and, ultimately, to justice and equality.

Even in sports beloved and passionately supported by fans, the abusers are ready to pounce. Following the Women's Euro 2020 Final, HateLab,[2] a global hub for data and insight into online and offline hate crime, tracked online misogynistic and homophobic abuse against England's team (Cullen and Williams 2022). HateLab's analysis revealed that over 90% of the team were directly targeted for abuse at the time of the tournament. 96% of the hate speech was misogynistic, 4% was homophobic, and 91% of abusive Twitter posts were sent by users who identified as men. 20% of the players received 50% of the abuse, Beth Meath (forward) receiving the most, followed by Ellen White (striker), Ella Toone (midfielder) and Lucy Bronze (defender). Cullen and Williams (2022: 10) posit that Beth Meath was singled out because of her high profile and many successes during the tournament (she won the Golden Boot, for example) and raised the profile of the women's game. She is a successful player in a game that was traditionally the bastion only of men.

As a 'pernicious social problem' (Cullen and Williams 2022), misogyny is the most prevalent category on social media because women account for more than half the population, while other victims of hate are minorities. To add to the standard array of misogynistic practices, is the culture of misogyny that festers among 'incels', involuntary male celibates who blame women for their celibacy, and other all-male communities, including right-wing extremist groups, who call for the rape and murder of women. Misogyny would probably attract the highest number of hate-crime prosecutions, except that it is not a hate crime in the UK, nor yet in the European Union.

3   A Feminist Conceptual, Descriptive, and Analytical Definition of Misogyny

Conceptually, descriptively, and analytically, misogyny uniquely connotes gender-based oppression. Conceptually, the question to ask is: what is misogyny? When we discuss it descriptively, we ask: what are its properties? (How is it used

---

[2] HateLab is a data lab funded by the Economic and Social Research Council in the UK and developed by Mathew Williams at Cardiff University. HateLab developed and uses hate speech detection algorithms that classify misogynistic and other hateful content in real time. In men's football, HateLab find that ethnic minority players receive most abuse. See https://hatelab.net/. Accessed 9 December 2022.

empirically?); and analytically, we ask: what is the point of the term? (How can we use for liberatory purposes, to help women and girls escape it on- and off-line?). These questions may form the basis of a feminist analysis of this pernicious social harm.

The common or naive understanding of misogyny is that it is individual hatred of, or hostility felt towards women *as* women. In this narrow conception, misogynists regard all women with contempt, disgust, and derision. They believe women to be less intelligent, less reliable, less rationale, less capable, and more emotional than men. Women are, further, conceived of as mindless but useful sex objects who should know their place (the home, kitchen, and the bedroom). Misogynists tend see women as threats to men: they will, if given rein, emasculate men, undermining their status, stature, and position, while eroding the family and its values. Inappropriately empowered women will not show men the right kind of respect. In this conception, the hatred of and hostility towards women is an individual pathology that can be explained by the psychology of the person.

However, as Manne (2017) has convincingly argued, a narrow psychological understanding of misogyny obscures the objective structures that support and diffuse misogyny throughout society and the online environment. The conception of misogyny as individual pathology makes it difficult to diagnose it as misogyny, for how can we *know* with certainty that the misogynist acted from his hatred of women? (The epistemological problem.) The other and significant problem is how women can make sense of the hatred if they cannot be certain that the hostility is in fact misogynistic: it could simply be that the individual man dislikes her *as* her, not because she is a woman. Naïve conceptions of misogyny put women at a disadvantage not only because misogyny is structural, inheritable and reproductive, but also because they lack the interpretive resources to make an affirmative diagnosis of the malaise (the hermeneutical problem) (Fricker 2007). Improper recognition of the source of misogyny, namely that it is objectively structural, means that women, collectively, cannot (confidently) call it out. The individuals who are, in fact, misogynistic, may be diagnosed as having depression, or be excused as having said things only in jest or that it was merely banter (see MacKenzie 2022). The harm of the naïve conception that women remain silent, ignorant of what it is, and or experience credibility shortfalls when they diagnose it is as structural misogyny.

The naïve conception is also blunt. It obscures the idea that the misogynist does not always hate all women, as Manne (2017) has argued. There are women who do not arouse or incite misogyny but male admiration, and Margaret Thatcher, the former British Prime Minister, exemplifies such a woman.[3] These women do well in patriarchal structures, mainly because they do not seek to undermine patriarchal structures but to uphold them. A realist view of misogyny recognises that he might

---

[3] Thatcher, though the first female Prime Minister, was no friend to feminism and was indifferent to women's concerns. Her devotion was to the Conservative Party and to ridding the UK of the scourge of trade unionism. She reportedly stated that she 'hated' feminism, that it was 'poison'. As Petri (2013) in The Washington Post concluded: 'Conservative icon? No question. Feminist icon? She's the hole in the list.'

only hate or deride *particular* women and particular *kinds* of women (Manne 2017), and that it is a political as well as a dispositional phenomenon (being socialised into having a low opinion of most women).

Misogyny, realistically defined, is the manifestation of patriarchal ideology. It is, as Manne suggests, 'the system that operates within a patriarchal social order to police and enforce women's subordination and to uphold male dominance' (2017: 19). The patriarchal order operates with 'intersecting systems of oppression and vulnerability, dominance and disadvantage' (Manne 2017: 19–20). Women face hostility, derision, or humiliation because they fail to uphold patriarchal standards and challenge men in their own environments – politics, gaming, football, the military, police, and the online world, of course. It is a selective group of women who become the active targets of misogyny – the ones who speak out especially, as the UN Special Rapporteur on violence against women reported to the UN Human Rights Council (2018).

The reasons for the hostility may reside in the psychology of the person (individual pathology), or they may be sourced to the actions, practices, policies of social institutions – the police, the Royal Navy or the Fire brigade – they are usually both. In the UK, reports found damning evidence of institutionalised misogyny in these three institutions: sexual abuse and violence, daily degrading and humiliating comments, viewing porn at work, posting sexist and misogynistic and sexist comments and pictures on WhatsApp groups and online, and views that women do not belong in the forces or the fire service. These oppressions intersected with racism and homophobia (see Afzal 2022; Independent Office for Police Conduct 2022; Badash 2022).[4] These will not be the only institutions in which misogyny will be found, especially where they have been until recently male dominated professions. A further source for misogyny is the social imaginary (Fricker 2007), the repository of stereotypes about women and their place in the socio-political structure, and how they are to be punished, condemned, or subordinated if they pose a threat to the patriarchy. As I argued above, the online environment is exemplary in enforcing patriarchal mechanisms expressed as misogyny.

---

[4] 'The head of the Royal Navy has ordered an investigation into 'abhorrent' allegations of inappropriate behaviour in the submarine service and declared that sexual assault and harassment has no place in the fleet.

It follows whistleblowers making harrowing allegations about misogyny, bullying, and sexual harassment of female members.

According to the Daily Mail, the abuse took place in the submarine service for more than a decade after the branch lifted its ban on female recruits in 2011.

One of the allegations is of submariners compiling a "crush depth rape list", in which women were ranked in the order they should be raped in a catastrophic event.' (Badash 2022)

3.1   Patriarchal Enforcement Mechanisms

Patriarchal enforcement mechanisms persist because of the internalisation of social norms about women's innate capacities and preferences, the lauding of women's care work as rewarding and natural, and beliefs that women are naturally disposed to certain emotional expressions – being loving, devoted, compassionate, caring wives, mothers, sisters or girlfriends. The mechanisms for enforcing the norms vary from surprised disapproval (what we might regard as soft coercion) to violent enforcement (threats of rape, revenge porn, or death). These 'coercive enforcement mechanisms' are the 'functional essence of misogyny' (Manne 2017: 47).

Narrow misogyny, if it ever to existed only in this form, would be highly disadvantageous to the misogynist. Women are essential to the good functioning of the family and society. Their work is invaluable: their emotional labour is essential for healthy nurture and care, and in their roles as wives, mothers, lovers, cleaners and who serve the interests of men (Kittay 2019). Women are integrated to greater or lesser degrees into social, political, and economic structures, which is why, if men hate all women and want to banish them from what were, once, male environments, it would be difficult to achieve (but not impossible. To wit: Afghanistan and Iran). Men are the beneficiaries of women's loving, caring and attentive ministrations (daughters, sisters, friends, too). They may love their mothers, sisters, girlfriends, and wives, and get on well with their female colleagues. If misogyny merely meant the universal hatred of all women, then misogynists would fail to value what women do in their interests. Why, therefore, would men hate all women? A psychologistic interpretation of misogyny reduces it to a phobia or a pathology when it is, instead, a systematic and predictable manifestation of social power relations that are governed by patriarchy (Manne 2017).

Systemic misogyny targets those women who fail in their roles as loving, caring, attentive, sensitive, subordinates. Such women will be described variously as harsh, shrill, unbecoming, unfeminine, bad, deviant … and when it gets particularly vitriolic and abusive, they will be reviled as whores, sluts, and bitches. The kind of women who attract the hostility of men will be those who enter male dominated professions, ascend the ranks, attain power over men, and who refuse to be subservient or subordinate. Some women, of course, may become the symbolic representation of all that is wrong with the progressive movement of women to equality with men, to feminism – and Hillary Clinton, former Senator and First Lady of the United States, is arguably the archetypal representation of a woman who does not behave as (is) a woman should: she was (is) a high powered, agentic, competent and successful politician, who was willing to compete with men in their high-stakes world.[5]

---

[5] Hillary Clinton first faced hostility when Bill Clinton became governor of Arkansas in 1978 because she insisted on keeping her maiden name and was an unashamed feminist. When she entered onto the Presidential stage in 1991, the largely male press corps distrusted her feminism and ambition which they thought was a threat to her husband's Presidency, and was no doubt

Misogyny may be the product of collective activity (we see this with online pile-ons or online campaigns against women). It may be the product of institutions and social practices, respect for which women fail to express, sometimes just for believing that they, like men, may be good firefighters, submariners, or policewomen. Or misogyny may be expressed or revived by powerful people who prey on the insecurities of disenfranchised or marginalised communities (incels), and this is especially vivid where socially progressive movements have made their mark (I take the repeal of Roe vs Wade in the US, the right of women to reproductive care, to be one such example). Manne (2017: 63) proposes that misogyny is the 'law enforcement branch' of patriarchy whose job it is to police and enforce its governing ideology.

Misogyny, Manne argues, is constituted of the following:

1. Hostile forces faced by a relevant class of girls and women because of their particular socially situated position.
2. These hostile forces will police and enforce patriarchal order along with other intersecting systems of domination, such as racism, classism, transphobia, etc.
3. And will substantively target women and girls for 'actual, perceived, or representative challenges to or violations of applicable patriarchal norms and expectations … in conjunction with applicable intersecting oppressive forces.' (Manne 2017: 63)

Misogynistic hostility can be expressed by individual agents, through collective activity and purely structural forces. Misogyny can be particular, general, and non-uniform. It can be punitive or act as a deterrent, and manifest as: blame, belittlement, condescension, disgust, humiliation, mockery, ridicule, vilification, silencing, and slurred; being infantilised, sexualised, desexualised, intimidated, maligned, shunned, patronised, or threatened; exposure to threats of violence, such as rape, assault, death, and many other negative generalisations. What helps mark out these hostilities as misogynistic are the levels of intensity, durability, prevalence, quality, and quantity of the attacks. The aim of these attacks is to coercively reinstate or restore patriarchal social norms.

Misogyny, then, suggest Manne (2017: 64) 'primarily targets women because they are in a man's world … rather than because they are a woman in a man's mind, where that man is a misogynist'. Misogyny can be thought of as 'aggrieved entitlement' (Kimmel 2013: 18) – and may be narcissistic and delusional.

Sexism, by contrast, works on the assumption that there are natural differences between women and men, but validates patriarchal social arrangements in conjunction with misogyny. Sexism justifies the subordination of women as a group to men as a group, in contrast to misogyny which targets particular kinds of women who fail to comply with patriarchal standards (however, all women are liable to become targets of misogynistic hostility simply because they are women). Both

---

unseemly for a First Lady. She is also formidably intelligent, assertive, and confident, and has been dogged by scandal and right-wing conspiracy theorists throughout her political life. Hillary Clinton was also a competent politician, another threat, perhaps, to male prowess. Clinton may have paid a 'social dominance penalty' for competing agentically with men. See Rudman et al. (2012).

have a common goal: to retain the patriarchal social order. Sexism works symbiotically with misogyny to sustain the order.

3.2 Explaining the Systemic Nature of Misogyny: An Epistemic Analysis

Misogyny is an endemic feature of patriarchy and will persist as long as patriarchy persists. What are its features in addition to those outlined above? Here, I turn to the epistemic dimensions of misogyny's grip on socio-political organisation (but which will seep into online socio-political structures). Patriarchy is a power, and power is a capacity which can operate actively and passively (Fricker 2007): it is in operation even when it is not realised in action. Misogyny is, therefore, both agential and structural, and is disseminated throughout patriarchal structures. It exists even when no particular agent is being misogynistic – and so is subjectless until it is activated by an agent. Structural misogyny is socially situated and is a socially coordinated power, in which meanings, pathologies, beliefs, activities, assumptions, and so on, are shared; they draw from the social imaginary. The operation of social power is to 'effect social control'– and there is always a group whose actions are being controlled – women – 'even while that control has no particular agent behind it, for purely structural operations of power are always such as to create or preserve a given social order' (Fricker 2007: 13).

The practical social co-ordination of power in which misogyny inheres is also dependent on imaginative social coordination, on shared conceptions of social identity, such as what it means to be a man or a woman, a woman of a certain class or education. When this is present, Fricker (2007) calls it 'identity power'. Identity power, like social power, can be active or passive. It is active when a man uses his identity to influence the actions of a woman; he can bring about a desired action because he has the power to do so. Identity power is passive when a man does not need to do anything; that he *is* a man is power enough to realise the desired outcome. The effective coordination of the social imagination depends on the degree to which we have shared conceptions of what it means to be a man or a woman, even when there is not belief that the conception is actually true. Its power depends on the existence of collective social imagination on which we often automatically, even unthinkingly, draw on stereotypes (Fricker 2007: 15) – these constitute our shared imaginative resources, the hermeneutical dimension of power (and injustice).

Identity power controls how we impart and receive knowledge, and how we assess the credibility of the speaker, often using spontaneous judgements or stereotypes. Our ability to convey or exchange knowledge is integral to our communicative and ethical lives. The extent to which we can successfully to do so will depend on a number of contextual and general factors, among them the 'operation of social power in our epistemic interactions' (Fricker 2007: 1) – in other words, our day-to-day conversations or communications. Levels of trust, operations of silence, forms of ignorance, reliance on reputation, appraisals of worth, or the influence of prejudicial stereotypes, for example, intervene to inflate, deflate, even subvert the credibility of the speaker. The assessment is both socially situated and structurally mediated.

In Fricker's (2007) influential construction of epistemic injustice, this analysis takes us to a distinctively epistemic forms of injustice by which a person is fundamentally and specifically wronged in her 'capacity as a knower' (1): testimonial and hermeneutical injustices. Defined simply, testimonial injustice occurs when 'prejudice causes a hearer to give a deflated level of credibility to a speaker's word' (1). Hermeneutical injustice occurs because of structural injustice whereby the speaker is at an unfair disadvantage because there are insufficient interpretive resources to make sense of, or to intelligibly convey, a social experience, or to give a causal account of the experience, such as being able to recognise and name misogyny.

An example of testimonial injustice is when a well-known woman's account of rape is discredited because of the identity of the accused (let's say he is a wealthy, powerful, operator). She, despite her own fame, is not judged to be a reliable witness because she is unable to give a precise and coherent account. What is likely to happen is that a vilification campaign will begin: she is the abuser, is histrionic, faking it and making things up; she is a money grabber and an attention seeker. The victim is exposed to hermeneutical injustice because the victim is judged in ignorance (the ignorance may be willed or cultivated) of the role of rape mythologies, systemic sexism, and misogyny, and the effects of violence on memory function and flight responses. There are, in other words, few socially interpretive resources to assist the victim or the accusers in coming to a fair judgement.

While hermeneutical injustice is not perpetrated by individuals, its effects influence testimonial exchanges as when, for example, the complainant is accused of pursuing the accused for ulterior motives. These negative prejudicial stereotypes, which embody abiding systemic prejudices, are called forth when the status of powerful (successful, attractive, wealthy, influential) is threatened: the women are not conforming to patriarch expectations (Rudman et al. 2012). The demeaning stereotypes may also emerge from a pervading sense of aggrieved male entitlement that render sexism and misogyny normal. According to Fricker, testimonial injustice 'is caused by prejudice in the economy of credibility' (it is person-to-person) while hermeneutical injustice is brought about by 'structural prejudice in the economy of collective hermeneutical resources' (148).

In Fricker's (2007) conception of hermeneutical injustice, dominant social groups tend to have the power to define or influence collective forms of social understanding, such as how women should behave. This power gives the powerful the right understandings of their own experiences, while the powerless are more likely to have 'ill-fitting meanings' (148) to draw on to make sense of a shared collective experience. Men, with the support of patriarchal women, have traditionally defined the appropriate understandings and punishments for women who fail to conform to patriarchal norms, as they have traditionally defined what a good woman is and does. This is a classic consequence of asymmetrical gendered power relations.

Women and girls in online environments can struggle not only to make sense of their own experience of hostility, but also to convey that experience without fearing an onslaught of abuse. Women do, of course, fill in the hermeneutical gaps to name a collective experience that is causing them harm as individuals and as a social group. We can name image-based sexual abuse, online stalking, doxing, ICT facilitated surveillance, and so on – but even despite the fact that these harms are recognised, appear in human rights protocols, journalism, women's magazines, or on BBC Radio 4 Woman's Hour,[6] still there will be women who don't realise that they are the victims of these harms (because of slow, insidious coercive control, gaslighting or shame at acknowledging that they are a victim). Up until the point of naming, describing, and calling out obscure, or even well-known harms, women will be hermeneutically marginalised. Women still unequally participate in politics, journalism, law, senior leadership positions, which means that they are often disabled from contributing to the collective hermeneutical resource – getting to assert what constitutes misogyny or insisting that what they experienced was sexism and not good-natured banter.

This marginalisation is epistemically unjust because the hermeneutical resource is 'structurally prejudiced'. The collective hermeneutical resource enables interpretations of a social experience (online sexual harassment) that are biased because 'insufficiently influenced by the subject group, and therefore unduly influenced by more hermeneutically powerful groups' (Fricker 2007: 155). When men decide the interpretation of sexual harassment as 'good old-fashioned flirting' or assert that they cannot be misogynistic because they love their mothers, sisters, or girlfriends, the imbalance in hermeneutical interpretation is clear: misogyny is a psychological deficit, not a structural manifestation of gendered based discrimination. Women will, most often, give very different interpretations of these oppressive misogynistic and sexist norms that regulate hermeneutical and epistemic practices. Identity power sustains these structural prejudices and oppressive harms.

Such marginalisation is unjust. It is discriminatory and will prejudicially impact the legitimate interests of the powerless as a social type. Legislation to hold Big Tech accountable for what its platforms enable, specific codes of practice which accompany online safety bills, delineating at least what constitutes online harm is essential if women are to operate in digital and cyber spaces equally with men, in safety, and with their dignity intact. I discuss this next.

---

[6] Woman's Hour is a radio magazine programme that has been broadcasting since 1946. It discusses women's lives, experiences, issues, campaigns, and so on often raising issues that are not common currency, such as the menopause, period poverty, stalking (before it was recognised in law), and marital rape (before it was criminalised). See https://www.bbc.co.uk/programmes/b007qlvb. Accessed 9 December 2022.

4 Keeping Patriarchy in Check by Digital Acts and Legislative Means

In the preceding discussion I sought to show why an analysis of misogyny is a critical component of feminist postdigital philosophy. Postdigital feminist philosophy, as a research method, enables us to engage with the inventive and persistent ways in which ancient harms find new guises in or channels by which to continue the pursuit of male power and to keep women advantageously ministering to men. The postdigital condition offers infinite variety for patriarchy to keep its structures of power and privilege intact.

The European Union (EU) recently agreed to the Digital Services Act (2022), which will regulate the digital landscape in Europe to protect children from online harms and end self-regulation by Big Tech.[7] The DSA also proposes to safeguard women online. As yet, however, there is no specific EU legislation that comprehensively addresses cyber violence against women. The European Commission (2022) Directive on Combatting Violence Against Women and Domestic Violence will be the first act to address this type of violence and includes measures to ensure the 'removal of online content in relation to offences of cyber violence, and a possibility of judicial redress for the affected users' (4). The Directive complements the DSA and Member States will criminalise and prosecute non-consensual sharing of intimate or manipulated material (Article 7), cyber stalking (Article 8), cyber harassment (Article 9) and cyber incitement to violence of hatred (Article 10) as criminal offences (European Commission 2022: 17).

The United Kingdom too is making legal efforts to hold the platforms accountable for some of their harms. The British Government's Online Safety Bill (2022/2023),[8] for example, promises to make the UK the 'safest place in the world' to be online while guaranteeing freedom of expression. The Bill places a duty of care on tech firms to protect users from harmful content. That duty of care is broadly split into three parts: to limit the spread of illegal content such as child sexual abuse images, terrorist material and encouraging suicide; ensure children are not exposed to harmful or inappropriate content; and, for the big platforms like Facebook, Twitter and TikTok, protecting adults from 'legal but harmful content' (such as cyberbullying and eating disorder-related material), though that requirement has been dropped because defining what is legal and harmful is contentious and messy, and could threaten free speech.

---

[7] The DSA will protect the rights of children online in recognition of UN Convention on the Rights of the Child. It is anticipated the Act will come into effect by January 2024. Further specifics on the landmark legislation can be found here: https://www.weforum.org/agenda/2022/06/eu-digital-service-act-how-it-will-safeguard-children-online/. Accessed 9 December 2022.

[8] The Bill is going through the House of Commons (UK Parliament). It will be sent for a third reading (in the relevant committee) when it has been reported to the House of Commons where Members of Parliament debate and propose further amendments to the Bill. It may become law in 2023.

The legislation will be overseen by Ofcom, the communications regulator, which will have the power to impose fines of £18 m or 10% of a company's global turnover for breaches of the act. In extreme cases, it can also block websites or apps. However, the Bill has been criticised a 'Frankenstein monster of legislation' (Stokel-Walker 2022), in part because UK politics has been chaotic.[9] The Bill in its current form puts the onus on tech firms to moderate its content, which past experience shows it will not do. Platforms are not willing to prioritise online safety over profit because it erodes profit (McKay 2021; The Centre for Humane Technology 2022).

The Bill, however, does not fully address the sexism, misogyny or violence against women and girls perpetrated in the digital sphere, though it promises to criminalise controlling or coercive behaviour and non-consensual deepfake pornography. The Bill as currently drafted (more provisions may be added or removed as it goes through parliament) will require social media platforms to provide users with tools to protect them from seeing harmful content that, for example, incites hatred on the basis of race, class, sex, sexual orientation or gender realignment. These tools include user verification processes, settings and functions which allow users to choose which kind of content they want to see and imposing stronger reporting mechanisms to report bullying and harmful content (Gov.UK 2022).

A coalition of UK experts on Violence Against Women and Girls had asked the British Government to amend the Bill and include a Code of Practice which specifically addresses violence against women and girls, to make this issue its top priority, and recognise VAWG as a specific harm. The Code of Practice will give guidance to tech companies on their obligations to protect users against adverse human rights abuses arising from the design, development, deployment and use of its products or services (McGlynn and Woods 2022). Because the pervading and pervasive presence of the digital pose considerable ethical and moral questions on what it means to be, for example, an autonomous, agentic online woman, A Code of Practice is important to safeguarding young women and girls online against adverse human rights abuses.

5 The Code of Practice

There are few resources to combat online hate and there is no money to stop it. Generating hate is profitable, it keeps people engaged, and attention makes money (The Centre for Humane Technology 2022). VAWG cannot dealt with by online platforms in isolation. The Code of Practice is necessarily a living document which will be revised as the Bill continues through the UK parliament. The Code has 13 sections, each of which details specific duties, responsibilities and actions by which Big Tech should abide by. For example:

---

[9]Writing this in December 2022, the country is on its fourth prime minister since 2016. The UK has had three Prime Ministers in 2022 alone; five Secretary of States and seven Digital and Culture Secretaries, who has overall responsibility for the Bill.

5.1 Responsibility, Risk Assessment and Remediation

Regulated services should have a specific policy commitment to prevent and take action to combat VAWG arising on their service. This commitment should be endorsed by the UK leadership of the organisation and a board member, or person reporting into the board, appointed to be accountable for delivering it. The policy should be informed by specialist VAWG expertise (7).

5.2 Safety by Design

Regulated providers must implement appropriate 'safety by design' technical and organisational measures.

Taking an appropriate and proportionate approach to the principle of knowing your client [KYC] to address VAWG harms spread by those using multiple, false, or anonymous identities.

b) Ensuring that young users' settings are set to safety by default.

c) Ensuring algorithms used on the service do not cause foreseeable harm through promoting hateful content, for example by rewarding misogynistic influencers with greater reach, causing harm both by increasing reach and engagement with a content item (11).

d) That speed of transmission has been considered, for example methods to reduce the velocity at which intimate images can be non-consensually shared and therefore the risk of cross-platform contamination (12).

e) Actors cannot take advantage of new or emerging tools to cause harms to women and girls. For instance: deep fake or audio-visual manipulation materials; nudification technology; bots and bot networks; content embedded from other platforms and synthetic features such as gifs, emojis, hashtag (McGlynn and Woods 2022: 12).

Other codes include Moderation; Transparency; and Victim support and mediation (McGlynn and Woods 2022). The code is comprehensive and would go a significant distance were all its codes taken up by companies working in the digital sphere and incorporated into the Online Harms Bill.

Women and girls' human rights should be protected off-and online. To ensure their protection, comprehensive action needs to be taken that includes cooperation between States, Intermediaries, Non-Governmental Organizations and National Human Rights Institutions to make online human rights protections operational with all international human rights frameworks.

6 Conclusion

Our postdigital condition describes an era of ubiquitous connectivity and rapidly evolving technology that means that perpetrators will find new ways to commit old harms in new ways. Technology has transformed how gender-based violence can be perpetrated in the digital and online sphere. VAGW can now be perpetrated across distance, beyond borders, without physical contact, by many, in many forms, at all times repeatedly. Creating safer online spaces with the co-operation of Internet intermediaries is a necessary step towards the full realisation of women's human rights and development. This is a postdigital moral and ethical necessity.

Feminist scholarship continues to expose how cultural traditions, dogma about gender, gender identity, woman/womanhood, epistemic credibility, sexual ethics, and so on, and invigorate lines of enquiry. Epistemic injustice is one such line of critical enquiry in the elucidation of women's oppression and for developing, one hopes, effective solutions, and strategies. Evidence for the deflation of epistemic credibility is abundant and obvious to see once women (and men) have the analytical tools to understand how testimony is inflated or degraded, depending on the status of the speaker and how she is socially situated. Postdigital feminist analysis, as I term it, is a contribution to that line of inquiry.

This line of enquiry helps us understand, along with human rights, feminist, LGTBQ+ activism, how women and girls are undermined in their capacity as *knowers* of their own social online experience and are stymied from conveying knowledge to those who have the power to protect their freedom to be equal online participants and contributors. Patriarchy and its legal enforces, misogyny and sexism, have settled easily and comfortably online, and its harms are as real and significant there as they are offline. It also has the same real power to define their own and women's reality. Postdigital feminist analysis, then, is a method by which to expose, scrutinise and challenge very bad old habits in very modern digital environments, to critique the postdigital condition to which Jandrić et al. (2019) have alerted us.

Feminist postdigital analysis then, such as the one used here, points to a research method whereby sexism, misogyny, inequality, and injustice in the online environment can be identified, named, exposed, and critiqued. The object of critique can obviously vary and here I chose to take misogyny, a systemic and structural practice, and examine it conceptually, descriptively, and analytically. In the process of such scrutiny, in so far as I have been successful, questions about beliefs about women inevitably surface: their source, content, justification, and reasons for the persistence of such beliefs. The epistemic and ontological investment in false beliefs about women – that they are a particular kind of human being, who have particular kinds of duties and responsibilities to others on account of their innate or natural natures – by the needy powerful and privileged mean that uprooting an enduring harm is very difficult. But this investment must be challenged if women are to engage in fair and just practices on a basis of equality with men off-and online. This challenge is, I suggest, integral to a feminist postdigital analysis – and hence, to a feminist postdigital research method.

References

Afzal, N. (2022). Independent Culture Review of London Fire Brigade. https://www.london-fire.gov.uk/media/7211/independent-culture-review-of-lfb-report953f61809024e20c7505a869af1f416c56530867cb99fb946ac81475cfd8cb38.pdf. Accessed 3 December 2022.

Amnesty International. (2017). Online Abuse of Women is Widespread in UK. London: Amnesty International. https://www.amnesty.org.uk/online-abuse-women-widespread. Accessed 26 November 2022.

Amnesty International. (2018). Troll Patrol Findings. London: Amnesty International. https://decoders.amnesty.org/projects/troll-patrol/findings. Accessed 26 November 2022.

Bailey, M. (2010). They aren't talking about me. The Crunk Feminist Collection, 14 March. http://www.crunkfeministcollective.com/2010/03/14/they-arent-talking-about-me/. Accessed 5 December 2022.

Badash, N. (2022). Royal Navy chief orders inquiry into sexual assault claims in submarine service. The Guardian, 20 October. https://www.theguardian.com/uk-news/2022/oct/28/royal-navy-chief-orders-investigation-into-abhorrent-allegations-of-bullying-misogyny-and-sexual-harassment. Accessed 26 November 2022.

Cullen, A., & Williams, M. (2022). Online Hate Speech Targeting the England Women's Football During the UEFA Women's Euro 2022. HateLab. https://orca.cardiff.ac.uk/id/eprint/153061/1/Online-Hate-Speech-WEURO-2022.pdf. Accessed 26 November 2022.

Eaton, A. A., Ramjee, D., & Saunders, J. F. (2022). The Relationship Between Sextortion During COVID-19 and Pre-pandemic Intimate Partner Violence: A Large Study of Victimization Among Diverse U.S Men and Women. *Victims and Offenders*. https://doi.org/10.1080/15564886.2021.2022057.

European Commission. (2022). Proposal for a directive of the European Parliament and the of the Council on combating violence against women and domestic violence. 8.3.2022, COM(2022) 105 final, 2022/0066 (COD). Strasbourg: European Commission. https://ec.europa.eu/info/sites/default/files/aid:development_cooperation_fundamental_rights/com_2022_105_1_en.pdf. Accessed 30 November 2022.

Feenberg, A. (2019). Postdigital or Predigital? *Postdigital Science and Education, 1*(1), 8–9. https://doi.org/10.1007/s42438-018-0027-2.

Fricker, M. (2007). *Epistemic Injustice. The Power and Ethics of Knowing*. Oxford: Oxford University Press.

Girlguiding. (2021). Girls' attitude survey 2021. https://www.girlguiding.org.uk/globalassets/docs-and-resources/research-and-campaigns/girls-attitudes-survey-2021-report.pdf. Accessed 26 November 2022.

Gov.UK (2022). New plans to protect people from anonymous trolls online. Press release, 25 February. https://www.gov.uk/government/news/new-plans-to-protect-people-from-anonymous-trolls-online#:~:text=The%20first%20duty%20will%20force,out%20of%20seeing%20harmful%20content. Accessed 5 December 2022.

Grevio. (2021). Grevio general recommendation No. 1 on the digital dimension of violence against women. Council of Europe, 20 October. https://rm.coe.int/grevio-rec-no-on-digital-violence-against-women/1680a49147. Accessed 26 November 2022.

Independent Office for Police. (2022). Operation Hotton: Learning report. https://www.police-conduct.gov.uk/sites/default/files/Operation%20Hotton%20Learning%20report%20-%20January%202022.pdf. Accessed 5 December 2022.

Jandrić, P. (2022). History of the Postdigital: Invitation for Feedback. *Postdigital Science and Education*. https://doi.org/10.1007/s42438-022-00345-w.

Jandrić, P., Knox, J., Besley, T., Ryberg, T., Suoranta, J., & Hayes, S. (2018). Postdigital Science and Education. *Educational Philosophy and Theory, 50*(10), 893–899. https://doi.org/10.1080/00131857.2018.1454000.

Jandrić, P., Ryberg, T., Knox, J., Lacković, N., Hayes, S., Suoranta, J., Smith, M., Steketee, A., Peters, M. A., McLaren, P., Ford, D. R., Asher, G., McGregor, C., Stewart, G., Williamson, B., & Gibbons, A. (2019). Postdigital Dialogue. *Postdigital Science and Education, 1*(1), 163–189. https://doi.org/10.1007/s42438-018-0011-x.

Jandrić, P., MacKenzie, A., & Knox, J. (Eds.). (2023a). *Postdigital Research: Genealogies, Challenges, and Future Perspectives*. Cham: Springer. https://doi.org/10.1007/978-3-031-31299-1.

Jandrić, P., MacKenzie, A., & Knox, J. (Eds.). (2023b). *Constructing Postdigital Research: Method and Emancipation*. Cham: Springer. https://doi.org/10.1007/978-3-031-35411-3.

Jopling, M. (2023). Postdigital Research in Education: Towards Vulnerable Method and Praxis. In P. Jandrić, A. MacKenzie, & J. Knox (Eds.), *Postdigital Research: Genealogies, Challenges, and Future Perspectives* (pp. 155–171). Cham: Springer. https://doi.org/10.1007/978-3-031-31299-1_9.

Kimmel, M. (2013). *Angry White Men: American Masculinity at the End of an Era*. New York: National Books.

Kittay, E. (2019). *Love's Labor: Essays on Women, Equality and Dependency*. New York and London: Routledge. https://doi.org/10.4324/9781315108926.

Manne, K. (2017). *Down Girl: The Logic of Misogyny*. Oxford: Oxford University Press.

Mijatović, D. (2022). No space for violence against women and girls in the digital world. Human Rights Comment. Council of Europe, Commissioner for Human Rights, 15 March. https://www.coe.int/en/web/commissioner/-/no-space-for-violence-against-women-and-girls-in-the-digital-world. Accessed 30 November 2022.

MacKenzie, A. (2022). Why didn't you scream? Epistemic injustice of sexism, misogyny and rape myths. *Journal of Philosophy in Education*. https://doi.org/10.1111/1467-9752.12685.

MacKenzie, A., Rose, J., & Bhatt, I. (Eds.). (2021). *The Epistemology of Deceit in a Postdigital Era: Dupery by Design*. Cham: Springer. https://doi.org/10.1007/978-3-030-72154-1.

McGlynn, C., & Woods, L. (2022). Violence Against Women and Girls (VAWG) Code of Practice. https://www.endviolenceagainstwomen.org.uk/wp-content/uploads/2022/05/VAWG-Code-of-Practice-16.05.22-Final.pdf. Accessed 4 December 2022

McKay, T. (2021). Facebook whistleblower Frances Haugen releases her 8 damning SEC complaints. Gizmodo, 5 October. *https://gizmodo.com/facebook-whistleblower-frances-haugen-releases-her-8-da-1847802360*. Accessed 9 December 2022.

Petri, A. (2013). Margaret Thatcher, Iron Lady, unusual feminist suspect. Washington Post, 8 April. https://www.washingtonpost.com/blogs/compost/wp/2013/04/08/margaret-thatcher-iron-lady-unusual-feminist-suspect/. Accessed 26 November 2022.

Peters, M., & Besley, T. (2019). *Critical Philosophy of the Postdigital. Postdigital Science and Education, 1*(1), 29–42. https://doi.org/10.1007/s42438-018-0004-9.

Rudman, L. A., Moss-Racusin, C. A., Phelan, J. E., & Nauts, S. (2012). Status Incongruity and Backlash Effects: Defending the Gender Hierarch Motivates Prejudice Against Female Leaders. *Journal of Experimental Psychology, 48*(1), 165–179. https://doi.org/10.1016/j.jesp.2011.10.008.

Ruvalcaba, Y., & Eaton, A. A. (2020). Nonconsensual Pornography Among U.S. adults: A Sexual Scripts Framework on Victimization, Perpetration, and Health Correlates for Women and Men. *Psychology of Violence, 10*(1), 68–78. https://doi.org/10.1037/vio0000233.

Savin-Baden, M., & Burden, J. (2019). Digital Immortality and Virtual Humans. *Postdigital Science and Education, 1*(1), 104–108. https://doi.org/10.1007/s42438-018-0007-6.

Sinclair, C., & Hayes, S. (2019). Between the Post and the Com-post: Examining the Postdigital 'Work' of a Prefix. *Postdigital Science and Education, 1*(1), 119–131. https://doi.org/10.1007/s42438-018-0017-4.

Stokel-Walker, C. (2022). While EU regulators take on Elon Musk, Britain's online safety bill is a beacon of mediocrity. The Guardian, 5 December. https://www.theguardian.com/commentisfree/2022/dec/05/eu-regulators-elon-musk-britain-online-safety-bill-big-tech-brexit. Accessed 5 December.

The Centre for Human Development. (2022). The ledger of harms. https://ledger.humanetech. com/. Accessed 9 December 2022.

UK Parliament. (2022/2023). Online safety bill. London: UK Parliament. https://publications. parliament.uk/pa/bills/cbill/58-03/0121/220121.pdf. Accessed 5 December 2022.

United Nations General Assembly. (2018). Report of the Special Rapporteur on violence against women, its causes and consequences on online violence against women and girls from a human rights perspective. Human Rights Council, thirty-eighth session, 18 June-6 July 2018. A/HRC/38/47. https://documents-dds-ny.un.org/doc/UNDOC/GEN/G18/184/58/PDF/ G1818458.pdf?OpenElement. Accessed 26 November 2022.

Women's Aid. (2021). Online and digital abuse. https://www.womensaid.org.uk/information-support/what-is-domestic-abuse/online-safety/. Accessed 26 November 2022.

Images of Incoming: A Critical Account of a (Mostly) Postdigital Photovoice Project with Rural Migrant Women in Northern Ireland and Canada

Tess Maginess, Amea Wilbur, and Elena Bergia

1 Prologue

As a consequence of a large war many millions of people who never before had fired a shot will have acquired the skills to operate a gun. As a consequence of an extensive plague, many millions will have gained skills and knowledge in forms of communication beyond the physical. As a result of migration becoming a more pervasive feature of the contemporary world (though migrations have always occurred), millions of people have gained skills and knowledge through perilous navigations. It is 'a truth universally acknowledged' that existential 'limit situations' can lead to the painful accelerated acquisition of survival knowledges and skills which make possible 'paradigm shifts' – including the realisation that, wherever people have come from, they are now in a postdigital space. We follow Jandrić (2020: 85) in defining 'that uncanny space that some of us like to call postdigital' as a space constructed upon the ethos of what Peters (2021) has called 'knowledge socialism' – a fundamentally social enterprise which is collaborative and for the public good.

We offer a critical account of one postdigital, arts based, co- research project with rural migrant women in Canada and Northern Ireland. It is likely that such a project could not have been possible 20 years ago. The limit situations of the last few years, including Covid-19, have, in 'fast-tracking' digital competence, enabled many of the migrant women and the academics to inhabit the online 'home' of the project. Yet, not all elements were online, some of the engagement was face-to-face,

T. Maginess (✉) · E. Bergia
Queen's University Belfast, Belfast, UK
e-mail: t.maginess@qub.ac.uk; ebergia01@qub.ac.uk

A. Wilbur
University of the Fraser Valley, Abbotsford, BC, Canada
e-mail: Amea.Wilbur@ufv.ca

P. Jandrić et al. (eds.), *Constructing Postdigital Research*, Postdigital Science
and Education, https://doi.org/10.1007/978-3-031-35411-3_15

recognising that digital inequality as a reality for many of the participants, especially those from the global south.

The overarching research question was how can we create a postdigital arts-based co-research model which can offer migrant women a voice to articulate experiences of exclusion and to reveal what belonging means? We did not assume that all the participants would experience negative stereotyping or, indeed, exclusion. Rather, we believed that co-research with rural migrant women was an underexplored field. However, we aimed to enact postdigital research that, as Knox (2019) warned, would not end up amplifying inequality but, rather, offer a forum in which women migrants could enact agency, to empower themselves through an inherently dialogic co-learning and co-research process.

2 Background

In line with an ethos that is about producing research which has direct benefits to participants and which, in terms of social justice, is not just about considering the more traditional academic emphasis on theorisation, we wish also to offer an account of *how* we did the project, so that this might offer a critical model for other groups concerned more primarily with practice. Thus, we hope to offer an account that combines both in offering a model of praxis.

'Images of Incoming: A Photovoice project exploring belonging and exclusion with newcomer and migrant women in rural areas' engaged nearly 70 women from Northern Ireland and Canada. The partnership was created between Queen's University Belfast's Open Learning (Adult Education) Programme and the University of the Fraser Valley, British Columbia's Faculty of Education, Community and Human Development (Social Work and Adult Education Department). Both teams were experienced in delivering projects with a range of marginalised groups. The University of Atypical, Northern Ireland's arts and disability network, later joined us to curate a high-quality exhibition of photographs from participants, including incorporating a virtual tour, signed in British, Irish and American sign language, facilitate the creation of an accessible website, and make a documentary film – recognising the postdigitality of accessible dissemination and impact.

In proposing this project, we embedded holistic outcomes for participants such as: improved digital literacy through the online medium of teaching, learning and research, and, for some, English language and literacy skills, increased self-confidence, intercultural awareness, self-awareness, an empowering, agentic ethos. Both universities were very supportive with funding, seeing the project as part of their vision as an engaged university and how it met key SDG aims. The United Nations has formulated 17 Strategic Development Goals (United Nations 2022). Of especial relevance to this project are gender equality (5), quality education (4) and working for the goals through partnership (17).

It was agreed that the process should follow the natural *modus operandi* of each partner. In each country the participants would take a series of digital photos which would convey how they felt they belonged and how they felt alienated or excluded. The women would come together, then, to discuss and comment on their photos with the project facilitators. In Northern Ireland, after a number of months' development work, we were able to arrange pre-project meetings and enrol 33 incomer women. In Canada, the process of engaging with participants was done through outreach to community organisations and 34 participants engaged. Two of the researchers, Dr. Tanis Sawkins and Dr. Amea Wilbur, had worked extensively in the sector before entering the academy and were able to reach out to contacts. Community facilitators also supported the recruitment of the participants. In Northern Ireland, we were able to enlist a number of community facilitators from a range of voluntary groups in Northern Ireland working with migrants and they played an invaluable role in helping to persuade women to participate.

Not all the initial connections with groups came to fruition, but, on the other hand, we created an important partnership with the First Steps Women's Group in Dungannon – a rural town 40 miles southwest of Belfast with a large incomer population. The Dungannon group included both incomer women and local women, which was an angle we had not thought of, and here the workshops were delivered face-to-face to suit the needs of the group. For the in-person participants in both countries, childcare was provided to the participants, as well as transportation and, in some cases, food.

In Northern Ireland, after a number of months' development work, we were able to arrange pre-project meetings and enrol 33 incomer women. In Canada, the process of engaging with participants was done through outreach to community organisations and 34 participants engaged.

In Northern Ireland, the project was platformed as two consecutive workshop courses (5 × 2 h each) within the Open Learning Programme and participants were able to obtain 10 credit points (at the equivalent of first year university study). No prior qualifications were needed. The aim of this was that participants would be able to add to the skills they have which could benefit them in applying for educational courses or jobs. In Northern Ireland, there were three groups, two online and one face to face. The approach in Canada was more informal and involved two workshops (2.5 h each) throughout the Lower Mainland of British Columbia or in an online or in person environment. While the initial intention was to deliver the project in a completely postdigital mode, it was vital that we met the needs of a variety of participants (Knox 2019). Women coming from global south or/and women with poor access to education or living with disabilities can find themselves oppressed and excluded in the postdigital domain others rule over.

In Northern Ireland, the first series of workshops began at the end of January 2022. At the request of participants, we scheduled two online, digital workshop 'slots'; one on Tuesday mornings and the other on Thursday evenings. The third group met face-to-face in Dungannon for the first series and then joined the second digital series. We believe that this kind of learner–focused orientation is essential in enacting the kind of democratic and humanistic postdigital pedagogy advocated by Knox (2019 and Harman and Varga-Dobai (2012), which we will discuss a little later with reference to the theoretical frameworks guiding the project. In Canada, at the first meeting with participants, the researchers explained what Photovoice and then explored the methodology in practice. The University of the Fraser Valley researchers took the participants through the process of analysing photos during both the first and second meetings.

It was agreed that the two groups of participants – in Canada and Northern Ireland – would then come together for 5 × 2 h online 'exchange workshops'. This would create digital connectivity between the women and further enhance the international element. The second series of workshops, March–May, brought together participants from Northern Ireland and Canada. While the first series was designed to give all the women space and time to discuss their photos, creating a commentary and interacting with the other women in the group, the second international exchange series was more about comparing, and contrasting migrant experiences and also, indirectly getting a sense of the contrasting policy and practice in each country. In that sense, the project was very much about building a postdigital community of practice with an empowering and inclusive ethos, as indicated by an independent ethnographic evaluator, Elena Bergia in her analysis:

> The approach is a collaborative one: both educators/researchers and learners are involved in all the phases of the project. An important goal of this photovoice project was to create a community of practice, raising awareness through and within this community, and effecting change.

We accepted that not all those who took an initial interest were going to complete the project. We do not regard this as a failure because every woman was able to engage on her own terms without any pressure. Some women produced a set of images or gallery but were not able to attend the workshops and so there were no commentaries. We included all their photos on the project website. Other women could only attend the series offered in their own country and were not able to also engage in the international workshops.

While the first phase, which was about collecting 'data' with the participants about their experiences as incomer women, the next phase was a meta-analysis of the project, undertaken primarily by participants in a co-research methodology to create a critique of the process which might be useful for other groups. The meta-analysis began in tandem with organising exhibitions, website and documentary.

3   Theoretical Frameworks

3.1   Postdigital Democratic Research

Our research positioning was very much in line with Peters (2021) in challenging neoliberal concepts of ownership and privatisation of knowledge with an ethos that research should not just be for the common good, but should be empowering, democratic, and agentic. This is sometimes referred to as Responsible Research and Innovation (Tassone et al. 2018). Hayes and Jandrić (2021) argue that postdigital practices can constitute a form of resistance to political and economic 'illusions' of democratic forms of public culture found across the internet, and can address issues pertaining to power, exploitation and emancipation'. Following Knox (2019), we view the 'post' in postdigital as a parallel to terms like postcolonialism in which a critical perspective on digital education is foregrounded. Similarly, our outlook echoes that of Bothwell and Stewart (2020) that the artwork produced in the project should respond to the digital age by being socially engaged, co-authored and participatory. Correspondingly, the 'outputs' of the project embody 'new methods of knowledge circulation' (Bothwell and Stewart 2020: 278).

3.2 Critical Pedagogy

Such an ethos lies behind and, arguably, emerges from a theoretical tradition known as critical pedagogy, which had its roots in Freire's *Pedagogy of the Oppressed* (1970) and has been developed by scholars like Nagda et al. (2003). Of especial relevance to this project, is the work of Harman and Varga-Dobai (2012), as it focuses specifically on critical pedagogy approaches with migrant learners on local immigration issues.

McLaren (2020: 1244) trenchantly argues for critical pedagogy as 'a moral compass for the way we treat each other in the classroom and by contributing to the epistemological, ontological and axiological, stances, we take in the production of knowledge. The importance of openness, respect and compassion is crucial'. The logic, not always, perhaps apparent, is to welcome participants – as experiential experts – as co-researchers. In this we drew on many years' experiences of Participatory Action Research (Maginess 2017a).

For groups so often rendered subject and passive, it is vital not to reproduce a further unthinking power imbalance in the research process and to move away from the unreflecting nomenclature of imperialising terms like research 'subjects'. Extending a pedagogy of co-production of knowledge through respect, openness, and compassion, into the domain of research, was, therefore, not just a way of erasing the growing academic dialectic between teaching and research, but a much more natural and organic approach for participants in 'the real world'. Breaking down the barriers between teaching, learning, pedagogy and research, and questioning traditional assumptions about who is expert, who has authority, was central to our approach. Bergia drew upon Freire, whose 'pedagogical theories rest on the radical assumption that 'knowledge already lies with the people' (Jarldorn 2019: 29).

3.3 Arts-Based Approaches

For the past several decades scholars have maintained, and it has become increasingly accepted, that a shift in methodology towards infusing arts into research can bring tremendous insight and create solutions that may not be possible through descriptive and linear language (Butterwick and Roy 2016; Maginess 2017a; Barone and Eisner 2012; Sinner et al. 2006). Using art with migrant women who may have lower levels of English language and literacy provides an alternative mode of expression which centres the women's experience. Images can also stimulate dialogue with others.

Photovoice is a method often used with marginalised communities (Brigham et al. 2018; Stack and Feng 2018; Lenette 2019) emphasising through visual images participants' realities, stories, and collective meaning making. Participants use photographic images, often taken on mobile phones or digital cameras, to explore and reveal their attitudes towards a key aspect of their lives – in this case, how they felt excluded or a sense of belonging as migrant women.

Wang et al. (2017) have foregrounded the connection between arts-based methods and socially engaged research practice, thus echoing the goals of postdigital democratic research. We aimed to live up to the values articulated by Jackson et al. (2007), including a humanistic approach objectivity, ethical diligence, and rigour. Sullivan (2006) usefully argues that this kind of research is both personal and public. From a more pedagogic perspective, Topolovčan (2016) identifies arts-based research as emerging from a constructivist, participatory pedagogy.

4 Methodology

4.1 Research Paradigm

The overall research paradigm for the project was qualitative. We follow Aspers and Corte (2019) in their conclusion that this paradigm oscillates between theory and practice, is concerned with getting closer to the actual experience of people, and about improved understanding – of, we may add, hidden or erased realities. And we hoped to fulfil the ideals adumbrated by Jackson et al. (2007) in embodying a humanistic ethos, ethical diligence, objectivity, and rigour. Qualitative research is a methodology for challenging hegemonic and stereotypical characterisations of migrant people, so often represented in crude quantitative terms implying that thousands of migrants are 'swamping' developed countries and that, most of them are, in any case, not 'real' refugees and asylum seekers but 'economic migrants'. As if the vast majority of migrants over the centuries have not, in fact, been economic migrants seeking a better life. That they have come to countries whose wealth has been sometimes built on colonial exploitation is conveniently forgotten. In line with the theoretical frameworks outlined above, the methodological engine was a co-learning and co-research ethos. The participants were agentic in choosing their own images and talking about them not to some pre-ordained academic agenda, but on their own terms.

4.2   Data Analysis

The project generated two kinds of analysis; the first kind was the commentaries of the participants about the photographs they took. These were generated in the workshops, recorded (both online and in transcripts prepared by facilitators and moderators), checked with each participant, and then saved with each set of photographs from each participant into a proto website gallery. While these commentaries to the photographs can be regarded as the primary data of the project, revealing the views of participants on their experience of exclusion, and belonging, the meta-analysis constituted another dimension to the co-research; enabling all those involved to comment critically on the process of the project. This panoptic critical pedagogy perspective was very important in enabling all of us there to evaluate the strengths and weaknesses of the Photovoice models we had created if there is to be impact and the potential for developing further projects which start to build sustainability and empowerment.

In analysing the commentaries from participants in both countries and, subsequently, in the meta-analysis, the views expressed by all those involved in the project, we used thematic analysis, which, as Maguire and Delahunt (2017) argue, allows themes to emerge from the data, rather than imposing a preset structure. In this chapter we will confine ourselves to discussing the postdigital aspects. Just as the participants were researchers of their own experiences in creating their galleries and critical commentaries, they were also central to the meta-analysis.

After the first phase was complete, 15 interviews were conducted with and, in many cases, by participants. The meta-analysis was conducted over several months and the project. The views of the project coordinator were also included. University stakeholders offered their perspective in their recorded addresses to the exhibitions. A further welcome incidental connection with Dr. Elena Bergia, an Italian anthropologist who was, herself an incomer in Northern Ireland, resulted in an additional ethnographic analysis of the project, considering, among other things, how the project constituted a community of practice. Almost all the views were collected through online interviews, but participants were interviewed in person if that suited them better. Ethical approval was obtained and participants were given codenames, as neutral as possible to avoid identification and assumptions about colour, background and status.

We now look at the first form of data analysis – the commentaries provided by the participants on their photos.

5   Findings

5.1   Participants' Commentaries

Responses in relation to the poles of exclusion and belonging highlighted the presence of racism, stereotyping and microaggressions, especially for women of colour in small towns and villages where they 'stand out', as attested by Northern Irish and

Canadian participants (Fig. 2). Some identities are valued, and some were not. Language or and associated lack of digital proficiency was also cited as a barrier, impeding belonging. For others, the lack of recognition of their credentials created barriers to accessing the job opportunities for which they were qualified (Fig. 1). The findings reveal how postdigital research can uncover issues of power and exploitation (Hayes and Jandrić 2021) through the testimonies of participants.

Identity emerged, not surprisingly, as a key theme; complex and even contradictory and unstable, changing over years. Belonging and exclusion were relative and often predicated upon people's circumstances and status, so the experience of

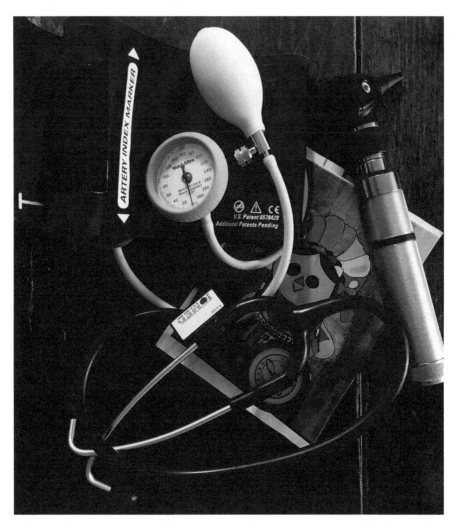

Fig. 1 I was a doctor back home but based on my immigration status and lack of language skills, I am not able to be a doctor in Canada. The lack of credential education recognition is a huge barrier to be certified as doctor. (Camilla, Canada)

Fig. 2 Gemma, Northern Ireland

migration was very different for 'high status' migrants, coming to a well-paid post in contrast to an asylum seeker. Gemma, living in Northern Ireland, expressed the views of many of the women in expressing a sense of having two identities, 'two' souls'. Amy, a Canadian-Chinese woman living in Northern Ireland, who was conflicted about her identities, saw the project as 'providing a space' to think about 'what was at the back of my mind, but I did not feel safe talking about it'. She experienced a tension or self-division between two identities– one relating to the originating culture and the other relating to the desire to be accepted in the new culture. This led to a feeling of being excluded from two cultures.

Some participants, like Helen, wanted to belong but felt they did not fit in:

I love Canada and I choose to see the big picture on the positive sides, trying to fit but not exactly getting that understanding the culture or something. But when I listened to other participants, it made me realise like an alarm; it is not okay that somebody belittle you or bully you for your accent or for not knowing language. And when listening to the other participants, I think all those things happened to me too. [The Canadians] they don't know, they don't understand that they don't know what we have been through. Seeing other participants and hearing their point of view, actually I understand they struggle to, so we are not alone.

[We are] working hard, triple hard and trying to fit in this society, which is not, not easy … Probably if I was in their position here I wouldn't have understood either.

The project helped us to understand each other better, and in a way to empower us too – not to feel like intimidated, to feel free, we are a part of this country, the fabric of this society, but I sometimes feel like I'm in somebody's space…

Belonging and exclusion also related to digital access and competence (Fig. 3). While we may be said to occupy a postdigital space, the reality is that people do not have equal access or training in postdigital 'literacy'. Canadian Research assistant, Sarah-Ann Wijngaarden, commented that one person might have a laptop which helped their sense of belonging, but another person might not have one or did not know how to use it so that could be very excluding. Within the project, we acknowledged this by conducting one group face to face and in inviting one participant to join the online workshops in the home of another person involved.

It should also be pointed out that a kind of internal exile can also occur with people growing up in 'advanced' societies who, for a variety of reasons, often economic and social, are most definitely not entering postdigital spaces. We may extrapolate from Knox (2019) that a critical perspective on words like 'postdigital' and other 'posts' like 'postcolonial', may imply a state of disadvantage or oppression and, often they who are marginalised, experience multiple disadvantage – in this case as migrants, as women, and in many cases, as women of colour. The co-research findings also clearly exposed the power imbalances and exploitation of the incomer women (Hayes and Jandrić 2021).

Participants articulated the complexity of foreignness and belonging, by talking a lot about foods that they could not get in the new country or how they had learned to adapt with the ingredients available (Fig. 2). Food also served as a way of bringing people together – either form one migrant community or between different communities. In addition, clothes and other cultural products were invested with great significance as a way of maintaining connection with the original country.

For young migrant women, body image and dress became a further troubling and complex issue (Fig. 4). Adaptation and the differing views of first- and

Fig. 3 My problem is I can't do [computer work] as fast as other people. When I go to library, or at school to do work, other people do it fast, for me it's slow. [I feel] very sad, because the people did it very fast. I [can't] go to school for a career. I had a newborn 2 years ago. If I find a program [that runs on weekends], I'm okay because my husband is off, otherwise I can't go. (Ayanna, Canada)

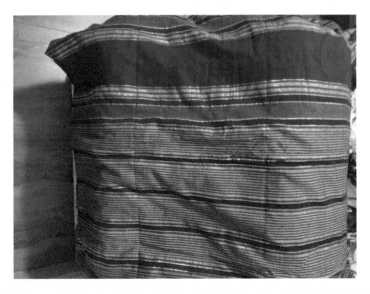

Fig. 4 This is a scarf or sari ... this is a traditional cloth. When I wear it and I'm in the Somali community, I feel belonging, I'm proud of it. But [sometimes] when I'm outside the house in Canada, I feel exclusion because I feel different, or I wear different [clothes] when I see other people wearing pants. (Bilqiis, Canada)

...the beauty of Northern Ireland, the natural side of it.

This is me walking in the garden.
It symbolises knowing what independence is,
versus always being surrounded by family.

Fig. 5 Rose, Northern Ireland

second-generation migrants was a related theme. Lisa, living in Northern Ireland, felt there was a need for migrants to 'avoid being critical of other migrants' – sometimes this is generational, as when second or third generation migrants support anti-immigration policies. This answers another aspect of McLaren's (2020) call for openness and research – in this case how the co-researchers develop critical awareness and intercultural understanding of other migrant groups and experiences.

Research assistant, Serrah Sidhu, who has Punjabi heritage, observed another interesting theme which emerged; participants spoke about having a family here but also having a family in their home country and how that might be both comforting and anguishing. And she said, 'until someone else said it, I thought it was just me'. Sarah, who is of Dutch heritage, concurred, 'the heart is in multiple places'.

Many women talked about the positive effect of nature (Figs. 5 and 6), eloquently articulated by Belfast based facilitator Asma Niazi, herself an incomer:

> ...it provides that kind of *space*. Because the population here is not too much, so when you go to open places, you *can* have that place to your own self, and I think that sense of belonging, you feel it with the land itself. Many women have talked about nature, and how they connect with nature, they have talked about the sea and the hills and different places. I feel that when people are not around, these places, these voids provide that sense of belonging that we *want* [author's own emphasis] to feel to a place. And nature gives us this connection. You need that kind of anchor to a place you come to, and I think that nature provides that kind of anchor here in Northern Ireland. I don't know about other places.

Stone is sometimes in your way.
That day I took the picture, it was warm,
and I stood on the cool stones.
When I came here. I had to learn the hard way,
it took me quite a few years to get back on my feet.
But everything happened as it should.
Even in my private life,
I never regretted that I made the decision.
My partner is very supportive, and I met him here.

Tomatoes; my parents are very much into gardening.
I never liked it. But now I somehow like the idea and I have
become like my mum. I have a little greenhouse.
This year it has improved but last year it was not that good
and we have started allotment together with my friend,
building together, grown so many things together, raised beds
and it was quite fun.
I hated it when my parents did, but when I started now,
I had the knowledge, and it came back to me.
It reminds me of my roots.
I learned a lot, I was not aware of what I knew.

Fig. 6 Brigit, Northern Ireland

Another important theme was the experience of older migrant women, often over-looked and disconnected and, on the other end of the scale, difficulties facing young people – children of migrants – with high expectations placed upon them.

5.2 Meta-analysis

5.2.1 Delivering the Project: Critical Pedagogy and Co-research

Within the framework of Responsible Research and Innovation (Tassone et al. 2018), the women were not traditional research 'subjects' but respected experts; as such, their capacity to become agentic (Peters 2021) was, concomitantly, enhanced. While the first level of data creation constituted a base, the meta-analysis added another dimension to the agentic potential of this kind of project. Rarely are research 'subjects' ever asked what they thought of the whole operation.

All participants testified that the particular pedagogy and approach of the project had helped them to think more imaginatively and critically about belonging and exclusion. Helen, who has lived in Canada for many years commented:

[It]was nice of you to ask these questions about belonging and exclusion, because in 23 years, nobody asked us. Somebody from government ought to, I thought, maybe they might have seen we are doing good, because we were paying taxes, contributing. We wanted somebody to evaluate us after five years, after 10 years, to say, 'you came a refugee from war, how are you doing?'

All participants emphasised the importance of the process of the project itself, especially listening to other participants and respecting their opinions in a safe environment. All participants testified that they were very much made to feel welcome and included and that their culture and beliefs were very much respected, in line with McLaren's (2020) exhortation and with enacting a humanistic postdigital pedagogy and also a Freirean ethos of empowerment and constructing a dialogic relationship between all those concerned and, as Bergia observed, 'on Freire's assumption that knowledge/awareness lies in the learners' lived experiences (Jarldorn 2019: 32).

Marcella Mancilla Fuller, one of the Canadian community facilitators, considered that the project was important as a way that she could 'support and empower the immigrant women she works with'. The notion of Frierian agency was key to the aims of the project. She also thought that the project was beneficial in creating reconciliation within a multicultural society.

Elena Bergia commented that the women were not necessarily looking for friendship but rather to share learning and get help from others about practical issues. This is an important observation; the postdigital space in which the project was enacted was a place for useful learning, a safe space for discussion of complex and often painful issues and also a space for learning about the otherness of other migrants, of debate, of difference.

It could be said that the participants, facilitators, and moderators rather constituted a community of practice, which was mostly, but not completely postdigital, thus recognising that such projects need to avoid reproducing the oppression that many migrant women experience as some of the women did not have access to computers or did not feel proficient in using them (see Fig. 3). Thus, while the development of critical thinking among participants is an academic desideratum, we would suggest that, perhaps contrary to prevailing views that everybody has been brainwashed by the Dark Web, there is no shortage of critical thinking. Hatred and fear can be monetised in a cynical pitch for free speech in which the very word 'critical' has shirked any academic connotation of profound analysis and has reverted to its simple definition of 'hostile'. The shortage is, rather, of visible, public postdigital spaces where we can criticise the status quo, weigh its faults and strengths. And the outsiders' perceptions, what, in the case of this project, rural migrant women see, is often the most necessary set of images for us all, defamiliarising the place we take for granted (Bothwell and Stewart 2020).

Operating in the postdigital spaces is not, for many adults, smooth or easy at the beginning. But what if you have no support structure to help you negotiate this new postdigital space, to help you, puzzled and estranged, in that cold universe. Amy remarked on how, at the beginning, she felt reluctant at first to contribute and express her views, that later, 'even outside the meetings, I was thinking about the brief'. This registers how hard the process of engaging with adult learning is. But it also attests to how the participants *affected each other* in that postdigital space in terms of releasing and building confidence, trust and critical thinking. Critical pedagogy is surely also centrally about peer learning, about co-learning.

It would appear from participants' commentaries on the photos and what they said in the workshop exchanges, that the project offered them a postdigital 'inside track'. It can be argued that online teaching and learning tends to promote an informal, active pedagogy, the moderators, and facilitators, drawing upon their experience of co-learning with adults, were very aware that the whole ethos of adult education is about valuing and centring the expertise of the learners (Maginess 2017b). Participants, in effect, created the curriculum for the workshops through their commentaries on their photos, so it was the issues of importance to the participants which were foregrounded.

Rose, an incomer to Northern Ireland, says: 'I got flashbacks taking the pictures, of the good and bad experiences and the long way I have come.' This poignantly attests to how an arts-based approach was condign for incomer women who were marginalised (Brigham et al. 2018; Stack and Feng 2018). The focus was not on some preordained research agenda but, following Lenette (2019), enabling participants to articulate their realities, stories and to create complex collective meaning making.

Importantly, especially for women who had not had the opportunity to become fluent in written English, Photovoice as an approach proved especially effective, creating a kind of visual bridge to what could be then spoken of in the commentaries (Brigham et al. 2018; Stack and Feng 2018). Elena Bergia concluded that the photovoice approach was, in Freirean terms, transformative:

> It seems like, through the project, the participants gained a greater awareness of their own difficulties, struggles, as well as personal successes and achievements. Hannah pointed out that the *method* [author's own emphasis] adopted in the project – taking photos and talking about your photos, as she put it – was a brilliant idea. Photos are a good way to start a conversation because 'the pictures allowed you that kind of baseline, from where you could build your story and talk about things you had come across.

Canadian Research Assistant, Sarah-Ann, registered the effect of the project on her perspective in saying that the project made her notice where she could improve, in terms of her own attitudes. It made her question and reflect; 'how, as an educator, am I hearing?' This reflected the commitment to a humanistic, Freirean, self-critical research positioning. As Elena Bergia commented, for a truly Freirean ethos to be embedded, 'educators/teachers must be prepared and open to question their own assumptions, positionalities, and practices'.

5.2.2   Postdigital Teaching and Research: Challenges and Opportunities

Most of those who were engaging online with the project thought this was an effective learning and teaching mode. Gemma commented that 'people were able to see verbal and non-verbal clues'. She added that 'people communicated well what they wanted to say'. Importantly, she stressed the empathic connection between participants; '[w]e sympathised with each other. We laughed together.'

It must be added that the face-to-face workshops in Dungannon produced a fair amount of hilarity. The point, though, is not lost, for participants were perhaps surprised that humour could be a facet of postdigital co-learning and co-research. Hannah remarked that the experience of this arts-based learning and research was 'not like the classroom'. Yet, this is precisely the environment in which adult education, at its best, comes to life, drawing upon the ironies of survival with compassion and wry humour. So, returning to the prologue, the project reflected the painful accelerated acquisition of survival knowledges and skills which make possible 'paradigm shifts', tiny and insignificant as they sometimes seem.

The decision in the Northern Irish cohort to use disposable digital cameras, while protecting the anonymity of participants – a key concern for some of the women – offered some other challenges. The business of getting the disposable cameras out to each woman and getting them back, was sometimes very challenging as many did not have transport. And in the printing and digitising process, there were some technical problems. In the operation of the workshops, technical issues were vexatious. In Canada mobile phones were used.

There is no doubt that the postdigital medium enables international projects to take place in an affordable way and so opens the potential for qualitative, engaged research which, for many, could not be possible due to the cost of bringing academics from one location to another. More importantly, the postdigital medium really overcame the far more complex economic and legal issues involved in trying to create physical exchanges between over 60 migrant women in two distant countries. The internationality of the project was, for participants and researchers, an important facet and there is, therefore, much to learn about how internationally oriented research, enacted within a democratic and Freirean focus on global disparities in this case, the very engine for south-north migration, can gather data in postdigital mediums that would be far too expensive and logistically demanding to achieve using a traditional research nexus. For others, the internationality enabled them to see ways of doing things that were still nascent in their own country.

The convenience of the postdigital *mise en scene* was important for some participants. Again, genuinely engaged and responsible research has practical implications in terms of making participation easy and enjoyable for the participants. Rose confessed, 'I was in my pyjamas without anybody knowing. And after [the workshops] you just start whatever, you have to do in the house.' Furthermore, there was no need for transportation or parking as Lisa noted. The postdigital mode also made the project accessible for women with small children and other caring responsibilities and for women with health issues or disabilities, in line with Brigham et al. (2018) and Stack and Feng (2018). Equally, the flexibility of the timetable was very much appreciated by all participants in the Northern Irish version because there were two online sessions, one morning and one evening. Participants could attend either session.

A further important advantage of the online postdigital *modus operandi* was that we were able to record all sessions. This was crucial in enabling the moderators and facilitators to create transcripts, both of the workshop commentaries and of all the meta-analysis interviews. Thus, from a research perspective, data collection was much more affordable and allowed the participants to be at the centre of the research process as interviewers, interviewees and desk researchers. In turn, the recordings provided 'materiel' for the website and documentary, accessible, postdigital products and dissemination for the project. As Gemma expressed it: 'We will have an impact if our voices are heard.' So, in thinking of postdigital projects in terms of influencing policy and in terms of the agentic potential, we need to carry through the logic of how we can maximise impact and accessibility in dissemination by imagining and incorporating less narrowly academic channels.

5.2.3   Postdigital Partnership Working

There were partnerships formed at every level of the project – between the two universities, between the universities and the University of Atypical, and a range of voluntary sector groups. In terms of the research agenda and how the research is done – 'to' the research 'subjects' or with people as co-researchers, participants appreciated how the universities had 'reached out'; 'it shows what we can strive for and achieve.'

The project coordinator noted that 'in hindsight, a WhatsApp/Facebook group (after receiving people's consent) could have been useful for participants to engage in an informal and more spontaneous way between sessions'. And it might have been better to have set up a project website from the beginning to familiarise participants with the postdigital 'atmosphere', though this would not have benefited participants engaging face-to-face rather than online. And, had we had more funding, we could have trained all participants in postdigital learning and research, but access to computers could have still been a problem for some. So, perhaps a hybrid form, allowing both postdigital and face-to face is a better model of praxis in recognising the situation of the potential participants.

5.2.4   Future Directions

The project coordinator, Federica, commented:

> I would suggest to dedicate a longer time, at the very beginning, to consult with migrant communities and understand the format that could best work for them, meet with potential participants in person and explain the project better, and also work on a simple and clear explanatory website and video to circulate on social media.

Gemma said she would be keen to work on more projects involving Muslim women and migrant women; the most important thing was to 'be taken seriously by the lawmakers'. Hannah believed the project was important as a way of combating racism. The agentic imperative here is clear (Peters 2021). More opportunities for both postdigital and face-to face intercultural exchange were also recommended by the women, for example, through having more cultural fairs and festivals 'so that migrant people could connect to the wider community', as Hannah put it. A recognition that postdigital approaches were not always condign was implicit in a Serrah's proposal for a project where the two partners would work with older Punjabi women, delivered in person.

Some participants were keen to develop and build on their achievements with another postdigital project. In a similar vein, Helen, living in Canada, commented that she would like to work on a project involving collecting the stories of incomers– funny stories maybe too. She also suggested that such a collection would be useful for new incomers, helping them to recognise some of the same problems.

Sarah-Ann was keen on developing the community of practice; 'a kind of forum or connection point between the women, where they could talk to each other informally when they needed advice or wanted to share new information'. For the Dungannon group, as Maria expressed it, the aim for the future would be to make better known the women's group as a resource for migrant women. Emphasising the agentic dimension (Peters 2021), how the project had given women more understanding and confidence about what was needed practically, suggestions included a guide for newcomers – which could be both postdigital and translated as a booklet. Related to this was a proposal for bringing greater awareness into schools, as Rose, living in Northern Ireland, poignantly noted; 'because when I was assaulted by pupils, there was no awareness'.

Again, postdigital modes could be used or greater deployment of people with lived experience of being a migrant could be deployed as ambassadors within schools. Canadian community facilitator, Marcella, suggested that there needed to be more engagement between formal education and communities. There is a role here for schools, but also for universities in dedicating sustained resources to enable academics to reach out far more proactively with their communities to genuinely fulfil the common mission of the engaged university, as noted earlier and deliver partnership and co-learning and research with marginalised communities.

Canadian facilitator, Huda Bolow, suggested that the organisers ask participants in this and future projects, 'how can I identify what you need and how can I help? Behind this is the importance of continually seeking what is needed rather than presuming and designing grandiose projects which are not benefiting people who are marginalised and oppressed. And, equally, how universities, communities and policy makers connect is key: as, Federica, the project co-ordinator, commented:

> The project output needs to be shared with political stakeholders, to give migrant communities a real opportunity to take part in decision-making processes. Also, the project should be repeated on a yearly basis to create a longer-term perspective of continuity with participants, to secure this safe space where women can continue to share their lived experience and ask stakeholders to act on the project findings, year after year, to reflect a society that is nowadays based on many, many colours.

Marcella argued that there needs to be more engagement between educational institutions and communities to increase the impact on policy. 'We need to ask how we can continue to bring these voices forward.' In relation to enacting such connections, Sarah-Ann proposed a scholarship fund, which could attract funding from major Irish-Canadian Foundations and cultural organisations to support education and opportunities for migrant women. Another practical suggestion from Amy was that educational institutions should offer more assistance with English language and qualifications conversion and bridging courses.

6   Concluding Reflections

At the time of writing, we launched successful exhibitions in each country and the website[1] and documentary are almost complete. We are also seeking funding for other projects to build on the momentum of this project. By documenting and evaluating all along, we created a rich reservoir of material which can be disseminated in democratic postdigital channels and thus become available to others, beyond academia and within it, who want to work in arts-based postdigital co-research. This reflects Lisa's view that 'the research could be replicated because, there are immigrants in every country'.

This project was informed by critical pedagogy enabling the participants to contemplate the meaning of their lived experience, foster mutual understanding, develop shared meaning making and enhance their digital competencies. By sharing their photographs and stories in different ways in postdigital platforms, the participants raised awareness of the complexity of belonging and exclusion as incomers/newcomers. They were able to build skills including collaboration, cross/inter-cultural awareness and felt more empowered to articulate their own experience and develop agency.

The research approach served as a tool to create social solidarity across multiple contexts both locally and internationally. Through the dissemination events in both Northern Ireland and Canada, participants were able to share their photographs and their settlements experiences with policy makers, university leaders, educators, NGOs, and academics. As one distinguished guest, Dr. Mary Gene Saudelli, said at the photo exhibition and dissemination event on 23 September 2022 in Canada: 'This project really speaks to the power of arts-based activism, which is sensory, evocative, and powerful. The exhibit speaks to what should be doing and thinking about today.'

In the research process, the participants, community facilitators and research assistants had input determining the themes, the dissemination process and how to speak to the research findings. The nature of this type of postdigital project required flexibility and adaptability working across cultural differences, digital divides, time zones, Covid-19 restrictions, and different funding bodies' requirements. The shared enthusiasm for the project helped build a sense of community and a commitment to continue to work together as a community of practice to build more inclusive, equitable and democratic spaces. We very much hope that we can build on the work.

---

[1] See https://www.qub.ac.uk/sites/photovoice-project. Accessed 15 December 2022.

References

Aspers, P., & Corte, U. (2019). What is Qualitative in Qualitative Research? *Qualitative Sociology, 42*(2), 139–160. https://doi.org/10.1007/s11133-019-9413-7.

Barone, T., & Eisner, E. W. (2012). *Arts Based Research*. Los Angeles, CA: Sage.

Brigham, S. M., Baillie Abidi, C., & Calatayud, S. (2018). Migrant Women Learning and Teaching Through Participatory Photography. *Canadian Journal for the Study of Adult Education, 30*(2), 101–114.

Bothwell, D. M., & Stewart, P.A. (2020). Knowledge Exchange and Knowing: The Self, Art Practice and the Digital. In M. A. Peters, T. Besley, P. Jandrić, & X. Zhu (Eds.), *Knowledge Socialism: The Rise of Peer Production: Collegiality, Collaboration, and Collective Intelligence* (pp. 277–297). Singapore: Springer. https://doi.org/10.1007/978-981-13-8126-3_14.

Butterwick, S., & Roy, C. (Eds.). (2016). *Working the Margins of Community-based Adult Learning: The Power of Arts-making in Finding Voice and Creating Conditions for Seeing/ Listening*. Rotterdam: Sense.

Freire, P. (1970). *Pedagogy of the Oppressed*. London, UK: Penguin.

Harman, T., & Varga-Dobai, K. (2012). Critical Performative Pedagogy: Emergent Bilingual Learners Challenge Local Immigration Issues. *International Journal of Multicultural Education, 14*(2), 1-17.

Hayes, S., & Jandrić, P. (2021). Postdigital Artistic Positionality and its Potentials for Cultural Education. In J. Ackermann & B. Egger (Eds.), *Transdisziplinäre Begegnungen Zwischen Postdigitaler Kunst und Kultureller Bildung* (pp. 17–28). Wiesbaden: Springer VS. https://doi.org/10.1007/978-3-658-32079-9_2.

Jackson, R. L., Drummond, D. K., & Camara, S. (2007). What is Qualitative Research? *Qualitative Research Reports in Communication, 8*(1), 21-28. https://doi.org/10.1080/17459430701617879.

Jandrić, P. (2020). Postdigital Knowledge Socialism. In M. A. Peters, T. Besley, P. Jandrić, & X. Zhu (Eds.), *Knowledge Socialism: The Rise of Peer Production: Collegiality, Collaboration, and Collective Intelligence* (pp. 81–98). Singapore: Springer. https://doi.org/10.1007/978-981-13-8126-3_5.

Jarldorn, M. (2019). *Photovoice Handbook for Social Workers. Methods, Practicalities, and Possibilities for Social Change*. Cham: Springer International Publishing. https://doi.org/10.1007/978-3-319-94511-8.

Knox, J. (2019). What Does the 'Postdigital' Mean for Education? Three Critical Perspectives on the Digital, with Implications for Educational Research and Practice. *Postdigital Science and Education, 1*(2), 357–370 https://doi.org/10.1007/s42438-019-00045-y.

Lenette, C. (2019). Arts-*based Methods in Refugee Research: Creating Sanctuary*. Singapore: Springer. https://doi.org/10.1007/978-981-13-8008-2.

Maginess, T. (2017a). Crossin' the Bridge: A Participatory Approach to Filmmaking. *New Directions for Adult and Continuing Education, 154*, 39–48. https://doi.org/10.1002/ace.20229.

Maginess, T. (2017b). *Enhancing the Wellbeing and Wisdom of Older Learners: A Co-research Paradigm*. London: Routledge.

Maguire, M., & Delahunt, B. (2017). Doing a Thematic Analysis: A Practical, Step-by-Step Guide for Learning and Teaching Scholars. *All Ireland Journal of Higher Education (AISHE-J), 9*(3), 3351–33514.

McLaren, P. (2020). The Future of Critical Pedagogy. *Educational Philosophy and Theory, 52*(12), 1243–1248. https://doi.org/10.1080/00131857.2019.1686963.

Nagda, B. R. A., Gurin, P., & Lopez, G. E. (2003). Transformative Pedagogy for Democracy and Social Justice. *Race, Ethnicity and Education, 6*(2), 165–191. https://doi.org/10.1080/13613320308199.

Peters, M. A. (2021). Knowledge Socialism: The Rise of Peer Production – Collegiality, Collaboration, and Collective Intelligence. *Educational Philosophy and Theory, 53*(1), 1–9. https://doi.org/10.1080/00131857.2019.1654375.

Sinner, A., Leggo, C., Irwin, R. L., Gouzouasis, P., & Grauer, K. (2006). Arts-based Educational Research Dissertations: Reviewing the Practices of New Scholars. *Canadian Journal of Education, 29*(4), 1223–1270.

Stack, M., & Wang, F. (2018). Students' Perceptions of Belonging: A Photovoice Participatory Action Research Project. *Canadian Journal of Action Research, 19*(1), 48–66. https://doi.org/10.33524/cjar.v19i1.375.

Sullivan, G. (2006). Research Acts in Arts Practice. *Studies in Art Education, 48*(1), 19–35. https://doi.org/10.1080/00393541.2006.11650497.

Tassone, V., O'Mahoney, C., McKenna, E., Eppink, H., & Wals, A. (2018). (Re-)designing higher education curricula in times of systemic dysfunction: a responsible research and innovation perspective. *Higher Education, 76*(2), 337–352. https://doi.org/10.1007/s10734-017-0211-4.

Topolovčan, T. (2016). Art-Based Research of Constructivist Teaching. *Croatian Journal of Education, 18*(4), 1141–1172. https://doi.org/10.15516/cje.v18i4.2074.

United Nations. (2022). The 17 Goals. https://sdgs.un.org/goals. Accessed 1 December 2022.

Wang, Q., Coemans, S., Siegesmund, R., & Hannes, K. (2017). Arts-based Methods in Socially Engaged Research Practice: A Classification Framework. *Art/Research International: A Transdisciplinary Journal, 2*(2), 5–39. https://doi.org/10.18432/R26G8P.

Future Workshops as Postdigital Research Method

Juha Suoranta ⓘ **and Marko Teräs** ⓘ

1 World Gone Mad

After the Second World War, a diverse and unrelated group of social scientists and philosophers noticed that technological advantages did not serve the good life of all people. Quite the reverse. In the 1930s and 1940s, critical theorists of the Frankfurt School described the flipside of modern progress leading to human alienation, loss of agency, and eventual submission to authoritarianism. Thinkers as diverse as Martin Heidegger, Herbert Marcuse, Jacques Ellul, Lewis Mumford, Hannah Arendt – and even Marshall McLuhan – were sceptical of the possibilities of technological 'solutions' to the problems of the post-war world (see Andersson 2018; Feenberg 1999, 2002; Kaiserfeld 2015; Winner 1978). In their view, technology dominated all forms of modern thought and activity.

John Kenneth Galbraith, the leading economist of his time, stated 'that we are becoming the servants in thought, as in action, of the machine we have created to serve us' (1972: 27). The postdigital era faces similar challenges and even more pressing problems with the advancements of digitalization, such as digital surveillance and algorithmic control affecting different areas of life, from military and war to health care, democracy, and education (Aitken 2021; Jandrić 2022; Knox 2019; Lacković 2021; Mirrlees 2009).

Sociologist C. Wright Mills was among the critics of modern industrial technostructure and social engineering. In his 1950s book, *The Power Elite* (2000a), Mills analysed how ordinary people were catapulted into the modern era without the possibility of making up their minds. They had to adapt to the ready-made social conditions and learn to behave as 'cheerful robots'. There was, however, a group that made big decisions and changed the world: the power elite.

J. Suoranta (✉) · M. Teräs
Tampere University, Tampere, Finland
e-mail: juha.suoranta@tuni.fi; marko.teras@tuni.fi

© The Author(s), under exclusive license to Springer Nature   317
Switzerland AG 2023
P. Jandrić et al. (eds.), *Constructing Postdigital Research*, Postdigital Science
and Education, https://doi.org/10.1007/978-3-031-35411-3_16

Many other thinkers thought the idea of a technology-driven future had become hollow. In Andersson's words (2018: 1), the views of the future 'born in an interwar romance with machines, science, and technology had developed into the ideology of totalitarianism, the totalizing nature of which lay precisely in its grasp on the human future'. To these thinkers, the arms industry, the cold war, nuclear threat, atomic science, overpopulation, lonely crowds, computing, famine, and ecological catastrophe were signs of technological determinism that eventually led to the extinction of the human species and the end of the world. The critics were utterly worried about the state of democracy as a method of political governance, deliberation, and a way of life.

German-born Robert Jungk, a pioneer of future studies, and his colleague Norbert Müllert, addressed these problems from the 1960s onward. They wanted to search for solutions to technological modernity's blind alleys and claimed that technologically advanced societies suffer not only information and power privileges but also imaginative and planning privileges (Jungk and Müllert 1987). Like Mills, they thought those privileges were owned and availed of by the influential political and business elite with the help of an expert army. The elite is small in numbers but makes far-reaching decisions for the people's majority.

Therefore, Jungk and Müllert (1987) stressed the essential role of ordinary people's creative imagination in creating a sustainable future democracy. At that time, it was generally believed that, as Andersson (2018: 159) puts it, 'art, phantasy, and imagination could bring about a new 'state of mind' capable of conjuring a different future'. The North American pragmatist John Dewey had already earlier developed these same ideas of living and participatory democracy. His philosophy emphasized democracy as a radical way of life (Putnam and Putnam 2017). In 1939, Dewey stated that democracy is more than a fossilized system or automatic political mechanism. It is 'a way of personal life controlled not merely by faith in human nature in general but by faith in the capacity of human beings for intelligent judgment and action if proper conditions are furnished' (Dewey 1988: 228).

Dewey also pointed out that, fundamentally, democracy 'springs from a living faith in our common human nature and in the power of voluntary action based upon public collective intelligence' (Dewey 1987: 300). In sum, Deweyan idea of democracy is 'a never-ending process where the conditions for democracy have continuously to be exercised and refined' (Bartenberger 2015: 5; see also Eskelinen 2020).

These are the foundations of the democratic belief that we should consider in looking for those research methods and methodologies that respect social scientists' and ordinary people's wit, abilities, and imaginations to provide solutions to small and large-scale social problems.

2   Towards Imaginative Methodologies

Unfortunately, the capitalist university and its neoliberal management have forced many social scientists into the role of reliable producers who deliver education and knowledge, whereas ordinary people have adopted the positions of cheerful consumerists and passive recipients of higher commands. Social scientists feel that the university administration no longer treats them as critical and creative world-makers who contribute to changing the world using their imagination, as Jungk and Müllert (1987) hoped they would. Instead, they feel that they operate only as extensions of a global business elite and the rule of money that emphasizes technical rationality and favors quick research outputs (Back and Puwar 2012b) in the name of global competitiveness in the knowledge economy (Poutanen 2022). In this respect, in the last few decades, universities have not been the best places for using imagination.

Under the circumstances, it has been possible to forget, as Graeber (2010: 47) put it, that the world 'is something that we make, and could just as easily make differently' and by using the human imagination, we can find alternatives to how things are and how to change them. Still, many scholars would like to be ethically engaged, to represent people's lived experiences, and their problems and to make them public issues – to act as public sociologists (Burawoy 2005; Brewer 2013) and follow Mills' (2000a: 6) maxim 'to grasp history and biography and the relations between the two within society'.

Imagination is a human characteristic that even dire social conditions cannot destroy entirely (Graeber 2015). As an individual capacity and collaborative tool to plan and foresee, imagination is necessary for grasping history and biography and their oft-complicated relations. For the social sciences, the original idea for what the imagination is, or can be understood as, came from Marx (1887: 127), who wrote that 'what distinguishes the worst architect from the best of bees is this, that the architect raises his structure in imagination before he erects it in reality'. Naturally, we cannot thoroughly know how bees construct architecture in imagination. Still, we know we can foresight our plans and actions as human beings.

For their part, Jungk and Müllert (1987) argued that imagination is humanity's most untapped energy source. Yet, technological society and educational institutions restrict the scope for imagination and hope and replace them with consumerism. Imagining the future appears reserved for the well-off and well-educated who have access to resources and opportunities to explore their imagination. To ordinary citizens, the elite's technologically managed society seems openly hostile: they are not allowed to use their capacity to imagine and voice their hopes and dreams. Jungk and Müllert aspired to change that with their method of future workshops.

A prominent proponent of imagination's power in the social sciences was C. Wright Mills, who believed that imagination is a quality of mind needed by researchers (Mills 2000a). Along with Mills, many other social theorists and philosophers have applied and developed the concept and the use of imagination (e.g., Appadurai 2000; Bloch 1995; Castoriadis 1987; Eskola 1988; Freire 2005; Fromm 1968; Graeber 2007; Jandrić and McLaren 2020; Mills 2000a, b; Rorty 1999; Stetsenko 2020). There has also been a growing movement in developing imaginative and creative methodologies (see, e.g., Back and Puwar 2012a; Gergen and Gergen 2012; Jacobsen et al. 2016; Elliott and Culhane 2017; Kara 2015; Lackey 1994; Ross 2023).

The common feature in these methodological developments has been a search for new ways to approach changing social reality. The authors have claimed that traditional methods cannot capture the new multiple worlds. Social scientists must reach beyond their disciplinary boundaries and find creative branches of social investigations. In addition, they need to invent methodological practices to replace the old ones. As Gergen puts it,

> in a world of rapid and unpredictable flux, the focus on what is the case has limited potential. The challenge is that of rapidly synthesizing multiple sources of information, and moving improvisationally in a context of ambiguity. Required is a more fully developed account of education as a continuous enrichment in capacities for skillful innovation, not in the service of adaptation, but in terms of bringing about a viable future. (Gergen 2015: 14)

These developments are part of the methodological continuum from Mills and the 1960s critical wildcat sociology. Through various methodological turns such as discursive-linguistic-rhetorical, pragmatic-critical, and participatory-action, the social sciences have entered the current era, which Lincoln and Denzin (2005) describe as fragmented. Lincoln and Denzin also predicted that social scientists would divide into two 'tribes' regarding research methodologies. One tribe will conduct its research with quasi-experimental setups and sophisticated statistical analysis. The other tribe will pursue 'a socially and culturally responsive, communitarian, justice-oriented set of studies' (Lincoln and Denzin 2005: 1123).

In the latter tribe's work, as Alvesson (2013: ix–x) has argued, social critique and critical insights are among the most valuable contributions, 'in particular when problems are deeply embedded in culture, and there are no easy policy or technical fixes'. Therefore, there is a critical edge in justice-oriented social research that calls to 'change the world and to change it in ways that resist injustice while celebrating freedom and full, inclusive, participatory democracy' (Denzin 2017: 9).

As we write this chapter in late 2022, fragmentation seems to be amplified even more. The profit-making, speeded-up competitive university demands fast-track publishing using statistics and mainstreamed publishing standards. On the other hand, there are pockets of methodological resistance, where scholars develop inventive ways to study social reality in its diversity (Denzin and Giardina 2022). In the task of methodological invention, it might be helpful to think as Robert Nisbet, who suggested long ago that social sciences arise from 'precisely the same kinds of creative imagination which are to be found in such areas as music, painting, poetry, the novel, and drama' (Nisbet 1976: 9).

In what follows, we join Lincoln and Denzin's (2005) latter tribe by emphasizing the need to develop new research methods, especially *research collaboration with the people* that fit the experimental postdigital research agenda. In this task, the concepts of sociological and methodological imagination are fundamental. We are convinced that the social scientist of the future will find the real Holy Grail of their work in collaboration with various groups of people. Thus, in collaborative social research, we need to join with those people's experiences, conceptions, and reflections who make and remake everyday postdigital worlds.

In various postdigital practices, e.g., in the digitalization of higher education (Ball and Savin-Baden 2022; Lamb et al. 2022), digitalization can be taken for granted. Higher education management may assume that digital tools are necessary without further inspection, requesting employees' approval, or engaging their experience. Similar to the remarks by Jüngk and Müllert (1987) on the rising wave of information technology, today's technological experts tend to ignore people who use digital technologies. It is as if digitalization would be a wonder cure that somehow works outside people's social milieu or the social construction of their work culture.

Therefore, in what follows, we introduce a method called *Future Workshops* as an appropriate means for imaginative and collaborative social research, or what Paavola and Hakkarainen (2005) have termed 'knowledge-creating learning'. The focus is not on individuals or their interaction but on their collaboration and development of mediating objects and artifacts and generating new ideas and insights. In the latter respect, the method of future workshops shares the aim of democratization of social research (Edwards and Brannelly 2017).

3   Future Workshop, or 'Turning the Affected into the Involved'

In this section, we will introduce the intellectual roots of the future workshops as a postdigital research method that 'can turn the affected into the involved', as the founder of the approach, Robert Jungk, called it (Spielmann n.d.). Jungk introduced the method in *Zukunftswerkstätten* (1981), which he co-authored with Norbert Müllert. A few years later, the book was translated into English as *Future Workshops* (1987).

During his life, Robert Jungk experienced much of the period Eric Hobsbawm (1995) named the Age of Extremes.

> When Hitler came to power Bob Jungk was a nineteen-year-old student in Berlin. Following the Reichstag fire he was arrested for anti-Nazi activities and deprived of his citizenship. With luck and the help of friends he was released, went to the Sorbonne in Paris, but later returned illegally to Germany to work for a subversive press-service. Before long he was forced to flee to Czechoslovakia. The fall of Prague took him to Paris and the fall of Paris to Switzerland. Even here he was again jailed for his outspoken condemnation of the Nazis. After the war he returned to Germany, took a degree at Zurich and travelled widely. (Slaughter 2010)

Jungk's adversities in Nazi Germany taught him to fight against oppression, the arms race, and the use of advanced technology in the arms and nuclear industry. He published books on the dangers of nuclear armament, atomic science, and the possibilities of peace (Jungk 1954, 1958, 1961, 1976, 1979); was active in the international anti-nuclear weapons campaign, and eventually became an icon of the West European peace movement (Nehring 2004; Andersson 2012, 2018). Jungk feared that the US-led military-industrial complex would create a monstrous future dominated by technology, eventually leading to omnicide.

Jungk was not alone in his fear. The political philosopher Hannah Arendt suspected in her 1958 book *The Human Condition* whether technology and 'machines still serve the world and its things, or if, on the contrary, they and the automatic motion of their processes have begun to rule and even destroy the world and things' (Arendt 1998: 151). Andersson summarizes Arendt's thinking as follows:

> This empty future was the starkest sign, to Arendt, of a pervasive crisis of Man. In its magnanimous belief in science and technology, humanity had replaced all eschatological and moral notions with the totalizing idea of constant progress. In such a futuristic world, no future was possible ... humanity existed in a void. This void was a gulf created by two opposing forces: on the one hand, the extension of the reach of instrumentalist human rationality, and on the other, the diminishing moral capacities of human beings to control their actions over time. (Andersson 2018: 1, 30)

Perhaps humanity stood on the brink of an abyss. Nevertheless, Jungk wanted to find a way to activate people to imagine an alternative future for atomic warfare and nuclear catastrophe and found inspiration in two separate sources.

First, for ideas of democratic participation and non-hierarchical and collective decision-making that did not reflect the power elite's repressive and mind-numbing methods, Jungk drew from anarchist socialist groups he had worked with as a filmmaker during the Spanish Civil War. These ideas also included the importance of critique (thus, the method consists of a critical phase). Secondly, Jungk had come across Alex Osborne's work on creative problem-solving. Osborne had invented a well-known brainstorming technique from which Jungk developed another phase for the future workshop, namely the fantasy phase. In this phase, Jungk assumed, it was possible to activate people's intuition and find their synergies and critical potentials to generate alternatives (Vidal 2005: 3).

Jungk thought that future workshops could counter the catastrophic politics of the power elite and the military-industrial complex: 'they would evoke peoples' self-confidence and create a source for the support of citizens' initiatives, actions, and broad involvement in the transformation of society' (Robert-Jungk-Bibliothek für Zukunftsfragen 2022). Jungk had a keen interest in futurology and developed his idea in the radical atmosphere of the 1960s.

The radicalized climate had an impact on futurology which took the form of a humanist critique of modernity and of the existing technological-economic basis of futurology. The critique was based on the social sciences, philosophy, and history, and.

> it contained a strong critique of the prevalent concept of progress and of historicist narratives of change as a linear development over time. Instead, it emphasized the question of choice and change. ... The technologies and methods of futurology, and its bias towards industrial and military interests, were accused of anti-democratic tendencies, technological determinism, and the unproblematized extrapolation of trends from present conditions. Its dystopic elements were said to create self-fulfilling prophecies and feelings of helplessness by presenting the future as a paved road to destruction. (Andersson 2006: 281)

The method of the future workshops belongs to the family of methods that cherishes human imagination, people's togetherness, and the idea of collective world-making. It has a family resemblance with Freirean pedagogy of the oppressed (Freire 2005), participatory action research (Kemmis et al. 2014), C. Wright Mills's critical sociology (Mills 2000a, b), Fromm's sociological and sociopsychological analysis (Fromm 1968, 1994; see also Fuchs 2020), and other critical theorists of the Frankfurt School. It has been used in various academic fields such as adult education and training (Nielsen et al. 1996), peacebuilding (Boulding 1988, 2000), computer science and system design (Kensing and Halskov Madsen 1991; Kensing 1987), future studies (Inayatullah 2013), and youth studies (Alminde and Warming 2020).

The future workshop allows participants to unleash their imagination and create possible future scenarios concerning any area of their life; that is, to construct, in the imagination, a model or blueprint of their lives or some aspect of it. Ideally, it can open eyes to 'the real possibilities we have in this world, but which can only be foreseen by the power of imagination and be carried into effect through action' (Eskola 1988: 256–261).

The future workshops in the 1950s aimed to activate ordinary citizens to critique prevailing societal conditions and to plan suggestions for a desirable future (Jungk and Müllert 1987). Hence, the workshops were about promoting and reviving grassroots democracy, inspiring people for social innovations, and making political initiatives instead of submitting to experts' and politicians' decisions. Jungk and Müllert (1987) meant the future workshops to battle alienation and restore hope and human agency. Furthermore, one of the critical aims was to encourage those who do not have the language to speak about the theme at hand.

> The first documented workshop was held at a music festival in Klagenfurt, and concerned how music could be given a transformative role in capitalist society. From 1968 on, Jungk held workshops with his protesting students in the sit-ins at Freie Universität in Berlin, and Zukunftswerkstätten then became a veritable social movement of their own in Austria and Germany, as Jungk led workshops for employees of large companies, habitants of areas targeted by urban regeneration, hospital patients, etc. From the 1970s on, Jungk clearly thought that he had invented a technology that could solve key problems of participatory democracy and visited not only RAND, but also the research department at IBM in order to tie the future workshop to emerging information communication technologies. (Andersson 2018: 180–181)[1]

Among other early examples are workshops in Nordrhein-Westfalen, Germany, in which some 500 people participated to pursue ideas for the design of human-friendly information and communication technologies (Vidal 2005: 3).

Jungk's thinking highlighted his general care for the future world. Jungk was confident that everyone could contribute to the future's democratization. It was not enough to only leave the world's future to the experts and policymakers; Jungk believed that every person could be part of co-creating the future. Other cornerstones

---

[1] RAND is an American nonprofit global policy think tank created in 1948 by the Douglas Aircraft Company to offer research and analysis to the United States Armed Forces. See https://www.rand.org/. Accessed 22 November 2022.

of democracy were social criticism and public debate; only they could guarantee a healthy social environment for all and formation of lively togetherness (Spielmann n.d.).

Jungk criticized the power of the scientific and military complex and its technological utopias, particularly in nuclear- and biotechnology. In his evaluation, they limit people's self-determination and cause a significant threat to the future of humankind and the planet. Therefore, independent media, scientific research, and well-informed citizens should offer countermeasures. They should control technological apparatus and contribute to serving the interests of the powerless and the oppressed (Spielmann n.d.).

Jungk was also committed to saving the Earth as a living planet. He believed that the solution was not technological but social. People needed places to use their social imagination and creativity to develop sustainable living conditions. New informal and social cooperation methods in living, culture, work and leisure should develop and improve in dialogues and Future Workshops. Artists had a unique role in these creative processes, but Jungk thought every adult possessed creative potential. The future workshops were a method to awaken this potential (Spielmann n.d.).

The method of future workshops combines people's creativity with future research for emancipatory aims. The method connects to futurology, which already lends a specific ethical stance to it, i.e., the purpose of removing war, hunger, and exploitation of humans and nature from the world. The basic argument is that the future is not a prediction question but of making. Therefore, future workshops are also about inducing hope and are part of utopian objectives and methods (e.g., Bloch 1995; Levitas 2013).

Jungk and Müllert (1987) summarize the main problem with experts' visioning of the future: projects that concern people's future do not engage people in the actual planning of their future. Still, people are told about their future when the plans are already underway, or experts can hear them. Information technologies are a case in point. They appear in organizations like ghost ships from the fog, without one or only a few knowing where they come from and why. Still, people have to deal with them and submit to their use.

As Jungk and Müllert (1987) write, the people affected by these decisions are usually only involved after politicians have already made the decision and when it is too late to affect the course of action or invent alternatives. The majority's role is to react to reforms and innovations, but they are not part of preparing them. As such, what was just one possibility yesterday, is a necessity today. Therefore, those excluded from initial planning processes must develop futures that can compete with or at least contrast the dominant future visions.

4   The Method of Future Workshop

In its basic form, the future workshop has four phases (Jungk and Müllert 1987; Kensing and Halskov Madsen 1991; Lauttamäki 2014): *preparation, critique, fantasy,* and *implementation.* The object of future workshops is usually a shared question or a problem. However, no one should decide on the theme in advance, for it is the participants' task to discuss and choose it. The world is increasingly global, and those forces affect local contexts. Still, future workshops are usually used 'by local groups to deal with local problems and find alternative solutions to the one proposed by the establishment' (Vidal 2005). These are more concrete and can set free social imagination to develop alternative local futures.

The preparation phase introduces the workshop method and its rules. During the preparation phase, participants decide on the theme and prepare the workshop space with tools such as pens, paper, pinboards, and flip charts to draft and jot down ideas. Tables that separate the participants from one another are put aside so that the participants will sit in an open circle to interact and use the pinboards comfortably (Apel 2004).

The critique phase introduces the problem and the problematic aspects of the theme, which participants then criticize. If the group is large, they can form smaller groups to brainstorm their ideas, then come together, write all the criticism down, and organize it into topics or clusters. In the group work, one rule applies, according to Apel:

> no excessive discussions, associative linking to ideas already existent, no 'killer phrases,' quantity has priority (collecting), etc. … Occasionally, it is also useful to intensify the collection of critique points in a second phase. Here, a change of method is possible, so that also a reflective discussion can be performed, but as well with the obligation to visualize the results in the end. (Apel 2004)

The fantasy phase directs the participants to respond to the critique with their hopes, dreams, and alternative ideas (of the future). Jungk and Müllert (1987) write about the hindrances of imagining the future, which could be summarized as the 'totalitarianism of facts'. It means that, too often, the establishment – 'the captains of destiny' – convinces people that the chosen political decisions are based on facts and 'reality' and that there are no alternatives. Thus, it is essential in social research to check these 'facts' provided by the all-mighty and powerful, reveal their ideological biases, and search for alternatives.

The first lesson in the critical path is to realize that elite does not seek the common good but, through its mythmaking, tries to guarantee its privileges (Freire 2002). Thus, as Chomsky (2011: 107–108) advises, social scientists and intellectuals need 'to join with the kind of people who are willing to commit themselves to overthrow power, and listen to them. They often know more than we do'. At the same time, it is necessary not to mix authentic, just, and humane alternatives to change the world for the better (or proven facts) with so-called alternative facts, fake news, or outright lies (MacKenzie and Bhatt 2020).

In the fantasy phase, the participants should not be tied down by 'obvious facts' but should draw from their frustrations and experience. They should try to think the impossible and leave their assumptions behind, to be curious, wild, and responsive to the unknown. The aim is to ask, e.g., 'what if the workplace could be organized differently?' (Kensing and Halskov Madsen 1991: 157), despite the 'known' and 'existing' reality. After drafting the ideas, the participants will select the most exciting ones and formulate them as suggestions for further development.

Participants should be as relaxed as possible, 'free from inherent necessities and may use brainstorming techniques and creative games to find and reflect utopian solutions' (Apel 2004). Ideally, the way they present their findings (fantasies) should differ from rationally oriented problem-solving:

> All ideas are collected and put into an 'idea store,' regardless of their practicability. In a second step (which can also be performed later in the implementation phase), all those ideas have to be 'transformed', that is, they must be reduced to a practical and realizable core. According to Robert Jungk, the social fantasy of the participants is developed in this phase. Or, to be more pragmatic, it is the point to alienate a problem solution and to present it in 'false,' 'untypical' and not strictly rational forms and/or texts like, e.g., painting, role plays, sketches, reports, and so on. This has a creativity-promoting effect, because here, in a very relaxed atmosphere, far away from the stress of everyday life and profession, expression forms can be found, and things and ideas may outcrop which could possibly not be figured out by using a direct and 'rational' approach. (Apel 2004)

Finally, participants return to the present social order and its power relations and structures in the implementation phase to critically determine possible obstacles and required actions for the desired future. At this phase, each group presents their 'utopia' and, if possible, more detailed plans. If the previous phases emphasize the free play of fancy and not holding back ideas, the implementation phase requires the participants to evaluate the practicality of their ideas (Apel 2004).

Future workshops is not necessarily an easy method to use. There may be practical problems, such as people's willingness to participate in a future workshop. If they do participate, it can be challenging to get them to speak and voice their views in the first place (Jungk and Müllert 1987). The method is also rather time-consuming, and people's unwillingness to participate can be due to the pressures in the work-life or everyday life's overall rush.

Those participating may feel that the method needs to be simplified and cannot imagine alternatives (see Markham 2021). They can suffer from a lack of imagination and feel helpless. This was the case in Markham's participatory intervention, in which she noticed that even though people could develop a critical stand towards digital platforms, they could not imagine alternatives. It was as if they felt that certain developments were inevitable (Markham 2021: 382). However, imagining can be re-engaged. People only 'have to be encouraged to image, taught to exercise a capacity they are unaccustomed to using in a disciplined way' (Boulding 1988: 21).

5   Conclusion

Social scientists' task is to use their social imaginations and invent new social imaginaries of the postdigital with others. The concept of postdigital is far from clear (Jandrić et al. 2018). Still, as such, it provides a fruitful opportunity for scholars to use their creative imagination for methodological experimentation. As 'postdigital theory understands knowledge as socially constructed, contextual, always in flux' (Jandrić 2022: 204), it offers a conceptual platform for scholars to switch from what is to what is not yet, but what could be. Our aim 'is not to keep a mirror in front of people's faces and show them how they look, but to explore ideas and thinking' (Eskola 1984: 29). Alternatively, in Gergen's (2015: 294) words, '[t]he aim of research would not be to illuminate *what is*, but to create *what is to become*. Herein lies the essence of a future forming orientation to research' (emphasis from the original).

Future forming research aims to explore ideas, think, and act with people. Furthermore, it is to invent practical research methods that researchers and people can use to bring up their personal and communal problems, connect them with more significant structural and sociopolitical issues, and find solutions. Collaborative methodological work can lead to what Gergen (1973) has called *enlightenment effects:* through collaborative research processes, people learn to 'read' the world and act in the world in fresh ways. Social scientists cannot leave the university, or any other social institution, in the hands of elites and bureaucrats and follow their (neoliberal) orders simply because it would be stupid and even lethal to the world. As Graeber aptly puts it:

> At a moment when the capitalists' collective refusal to even consider rethinking any of their basic assumptions about the world might well mean not just the death of capitalism, but of almost everything else, our only real choice is do it ourselves – to begin to create a new language, a new common sense, about what people basically are and what it is reasonable for them to expect from the world, and from each other. A case could well be made that the fate of the world depends on it. (Graeber 2010: 10)

At best, social scientists can serve as *curators* and *inventors* of the lived experience and not-yet-lived worlds, searching for alternatives with interest groups. One way to do this is to invent new imaginative research methods which, in the spirit of Jungk, Müllert and C. Wright Mills, nurture social scientists and the general public's imagination and allow them to outline alternatives to the current mindset, politics, and practices.

As we have outlined, the future workshop belongs to the methodological family of collaborative methods. It fulfils at least the following aspects of future-transforming research methods: it permits 'real-time' and 'live' investigation, develops participants' capacities to see the whole without a totalizing perspective, produces thinking and action, and affects and reactions that re-invent our relations to the social and environmental spheres, and engages 'political and ethical issues without arrogance or the drum roll of political piety' (Back and Puwar 2012b).

The future workshop is a research method and a pedagogical technique based on radical democracy; everyone's equal access to participation aims for the emancipation of all, social innovations, and social transformations. The method of future workshops is a systematic attempt to restore peoples' small margin of freedom and to build proper conditions for creative democracy, which is disobedient to the tyranny of the markets, authoritarian regimes, and technological determinism. It is the one Jungk and Müllert, Hannah Arendt, C. Wright Mills, John Dewey, and many others before and after them have long sought.

References

Aitken, G. A. (2021). Postdigital Exploration of Online Postgraduate Learning in Healthcare Professionals: A Horizontal Conception. *Postdigital Science and Education, 3*(1), 181–197. https://doi.org/10.1007/s42438-020-00103-w.

Alminde, S., & Warming, H. (2020). Future workshops as a means to democratic, inclusive and empowering research with children, young people and others. *Qualitative Research, 20*(4), 432–448. https://doi.org/10.1177/1468794119863165.

Alvesson, M. (2013). *The Triumph of Emptiness*. Oxford: Oxford University Press.

Andersson, J. (2006). Choosing Futures: Alva Myrdal and the Construction of Swedish Futures Studies, 1967–1972. *International Review of Social History, 51*(2), 277–295.

Andersson, J. (2012). The Great Future Debate and the Struggle for the World. *American Historical Review, 5*(117), 1411–1430. https://doi.org/10.1093/ahr/117.5.1411.

Andersson, J. (2018). *The Future of the World. Futurology, Futurists, and the Struggle for the Post-Cold War Imagination*. Oxford: Oxford University Press.

Apel, H. (2004). The Future Workshop. Bonn: Deutschen Instituts für Erwachsenenbildung. http://www.die-bonn.de/esprid/dokumente/doc-2004/apel04_02.pdf. Accessed 22 November 2022.

Appadurai, A. (2000). Grassroots Globalization and the Research Imagination. *Public Culture 1*(12), 1–19. https://doi.org/10.1215/08992363-12-1-1.

Arendt, H. (1998). *The Human Condition*. Chicago, IL and London, UK: The University of Chicago Press.

Back, L., & Puwar, N. (2012a). *Live Methods*. Cambridge: Wiley-Blackwell.

Back, L., & Puwar, N. (2012b). A Manifesto for Live Methods: Provocations and Capacities. *The Sociological Review, 60*(S1), 6–17. https://doi.org/10.1111/j.1467-954X.2012.02114.x.

Ball, J., & Savin-Baden, M. (2022). Postdigital Learning for a Changing Higher Education. *Postdigital Science and Education, 4*(3), 753–771. https://doi.org/10.1007/s42438-022-00307-2.

Bartenberger, M. (2015). John Dewey and David Graeber. Elements of Radical Democracy in Pragmatist and Anarchist Thinking. *Politix, 37*, 49. https://doi.org/10.2139/ssrn.2408571.

Bloch, E. (1995). *The Principle of Hope*. Cambridge, MA: The MIT Press.

Boulding, E. (1988). Image and Action in Peace Building. *Journal of Social Issues, 44*(2), 17–37. https://doi.org/10.1111/j.1540-4560.1988.tb02061.x.

Boulding, E. (2000). Designing Future Workshops as a Tool for Peacebuilding. In L. Reychler & T. Paffenholz (Eds.), *Peacebuilding. A Field Guide*. Boulder, CO: Lynne Rienner.

Brewer, J. (2013). *The Public Value of the Social Sciences*. London: Bloomsbury.

Burawoy, M. (2005). For Public Sociology. *American Sociological Review, 70*, 4–28. https://doi.org/10.1177/000312240507000102.

Castoriadis, C. (1987). *The Imaginary Institution of Society*. Cambridge: Polity Press.

Chomsky, N. (2011). *Power and Terror. Conflict, Hegemony, and the Rule of Force*. Boulder, CO and London, UK: Paradigm. Publishers.

Denzin, N. (2017). Critical Qualitative Inquiry. *Qualitative Inquiry, 23*(1), 8–16. https://doi.org/10.1177/1077800416681864.

Denzin, N., & Giardina, M. (Eds.). (2022). *Transformative Visions for Qualitative Inquiry*. New York and London: Routledge.

Dewey, J. (1987). Democracy is Radical. In *The Collected Works of John Dewey, 1882-1953. (2nd Release). Electronic Edition. The Later Works of John Dewey, 1925-1953. Volume 11: 1935-1937, Essays, Liberalism and Social Action*. Carbondale and Edwardsville, IL: Southern Illinois University Press.

Dewey, J. (1988). Creative Democracy – the Task Before Us. In *The Collected Works of John Dewey, 1882-1953. (2nd Release). Electronic Edition. The Later Works of John Dewey, volume 14*: 1939-1941, Essays. Carbondale and Edwardsville, IL: Southern Illinois University Press.

Edwards, R., & Brannelly, T. (2017). Approaches to democratising qualitative research methods. *Qualitative Research, 17*(3), 271–277. https://doi.org/10.1177/1468794117706869.

Elliott, D., & Culhane, D. (2017) (Eds.). *A Different Kind of Ethnography. Imaginative Practices and Creative Methodologies*. Toronto: Toronto University Press.

Eskelinen, T. (Ed.). (2020). *The Revival of Political Imagination: Utopia as Methodology*. London: Zed Books.

Eskola, A. (1984). *Uhka, toivo ja vastarinta* [Risk, hope and resistance]. Helsinki: Kirjayhtymä.

Eskola, A. (1988). *Blind Alleys in Social Psychology*. Amsterdam: North-Holland.

Feenberg, A. (1999). *Questioning Technology*. London and New York: Routledge.

Feenberg, A. (2002). *Transforming Technology*. Oxford: Oxford University Press.

Freire, P. (2002). *Education for Critical Consciousness*. New York: Continuum.

Freire, P. (2005). *Pedagogy of the Oppressed*. New York: Bloomsbury.

Fromm, E. (1968). *The Revolution of Hope: Toward a Humanized Technology*. New York: Harper and Row.

Fromm, E. (1994). *Escape from Freedom*. New York: Henry Holt.

Fuchs, C. (2020). Erich Fromm and the Critical Theory of Communication. *Humanity & Society*, *44*(3), 298–325. https://doi.org/10.1177/0160597620930157.

Galbraith, J. K. (1972). *The New Industrial State*. London: Penguin.

Gergen, K. (1973). Social Psychology as History. *Journal of Personality and Social Psychology*, *26*(2), 309–320. https://doi.org/10.1037/h0034436.

Gergen, K. (2015). From Mirroring to World-Making: Research as Future Forming. *Journal for the Theory of Social Behaviour*, *45*(3), 287–310. https://doi.org/10.1111/jtsb.12075.

Gergen, M., & Gergen, K. (2012). *Playing with Purpose. Adventures in Performative Social Science*. London and New York: Routledge.

Graeber, D. (2007). *Possibilities. Essays on Hierarchy, Rebellion, and Desire*. Oakland, CA: AK Press.

Graeber, D. (2010). *Revolution in Reverse*. Brooklyn, NY: Minor Compositions.

Graeber, D. (2015). *The Utopia of Rules*. London: Melville House.

Hobsbawm, E. (1995). *The Age of Extremes. The Short Twentieth Century*. London: Abacus.

Inayatullah, S. (2013). Learnings From Futures Studies: Learnings From Dator. *Journal of Futures Studies, 18*(2), 1–10.

Jacobsen, M., Drake, M., & Petersen, A. (Eds.). (2016). *Imaginative Methodologies in the Social Sciences. Creativity, Poetics, and Rhetoric in Social Research*. Abingdon and New York: Routledge.

Jandrić, P. (2022). Postdigital Warfare: A Plea for Dialogue. *Postdigital Science and Education, 4*(1), 201–206. https://doi.org/10.1007/s42438-022-00301-8.

Jandrić, P., & McLaren, P. (2020). Postdigital Cross Border Reflections on Critical Utopia. *Educational Philosophy and Theory, 52*(4), 1470–1482. https://doi.org/10.1080/00131857.2020.1731687.

Jandrić, P., Knox, J., Besley, T., Ryberg, T., Suoranta, J., & Hayes, S. (2018). Postdigital science and education. *Educational Philosophy and Theory, 50*(10), 893–899. https://doi.org/10.1080/00131857.2018.1454000.

Jungk, R. (1954). *Tomorrow is Already Here: Scenes from a Man-Made World*. London: Rupert Hart-Davis.

Jungk, R. (1958). *Brighter than a Thousand Suns*. New York: Harcourt Brace.

Jungk, R. (1961). *Children of the Ashes*. New York: Harcourt, Brace and World.

Jungk, R. (1976). *The Everyman Project*. London: Thames and Hudson.

Jungk, R. (1979). *The New Tyranny*. New York: Warner.

Jungk, R., & Müllert, N. (1981). *Zukunftswerkstätten*. München: Heyne.

Jungk, R., & Müllert, N. (1987). *Future workshops: How to create desirable futures*. London: Institute for Social Inventions.

Kaiserfeld, T. (2015). *Beyond Innovation: Technology, Institution and Change as Categories for Social Analysis*. London: Palgrave Pivot. https://doi.org/10.1057/9781137547125.

Kara, H. (2015). *Creative Research Methods in the Social Sciences: A Practical Guide*. Bristol: Bristol University Press.

Kemmis, S., McTaggart, R., & Nixon, R. (2014). *The Action Research Planner. Doing Critical ParticipatoryActionResearch.* Singapore: Springer. https://doi.org/10.1007/978-981-4560-67-2.

Kensing, F. (1987). Generation of visions in systems development. In P. Docherty, K. Fuchs-Kittowski, P. Kolm, & L. Mathiassen (Eds.), *Systems design for human and productivityParticipation and beyond* (pp. 285-301). Amsterdam: North-Holland.

Kensing, F., & Halskov Madsen, K. (1991). Generating Visions: Future Workshops and Metaphorical Design. In J. Greenbaum & M. Kyng (Eds.), *Design at Work* (pp. 155–168). Boca Raton, FL: CRC Press.

Knox, J. (2019). What Does the 'Postdigital' Mean for Education? Three Critical Perspectives on the Digital, with Implications for Educational Research and Practice. *Postdigital Science and Education, 1*(2), 357–370. https://doi.org/10.1007/s42438-019-00045-y.

Lackey, C. (1994). Social Science Fiction: Writing Sociological Short Stories to Learn about Social Issues. *Teaching Sociology, 22*(2), 166. https://doi.org/10.2307/1318562.

Lacković, N. (2021). Postdigital Living and Algorithms of Desire. *Postdigital Science and Education, 3*(2), 280–282. https://doi.org/10.1007/s42438-020-00141-4.

Lamb, J., Carvalho, L., Gallagher, M., & Knox, J. (2022). The Postdigital Learning Spaces of Higher Education. *Postdigital Science and Education, 4*(1), 1–12. https://doi.org/10.1007/s42438-021-00279-9.

Lauttamäki, V. (2014). Practical guide for facilitating a futures workshop. Turku: Finland Futures Research Centre. https://www.utu.fi/sites/default/files/public://media/file/Ville-Lauttamaki_futures-workshops.pdf. Accessed 22 November 2022.

Levitas, R. (2013). *Utopia as Method: The Imaginary Reconstitution of Society.* London: Palgrave. https://doi.org/10.1057/9781137314253.

Lincoln, Y., & Denzin, N. (2005). Epilogue. The Eight and Ninth Moments–Qualitative Research in/and the Fractured Future. In N. Denzin & Y. Lincoln (Eds.), *The Sage Handbook of Qualitative Research.* 3rd Ed. (pp. 1115–1126). Thousand Oaks; CA: Sage.

MacKenzie, A., & Bhatt, I. (2020). Opposing the Power of Lies, Bullshit and Fake News: The Value of Truth. *Postdigital Science and Education, 2*(1), 217–232. https://doi.org/10.1007/s42438-019-00087-2.

Marx, K. (1887). *Capital. A Critique of Political Economy Volume I.* https://www.marxists.org/archive/marx/works/download/pdf/Capital-Volume-I.pdf. Accessed 27 September 2021.

Markham, A. (2021). The limits of the imaginary: Challenges to intervening in future speculations of memory, data, and algorithms. *New Media & Society, 23*(2), 382–405. https://doi.org/10.1177/1461444820929322.

Mills, C. W. (2000a). *Sociological Imagination.* Oxford: Oxford University Press.

Mills, C. W. (2000b). *The Power Elite.* Oxford: Oxford University Press

Mirrlees, T. (2009). Digital Militainment by Design: producing and playing SOCOM: U.S. Navy SEALs. *International Journal of Media and Cultural Politics, 5*(3), 161–181. https://doi.org/10.1386/macp.5.3.161_1.

Nehring, H. (2004). Cold War, Apocalypse and Peaceful Atoms. Interpretations of Nuclear Energy in the British and West German Anti-Nuclear Weapons Movements, 1955–1964. *Historical Social Research / Historische Sozialforschung, 29*(3), 150-170. https://doi.org/10.12759/hsr.29.2004.3.150-170.

Nielsen, B., Nielsen, K., & Olsén, P. (1996). 'Industry and Happiness.' Social Imagination as the Basis of Democratic Innovation Society. In H. Olesen & P. Rasmussen (Eds.), *Theoretical Issues in Adult Education* (pp. 41–64). Roskilde: Roskilde University Press.

Nisbet, R. (1976). *Sociology as an Art Form.* London: Oxford University Press.

Paavola, S., & Hakkarainen, K. (2005). The Knowledge Creation Metaphor – An Emergent Epistemological Approach to Learning. *Science & Education, 14,* 535–557. https://doi.org/10.1007/s11191-004-5157-0.

Poutanen, M. (2022). Competitive knowledge-economies driving new logics in higher education – reflections from a Finnish university merger. *Critical Policy Studies.* https://doi.org/10.1080/19460171.2022.2124429.

Putnam, H., & Putnam, R. (2017). *Pragmatism as a Way of Life. The Lasting Legacy of William James and John Dewey*. Cambridge, MA and London, UK: Harvard University Press.

Robert-Jungk-Bibliothek für Zukunftsfragen. (2022). Salzburg: Robert-Jungk-Bibliothek für Zukunftsfragen. https://jungk-bibliothek.org/future-workshops/. Accessed 22 November 2022.

Rorty, R. (1999). *Philosophy and Social Hope*. London: Penguin Books.

Ross, J. (2023). *Digital Futures for Learning: Speculative Methods and Pedagogies*. New York: Routledge. https://doi.org/10.4324/9781003202134.

Slaughter, R. (2010). Robert Jungk: one man revolution. https://foresightinternational.com.au/wp-content/uploads/2015/04/RJ_One_Man_Revolution_1992.pdf. Accessed 10 November 2022.

Spielmann, W. (n.d.). Some Key Theses of Robert Jungk's Work. https://jungk-bibliothek.org/some-key-theses-of-robert-jungks-work/. Accessed 23 September 2022.

Stetsenko, A. (2020). Hope, political imagination, and agency in Marxism and beyond: Explicating the transformative worldview and ethico-ontoepistemology. *Educational Philosophy and Theory, 52*(7), 726–737. https://doi.org/10.1080/00131857.2019.1654373.

Vidal, R. (2005). The Future Workshop: Democratic problem-solving. Informatics and Mathematical Modelling. Lyngby: Technical University of Denmark. http://www2.imm.dtu.dk/pubdb/edoc/imm4095.pdf. Accessed 10 November 2022.

Winner, L. (1978). *Autonomous Technology. Technics-out-of-Control as a Theme in Political Thought*. Cambridge, MA: MIT Press.

Understanding Digital Inequality: A Theoretical Kaleidoscope

Caroline Kuhn ⓘ, Su-Ming Khoo ⓘ, Laura Czerniewicz ⓘ, Warren Lilley ⓘ,
Swati Bute, Aisling Crean, Sandra Abegglen ⓘ, Tom Burns ⓘ,
Sandra Sinfield ⓘ, Petar Jandrić ⓘ, Jeremy Knox ⓘ,
and Alison MacKenzie ⓘ

1 Introduction

Internet and Information and Communication Technologies (ICTs) have become ubiquitous in workplaces and homes, through either their visible existence or their invisible impact. The widespread existence of ICTs has given rise to what Castells (2001) and others (e.g. Van Dijk 2001: 3) call the network society: 'an information society with a nervous system of social and media networks shaping its prime modes of organisation and more important structures'. For the human body, a

Republished Chapter

The last chapter in Constructing Postdigital Research: Method and Emancipation was originally published as: Kuhn, C., Khoo, S.-M., Czerniewicz, L., Lilley, W., Bute, S., Crean, A., Abegglen, S., Burns, T., Sinfield, S., Jandrić, P., Knox, J., & MacKenzie, A. (2023). Understanding Digital Inequality: A Theoretical Kaleidoscope. Postdigital Science and Education. https://doi.org/10.1007/s42438-023-00395-8. We are grateful to Springer publishers for the permission to republish.

C. Kuhn (✉)
Bath Spa University, Bath, UK
e-mail: c.kuhn@bathspa.ac.uk

S.-M. Khoo
National University Ireland Galway, Galway, Ireland
e-mail: suming.khoo@universityofgalway.ie

L. Czerniewicz · W. Lilley
University of Cape Town, Cape Town, South Africa
e-mail: laura.czerniewicz@uct.ac.za; Warren.Lilley@uct.ac.za

S. Bute
Jagran Lakecity University, Bhopal, India

A. Crean
University of St. Andrews, St. Andrews, Scotland, UK
e-mail: apc2@st-andrews.ac.uk

P. Jandrić et al. (eds.), *Constructing Postdigital Research*, Postdigital Science
and Education, https://doi.org/10.1007/978-3-031-35411-3_17

healthy nervous system is critical for a fully functional life. Similarly, access to this 'nervous system' of social and media networks is paramount for individuals to be fully able to participate in the different realms of this networked society.

Unfortunately, it became evident during the Covid-19 pandemic how precarious the nervous system of the networked society is as more than a third of all students globally were unable to access education, detrimentally affecting their present and future life (UNESCO 2021; Jandrić et al. 2021) and further reinforcing already well-known historical inequalities. Researchers recognised this reality early on, as a review of teaching and learning research during the first year of the pandemic found that inequality was a key focus of research interest (Stewart 2021).

1.1 Why Does Digital Inequality Matter?

High levels of inequality negatively affect society as a whole, not just the less advantaged. More unequal societies have higher crime rates, weaker property rights, skewed access to social services, less influence on decision-makers, and slower transitions to democracy (Helsper 2021; Wilkinson and Pickett 2009). Individuals can only flourish if all other individuals are doing so. Thus, finding ways to address and alleviate the stark and ever-increasing digital inequality that, although not new, has been crudely exposed during the pandemic is vital to us all. What has been clear from multiple studies is that the links between technology and inequality are highly complex and multifaceted (Eynon 2022: 1); one could even argue, super complex (Barnett 2000a, b; Abegglen et al. 2020a).

Experiences and effects are diverse, multiple, and often contrasting, with frames of reference intersected by uncertainty, unpredictability, and fragility. Thus, we need to discuss not just the technology itself but the practices surrounding its use for teaching and learning. This includes taking a critical stance and questioning the structures and processes that facilitate/constrain students' and educators' ability to

S. Abegglen
University of Calgary, Calgary, Canada
e-mail: sandra.abegglen@ucalgary.ca

T. Burns · S. Sinfield
London Metropolitan University, London, UK
e-mail: t.burns@londonmet.ac.uk; s.sinfield@londonmet.ac.uk

P. Jandrić
Department of Informatics and Computing, Zagreb University of Applied Sciences, Zagreb, Croatia
e-mail: pjandric@tvz.hr

J. Knox
Moray House School of Education and Sport, University of Edinburgh, Edinburgh, UK
e-mail: jeremy.knox@ed.ac.uk

A. MacKenzie
SSESW, Queen's University Belfast, Belfast, UK
e-mail: a.mackenzie@qub.ac.uk

participate and take action. As Barnett (2000a, b) argues, the main pedagogical task of a university is not to transmit knowledge but to develop students' attributes appropriate to the conditions of supercomplexity, and we add, to the conditions of the postdigital (Jandrić et al. 2018), which is to treat digital and human social life as fundamentally intertwined.

Historically, the supercomplex nature of digital inequality has been underplayed and under-theorised. Traditional accounts of digital inequality have centred on the lack of access to ICTs, framing the discussion in terms of the 'haves' and 'have-nots' (see Light 2001; van Dijk 1999, 2006; DiMaggio and Hargittai 2001), and have also concentrated on the technology as such, emphasising these devices as neutral within the contexts they are placed, overlooking the fact that they are impacted by greater socio-cultural constraints and users' agency, as well as new articulations of uneven power relations.

In relation to the postdigital condition, it is important to note that the prefix 'post' has nothing to do with the digital being over, but that the digital has progressed from a discrete point of departure to an ongoing condition, a way of life everyone is part of, even the disconnected, who unknowingly contribute digital data to socio-technical infrastructures. Cramer (2015) believes, as we do, that the postdigital means that new power structures become less evident, but not less insidious as they continue to govern such socio-technical infrastructures as well as geopolitics, and markets. For this reason, it is vital to find tools that allow us to shed light on such invisible and pervasive power structures and the consequences of their exercise in the daily lives of so many.

Currently, governments, organisations, and individuals are wrestling with what digital inequality means in an increasingly digitalised, postdigital, and post-pandemic world and how they can confront it. Unfortunately, interventions guided by simplistic, uncritical, and apolitical accounts of digital inequality are more likely to entrench inequality than find pathways for equitable transformation, especially in education (see Lilley 2022).

1.2   Why Different Theories to Understand Digital Inequalities?

Our starting point is that digital inequality is a complex phenomenon and that different theoretical approaches may help to diagnose different aspects of what is wrong and why. If an injustice is misdiagnosed, it can lead to strategies which may not only be ineffective, but potentially create further injustices. Guided by Lewin's maxim that nothing is as practical as a good theory (McCain 2016), we believe it is important to elucidate what different approaches can be offered, which might be helpful to answer particular questions to address particular injustices but not others. Given that digital inequality is a supercomplex social phenomenon, stratified, and multidetermined, it is our contention that different ways of theorising can clarify a greater range of structural solutions to the social problem of inequities.

2 A Theoretical Kaleidoscope

We use the metaphor of a kaleidoscope to describe the need for different theories, or sometimes, the intersection of multiple theories, to unpack and understand the complexity of digital inequality. When discussing the relationship between theory and research, 'theoretical lenses' are posited to help showcase how a particular theory provides specific concepts when examining any social phenomenon. Kaleidoscopes are different. This optical instrument uses two or more mirrors/lenses, angled at particular points, which, when rotated, allow the viewer to see an increasing array of complex patterns that would be hard to see with our naked eye. It is important to note that with each modest turn of the kaleidoscope, the image shifts slightly, offering a different perspective, colour, or intricacy. The kaleidoscopic image is shaped by the number of mirrors in the kaleidoscope.

The mirrors in the kaleidoscope represent the theories chosen by the researcher depending on her/his/their needs. While all the theories centre on the importance of recognising digital inequality as a supercomplex phenomenon, each view is angled at a distinct point, highlighting specific patterns or features for the researcher to discern. Just like a kaleidoscope, as the reader turns to a new theory or the intersection of many, we aim to support them to appreciate and understand the nuanced nature of digital inequality that the theory or the intersection of them unveils as well as its relationship to previously discussed theories. In short, what the kaleidoscope does is serve as an analytical tool to examine, critique, and understand different dimensions of digital inequality and in so doing, we hope that a variety of alternatives and novel solutions can be found to address the insidious consequences of digital inequalities.

For example, Eynon (2022) points out that in academic research, the relationships between individual Internet use and social opportunities are typically understood within the classic sociological problem of structure versus agency, pointing out that digital inclusion scholars have tended to privilege either structure or agency. When structure and agency are conflated, problems can seem circular and difficult to break open and understand. Similar to other work in this domain, it is clear that outcomes of Internet use should not only be understood as the product of access and skills, but it is crucial to attend to socio-cultural structural conditions (Eynon 2022).

Therefore, using a social theory that allows us to study the interplay of structure and agency (e.g. see the 'Critical Realism and Realist Social Theory' section) rather than conflating both or privileging one over the other will be useful to acknowledge the importance of both people's actions–agency–and the role of social structure in constraining or enabling those actions. Other theories will focus more on the person in all their humanity–their strengths, frailties, hopes, and fears. For example, critical pedagogical theories can be used to look into more human dimensions of the phenomenon. They can, amongst other things, help develop an emancipatory 'sociological imagination' (Mills 2000).

2.1 Why a Collaborative Piece?

Collective writing aims to organise diversity rather than replicate uniformity (Peters et al. 2021). Coming together to write seemed a positive, constructive way to approach digital inequality. Our conversation as a group of authors began in an international online event on digital inequality, followed by our mutual explanations regarding which theories we had each found useful in our own research and why. Through our shared experiences, it became obvious that inequality can be explored in different ways using different lenses, each with advantages and limitations. The joint unravelling of the complex nature of digital inequality created an energy, a collective generativity, of doing something together that was multifaceted.

Collaborative writing is a form of 'resistance' in itself. Greene (2007) considers it an approach that is sometimes deemed countercultural since the academic norm, particularly in the humanities, is the lone scholar, and the 'gold standard' writing product is the single-authored monograph. Collaborative writing has particular pragmatics and ethics: as a 'coming together', as an observational tool (Magnusson 2021), and as a method of inquiry (Gale and Bowstead 2013), pushing us towards a different understanding, a continuous struggle for meaning-making (Jandrić et al. 2022a, b). Starting from where we are, we acknowledge the problems as we generate a shared sense of, and hope for, higher education 'otherwise'. By working with each other and creating an assemblage, the act of writing evokes something new, which provokes and touches–an emergent praxis of enquiry (Gale 2014; Gale et al. 2012).

Collaborative writing goes beyond a simple, efficiency-driven division of labour (cooperative writing). It requires the co-authors to be involved in all stages of the writing process, sharing the responsibility for and the ownership of the entire text produced (Storch 2019). The pragmatics begin the work of collaborative writing through call and response (being asked to write sections) and collective crafting (deciding who will do what, the order of things, weaving together). The ethics of collaboration emerges from the process, the situated experiences of trying to understand and appreciate what each contributor brings, to structure our contributions and seek responses. We consider, thus, it is a more 'response-able' approach to navigating the ethics of various facets of digital inequalities, respecting the many-sided character of the complex inequalities involved in its apprehension.

2.2 A Brief Overview of the Theories Presented to Craft the Kaleidoscope

To answer the questions and concerns above, we assembled a group of theoretical approaches that can address various dimensions of digital inequality. We recognise that the theories discussed in this article, and summarised below, can only provide a partial picture. At the same time, these theories are tried and tested in our work, and those of many others, hence the sharing of these lenses. We begin with the *capability approach* (Sen 1992; Nussbaum 2011; Robeyns 2017), which is mindful of people's differences by questioning what it means to offer equal access via digital means. In the capability approach, inequality is understood as unequal capabilities to do and be things that people have reasons to value. We follow with Bourdieu's *theory of practice* (1990), where inequality is understood through the key concepts of field, habitus, and capital. For Bourdieu, inequality goes beyond a person's goods and economic resources. Instead, it is linked to economic, cultural, and symbolic capital. Next, we touch on *cultural-historical activity theory* (CHAT) (Engeström 1987, 2011) which focuses on the socio-cultural structures and interdependent relationships between the individual and the community that enable and/or constrain the uptake of digital technologies.

Affective injustice (Srinivasan 2018; Whitney 2018) is another lens through which we might view our responses to the emotional lives of others as a distinctive source of social inequality and injustice. For example, due to status or stigmatising differences, the emotional lives of the less socially equal are given less weight than is appropriate. As a result, they are made to experience themselves as relationally inferior and are treated as such. For Jan van Dijk's *resources appropriation theory*, the problem of digital inequality starts with how people use digital media in their daily lives. Personal and positional differences generate inequalities in the distribution of resources (e.g., income, social network, status), resulting in disparities in the process of technology appropriation.

We also include *critical pedagogy* (Freire 1972/2018), an approach which problematises the notion that technology automatically grants access and enhances learning. Instead, educators and students need to learn how to harness digital education for liberatory purposes–for agency and 'action'. By including the work of Fraser (2008a, b), we offer a *tripartite model of justice* that provides a broader understanding of what injustice is by adding two dimensions besides distribution–cultural injustice and political injustice. This tripartite model offers the researcher a lens to look into digital inequality decentred from technology that focuses on issues of misrecognition and misrepresentation in the digital world but also outside of it. The theory provides concepts and ideas to address injustices derived from institutionalised hierarchies of cultural value and misrepresentation of political voicelessness.

Our final kaleidoscopic lens offered is *critical realism* (CR) and *realist social theory* (RST), which work in tandem to address the 'why', 'what', and 'under which circumstances' questions in social science. These theories bring attention to the interplay of structure, culture, and agency in inequality, particularly in social reproduction/change, i.e. morphogenesis/morphostasis. For CR proponents, the critical question is how digital inequality is produced, reproduced, and transformed, and what mechanisms and actions interact to arrive at the problematic event.

In the next section, we describe each theoretical lens in detail, exploring their advantages and sharing relevant examples where the theory has proved useful in shedding light on various aspects of digital inequality.

3 The Kaleidoscope of Theories to Study Digital Inequality

In this section, each author outlines a different theoretical approach they think may be helpful to research and understand issues related to digital inequality. The choice of the theories responds to the pertinence of the theory to study a particular dimension of the phenomenon and the expertise of the author using a particular theory or the combination of several.

3.1 Human Development and Capability Theory (Su-Ming Khoo)

Inequality is difficult to pin down because people are different–diversity complicates our understanding of equality. Therefore, we might consider what it means to offer 'equal access' via digital means.

The human development (HD) paradigm and the related capability approach (CA) are interested in people's entitlements, treating the distribution of goods and equality of opportunities as political and moral issues. CA is concerned with different individuals having unequal power to pursue well-being within their societies as a problem of injustice. Broadly, according to Sen (2009), the purpose of understanding inequality is to advance justice by reducing manifest injustices. Digital equity is achieved when digital technologies and spaces enable (and do not obstruct or reduce existing obstructions to) equitable development of different people's capabilities to do and be what they have reason to value as a matter of justice.

Most studies relating to the CA and technology form a subset of a more extensive literature on ICT for Development (ICT4D). This literature primarily derives from locations in the global South, e.g. Chile, as an example of a country with a 'successful digital agenda' (Kleine 2013). Digitalisation in these territories is seen as a technical solution to societal challenges, for example, offering inclusive, quality access to higher education (HE) in the face of financial constraints, social-economic inequalities, and exclusion. However, academic and popular discussions of digital technologies are often informed by a techno-utopian ideal, which assumes that technologies must be benevolent and progressive, sometimes obscuring the fundamental ethical and social challenges and complexities of a non-ideal world.

The HD/CA is an interdisciplinary human- or people-centred approach that is analytically detailed, systematic, and oriented towards justice. Here, we distinguish the HD/CA from analyses of firm and innovation 'capabilities', which do not have human capabilities or justice as their focus (e.g. Andrews et al. 2018)–the latter are not relevant here.

HD/CA is particularly interested in the condition of human diversity and questions of choice. It is a critical, ethical theory containing a critique of economism and explicitly distinguishing means from ends. It hopes to shift the referent object of development to the human person as ends, not means. HD redefines development as 'a process of expanding the real freedoms that people enjoy' (Sen 1999: 3). 'Real freedoms' mean having different capabilities to function (to be, to do) and make choices. In contrast, CA focuses on opportunities and processes which prioritise people as 'agents, not patients, in control of their own destiny' (Sen 1999: 11). Thus, the inaugural 1990 Human Development Report (HDR) states:

> People are the real wealth of a nation. The basic objective of development is to create an enabling environment for people to enjoy long, healthy, and creative lives. This may appear to be a simple truth. But it is often forgotten in the immediate concern with the accumulation of commodities and financial wealth. (United Nations Development Programme 1990: 9)

An HD/CA analysis differs from a human capital analysis, focusing not on the development of humans for the ultimate goal of economic production but on the development of functionings and capabilities that people have reason to value. It is intellectually and theoretically holistic and ambitious, claiming to be 'the most holistic model that exists today … a practical reflection of life itself' (ul Haq 2003: 21). A more modest view contained in 'Development as Freedom' promotes a policy focus on 'instrumental freedoms' which include social opportunities, economic facilities, transparency guarantees, security, and political freedoms (Sen 1999).

HD/CA is a liberal, pluralist vision of equality that recognises the fundamental diversity of human beings, yet upholds every person's equal capability for functioning and equality of effective freedom to achieve well-being. It can be described as a normative ethical perspective which offers a detailed approach to the states and activities a person 'has reason to value', and focuses on how to measure and evaluate progress using a wider range of indicators, such as multidimensional poverty, life expectancy, friendship, work satisfaction, happiness, and self-respect. In this way, HD/CA also pays attention to 'adaptive preferences' and 'conversion factors', which deform and structure choices to the detriment of the person in question. Moreover, HD/CA has been considered an option to enable systematic assessment of technological options that help bring questions of justice into the spotlight (see Hillerbrand et al. 2021).

Collective choice and agency are an important special topic, recognising that while HD/CA is an ethically individualist approach, individuals can generally only achieve choices in dialogue and concert with others. While some focus on 'basic capabilities' which map onto basic thresholds of needs and human rights, Nussbaum (2011) offers a specific approach to ten 'central capabilities' for a 'good' life: life, bodily health and integrity, senses, imagination and thought, emotions, practical reason, affiliation, other species, play, and control over one's environment.

3.1.1 Some Useful Examples

What relevant examples of HD/CA relate to ICT, and which types of questions have been addressed? Kleine (2013) applied the CA to ICT in a general way to develop a 'choice framework' for understanding ICT. Kleine's (2013) work was done in a rural community in Chile, studying the government's digital agenda and its uptake. The CA has been used in the past 30 years to understand poverty, especially multidimensional deprivation, but it has not been used much to evaluate technologies.

One recent example considers the digitalisation of energy networks (smart grids) and automated vehicles. This study employs both a Fraserian perspective on the three dimensions of justice: distributive, cultural-recognition, and political-representation. This theory is explained in detail in the section titled 'Tripartite Justice' (Hillerbrand et al. 2021: 338) and Nussbaum's (2011) 'central capabilities' to evaluate the potential positive and negative impacts of energy digitalisation and automated vehicles.

Further examples focusing especially on community-based participatory projects and epistemic injustice in Africa, Europe, and Latin America are richly described in a collective volume edited by Walker and Boni (2020). Some of these participatory research examples have a digital dimension, and the CA is the underlying framework of most of the case studies presented in this collection.

3.2 Theory of Practice (Laura Czerniewicz)

In this context, inequality connotes fairness or the same distribution and access, with likely different outcomes for different people, whereas equity connotes appropriate or proportionate fairness in access and outcomes.

Bourdieu's framework provides a way of describing students' practices through the key concepts of 'field', 'habitus', and 'capital'. The field explains and defines the structures or systems within which individuals attempt to achieve their outcomes. It is 'a structured system of social positions … the nature of which defines the situation for their occupants' (Jenkins 2002: 85). HE is one of a series of relatively autonomous worlds or fields whose complex interactions constitute society. Like all social fields, HE is a site of struggle over resources of all kinds, as it is 'a system of forces which exist between these positions … structured internally in terms of power relations' (Jenkins 2002: 85). Access to forms of capital is central, as 'positions [in the field] stand in relationships of domination, subordination or equivalence (homology) to each other by virtue of the access they afford to the goods or resources (capital) which are at stake in the field' (Jenkins 2002: 85). These positions are relational relative to specific forms of capital. Bourdieu explains that the structure of the distribution of the different types and subtypes of capital at a given moment in time represents the immanent structure of the social world, i.e., the set of constraints, inscribed in the very reality of that world, which durably governs its functioning, determining the chances of success for practices (Bourdieu 1990: 241).

Capital presents itself in four fundamental forms: economic, social, cultural, and symbolic. Economic capital refers to assets either in the form of or convertible to cash. Social capital is about connections, social obligations, and networks, i.e. who you know (or don't know), and the advantages or disadvantages of a person. Cultural capital occurs in three states. Embodied cultural capital refers to 'long-lasting dispositions of the mind and body' (Bourdieu 1990: 241), expressed commonly as skills, competencies, knowledge, and representation of self-image. Objectified cultural capital refers to physical objects as 'cultural goods which are the trace or realisation of theories or critiques of these theories' (Bourdieu mentions pictures, books, dictionaries, instruments, machines, etc.). Institutional cultural capital is the formal recognition of knowledge, usually in the form of educational qualifications. Finally, symbolic capital is appropriated when one of the other capitals is converted to prestige, honour, reputation, and fame–recognition, value, and status. Notably, one form of capital can be converted into another. The different forms of capital are various forms of power, but the relative importance of the other forms will vary according to the field.

Habitus is how all the different constructs come together, the dynamic and shifting relationship between particular fields and capitals. Bourdieu explains that habitus is a system of durable and transposable dispositions developed in response to determining structures. An individual's habitus is involuntary (outside of their control) and voluntary (changeable). Habitus is about identity, being in the world, and the intersection between structure and agency. It is, therefore, clear that while individuals can exercise agency, that agency is socially constrained and is exercised within existing social conventions, rules, values, and sanctions, negotiated specifically within the rules of the fields in which they operate (Czerniewicz and Brown 2012).

Bourdieu's impact has been wide-ranging, but certain concepts, in particular, have had significant resonance: the symbolic capital which particular forms of a language bring to their speakers while other forms do not; the symbolic power and violence through which the social norms of acceptable language are reproduced, sometimes with the complicity of the speakers who are led to conform; the habitus, which embodies (literally) the tension between individual agency and social forces and occupies a position in a field with other habitus, each defined by their difference from the others.

Bourdieu treats habitus essentially as 'a set of dispositions which incline agents to act and react in certain ways' (Thompson 1991: 12), dispositions that sediment within us through social interaction from childhood onward, and that becomes a physical part of our nervous system. These dispositions are inculcated into us from early childhood, and they generate regular practices without being governed by any 'rule'. The habitus is inhabited by an active human agent who is defined by the system but, crucially, is not merely its passive object. The agent engages in exchanges of symbolic power with other agents, each of whose habitus is linked to the rest in the shared field.

When Bourdieu deals with symbolic capital and power, his touchstone is often Max Weber, who described himself as a 'political economist'. Since the political is about power, and the economic is about capital, the reference is appropriate.

Bourdieu makes it clear that individuals can, in a wilful, active way, undo any identities into which they were socialised, where 'identities' are understood not as objective categories but as categories through which we are perceived by others with whom we come in contact, and in many cases, through which we perceive ourselves. These perceptions then affect how we are placed relative to others within a social hierarchy, or rather a network of social hierarchies. The word hierarchy itself implies an unequal standing, and it is into this standing that perceptions of us feed. Within a social field, the hierarchical positioning is determined by and determines what each of us possesses relative to others in terms of powers, goods, and rights–a combination of economic and symbolic goods. This constitutes 'capital' because possessing it automatically gives one the means of increasing it.

The dispositions constituting the cultivated habitus are only formed, only function, and are only valid in a field, in the relationship with a field which, as Gaston Bachelard says of the physical field, is itself a 'field of possible forces', a 'dynamic situation', in which forces are only manifested in their relationship with certain dispositions. This is why the same practices may receive opposite meanings and values in different fields, in various configurations or opposing sectors of the same field (Bachelard in Bourdieu 1990: 60).

For Bourdieu, habitus is a model for understanding how we act as agents, making deliberate choices within the parameters of a social field that accords a value to our acts, a value of which we develop an instinctive, corporeal cognition through sedimented experience (Joseph 2020).

3.2.1 Some Useful Examples

Bourdieu's framework is perhaps the most widely used to describe and analyse inequality and digital inequality, owing to its reasonable accessibility. Some scholars prefer the term resources rather than capitals because of the association with human capital theory. Theorisations of capitals based on Bourdieu's original framework have been accused of using a kitchen-sink approach, creating, and defining new capitals for every new interest of researchers. Similarly, scholars have debated whether digital capital is distinct from other forms of capital in the digital inequalities field or whether we should map digital onto traditional capitals (Ragenedda and Muschert 2013). Still, others contend it is not a primary capital but a secondary form of capital, similar to objects or status (Villanueva-Mansilla et al. 2015).

High-quality access is, therefore, not a separate digital capital but a secondary capital that individuals have primarily because of their economic capital (e.g. wealth). However, it can also be an outcome of cultural capital if aspects of their upbringing have socialised them into perceiving technologies to be significant (Helsper 2021). Czerniewicz and Brown (2012, 2013, 2014) offer valuable examples where Bourdieu's theory has been used to analyse digital inequality.

3.3 Cultural-Historical Activity Theory (CHAT) (Warren Lilley)

In this section, the potentials of cultural-historical activity theory (CHAT) are described to provoke novel insights into digital inequality within education and how this theory and its research methodologies can be harnessed towards realising more significant equity in how educators and students utilise digital technologies for teaching and learning.

The need for new approaches to addressing digital inequality is grounded in how much conventional insight overly simplifies digital inequality purely as an 'access' issue. These over-simplified framings often neglect the broader historical, social, and cultural aspects that perpetuate and influence how people utilise digital technologies in their diverse settings. By advocating the 'solution' as purely 'access' to more ICTs, there is a risk of further reproducing inequalities rather than finding ways to promote equity. Given this over-simplification, I discuss how CHAT can provide more nuanced insights into digital inequality as a multidimensional phenomenon in educational research.

As a concept, digital inequality is often seen as synonymous with the 'digital divide' (Mubarak et al. 2020; Robinson et al. 2020). This view of digital inequality is depicted as a 'divide' between those that have 'access' to use the latest ICTs (the 'haves') and those who do not have the same 'access' (the 'have-nots'). However, this 'access' framing has been increasingly found wanting. For example, Mervyn et al. (2014) comparison of two UK government mobile-technology initiatives designed to aid socially excluded citizens' access to governmental services demonstrated that merely providing mobile access did not benefit these communities to use these services. Instead, their study illustrated that by these initiatives not considering these citizens' social and cultural contexts as well as diverse literacy needs, these mobile interventions amplified social exclusion rather than mitigated it. Similarly, Hardaker et al.'s (2017) and Tsuria's (2020) research demonstrated how religious and gender norms could restrict women's ability to harness digital technologies despite their ability to access them.

These studies and a plethora of others (see Robinson et al. 2020) demonstrate that the unequal experience of digital technologies is more than mere differential 'access' to digital resources. Instead, these studies indicate that digital inequality is a socio-cultural phenomenon wherein an individual's potential capacity to utilise ICTs is tied to broader social structures, cultural norms, and beliefs. One theoretical approach that can account for this is CHAT, which stresses how an individual's intentional uptake of cultural tools is both afforded and constrained by socio-cultural structures and relationships (Engeström 1987).

Premised on Vygotsky's and Cole (1978) dialectical account of human development, CHAT emphasises the interdependent relationship between the individual and their wider community. To illustrate this, consider a formal learning environment with a teacher and students. Both have entered into this interaction to realise a socially derived motive. For the teacher, this could be financial compensation; for the student, this could be social mobility (amongst others). The key to this exchange is both parties' reciprocal interaction is premised on the other's participation to realise their aims: to learn, the student requires the teacher; to teach, the teacher needs the student.

Moreover, the agency of the teacher and the student to pursue these motives is afforded and constrained by various broader social and cultural factors beyond their control. For example, the teacher's agency to employ any digital resource to instruct the students depends on broader schooling infrastructure, school board policies, or appropriacy to mandated curricula. Similarly, the students' ability to direct the lesson or employ their digital device use is equally constrained by similar broader socio-cultural aspects, which, while not physically present, still constrain and afford their available actions within the exchange with a teacher.

Central to CHAT is that the socially derived motives for the teacher and learner and the broader socio-cultural aspects that enable or limit their actions have historically developed over time (Engeström 1987). For example, consider how classroom learning has evolved through the available tools, configurations, curricula, and learning goals–these have never stayed the same but have historically evolved to meet, realise, and challenge greater collective social motives (Säljö 2010). By underscoring both the historical and cultural aspects of human activity with semiotic and physical tools, CHAT promotes a nuanced understanding of the powerful ways in which access to digital technologies promotes unequal relationships and how these tools may further perpetuate historical and social inequalities in their use and uptake.

3.3.1 Some Useful Examples

In this regard, a notable CHAT study can be seen in Mnyanda and Mbelani's (2018) CHAT-informed analysis of critical literacy of Grade 9 learners in Eastern Cape township schools. In mapping teachers' and learners' activity towards developing critical literacy, the study demonstrated that unequal proficiencies in digital media made it difficult for teachers to develop learners' critical literacy in the classroom effectively. The study showcases how differential access, formal acknowledgement, and development of critical digital literacy skills for in-service and pre-service teachers may negatively impact critical literacy instruction within South African classrooms, especially in marginalised communities.

These insights become even more pronounced in Isaacs' (2020) CHAT analysis of South African (RSA) digital education policy. Their analysis highlights an evolving tension in the activity of RSA educational policy development which overemphasises market-driven, performative discourses necessitating digital infrastructure for administration over socially driven discourses aimed at transforming teaching and learning of marginalised communities. For example, while policies make explicit provisions for digital technologies in education administration, they undermine their use by teachers for meaningful teaching and learning activities. The analysis concludes by suggesting that should this tension in policy development remain unresolved and current market-driven understandings pursued, further exacerbation of experienced digital and social inequalities in RSA education will continue.

Another notable study of CHAT's ability to unearth digital inequalities can be seen in Mervyn et al. (2014) comparison of two UK government mobile-technology initiatives. By mapping the activity of these two social interventions, the researchers could showcase how these top-down approaches could not fully account for the diverse social-economic barriers and literacy needs of the marginalised communities they were aimed at. Furthermore, their analysis highlights how interventions centrally premised on the 'neutral' introduction of digital tools to overcome the 'digital divide' will likely always fall short of meeting the unique contextual inequalities designed to overcome.

This brief mention of contemporary studies illustrates that, as a research approach, CHAT can identify spaces where digital inequalities may be present when digital tools are introduced into human activities. However, what is less well-known about CHAT theory is that its dialectical understanding of development also captures a formative-research intervention methodology. As is often cited in contemporary digital intervention literature, top-down interventions fail to account for participants' life-world complexity as participants are usually not included in these interventions' designs or outcomes (Engeström 2011). To that end, CHAT's research methodology of Change Laboratories (CLs) emphasises participants' agency to direct the development and trajectory of the intervention in line with the unique demands of their context. In other words, these interventions aim to empower participants to find pathways to re-develop their activity in response to their social needs.

Several studies in digital education have found that the use of this formative-intervention research methodology was able to create more democratic, emancipatory practices with digital technologies which responded to the broader inequalities participants experienced (see Aagaard and Lund 2019; Juujärvi et al. 2016; Lund et al. 2019; Lund and Rasmussen 2008; Rasmussen and Ludvigsen 2009). If digital inequality research is premised on finding how individuals are disenfranchised from the benefits of digital technologies (Robinson et al. 2020), then digital equity research should be premised on finding socially responsive ways individuals can meaningfully benefit from their inclusion. To that end, I believe CHAT can facilitate research in both directions, which can genuinely help realise research towards a more equitable use of digital technologies.

3.4 Affective Inequality and Affective Injustice (Aisling Crean)

In the context of education, Kotzee (2017) explores varieties of epistemic injustice (injustices related to knowledge) that crop up in the classroom, while Bacevic (2021) considers the implications of a similar phenomenon that she labels 'epistemic positioning' for the sociology of knowledge in a higher education culture where the participation of women and ethnic minorities is low. However, our learning processes are not purely epistemic (Boud et al. 1985); they are charged with emotions like confusion, boredom, wonder, frustration, anxiety, curiosity, and love. Therefore, this section explains how our emotional lives when learning can be *loci* of social inequalities bound up with a family of injustices known as *affective injustices* (Srinivasan 2018), or injustices bound up with unfair attitudes to the emotional lives of others. It then explores the way algorithmic decision-making used by digital technologies in online learning spaces is implicated in generating *algorithmic* affective inequalities and injustices in digital education. In a nutshell, *algorithmic inequalities* result in affective inequalities and injustices in the context of digital education and these damage the process of learning.

In contemporary philosophy, the idea that our social and emotional lives might be *loci* of a distinctive family of injustices that Srinivasan (2018) calls *affective injustice* has been explored by Whitney (2018), Archer and Mills (2019), and Archer and Matheson (2020). Srinivasan notes that in day-to-day life, we can and do consider whether emotional responses, such as anger, are apt responses to how things are or whether our anger is 'a fitting response to how things are' (Srinivasan 2018: 6). She argues that emotions like anger are appropriate when (a) properly motivated by a personal reason to feel anger and (b) are a proportional response to a genuine moral violation, as opposed to being a violation of someone's wishes or desires that are not grounded in any moral values. But even when anger meets these criteria, it can be policed and silenced, discouraged, or ignored.

For example, victims of oppression are often advised to 'let go' of their anger or told straight out (usually by those in power) that it is 'inappropriate', 'uncivil', or simply 'unwise'. According to Srinivasan (2018), these kinds of responses to appropriate anger constitute what she calls *affective injustice*. Whitney (2018) identifies three types of injustice that involve the lack of uptake given to the emotions of oppressed groups: *affective marginalisation*, *affective exploitation*, and *affective violence*. Archer and Mills (2019) draw on research on emotion regulation to further elucidate the nature of *affective injustice*, illustrating the kind of work imposed upon people experiencing *affective injustice* and explain why it is harmful.

This work in philosophy is in tune with work by Lynch and McLaughlin (1995) in sociology that explores debates around the nature of work, especially two interrelated kinds of work: caring- and love-labour. Finally, Archer and Matheson (2020) discuss emotional imperialism, a kind of *affective injustice* involving a dominant group imposing its culture's emotional norms and standards on a less powerful or oppressed group. The following section discusses examples of more sophisticated digital *affective* inequalities imposed on learners by data-intensive technologies and algorithmic decision-making in the context of digital education, and frames these inequalities in terms of *affective injustice* to conceptualise and elucidate the extent of their negative impact on learning.

3.4.1 Some Useful Examples

In the context of digital education, algorithmically driven facial recognition systems are increasingly being used for securing young people's safety, attendance monitoring, proctoring, and authenticating online learners to control access to educational content, as well as being used as indicators of student engagement and support for pedagogical practices putatively connected to concerns about well-being (Andrejevic and Selwyn 2020: 118–119). Such algorithmically driven systems are not just abstract computational processes; they also have the power to enact material realities by shaping social life to various degrees (Beer 2013; Kitchin and Dodge 2011). Beer (2017) reflects on the role of such algorithms in shaping how people are treated and judged and how, as a result, they affect outcomes and opportunities for people, while Bucher (2017) explores 'how algorithms make people feel', elaborating on the details of people's personal stories of algorithms and their effects on their lived experiences, their friendships and memories, and their sense of self.

In 2020, the proctoring company ExamSoft told Black students taking exams in the USA that its software could not identify them due to 'poor lighting' (Chin 2021). In fact, there were usually no problems with lighting and the problem was not replicated for White students working in similar conditions; rather, racial bias working against Black skin tones was baked into the algorithm. Characterising this situation with ExamSoft as one of mere algorithmic bias against Black students underplays the character and significance of the inequality of treatment for the learning of Black students in contrast with that of White students since it ignores the affective injustice of the attendant emotional fallout for Black students and its consequences for their learning and sense of belonging. Prospective law students using proctoring software have described the emotional fallout of racially based inequality treatment by algorithms while attempting mock bar exams in stark terms (Harwood 2021). One student described how emotionally stressful the difficulties she faced were, how they interfered with her ability to perform, and how, ultimately, they left her questioning whether the law profession was for her and wondering whether it would recognise her as a person when she entered it.

If we understand such algorithms as, effectively, being optimised for Whiteness, we can see that the specific *kind* of algorithmic injustice these algorithms inflict is of a piece with the affective injustice that Whitney (2018) and Srinivasan (2018) describe [in this particular instance, Whitney (2018) characterises it as *affective marginalisation*] but is, in contrast, the result of algorithmic, rather than human, decision-making. In being optimised for Whiteness, proctoring algorithms de-prioritise and marginalise Blackness, resulting in what Whitney (2018: 495) calls 'disabl[ed] affective sense-making in marginalised persons'. This causes significant damage to a learner's socio-emotional learning processes, often leaving them feeling like they do not belong.

3.5 Resources Appropriation Theory (Swati Bute)

Digital inequality can be understood as the unequal or differentiated use of the available technology, infrastructure, services, facilities, and information. It prominently exists socially, economically, educationally, culturally, and in geographically diverse societies. Digital equality, instead, is a deliberate and dedicated effort to provide digital technology, infrastructure, services, facilities, and information at a minimum cost to all citizens so that they can be informed and participate in the growth and development of their society. In such a society, the distribution and availability of digital technology, infrastructure, and services are insured without any military, geographical, or economic agenda.

Accessing technology is one thing but understanding and using that technology is another. The ability to use technology depends on the structure and setup of the society, as how and for what purpose they use technology are central aspects of understanding and achieving digital equality. What impact the technology makes on society and people is a different aspect of achieving digital equality. Therefore, digital equality is not a linear process but is multifaceted in its nature.

Jan van Dijk (2006) developed his resources and appropriation theory to better understand the concept of the digital divide, inextricably linked to digital inequality. Research within the theory can be categorised into two distinct phases: the first concerns physical access to technologies, which characterised early research (van Dijk 2006). However, as digitisation increased, the concept of access needed to move beyond the mere appropriation of digital resources and to take account of the inequalities experienced as these technologies entered people's daily life–a concept coined the *second level divide* (van Dijk 2017). This 'deepening divide' emphasises that digital inequality does not end after physical access has been attained. Instead, digital inequality is further exacerbated by how individuals and communities incorporate technology shaped by different sociological dimensions such as gender, age, education, and ethnicity (Ragenedda and Muschert 2013).

The theory proposes that four main factors contribute to the quality of digital access: the dimension of motivation, physical access, cultivation of skills, and usage typologies–personal categories (e.g. age, sex, gender, ethnicity), positional categories (e.g. labour, education, household), and resources. Van Dijk (2017) distinguishes four types of access:

- Lack of any digital experience caused by lack of interest, computer fear, and indifference to new technology
- No possession of computers and network connection (material access)
- Lack of digital skills caused by insufficient user friendliness and inadequate education or social support (skill access)
- Lack of significant usage opportunities (usage access) (van Dijk 2017).

3.5.1 Some Useful Examples

A small 2020–2021 empirical study (not yet published) conducted by Swati Bute at Jagran Lakecity University in Bhopal, India, involving undergraduate and postgraduate students of journalism and communication will serve as an example. The findings are based on daily online interactions with students (e.g. participation in online classes, observation of assignment submission, and students' exam performance). The study's results shed light on a few critical points. At the first level of the digital divide, the participants struggled with multiple factors in accessing the infrastructure and services required to attend and participate in the online class. For example, many students could not attend classes, submit assignments, and appear in online exams because of electricity supply, not having digital devices, and not having a stable Internet connection. Some of the students were from rural areas, so they faced many infrastructure-related problems and availability of essential services-related problems.

At the second level of the digital divide, students' behavioural and contextual issues were responsible for the lack of interest in online classes. Not attending online classes regularly had sometimes to do with household atmosphere and household work; not participating in the online classes, e.g. keeping camera and audio off during the classes, was due amongst other things to household issues as well as economic constraints; giving wrong reasons for late submission of assignments and online exam papers; saving mobile data for other personal online activities; and remaining active on social media platforms were some of the behaviours observed. In addition, during the first phase of the pandemic, due to uncertainty, students were shocked, fearful, and traumatised. Many students were infected by the virus during the second phase of the pandemic; and some students had lost family members, no wonder that students remained silent and invisible.

3.6 Critical Pedagogy and Digital Liberation: A Freirean Approach (Sandra Abegglen, Tom Burns, and Sandra Sinfield)

> The [online] classroom remains the most radical [online] space of possibility in the academy. (hooks 1994: 12)

In this section, we continue the discussion on understanding digital inequality through Paulo Freire's lens and his idea of critical pedagogy. We are building on the premises presented in the 'Critical Realism' and the 'Human Development and Capability Theory' sections that put forward that digital inequality is multifaceted and part of larger social inequalities, positing that it is useful to think about what it means to have 'equal access', not just in terms of access to technology and broadband, but access to the academic and cultural capital that allows educators and students to use the digital for research, study, voice, and liberation. We ask what it means to be an academic and student in a world that relies on digital technology, problematising the notion that technology automatically grants access and enhances teaching and learning (Bayne 2015), suggesting instead that both educators and students need to learn how to harness digital education for liberatory purposes (Freire 2018; Stommel 2014)–for agency and 'action'.

As outlined in the 'Introduction' section of this article, education takes place in a supercomplex world (Barnett 2000a; Abegglen et al. 2020a, b). Thus, as Barnett (2000a, b) asserts, the main pedagogical task of a university is not to transmit knowledge but to develop students' attributes appropriate to the conditions of supercomplexity. In a later paper, Barnett (2004) calls for a pedagogy that prepares learners for an unknown future, a pedagogy that fosters and supports human qualities that help students in standing up to the world and engaging with it purposefully. 'What is called for, therefore, is a creative knowing in situ.' (Barnett 2004: 251) Concerning digital education, then, we need to problematize the way that we discuss digital inclusion and equality–to help us rethink learning and teaching itself in more equal terms.

Paulo Freire, the Brazilian educator and philosopher, was a fierce advocate of critical pedagogy, a philosophy of education and a social movement that developed and applied concepts from critical theory and related traditions to the field of education and the study of culture, proposing a more equal relationship between teacher, student, and society. While most of Freire's work, including *Pedagogy of the Oppressed* (2018), was written before digital technology and the Internet entered the classroom, the writing offers valuable pointers for rethinking digital inequalities in education (see, for example, Johnston et al. 2021).

Freire (1972/2018) posits that education, as with technology, is not neutral, objective, measurable, and apolitical. Those who are oppressed need to be given the freedom to express themselves, in their own words, in their own spaces. There is something profound in Freire's attempt to help the oppressed fight back to regain their power–to find their words–to have their humanity recognised. If we apply this to digital inequalities, we can conceive of an approach that does not construct an idealised model of a 'technology-tooled-up' student, a digital native, able to afford and navigate the World Wide Web seamlessly, but rather an approach that acknowledges that that particular idealised model is itself not 'neutral' but serves to dehumanise further and disempower those on the other side of the digital divide. Only when that shift has been made can we start creating digital equity.

If we are to truly create equal access to the digital and the digital world, we perhaps should start as Freire started, with the actual students in all their humanity, their strengths, their frailties, and their burning hopes and fears (Farag et al. 2021). If we allow lecturers to set challenges and tasks that enable students to play with and experiment with the digital for self-expression, exploration, and creative emergence, then students learn to use the tools they have for themselves–they start to become digital more on their terms.

If we apply this perspective – together with a liberatory thrust – to digital inequality, rather than viewing the students only in terms of what they are not: not traditional, not prepared for higher education, not in a position of privilege or advantage' (Smit 2012: 370) – and not digital natives – we can tackle digital equality more positively. We bridge the digital divide not by 'remediating' students' lack of digital proficiency but with a 'minimally invasive education' (Mitra and Rana 2001) process akin to Sugatra Mitra and his Hole in the Wall (Mitra 2012) experiment.

3.6.1 Some Useful Examples

In 1999, Mitra and his team at NIIT University, Kalkaji, New Delhi, India, literally carved a 'Hole in the Wall' that separated the university from the slum next door (Mitra 2012). Through the hole, slum children had free access to a computer. With no prior experience but driven by their curiosity and the freedom to explore, students learned to use the computer, surf the web, and develop knowledge and skills– without the intervention of a teacher. If we apply Mitra's philosophy to our students and their agency concerning developing digital literacy more on their terms, yes, we need to provide access to computing equipment, but more importantly, we need to accept the students as capable of driving their own learning, without the need for an all-knowing lecturer. This leads us to discuss our own 'Develop a Digital Me' project (Burns et al. 2018).

In our undergraduate teaching, we challenged our students with developing a 'Digital Me' (Burns et al. 2018). Rather than quizzing students about their digital knowledge and skills, we asked them to use an unfamiliar digital tool to make a digital artefact that would introduce them to the other students in the group. This task was deliberately evasive–students could introduce themselves digitally, or they could introduce their digital selves, or some combination of the two. We built class time in the computing labs, supplied some senior students as mentors, and asked the students to be creative and have fun. Near Christmas, rather than an assessment point, we had a celebratory 'party' that incorporated an exhibition of their digital artefacts. The students enjoyed showcasing their work–they entertained and supported each other– and they delighted and surprised us. Most importantly, however, they engaged them-selves in authentic digital education–as a liberatory endeavour.

We are situated within and confronted by an education system that labels our students–and often ourselves–as 'deficit' and in need of 'training', especially in digital literacies. We argue that the twenty-first-century educators need to make the space and place in the curriculum for creative opportunities for emergent learning to counter current educational narratives–especially with respect to who is included seamlessly in academia and who is systematically 'othered' and excluded. As Sugata Mitra (2012) has demonstrated, and as we argue, we cross the digital divide by believing in learners–and recognising them as the creative human beings they are.

Why does this matter? It matters because the supercomplexity of the world and of education (Abegglen et al. 2020a) is more challenging to those marginalised and on the periphery. It matters to those students who come from 'non-advantaged' backgrounds; they, and their parents, are more prone to zero-hour contracts and minimum wages and more marginalised even than in traditional manual labour jobs. It matters that when talking about students, we cannot refer to them as a single, homogenous, unified group. Instead, we need to acknowledge that there is an element of uncertainty and fragility and thus strangeness about our unequal students (Lillis 2001).

This demands imagination, creativity, openness, and ingenuity on the part of the staff on the ground and of institutions themselves. We need structures and processes that facilitate the student's ability to participate and make their accommodations with discourses of power and exclusion. Thus, we need a more significant ontological shift in pedagogy–and digital pedagogy and access. We need a practice that is supportive of difference and allows us to holistically include students–all students– so that they can participate with agency while successfully holding on to their subjectivity in the supercomplex reality we all live in.

3.6.2 Tripartite Justice (Caroline Kuhn)

This approach to social justice, envisioned by Nancy Fraser (2008a, b), aims to achieve participation parity encouraging a multidimensional perspective to addressing social injustice. Distinguishing different kinds of injustices–economic, cultural, and political–is critical because they need to be challenged through different kinds of tactics. In Fraser's view, the threat of injustice is to the ability of people to participate as a legitimate member of society, at equal footing with others. She defines participatory justice in education as:

> Social arrangements that permit all to participate as peers in social life. On the view of justice as participatory parity, overcoming injustice means dismantling institutionalised obstacles that prevent some people from participating on a par with others, as full partners in social interaction. (Fraser 2007: 27)

Economic injustices are derived from the economic structure; thus, they require a politics of redistribution. They involve exploitation and economic marginalisation, e.g. being confined to work that is undesirable and poorly paid, or not having work and being deprived of an adequate living standard. Therefore, people are indirectly being denied from having meaningful connectivity (a measure of whether someone can regularly access the Internet on an appropriate device with sufficient data and a fast connection) (Namakula and Nsekanabo 2020).[1] Cultural injustices prevent people from interacting in terms of parity by institutionalised hierarchies of cultural value related to cultural domination and non-recognition, that is, being invisible by hegemonic representational, communicative, and interpretative practices (Power 2012). They can be addressed through a politics of recognition.

Lastly, political injustices are a consequence of the former two injustices because people who are mis-recognised and endure material maldistribution are unlikely to engage in civic and political activities. Misdiagnosis of an injustice can result in strategies that may not only be ineffectual but also have the potential to produce

---

[1]This work is explained in more detail by The Web Foundation. See https://webfoundation.org/research/2022-meaningful-connectivity-report/. Accessed 24 December 2022.

additional injustices. Fraser (2008a, b) argues that these forms of injustices rarely exist in their pure form but separating them provides heuristic advantages to understand, for example, the match or mismatch between inequalities and existing strategies to address them (Power 2012).

By using Fraser's (2008a, b) theory of participatory parity, we can attend to different kinds of injustices, and it is possible to craft a normative decentred framework that does not privilege technology but structural injustices that are connected to larger systems of institutionalised oppressions. The aim of using this theory in a datafied society, for example, is to decentralise big data and data-driven technologies from the debate on discrimination and recognise the broader forms of systemic oppression and injustices that produce both mediated and unmediated forms of discrimination.

Fraser (2008a, b) considers that injustices are historically contingent ideas, and it is critical, therefore, to not only focus on what is unequal but more so on 'who' is unequal/unjust and 'how' inequality is imbued in political institutions. This entails a relational understanding of justice. With this broader understanding, it will be possible to offer a normative model that is decentred from the technology and thus, permits a broader understanding of injustices supporting individuals to participate on equal footing in social life. Fraser (2008a: 405) argues that 'overcoming injustice means dismantling institutionalised obstacles that prevent some people from participating on par with others, as full partners in social interaction'.

This model can be useful for understanding technology-mediated discrimination (Peña Gangadharan and Niklas 2019), e.g. algorithmic discrimination that is not centred on the technology per se but on the power relations that define the value structure of society at large. Thus, discrimination is not seen only through technology even though technical discrimination matters. Discrimination mediated by technology exists alongside other forms of discrimination that contribute to the systemic marginalisation of individuals and groups marked by social differences. Problems related to data-driven technologies, thus, data justice, are examples of such multifaceted issues.

3.6.3 Some Useful Examples

Data-driven technologies can be conceptualised as one amongst many discrimination mechanisms, and data-driven discrimination is one facet of an unjust society. Peña Gangadharan and Niklas (2019) questioned in their study to what extent does a decentred (of the technology) discourse exist in the real world? Their research explored how European civil society understands data-driven discrimination and connects between data, discrimination, and inequalities. For that, they analysed 'the terrain and texture of civil society discourse on data and data-driven technologies, including when and how technology plays a role in civil society organisation's work on discrimination as well as who is impacted and how discrimination can be prevented' (Peña Gangadharan and Niklas 2019: 887). To answer the question of how European civil society understands and encounters automated computer systems, data, and discrimination, and to what extent maldistribution, misrecognition, or/and misrepresentation factors play a role on these understandings or encounters, they use Fraser's (2008a) tripartite social justice model.

Focusing on the technology seems to prioritise technical forms of discrimination or unfairness at the expense of other non-digital discriminatory techniques faced by individuals or groups who systematically bear the risks and harms of a discriminatory society. So, while techniques may vary over time, discrimination's target may stay unchanged. What remains constant is the marginality and deprivation experienced by socially silenced groups. 'Who' matters as much as 'how' as Fraser (2008a) insists. In other words, unmediated discrimination exists alongside technologically mediated techniques of discrimination. Algorithmic discrimination and exclusionary automated systems represent one element of a larger ecosystem of discriminatory practices and procedures, and any diagnosis of problems or prescription for remedies would benefit from some measure of reflexivity concerning this ecosystem (Peña Gangadharan and Niklas 2019: 887).

Another example is explained in 'Participatory Parity and Emerging Technologies' (Bozalek 2017).

> Students who make use of their own devices may find themselves excluded by the banning of mobile devices such as mobile phones in lecture theatres, for example. Or those who do not have access to Internet services in their homes may find themselves being excluded from courses, which are blended or offered fully online. (Bozalek 2017: 92)

Following Fraser (2003), injustices can be addressed through affirmative or transformative social arrangement; the former facilitates the outcomes and the latter addresses the structural causes of the injustice. From an affirmative perspective, socially just pedagogies would be achieved by addressing education inequitable outcomes by making ameliorative changes to how teaching and learning are practised. In other words, the changes that the socially just pedagogies would affect would not disturb the underlying structures that generate social inequities but would address what Fraser (2003: 74) refers to as the 'end-state outcomes'.

On the other hand, transformative approaches to socially just pedagogies would involve practices which address the root causes of maldistribution, misrecognition, and misrepresentation in the three dimensions. Examples of affirmative arrangements can be the case of the lecturer that brings their device to solve the problem of lack of technology. Whereas some other teachers made rather transformative arrangements, such as ensuring that the institution provided adequate Internet access to all students in his/her/their class and to all devices that they brought themselves, by insisting that the institution install a wireless router in the classroom (Fraser 2003: 98).

3.6.4 Critical Realism and Realist Social Theory (Caroline Kuhn)

An essential aspect of digital inequality is studying and intervening in the organisation of social structures embedded in digital technology infrastructures. However, this is not a straightforward endeavour for many reasons, one of which is the invisibility of social structures, power relations, and the prominent presence of 'commonsensical' ideas, so commonly deployed in the world of technology use. Critical realism (CR) is a philosophical approach to understanding (social) science initially developed by Roy Bhaskar (1998, 2008). In contrast to positivism's methodological foundation and poststructuralism's epistemological foundation, CR argues that (social) science should be built from an explicit ontology. In this respect, critical realists start any investigation by acknowledging that the world exists independently of the knower. Our knowledge of the world is historical, partial, and fallible. Knowledge only describes the world partially and at a particular moment in time. Therefore, any critical realist research starts from the premise that social reality is much more than what catches the eye and what the researcher can observe and grasp from the empirical data collected.

An illustrative example of the transitive nature of any knowledge that seeks to understand the world is the shift from a geocentric model of the universe to a heliocentric one. Before Copernicus, the system of the universe was explained using a geocentric model. Still, given the creation of more powerful telescopes and the availability of systematic data from former astronomers, Copernicus discovered and created a model of the Universe that revolutionised science and was later refined by Galileo. This story is more complex than this, but the point I want to make is that our knowledge is historical and theory/concept dependent, thus, transitive, unlike the existence of the world, which does not depend on any theory or knowledge that seeks to explain it. The world exists, waiting to be explored but never fully understood.

CR conceives social reality as stratified, emergent, constantly transformed, and/ or reproduced by agents (Archer 2007). Structure, for CR, precedes agents but are consistently reproduced or transformed by agents. The world has different stratas, i.e. the empirical, the actual, and the real. An iceberg is a helpful metaphor for understanding the stratification of the world. The tip of the iceberg represents only 10% of the whole mass of the iceberg, and it is the empirical layer that the knower can observe through the senses. Underneath the water lies 90% of the rest of reality. The actual level consists of the events that occur independently of them being observed by the knower. The deepest level is the real, constituted by what critical realists call generative mechanisms or powers. These generative mechanisms interact in myriad ways to produce the events at the actual level and observed at the empirical level. These mechanisms or generative powers are the properties of social and cultural structures that emerge when individuals or groups interact with society. These mechanisms are relatively enduring and make things happen in the world, namely in the social world of our concerns.

At its core, critical realism offers a theory of being and existence (ontology), but it takes a more open position to the theory of knowledge (epistemology) used to explain social phenomena.[2] Therefore, an array of approaches has developed that

---

[2] Considering that CR is a philosophical approach to social science, it devotes more space that this paper does not have. Thus, we refer the interested reader to look for more information at https://criticalrealismnetwork.org/webinarvideos/. Accessed 18 January 2023.

offers a theoretical framework for social research. Because they are not theories in specific disciplines nor theories relating to particular aspects of society, these approaches are generally known as 'meta-theories' (Archer 2013). Critical realist social theories include but are not limited to the transformational model of social activity (Bhaskar 2016); the morphogenetic approach to the interplay of structure, culture, and agency (Archer 1995, 2013); critical discourse analysis (Chouliaraki and Fairclough 1999); critical realist feminism (Van Ingen et al. 2020); and critical realist Marxism (Brown et al. 2002). In short, under a CR framework, the researcher has an array of social theories to choose from. However, the choice is contextual, historical, and contingent.

For example, in the context of online learning during the pandemic, different barriers must be addressed if online learning were to become an equaliser. It is not only about accessing online learning through a device but also providing socio-cultural and economic support to overcome different constraints emerging from the context. It is known that students' social-economic status and access to learning are connected to structural issues in society: poverty, social disadvantage, gender, and race, amongst others. To address equity in access to education and its transformative capacity, it is vital to uncover these structural aspects that constrain learners' needs. CR and the chosen theory can aid in this process. This will allow us to design strategies that can be put in place to tackle these structural issues of inequity.

3.6.5 Some Useful Examples

To understand students' lack of reflexive engagement with open and participatory tools in an academic setting (HE), Kuhn (2022) used a kaleidoscopic approach. The instrument was built with a number of mirrors to shed light on 'why' and 'how' questions. The kaleidoscope combined a CR understanding of the world together with realist social theory (Archer 1995) to explore students' interaction with the technologies at the institution. In addition, it integrated the transformational model of technical activity (Lawson 2007) and the capability approach (Sen 1999; Nussbaum 2000) to come up with two causal pathways that explained which are the possible mechanisms responsible for students' lack of reflexive digital engagement.

Figure 1 presents one of the causal pathways that illustrates the combination of a number of mechanisms; amongst them is the culture of the institution (lecturers' false beliefs about young people being digital natives and the culture of assessment prevalent in the School where the study was made). It also shows how the sociality of open and participatory tools within the institution (the position of these tools in the institution's context of use), the valued goals of students and their conflicting emotions towards novel digital practices, interact. These interactions produce as an outcome a lack of reflexive engagement with open and participatory tools.

The focus of the study was not the tools per se but the social and cultural conditions with which students interacted that led to the outcome observed, i.e. a lack of reflexive engagement with open and participatory tools in the university context. The use of the capability approach served to conceptualise and point out the

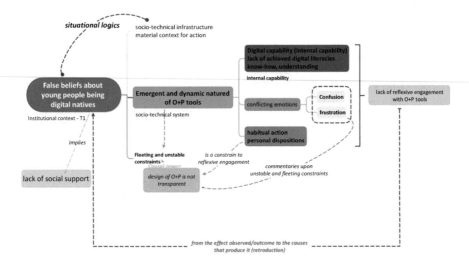

Fig. 1 Causal pathways of students' lack of engagement with open and participatory tools in HE. (Kuhn 2022)

importance that having a valued goal has for the student, as a force to overcome different socio-technical constraints.

Another interesting example is presented by Eynon (2022), who explores the relationship between Internet use and social inequality. The study explores how people use the Internet, how people can exert agency by harnessing the affordances of the Internet, and the structural conditions that constrain or enable what people can achieve. In this study, using CR and RST, it was possible to understand the complex interplay of agency and structure to explain the outcomes of Internet use for different individuals. The advantage of such findings is that it promotes a focus beyond access and skills in digital inclusion policies.

4   Discussion

A kaleidoscope can serve as an analytical tool to examine and critique the constitutive elements of digital inequalities using the intersection of different theories and finding generative connections to shed light on different dimensions of digital inequality so that we can decentre our attention from emerging technologies without dismissing them. For example, when turning the kaleidoscope, we might shed light to issues that have not much to do with the digital technology as such, but with social issues of misrepresentation and misrecognition of vulnerable individuals. This, in turn, constraints people's access to and participation in the digital economy, e.g. in endeavours of knowledge production so germane to education.

For this, we would need to craft a kaleidoscope using three mirrors (theories), e.g. one being the tripartite justice model proposed by Fraser (2008a, b) that sheds light on the cultural (misrecognition) and political (misrepresentation) injustices. The other mirror could be the human development and capability theory to critique the consequences of being denied one of the most central capabilities, namely, being capable to make meaningful epistemic contributions to the common pool of knowledge. The other theory could be critical pedagogy to find alternative pedagogical approaches to remedy such injustices. In crafting this kaleidoscope using this particular intersection of theories, we are able to connect injustices that are not necessarily related only with the digital but which consequences affect the participation in the digital sphere. Thus, the kaleidoscope aids researchers to explore and understand the tensions between the social, the political, and the technological.

It becomes evident that such a complex situation like the one described above epitomises a critical attitude whereby the researcher inquiries into the digital world but is not only concerned with the digital. Instead, they scrutinise how more pervasive and elusive power relations are partially responsible for the misrepresentation and misrecognition of those who might choose or are forced to dwell on the periphery, as well as how that situation excludes them from participating in the digital knowledge economy. It is now well understood that digital inequality and exclusion cannot be analysed apart from the offline circumstances of individuals and groups. Thus, the specific forms of digital exclusion map onto particular kinds of offline disadvantage. This is what the postdigital stresses: digital/analogue and human/machine cannot be separated anymore; instead, they are in constant tension and entangled, shaping one another. Therefore, being able to explore the interplay between offline/online and human/machine can be helpful to postdigital educational research.

In this article, through using collaborative writing, we have put together a toolkit for researchers who want to choose a kaleidoscopic approach to studying digital inequality. We have presented an overview of some theories and the possibility of finding generative intersections and connections to craft a powerful kaleidoscope that serves to inquire into the world of digital inequalities examining and critiquing its constitutive elements, its theoretical approaches, and its consequences for society more generally. In addition to the detailed description of the theories, we present the reader with a table that summarises the usefulness of each theory so that choosing which to use for your kaleidoscope can become clearer.

The mirrors (how many and which) you will use to craft your kaleidoscope is a matter of professional choice shaped by the nature of the problem and your positionality. Taking inspiration from Ursula Franklin (1999), we have envisioned the kaleidoscope not as a prescriptive but as a holistic tool. Holistic tools, Franklin argues, are tools related to the notion of craft, where the artisan controls the process of their own work. Artisans, as researchers, make decisions on their own terms drawing on their experience and positionality. In short, the theoretical kaleidoscope is a holistic tool for the researcher to be as much in control as possible of their work. We cannot forget that anybody's perspective will necessarily be limited by consideration of scope, feasibility, and context. A perspective by definition is a *particular* way of considering something.

We need to be reminded that digital inequalities, in postdigital times, are complex and they entail nuanced, thus hard to grasp tensions between offline and online, human and machine, and analogue and digital. Although we present a number of theories for reasons we have explained above, we do not argue that these are the only ones that are available to the researcher. There are many others to explore, and depending on the nature of the problem and the context, as well as the experience of the researcher, some intersections of theories will work better than others. You are the artisan, you are in charge of your kaleidoscope!

In Table 1, we illustrate the strengths and key aspects of the different theories that the researcher can choose to assemble their kaleidoscope.

Table 1 An overview of theories for understanding digital inequality

Theory	Description
Capability Approach	Accommodates diversity and plurality of needs and outcomes. Asserts ethical individualism (every person matters) while appreciating the embeddedness of each person in relationality and context. Distinguishes means and ends. Focused on evaluative judgement (are things getting better or worse?). 'Thick' conception of ethics focused on human well-being and flourishing. The integration of feminism and decoloniality challenges the universalism of the HD/CA's humanistic perspective (e.g., Khader 2018).
Theory of Practice	Demystifies the link between hardworking people and success. Social and cultural capital is useful to shed light to injustices that are related with the context of people and how differences in education lead to other differences in life, e.g., digital inequality. Theory of habitus stresses the huge influence of education upon one's ability to attain success. Helps to show that inequality is not a naturally occurring phenomena but it is related to a lack of social/cultural/economic/symbolic capital.
Cultural Historical Activity Theory	Emphasises the interdependent relationship between the individual and their wider community. Sees digital inequality as a cultural-historical phenomenon. Highlights how no 'tool' (whether digital or physical) is 'neutral'. Promotes research aimed at exploring how digital inequality is experienced. Methodology of Formative-Research Interventions aimed at equity. Intervention based on contradiction surfaced by community members; that is, not imposed and therefore likely to last longer and gain more traction. Dialectical rather than binary logic; contradictions as a site of dynamic change. View of contradictions as progressive.

(continued)

Table 1 (continued)

Theory	Description
Critical Pedagogy and Digital Liberation	Highlights digital inequality as part of larger social inequalities. Sees technology as not neutral and not a panacea: it requires interrogation and creative approaches to utilise digital education for laboratory purposes. Allows students to drive their learning via authentic and engaging co-created digital 'tasks'. Is not just about access to technology but about harnessing technology for agency. If approached this way, it does not privilege traditional academic or cultural capital but increases access and inclusion. Links with bell hooks (1994) and education as a process of hope and freedom. Is aspirational and emergent - suitable for a supercomplex world - and the often supercomplex positionalities and experiences of students.
Resource Appropriation Theory	Talks about different levels of the digital divide. This plays an essential role in addressing the nuances of the phenomenon, and thus, it supports the researcher in making informed choices in society. Posits that the digital divide is not a static and a permanent condition but fluid. Stresses the need to study digital inequalities in different situations and societies, that is, in different settings.
Tripartite Justice	Offers the possibility to study inequalities decentering the study from technology. Focuses the attention on deeper socio-cultural structures. Entails a multidimensional understanding of justice which aids the researchers in addressing the multifaceted nature of discrimination by into the social arrangements that underlie the many injustices. Allows the researcher to recognise other wrongdoings related to questions of 'who' perpetuates the injustice and 'how' different injustices occur.
Critical Realism and Realist Social Theory	Answers questions of why and how attempting to address the root cause and not so much the symptoms of the problem. Explores the interplay of culture, structure, and agency. Addresses structural issues in society.
Affective Inequality and Affective Injustice	Stresses the affective or emotional dimensions of learning and shows how emotional dimensions of learning, like our emotional lives more generally, can be *loci* of injustice. Helps explore effective inequalities and injustices when using data-intensive technologies for digital education. Allows a more sophisticated analysis of cases where digital technologies used for proctoring are not simply biased, but have inflicted specifically affective injustice on already marginalised people, especially people of colour.

5   Conclusion

Digital inequality is a pluralistic construct, multidimensional, and contextual. Each turn of the kaleidoscope allows the researcher to examine and critique the constitutive elements (online and offline which are not exclusive but intertwined). We acknowledge as do Peters and Besley (2019: 30) that the postdigital is not a chronological term but rather a critical attitude to examine 'the ideology of digitalism', its concomitant inequalities, and the huge losses it entails for human flourishing.

Digital inequality is nothing new, but its significance has augmented in the sector of HE during and after the pandemic. We believe, as do White (2009) and others (see Hayes 2021; Jandrić et al. 2018; Knox 2019), that when considering the digital, its pitfalls, and affordances, a robust toolkit that aids the researcher to focus on the broader socio-cultural questions regarding people's lack of access to economic, cultural, social, and political power is needed.

We further argue, in line with Knox (2019), that there is a need to broaden the scope of educational research on socio-technical systems within which the project of digital education is constituted. This requires mobilising the intersection of different theoretical perspectives through a kaleidoscopic approach that allow us to transcend the tendency to understand technology, in particular educational technology, in terms of the newest gadget and the prevailing idea of an outdated educational system that needs to constantly catch up with the latest trend in technology. The educational system will always be running to understand the implications of the postdigital scenario in a way that remains open to different possibilities for humanity.

Instead, what is required is to explore, at a relational level, how power relations are (mal)distributed, shaping people's experience when engaging in uneven ways with technologies. As Wakunuma (2019) upholds, despite the positives of the digitisation agenda, there are also negative aspects which have to be addressed in the form of ethical concerns. In particular, we argue in line with Wakunuma for an urgent need to explore the aspect of power in light of the digital transformation of the Global South. This, we sustain, is a critical task if we wish to shed light on the stark injustices and inequalities that are taking place now but are not new; they have only become more prevalent and urgent since the pandemic. We ought, as researchers, to transcend the idea of a tempting and seductive novelty and linear progress that seems to be implicit in the digital if our aim is to strengthen the social justice agenda in HE in the Global South or North, as both are in the midst of a severe crisis concerning digital injustices and its accompanying consequences for education.

For doing this, we have envisioned a toolkit for researchers consisting of some theories (it is not an exhaustive list), useful examples, and a summary of practical advantages of each theory. It will be the researcher, given her/his/their positionality and professional experience, that will craft the kaleidoscope in a particular way, to shed light on the problem at stake. Looking through a kaleidoscope can seem to be slippery and tricky; sometimes you do not see what you expect but even then it is a matter of keep on trying. Maybe you need to use different theories, maybe you need two instead of three, or maybe you need to change the object of analysis. The kaleidoscope is not the only tool to use in your research project; you also need to choose the right ontological and epistemological approach, the best methods to generate valuable data that you can then introduce into your kaleidoscope to see what unexpected patterns, and incredible images you can create. It is a holistic process where the kaleidoscope can serve your purpose to discover some of the tensions that have been overlooked perpetuating insidious injustices in society. We are not suggesting that with the kaleidoscope researchers will be able to understand and uncover everything. Instead, it is a tool to enable us to see more dimensions of digital inequality that have remained rather invisible and therefore difficult to understand and address.

6 Open Review 1: The Glitter and Gloom of Kaleidoscope Research (Petar Jandrić)

When I received an early idea for this article from Caroline Kuhn and the co-authors, I immediately fell in love. Kaleidoscope research is a breath of fresh air in often-stale literature on research methods: highly creative, visually attractive, and above all pedagogical. Reminiscence of my own childhood play with kaleidoscope toys brought about some warm feelings. I even tried to find a new kaleidoscope for my 9 years old son Toma! While I could not find a new kaleidoscope in Zagreb's toy shops, my Mum managed to find a couple of old, half-broken kaleidoscopes in the attic. A hipster move, perhaps, but Toma at least managed to taste a bit of history.

While we played with the toys, Toma asked: So each kaleidoscope is different, right? I wasn't sure of the answer, so I quickly looked it up.

> A kaleidoscope (/kəˈlaɪdəskoʊp/) is an optical instrument with two or more reflecting surfaces (or mirrors) tilted to each other at an angle, so that one or more (parts of) objects on one end of these mirrors are shown as a regular symmetrical pattern when viewed from the other end, due to repeated reflection. (Wikipedia 2023)

Sharp little fellow has hit the nail on the head. A kaleidoscope can provide an almost indefinite number of different images. Nevertheless, those images depend on the reflecting surfaces, angles, and objects in the kaleidoscope. However rich and varied, these images are indeed predefined by the physical setup of the kaleidoscope.

Back to work, researchers' choice of approaches and theories in a kaleidoscope will always create a unique optic. However varied, this optic will be based on approaches and theories that we include and will not be based on those that we excluded (or, will be based by absence). The main theme of this paper, inequality, is also about inclusions and exclusions. Back to square one, the kaleidoscope approach to postdigital research does not escape the eternal dichotomy between inclusion and exclusion. However, it does reconfigure this dichotomy, and I believe that this reconfiguration is important in several ways.

First, typical (postdigital) research is based on one or two methodologies; studies that intersect three or more research approaches are few and far in between. With full recognition of issues arising from commensurability of research methods (see Jandrić 2021), the kaleidoscope pushes researchers towards more varied approaches—and that's a good thing.

Second, the kaleidoscope offers many ways of combining chosen methodologies. Carefully avoiding the mixing of proverbial apples and oranges (another shout-out to commensurability), it still offers an inspiration to develop fresh and unusual mixes, perhaps those that we would not think of otherwise.

Third, the kaleidoscope is (at least in my aged mind) such a beautiful picture, which is itself deeply pedagogical. Displaying links and connections between approaches and methods that I never thought of, it helped me think of postdigital research in a new way. Cannot wait to test it with my students on Research Methods course!

While I could continue this praise for much longer, I do feel responsible to end with some words of caution. One is the need to beware of various inclusions and exclusions inherent in the method (see Bayne in Networked Learning Editorial Collective et al. 2021). The other is the need to resist definitions of the kaleidoscope research method (see Jandrić and Ford 2022; Jandrić 2022). Yet another is to beware of the apparent infinity of kaleidoscopic opportunity–all that glitters is not gold (Jandrić et al. 2022a, b). And yet another is to think carefully through connections between this theoretical richness and practical reality (hopefully through the concept of critical praxis) (McLaren and Jandrić 2020).

We should not get too infatuated by the glaze and glitter of kaleidoscopic research methods and we should neither be put off by their gloom(ier) sides. A proper response, especially for a reviewer, usually lies somewhere around a moderate middle. Yet I cannot help my excitement with the new, shiny metaphor that evokes such warm feelings. For better or worse, I do wish to explore it further in my future work!

7 Open Review 2: David Brewster's Kaleidoscope: Precision and 'Supercomplexity' (Jeremy Knox)

The assembled group of theoretical approaches in this article appears to offer much for the study of digital inequality, including the *capability approach*, which emphasises the 'distribution of goods and equality of opportunities as political and moral issues', to *cultural-historical activity theory*, which draws attention to 'historical and social inequalities'. In each of the eight theoretical contributions, a succinct outline is followed by concise examples, resulting in a clear sense of the potential value to the study of digital inequality. The proposition that warrants further reflection in this paper, however, is not contained within any one of these theoretical frameworks, but in the titular suggestion of their methodological combination, through the analogy of the 'kaleidoscope'.

It seems pertinent, as I write this open review in my office at the University of Edinburgh, to acknowledge that the kaleidoscope was invented in the early 1800s by a Scotsman, David Brewster, who was not only an alumnus of the university in which I now sit, but also later in his life, the Principal. Not far from the view outside my window is the Royal Society of Edinburgh, where a prototype of the device was first introduced. That Brewster could engage such audience was because he was a relatively prominent scientist of the time, working in the field of wave optics, in which he is credited with several discoveries, including 'Brewster's law', which defined relationships between light waves. As I ponder the value of a 'theoretical kaleidoscope', I am conscious that some of the very first kaleidoscopic views were perhaps of the very same Edinburgh skyline that presents itself before me now.

The scientific approach underpinning the invention of the kaleidoscope (Brewster's idol was apparently Sir Isaac Newton, but he was curiously an anti-Darwinist) suggests to me two brief reflections (no pun intended). First is the precision. As Brewster's *Treatise on the Kaleidoscope* (1819) makes clear, the device required a meticulous positioning of three key elements: the reflectors, the object, and the eye of the viewer. Of the latter, he suggests: 'That out of an infinite number of positions for the eye, there was *only one* where the symmetry was perfect' (Brewster 1819: 5) (emphasis original). The complex images produced by a kaleidoscope, in other words, do not result from much in the way of 'creative licence' with the arrangement of its key elements. If the theories outlined in this paper are the reflectors of the kaleidoscope, as suggested, they may need to be positioned and aligned in very precise and predefined orientations in order to produce the proposed beauty of a kaleidoscopic insight. Such precision suggests a rigour in the combination of theory that may be antithetical to the study of 'supercomplex phenomenon'.

And this leads to the second reflection: complexity. Brewster's fastidious composition of reflectors, object, and eye seems to imply a quite rigid relationship between the three, and a rather dualistic distinction between subject and object. Furthermore, the complex image one encounters by using the device is assumed to derive, not from the object itself, but from the array of reflections produced by reflectors. In other words, the object is *made* complex, rather than being assumed to be complex itself. Brewster states:

> The fundamental principle, therefore, of the Kaleidoscope is that it produces symmetrical and beautiful pictures, by converting simple into compound or beautiful forms, and arranging, by successive reflections, into one perfect whole. (Brewster 1819: 17)

For Brewster then, the kaleidoscope converts the simple into the compound, and the results are undeniably beautiful. However, interpreted thusly, the kaleidoscope does something fundamentally different from what is proposed in this paper, which is to assume 'supercomplexity' as intrinsic to the object itself (in this case digital inequality), and to draw on multiple theoretical frameworks to discern its intricacy, nuance, and convolution. The cautionary tale for the mixing of theories here would then be one in which the mixture itself becomes the focus of complexity, difficulty, and attention, rather than the object of study itself.

8 Open Review 3: Not the Observation of 'Beautiful' Forms, But How to Undertake a Theoretical Kaleidoscope of Inequality (Alison MacKenzie)

I have often thought how valuable it would be to look at an issue of injustice from several theoretical or applied philosophical perspectives. In my own master's teaching, that's the approach I take but over three modules each one dedicated to the capabilities approach (Nussbaum's version), epistemic injustice (Fricker 2007), and deconstruction using Bourdieu and Foucault. The students are free to choose any injustice and they are varied. The popular ones are disability, sexual violence and harassment, and medical–endometriosis or the menopause, for example. The students are free to examine the same injustice in each module in order to develop a deep understanding of the varieties of injustice, how entrenched and invisible they can be, and why. Injustice serves some people very well. They enjoy privilege, status, wealth, and power. The privileged have many means to keep the injustice alive or obscured: subjugation, suppression, denigration, threats, and so on. So, I was intrigued when Petar asked me to review this article.

I like the approach and I like the idea of a kaleidoscope. I had one as a child. I recall my endless fascination of, and absorption in, the changing colours and shapes. I thought it was beautiful and mysterious. Kaleidoscope is formed from three Greek words–*kalos* which means beautiful, *eidos* which means form, and *scopeo* which means to examine–and denotes the observation of beautiful forms. As a concept, it is charming, denoting childlike curiosity at how the world can change just by looking down the eyepiece and rotating the cylinder to observe an infinite variety of forms shift into view.

'Kaleidoscope' might, then, seem an odd choice of word to describe the authors' approach because inequality is not charming, it is not beautiful or innocent, and its form changes only insofar as technology or progress finds new ways for inequality to persist. Standardly, we use it to mean 'constantly changing' or 'shifting patterns'. It refers to kaleidoscope of theories. Understanding the 'supercomplexity' of inequality, as Kuhn et al. aptly describe it, is not easy, mainly because as researchers we tend to look at inequality one theory at a time or through only one theory over the course of one's academic life (as Marxists, Foucauldians, capabilitarians, for example). We do need to understand inequality and injustice from multiple perspectives in one place.

What is the best way to do this? Not in articles for journals. The standard wordcount does not permit good quality analysis of injustice and inequality from anything more than one perspective as academics have no taste for theoretical 'soups'. Even if writers have nearly double the word count, as the authors do here, all they can achieve is a proposition on what could be done, to give the briefest indication of what such an analysis might look like. This also relies on the reader having some background knowledge to appreciate what the kaleidoscopic approach is presenting to our minds. For full-scale treatment, it requires a detailed exposition of the theory and then its application to the issue–and that needs about 8000 words.

But this provides an opportunity if the authors of this article were interested in taking their idea further, a book. A single issue–digital inequalities–explored over eight chapters from eight perspectives, with a final chapter that concludes on the insights of digital inequality from a capabilities approach, critical realism, affective injustice, and so on. This could be a compelling and important contribution to the Postdigital Science and Education book series.[3]

---

[3] See https://www.springer.com/series/16439. Accessed 3 February 2023.

Acknowledgement This chapter was first published as Kuhn, C., Khoo, S.-M., Czerniewicz, L., Lilley, W., Bute, S., Crean, A., Abegglen, S., Burns, T., Sinfield, S., Jandrić, P., Knox, J., & MacKenzie, A. (2023). Understanding Digital Inequality: A Theoretical Kaleidoscope. *Postdigital Science and Education.* https://doi.org/10.1007/s42438-023-00395-8. The original text is reproduced verbatim.

References

Aagaard, T., & Lund, A. (2019). *Digital Agency in Higher Education: Transforming Teaching and Learning.* London: Routledge. https://doi.org/10.4324/9780429020629.

Abegglen, S., Burns, T., Maier, S., & Sinfield, S. (2020a). Global university, local issues: Taking a creative and humane approach to Learning and Teaching. In E. Sengupta, P. Blessinger, & M. Makhanya (Eds.), *Improving classroom engagement and international development programs: International perspectives on humanising higher education* (pp. 75–91). Emerald Publishing Limited. https://doi.org/10.1108/S2055-364120200000027007.

Abegglen, S., Burns, T., Maier, S., & Sinfield, S. (2020b). Supercomplexity: Acknowledging students' lives in the 21st century university. *Innovative Practice in Higher Education, 4*(1), 20–38.

Andrejevic, M., & Selwyn, N. (2020). Facial recognition technology in schools: Critical questions and concerns. *Learning, Media and Technology, 45*(2), 115–128. https://doi.org/10.108 0/17439884.2020.1686014.

Andrews, D., Nicoletti, G., & Timiliotis, C. (2018). Digital Technology Diffusion: A Matter of Capabilities, Incentives or Both?, OECD Economics Department Working Papers, No. 1476. Paris: OECD Publishing. https://doi.org/10.1787/7c542c16-en.

Archer, A., & Matheson, B. (2020). Commemoration and Emotional Imperialism. *Journal of Applied Philosophy, 39*(5), 761–777. https://doi.org/10.1111/japp.12428.

Archer, A., & Mills, G. (2019). Anger, affective injustice, and emotion regulation. *Philosophical Topics, 47*(2), 75–94. https://doi.org/10.5840/philtopics201947216.

Archer, M. (1995). *Realist Social Theory.* Cambridge: Cambridge University Press.

Archer, M. (2007). *Making our Way through the World: Human Reflexivity and Social Mobility.* Cambridge: Cambridge University Press.

Archer, M. (2013). Social Morphogenesis. Springer book series. https://www.springer.com/series/11959. Accessed 18 January 2023.

Bacevic, J. (2021). Epistemic injustice and epistemic positioning: towards an intersectional political economy. *Current Sociology.* https://doi.org/10.1177/00113921211057609.

Barnett, R. (2000a). *Realising the University in an Age of Supercomplexity.* London: Open University Press.

Barnett, R. (2000b). Supercomplexity and the curriculum. *Studies in Higher Education, 25*(3), 255–265. https://doi.org/10.1080/713696156.

Barnett, R. (2004). Learning for an Unknown Future. *Higher Education Research & Development, 23*(3), 247–260. https://doi.org/10.1080/0729436042000235382.

Bayne, S. (2015). What's the Matter with 'Technology-enhanced Learning'? *Learning, Media and Technology, 40*(1), 5–20. https://doi.org/10.1080/17439884.2014.915851.

Beer, D. (2013). *Popular Culture and New Media: The Politics of Circulation.* London: Palgrave Macmillan. https://doi.org/10.1057/9781137270061.

Beer, D. (2017). The social power of algorithms. *Information, Communication, and Society, 20*(1), 1–13. https://doi.org/10.1080/1369118X.2016.1216147.

Bhaskar, R. (1998). *The Possibility of Naturalism: A Philosophical Critique of the Contemporary Human Sciences.* 3rd Ed. London: Routledge.

Bhaskar, R. (2008). *A Realist Theory of Science.* London: Verso.

Bhaskar, R. (2016). *Enlightened Common Sense. The Philosophy of Critical Realism*. London: Routledge.

Boud, D., Keogh, R., & Walker, D. (1985). Promoting reflection in learning: a model. In D. Boud, R. Keogh, & D. Walker (Eds.), *Reflection: Turning Experience into Learning*. London: Kogan Page.

Bourdieu, P. (1990). *The Logic of Practice*. Cambridge: Polity Press.

Bozalek, V. (2017). Participatory Parity and Emerging Technologies. In M. Walker & M. Wilson-Strydom (Eds.), *Socially Just Pedagogies, Capabilities and Quality in Higher Education*. London: Palgrave Macmillan. https://doi.org/10.1057/978-1-137-55786-5_5.

Brewster, D. (1819). *Treatise on the Kaleidoscope*. Edinburgh: Archibald Constable & Co.

Brown, A., Fleetwood, S., & Roberts, J. M. (2002). *Critical Realism and Marxism*. London: Routledge.

Bucher, T. (2017). The algorithmic imaginary: Exploring the ordinary affects of Facebook algorithms. *Information, Communication & Society, 20*(1), 1–15. https://doi.org/10.108 0/1369118X.2016.1154086.

Burns, T., Sinfield, S., & Abegglen, S. (2018). Case study 4: Digital storytelling. *Journal of Writing in Creative Practice, 11*(2), 275–278. https://doi.org/10.1386/jwcp.11.2.275_7.

Castells, M. (2001). *The Internet Galaxy*. Oxford: Oxford University Press.

Chin, M. (2021). ExamSoft's proctoring software has a face-detection problem. The Verge, 6 January. https://www.theverge.com/2021/1/5/22215727/examsoft-online-exams-testing-acial-recognition-report. Accessed 12 December 2022.

Chouliaraki, L., & Fairclough, N. (1999). *Discourse in Late Modernity: Rethinking Critical Discourse Analysis*. Edinburgh: Edinburgh University Press.

Cramer, F. (2015). What is 'post-digital'? In D. M. Berry & M. Dieter (Eds.), *Postdigital aesthetics: Art, computation and design* (pp. 12–26). New York: Palgrave Macmillan. https://doi.org/10.1057/9781137437204_2.

Czerniewicz, L., & Brown, C. (2012). Objectified Cultural Capital and the Tale of Two Students. In L. Dirckinck-Holmfeld, V. Hodgson, & D. McConnell (Eds.), *Exploring the Theory, Pedagogy and Practice of Networked Learning* (pp. 209–219). New York: Springer. https://doi.org/10.1007/978-1-4614-0496-5_12.

Czerniewicz, L., & Brown, C. (2013). The Habitus of Digital 'Strangers' in Higher Education. *British Journal of Educational Technology, 44*(1), 44–53. https://doi.org/10.1111/j.1467-853 5.2012.01281.x.

Czerniewicz, L., & Brown, C. (2014). The Habitus and Technological Practices of Rural Students: A Case Study 1. *South African Journal of Education, 34*(1). 10.15700/201412120933.

DiMaggio, P., & Hargittai, E. (2001). From the 'Digital Divide' to 'Digital Inequality': Studying Internet Use as Penetration Increases. Working Paper No. 47. Princeton, NJ: Princeton University, School of Public and International Affairs, Centre for Arts and Cultural Policy Studies. https://econpapers.repec.org/paper/pricpanda/15.htm. Accessed 12 December 2022.

Engeström, Y. (1987). *Learning by Expanding: An Activity-Theoretical Approach to Developmental Research*. Helsinki: Orienta-Konsultit.

Engeström, Y. (2011). From Design Experiments to Formative Interventions. *Theory & Psychology, 21*(5), 598–628. https://doi.org/10.1177/0959354311419252.

Eynon, R. (2022). Utilising a Critical Realist Lens to Conceptualise Digital Inequality: The Experiences of Less Well-Off Internet Users. *Social Science Computer Review*. https://doi.org/10.1177/08944393211069662.

Farag, A., Greeley, L., & Swindell, A. (2021). Freire 2.0: Pedagogy of the Digitally Oppressed. *Educational Philosophy and Theory, 54*(13), 2214–2227. https://doi.org/10.1080/0013185 7.2021.2010541.

Franklin, U. (1999). *The Real World of Technology*. Toronto: House of Anansi Press.

Fraser, N. (2003). *Redistribution or Recognition? A Political and Philosophical Exchange*. Trans. J. Golb, J. Ingram, & C. Wilke. London: Verso.

Fraser, N. (2007). Feminist Politics in the Age of Recognition: A Two-Dimensional Approach to Gender Justice. *Studies in Social Justice, 1*(1), 23–35. https://doi.org/10.26522/ssj.v1i1.979.

Fraser, N. (2008a). Abnormal Justice. *Critical Inquiry, 34*(3), 393–422. https://doi.org/10.1086/589478.

Fraser, N. (2008b). Reframing Justice in a Globalising World. In K. Olson (Ed.), *Adding Insult to Injury: Nancy Fraser Debates her Critics.* London and New York: Verso.

Freire, P. (1972/2018). *Pedagogy of the Oppressed.* London: Bloomsbury.

Fricker, M. (2007). *Epistemic Injustice. The Power and Ethics of Knowing.* New York: Oxford University Press.

Gale, K. (2014). Call and Response on Email Within and Between the Two. In J. Wyatt & J. Speedy (Eds.), *Collaborative Writing as Inquiry* (pp. 34–41). Newcastle on Tyne: Cambridge Scholars.

Gale, K., & Bowstead, H. (2013). Deleuze and collaborative writing as a method of inquiry *Journal of Learning Development in Higher Education, 6*, 1–15. https://doi.org/10.47408/jldhe.v0i6.222.

Gale, K., Pelias, R. J., Russell, L., Spry, T., & Wyatt, J. (2012). *How Writing Touches.* Newcastle on Tyne: Cambridge Scholars.

Greene, M. (2007). The demise of the lone author. *Nature, 450*(7173), 1165. https://doi.org/10.1038/4501165a.

Hardaker, G., Sabki, A., Qazi, A., & Iqbal, J. (2017). Differences in Access to Information and Communication Technologies: Voices of British Muslim Teenage Girls at Islamic Faith Schools. *International Journal of Information and Learning Technology, 34*(4), 351–366. https://doi.org/10.1108/IJILT-05-2017-0029.

Harwood, Z. (2021). Surveillance U: Has Virtual Proctoring Gone Too Far? YR Interactive Media. https://interactive.yr.media/has-virtual-proctoring-gone-too-far. Accessed 13 April 2022.

Hayes, S. (2021). *Postdigital Positionality: Developing Powerful Inclusive Narratives for Learning, Teaching, Reseearch and Policy in Higher Education.* Leiden: Brill.

Helsper, E. (2021). *The Digital Disconnect. The Social Causes and Consequences of Digital Inequalities.* SAGE Publications.

Hillerbrand, R., Milchram, C., & Schippl, J. (2021). Using the Capability Approach as a Normative Perspective on Energy Justice: Insights From Two Case Studies on Digitalisation in the Energy Sector. *Journal of Human Development and Capabilities, 22*(2), 336–359. https://doi.org/10.1080/19452829.2021.1901672.

hooks, b. (1994). *Teaching to transgress: Education as the Practice of Freedom.* New York: Routledge.

Isaacs, S. (2020). South Africa's (Unequal) Digital Learning Journey: A Critical Review. In C. K. Looi, H. Zhang, Y. Gao, & L. Wu (Eds.), *ICT in Education and Implications for the Belt and Road Initiative* (pp. 187–211). Singapore: Springer. https://doi.org/10.1007/978-981-15-6157-3_11.

Jandrić, P. (2021). The postdigital challenge of critical educational research. In C. Mathias (Ed.), *The Handbook of Critical Theoretical Research Methods in Education* (pp. 31–48). Abingdon and New York: Routledge.

Jandrić, P. (2022). History of the Postdigital: Invitation for Feedback. *Postdigital Science and Education.* https://doi.org/10.1007/s42438-022-00345-w.

Jandrić, P., & Ford, D. (2022). Postdigital Ecopedagogies: Genealogies, Contradictions, and Possible Futures. *Postdigital Science and Education, 4*(3), 672–710. https://doi.org/10.1007/s42438-020-00207-3.

Jandrić, P., Bozkurt, A., McKee, M., & Hayes, S. (2021). Teaching in the Age of Covid-19 - A Longitudinal Study. *Postdigital Science and Education, 3*(3), 743–770. https://doi.org/10.1007/s42438-021-00252-6.

Jandrić, P., Knox, J., Besley, T., Ryberg, T., Suoranta, J., & Hayes, S. (2018). Postdigital Science and Education. *Educational Philosophy and Theory, 50*(10), 893–899. https://doi.org/10.1080/00131857.2018.1454000.

Jandrić, P., Luke, T. W., Sturm, S., McLaren, P., Jackson, L., MacKenzie, A., Tesar, M., Stewart G. T., Roberts, P., Abegglen, S., Burns, T., Sinfield, S., Hayes, S., Jaldemark, J., Peters, M. A., Sinclair, C., & Gibbons, A. (2022a). Collective Writing: The Continuous Struggle for Meaning-making. *Postdigital Science and Education.* https://doi.org/10.1007/s42438-022-00320-5.

Jandrić, P., MacKenzie, A., & Knox, J. (2022b). Postdigital Research: Genealogies, Challenges, and Future Perspectives. *Postdigital Science and Education*. https://doi.org/10.1007/s42438-022-00306-3.

Jenkins, R. (2002). *Pierre Bourdieu*. London: Routledge.

Johnston, B., Macneill, S., & Smyth, K. (2021). Paulo Freire, University Education and Post Pandemic Digital Praxis. The Post-Pandemic University, 9 November. https://postpandemicuniversity.net/2021/11/09/paulo-freire-university-education-and-post-pandemic-digital-praxis/. Accessed 18 January 2023.

Joseph, J. (2020). The Agency of Habitus: Bourdieu and Language at the Conjunction of Marxism, Phenomenology and Structuralism. *Language and Communication, 71*, 108–122. https://doi.org/10.1016/j.langcom.2020.01.004.

Juujärvi, S., Lund, V., & Darsø, L. (2016). Enhancing Early Innovation in an Urban Living Lab: Lessons from Espoo, Finland. *Technology Innovation Management Review*, 6(1), 17–26. https://doi.org/10.22215/timreview/957.

Khader, S. (2018). *Decolonizing Universalism: A Transnational Feminist Ethic*. New York: Oxford University Press. https://doi.org/10.1093/oso/9780190664190.001.0001.

Kitchin, R, & Dodge, M. (2011). *Code/Space: software and everyday life*. London: The MIT Press.

Kleine, D. (2013). *Technologies of Choice? ICTs, Development and the Capabilities Approach*. Cambridge, MA: The MIT Press.

Knox, J. (2019). What Does the 'Postdigital' Mean for Education? Three Critical Perspectives on the Digital, With Implications for Educational Research and Practice. *Postdigital Science and Education, 1*(2), 357–370. https://doi.org/10.1007/s42438-019-00045-y.

Kotzee, B. (2017). Education and epistemic injustice. In I. J. Kidd, J. Medina, & G. Pohlhause Jr. (Eds.), *The Routledge Handbook on Epistemic Injustice* (pp. 324–335). London: Routledge.

Kuhn, C. (2022). An exploration of the Underlying Generative Mechanisms that Shape University Students' Agency in their Educational Digital Practices. PhD thesis. Bath: Bath Spa University. https://researchspace.bathspa.ac.uk/14650. Accessed 18 January 2023.

Lawson, C. (2007). Technology, Technological Determinism and the Transformational Model of Technical Activity. In C. Lawson, J. Spiro Latsis, & N. Martins (Eds.), *Contributions to Social Ontologies* (pp. 32–49). New York: Routledge.

Light, J. (2001). Rethinking the Digital Divide. *Harvard Educational Review, 71*(4), 709–734. https://doi.org/10.17763/haer.71.4.342x36742j2w4q82.

Lilley, W. (2022). Cultivating Locally Transformative Digital Pedagogies: The Need for Formative-intervention Research. In J. Olivier, V. A. Oojorah, & W. Udhin (Eds.), *Multimodal Learning Environments in Southern Africa - Embracing Digital Pedagogies* (pp. 9–30). Cham: Palgrave MacMillan. https://doi.org/10.1007/978-3-030-97656-9_2.

Lillis, T. M. (2001). *Student Writing. Regulation, Access, Desire*. London: Routledge.

Lund, A., & Rasmussen, I. (2008). The Right Tool for the Wrong Task? Match and Mismatch Between First and Second Stimulus in Double Stimulation. *International Journal of Computer-Supported Collaborative Learning, 3*(4), 387–412. https://doi.org/10.1007/s11412-008-9050-8.

Lund, A., Furberg, A., & Gudmundsdottir, G. B. (2019). Expanding and Embedding Digital Literacies: Transformative Agency in Education. *Media and Communication, 7*(2), 47–58. https://doi.org/10.17645/mac.v7i2.1880.

Lynch, K., & McLaughlin, E. (1995). Caring Labour and Love Labour. In P. Clansy, S. Drudy, K. Lynch, & L. O'Dowd (Eds.), *Irish Society: Sociological Perspectives*. Institute of Public Administration.

Magnusson, S. (2021). Establishing Jointness in Proximal Multiparty Decision-making: The Case of Collaborative Writing. *Journal of pragmatics, 181*, 32–48.

McCain, K. W. (2016). Nothing as Practical as a Good Theory. Does Lewin's Maxim Still Have Salience in the Applied Social Sciences? *Proceedings of the Association for Information Science and Technology Computer Science, 52*(1), 1–4. https://doi.org/10.1002/pra2.2015.145052010077.

McLaren, P., & Jandrić, P. (2020). *Postdigital Dialogues on Critical Pedagogy, Liberation Theology and Information Technology*. London: Bloomsbury.

Mervyn, K., Simon, A., & Allen, D. K. (2014). Digital Inclusion and Social Inclusion: A Tale of Two Cities. *Information Communication and Society, 17*(9), 1086–1104. https://doi.org/10.108 0/1369118X.2013.877952.

Mills, J. S. (2000). *The Sociological Imagination*. Basingstoke: Palgrave Macmillan.

Mitra, S. (2012). The Hole in the Wall. Project and the Power of Self-Organized Learning. Edutopia, 3 February. https://www.edutopia.org/blog/self-organized-learning-sugata-mitra. Accessed 18 January 2023.

Mitra, S., & Rana, V. (2001). Children and the Internet: Experiments With Minimally Invasive Education in India. *British Journal of Educational Technology, 32*(2), 221–232. https://doi. org/10.1111/1467-8535.00192.

Mnyanda, L., & Mbelani, M. (2018). Are we teaching critical digital literacy? Grade 9 learners' practices of digital communication. *Reading & Writing-Journal of the Reading Association of South Africa, 9*(1), 1–9. https://doi.org/10.4102/rw.v9i1.188.

Mubarak, F., Suomi, R., & Kantola, S. P. (2020). Confirming the Links Between Socio-economicc Variables and Digitalisation Worldwide: The Unsettled Debate on Digital Divide. *Journal of Information, Communication and Ethics in Society, 18*(3), 415–430. https://doi.org/10.1108/ JICES-02-2019-0021.

Namakula, P., & Nsekanabo, S. (2020). Shifting from Main Access to Meaningful Connectivity. The Web Foundation, 30 October. https://webfoundation.org/2020/10/shifting-from-basic-access-to-meaningful-connectivity/. Accessed 15 July 2022.

Networked Learning Editorial Collective, Gourlay, L., Rodríguez-Illera, J. L., Barberà, E., Bali, M., Gachago, D., Pallitt, N., Jones, C., Bayne, S., Hansen, S. B., Hrastinski, S., Jaldemark, J., Themelis, C., Pischetola, M., Dirckinck-Holmfeld, L., Matthews, A., Gulson, K. N., Lee, K., Bligh, B., Thibaut, P., ... & Knox, J. (2021). Networked Learning in 2021: A Community Definition. *Postdigital Science and Education, 3*(2), 326–369. https://doi.org/10.1007/ s42438-021-00222-y.

Nussbaum, M. (2000). *Women and Human Development. The Capability Approach*. Cambridge: Cambridge University Press.

Nussbaum, M. (2011). *Creating Capabilities*. Cambridge, MA: The Belknap Press.

Peña Gangadharan, Z., & Niklas, J. (2019). Decentering Technology in Discourse on Discrimination. *Information, Communication & Society, 22*(7), 882–899. https://doi.org/1 0.1080/1369118X.2019.1593484.

Peters, M. A., Tesar, M., Jackson, L., Besley, T., Jandrić, P., Arndt, S., & Sturm, S. (2021). *The Methodology and Philosophy of Collective Writing*. Abingdon and New York: Routledge.

Peters, M., & Besley, T. (2019). Critical Philosophy of the Postdigital. *Postdigital Science and Education, 1*(1), 29–42. https://doi.org/10.1007/s42438-018-0004-9.

Power, S. (2012). From Redistribution to Recognition to Representation: Social Injustice and the Changing Politics of Education. *Globalisation, Societies, and Education, 10*(4), 473–492. https://doi.org/10.1080/14767724.2012.735154.

Ragenedda, M., & Muschert, G. (2013). *The Digital Divide. The Internet and Social Inequality from an International Perspective*. London: Routledge.

Rasmussen, I., & Ludvigsen, S. (2009). The Hedgehog and the Fox: A Discussion of the Approaches to the Analysis of ICTs Reforms in Teacher Education by Larry Cuban and Yrjö Engeström. *Mind, Culture, and Activity, 16*(1), 83–104. https://doi.org/10.1080/10749030802477390.

Robeyns, I. (2017). *Well-being, Freedom, and Social Justice*. Cambridge, UK: Open Book Publishers.

Robinson, L., Ragnedda, M., & Schulz, J. (2020). Digital Inequalities: Contextualising Problems and Solutions. *Journal of Information, Communication and Ethics in Society, 18*(3), 323–327. https://doi.org/10.1108/JICES-05-2020-0064.

Säljö, R. (2010). Digital Tools and Challenges to Institutional Traditions of Learning: Technologies, Social Memory and the Performative Nature of Learning. *Journal of Computer Assisted Learning, 26*(1), 53–64. https://doi.org/10.1111/j.1365-2729.2009.00341.x.

Sen, A. (1992). *Inequality Reexamined.* Cambridge, MA: Harvard University Press.

Sen, A. (1999). *Development as Freedom.* Oxford: Oxford University Press.

Sen, A. (2009). *The Idea of Justice.* London: Allen Lane.

Smit, R. (2012). Towards a Clearer Understanding of Student Disadvantage in Higher Education: Problematising Deficit Thinking'. *Higher Education Research & Development, 31*(3), 369–380. https://doi.org/10.1080/07294360.2011.634383.

Srinivasan, A. (2018). The Aptness of Anger. *Journal of Political Philosophy, 26*(2), 123–44. https://doi.org/10.1111/jopp.12130.

Stewart, W. H. (2021). A Global Crash-Course in Teaching and Learning Online: A Thematic Review of Empirical Emergency Remote Teaching (ERT), Studies in Higher Education during Year 1 of COVID-19. *Open Praxis, 13*(1), 89–102. https://doi.org/10.5944/openpraxis.13.1.1177.

Stommel, J. (2014). If Freire made a MOOC. Open Education and Critical Digital Pedagogy. https://www.slideshare.net/jessestommel/if-freire-made-a-mooc-open-education-and-critical-digital-pedagogy. Accessed 13 January 2023.

Storch, N. (2019). Collaborative Writing. *Language Teaching, 51*(1), 40–59. https://doi.org/10.1017/S0261444818000320.

Thompson, J. B. (1991). Introduction. In P. Bourdieu & J. B. Thompson (Eds.), *Language and Symbolic Power* (pp. 1–32). London: Polity Press.

Tsuria, R. (2020). Digital Divide in Light of Religion, Gender, and Women's Digital Participation. *Journal of Information, Communication and Ethics in Society, 18*(3), 405–413. https://doi.org/10.1108/JICES-03-2020-0028.

ul Haq, M. (2003). The Human Development Paradigm. In S. Fukuda-Parr & A. K. Shiva Kumar (Eds.), *Readings in Human Development: Concepts, Measures and Policies for a Development Paradigm.* New Delhi: Oxford University Press.

UNESCO. (2021). Education: from Disruption to Recovery. https://www.unesco.org/en/covid-19/education-response. Accessed 18 January 2023.

United Nations Development Programme. (1990). Human Development Report 1990e: Concept and Measurement of Human Development. New York: United Nations. https://hdr.undp.org/system/files/documents/hdr1990encompletenostatspdf.pdf. Accessed 18 January 2023.

Van Dijk, J. A. G. M. (1999). *The Network Society: Social Aspects of New Media.* London: Sage.

Van Dijk, J. A. G. M. (2001). Netwerken, het Zenuwstelsel van Onze Maatschappij [Networks, the nervous system of our societies]. Inaugural Lecture. Twente: Enschede University of Twente, Department of Communication.

Van Dijk, J. A. G. M. (2006). Digital Divide Research, Achievements and Shortcomings. *Poetics, 34*(4–5), 221–235. https://doi.org/10.1016/j.poetic.2006.05.004.

Van Dijk, J. A. G. M. (2017). Digital Divide: Impact of Access. In P. Rössler (Ed.), *The International Encyclopedia of Media Effects.* Hoboken, NJ: John Wiley & Sons. https://doi.org/10.1002/9781118783764.wbieme0043.

Van Ingen, M., Grohmann, S., & Gunnarsson, L. (2020). *Critical Realism, Feminism, and Gender: A Reader.* London: Routledge.

Villanueva-Mansilla, E., Nakano, T., & Evaristo, I. (2015). From Divides to Capitals: An Exploration of Digital Divides as Expressions of Social and Cultural Capital. In L. Robison, S. R. Cotton, J. Schulz, T. M. Hale, & A. Williams, A. (Eds.), *Communication and Information Technologies Annual* (pp. 89–117). Emerald Group Publishing Limited.

Vygotsky, L. S., & Cole, M. (1978). *Mind in Society: The Development of Higher Psychological Processes.* Cambridge, MA: Harvard University Press.

Wakunuma, K. (2019). Power as an Ethical Concern in the Global South's Digital Transformation. *TATuP - Zeitschrift Für Technikfolgenabschätzung in Theorie Und Praxis, 28*(2), 29–34. https://doi.org/10.14512/tatup.28.2.s29.

Walker, M., & Boni, A. (Eds.). (2020). *Participatory Research, Capabilities and Epistemic Justice.* Cham: Palgrave. https://doi.org/10.1007/978-3-030-56197-0.

White, D. (2009). Postdigital: Escaping the Kingdom of the New? TALL blog. https://tallblog.conted.ox.ac.uk/index.php/2009/06/19/postdigital-escaping-the-kingdom-of-the-new/. Accessed 15 June 2022.

Whitney, S. (2018). Affective Intentionality and Affective Injustice: Merleau-Ponty and Fanon on the Body Schema as a Theory of Affect. *Southern Journal of Philosophy, 56*(4), 488–515. https://doi.org/10.1111/sjp.12307.

Wikipedia. (2023). Kaleidoscope. https://en.wikipedia.org/wiki/Kaleidoscope. Accessed 18 January 2023.

Wilkinson, R., & Pickett, K. (2009). *The Spirit Level: Why More Equal Societies Almost Always do Better.* London: Allen Lane.

Afterword: A Study of Growth

Christine Sinclair ⓘ

Introduction

When I started my career in distance education, the mediating medium was paper and delivery was by post. Between this postal past and the postdigital present, much has happened to me, to mediating media, to distance education, and to the world, which have all affected my reading of *Constructing Postdigital Research: Method and Emancipation* (Jandrić et al. 2023). The growth of change during this time has sometimes seemed exponential, a word I don't use lightly.

Taking a Position

In 1977, I was one of a team of editors in a correspondence college. We marked up texts in green ink to be turned into documents by typists. If it was a new text, the typists created a set of paper masters. For revised texts, they retrieved masters from a physical file, treated them with correction fluid, and typed over them. A build-up of correction fluid sometimes caused words to flake off the master copy and the typist would have to make a new one. This state of affairs certainly provided a strong rationale for the arrival, around 1980, of the word processor—a centralized one with a terminal for each typist. I was fascinated by it. By that time, I was the head of one of the correspondence schools, and I managed writers and tutors to support students across the world to study at home using printed texts.

A company computer soon joined the word processor. I observed that the needs of this computer would override my decisions about when materials should go out

C. Sinclair
University of Edinburgh, Edinburgh, UK
e-mail: christine.sinclair@ed.ac.uk

P. Jandrić et al. (eds.), *Constructing Postdigital Research*, Postdigital Science and Education, https://doi.org/10.1007/978-3-031-35411-3

to students. The correspondence college soon began laying off the workforce in sizable swathes, and I was in the third of these—a distressing but life-changing time. My interest in the potential of technology and its unanticipated harmful effects then followed me through various university positions in the following four decades. I returned to distance education several times: as a developer, writer, and course designer. In the early 2000s, I became a distance student again and eventually a teacher, researcher, and programme director in digital education. Now, as a retired but not disinterested onlooker, I have relished the lifetime reverberations from this explosive book.

During this time, word processing has changed beyond recognition, typists have disappeared, and universities have developed and researched online education. Text has been 'troubled' (Bayne et al. 2020) but still exists and has taken on new guises (as shown by Engman et al. 2023 with their use of maps as method). Commercial distance education has expanded and has infiltrated schools and colleges, particularly through vocational education along with other EdTech businesses (see Hillman 2023). In universities, the changes in the ways academic staff and their students engage with various technologies for learning and research have been phenomenal— far more than I could imagine when, in a futures-based staff development workshop in the 1990s, I enthused that I was looking forward to 'new methods and new media'. I would like to compare that experience with the Future Workshops described by Suoranta and Teräs (2023). Like many other university employees, during the late 1980s and 1990s, I learned much from 'playing' and making mistakes with word processors, mainframe and personal computers, various software packages, and eventually the Internet, just to find out what they could do. It did not take long to realise how important this playful time is, and I agree with Greta Goetz (2023) that it is dangerous to let technology prevent this from happening by doing it all on our behalf.

In the 1990s, I was also a student, making an autoethnographic study of my responses to an unfamiliar academic discourse. My experiences as a part-time mechanical engineering student and later as an online digital education one, bring additional resonances to my reading of this book. For example, the use of the kaleidoscope (Kuhn et al. 2023) reminds me of my struggles to understand the workings of another optical instrument, the interferometer, and I return to this later. As a PhD student at the same time, I had serious issues with establishing my research paradigm and methods of analysis. The dominant methodology in my field at the time (phenomenography) did not quite suit my autoethnographic study; Cultural Historical Activity Theory (CHAT) did. I was so pleased to see it in the kaleidoscope!

No-one comes to an academic book without current and past issues entangling with its messages and our interpretations of them. Most readers, however, will come to it a chapter at a time. A reviewer or Afterword writer must attempt to read it as a whole. I've noted previously, when reading a book in the Postdigital Science and Education series, that it was rewarding to follow the editors' sequence (Sinclair 2022), and this time I have found it to be spectacularly so. It has explained why I started to sense that the expansion of ideas and methods was accelerating, approaching the likelihood of a combinatorial explosion as I read each chapter in sequence. The book's final chapter (Kuhn et al. 2023) illuminates the reason: some contemporary issues need multiple theoretical lenses. Whether the focus is on digital inequalities, postdigital research, or the construction of that research (and every chapter considers all three), this volume contains multiple theoretical lenses. The postdigital condition may entail an exponential growth in theory and praxis. However, exponential growth is ultimately worrying.

Expanding the Focus

I am not reviewing the book here; my aim is rather to comment on what it has stimulated in one of its readers. However, I explore evidence of expansion in each chapter and will comment on other things I have noticed, especially those that support my proposition that we may be experiencing exponential growth. Expansion pervades the book from the beginning.

Postdigital Positionality: Multiple Theories, Extending and Combining

Hayes' (2023) important construction of postdigital positionality is explored from both an individual and community perspective and her chapter asks whether 'multiple theories of change' are needed for postdigital research. Pallitt and Kramm (2023) expand positionalities to include non-human and more than human. Hayes (2023) does actually consider these too, though I can understand why Pallitt and Kramm (2023) want to highlight them in building on Hayes' earlier work on positionality (Hayes 2021), especially as they are speculating about the impact of AI. They also introduce a range of theoretical perspectives to novice postdigital researchers and ask in a prompt what studies of AI might look like according to the different paradigms. I enjoyed their well-crafted prompts and this one resonated with my own struggles with research paradigms. A later prompt expanded my own thinking about why I feel the need to be polite and respectful in my communications with ChatGPT.

The mapping exercises in the chapter by Engman et al. (2023) demonstrate how 'dragging' postdigital conditions into analogue metaphorical maps can open up alternative views on the academic terrain and positionalities. The activity is also playful, stimulating, creative, and above all, generative of new ways of seeing. However, the act of creating a map also has the useful effect of disrupting the speedy expansion I had already been picking up on; the authors write of the value of holding still, and freezing so that they can take a position on everything that is emerging.

Constructing Postdigital Research: Multidisciplinarity, Complexity, Expansion, and Immersion

Part II begins with two chapters that illustrate how design-based research and knowledge can be applied in conditions of pervasive technological mediation. It was the second of these that confirmed to me that there is a process of expansion in the sequencing of chapters. First, there is a look at how to research complex interdisciplinary and multidisciplinary activity using the well-established ACAD (Activity-Centred Analysis and Design) framework (Goodyear et al. 2023) I felt in safe hands as I read this: respected researchers offering useful analysis and ways of looking at change affecting real people in real work situations. Looking at the case study sites, though, there is a lot going on. The authors write of 'zooming in' with different theoretical lenses and then out again to see what is connected and emergent. There are multiple theories at play again here, as would be expected in multidisciplinary work, but the authors are careful to delineate how they are used. As in the following chapter, research can not only depend on design, but can also be itself part of the design.

Tzirides et al. (2023) offer a 'synthesis and extension' of approaches to integrate educational research into agile software development—cyber-social learning. Again, there is a lot happening in the case study of the CGMap tool and it seems to be expanding, especially with the role of AI in providing feedback. Lamb (2023) observes much digital and other activity in any lecture theatre and shows how a 'postdigital research sensibility' can take us further than a sociomaterial approach to establish what is happening, and also to reflect on our researcher selves. A postdigital lens does certainly support the idea of expanding other research; perhaps never more so than in the following chapter where a researcher can be 'a participant that can inhabit and reactivate the data immersively' (Davidsen et al. 2023). This takes earlier themes of situated research with real people into a new space, with researchers going beyond passive spectator roles, automation, or relying on data-based abstractions from an educational situation. Though there have been some precedents with immersive approaches to research, this 'scenographies' angle did make me feel I was being whisked into another dimension. The chapter also set me up for thinking about data and algorithms.

Postdigital Data and Algorithms: What's Missing and What Might Be Lost in the Mass of Data?

Part III's focus on datafication reveals an interesting tension in all this talk about growth: the exponential expansion of data is also associated with the reproduction of the status quo, which suits some powerful vested interests. Paul Prinsloo (2023) reveals some uncomfortable predigital analytics arising from the obsession with retention of student bodies in the system, and assumptions about bodily characteristics—an obsession that remains today in its 'flesh-electric' form (the assumed inseparable nature of analog and digital data). Prinsloo also makes the first of only four explicit references in the book to exponential growth, reminding us that measurements resulting in educational data have been happening since the 1850s, and their growth became obviously exponential a century later. Prinsloo finds that with learning analytics those earlier ways of measuring have been superseded by digitisation, and now only the digitally generated analytics count, further depriviliging those students who have scant access to the digital. While datafication can contribute to exponential growth, the analytics may be missing out important dimensions of the student journey on the way. Embedded into these analytics too are deficit models of students and bias in the data that count as evidence – a point highlighted and expanded in the following two papers.

Velislava Hillman (2023) applies a Bourdieusian analysis to an urgent need for research focus on what EdTech businesses are doing through not only mediating but determining educational practices. Through gathering and repurposing of data, they are potentially gaining a monopolistic hold on education to benefit the needs of industry rather than society as a whole. And as industry becomes more automated, there are stark warnings from Greta Goetz (2023) about the dangers of the entropy of knowledge because of mnemotechnic tools (memory aids) that become too abstract and bypass human understanding. Building on the philosophy of Bernard Stiegler, Goetz (2023) calls for the need to augment human capabilities rather than replace them with today's 'tool most capable of the greatest combinatorial proliferation of meanings'. That 'tool' is AI. The word 'combinatorial' alarmed me, as does Goetz' important question about the 'research observer' —who or what is this? If it is no longer human, will we start to lose our ability to research, or even to think?

Exclusions and Inclusions: Triggering Needs for More Theory, Legislation, and Teaching

In the light of all this expansion of ideas and theoretical lenses, and worries about what might be lost, it seems appropriate that Part IV begins with a question about validity. Felicitas Macgilchrist (2023) asks how to engage with reviewers whose ideas about what is valid might be at odds with the everyday postdigital practices with blurred boundaries that are being researched in novel ways. There are many important insights in this chapter but it is Macgilchrist's conclusion that interests me from the perspective of my proposition about exponential growth. She suggests that postdigital research actually 'reworks' validity towards the need for further theory and practice. The search for validity, then, may be a trigger for further growth.

Selman Özdan (2023) applies the idea of exponential growth to the global need for leadership on human rights. This is presumably in response to the exponential growth in problems, and it can certainly be seen in relation to his theme of AI and human rights where he lists a number of specific threats. He makes fascinating and alarming points about the need for an AI entity to have both rights and responsibilities via a legal personality. At this point in the book, I began to realise that we need exponential growth in thinking, critique, research, and education (as well as leadership and legislation) in order to counter exponential growth in injustices and fake news. The following chapter illustrates why: Amy Hanna (2023) shows that children are now exposed to massive amounts of information, disinformation, and silences both online and offline. They need the critical skills that will enable them to discern fake news and omissions and engage fully with their rights to information.

Method and Emancipation: Survival Skills, Imagination, and a Kaleidoscope of Methodologies

Alison MacKenzie (2023) adopts the 'capacious' idea of the postdigital to examine the problem of misogyny and its harms, which are exacerbated by the 'exponential speed at which information passes'. This is not hyperbole: there is also an exponentially growing torrent of abuse triggered by (mis)information and opinions passing through different social media. But the abuse itself is not new, as MacKenzie makes clear; there is just more of it. Although each abusive comment comes from an individual, the problem lies particularly with the patriarchal structures which the misogyny upholds. These harms and injustices serve to protect the status quo—a recurring theme throughout this book.

By the time I reached the final three chapters, I was primed to recognise instances of growth, although these chapters are more geared to offering inclusive and imaginative approaches to engaging with research. This is especially apparent in Maginess et al. (2023), where the researchers' specific voices are heard, in keeping with the book's stress on positionalities. The participants in the study of Images of Incoming, have themselves had to deal with 'painful accelerated acquisition of survival knowledges and skills', so acceleration is sadly never far away. It is present too in the next chapter (Suoranta and Teräs 2023), when the authors discuss imagining an alternative future to the amplification of fragmentation in the university. The consequences of exponential growth also seem present in the comparison with the resistance to the technological determinism and negative thinking following the second world war.

A combinatorial explosion has seemed likely in the final chapter (Kuhn et al. 2023) where I share the reviewers' delight and concerns with the kaleidoscope metaphor. This is the subject of my concluding section.

Repositioning

Learning When Metaphors Break Down

When I was a mechanical engineering student, I could not grasp the idea of interferometry. We had a demonstration of an interferometer (an instrument for measuring based on the way beams of light interfere with each other) in a lab with all the students crowded round. The lecturer talked us through the demonstration and I did not understand it at all. Like a kaleidoscope, this kind of interferometer uses mirrors to create its effects. In my assignment, I attempted to 'explain and use the concept of interferometry' but my actual 'learning outcome' was to paraphrase the notes I'd been given and could not follow, despite consulting other sources. A phenomenographic researcher with access only to my written answer or even an interview about my approach, might have concluded I had taken a surface approach to my studies, though I had actually spent about eight hours trying to understand this complex concept and had run out of time. I had no idea what I was looking at and what I was supposed to 'see'.

When I was writing about this incident for my PhD in Education, I used an excellent quotation that offered an explanation, from a (frequently misrepresented) pioneer of phenomenography and his colleague who had been studying school students' work in a physics laboratory to 'discover' properties of light:

> Learning in such contexts implies appropriation of accounts of the world that are neither out there in the objects themselves nor in our brains. Rather, they are cultivated in institutional settings for particular and sometimes highly specialized purposes. (Säljö and Bergqvist 1997: 402)

The authors' students could not 'just see' what was going on. Like me, they had not been inducted into the discursive practices necessary to guide understanding of the relationships involved.

A metaphor is a different kind of discursive practice, of course. In the last chapter, Kuhn et al. (2023) present their wonderful theoretical kaleidoscope using seven different theoretical 'lenses' to understand the problems of digitalism and inequality. Anyone who has used a kaleidoscope as a child would see what they were trying to say, and the different lenses certainly draw attention to different aspects of the problem. However, as the co-authoring reviewers indicate, there a need to be wary about claims about the emerging patterns that might be revealed. Because metaphors usually break down, it might seem to some readers that we don't really need to labour the point. In this case, though, the potential problems add an important dimension to the toolkit.

One of Jeremy Knox' comments (in Kuhn et al. 2023) resonates with the quotation above, about the object in the kaleidoscope not being the source of the complex image, the array of reflections itself causing the effect. This comment on the metaphor now leads me to ask whether the use of a particular theory or set of theories on a phenomenon (such as digital injustice) might just reflect aspects of the theory rather than a new angle on the phenomenon itself. I don't think this is the case, but it is a question worth asking. As for Alison MacKenzie's observation that a theoretical kaleidoscope needs a book of its own (in Kuhn et al. 2023), I thought this was an excellent idea but then asked: is that not what this current book has turned out to be? Figure 1 suggests an array of theoretical lenses being applied to a range of themes: though what would happen to the image with a kaleidoscopic turn, is beyond my ability to imagine.

Speculating When Exponential Growth Will Break Down

There are four references to exponential growth in the book and a further three to viral modernity. There is only use of the word 'combinatorial', so my claim to see a worrying trend in the expansion of postdigital research, methodologies, frameworks, and objects might be exaggerated. There are however over 100 mentions of messiness or entanglement, and these words can certainly be associated with exponential growth, which invariably breaks down because it reaches a natural limit.

Exponential growth occurs when the amount being added to a system is proportional to the amount already there. Thus if every paper in *Postdigital Science and Education* resulted in two further papers written by its readers, the editor would fairly quickly be overwhelmed. I am not an expert on exponential growth, but I am aware that it underpins a number of phenomena and practices: for example, chain letters/ emails, pyramid selling, the processing power of computers (usually associated with Moore's law), Internet memes, the spread of viruses such as Covid-19, economic growth, population growth, and the climate crisis. Sometimes people use the expression just to mean 'large', but true exponential growth can be quite small in its early stages, as the wheat/rice on the chessboard problem shows.[1] Unbounded exponential growth is not sustainable; despite the threats that terrible things will happen if you break the 'email chain', if no-one broke it, it would quickly

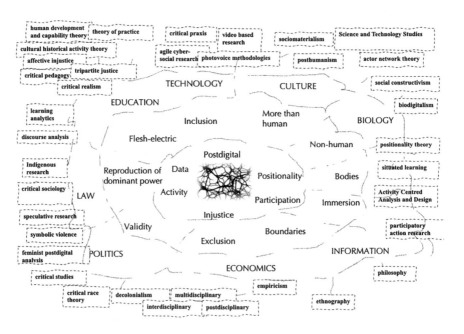

Fig. 1 An explosion of postdigital research lenses. (Central image: Neurons Altmann 2014)

---

[1] See https://en.wikipedia.org/wiki/Wheat_and_chessboard_problem. Accessed 23 April 2023.

run out of people (though the email system would have been overloaded before then). My fear of exponential growth is that things start to get out of hand very suddenly; I believe we can see it in the online abuse of women detailed by MacKenzie (2023).

A related concept is a combinatorial explosion, where the possible combinations of options available is unmanageable. If we tried to apply the lenses in Fig. 1, or even only the kaleidoscope (Kuhn et al. 2023), to all the issues that have emerged in the book, we would have more examples than we could cope with. If we then have to turn to AI to help us out, we could risk bypassing the human altogether as warned by, for example, Greta Goetz (2023), but having had that warning, we should be prepared. This book presents the reader with so many themes worth exploring and lenses to explore them with that it does all feel rather explosive, yet I feel optimistic that we can work with it effectively, without succumbing to the issues of growth I am finding.

References

Altmann, G. (2014). Neurons. https://pixabay.com/illustrations/neurons-brain-cells-brain-structure-440660/. Accessed 27 April 2023.

Bayne, S., Evans, P., Ewins, R., Knox, J., Lamb, J., Mcleod, H., et al. (2020). *The Manifesto for Teaching Online*. Cambridge, MA: MIT Press.

Davidsen, J., McIlvenny, P., & Ryberg, T. (2023). Researching Interactional and Volumetric Scenographies – Immersive Qualitative Digital Research. In P. Jandrić, A. MacKenzie, & J. Knox (Eds.), *Constructing Postdigital Research: Method and Emancipation*. Cham: Springer. https://doi.org/10.1007/978-3-031-35411-3_7.

Engman, M. M., Cushing-Leubner, J., & Ennser-Kananen, J. (2023). Mapping (Metaphorical) Journeys in And Against the Academy. In P. Jandrić, A. MacKenzie, & J. Knox (Eds.), *Constructing Postdigital Research: Method and Emancipation*. Cham: Springer. https://doi.org/10.1007/978-3-031-35411-3_3.

Goetz, G. (2023). Negotiating Mnemotechnic Re-presentation. In P. Jandrić, A. MacKenzie, & J. Knox (Eds.), *Constructing Postdigital Research: Method and Emancipation*. Cham: Springer. https://doi.org/10.1007/978-3-031-35411-3_10.

Goodyear, P., Markauskaite, L., Wrigley, C., Spence, N., Mosely, G., & Swist, T. (2023). Constructing Design Knowledge for Postdigital Science and Education. In P. Jandrić, A. MacKenzie, & J. Knox (Eds.), *Constructing Postdigital Research: Method and Emancipation*. Cham: Springer. https://doi.org/10.1007/978-3-031-35411-3_4.

Hanna, A. (2023). Understanding Children's Participation Rights Through A Postdigital Epistemology of Silence. In P. Jandrić, A. MacKenzie, & J. Knox (Eds.), *Constructing Postdigital Research: Method and Emancipation*. Cham: Springer. https://doi.org/10.1007/978-3-031-35411-3_13.

Hayes, S. (2021). *Postdigital Positionality: developing powerful inclusive narratives for learning, teaching, research and policy in Higher Education*. Leiden: Brill.

Hayes, S. (2023). Positionality in Postdigital Research: The Power to Effect Change. In P. Jandrić, A. Mackenzie, & J. Knox (Eds.), *Constructing Postdigital Research: Method and Emancipation*. Cham: Springer. https://doi.org/10.1007/978-3-031-35411-3_1.

Hillman, V. (2023). Algorithmic Systems Claim Education and The (Re)Production of Education. In P. Jandrić, A. MacKenzie, & J. Knox (Eds.), *Constructing Postdigital Research: Method and Emancipation*. Cham: Springer.

Jandrić, P., MacKenzie, A., & Knox, J. (Eds.). (2023). *Constructing Postdigital Research: Method and Emancipation*. Cham: Springer. https://doi.org/10.1007/978-3-031-35411-3.

Kuhn, C., Khoo, S.-M., Czerniewicz, L., Lilley, W., Bute, S., Crean, A., Abegglen, S., Burns, T., Sinfield, S., Jandrić, P., Knox, J., & MacKenzie, A. (2023). Understanding Digital Inequality: A Theoretical Kaleidoscope. In P. Jandrić, A. MacKenzie, & J. Knox (Eds.), *Constructing Postdigital Research: Method and Emancipation*. Cham: Springer. https://doi.org/10.1007/978-3-031-35411-3_17.

Lamb, J. (2023). Sociomateriality, Postdigital Thinking, and Learning Spaces Research. In P. Jandrić, A. MacKenzie, & J. Knox (Eds.), *Constructing Postdigital Research: Method and Emancipation*. Cham: Springer. https://doi.org/10.1007/978-3-031-35411-3_6.

Macgilchrist, F. (2023). Postdigital Validity: Peer Reviews on The Edges of Modernity. In P. Jandrić, A. MacKenzie, & J. Knox (Eds.), *Constructing Postdigital Research: Method and Emancipation*. Cham: Springer. https://doi.org/10.1007/978-3-031-35411-3_11.

MacKenzie, A. (2023). A Feminist Postdigital Analysis of Misogyny, Patriarchy And Violence Against Women and Girls Onlinee. In P. Jandrić, A. MacKenzie, & J. Knox (Eds.), *Constructing Postdigital Research: Method and Emancipation*. Cham: Springer. https://doi.org/10.1007/978-3-031-35411-3_14.

Maginess, T., Wilbur, A., & Bergia, E. (2023). Images of Incoming: A Critical Account of A (Mostly) Postdigital Photovoice Project with Rural Migrant Women in Northern Ireland and Canada. In P. Jandrić, A. MacKenzie, & J. Knox (Eds.), *Constructing Postdigital Research: Method and Emancipation*. Cham: Springer. https://doi.org/10.1007/978-3-031-35411-3_15.

Özdan, S. (2023). Don't Leave Artificial Intelligence Alone: It Could Hurt Human Rights. In P. Jandrić, A. MacKenzie, & J. Knox (Eds.), *Constructing Postdigital Research: Method and Emancipation*. Cham: Springer. https://doi.org/10.1007/978-3-031-35411-3_12.

Pallitt, N., & Kramm, N. (2023). Beyond A 'Noticing Stance': Reflecting to Expand Postdigital Positionalities. In P. Jandrić, A. MacKenzie, & J. Knox (Eds.), *Constructing Postdigital Research: Method and Emancipation*. Cham: Springer. https://doi.org/10.1007/978-3-031-35411-3_2.

Prinsloo, P. (2023). Postdigital Student Bodies – Mapping the Flesh-Electric. In P. Jandrić, A. MacKenzie, & J. Knox (Eds.), *Constructing Postdigital Research: Method and Emancipation*. Cham: Springer. https://doi.org/10.1007/978-3-031-35411-3_8.

Säljö, R., & Bergqvist, K. (1997). Seeing the Light: Discourse and Practice in the Optics Lab. In L. Resnick, R. Säljö, C. Pontecorvo, & B. Burge (Eds.), *Discourse, Tools and Reasoning* (pp. 385–405). New York: Springer. https://doi.org/10.1007/978-3-662-03362-3_17.

Sinclair, C. (2022). Review of Petar Jandrić and Derek R. Ford (Eds.). (2022). Postdigital Ecopedagogies: Genealogies, Contradictions and Possible Futures. *Postdigital Science and Education*, 4(3), 1069–1082. https://doi.org/10.1007/s42438-022-00339-8.

Suoranta, J., & Teräs, M. (2023). Future Workshop as Postdigital Research Method. In P. Jandrić, A. MacKenzie, & J. Knox (Eds.), *Constructing Postdigital Research: Method and Emancipation*. Cham: Springer. https://doi.org/10.1007/978-3-031-35411-3_16.

Tzirides, A. O., Saini, A. K., Cope, B., Kalantzis, M., & Searsmith, D. (2023). Cyber-Social Research: Emerging Paradigms for Interventionist Education Research in the Postdigital Era. In P. Jandrić, A. MacKenzie, & J. Knox (Eds.), *Constructing Postdigital Research: Method and Emancipation*. Cham: Springer. https://doi.org/10.1007/978-3-031-35411-3_5.

Index

A

Academic labour, 10, 47, 57
Academic publishing, 217, 222
Academic terrain, 40, 42, 46, 47, 377
Academic writing, 33, 34, 44
Actionable knowledge, 65, 74, 80
Agency, xiv, 23, 25, 31, 32, 34, 36, 100, 109,
 125, 126, 148, 151, 152, 163–165, 169,
 170, 173, 196, 215, 220, 277, 296, 308,
 313, 317, 323, 335, 336, 338, 340, 342,
 345, 346, 351–353, 357, 358, 361
Agile software development, 87, 89, 377
Anthropocene, 196
Artificial intelligence (AI), vi, 4, 10, 17, 23,
 26, 28, 32, 35, 79, 98, 120, 123, 132,
 169, 171, 183, 184, 186, 188, 191, 193,
 196–198, 202, 227–246, 278,
 377–379, 383
Arts-based approaches, 299–300, 309
Attrition, 139, 140, 153

B

Bias, 4, 5, 9, 17, 98, 141, 166, 216, 234, 235,
 240, 322, 348, 379
BigSoftVideo, 126
Biodigital, 12
Bullshit, 252, 262

C

CGMap, 92–95, 97–99, 378
Children, xvi, xvii, 54, 161, 163–165, 169, 230,
 246, 251–267, 288, 307, 310, 352, 380

Children's rights, 251, 252, 255, 257, 260,
 261, 264–266
Collaborative writing, 337, 359
Combinatorial, 202, 377, 379, 380, 382, 383
Community, xiii–xv, 3–6, 8, 9, 11, 13–18,
 23, 29, 34–36, 41, 66, 71, 74, 92, 95,
 164, 165, 168, 171, 195, 200, 216,
 220, 222, 235, 239, 241, 254, 280,
 284, 296–298, 300, 301, 304, 305,
 308, 311–313, 338, 341, 344–346,
 349, 360, 377
Co-research, 95, 100, 296, 298, 300, 301, 304,
 307–309, 313
Critical pedagogy, xix, 266, 299, 301,
 307–309, 313, 338, 350–359, 361
Cybernetics, vii, 197
Cyber-social research, xv, xvi, 85–100

D

Data, 4, 30, 41, 70, 90, 105, 120, 140, 160,
 211, 229, 280, 298, 335, 384
Datafication, xvi, 111, 140, 143, 150, 160,
 163, 378, 379
Deceit, xvii, 255, 260, 266, 267
Decolonisation, 4, 7, 41
Design-based research, 88–92, 98, 99, 378
Design knowledge, xv, 65–80
Digital inequalities, xvii, xviii, 30, 36, 142,
 148, 296, 333–366, 377
Digital research environments,
 121–123, 125–132
Disinformation, xvii, 232, 233, 241, 256, 260,
 261, 264–267, 380

Printed by Printforce, United Kingdom